N. C. EDSALL
1920

THE
CAMBRIDGE
ECONOMIC HISTORY

GENERAL EDITORS: M. POSTAN, Professor of Economic History
in the University of Cambridge, and H. J. HABAKKUK, Chichele
Professor of Economic History in the University of Oxford

VOLUME VI, PART I

THE
CAMBRIDGE
ECONOMIC HISTORY
OF EUROPE

VOLUME VI

THE INDUSTRIAL REVOLUTIONS
AND AFTER:
INCOMES, POPULATION AND
TECHNOLOGICAL CHANGE (I)

EDITED BY

H. J. HABAKKUK

*Chichele Professor of Economic History in the
University of Oxford*

AND

M. POSTAN

*Professor of Economic History in the
University of Cambridge*

CAMBRIDGE
AT THE UNIVERSITY PRESS
1966

PUBLISHED BY
THE SYNDICS OF THE CAMBRIDGE UNIVERSITY PRESS

Bentley House, 200 Euston Road, London, N.W. 1
American Branch: 32 East 57th Street, New York, N.Y. 10022
West African Office: P.M.B. 5181, Ibadan, Nigeria

©

CAMBRIDGE UNIVERSITY PRESS
1965

First Published   1965
Reprinted   1966

Printed in Great Britain at the University Printing House, Cambridge
(Brooke Crutchley, University Printer)

PREFACE

The present volume is the first of a group of three designed to cover the economic history of the western world during and since the Industrial Revolution. As the main theme of the volume is the rise and development of the modern industrial system, and as that system arose and developed at different times in different countries, the editors did not set these volumes within any precise terminal dates. But broadly speaking most of the essays in this and the subsequent two volumes will be found to deal with the economic history of the nineteenth and the twentieth centuries.

In planning these volumes the editors have endeavoured to break away from the time-honoured division of the subject into separate parts, respectively devoted to agriculture, industry and trade. This traditional division of the subjects does not relate well to the issues of economic development as formulated and discussed by non-historians; it also makes it difficult to find room for subjects common to the economy as a whole, such as population, national incomes, or transport. The editors have therefore tried so to define the main themes of the separate volumes as to focus attention on topics directly relevant to the current discussions of economic growth and also to enable the authors to deal with salient features of the modern economy treated as a whole.

In accordance with this plan the first volume deals with factors of economic development which are so to speak 'external' to the economic system narrowly defined, and which in economic analysis are frequently treated as social 'parameters', or assumed conditions of the economic process: viz. population, territorial expansion, transport and, above all, technological change. The second volume will concern itself with the factors of production, the entrepreneurial and managerial functions and related topics. The third volume will be devoted mainly to economic and fiscal policies and perhaps also to the social changes involved with the economic development of the modern world.

This scheme must be borne in mind in reading the present volume. Some of its chapters may underemphasize certain topics which are commonly brought into the economic history of the period. With the possible exception of Professor Gerschenkron's contribution, the chapters may appear to disregard such important themes as labour movements, taxation, or changes in social structure. The fault, if fault it be, is not the authors' but the editors', who encouraged the contributors to skim lightly over subjects which the editorial plan has reserved for more detailed treatment in later volumes.

The actual table of contents does not require much explanation.

The first chapter, Mr Cole's and Miss Deane's, dealing with national income, is in a sense an introduction to the series as a whole. Professor Glass's and Professor Grebenik's chapter on population, Professor Girard's chapter on transport and Professor Youngson's chapter on migrations, deal with separate 'external' changes. The technological changes, however, are so closely involved with the story of industrialization, and differ so much from country to country, that the editors have been compelled to provide for the separate treatment of western Europe, America and Russia. In this triad of chapters—Professor Landes's, Professor North's and Professor Portal's—the central position is naturally occupied by Professor Landes's essay on the technological aspects of the industrial development of western Europe. Professor Dovring supplies a parallel story for agriculture, while Professor Gerschenkron tells separately the history of Russian agrarian policies as they enter into the story of Russian economic development. The editors decided to make this separate provision for Russian agrarian policies not only because the social background of Russian agricultural history is radically different from that in western Europe, and is less familiar to western readers, but also because in Russia more than in any other country government attitudes to agriculture and to rural society were directly related to the prospects and the progress of industrialization.

As in the previous volumes of the *Cambridge Economic History*, the editors have done nothing to enforce on their contributors a common point of view. The reader will therefore notice, and, let us hope, welcome occasional conflicts of opinion in different parts of the volume. As in other volumes, the editors have also left to the discretion of the authors the use of footnotes. In general, it is the policy of the editors not to require the footnoting of chapters, or of sections within chapters not based on original research. Some of the authors have, however, felt that liberal references to authorities in footnotes would enable them to present their views more definitely, and even more adventurously. The editors have adopted a similarly *laissez faire* attitude to bibliographies. To quote a preface to an earlier volume

The subjects of individual chapters are disparate; some cover the whole of western Europe, others are regional; some deal with well-worn topics abundantly served by books and articles, others tread new ground hardly traversed by earlier writers. The bibliographies therefore differ in both length and arrangement. But, every care has been taken to make the references to books and articles uniform in accordance with scholarly practice prevailing in this country.

H. J. H.
M. M. P.

CONTENTS

PART I

CHAPTER IV

Transport

By L. GIRARD, Professor of Modern and Contemporary History,
University of Paris

CHAPTER V

Technological Change and Development in Western Europe, 1750–1914

By DAVID S. LANDES, Professor of History and Economics,
University of California

PART II

CHAPTER VI

The Transformation of European Agriculture

By FOLKE DOVRING, Professor of Agricultural Economics,
University of Illinois

CHAPTER IX

The Industrialization of Russia

By ROGER PORTAL, Professor, Institut d'études slaves, University of Paris

CHAPTER X

The Industrialization of the Far East

By G. C. ALLEN, Professor of Political Economy, University College London

CHAPTER I

The Growth of National Incomes[1]

THE characteristic which distinguishes the modern period in world history from all past periods is the fact of economic growth. It began in western Europe and spread first to the overseas countries settled from Europe. In a gradually increasing number of countries the product of economic activity began to expand and to generate the momentum of its future expansion. For the first time in human history it was possible to envisage a sustained increase in the volume of goods and services produced per unit of human effort or per unit of accessible resources.

Wherever this enlargement of the productive horizon of the ordinary man appeared it involved a distinctive transformation of the economy concerned. A predominantly agricultural, family-based system of economic organization began to give way to a predominantly industrial system in which the representative unit of production was necessarily larger than the family. The international economy began to shape national patterns of economic activity which had hitherto been largely focused on domestic needs and opportunities. Individuals and nations specialized in a narrowing range of occupations and industries in order to satisfy a widening range of everyday needs.

I. *The Origins of Sustained Growth*

The effective beginnings of the transformation can be placed in eighteenth-century Europe. To be sure, there had been significant developments in overseas trade, industrial organization and specialization of labour before then. Elizabethan policy-makers and their

[1] One of the most convenient ways of analysing the gamut of changes involved in the process of economic growth is to discuss them in terms of the shifts in the level or structure of national income to which they give rise. Unfortunately, historical estimates of national income are conceptually and statistically imprecise even for those countries and periods where the underlying data are relatively reliable and complete. Frequently the available estimates are little more than quantitative illustrations of the opinion of a well-informed observer or scholar. Sometimes they are very much less than this and degenerate into being instruments of propaganda or mechanistic aggregations of incomplete statistics. The estimates on which this chapter depends have been selected from recent reputable studies and only occasionally do we pause to discuss their reliability. It must be remembered, however, that historical national income research is still actively in progress in most countries so that the acceptable figures now available are provisional and liable to extensive revision on the basis of later research.

continental contemporaries were aware of the fact that a nation drew
much of its economic (and hence military) strength from its share in
world trade. The growth of large-scale industry and capitalistic enterprise in Britain has been traced back to the middle of the sixteenth
century. Cities grew and trade and industry developed in earlier
centuries. Technological change did not begin with the spinning-jenny
and the steam-engine.

The economic advances of pre-industrial societies, however, were
different in kind, in magnitude and in continuity from the economic
growth that springs from an industrial revolution. In so far as they
were sufficiently far-reaching to affect whole nations, and not merely
favoured regions or cities or social groups, their benefits were readily
cancelled by the disasters of wars or epidemics and by the brute fact of
population pressure. The statistical evidence for early periods of
economic growth is of course scanty. The broad trends must be deduced
from incomplete records for particular places and branches of economic
activity. But a study of wage and price data from a number of countries
over some seven centuries confirms the view that pre-industrial
standards of living depended more than anything else on population
trends.[1] Between the Black Death and Agincourt the commodity
equivalent of an English builder's wage roughly doubled and held that
level for nearly a century. The same rise in economic prosperity seems
to have followed the Black Death elsewhere in Europe. Then, in
southern England, France and Alsace, in Münster, Augsburg, Vienna
and Valencia the basketful of goods which a builder's labourer could
buy with a day's pay shrank back in the course of the sixteenth century
to less than half of what it had been in the fifteenth, and recovered only
where plague, wars and harvest failures relaxed the population pressure. The significant variable in the long pre-industrial secular swings
in productivity seems to have been the rate of population growth.
When population rose product per head fell: when population fell
product per head rose.

The upward trend in material welfare that had its origins in the
eighteenth century and was associated, wherever it appeared, with
industrialization differed from all earlier experience of this kind in that
it proved to be irreversible in the long run. Nor is this just a question of
hindsight. The improvement in human productivity brought about by
transforming the economic system into its modern form represents a
level which is within the grasp of every succeeding generation. Thus,
although an industrialized country's rate of economic growth may

[1] See E. H. Phelps Brown and Sheila V. Hopkins, 'Builders' Wage-rates, Prices and
Population: Some further evidence', *Economica* (1959) and earlier articles by the same
authors in *Economica* for 1955, 1956, and 1957.

fluctuate, stagnate, and even be forced into temporary reverse by the destructive catastrophe of modern war, recovery is inevitable because the system carries within itself the seeds of its own resurgence. Its capacity for producing material things is no longer dependent solely on its heritage of physical resources.

It is probably not coincidence that the region which experienced the first industrial revolution had already developed to a relatively high level the kind of economic institutions and systems of economic organization that were essential to successful industrialization. For Europe the development of the market economy, the growth of cities and the elaborate trading connections with the rest of the world were familiar features of the economic system before the end of the seventeenth century. When Gregory King drew up his tables of English income and expenditure for the year 1688, the subsistence sector of the economy (the cottagers and paupers) accounted for less than 30 per cent of the nation's families and received only about 6 per cent of its income. About a quarter of the population of England and Wales lived in 'cities and great towns'. Industry was still largely at the domestic stage in which it constituted an auxiliary occupation to agriculture, but over 14 per cent of the population was supported by economic activities which did not result in the production of physical commodities, that is, in commerce or the professions or in the service of Church or State. More important still perhaps, as an indicator of the way in which the economy was already being transformed was the change in men's attitudes to enterprise, the enlargement of their concept of wealth. No longer was economic wealth a purely physical thing—land and buildings, a store of gold or commodities. Between *circa* 1689 and 1695 the paid-up capital of British joint-stock companies (including the newly formed Bank of England) expanded from about £630,000 to about £3½ millions.[1] In the following quarter-century, which ended with the South Sea Bubble, the connection between tangible and intangible forms of wealth was strained to the point of disaster, but the business community was learning from experience to adapt itself to new economic horizons.

By comparison with many present-day pre-industrial economies in Africa and Asia, therefore, the English economy of the late seventeenth and early eighteenth centuries had reached a relatively advanced stage of economic organization. So too, no doubt, had certain other European countries. When Gregory King made his calculations of national income for 1688 he estimated the average annual income in Holland at £8. 1s. 4d., and in France at £6. 3s., compared with an English average of

[1] W. R. Scott, *The Constitution and Finance of English, Scottish, and Irish Joint Stock Companies to 1720* (1911), I, 328.

£7. 18s.[1] Nearly a century later Adam Smith ranked the three leading countries in the same order by naming England as 'perhaps the second richest country in Europe' and 'Holland in proportion to the extent of the land and the number of inhabitants by far the richest country in Europe'.[2]

If Holland, England, and France were the leading countries of Europe in terms of the levels of living of their inhabitants in the first half of the eighteenth century, we can take it that they were the leading countries of the world. International disparities in income levels were very much narrower than they are today, largely because there was no country in which the average individual lived far above the poverty line, while the bare essentials of human subsistence are basically similar in all places and at all periods. Nevertheless, there were significant contrasts between 'rich' and 'poor' and between 'barbarous' and 'civilized' countries, even at this stage, and it is interesting to note that the European lead seems to have been a relatively recent phenomenon.

In medieval times the accounts brought back by Marco Polo had suggested that China was economically in advance of Europe. In the seventeenth and eighteenth centuries French missionaries continued to bring back glowing reports of the superior wealth of China, of its large cities alive with trade, its high agricultural yields, its extensive system of canals and highways, its high educational attainments and its growing population. As late as 1819 a French scholar described the internal trade of China as being greater than that of all Europe, its labourers as being better educated, and its cities much larger.[3] Most British accounts of the Chinese Empire grew less admiring as the eighteenth century wore on. Adam Smith referred to a long period of Chinese economic stagnation and pointed out that some sections of the Chinese people were poorer than 'the most beggarly nations in Europe'. Nevertheless, writing on the threshold of the Industrial Revolution and looking back with conviction on a perceptible recent growth in English real income and population he thought that 'in manufacturing art and industry, China and Indostan, though inferior, seem to be not much inferior to any part of Europe'.[4] On balance it seems likely that if Adam Smith had been addicted to 'political arithmetic' and had been disposed to make national income comparisons between Europe and China he would have put national income in the latter far above that of any European country and would have put its average

---

[1] Gregory King, *Two Tracts*, edited by George E. Barnett (Baltimore, 1936), p. 55.

[2] Adam Smith, *The Wealth of Nations* (Cannan edition), I, 353.

[3] M. l'Abbé Grosier, *De la Chine* (Paris, 1818–19), v, 202–4.

[4] *Op. cit.* I, 206.

national income lower but not greatly below the European average. By then, that is in the 1770's, China's expanding population is estimated to have been in the region of 260 millions: which was nearly twice that of the contemporary population of Europe.

In Europe the economically advanced nations were those in the north-west whose trading horizons extended to the New World in the West and to the Indies in the East. At some point during the eighteenth century the British outstripped the Dutch in terms of average incomes per head and took the lead. In absolute terms, of course, Holland, with less than half the population of England, was a less powerful economy at the beginning of the century. The statistics are not complete or continuous enough to give a clear indication of the date at which the English average drew ahead of the Dutch. Probably the gap between the two narrowed steadily through the first three quarters of the century as the Dutch share in the growing volume of world trade declined and the British share rose. By 1780 the powerful Dutch commercial corporations were in serious difficulties and Dutch industry and trade was in a deplorable condition. Moreover, since British overseas trade was based far more than the Dutch on a widening range of domestic manufactures its expansion presumably had a relatively greater impact on industrial conditions at home. On the other hand, the Dutch financed a large proportion of the growing world trade and lent capital to the expanding economies of Europe. Their invisible incomes from finance may therefore be presumed to have grown more rapidly than their income from the carrying trade.

Taken overall, however, the evidence suggests that the Dutch economy stagnated during the eighteenth century. This view is confirmed by the contemporary national income estimates which imply an increase of barely 14 per cent in national incomes per head over the century or so between 1688 and 1792: and even this slight advance was rapidly reversed by the French wars and the Continental System which killed both the Dutch carrying trade and the financial supremacy of Amsterdam.[1] At this stage there was no doubt of the British lead.

There is little evidence for an appreciable rise in output per head in France during the century preceding the revolution. For a predominantly agricultural community the progress of agriculture is probably as good an index as can be found of the changing levels of living. Estimates of French agricultural production suggest an increase averaging about 0·6 per cent per annum over the period 1700–90 in relation to

[1] The estimates by Gregory King for 1688, Meterlerkamp for 1792 and Keuchenius for about 1800 are compared and discussed by H. C. Bos in 'Economic Growth of the Netherlands', an unpublished paper presented to the Sixth European Conference of the International Association for Research in Income and Wealth, Portoroz, 1959.

a population increase of a little more than 0·3 per cent.[1] This represents a barely appreciable rate of growth in average incomes per head. In the industrial sphere the English manufacturers may have been technically superior to the French even before the spectacular innovations of the last quarter. Certainly the French made persistent efforts to attract skilled workers from England and to imitate English industrial techniques from before the middle of the eighteenth century, though it was probably not until after the introduction of the spinning-jenny, the steam-engine and Cort's puddling process that English industry became absolutely larger as well as relatively more efficient than its French counterpart. On the other hand, Nef has argued (on the basis of estimates of French coal and iron output) that 'between 1735 and 1785 the rate of growth in industrial output and large scale industry in France was apparently at least as rapid as in England and possibly more rapid'.[2] In absolute terms, of course, the scale of French economy kept French industry larger than British over most of the eighteenth century. As late as 1801, after several decades of rapidly expanding numbers in Britain, the latter's population, at nearly 11 millions, was less than half the French population which exceeded 27 millions. Hecksher's estimates for the iron industry, for example, indicate that French pig iron output was twice the volume of British output in 1789: and although British output of cotton manufactures was one and three quarters French output in 1789 this was apparently a recent phenomenon, attributable to the spectacular success of the English textile inventions which came into effect in the 1770's.[3] On balance then, it seems likely that the gap between English and French levels of national income per head widened during the eighteenth century, probably at an accelerating rate, but the evidence is by no means conclusive.

The statistical evidence on the British economy of the eighteenth century is fragmentary, too incomplete to permit an unambiguous measure either of the rate of growth or of its chronological variations; but it points conclusively enough to the facts of economic change and economic growth. What is significant in the light of all past experience is that this economic expansion was associated with a population upsurge of unprecedented vigour. Because the figures of baptisms, burials and marriages which the English clergy extracted from their parish registers at the bidding of the first census enumerators in 1801 do not constitute an annual series—for most of the century they were for

[1] J. C. Toutain, 'Le produit de l'agriculture française de 1700 à 1958' in Histoire Quantitative de L'Economie Française (1), *Cahiers de l'Institut de Science Economique Appliquée*, no. 115 (Paris, 1961), p. 215.
[2] John Nef, 'The Industrial Revolution Reconsidered', *J. Econ. Hist.* III (1943).
[3] E. Hecksher, *Mercantilism*, I, 200-1.

isolated years at decade intervals—they cannot give a clear indication of the turning-point. It looks as though the beginnings of the rising trend in English population can be traced back to the 1740's. There is nothing startling about the rise suggested by the 1741 and 1751 data but between about 1751 and about 1801 there was apparently an increase of the order of 50 per cent. Probably the Scottish population expanded less strongly—comparison of the 1801 census returns with the results of Webster's 1755 enumeration suggests an increase of less than a third over the half century. Possibly the potato-eating Irish multiplied even faster—by nearly two-thirds according to recent estimates[1]—though there is no firm basis for an estimate of Irish population before 1821. Making due allowance, however, for the uncertainties of the statistics there seems good reason to believe that the population of the British Isles was growing at an accelerating rate in the second half of the eighteenth century and that by 1801 it was roughly half as numerous again as it had been in mid-century.

A more impressive rate of growth emerges from the statistics of British commerce with the rest of the world. As is well known, the eighteenth-century records of overseas trade valued and aggregated the merchandise at fixed official rates which were, for the most part, based on the prices prevailing at the end of the seventeenth century. They tell us nothing about the changing value of British trade: but they provide an acceptable indicator of the trends in its volume: and since the trade figures are the only statistical series which reflect the joint experience of a wide range of industries and economic activities they must constitute a crucial part of the evidence in any attempt to assess the overall development of the economy. The evidence is summarized in Table 1 where it is seen against the trend in population.

Over the first four decades of the century while population stagnated English purchases on world markets expanded some 40 per cent. It is difficult to believe that this could have occurred without some growth in English average incomes though this may have been largely limited to certain rather narrow groups in the population. The output of those who were producing for export, for example, rose by about 60 per cent and the merchants and seamen engaged in the re-export trade more than doubled the volume of their business. Thus, unless overseas trade expanded at the expense of internal trade (and there is no reason to suppose it did) we may deduce that there had been some advance in English real incomes per head over this period. But it could have been very small indeed. When Gregory King was making his calculations of national income at the end of the seventeenth century it is doubtful whether the incomes received from foreign trade accounted for much

[1] K. H. Connell, *The Population of Ireland, 1750–1845* (1950).

more than 11 per cent of the total national product. So that, of itself, the trade expansion in the first four decades cannot have accounted for an increase in average real incomes which was large enough to impress itself on the ordinary man. We need not be surprised therefore to find that contemporary analysts who argued in terms of national income in the second quarter of the century were content to adopt, without adjustment, the estimates compiled by Petty or King fifty to seventy years previously. Nor that an attempt to combine all the available statistical indicators (trade returns, production and excise data, etc.) into a single indicator of national product yields an estimated overall rate of growth for this period of not more than 0·3 per cent per annum.[1]

Table 1. *Indices of English Population and Trade in the Eighteenth Century*

Indices of overseas trade 1779/83 = 100

	Index of population (1781 = 100)	Total imports	Domestic exports	Re-exports
1701	77	47	45	40
1711	79	43	54	43
1721	80	55	58	60
1731	79	68	66	72
1741	79	67	73	83
1751	82	73	108	81
1761	87	87	124	98
1771	94	112	122	124
1781	100	100	100	100
1791	110	161	177	131
1801	122	252	280	344

SOURCES. Population index based on Brownlee's estimates in 'History of Birth and Death Rates in England and Wales', *Public Health* (1916).

Trade indices based on quinquennial averages centering on years suggested for England and Wales 1699/1703 to 1779/83 and Great Britain 1779/83 to 1799/1803. The statistics are given annually in B. R. Mitchell, *Abstract of British Historical Statistics* (1962).

The expansion that began in the 1740's was more marked. Between about 1741 and 1771, when English population grew by nearly a fifth, the volume of imports and of domestic exports increased by roughly two thirds. This was a solid achievement though it is still doubtful whether it brought with it much increase in the rate of growth of incomes per head. An estimate of the overall trend in national product suggests a trebling of the rate of growth of national product in the absolute (0·9 per cent per annum between 1741 and 1771 compared

[1] See Phyllis Deane and W. A. Cole, *British Economic Growth, 1688–1959* (1962), for a description of the methods used to arrive at this overall index.

with 0·3 per cent in the period before 1741), but little or no increase in
the rate of growth in real product per head by comparison with the
0·3 per cent per annum calculated for the period 1701–41. It is notable,
however, that by the 1770's the rate of growth was sufficient to impress
itself on contemporaries. When Arthur Young made his national
income calculations for about 1771 he produced estimates which, when
compared with Gregory King's figures, implied a doubling of average
real incomes since 1688.[1] No doubt Young exaggerated, but he was not
alone in recognizing the existence of national economic growth. When
Adam Smith, for example, wrote of England that 'the annual produce
of its land and labour is, undoubtedly, much greater at present than it
was either at the restoration or the revolution',[2] he was expressing a
view of economic progress which might have surprised the political
arithmeticians though it was common enough in the third quarter of
the eighteenth century.

Whether the economy was already launched on the path of sustained
growth by the early 1770's it is difficult to say. The stream of British
domestic exports had broadened to more than two and a half times
their volume at the beginning of the century. Agricultural output is
estimated to have expanded by about a fifth. The evidence for the textile industries suggests that their output may have doubled. The population of Birmingham (the centre for the metal industries) had quadrupled.
In effect, there is a considerable weight of evidence in favour of the
hypothesis that the process of economic development had gathered a
formidable momentum in Britain before the industrial revolution took
shape.

By the turn of the century it was clear that, in spite of the wastes and
distortions of war and inflation, what was happening to the British
economy was something new in human experience. Within roughly the
space of a generation the output of the cotton industry multiplied
tenfold, and that of the iron industry fourfold. The population of Manchester and Glasgow trebled. The steam-engine was opening up opportunities for reducing costs in a wide range of industries. More than
half a million acres of agricultural land were statutorily enclosed in the
last three decades of the century and some £7 or 8 millions of private
capital were spent in the construction of a canal system. Finally, when
attempt is made to reduce the accessible statistics to a single index of the
trend in national product, it suggests that before the end of the century
national output was growing in global terms at a compound rate of
2 per cent per annum and in per head terms at nearly 1 per cent per
annum.

[1] Arthur Young, *Political Arithmetic* (1774–9).
[2] Adam Smith, *Wealth of Nations* (1774) (Cannan edition), 1, 327.

The revolutionary character of the changes which took place in the last two or three decades of the eighteenth century is not in question. This is the period in which the first industrial revolution is generally agreed to have taken shape. Whether it was in some sense completed is another matter. Whether the changes which gave it shape became self-perpetuating, so that by the early years of the nineteenth century the British economy could be said to have reached a point at which economic growth—in the sense of increasing real incomes per head—became more or less automatic, is disputable. The fact that in the industrialized countries growth has been sustained over the long run does not prove that the first phase of industrialization makes growth automatic in any meaningful sense of the term. Nor is the controversy about the concept of a 'take-off' merely a dispute about words and definitions. For countries which have not yet begun to enjoy the benefits of rapid economic growth the question of whether it is possible to define a 'take-off' stage in the growth process, to identify a period and con-catenation of events which, once successfully completed, ensure a perpetual tendency for real incomes per head to increase, is obviously a question of peculiar interest.

II.   *The Spread of Economic Growth in Western Europe*

It is generally agreed that it was the industrial revolution, in the sense of the general adoption of improved techniques of production based on the deliberate application of scientific knowledge to a wide range of agricultural and industrial problems, that permitted the relatively rapid and continuous growth of real incomes per head in countries that are today regarded as 'advanced' or 'developed'. The way in which the relevant transformation in methods of production and economic organization was achieved has varied considerably, however, for different countries. In the case of Britain, for example, it can be said (without begging the question of whether its later development was automatic) that what happened in the last quarter of the eighteenth century represented a change of direction, the implications of which were to determine the future development of the economy for the next half century or more. In other countries also there have been similarly striking concentrations of crucial innovation and change within a relatively short period of time: but not in all countries. The idea that an industrial revolution is a transformation which can be given an effective impetus in the course of a single generation does not receive much support from the French experience, for example.

Apart from Belgium, for which we unfortunately do not possess any relevant evidence, France was the first country to follow the British lead. At the outbreak of the revolution (and perhaps for the whole of the preceding century) it was lagging behind its smaller neighbour in average productivity. But the gap was not wide by modern standards. The two countries enjoyed the same western European cultural and social heritage. If it makes sense to think in terms of 'stages' of economic development then it is arguable that France and Britain were at essentially the same stage in the 1780's. In some respects the French were in a position of advantage. They were already building on a strong scientific tradition. The setting up in 1794 of the Ecole Polytechnique, the first college of applied science in the world[1] and later (in 1829) of the Ecole Centrale des Arts de Manufactures to train factory owners and managers in the principles of scientific industry were only two of the ways in which the French seemed at times to be more progressive in their approach to economic development than the British. During the war itself the measures adopted by the administration to stimulate the chemical industry transformed it from a few small and scattered plants into a large and diversified industry.[2]

These advances could have been turning-points. In the event they were either isolated or abortive. When peace opened up the European market the British heavy chemical industry rapidly caught up with and outstripped the French. Neither the Ecole Polytechnique nor the Ecole Centrale des Arts proved seminal institutions. As late as the early 1850's more than half of the output of the French iron industry was produced by charcoal furnaces and it was not until after the crisis of 1856 that the output of the latter went into decline. It has been estimated that there were fewer than 5000 steam-engines, with a horse-power of only 62,000, in the whole of French industry in 1847.[3] Not until the 1830's did the domestic cotton industry begin to wilt before the competition of the factories. Even the railway age developed hesitantly. At the end of the first railway boom in 1845 France had only some 1200 miles of track open for use.

In effect, the most striking characteristic of the industrial revolution in France was the gradual way in which it developed. In terms of any index of industrialization she was passed by the United States, Germany and Belgium before the beginning of the twentieth century. Agriculture, which has been estimated to have accounted for 59 per cent of national income in 1789 and 46½ per cent in 1845, was still about 35 per

[1] D. S. L. Cardwell, *The Organisation of Science in England* (1957), p. 21.
[2] L. F. Haber, *The Chemical Industry during the Nineteenth Century* (1958), p. 42.
[3] S. B. Clough, *France, A History of National Economics (1789–1939)* (1939), p. 153. He gives a figure of 375,000 for England in 1826.

cent of the total in 1890.[1] It is doubtful whether in Britain the agricultural group of industries had more weight than this at the beginning
of the nineteenth century. As late as 1954 when agriculture accounted
for about 14 per cent of the French gross national product the country
was less industrialized, in terms of industrial output per head, than
Sweden, Norway, and Switzerland and barely more so than Denmark.

In the long run, of course, there have been substantial changes in the
structure of the French economy, though the transformation has been
gradual and has not gone so far as in Britain and many other industrial
countries. Yet at first sight it may seem surprising that the disparity
between French and British income levels does not appear to have
widened in the past two hundred years. It is true that the rate of growth
of *aggregate* incomes has been much lower in France than Britain, but
so, too, has the rate of population growth. The evidence suggests that,
despite the relative backwardness of French industry, *average* real
incomes have increased by roughly the same amount in both Britain
and France. The rhythm of growth has, indeed, been somewhat different in the two countries. As we have already suggested, the French rate
of growth was probably lower than the British for much of the
eighteenth century, and almost certainly so during the first phase of the
Industrial Revolution from 1780 to 1830, but in the next thirty years it
seems to have been higher. At the end of the nineteenth century,
Britain again forged ahead of France, only to fall behind again at the
beginning of the twentieth. Today, Britain is a somewhat richer
country than France, but in *per capita* terms this was also true at the end
of the seventeenth century, and in so far as it is possible to judge from
the statistical evidence, it does not appear that the relative position of the
two countries has changed substantially in the intervening period.[2] The
reasons for the maintenance of the French position are obscure. It may
be that until the latter part of the nineteenth century, it was achieved by

---

[1] I.S.E.A. La Croissance du Revenu National Français depuis 1780. *Cahiers de
l'Institut de Science Economique Appliquée*, Serie D; 7 (1957).

[2] For the data on which these remarks are based, see Deane and Cole, *British
Economic Growth, op. cit.* and, for France, F. Perroux, 'Prise de Vues sur la Croissance de
l'Economie Française, 1780–1950', in *Income and Wealth, Series V*, ed. Simon Kuznets
(1955), pp. 41–78 and J. Marczewski, 'Résultats Provisoires d'une Etude sur la Croissance de l'Economie Française, 1700–1958', a paper presented to the Portoroz conference of the International Association for Research in Income and Wealth in August
1959. The figures suggest that since 1780 the long-term rate of growth has averaged
about $1\frac{1}{4}\%$ per annum in both countries. Before 1780 the figures at present available
are too unreliable to make comparisons possible but since the rates of growth in both
countries in the eighteenth century were in any case only a fraction of one per cent per
annum, the difference between them would not have had a substantial effect on the
relative levels of incomes per head.

a comparatively high level of savings and investment in France,[1] though the evidence does not suggest that this has been the case since that time. But it seems likely that thereafter part of the explanation at least should be sought in a relatively greater input of labour. In Britain and France, as in other industrial countries, increasing productivity has been reflected not only in rising real incomes, but in a shortening of the working day. But France, unlike Britain, is still predominantly a country of small independent producers who have been little affected by the social changes which have brought increasing leisure to the wage-earning population. If incomes per head have risen as much in rural France as they have done in industrial Britain, this may simply mean that more of her people have continued to toil for long hours in the shops and cafés, on small peasant farms and in industrial workshops, to earn those incomes.

A similarly gradual process of development seems to have taken place in Holland and here too the rate of growth has until recently been comparatively low. In terms of occupational structure the Dutch economy was more highly developed than the British in the mid-eighteenth century. It stagnated nevertheless. After the disasters of the French occupation and the Continental System had been weathered the economy began to grow, but not until the middle of the twentieth century is there evidence of any marked acceleration in the rate of change. The rate of growth in real incomes per head over the period 1800–1910 was apparently almost exactly the same as the rate for the first half of the twentieth century, that is, at rather less than 0·9 per cent per annum.[2] The associated structural changes were also slow to develop. The census returns suggest that about 40 per cent of the working population was engaged in agriculture in 1849 and 28 per cent in the manufacturing group of industries; half a century later the share of agriculture had fallen to 30 per cent and that of manufacturing had risen to 34 per cent: within half a century again the corresponding proportions had shifted to 20 per cent and 37 per cent precisely. But within less than a decade 1947–56 the percentage employed in agriculture had fallen from 20 per cent to 11 per cent and that engaged in manufacture had risen from 37 per cent to 42 per cent while real incomes per head were increasing at about 3 per cent per annum.

We must beware, of course, of assuming that the completion of the industrial revolution involves the virtual disappearance of agriculture or of equating economic growth with industrialization in the narrow

[1] Cf. p. 439 below.
[2] For estimates of national income, 1800 and 1910, see H. C. Bos, 'Economic Growth of the Netherlands' (an unpublished paper). For annual estimates, 1900–59, see Centraal Bureau voor Statistiek, *Nationale Rekeningen* (1959).

sense of a growth of manufacturing industry. There is a direct connection between these developments in that agricultural incomes
tend in all countries to be lower than industrial incomes, so that
a structural change in favour of industry leads automatically to a rise
in incomes per head; and also in that technological progress in the past
(though not necessarily in the future) has generally been more rapid
and continuous in industry than in agriculture. But it should be
remembered that increasing industrialization brings with it developments that push up the national income in ways that are not indicative
of increased welfare. Prices and hence incomes are almost invariably
higher in urban areas than in rural areas. The need for an elaborate
system of transport to carry food to city consumers, or workers to
places of production, does not represent a net addition to individual
well being or at any rate not to the extent that it raises national incomes.
In assessing levels of national incomes per head in different countries
these fictitious discrepancies can only be noted: they cannot be measured. For while national income aggregates, as generally conceived,
purport to measure the net flow of goods and services produced they
do not measure the net flow of goods and services consumed.[1]

This, of course, is only one of a variety of conceptual and practical
problems which complicate the attempt to assess economic growth in
terms of national income estimates. Even where the basic statistics are
reasonably complete and conclusive—and the farther we go back in
time the less likely is this to be so—the changes in the content of the
national economy are such that we can never be certain of comparing
like with like. It is of the essence of economic development that the
flow of goods and services should change in character, in quality and
in the relative values attributed to them by the community in question.
If we measure the percentage change in real national income as between
one year and another by the usual method of valuing its components at
constant prices the figure we get will differ according to which year's
prices we apply. The wider the span of time, the greater the intervening
economic changes, the larger is the area of uncertainty marked out by
these differing answers. Nor is this all. New goods appear in the system
and old goods change in quality (the hand-made good may be inferior
or superior to its machine-made substitute) or in character (men may
eat wheat instead of rye or oats as their staple food). What it amounts
to is that long-term national income series can never be a precise
measure of economic development. At best they are a rough guide to
orders of magnitude in economic activity and to directions and rates of
change.

[1] For further discussion of this point see Simon Kuznets, *Economic Change* (1954),
pp. 176 ff.

Discussion of a country's economic experience in terms of its national income is based, implicitly if not always explicitly, on the assumption of a certain measure of economic unity, on the existence of something approaching a national market. Neither in theory nor in practice does it make sense to aggregate the money value of goods and services for an economy which contains more than one effective system of prices and within which the free movement of factors of production and commodities is restrained by more than the natural factors of distance and inertia. It is arguable that this lack of national economic unity severely limits the applicability of the national income concept to eighteenth-century England before the network of roads and canals became reasonably effective. Certainly the sharply differing structure of Ireland and its unique demographic and economic experience makes it difficult to interpret nineteenth-century estimates of national income for the United Kingdom, at any rate until the process of population decline had appreciably reduced the weight of the Irish component. Still more is it difficult to apply the national income yardstick to those European countries which, like Germany for most of the nineteenth century, were not even administratively unified.

Yet if we are looking for the origins of sustained economic growth in the German Empire we must go back before its unification in 1871 for the industrial revolution took shape in earlier decades. We can trace the beginnings of industrial change to direct imitation of the British example at the end of the eighteenth century. There were Germans as well as French and Belgians infiltrating into English factories in the 1780's and 1790's and smuggling back the secrets of the new technology to their homeland. Henderson cites several examples of new German textile factories equipped with British machinery and operated by British workmen at this early date.[1] But these were isolated developments. In spite of state subsidies, energetic entrepreneurs, and promising experiments, German industry remained essentially primitive and small-scale until the second half of the nineteenth century. Its development could have had little direct impact on national standards of living before mid-century.

In the agricultural sector, on the other hand, the transformation was more radical and far-reaching in its effects during the first half of the nineteenth century. The breaking of the traditional mould of German agriculture by the emancipation of the peasantry, for example, permitted an agricultural and a demographic revolution. Emancipation was complete by 1850: it had been largely accomplished in West Germany by 1830 and in East Germany by 1840. Its effect can be seen in a half-century of expansion in agricultural productivity. It has been

[1] W. O. Henderson, *Britain and the Industrial Revolution 1750-1870.*

estimated that between 1816 and 1865, partly as a result of the extension of the cultivated area and partly due to the more intensive and efficient methods of cultivation which emancipation made possible, the output of livestock increased by 213 per cent and of crops by 62 per cent—in relation to a population increase of about 59 per cent.[1] Since agriculture was by far the principal economic activity this points to an appreciable increase in average real incomes.

The stimulus to agriculture seems to have spent itself by the 1860's. Between 1865 and 1890 agricultural output is estimated to have expanded more slowly than population and at less than half the rate of the preceding half-century. It may have contributed to the initiation of a process of sustained growth, but it is not obvious that it formed part of such a process. In effect, for evidence of the origins of sustained growth, we need to look at developments in the non-agricultural sectors of the economy. Here the statistical series seems to exhibit two turning-points—one dating from the formation of the Zollverein in 1834 and one from the cyclical recovery of the 1850's.

The Zollverein came into action on 1 January 1834 and was gradually extended. It took the first major stride towards the economic unity of Germany and effectively brought the 23½ million people in the German states concerned into the international economy. In 1835, for example, the German mercantile tonnage was barely larger than its 1816 level. Within twenty years it had more than doubled and by 1870 it was three and a half times the 1816 level. Also in 1835 the German railway network began to be constructed. By 1851 3761 miles of railway had been built and by 1871, 12,253 miles—which was 25 per cent more than in France, despite the less propitious and unco-ordinated beginnings of the German system. These were substantial developments and may be presumed to have had repercussions which spread far beyond the industries concerned. The railways, in particular, created a powerful direct demand for capital, labour, and raw materials while under construction, and as soon as they were operative made markets and materials accessible to a wide range of industries. It was in the 1860's that Germany drew ahead of her continental rivals (France and Belgium) as a coal producer.

The industrial revolution seems to have gathered momentum in the quarter-century preceding unification. In the 1840's the typical German manufacturer was the peasant or the handicraftsman. As late as 1861 69·3 per cent of the population of Prussia was classified as rural—the corresponding proportion for 1816 was 73·5 per cent. But the rush to the towns and the transition to factory conditions and powered machines had begun in earnest. The cotton industry began to replace linen. By

[1] Estimates by W. G. Hoffmann, see W. W. Rostow (ed.) *The Economics of Take-off into Sustained Growth* (1963), p. 103.

the quinquennium 1871/5 the Empire's consumption of raw cotton had reached an annual average of 116,000 tons, which was more than the British average for 1825–30. The railways brought Germany's enormous coal and iron resources within the grasp of her industrialists and made large-scale operations a practical possibility at a relatively early stage in the industrial revolution.

The developments of the 1850's and the 1860's show up strongly in most of the existing statistical series and, significantly, in the national income estimates. Between 1851 and 1855 and the quinquennium which preceded unification total real national income (that is, national income measured at constant prices) expanded by a quarter. In terms of real incomes per head of the population this represented an annual rate of growth of about 0·8 per cent. At this rate the nation's productivity would have doubled in about ninety years. In fact, however, it doubled in less than half that time—in about forty years. For in the 1870's and 1880's the German economy was expanding at a rate which was beyond all previous experience and—as it happened—beyond all later experience even including the spectacular post-war recovery of the 1950's.[1] In the twenty years or so following the quinquennium 1871/5 the total real national income of the German Empire more than doubled and it was to increase by another 70 per cent before the outbreak of the First World War. By 1913 a nation of more than 66 million people, three-fifths of them townsmen, Germany was the leading industrial country of Europe.

There were two features of the German industrial revolution which distinguished it from its predecessors in Europe. The first was the vigour and rapidity with which it developed. The second was the degree to which it was dependent on political factors. The influence of the Zollverein and the unification have already been stressed. But more than this, German industrialization was a deliberate act of policy. The changes in the rate of growth of national income can be largely traced back to the conscious decisions of German economic policy makers.

The tradition of government interference in the economic system, indeed of direct participation in industry, was an old one. The Prussian government operated iron and leadworks and coal mines in the nineteenth century.[2] The German states brought in foreign technicians, protected local industry and provided much of the capital for the long-term financing of the railroads. In 1840, for example, 92 per cent of the

[1] Estimates of German national income for the century following 1850 were made by W. Hoffmann and J. H. Müller and published in *Das Deutsche Volkseinkommen 1851–1957* (Tübingen, 1959).
[2] Nationalized coal production is estimated to have accounted for a fifth of total Prussian coal output in 1851. W. O. Henderson, *The State and the Industrial Revolution in Prussia, 1740–1870* (1958), p. xviii.

Prussian railway lines were operated by private companies, in 1850 65 per cent and in 1860 5·5 per cent.[1] At the height of the international enthusiasm for free trade the ideal was abandoned in Germany long before the goal was reached. The significance of the industrial revolution, the extent to which it represented the application of scientific know-ledge to productive processes seems to have been more completely appreciated in Germany than anywhere else. German polytechnics and universities were generously supported state institutions from the first and provided the relatively rich resources of technical skill to which the rapid development of the German chemical and electrical industries was unquestionably due.

Neither of the two outstanding features of the German industrial revolution was, of course, peculiar to Germany. On the contrary, both have proved to be characteristic of most, if not all, late-comers to the industrial stage. Nor is it surprising that this should be so. In the first place, although German political traditions were undoubtedly import-ant, they were by no means the only factor which tended to enhance the role of the State in the process of industrialization, and there were more significant forces working in the same direction. It was natural enough that in countries where the conditions for rapid economic growth did not develop spontaneously, as they had done in Britain, men should seek to create them by conscious design, since both the economic and the politico-military implications of the industrial revolution pro-vided countries less favoured by nature and history with a powerful incentive to emulate the British example. As will be seen elsewhere in this volume, British achievements exercised a profound influence on German thought in the nineteenth century, and in much the same way the impact of the growing number of industrial powers has stimulated the demand for industrialization in the underdeveloped lands of today.

III. *The Late-comers to Industrialization in Europe*

But if the desire to promote economic development by political means was increased by the challenge of industrialization elsewhere, so, too, was the need. It was not simply a question of governments seeking to accelerate the pace of historical change by the removal of the political and social barriers to growth and the protection of nascent industries. For as time passed, it became less likely that economically backward countries would ever follow in the footsteps of the pioneers unless the state played a more direct part in the economic process, both as pro-ducer and customer. On the one hand, both the size of the market and

[1] Hoffmann, in W. W. Rostow (ed.), *op. cit.* p. 113.

the supply of capital were limited in backward countries by the low level of incomes, while on the other the continued progress of technology in the advanced countries meant that the capital required to initiate industrial projects and the market necessary to absorb their products became progressively larger. Not only did capital equipment increase in size and cost, but at the same time the focus of investment tended to shift from textiles and other consumer goods industries where capital costs per unit of output were relatively low, to industries where they were relatively high. Professor Hoffmann's index of industrial production suggests that in Britain, until the advent of the railway, the output of consumer goods industries increased at roughly the same rate as that of producer goods, but that after 1830 the latter forged ahead.[1] It seems likely that a similar pattern was followed in other countries for which statistics are lacking: certainly it is true that in most European countries in the nineteenth century the new technology was applied first in the textile industries, and particularly cotton. But two qualifications should be noted. In the first place, the late-comers had either to import machinery or to develop their capital goods industries relatively early if they were to install up-to-date plant and equipment which would enable them to compete on equal terms in world markets. Secondly, and perhaps more important, whereas in Britain a substantial increase in output and incomes took place before the country incurred the heavy capital expenses involved in railway building, in countries which did not enjoy Britain's natural advantages in respect of water transport, the process of growth could not gather momentum until an adequate transport system was already under construction. Hence the importance of railway building in the first phase of rapid economic growth in western Europe in the 1830's and 1840's, to which we have already referred, and hence, too, the importance which the producer goods industries, notably coal and iron, quickly assumed in the process of growth. It has been estimated that in Germany between 1835 and 1860 the output of producer goods grew more than three times as fast as that of consumer goods.[2]

Such considerations also help to explain why industrial development, once started, has usually proceeded more rapidly in the case of the late-comers than it did in the older industrial countries. For technological progress laid the basis for a more rapid rise in productivity than had been possible with the relatively primitive techniques available to the pioneers. And, although expensive investment in transport and heavy industries involved an immediate burden on limited resources, it also

[1] Walther G. Hoffmann, *British Industry, 1770–1950*, translated by W. O. Henderson and W. H. Chaloner (Oxford, 1955).
[2] Hoffmann, in W. W. Rostow (ed.) *op. cit.* pp. 106–8.

tended to increase the potential for long-term growth more rapidly
than concentration on industries catering mainly for the needs of consumption. Nor was the correlation between the extent of state intervention and the pace of industrial development simply a reflection of the
fact that the former was necessitated, and the latter caused, by the
increasing importance of capital-intensive industries in the initial stages
of industrialization. In so far as state intervention was inspired by
political and military motives, this was itself likely to accentuate the
emphasis on 'growth-potential' industries, since these industries also
constituted the foundation of the military power of the state. In Europe,
state enterprise had traditionally been associated with the armaments
industries and hence with mining and metallurgy, and nineteenth-
century government control was important in the construction and
operation of railways and public utilities.

   In the later cases of industrialization, the direct role of the state has
usually been much more in evidence than it was anywhere in western
Europe, and as we might expect most of these late-comers have achieved
even higher rates of industrial growth. It does not follow, however,
that they also exhibit unusually high rates of *economic* growth, as the
example of Tsarist Russia clearly shows. Until the latter part of the
nineteenth century modern industry was conspicuously absent in
Russia. In the eighteenth century, to be sure, she had ranked in
absolute, if not *per capita* terms, as a major industrial power. But with
the Industrial Revolution in England, Russia began to lose ground, and
in her case the period of stagnation and relative decline lasted much
longer than in the countries of western Europe. In 1860 she was by far
the most backward of the major European powers. Average real
incomes were probably roughly comparable with the Italian and,
according to one estimate, not more than half, and according to another
estimate less than one-third, the American level.[1] Only about 860,000
out of a total population of 74 millions were employed in industrial
establishments, and well over half of the national income was produced by a serf-worked agriculture, which absorbed an even larger
percentage of the working population. In the closing decades of the
nineteenth century there were, indeed, signs of significant changes in
the Russian economy. As in western Europe, these arose out of the

   [1] Raymond W. Goldsmith, 'The Economic Growth of Russia, 1860–1913',
Economic Development and Cultural Change, IX (April 1961), 475. Goldsmith's
estimate was derived by extrapolation from those given by Colin Clark in *Conditions of
Economic Progress* (1951 edition), for the eve of the First World War. If Prokopovicz's
estimate is taken as a basis, it would seem that in 1860 Russian incomes per head were
only about 30% of the American. As late as 1897, 75% of the population were
attached to agriculture, according to the (unreliable) census taken in that year.

gradual dissolution of the traditional agrarian structure and the development of a modern transport system. The first railway was built in 1836, but it was not until after Russia's defeat in the Crimean War that railway construction was undertaken on a large scale. Between 1855 and the 1880's the length of track increased from 850 miles to about 17,000, and the main period of activity came in the 1890's when about a third of the entire railway network built before 1900 was constructed. With the completion of the Trans-Siberian railway in 1904, the tempo slackened, but by 1914 Russia had 48,000 miles of track in use.

The construction of railways was accompanied by rapid industrial development which was most marked in the heavy industries, notably, coal, oil, iron and steel. Although the consumer goods industries, and particularly textiles, were absolutely larger throughout the period down to 1914 the bulk of new investment went into the heavy industries and these showed the highest rates of growth. Many of the new enterprises established during this period were up to date in organization and technique and were characterized by a remarkably high degree of concentration. Over half Russian factory workers were employed in enterprises with more than 500 operatives compared with a third or less in the United States. The small charcoal furnaces of the old Urals iron industry had given way to the new coke-fired furnaces in the Ukraine which were bigger than their German counterparts, 50 per cent larger than the comparatively antiquated plants still in use in Britain and about three-fifths the size of the huge furnaces employed in the United States. Moreover, Russian industry was becoming highly mechanized: by the eve of the First World War, Russia had already overtaken France and Germany in terms of horse-power per head of the industrial population, though she still lagged behind England and the U.S.A.[1]

These developments are reflected in the statistical series which point to a rapid expansion in the volume of Russian industrial output during this period. The scattered indices available suggest that between 1845 and 1863 industrial production was growing at the rate of $3\frac{1}{2}$–4 per cent per annum. Thereafter it gradually accelerated, reaching a peak of about 7 per cent in the great industrial boom in the last decade of the nineteenth century. It fell between 1900 and 1905, but rose sharply again in 1906 and continued to rise until 1914. Over the whole of the period from 1860 to 1913 it probably averaged about 5 per cent per annum or over 3 per cent per head of population.[2] These rates of

[1] P. I. Lyashchenko, *History of the National Economy of Russia to the 1917 Revolution* (New York, 1949), pp. 669 ff., cited by M. H. Dobb, *Soviet Economic Development since 1917* (1948), p. 34.

[2] Goldsmith, 'The Economic Growth of Russia, 1860–1913', *op. cit.* The figures are somewhat lower than those sometimes quoted—for example, by Alexander

growth were not exceptionally high in international comparison, but they were somewhat higher in relation to the rate of population growth than those obtaining in Germany and the United States at the time, and substantially greater than anything achieved in Britain even during the period of most rapid industrialization in the first half of the nineteenth century. The extent to which these developments in the industrial sector were reflected in increases in national income is somewhat obscured by the uncertainty as to the levels of national income in mid-century. If that level was as high as half of the contemporary American level, as some authorities believe it to have been, then the estimated rate of growth of aggregate national income in Russia between 1860 and the 1914 war was about $2\frac{1}{2}$ per cent per annum, and since the rate of population growth was comparatively high, it appears that the annual rate of increase of real incomes per head would in that case average about 1 per cent. If, on the other hand, the average *per capita* income in 1860 was, as other authorities believe it to have been, only one-third of the American, the rate of growth of aggregate national income between 1860 and 1914 might have exceeded $3\frac{1}{2}$ per cent per annum. Both figures, however, are comparable with those achieved in the early stages of the industrial revolution in older industrial countries, and even the higher figure is below the comparable rates of growth over certain periods in countries like the U.S.A. and Japan. Hence it seems likely that, despite the growth of industry in Russia, the gap between her and the advanced countries in the west in terms of incomes per head may not have appreciably narrowed and on some assumptions may even have widened during this period.

The reason is not far to seek. In view of the overwhelming predominance of the agricultural sector in the Russian economy at the beginning of the period, the growth of national income was still largely determined by the fortunes of agriculture. As late as 1913 approximately two-thirds of the population was engaged in agriculture and nearly half of the national income was derived from it. The rate of growth of agricultural output, which is estimated to have averaged 2 per cent per annum over this period, was not low compared with other countries, but it was substantially less than the growth of industrial output, and given the strong population increase it was not sufficient to produce a substantial rise in *per capita* incomes. The rural population grew nearly as fast as agricultural output during this period and

Gerschenkron, 'The Rate of Industrial Growth in Russia since 1885', *J. Econ. Hist.* Supplement VII (1947), 144–74. The higher estimates are derived from the index of Russian industrial production prepared under the direction of Kondratiev in the 1920's, which was based on a geometric, instead of an arithmetic mean of volume relatives, and is therefore less comparable with those available for other countries.

although the number of factory workers increased from 860,000 to about 3 million, industry still absorbed only about 5 per cent of the working population. In the long run, no doubt, the emancipation of the serfs in 1861 prepared the ground for a transformation of Russian agriculture no less fundamental than that which had taken place in other countries, but owing to the traditions of Russian society and the form which emancipation took these changes were slow to take effect. Even in 1913 the use of agricultural machinery, fertilizer and scientific methods was only just beginning and was limited mainly to some of the western provinces and to the agricultural crops. After being accelerated by Stolypin's reforms after the 1905 revolution, the incipient agricultural revolution was cut short by the outbreak of war and the Bolshevik revolution of 1917.

It is indeed open to question whether the process of industrialization had gone far enough to generate sustained economic growth in Russia before 1914. So long as the bulk of the Russian population was tied to a primitive agriculture, the industrial enclave was bound to remain small and its progress impeded by a limited home market and inadequate supplies of domestic capital. It is not surprising that the salient feature of the 'industrial revolution' in Tsarist Russia, apart from its dependence on the state, was its reliance on foreign capital and foreign technical and managerial personnel. It may be that this dependence began to diminish in the opening years of the twentieth century, but down to 1914 Russia remained in many ways an economic appendage of western Europe.

In some respects, industrialization was made more difficult by the revolution of 1917. It was not simply that by 1920, war, revolution and civil war resulted in a catastrophic fall in industrial production to about one-fifth of the 1913 level, which took some seven years to recover. More important, the break-up of the large estates and official hostility to the wealthier peasants, or kulaks, led to the proliferation of small-scale, uneconomic, peasant farms and a decline in production for the urban and foreign market. In 1926–7, when grain production was about 90 per cent of the pre-war level, the amount placed on the market outside the village was more than 50 per cent less.[1] It was this problem which the collectivization programme was designed to meet. There is little evidence that the introduction of a socialized agriculture and the development of large-scale mechanized farming resulted in an immediate increase in agricultural output.[2] But it did produce a marked

[1] M. Dobb, *Soviet Economic Development since 1917*, p. 217.
[2] Until 1938 official Soviet statistics claimed an increase of 50% in grain production between 1928 and 1937. But 1937 was a good year and the figures are misleading owing to changes in the methods of computing yields. Moreover, it is important to remember

increase in agricultural productivity which both released workers for other employment and made it possible to feed them. It appears that the absolute number employed in agriculture declined by 10–20 per cent between 1926 and 1939, while the proportion of the total population dependent on the land for their livelihood fell from 75 or 80 per cent to about 56 per cent.[1]

The change in the distribution of the working population would of itself have resulted in a substantial rise in the national income. In addition the growth of the economy was promoted during this period by an exceptionally high level of investment in heavy industries at the expense of a potential increase in current consumption. Unfortunately, a precise assessment of the outcome of this policy is rendered impossible by the nature of the statistical materials available. According to the official Soviet figures, aggregate national income was expanding during the first two Five-Year Plans (1928–37) at the unparalleled rate of 16 per cent per annum. The estimates of national income purport to be based on 1926–7 prices, but new commodities were at first valued at the price prevailing when they were introduced; and since the number of new commodities was large and prices were rising sharply in the 1930's, this alone may impart a marked upward bias to the figures. An attempt by a western critic to produce revised estimates in terms of 1926–7 prices yielded an average rate of growth during this period of about 8 per cent per annum.[2] Nor is this the only source of upward bias in the national income estimates. By adopting 1937 as the base year, another writer, using the same materials, arrived at an estimated growth rate of only 5 per cent.[3] More recent work in this field suggests that

that large numbers of livestock were slaughtered by the peasantry during the collectivization drive. According to the latest Soviet estimates, gross agricultural output in 1937 was only 8 % above, and in every other year before 1940 was below, the 1928 level. See E. Zaleski, *Planification de la Croissance et Fluctuations Economiques en U.R.S.S.* (Paris, 1962), pp. 350–4, where various Soviet and Western estimates are conveniently tabulated.

[1] Measurement of the decline in the agricultural population is complicated by changes in classification. For estimates of the actual numbers, see, *inter alia,* F. Lorimer, *The Population of the Soviet Union* (Geneva, 1946), p. 105; N. Jasny, *The Socialised Agriculture of the U.S.S.R.* (Stanford, California, 1949), p. 713.

[2] N. Jasny, *The Soviet Economy during the Plan Era* (Stanford, California, 1951).

[3] Gregory Grossman on 'National Income' in *Soviet Economic Growth,* Abram Bergson (ed.) (Evanston, Illinois, 1953), pp. 1–23. This, of course, reflects the familiar 'index number problem'. In an industrializing economy changes in prices and output tend to be inversely related, so that it is the goods whose output expands most rapidly that experience the steepest price declines. Hence a rate of growth calculated by evaluating national output in terms of the prices of the first year of the period under consideration will automatically be higher than the rate suggested by using the prices of the final year.

these estimates may be too low.[1] The fact that it is possible to obtain such wide discrepancies in the results for such a short period by choosing a different base year, however, illustrates the overwhelming difficulties involved in any attempt to measure the precise rate of change. The most that can be said is that the Soviet economy of the late 1920's and the 1930's was expanding with extraordinary rapidity and that the gap between its productivity and that of the western world was narrowing markedly.

Table 2. *Percentage Distribution of the World's Manufacturing Production*

Percentage of world total

	1870	1913	1936–8
U.S.A.	23·3	35·8	32·2
Germany	13·2	15·7	10·7
U.K.	31·8	14·0	9·2
France	10·3	6·4	4·5
Russia	3·7	5·5	18·5
Italy	2·4	2·7	2·7
Canada	1·0	2·3	2·0
Belgium	2·9	2·1	1·3
Sweden	0·4	1·0	1·3
Japan	} 11·0	1·2	3·5
India		1·1	1·4
Other countries		12·2	12·7

SOURCE. League of Nations, *Industrialization and World Trade* (1945). The 1936–38 percentages are approximations which should be used with reserve, for by then Russian output was large enough for possible errors in the statistics relating to it to obscure the distribution substantially.

By the outbreak of the First World War the great powers of Europe had either achieved an industrial revolution or had taken significant strides in the direction of industrialization. In 1870 there had been only five industrialized or seriously industrializing countries, four in Europe (the United Kingdom, France, Belgium, and Germany) and one outside Europe (the United States). These five countries are estimated to have accounted together for over four-fifths of the world's output of manufactures in 1870. By 1913 their share had fallen to under three quarters (see Table 2).

The other areas of Europe which had begun seriously to industrialize before the First World War and had accordingly begun to enjoy the

[1] Abram Bergson, *The Real National Income of Soviet Russia since 1928* (Cambridge, Mass., 1961), especially pp. 195–203 and 217. See also Bergson's comments on Grossman's paper in *Soviet Economic Growth, op. cit.* pp. 33–4. In the former book Bergson estimates the rate of growth for the period 1928–37 at only 5·5% in 1937 prices but at 11·9% in 1928 prices.

'mixed blessings of compound interest' were Italy and Scandinavia. The Italian case seems at first sight to disprove the thesis that the late starters tend to achieve a higher rate of growth than their predecessors for it grew in product per man year by only 0·7 per cent per annum over the period 1863–1913 and by no more than 1·7 per cent over the succeeding period, 1913–59. But the Italian case is complicated by the divergent experience of north and south. It was the north which led the way in industrializing and the south which exercised a powerful brake on the national rate of growth. At the time of unification the difference between north and south was more cultural and social than economic

Table 3. *Annual Percentage Rates of Growth*

	Starting year of data	Starting year to 1913		1913–59	
		Total product	Product per man year	Total product	Product per man year
Japan	1880	4·4	3·4	3·8	2·6
U.S.A.	1871	4·5	2·2	3·1	1·8
Canada	1872	4·0	1·9	3·1	1·5
Sweden	1863	3·1	2·4	2·4	1·7
Denmark	1872	3·2	2·1	2·2	1·2
Norway	1865	2·1	1·3	2·8	1·9
Germany	1853	2·6	1·5	2·4	1·4
France	1855	1·7	1·5	1·3	1·5
Italy	1863	1·4	0·7	2·2	1·7
U.K.	1857	2·6	1·6	1·3	0·8
Netherlands	1900	2·2	0·7	2·6	1·3

SOURCE. *National Institute Economic Review* (July 1961).

though it has been estimated that average taxable income in the south was approximately 21 per cent below that of the north in 1890.[1] In 1871, however, it is doubtful whether the gap in average incomes was very marked over the two regions. Structurally they were quite similar. In 1871 the percentage of adult males engaged in agricultural occupations was 55 per cent in the north, 54 per cent in the centre and 52 per cent in the south (which however had an appreciable number of fishermen): but by 1936 the agricultural proportion had fallen to 36 per cent in the north, 41 per cent in the centre and was still 45 per cent in the south (again excluding fishermen). By 1951 average taxable income in the south was barely a fifth of that in the north. So that for Italy the national rates in Table 3 cloak unduly disparate regional rates, ranging from a virtually stationary state in the stagnant south to a relatively

[1] H. Saville, 'Statistical Sampling: An Adaptation to Italian Economic Development', *Econ. Hist. Rev.* (1956).

rapid growth in productivity in the industrializing north. And if the comparison between Italy and the United Kingdom in Table 4 shows little change in real product per head over the eight or nine decades following unification this provides no indication of the change in relative average productivity in the industrial north of Italy.

Table 4. *Level of Real Product per Head in Relation to that of United Kingdom*

	1871/5	1900/4	1909/13	1938	1959
U.K.	100	100	100	100	100
U.S.A.	84	116	126	129	181
Canada	74	89	101	86	121
France	—	—	91	82	95
Netherlands	—	76	77	80	92
Denmark	66	71	85	93	100
Norway	66	52	58	87	99
Sweden	61	63	76	97	124
Germany	61	68	73	82	96
Italy	54	38	42	48	55
Japan	—	11	12	24	26

SOURCE. *National Institute Economic Review* (July 1961).

The beginnings of sustained growth in the Scandinavian countries can be traced back to the 1850's and 1860's when British free trade policy opened up a new range of opportunities in overseas trade. Sweden, which had the iron, if not the coal, demanded by the old industrialism of the nineteenth century, set the pace. A railway boom got under way in the 1870's and domestic gross capital formation rose from under 6 per cent in the 1860's to nearly 14 per cent in the 1890's. The expansion thus begun continued after the railway boom had died down and the industries which justified it—timber and iron—had come up against falling world prices, foreign tariff walls and growing international competition. New industries took over from the declining ones—pulp-making from timber, planed wood and matches from unplaned boards, refined steel and engineering industries from the old pig iron trade. Hydro-electric sources of power were systematically exploited in the early twentieth century. Meanwhile, the agrarian population declined from 75 per cent in 1861 to 61 per cent in 1891 and then to 48 per cent in 1911, by which time the decline in absolute numbers in agriculture had already begun. With this rapid transformation to an industrial system went a high rate of economic growth. In the half-century preceding 1913 Sweden's rate of growth in product per man-year seems to have been faster than that of any other European or North American country and before the beginning of the Second World War her level of real product per head was not far short of that of the United Kingdom and apparently above that of either Germany or France.

When Swedish industry began to quicken and expand in the mid-nineteenth century Denmark was probably a more advanced country in terms of agricultural and commercial productivity. Like Britain she had enjoyed a brilliant expansion in commerce and agriculture at the end of the eighteenth century while the great European powers were pinned down by war, but her disastrous entry into the war in 1807-14 brought this expanding phase to an abrupt conclusion. Most of her merchant marine fell into the hands of the enemy, her overseas connections were broken, her government went bankrupt and after the war agriculture itself was hit by falling prices. It was in the middle of the century when the British market opened up to Danish grain, butter and livestock that expansion was strongly resumed and in the four decades before the First World War her aggregate national product was growing as fast as that of Sweden and her product per man-year roughly as fast. By the end of the nineteenth century 38 per cent of her population lived in towns, agriculture contributed less than 30 per cent of her domestic product and about 13 per cent of the national product went to capital formation.

Something in the nature of an industrial revolution was taking shape in Denmark in this period though, paradoxically enough, the technological breakthrough came in agriculture rather than in industry. Denmark, with no tradition of factory industry, and no mineral or water resources, was at a serious disadvantage in terms of the conventional industrial revolution of the nineteenth century. So when the 1870's brought increasing competition from American and Dutch grain exports in British markets, she applied to agriculture the crucial, cost-reducing innovations which must underlie an increase in national product per head. In the 1880's and 1890's Denmark became a net importer of grain and concentrates, mechanized and reorganized her dairy industry on a co-operative basis and turned agriculture into a kind of processing industry. Agriculture, which accounted for 60 per cent of Danish exports by the turn of the century, provided the foreign exchange necessary to finance social overhead capital such as railways and port equipment, and stimulated urbanization and industrialization by providing a direct demand for construction activity and distribution services and an expanding rural market for manufactured consumer's goods.

Norwegian experience in the nineteenth century was parallel in some respects to Denmark and in some respects to Sweden. Being politically united to Denmark until 1814 it shared in the liberal trade expansion up to 1807 and the disastrous war with England. Like both Denmark and Sweden it revived with British free trade in the late 1840's and 1850's. But its technological breakthrough was delayed until the early twentieth century when the progress in hydro-electric technology compensated for its lack of coal by turning its waterfalls into potential energy. Between 1865 and 1913 Norway's average national product is estimated to have grown appreciably more slowly than for the other Scandinavian countries, but in the following four or five decades she took the lead. So that by 1959 her level of product per head appears to have been much the same as for the United Kingdom, France, Germany or Denmark though probably lower than that of Sweden.

IV. *Economic Growth for Europe's Overseas Descendants*

Before the end of the nineteenth century, the industrial revolution had begun to spread and to generate sustained growth outside Europe. It spread first to the overseas descendants of Europe. In the story of the international spread of the industrial revolution the experience of the countries which were largely peopled from western Europe—North America and Australasia and parts of South America and Africa, for example—differs markedly from that of the rest of the world. They differed in the starting-point from which they began to industrialize, in the way they achieved the transformation to an industrial system and in the levels of real income to which it carried them. It might almost be said of some of them that they brought over the essentials of an industrial revolution—pre-fabricated as it were—as part of their cultural heritage from the countries from which they came and that it merely remained for them to put it into practice in a new resource environment. Certainly they made their adaptation more expertly and less painfully than their European ancestors or ex-compatriots and they achieved standards of living which were well above European levels in the countries from which they came.

The United States is of course the outstanding example of successful industrialization by the descendants of western Europe. It is pre-eminent among the countries which have been described as 'born free'. It achieved its nationhood at a time when the first steps in the transition to an industrial society had already been taken in the Old World: and many of its subsequent settlers came from the new industrial order. Being a new country it offered few of the obstacles to industrial growth which were encountered in communities with strong pre-industrial traditions—save possibly in the southern states where a slave-based plantation economy was firmly entrenched at an early stage.

Throughout the period since the United States came into existence its high productivity and evident growth potential had been a source of European amazement and envy. Even before independence the Americans seem to have discovered the secret of economic growth. Adam Smith, for example, writing on the threshold of the first industrial revolution commented on the high wages and low prices enjoyed by the American colonists. At that stage the American colonies contained nearly 2½ million inhabitants (that is, roughly a quarter of the population of Great Britain) and accounted for about a sixth of British overseas trade. This little population had doubled by the end of the century and doubled again by 1825—largely as a result of natural increase. It was still largely peopled by the descendants of British migrants and nearly half of its exports went to Britain, which provided about 40 per cent of its imports.

It is unlikely that the new nation grew rapidly in productivity in the first half-century of its existence, but in absolute terms its growth was impressive for its population was doubling every generation. The French wars opened up golden opportunities by giving the United States control of a substantial part of the world carrying trade and of the lucrative tropical trades. Then, as later, in the twentieth century, the United States benefited from European internecine conflicts and its rate of growth shot up as its European competitors battled desperately for survival. The prices of United States exports and freight rates earned by United States shipping soared while the prices of British manufactures to the United States rose only moderately. The expansion in foreign trade stimulated the growth of ports (urbanization increased from 5 to 7 per cent), of turnpikes and of subsidiary industry (shipbuilding, railmaking, rope-making, etc.). The economy remained essentially pre-industrial however for the first few decades of the nineteenth century. Seventy-three per cent of the gainfully-occupied population was estimated to have been engaged in agricultural activities at the turn of the century and four decades later, in 1840, the proportion was still about 69 per cent. Meanwhile, American average income grew[1]—sometimes

[1] R. F. Martin's estimates indicating a continuous fall in real incomes per head over the period 1799–1839 do not stand up to the criticism of later scholars, but progress was erratic and North, for example, has concluded that 'although Martin's methods will not stand scrutiny, his conclusion that *per capita* real income was higher in 1799 than it was to be again for half a century appears to be correct'. See Robert F. Martin, *National Income in the United States 1799 to 1938* (1939). Simon Kuznets, 'National Income Estimates for the period prior to 1870', *Income and Wealth of the United States, Trends and Structure* (Income and Wealth Series, II, Cambridge, 1952). William Nelson Parker and Franklee Whartenby, 'The Growth of Output before 1840', *Trends in the American Economy in the Nineteenth Century* (Studies in Income and Wealth, XXIV, Princeton, 1960). Douglass C. North, 'Early National Income Estimates of the

quite rapidly, as in the early 1800's; sometimes very slowly as in the period following Waterloo when it had to adjust to a recrudescence of European competition on the high seas and to falling freight rates. But it seems unlikely on the whole that average national income was growing at more than half of one per cent per annum in the first half-century or so after independence.[1] The turning-point seems to have come in the late 1830's when the industrialization that was already developing in New England in the 1820's began to gather a massive momentum. It was then that the economy graduated from what Schumpeter has called 'simple expansion along obvious lines'[2] and began to exhibit the flexibility, the drive and the immense adaptability that were to be the special characteristics of American economic growth.

There were three main characteristics by which the economic growth of the United States has been distinguished from that of other countries over the past century or so. The first was its vigour, the second its secular steadiness and the third its internal variety. The almost legendary 'dynamism' of American growth was already evident by the middle of the nineteenth century. Over the period 1839–79 the gross national product of the United States was estimated to have been growing at the remarkable rate of 4·3 per cent per annum, and in per head terms at slightly over 1½ per cent per annum.

Other countries (notably Japan, Russia and Sweden) were to achieve comparable rates of long-term growth, but always from a much lower starting-point. The extraordinary feature of the fast United States rates is that they soared from levels which were already high in the international spectrum. Contemporary estimates of domestic product per head about 1840 show the United States at second place tied with Holland and Belgium, with the French average 20 per cent below.[3] By 1879 it is doubtful whether the United States was second even to the United Kingdom and by the 1890's it was unquestionably the richest country in the world.

In aggregate terms of course the real national product of the United States grew rather more slowly than this in ensuing periods—at about 3·7 per cent per annum over the next forty years, 1879–1919 and at almost 3 per cent per annum from 1919 to 1959. But the deceleration

United States', *Essays in the Quantitative Study of Economic Growth* (*Economic Development and Cultural Change*, vol. IX, no. 3, April 1961).

[1] See the testimony of Raymond Goldsmith in United States Congress, Joint Economic Committee, Employment, Growth and Price Levels. Hearings (86th Congress 1st Session), part II (Washington 1959), p. 271.

[2] J. A. Schumpeter, *Business Cycles*, I, 285.

[3] Ezra Seaman's estimates quoted by Robert E. Gallman 'Estimates of American National Product made before the Civil War', *Essays in the Quantitative Study of Economic Growth*, p. 40.

was due to a slackening of the rate of population growth. In terms of incomes per head the trend over the 120 years 1839–1959 varied little although there was some acceleration in the middle period when it reached 1·76 per cent per annum compared with 1·55 per cent in 1839–79 and 1·64 per cent in 1919–59.[1]

This overall steadiness, however, masks wide regional disparities in income levels and rates of growth. The changing regional distribution of aggregate incomes reflects the westward expansion of industry. In 1840, for example, 58 per cent of the nation's personal incomes were earned in the eastern region, the cradle of American industry, 28½ per cent in the southern states and 13½ per cent in the central and west regions. By 1900 the states of the centre and west accounted for 44 per cent of the nation's incomes and the south for under 15½ per cent. By 1950 the share of the south had begun to rise, to 20½ per cent, and that of the centre and west had expanded to 46½ per cent.[2] More striking, however, were the regional differentials in incomes per head and in the corresponding rates of growth. These are illustrated in Table 5. In the first half of the nineteenth century it was the north-east that took the initiative and set the pace. It accounted for three quarters of employment in manufacturing in 1850[3] and its rate of growth was well above the national average. In 1840 average incomes in the New England and Middle Atlantic states were about a third above the national average and the South Atlantic states 70 per cent of it. By 1880 the New England and Middle Atlantic states had raised their level to 141 per cent of the national average and the South Atlantic average had sunk to 45 per cent. Since 1920 levels of incomes per head have tended to converge as the southern states have accelerated and the north-eastern states slackened their rates of growth. Between 1929 and 1957 average incomes in the south-eastern and south-western states were growing at almost 3 per cent per annum which was twice the rate of New England and the Middle Atlantic states.[4] Thus the relatively steady national rate of growth in the United States has been achieved by handing on the torch to a succession of industrializing regions.

At the beginning of the twentieth century, there were five or six countries which could be said to have undergone an industrial revolution. They were the United Kingdom, the United States, Germany,

[1] Raymond Goldsmith, *loc. cit.*
[2] Richard A. Easterlin, 'Interregional Differences in *per capita* Income, Population and Total Income, United States, 1840–1950', *Trends in the American Economy in the Nineteenth Century, op. cit.*
[3] Douglass C. North, 'Industrialization in the United States, 1815–1860' (paper presented to a conference of the International Economic Association, September 1960).
[4] Raymond Goldsmith, *loc. cit.*

France, Belgium and possibly Holland, though France and Holland were still far from being industrial countries. A handful of other countries—the Scandinavian countries, Japan and Russia for example—were evidently in the early stages of transformation to the industrial system. In Italy the industrial spurt stimulated by the railway boom of the 1880's had failed to gather momentum. The only signs of modern economic development in the Iberian peninsula at the turn of the century were between 8000 and 9000 miles of railway track, mechanization of the textile mills of Catalonia and a few Spanish steel mills which had taken advantage of the cheap coal brought by English ships in search of Spanish ore.

Table 5. *Personal Income per Head in each Region of the United States*

As percentage of United States average 1840–1950

Regions	1840	1860	1880	1900	1920	1940
United States	100	100	100	100	100	100
North-east	135	139	141	137	132	124
New England	132	143	141	134	124	121
Middle Atlantic	136	137	141	139	134	124
North Central	68	68	98	103	100	103
East N. Central	67	69	102	106	108	112
West N. Central	75	66	90	97	87	84
South	76	72	51	51	62	65
South Atlantic	70	65	45	45	59	69
East S. Central	73	68	51	49	52	55
West S. Central	144	115	60	61	72	70
West	—	—	190	163	122	125
Mountain	—	—	168	139	100	92
Pacific	—	—	204	163	135	138

SOURCE. Richard A. Easterlin, 'Regional Income Trends 1840–1950', *American Economic History*, ed. Seymour Harris.

If the industrial revolution had taken shape in a relatively few countries by the end of the nineteenth century it had already had a decisive impact on world economic growth. Countries which could supply the primary products required by expanding markets in the industrialized countries could enjoy some of the benefits of the transformation to an industrial system at second hand, and could achieve quite rapid rates of growth at pre-industrial levels of economic organization. Canada was an outstanding example, for the Canadian colonies were able to attach themselves simultaneously to two of the world's leading industrial economies. The breakdown of the British imperialistic trading system in the 1840's forced them to reassess their international trading opportunities and in so doing they accepted a stake in their vigorously expanding neighbour to the south. Confederation in 1867 created a nation which was strong enough to maintain its political independence and so retain a choice in the nature of its economic dependence. For most of the second half of the nineteenth century 35–60 per cent of Canada's exports flowed either to the United Kingdom or to the United States, while less than 12 per cent went to other destinations. These two great markets gave Canada access to a wide range of economic opportunities. Her total exports expanded from about $10\frac{1}{2}$ per cent of gross national product in 1851 to about $18\frac{1}{2}$ per cent in 1900.[1]

By developing an export trade of these dimensions Canada was able to begin the rapid climb to higher standards of living without making any substantial change in the degree of her own industrialization. Over the same half-century the share of the manufacturing group of industries rose from about $18\frac{1}{2}$ per cent of Canada's gross national product to about 21 per cent. Yet from the 1850's when the railway building and real estate boom marked the economy's emergence from the 'wood and water' stage of development, the rate of growth has been high by pre-industrial standards. The volume of goods and services produced is estimated to have grown at an average (compound) rate of rather more than 3 per cent per annum over the period 1851–1900: in per head terms the corresponding rate was a little over $1\frac{1}{2}$ per cent per annum.

When the First World War began, however, the process of transformation to an industrial system, and all that it implies, was well under way in Canada. In the 1890–1910 period the number of persons working in manufacturing doubled, real output rose 130 per cent and fixed capital employed in industry increased $2\frac{3}{4}$ times in real value. Between 1901 and 1911 machinery used on farms more than doubled and the number of gainfully-occupied agricultural workers per thousand acres of farmland declined by 32 per cent. By 1910 $45\frac{1}{2}$ per cent of the population lived in urban areas. In this first decade of the twentieth century the Canadian economy surged forward into rapid industrialization. Its population was increasing at the rate of about 2·9 per cent per annum and its labour force at nearly 4·2 per cent. By 1913 its output of goods and services was more than twice its volume in 1899. In effect, over the four decades ending in 1913 Canada's product per man-year grew faster than that of the United Kingdom and not much more slowly than that of the United States.

In Australia too there was rapid expansion of the national income in

[1] For quantitative evidence on Canada's economic growth and changing structure, 1850–1935, see the estimates of O. J. Firestone in 'Canada's Economic Development 1867–1953', *Income and Wealth, Series VII* (1958) and 'Canada's Changing Economy in the Second Half of the Nineteenth Century', *Studies in Income and Wealth*, vol. XXIV, *Trends in the American Economy in the Nineteenth Century* (1960).

the second half of the nineteenth century and the British migrants managed to achieve standards of living which were on the average probably well above those of their contemporaries in the British Isles. Many of them owed their good fortune to the gold rush of the 1850's but even in the 1840's the average Australian enjoyed a standard of living which compared favourably with that of the ruling classes in the mother country. He ate better and was taller, heavier and healthier than his British counterpart. Transportation to the eastern mainland was abolished in 1840 and in the second quarter of the century some 223,000 free immigrants arrived in Australia. A simply organized pastoral industry supported a growing population on the strength of the increasing world demand for industrial raw materials. By 1851 with 438,000 inhabitants Australia had become the chief exporter of wool to world markets: her sheep numbered nearly 17½ million compared with fewer than ½ million in 1821. There are no national income estimates available for this period but it is evident that the national product grew at least in step with and probably appreciably faster than a population which increased tenfold between 1823 and 1850.

The gold discoveries jerked up this rapidly expanding economy to an entirely new level of activity and affluence. Within a decade the population almost trebled. In the eleven years 1851–61 gold to the value of at least £124 millions was raised in Australia. Nor was the expansion confined to the mining sector. The area under crop doubled itself within eight years and the value of wool exported more than doubled between 1850 and 1860. Freight rates on exports fell as the outward shipping space expanded with the growing import traffic in men and goods. Wages soared. The country had suddenly become rich, and for three more decades it went on growing richer. We cannot say what happened to average incomes per head over the turbulent years of the gold rush—except that they certainly rose substantially— but by 1861 it is estimated that the gross national income was running at a level that yielded an annual average of nearly £50 per head of the population.[1] This was a high income by contemporary standards even if it was somewhat erratically come by and somewhat unequally distributed. The corresponding average for the United Kingdom in 1861 was almost exactly half. And even if we leave out the Irish who were still battling with a legacy of disastrous poverty—the average annual income for the inhabitants of the industry state of Great Britain (then more advanced than any of its rivals) worked out at under £30.

It is hardly surprising then that Australia continued to act as a magnet to British labour and capital in the decades immediately following the

[1] N. G. Butlin, 'The Shape of the Australian Economy, 1861–1900', *Econ. Rec.* (April, 1958).

golden decade. In 1861 about 53 per cent of the population of Australia was United Kingdom born and over the next three decades the inflow continued at a brisk pace: about 733,000 immigrants arrived from the United Kingdom in the years 1860–89, more than half of them being government assisted. Perhaps it is also not surprising that a hopeful active population should have managed to sustain a relatively high rate of economic growth even when the industry which had filled their pockets had begun to decline. Yet for a country which depended so largely on the pastoral industry this was no ordinary achievement. Over the three decades following 1860 gross domestic product measured at constant prices rose at a compound rate of growth of 4·9 per cent per annum. Only the rapidly industrializing United States for which the corresponding rate was over 5 per cent grew faster during this period. In per head terms of course, the Australian rate of growth was much lower, because population itself was increasing at over 3½ per cent per annum. Nevertheless, the rise in national productivity in Australia was by no means negligible in the three expansive decades following the gold rush. In the period 1861–77 gross domestic product per head of the work force was growing at over 3 per cent per annum and over the whole period 1861–89 it was growing by 2·2 per cent which compares favourably with the pre-1913 long-term rates of growth in product per man-year for most of the industrialized or industrializing countries of Europe and North America.[1]

Australia, though expanding strongly, remained primarily dependent on the British economy for its capital, its labour force and its markets, however. It was still essentially at a pre-industrial stage of development but the value of its overseas exports fell from about 30 per cent of national product in 1861 to about 12½ per cent in 1887. When British investors became more cautious or diverted their funds to channels nearer home and when wool prices sagged, Australian producers, saddled with heavy burdens of debt and of excess capacity, found themselves in difficulties. The depression of the 1890's was severe and prolonged and it was not until 1909 that average real incomes regained their 1891 peak. The collapse of world trade and the virtual cessation of British overseas investment in the inter-war period brought fresh checks to Australian economic development. Although industrialization continued, so that by the outbreak of the Second World War the share of manufacturing in gross domestic product had reached 19 per cent and total national output was 40 per cent above its 1913 level, this was accompanied by a negligible rate of growth in real income per head.

[1] N.G. Butlin, *Australian Domestic Product, Investment and Foreign Borrowing, 1861–1938/39* (1962).

The seeds of modern economic growth carried overseas by Europe's migrants took root most effectively in the empty lands. Elsewhere the settlers constituted prosperous enclaves in economies whose growth depended on their ability to supply primary products to the industrial countries and where technical progress was virtually confined to the European sector. In South Africa, where there were immense resources of such valuable primary products as gold and diamonds, relatively high rates of growth were achieved. Real national income per head in the Union grew at an estimated rate of nearly 1·8 per annum on the average over the period 1911–38.[1] On the other hand, where—as in India—the innovating settlers were enormously outnumbered by the traditional communities the per head rate of economic growth received little stimulus from contact with the growing economies of the world. Whether average real incomes rose or fell in India over the century or so preceding independence is a matter of controversy. On the most optimistic assessment of the data, however, it is difficult to see how they can have grown over the long period at much more than half of one per cent per annum.[2] In the West Indian colony of Jamaica, where the white population was under 5 per cent of the total and declined to under 2 per cent, it is estimated that average product per head fell in the three or four decades following emancipation, and then rose at a slowly accelerating rate which ranged from 0·2 per cent per annum over the period 1870–90 to 0·7 per cent over the period 1910–30.[3]

It would appear then that the Europeans who shook the dust of the old world off their feet and started a new life in empty countries overseas had an advantage over those they left behind. Perhaps it was because emigration was a selective factor in itself and ensured that the settlers were on the whole more enterprising and more determined to make their fortunes than those who stayed behind and endured. Perhaps it was because it was destructive of out-worn institutions: those who moved were able to shed much of the traditional baggage of a pre-industrial society, many of the customs which were inhibiting to an industrial capitalistic mode of economic organization. Rostow, for example, has argued that, for the nations that were 'born free', 'the process of their transition to modern economic growth was mainly

[1] S. H. Frankel and H. Herzfield, 'An Analysis of the Growth of the National Income of the Union in the Period of Prosperity before the War', *South African J. Econ.* vol. XII (1944).

[2] In 'A Preliminary Study of the Growth of National Income in India 1857–1957', a paper presented to the Asian Conference of the International Association for Research in Income and Wealth, M. Mukherjee estimates that average *per capita* incomes rose at about 0·4 % per annum over the period 1857/63 to 1896/1904 and at 0·5 % per annum over the period 1896/1904 to 1946/54.

[3] G. Eisner, *Jamaica 1830–1930* (1961).

economic and technical. The creation of the pre-conditions for take-off
was largely a matter of building social overhead capital—railways,
ports and roads—and of finding an economic setting in which a shift
from agriculture and trade to manufacture was profitable.'[1]

But what about the other nations of the new world, the Latin
American countries? Some of those involved settlement by Europeans
in largely empty countries, though in some of the central American
countries there was a substantial indigenous Indian population. What
about Argentina, however, which effectively shook off the Spanish
yoke in 1810, but which was still relatively unindustrialized, relatively
poor, and stagnating in the middle of the twentieth century? When the
United Nations Statistical Office, for example, drew up a comparative
table of national incomes per head in the early 1950's, Argentina's
average worked out at about a quarter of that of the United States.

It is significant of course that the Latin American countries drew the
bulk of their population not from western Europe but from southern
Europe—mainly from the Spanish and Italian peninsulas. Perhaps it is
also significant that if we compare Latin American standards of living
as measured by the United Nations national income averages it appears
that they too are at a higher level than the countries from which their
settlers originated. A century ago, there were rather more than $1\frac{1}{2}$
million people in Argentina, most of them of Spanish origin. Between
1857 and the beginning of the First World War nearly $3\frac{1}{2}$ million
immigrants entered the country. A high proportion of them were
Spaniards—existing settlers exert a strong magnetic attraction to new
settlers from their country of origin. But between 1857 and 1926
$47\frac{1}{2}$ per cent of Argentina's migrants were Italians, many of them from
southern Italy. There were Germans and Russians and English and
Scots among the migrants who settled permanently in Argentina, in
the past century, but it is fair to say that the institutions, customs and
social values which are characteristic of the country are south European
rather than west European, Latin rather than Anglo-Saxon. There is
little doubt that average incomes in Argentina are somewhat higher
than those in southern Italy and Spain.

There is a considerable consensus of opinion to the effect that the
cultural heritage, the system of economic and social values and institutions passed on by Spain to her colonies was different in character and
result to the heritage of the western European settlements. This is
generally attributed to the fact that the Spanish moved in to the new
world before the traditional pre-industrial society had begun to break
up. Veblen, the American sociologist, put the point most strongly when
he referred to the fact that the Spanish and Portuguese colonizations

[1] W. W. Rostow, *Stages of Economic Growth*, pp. 17–18.

came at a time when 'these South Europeans were still living very busily in a more archaic and barbaric phase of the European culture, which belongs at a point in the sequence ante-dating the natural rights that make democracy' and described the Spanish and Portuguese colonizations as 'an enterprise in pillage, influenced and inflated by religious fanaticism and martial vanity'.[1]

During the turbulent half-century or so of military rule that followed independence there is no evidence to suggest that the Argentine economy was growing in productivity, though the aggregate national income probably expanded more or less in step with a slowly growing population. In the last quarter of the nineteenth century, however, after experiencing a decade or so of more enlightened and constitutional government, the Republic managed to reap some direct and indirect benefit from the technological progress associated with the industrial revolution in western Europe and North America. In 1872 a system of artificial refrigeration was invented and in 1882 a new freezing-plant was installed in Buenos Aires. By 1890 over 6000 miles of railroad stretched inland from Buenos Aires and, with the aid of British capital and Italian and Spanish immigrants, Argentina was able to supply fresh meat and cereals to growing industrial markets. During the half-century following 1875 Argentina's trade increased some eighteenfold. In the two decades preceding 1913 the area under cultivation increased nearly fivefold and the population doubled. By 1914, with 36 per cent of her population in towns of 20,000 or more, Argentina was one of the most urbanized countries in the world and one of the ten leading commercial countries.

Argentina's peak period of growth—perhaps the only period of sustained growth in incomes per head that the country has ever experienced —coincided with the secular export boom of 1880–1929 with which it was associated. For roughly half a century the economy expanded at a rate which may have exceeded $1\frac{1}{4}$ per cent per annum per head of the population.[2] It became the richest country in South America in terms of incomes per head and the most industrialized in terms of the percentage of national product earned in manufacturing and construction industry. But it had not achieved an industrial revolution and even in the 1950's after the forced industrialization and declining output of the past two decades the share of gross domestic product attributable to manufacturing industry was only about 23 per cent. And if its economic performance was superior to that of Spain it fell behind that of northern Italy.

[1] T. Veblen, *Absentee Ownership and Business Enterprise in Recent Times*, p. 121.
[2] Estimates made by the Economic Commission for Latin America suggest a rate of growth of $1\frac{1}{4}\%$ per annum in incomes per head over the period 1900/4 to 1925/29.

V.   *The Spread of the Industrial Revolution to other Non-European Nations*

Were it not for Japan it could be said that the Industrial Revolution was
a European phenomenon—confined in its incidence to the countries of
Europe and their overseas settlements. But Japan was the spectacular
exception to the rule. After a century and a quarter of isolation from
the rest of the world and virtually complete stagnation in both population and productivity the Japanese responded to the western example
and challenge with a rapidity and verve that are unequalled for any other
nation. They took their starting-point from a more primitive level of
economic organization than any European nation.

Until the Meiji Restoration of 1868, about one-fifth of Japan was
owned by the family and immediate vassals of the military dictators
who ruled the country, the Tokugawa *Shogun*, while the rest of the
land, as in medieval Europe, was held by the class of feudal lords, the
daimyo. Their retainers, the *samurai*, had once held land in return for the
performance of military service, but just as in Europe in the 'bastard
feudalism' of the later Middle Ages, the links between tenure and service had been broken, so in Japan in the sixteenth century the retainers
began to live in towns and to receive a maintenance in rice for themselves and their families from their lords. The bulk of the population
were peasants, who, like European serfs, were tied to the soil and paid
rent for their holdings in service and kind. In the towns, industry was
under the control of gilds, while in the countryside the domestic system
prevailed, though there were some small factories owned by the *Shogun*
and the feudal lords.[1] In these conditions, economic progress tended to
be slow and spasmodic and, again as in pre-industrial Europe, there
seems to have been a marked correlation between the ebb and flow of
economic activity and demographic trends. In the seventeenth century,
a growth in numbers, connected with an extension of the cultivated
area, had been checked, and in the eighteenth and early nineteenth
centuries a precarious balance between population and food supply had
stabilized the population at some 28–30 millions.[2]

In spite of attempts to prevent change, the traditional form of society
had for long been undermined by the slow development of a commercial economy, and when the country was forcibly opened by western
traders in the 1850's and 60's, the whole structure collapsed. After 1868

[1] For these and further details, see G. C. Allen, *A Short Economic History of Modern
Japan, 1867–1937* (1946), pp. 9 ff.

[2] W. W. Lockwood, *The Economic Development of Japan: Growth and Structural
Change, 1868–1938* (Princeton, New Jersey, 1954), pp. 3–4.

the Restoration government set to work to reconstruct the economy on western lines. Feudalism was abolished, foreign techniques were introduced, new enterprises were established, either by the state itself or with government assistance, communications were improved and foreign trade, which had formerly been subject to severe restrictions, was actively encouraged. In the early years the importance of the state was considerable, but as the process of growth gathered a momentum of its own, the direct role of the government in economic activities tended to diminish. In the ensuing decades, Japan underwent a transformation which has few parallels in modern history. It is unlikely that the rate of economic growth ever attained the remarkable proportions which characterized the Soviet economy in the era of the first Five-Year Plans. But it achieved a high level much earlier in time and was sustained over a longer period, since Japan did not suffer the disasters which the First World War and subsequent upheavals inflicted on the Russian economy. Estimates of the Japanese national income vary considerably and in recent years the tendency has been to revise the rates of growth deduced from them in a downward direction.[1] But on present evidence it seems that from about 1880 until the mid-twentieth century, the Japanese performance, in relation to her rate of population growth, which by then was considerable, was apparently without parallel in any other country.[2] Statistics of national income are not available before 1878, but it is probable that the upward movement had begun before that date. Foreign trade had been increasing since 1858, and it was in the 1870's that the first railways were built and new industrial enterprises began to be established. Thereafter the rate of growth of aggregate incomes almost certainly accelerated, reaching a peak of over 5 per cent per annum in the 1890's, before falling slightly in the opening years of the twentieth century. In the 1920's it again rose to over 5 per cent and maintained a level of over 4 per cent even in the depressed years of the early 1930's. Over the whole period from 1880 until the Japanese attack on China in 1937, the average rate of growth of aggregate real incomes was over 4 per cent per annum, or about 3 per cent per head of the population.

This achievement is the more remarkable when we remember that in the 1860's the proportion of the total population engaged in a primitive agriculture was as high as in Tsarist Russia. Moreover, the

[1] The earlier estimates are reviewed by Yuzo Yamada in 'Notes on Income Growth and the Rate of Saving in Japan', *Income and Wealth, Series V*, edited for the International Association for Research in Income and Wealth by Simon Kuznets (1955), pp. 224–42. For the most recent estimates at the time of writing, see K. Ohkawa and others, *The Growth Rate of the Japanese Economy since 1878* (Tokyo, Kinokumija, 1957).
[2] See Table 3, p. 26 above.

new Japan took over from the past a number of small-scale handicraft industries which proved to be singularly tenacious of existence in the new environment.[1] Nor was the country well adapted for a speedy development of the 'growth-potential' industries to which we referred earlier. While the textile industries, particularly cotton and silk, expanded swiftly, the producer goods industries, and especially iron and steel, remained small, and it was not until after the First World War that Japan substantially reduced her heavy dependence on imported capital equipment. Indeed, it is noteworthy that although the absolute level of investment was high, and rose steeply during and after the First World War, it was not particularly high in relation to the rate of economic growth, and in the decades before 1914 net investment seems to have averaged less than 10 per cent of the national income.[2]

How then are we to account for Japan's unusually high rate of economic growth? A large part of the explanation, at any rate in the earlier decades, must be sought in the rapid increase of productivity in agriculture. It has been estimated that in three decades, between the 1880's and the 1910's, output per head in Japanese agriculture more than doubled. In many European countries, the increase in agricultural productivity has been associated with the development of large-scale mechanized farming. Although it is in principle possible to secure a high level of output per head on small peasant farms, in arable cultivation at least it is usually easier to secure economies of labour on larger farms. But in Japan this was not so. In her case, both topographical conditions and the predominance of rice cultivation were favourable to the development of intensive farming. As a result, the size of the agricultural unit remained minute by European standards and the rise in output per head was brought about by an improvement in technical methods such as the introduction of new seeds and the increased use of fertilizers, whose capital cost was relatively low.

This increase in productivity made it possible not only for agriculture to make a significant direct contribution to the rising level of *per capita* incomes, but also to release a growing surplus population in the countryside for productive employment elsewhere. The output of six major

---

[1] It has been estimated that the modern sector of the economy (large-scale mechanized industry) absorbed a smaller proportion of the labour force in 1920 than the traditional occupations, the cottage industries, etc., which had survived virtually unchanged from the pre-Meiji era. See Henry Rosovsky, 'The Indigenous Elements in the Modern Japanese Economy', *Economic Development and Cultural Change* (April 1961), p. 48.

[2] Yamada, 'Notes on Income Growth and the Rate of Saving in Japan,' *op. cit.* p. 233; H. Rosovsky, 'Japanese Capital Formation: The Role of the Public Sector', *J. Econ. Hist.* XIX (1959), 350–75. According to Rosovsky's estimates, from 1889–1913 *gross* investment averaged 10·3% of the *net* national income.

crops, which are thought to represent fairly accurately changes in total agricultural production, increased by 77 per cent from about 1885 to 1915, while the population of the country rose by 44 per cent, so that the supply of foodstuffs per head increased by about 20 per cent.[1] At the same time, the numbers in the countryside, which in the late nineteenth century were still increasing, tended to remain stationary or even to decline slightly after 1900, with the result that the proportion of the population engaged in agriculture fell from an estimated 77 per cent in 1872 to 52 per cent in 1920.[2] This shift in the distribution of the labour force was undoubtedly one of the major factors in the rapid increase in output in the non-agricultural sectors in the economy. It has been estimated that until 1910 two-thirds of the increase in output in these sectors can be attributed to the growing size of the labour force and only one-third to rising output per head. The importance of this fact may be illustrated by a comparison with the experience of Tsarist Russia at the same period. For whereas the rate of growth of industrial output in Japan was even higher than in Russia, the increase in industrial product per worker was, if anything, lower. Indeed, it appears that although the increase in industrial productivity in Japan during this period was not low in international comparison, it was quite small in relation to developments in the agricultural sector. For it appears that, in sharp contrast to experience in other countries, the increase in output per head in agriculture was actually greater than that in both manufacturing and service industries. Nor does this exhaust the contribution of agriculture to Japanese economic growth. For although productivity increased less rapidly in the non-agricultural sectors the absolute level remained higher. Hence, as a result of the transference of population, the overall increase in output per head during this period was significantly greater than in any of the component sectors.[3]

One other feature of Japanese economic growth may perhaps be briefly noted here. The importance of the developments in agriculture was, of course, not confined to the supply side, for they also made their contribution to the growth of the Japanese home market. But there was also a rapid expansion in overseas markets during this period which made it possible for Japan to import the capital equipment and raw

[1] Bruce F. Johnston, 'Agricultural Productivity and Economic Development in Japan', *J. Political Economy*, LIX (1951), 498–513.
[2] G. C. Allen, *A Short Economic History of Modern Japan, 1867–1937*, pp. 57, 164. By 1936, the proportion had fallen to 44%.
[3] See the paper on 'The Pattern of Japanese Long-term Economic Growth' presented to the Asian Conference of the International Association for Research in Income and Wealth at the University of Hong Kong by K. Ohkawa in August 1960; and for the comparative Russian data, Raymond Goldsmith, 'The Economic Growth of Russia', *op. cit.*

materials on which her industrial development heavily depended. In the early years the world demand for raw silk, which at that time constituted a major item in her export trade, rapidly increased as a result of a contraction in the European supply, while during and after the First World War, Japan was able to make substantial inroads into the Asiatic markets of her European competitors. It has been pointed out that the expansion of her foreign trade was less important than has sometimes been supposed, at any rate after 1910, since the growth of her export trade was no greater than the increase in the supply of goods to the home market.[1] Moreover, it should be remembered that at the time of the Meiji Restoration the volume of Japanese foreign trade was comparatively small, and at no time during the next sixty or seventy years did foreign and colonial markets absorb more than 25–35 per cent of her manufacturing output. Nevertheless, the increase in trade was certainly remarkable. Between 1873 and 1934 the total volume increased no less than forty-fold. And whereas in 1880 her exports (excluding trade between Japan proper and her colonies) constituted only about 4½ per cent of the national income, by the 1930's the proportion had risen to 16 per cent. Indeed, it is doubtful whether foreign trade acted as a more powerful 'engine of growth' in any other major industrial country with the possible exception of England.

However, by 1959, in spite of her relatively rapid industrialization and sustained growth in national productivity, Japan had reached a level of economic performance which was still well below that of most of the European industrialized countries. The estimates in Table 4 suggest that Japanese real output per head was not much more than a quarter of that prevailing in western Europe. This low income level, after nearly a century of rapid economic change and growth reflects the low starting-point from which Japan began and from which present-day Asia has to make its structural transformation.

VI. *The Structural Changes associated with Economic Growth*

It is evident from what has already been said that modern economic growth implies more than a change in the scale of economic activity. Associated with the rise in real income per head for those countries which achieved sustained growth was a series of well-defined changes in economic structure. The growing economies have undergone broadly similar changes in the pattern of economic activity, in the organization of their factors of production and in the character of their

[1] Lockwood, *The Economic Development of Japan*, op. cit. p. 576.

relationships with the rest of the world. These three major categories of structural change were part cause and part effect of the national advances in real incomes per head.

The essence of the process was the adoption of the industrial system with all that this implies in specialization of economic function and integration of national markets. It is a well-established generalization that as a community develops economically the number of its workers engaged in agriculture tends to decline, at first relatively to those engaged in manufacturing or the provision of services, and later absolutely as more and more of its resources are devoted to the production of industrial goods. As average incomes rise above subsistence levels a smaller proportion is required to buy the staple foods and a correspondingly larger proportion becomes available to purchase manufacturing products to support a developing network of commercial, social and governmental institutions and to buy professional and personal services. Thus a familiar, if imprecise, indicator of the stage of economic development reached by a country and the level of real incomes enjoyed by its citizens is the proportion of its labour force tied to agricultural occupations.

The country which went furthest in the shift from agricultural to non-agricultural activities was Great Britain. In 1688, when Gregory King drew up his list of families classified by social and income groups for England and Wales, barely a fifth of them could be unequivocally attributed to non-agricultural occupations. For the most part industry was organized domestically as an off-season occupation of the agriculturist and his family. By the end of the eighteenth century this proportion had roughly trebled and probably less than 40 per cent of the labour force was primarily engaged in the agriculture–forestry–fishing group of industries. The percentage in agriculture continued to fall steadily in the first half of the nineteenth century and rapidly in the second half when the numbers began to decline absolutely as well as relatively, so that by 1901 only about $8\frac{1}{2}$ per cent of the British labour force was in the agricultural group of industries. Expressed in terms of the percentage of national product attributed to agriculture the fall was from probably 40–45 per cent in the mid-eighteenth century to about a third in the early decades of the nineteenth century, about a fifth in 1851 and about a tenth in 1881. Given the universal disparity of income levels in agricultural and non-agricultural occupations and given the more rapid rate of growth of manufacturing and commercial industries, it was no accident that the period of the most rapid exodus from agriculture, that is, the second half of the nineteenth century, was the period within which the British economy reached its most rapid rate of growth. For it is this shift of productive resources from low yielding

stagnant industries to relatively high yielding rapidly growing industries
that is the very mechanism of economic growth.

This pattern has been repeated, with differences in timing and
degree, in all countries which have taken the path of sustained growth.
Reference has already been made to the slow transformation of the
Dutch economy.[1] In the United States about 73 per cent of the gainfully occupied population was in agriculture at the beginning of the
nineteenth century: by 1850 the proportion was 64 per cent and by
1870 53 per cent. Thereafter the decline gathered momentum—to 43 per
cent in 1890 and 31 per cent in 1910. The decline in absolute numbers
engaged in agriculture seems to have begun during the First World
War. By 1940 the proportion had dropped to 17 per cent and in
absolute terms the numbers engaged in agricultural occupations had
fallen back to the levels of the 1880's.[2]

Countries which developed later and relatively rapidly exhibited a
correspondingly rapid decline in the agricultural proportion of the
labour force. In the rapidity of this transition lay part of the reason for
their speedy growth. In Sweden, for example, the agrarian population fell from 75 per cent in 1861 to 61 per cent in 1891 and then to
48 per cent in 1911—by which time the decline in absolute numbers
had already begun.[3] On the other hand, in Denmark, already showing
signs of economic growth in the early part of the nineteenth century,
the proportion of the labour force in agriculture had reached 52 per cent
by 1871, fell quite slowly to 40 per cent by 1911 and more rapidly again
to 28 per cent by 1939.[4] Reference has already been made to the extraordinarily rapid decline in the agricultural proportion of the Russian
labour force in the period 1926–39.[5]

Growth then involves changes in industrial structure, a shift from
slowly growing to rapidly growing industries. Sustained growth
requires a continuous succession of such shifts, so that each country's
long-term rate of growth depends basically on two factors: (a) its propensity to adopt innovations which increase the efficiency of individual
industries, and (b) its propensity to reorganize its productive resources
in favour of those industries which are innovating most effectively. In
general it is the shift from agriculture, operating in the traditional

[1] See above, p. 13.
[2] For estimates of the percentage gainfully occupied in agriculture in the
United States see Simon Kuznets, *Income and Wealth of the United States; Trends and
Structure*, Series II (1952), p. 224 and *Historical Statistics of the United States* (1960),
pp. 72–4.
[3] Erik Lindahl, Einor Dahlgren and Karin Kock, *National Income of Sweden, 1861–
1930* (1937), pp. 2–3.
[4] Kjeld Bjerke and Niels Ussing, *Studier over Danmarks Nationalprodukt 1870–1950*
(Copenhagen, 1958), pp. 142–3.   [5] See above, p. 24.

framework of diminishing returns, to manufacturing industry and steam transport enjoying rapidly increasing returns, which constitutes the first and most rewarding shift. In most developed countries it has been responsible for the peak long-term rates of growth: and for most countries there is evidence of some retardation of growth in the later stages of the transition to a fully industrial economy. Growth continues but the *rate* of growth tends to stop rising and in some cases to decline. Evidence of a significant slackening in the rate of growth of real incomes per head, for example, shows up in the national income estimates for the United Kingdom, the United States and Germany before the First World War.

There are a number of reasons why in the absence of an accelerating rate of technical progress an eventual retardation should be regarded as inevitable. As far as total product is concerned certain limits are set by the extent to which the community can expand its supply of land and labour. While the United States was able to open up new land resources and to bring in new labour to exploit them its growth potential was consistently high. The slowing down of population growth has been associated with the decline in the rate of growth of total output (though not necessarily of productivity) in nearly all industrialized countries.[1] And this slackening of the overall rate of growth may have had an impact on the rate of growth in real incomes per head. For it involves a narrowing of economic opportunities. On the one hand, markets expand less vigorously with a slowly growing community because consumers' demand is more easily saturated. On the other hand, there is less scope and less incentive for entrepreneurs to introduce technical innovations in a slowly growing industry, where the introduction of a new piece of equipment may involve the scrapping of plant which has not yet worn out, than in a rapidly growing industry where new units of production create an important part of the total demand for new methods and machines.

Moreover, as a country develops, it gradually exhausts the range of economic opportunities open to it and unless it becomes technologically more progressive it will grow less rapidly than before. Some physical resources (minerals, for example) are absolutely exhaustible. For others, such as labour supply, the very nature of development tends to contract the flow of new productive resources (for example, by reducing child labour or increasing leisure). In any case, the first country to take advantage of a new economic opportunity will find its rewards less easily won as soon as it attracts imitators.

[1] The exception is Russia, where a fall in the rate of population growth in the Stalin era was associated with the record rates of growth of national product under the Five-year Plans.

There is clear evidence of retardation also in the evidence for particular industries.[1] The revolutionary changes in technique which are associated with an industrial revolution have tended to be closely bunched in time and to have produced their strongest impact within a definable span of years. Few important textile inventions, for example, were made after 1860. The crucial and radical innovations which made the modern steel industry possible were largely concentrated in the period 1855–90. None of the improvements and refinements introduced in steady succession in the later history of these industries permitted quite such a revolutionary upsurge in productivity as emanated from the first breakthrough. *A fortiori* in the primary or extractive industries, confronted in any case with the gradual exhaustion of resources, the evidence on yields per acre or on output per worker have shown a tendency for the tempo of technical progress to decline after an initial sharp improvement.

In sum, then, modern economic growth involves an orderly and broadly predictable sequence of changes in the *content* of the national product. Also inherent in the process are certain related changes in the *organization* of production and this shows up most clearly in the changing roles of capital and labour. Adoption of the industrial system involved mechanization of manufacturing process, larger-scale construction of new routes and means of transport, and the building of cities and factories. In effect, it meant accumulation of capital on an unprecedented scale. Hence familiar indicators of the degree of industrialization or of the level of real incomes achieved by a country are the size of the capital stock available to each member of its labour force, or the relation of its capital formation to its national income. It has even been maintained that 'The central problem in the theory of economic growth is to understand the process by which a community is converted from being a 5 per cent to a 12 per cent saver.'[2] This may be an oversimplification, but there is no doubt that some such change as this has been part of the experience of all those countries which have achieved a sustained rate of growth in real incomes per head.

Little is known of pre-industrial levels of capital formation for the industrialized countries because for most of them our quantitative data do not go beyond the early stages of the industrial revolution—which itself may have demanded abnormally large capital outlays. Gregory King, looking back over the experience of the seventeenth century, thought that the nation's capital stock had been growing at an average rate of about $1\frac{1}{2}$ per cent per annum—rather faster at the end, however,

[1] Simon Kuznets, 'Retardation of Industrial Growth', *Economic Change* (1954), pp. 260 ff.
[2] W. A. Lewis, *The Theory of Economic Growth* (1955), p. 226.

than at the beginning. An attempt to express his figures—which are no more than a quantitative illustration of an informed opinion—in terms of an annual rate of productive capital formation suggests a long-term average of about 3 or 4 per cent of national income.[1] The stock thus being accumulated consisted largely of farm animals, buildings, traders' goods, ships and gold bullion. It was vulnerable to destruction by fire, war or natural disaster and its earning power was low and erratic. From the rapidity with which London was rebuilt after the fire and the ease with which the great trading corporations and the Bank of England were able to raise new funds at the end of the seventeenth century we may judge that the nation was able, when the occasion arose, to save more than it normally did. The operative cause of the characteristically low pre-industrial levels of capital formation was not an inability to save, but a dearth of sound opportunities for profitable investment; and in both England and France during the early eighteenth century the enthusiasm of savers disastrously outran the capacity of investors to turn their capital to productive account.

The English stock of capital in buildings, roads, bridges, navigations, docks, ships and breeding animals continued to expand at an accelerating rate during the eighteenth century: though whether it grew faster than the national income is dubious. There is evidence that the expansion of internal and external trade led to and was facilitated by increased investment in communications; and that eighteenth-century English farmers invested more in fencing, drainage and breeding stock, and in putting waste under crops than their predecessors had been wont to do. But the first stage in escape from stagnation, the effective beginnings of sustained growth, may well have been due more to a change in the *character* of the national capital—a shift to more productive uses—than to a change in the national propensity to save. It is not until the 1840's, when the railway age made its massive demands for capital that we find evidence of a marked rise in the *level* of capital formation. A similarly gradual transition from low to high rates of capital accumulation probably characterized the experience of France and the Low Countries.

Countries which industrialized later, on the other hand, often achieved the change to higher levels of capital accumulation more abruptly. For one thing the investment opportunities presented by imitation of the new technology were obvious and much of the costly trial and error stage could be by-passed by the late starters. Equally apparent were the implications of industrialization in terms of the social overhead capital and capital-intensive producers' goods required. It was logical to begin the process by massive applications of capital—obtained if necessary by borrowing from abroad. Sweden, for example, which

[1] Deane and Cole, *British Economic Growth, 1688–1959, op. cit.*

4

achieved one of the most effective late entries on to the industrial scene is estimated to have expanded its gross capital formation from 9 per cent of gross national product in the period 1861/90 to nearly 20 per cent in the period 1901/30: of this, domestic savings accounted for only two-thirds at the earlier period and 99 per cent at the latter.[1]

Outside Europe, in the large empty countries settled by Europe's enterprising migrants and enjoying relatively high levels of income per head, even in pre-industrial periods, the pattern was different. Massive doses of capital formation preceded the industrial revolution proper. In the United States, Australia and Canada, for example, the earliest recorded levels of capital formation are quite high and the process of industrialization did not appreciably raise these levels. In Australia and Canada there has even been some decline and in countries like Argentina, where the railway age did not succeed in stimulating the sequence of structural changes and the sustained rise in national income which are associated with an industrial revolution, the decline in the rate of capital formation has been quite sharp.[2]

In principle we might expect a decline in the level of capital formation to be associated with the retardation in the rate of population growth which has taken place in the industrially mature countries. The very rapid increases in population which have often been associated with the early stages of economic development exert a strong upward pressure on the level of investment. An expanding, urbanizing, population requires a growing stock of capital in new dwellings and other amenities; a growing labour force needs a correspondingly larger stock of productive equipment. When a new demographic equilibrium is achieved and the rate of immigration or of natural increase settles down to a new and lower level, this upward pressure is relaxed, and unless there are other forces maintaining the level of investment it may be expected to contract. In fact, however, there is no evidence that contraction has taken place for this kind of reason. The pre-industrially low rates of capital formation which characterized the mature economies in the inter-war period (in the United Kingdom and the United States, for example, the level of net investment fell well below 5 per cent) can be attributed to an abnormally depressed climate of business expectations.[3] After the Second World War there was a marked recovery of

---

[1] Simon Kuznets, *Six Lectures on Economic Growth* (1959), p. 82.

[2] H. S. Ferns, *Britain and Argentina in the Nineteenth Century* (1960).

[3] For U.S. estimates of net capital formation as percentage of net national product see Simon Kuznets, *Capital in the American Economy* (Princeton, 1961), pp. 92–3. Estimates based on the Department of Commerce concept of national product indicate that net capital formation fell below 2 per cent of the net national product over the decade 1929–38, compared with 10·4 per cent for the decade 1919–28.

pre-First World War levels and indeed in most of western Europe the latter levels were unprecedentedly high.

The increase in the stock of capital associated with industrialization was a major cause of the improvements in productivity and standards of living. It was not, however, the only cause. In the United States, for example, capital per head of the population roughly trebled between 1869/73 and 1949/53. Net product per head, on the other hand, roughly quadrupled.[1] Clearly there were other factors contributing to the great secular rise in productivity. There were improvements in the quality of capital (as of labour), there were innovations in technique (better layout of productive processes, for example, and more efficient social and industrial institutions) and there were the external economies and economies of scale which took effect as soon as output achieved a sufficient magnitude. It is usual to apply the term technical progress to this *mélange* of incommensurable forces which gave the process its cumulative momentum. The more mature the economy the more significant becomes the role of technical progress in determining the rate of growth.

The third group of structural changes which are inevitably associated with industrialization and growth is concerned with the nation's relationship with the rest of the world. Here again the broad features of the pattern can be generalized, while the details vary in the individual cases. The outstanding common feature, of course, is the development of a closer relationship with the rest of the world. The close integration of the international economy is paralleled by a corresponding integration at the national level. This generally involves an increase in the share of incomes from foreign trade in the total national income. It may precede, accompany or follow the industrial revolution proper. It may be a permissive or an operative factor in the growth process.

The British case is the classic prototype of an industrial revolution based on overseas trade. Gregory King's estimate for 1688 put English exports at 5 or 6 per cent of the value of national income. A century later the proportion had risen to 14 per cent. Roughly another century later they had reached an all-time peak of about 36 per cent in the early 1880's. The growth of English commerce in the eighteenth century provided a large part of the accumulated wealth necessary to finance nascent industry in the last quarter of the century. The opportunity to buy raw materials and sell finished products in foreign markets vastly extended the range of economic opportunity open to British industrialists. And in the second half of the nineteenth century it was the accessibility of cheap food then becoming available in bulk in the new

---

[1] Moses Abramovitz, *Resource and Output Trends in the United States since 1870* National Bureau of Economic Research, Occasional Paper 52 (1956).

world that turned the shift from agriculture to industry into a land-slide and permitted the economy to achieve its peak rates of growth.

Reference has already been made to the importance of foreign trade in facilitating Japanese industrialization.[1] For most other countries the relevant statistics do not extend far enough back to permit an acceptable assessment of the role of foreign trade over the full period of industriali-zation. But the existing data suggest that in most cases the foreign trade ratio followed a similar course, in direction, if not in degree, to the British one.[2] Except perhaps for the United States, which expanded its markets by importing people rather than by exporting commodities, there were few industrializing countries which did not derive a sub-stantial part of their initial impetus from the development of overseas trade.

These trends in the changing pattern of relationship between individual growing countries and the rest of the world are merely one aspect of a wider story. A significant aspect of modern economic growth is the course of development followed by the international economy itself. Indeed the fact that it is convenient to identify the international economy as a separate unit of analysis is a distinguishing feature of the modern period in world history. It constitutes a third dimension of growth. For in any one country growth depends on the opportunities presented by the international environment in which it finds itself as on the factors of production (people and things) within its national borders. An increased dependence on the rest of the world seems to be a condition of economic growth for economies based on private enterprise.

The extent of this dependence was sharply illustrated by the univer-sality of the world depression of the 1930's. It was emphasized again by the upward movement of nearly all the national growth rates in the period following the Second World War. But students of business cycles had noted the correlation between economic advance and inter-national interdependence before these two episodes impressed them-selves on the popular imagination. The international business cycle pattern can be traced back to the first half of the nineteenth century when Britain, France and the United States shared in the great financial crises. Germany joined them in the panic of 1857. It was during the second half of the century that the pattern began to develop its world-wide significance. 'The long depressions of the 1870's, the checkered fortunes of the 1880's, the revival of the middle 1890's, the boom of 1906-7, the calmer prosperity of 1912, the hectic activity of the war years, and the severe depression after 1920 had much the same inter-

[1] See above, pp. 43-4.
[2] Simon Kuznets, *Six Lectures on Economic Growth* (1959), pp. 100-7.

national character as the crises to which attention is commonly restricted.'[1]

Moreover, it was through the international economy that the benefits of technological progress implied in the industrial revolution were communicated to countries which did not themselves industrialize to any considerable extent. So that the industrial revolution in Europe widened the economic horizons of all countries, though its direct impact on standards of living and methods of economic organization for any particular region depended on the responsiveness of the inhabitants and the extent of economic contact with the industrializing countries. Primary producers who were in no way stimulated to industrialize gained some benefit from the cheaper manufactures flowing on to world markets and from an increased world demand for imports of food and industrial raw materials. Railways and steamships reached out into quite remote corners of the globe.

In effect, the half-century before the First World War was the period within which the international economy began its massive expansion. If we measure growth in terms of the increase in industrial output per head it appears that the international economy expanded more rapidly in the period 1870–1913 than ever before—or after for that matter, even if we include the recovery period of the early 1950's. Between 1876/80 and 1911/13 world manufacturing production increased three times as much as world population and the volume of commodities entering into world trade two and a half times as much: but between 1913 and 1948 the increase in manufacturing production was less than twice that of world population, while the quantum of world trade signally failed to keep pace with population.[2]

During the half-century before the First World War, however, there had been significant changes in the shape of the international economy. In the 1860's there was virtually only one industrial economy—the United Kingdom, which probably accounted for more than a third of the world output of manufactured goods. France and Belgium had had several decades of industrialization but the latter was small and both had a long way to go. Germany and the United States were still essentially agricultural countries though they had already begun to industrialize rapidly. Between 1870 and 1914 the United Kingdom was

---

[1] W. L. Thorp, *Business Annals* (NBER, New York, 1926), p. 89.
[2] Calculated on the basis of statistics given in P. Lamartine Yates, *Forty Years of Foreign Trade* (1959), pp. 30–1. By 1911/13 manufacturing production was estimated to be 378 % of the 1876/80 level and population 126 %. By 1956 manufacturing production was 355 % of the 1913 level and population 153 %; the corresponding figures for 1948 were 226 % of the 1913 level for manufacturing production and 132 % for population.

outweighed by both the United States and Germany in sheer volume of industrial production and the balance of industrial power shifted from western Europe to the world overseas.

Within Europe the balance of wealth and industrial power still lay in the north-west, however. In 1913 the United Kingdom, France and Germany accounted for more than seven-tenths of the continent's manufacturing capacity. The remaining three-tenths was scattered in specialist centres which depended heavily on the three industrial giants to provide the economic framework which made specialization possible and worth while.[1]

The First World War made havoc of the complex system of relationships on which European progress was based. It showed specialization to be perilous and put a premium on autarchy; it dried up the supplies of capital with which the great powers had been financing the industrialization of the small; it ran down equipment and earning power in the industries of peace and created excess capacity in the industries of war; it gave large competitive advantages to Europe's overseas rivals and an impetus to industrialization to Europe's customers. Calculations based on hypotheses of what might have been (for example, had there been no war and had Europe continued to advance at the pace set in the period 1880–1913) lead to the conclusion that the First World War set back Europe's economic growth by a total of eight years.[2]

The true extent of the setback cannot, of course, be measured. Certainly it was an unmitigated catastrophe for Europe, though for most of Europe's overseas descendants it provided a stimulus to industrialization and economic growth. Whereas in the United States manufacturing output had risen by 22 per cent over the 1913 level in 1920 and by 41 per cent in 1923, for Europe the manufacturing output index shows a decline of 23 per cent by 1920 and 18 per cent by 1923.[3] From these sunken levels growth was slow and erratic—over the whole of the inter-war period the rate of growth of industrial productivity in Europe (excluding Russia) probably did not exceed one per cent per annum. Measured over the longer period, including the First World War, industrial growth rates are still lower. Since agriculture stagnated more wretchedly even than industry, standards of living in Europe, taken overall, show little improvement in the quarter-century preceding the Second World War. It has been estimated that real incomes per head in Europe as a whole grew by an annual average of no more than 0·8 per cent between 1913 and 1938.[4]

These European averages, however, are heavily weighted by the

---

[1] Ingvar Svennilson, *Growth and Stagnation in the European Economy* (United Nations Economic Commission for Europe, Geneva 1954).

[2] *Ibid.* p. 19.   [3] *Ibid.* p. 18.   [4] *Ibid.* pp. 57–8.

slow-growing industrial giants—already well past the peak rates of growth associated with the industrialization process itself. Even in 1938 Germany, the United Kingdom and France (in that order of importance), still accounted for nearly seven-tenths of Europe's industrial output, excluding the Soviet Union.[1] Among the newly industrializing countries on the other hand there were some significant exceptions to the general impression of stagnation. The spectacular progress of the Soviet Union has already been discussed. Swedish manufacturing output rose faster (at an annual rate of over 5 per cent) in the period 1920–39 than it had in 1896–1913 when the rate was $4\frac{1}{2}$ per cent. By 1938 Sweden's output of goods per head of the population had reached a level comparable to (if not slightly higher than) that of the United Kingdom. A relatively rapid rate of growth (though at a much lower level) was also achieved by Finland in the inter-war period and Italy too escaped the general European stagnation.[2]

The inter-war advances in Russia, Italy and Japan were portents of fresh changes in the international economy and of a fresh wave of industrialization accelerated by the Second World War. Meanwhile, however, it is worth noting that at mid-twentieth century the industrial revolution and the modern economic growth to which it gave rise was still predominantly a product of western Europe though it was no longer geographically contained in the old world. The early twentieth-century shift in economic leadership was a shift from western Europe to its areas of overseas settlement. Only Japan in Asia and the Soviet Union in the rest of Europe were advancing at comparable rates. Taken together, western Europe and its overseas descendants in North America and Australasia have absorbed a steadily expanding share of the wealth of nations; with about 17 per cent of world population they accounted for an estimated 57 per cent of world incomes in 1938 and for nearly two-thirds in 1949.[3]

---

[1] U.N. Department of Economic Affairs, *Economic Survey of Europe in 1949* (ECE, Geneva, 1950), pp. 276–7.

[2] *Ibid.* p. 205.

[3] Simon Kuznets, 'Quantitative Aspects of the Economic Growth of Nations. I. Levels and Variability of Rates of Growth', *Economic Development and Cultural Change*, v, no. 1 (October 1956), 17. According to these estimates western Europe itself accounted for 27·7 % of world incomes in 1938 and U.S.A. for 25·9 %: the corresponding proportions in 1949 were 22 % and 41 %.

CHAPTER II

World Population, 1800-1950

A RECENT study has compared world population growth to 'a long thin powder fuse that burns slowly and haltingly until it finally reaches the charge and then explodes'.[1] The analogy is vivid, if a little strained. The 'explosion' referred to is, of course, the rapid rate of population growth which took place from the middle of the eighteenth century onwards. The nature and beginnings of this increase are very inadequately documented. Even today reliable population and vital statistics are available for only part of the world's population. In 1949 it was estimated that some 40 per cent of the world's population lived in areas in which population and vital statistics were 'poor' and only 23 per cent in areas with 'good' figures.[2] The further back in time, the larger is the proportion of the population living in areas with 'poor' data. Even to go back to 1800 means that many of the apparently firm figures are estimates, and that much of the discussion of world population becomes speculative.

At the beginning of the nineteenth century, census-taking on a nation-wide basis was in its infancy. Only in the Scandinavian countries did fairly reliable population estimates exist in the second half of the eighteenth century;[3] in the United States, the first census was taken in 1790; in Great Britain and France in 1801. In Austria-Hungary

[1] Kingsley Davis, 'The World Demographic Transition', *Annals of the American Academy of Political and Social Science* (January, 1945), p. 1.

[2] United Nations, *World Population Trends: 1920–47* (New York, 1949), p. 3. Since then, the various censuses taken around 1950 and around 1960 have extended the area covered by relatively reliable census statistics. But comprehensive and effective vital registration systems have not developed at a corresponding rate. Moreover, for one very large population—the population of China—it is at present difficult to estimate the reliability of the most recent census (1953), though there is reason to believe that it was more reliable than any of the previous twentieth-century 'censuses' of that population (see the discussion in J. S. Aird, *The Size, Composition and Growth of the Population of Mainland China* (U.S. Dept. of Commerce, Washington, D.C., 1961)). Since 1950, too, official estimates of the total population of the U.S.S.R. have again become available (for the size of the U.S.S.R. population after the First World War, see M. K. Roof, 'The Russian Population Enigma Reconsidered', *Pop. Studies*, XIV (1960)). According to the U.N. *Demographic Yearbook* (New York, 1956), p. 10, that volume contained census data relating to some 86% of the estimated total world population in 1955, as compared with a coverage of only about 66% at the end of 1948. See also the discussion in the U.N. *Demographic Yearbook*, 1960, 'How well do we know the present size and trend of the world's population?'

[3] Cf. H. Gille, 'The Demographic History of the Northern European Countries in the Eighteenth Century', *Pop. Studies*, III (1949), 3–65.

enumeration began in 1754,[1] but all other European countries began their regular censuses later in the nineteenth century.[2]

The position is even less favourable outside Europe. In South America, for instance, no censuses were taken in the nineteenth century in Bolivia, Ecuador or Paraguay and even the larger countries like Argentina, Brazil and Peru have scanty, and not always reliable population figures for the period between about 1870 and the 1930's or 1940's.[3] Africa is virtually *terra incognita* demographically throughout the nineteenth century,[4] as are large parts of Asia, particularly China, South-east Asia and the countries of the Middle East.[5]

The absence of census statistics does not, of course, mean that estimates of total population are impossible. Other sources of information, such as tax rolls, parochial registers, numbers of inhabited houses and counts of men of military age, provide bases for more or less informed guesses about the total population and many such estimates were made by contemporary writers. Estimates of this kind have been studied and combined by A. M. Carr-Saunders and W. F. Willcox,[6] who have both presented tables aiming to depict the growth of world population since 1650. These estimates differ slightly from one another, for reasons which are explained below. In a recent United Nations monograph, both sets of estimates are given,[7] and they are reproduced with some

---

[1] See H. Grossmann, *Die Anfänge und geschichtliche Entwicklung der amtlichen Statistik in Österreich* (Brunn, 1916); and S. Peller, 'Zur Kenntnis der städtischen Mortalität im 18. Jahrhundert...', *Z. Hygiene und Infektionskrankheiten* (1920), cx.

[2] For a list of censuses taken after 1800 see *Aperçu de la démographie des divers pays du monde, 1929–36*, published by the International Statistical Institute (The Hague, 1939), pp. 44 ff.

[3] See I. B. Taeuber (Director), *General Censuses and Vital Statistics in the Americas* (Washington, D.C., 1943).

[4] See R. R. Kuczynski, *A Demographic Survey of the British Colonial Empire*, 3 vols. (London, 1948, 1949, 1953), for an account of nineteenth-century statistics relating to British possessions in Africa and America.

[5] The existence of a series of censuses does not inevitably mean the provision of reliable population statistics. Such a series exists for Egypt, but it is evident that each census contains considerable errors and much detailed analysis is required in order to 'correct' for such errors. So far as the total number of sovereign countries taking censuses is concerned, there were only twenty-four in the period 1855–64, as compared with sixty-five in 1945–54 (see U.N. *Demographic Yearbook* (New York, 1956), p. 10).

[6] A. M. Carr-Saunders, *World Population* (Oxford, 1936), pp. 30–45; W. Willcox, 'Population of the World and its Modern Increase', *Studies in American Demography* (Ithaca, 1940), pp. 22–51. Professor Willcox modified his estimates from time to time; the paper cited is the last published estimate. See also his 'The Population of China, and its Modern Increase', *ibid.* pp. 511–40.

[7] U.N., *The Determinants and Consequences of Population Trends* (New York, 1953), p. 11.

Table 6. *Estimated World Population, 1800–1955*

(a) Carr-Saunders's estimate.　　　(b) Willcox's estimate.　　　(c) U.N. estimates.

(i) Numbers (in millions)

	1800		1850		1900		1920	1930	1940	1950	1958
	(a)	(b)	(a)	(b)	(a)	(b)	(c)	(c)	(c)	(c)	(c)
Africa	90	100	95	100	120	141	140	155	172	198	231
North America[a]	6	6	26	26	81	81	117	135	146	168	193
Latin America	19	23	33	33	63	63	91	109	131	163	197
Asia[b]	597	595	741	656	915	857	966	1072	1212	1376	1591
Europe and U.S.S.R.[c]	192	193	274	274	423	423	487	532	573	576	626
Oceania	2	2	2	2	6	6	9	10	11	13	16
Total	906	919	1171	1091	1608	1571	1810	2013	2246	2494	2854

[a] North America, north of the Rio Grande.　　[b] Excluding U.S.S.R.
[c] The figure for the population of the U.S.S.R. in 1950 and 1955 was obtained as a residual.

(ii) Percentage distribution

	1800		1850		1900		1920	1930	1940	1950	1958
	(a)	(b)	(a)	(b)	(a)	(b)	(c)	(c)	(c)	(c)	(c)
Africa	9·9	10·9	8·1	9·2	7·5	9·0	7·7	7·7	7·7	8·0	8·1
North America	0·7	0·7	2·2	2·4	5·0	5·2	6·5	6·7	6·5	6·7	6·8
Latin America	2·1	2·5	2·8	3·0	3·9	4·0	5·0	5·4	5·8	6·5	6·9
Asia	65·9	64·7	63·3	60·1	56·9	54·6	53·4	53·3	54·0	55·2	55·7
Europe and U.S.S.R.	21·2	21·0	23·1	25·1	26·3	26·9	26·9	26·4	25·5	23·1	21·9
Oceania	0·2	0·2	0·2	0·2	0·4	0·4	0·5	0·5	0·5	0·5	0·6
Total	100·0	100·0	100·0	100·0	100·0	100·0	100·0	100·0	100·0	100·0	100·0

(iii) Annual rate of increase per 1000

	1800–50		1850–1900		1900–20		1920–30 (c)	1930–40 (c)	1940–50 (c)	1950–58 (c)*
	(a)	(b)	(a)	(b)	(a)	(b)	(c)	(c)	(c)	(c)*
Africa	1·1	0·0	4·7	6·9	7·7	−0·4	10·2	10·4	14·7	19·0
North America	29·8	29·8	23·0	23·0	18·6	18·6	14·4	7·9	14·1	17·0
Latin America	11·1	7·2	13·0	13·0	18·6	18·6	18·2	18·6	21·4	24·0
Asia	4·3	2·0	4·2	5·4	2·8	6·1	10·5	12·3	12·7	18·0
Europe and U.S.S.R.	7·1	7·0	8·7	8·7	7·0	7·0	8·9	7·5	0·4	11·0
Oceania	—	—	—	—	—	—	16·8	8·3	15·7	22·7
Total	5·1	3·4	6·4	7·3	5·9	7·1	10·7	11·0	10·5	17·0

* Rounded to units only.

auxiliary calculations in Table 6, for the period 1800 to 1958. The
figures from 1920 onwards have been estimated by the United Nations,[1]
and Carr-Saunders's and Willcox's estimates have been adjusted by the
United Nations to fit with their own geographical classification.

The main differences between Carr-Saunders's and Willcox's esti-

[1] U.N. *Demographic Yearbook* (New York, 1956), p. 151. The figures given there
differ from those in earlier editions in taking account of the census of China taken in
1953, and of a new estimate of the population of the Soviet Union.

mates relate to Africa and Asia. Willcox believed that the population of Africa remained more or less stationary between 1650 and 1850. Carr-Saunders found it impossible to accept this contention. He pointed out that the intensity of slave raiding diminished in the early nineteenth century, and that the population of Egypt and other North African countries is known to have increased after 1800. It is clear that Carr-Saunders's figures for Africa are more closely in line with the United Nations estimates for the present century than are Willcox's; it is extremely unlikely that the population of Africa actually decreased between 1900 and 1920, and it is probable that Carr-Saunders's estimate for Africa is nearer the truth. The main discrepancy, however, relates to Asia, and within Asia to the population of China. Willcox states that the population of China had been studied by two kinds of scholars: those who knew a great deal about statistics and very little about China, and those who knew a great deal about China, and very little about statistics. There are many statistical series for China, but to use them effectively would involve detailed analysis and comparison of a kind which so far has rarely been undertaken.[1] At the moment, however, it should be noted that Carr-Saunders's estimates imply a slackening in the rate of population growth in Asia in the early years of the present century, a conclusion which is somewhat doubtful.

Whichever of the two sets of estimates is accepted, the same broad conclusions follow. In absolute terms, world population growth during the past 150 years is of a magnitude without previous parallel. Moreover, the rate of growth has itself increased fairly systematically since the end of the eighteenth century to reach the present level, estimated at about 1·7 per cent per year. This rate of growth does not constitute an 'explosion' in any technical sense. But it certainly means a massive expansion in numbers. Between 1900 and 1950, world population grew by more than 1000 millions—a larger absolute increase than had occurred in the preceding hundred years. At present levels of growth, a further 1000 millions would be added in less than a generation.[2]

Behind the overall growth rates, there have been wide differences between and within the various regions. The Americas and Oceania

[1] See A. J. Jaffe, 'A Review of the Censuses and Demographic Statistics of China', *Pop. Studies*, 1 (1947), 308; J. Durand, 'The Population Statistics of China, A.D. 2–1953', *Pop. Studies* XIII (1960), 209. It is to be hoped that, in the future, qualified Chinese scholars will devote some time to the analysis of the dynastic statistics and help to fill a major gap in our knowledge of world population growth. One example of a beginning in this direction is Ho Ping-ti, *Studies on the Population of China, 1368–1958* (Cambridge, Mass., 1959).

[2] An annual rate of growth of 1·7 % (17 per 1000 total population) would imply the doubling of a population in just over forty-one years.

have throughout shown rates of increase above the average for the world, but immigration has contributed significantly to those higher rates. Until the 1920's, the rate of growth of European populations consistently exceeded that of Asians and Africans. If the combined populations of Africa and Asia be taken as a rough estimate of the total world population of non-European stock, it accounted for about 75 per cent of the world total in 1800, but had fallen to 61 per cent by 1920. Thereafter the situation changed and Africans and Asians began to increase more rapidly than Europeans, so that by 1955 their proportion had risen to over 63 per cent. The reasons for this change, and some of its implications, will be considered later.

Before discussing the factors underlying the geographical variations in rates of increase, it will be convenient to examine in greater detail the statistics for one or two major regions. This will make it possible to show more clearly the basis of some of the estimates given in Table 6.

I. *Europe*

So many boundary changes have occurred since 1800, that it is extremely difficult to give fully comparable figures for the countries of Europe over the period 1800–1955. A collection of data from various sources is presented in Table 7. The estimates for 1800 are those given by Sundbärg, who extracted them from a number of publications, adjusting them when they were manifestly incorrect.[1] Nevertheless, many of the figures are simply estimates and cannot be regarded as providing more than an indication of the order of magnitude of the population. For the period 1850 to 1920, the figures are those contained in the collection published by the International Statistical Institute,[2] and generally relate to the censuses nearest in time to those points shown in the table. From 1920 onwards, United Nations estimates have been used.[3]

The figures in Table 7 do not always agree with those in alternative estimates[4] and there must inevitably be some degree of doubt about them. For the sake of completeness, Table 8 summarizes the annual rates of growth for different decennia of the nineteenth century, calculated by Sundbärg. The rates here relate to areas with 1906 boundaries, and therefore differ from those of Table 7.

[1] G. Sundbärg, *Aperçus statistiques internationaux* (Stockholm, 1906), p. 31.
[2] *Aperçu de la démographie des divers pays du monde.*
[3] The same source has been used for the beginning and end of a period for which a rate of growth is shown.
[4] Cf., for instance, J. Athelstane Baines, 'The Recent Growth of Population in Western Europe: An Essay in International Comparison', *J. Roy. Stat. Soc.* vol. LXXII (1909), for slightly different figures, some of which are difficult to reconcile with those given in Table 7.

Table 7. Estimated Population of European Countries, 1800–1955

	Population (in millions)											Annual rate of growth per thousand				
	1800	1850	1880	1890	1900	1910	1920	1930	1940	1950	1955	1850–1900	1900–20	1920–40	1940–50	1950–55
Denmark^a	0·9	1·6	2·1	2·3	2·6	2·9	3·2	3·5	3·8	4·3	4·4	10·4	11·1	8·4	10·9	5·5
Finland^b	1·0	1·6	2·0	2·4	2·7	3·1	3·4	3·4*	3·7	4·0	4·2	10·2	10·8	8·3	8·1	7·8
Norway	0·9	1·5^d	1·8^i	2·0	2·2	2·4	2·6	2·8	3·0	3·3	3·4	9·1	8·4	6·1	9·4	9·6
Sweden	2·3	3·5	4·6	4·8	5·1	5·5	5·9	6·1	6·4	7·0	7·3	7·8	7·0	3·9	9·9	7·0
Belgium	3·0	4·3^e	5·5	6·1	6·7	7·4	7·6*	8·1	8·3	8·6	8·9	8·1^m	—	5·3	2·9	5·2
France	26·9	36·5*	39·2	40·0	40·7	41·5	39·0	41·2	39·8	41·7	43·3	2·2	–1·4	1·0	4·8	7·3
Holland	2·2	3·1	4·0	4·5	5·1	5·9	6·8	7·9	8·9	10·1	10·8	10·3	14·9	13·3	13·1	12·3
U.K.^c	—	22·3	31·1	34·3	38·2	42·1	43·7	45·9	48·2	50·3	51·0	10·9	7·1	4·9	4·2	2·5
Italy	18·1	23·9*	29·6	31·7	33·9	36·2	37·0*	40·3	43·8	46·6	48·0	6·8^n	5·7	8·5	6·1	6·0
Portugal	3·1	4·2^f	4·6	5·1	5·4	6·0	6·0	6·8	7·7	8·4	8·8	7·2°	5·3	12·5	8·8	8·4
Spain	11·5	15·5^g	16·6^j	17·6^k	18·6	19·9	21·2	23·4	25·8	27·9	29·0	4·2^p	6·8	9·8	7·9	7·9
Austria	—	3·9	5·0	5·4	6·0	6·6	6·5	6·7	6·7	6·9	7·0	8·9	3·4	1·9	3·3	1·3
Czechoslovakia	—	—	—	—	—	—	13·0	14·0	14·7	12·4*	13·1	—	—	6·3	—	11·1
Germany	24·5	31·7*	40·2	44·2	50·6	58·5	61·8	65·1	69·8	68·0*	70·1	9·4	10·0	6·1	—	6·1
Hungary	—	5·0^h	5·3	6·0	6·9	7·6	8·0	8·6	9·3	9·3	9·8	10·1^q	7·6	7·8	0·5	9·9
Switzerland	1·8	2·4	2·8	2·9	3·3	3·8	3·9	4·1	4·2	4·7	5·0	6·5	7·9	4·3	10·6	11·7
Bulgaria	—	—	2·8	3·3*	3·7	4·3	4·8*	5·7	6·7	7·3*	7·5	—	—	13·7	—	7·5
Yugoslavia	—	—	—	—	—	—	11·9	13·8	15·8	16·2*	17·6	—	—	14·9	—	16·5

* Indicates a boundary change since the previous figure.

a Excluding Faroe Islands.
b Pre-1940 area for all figures prior to 1930.
c Excluding the Isle of Man and Channel Islands.
d 1855.   e 1846.   f 1864.
g 1857.   h 1869.   i 1875.
j 1867.   k 1877.   l 1855–1900.
m 1846–1900.   n 1880–1900.   o 1864–1900.
p 1857–1900.   q 1869–1900.

Although some of the fluctuations shown for different decennia cannot be taken at their face value, the table gives a generally valid impression of a considerable acceleration in the rate of population growth
during the last quarter of the nineteenth century. In addition, there was
undoubtedly a considerable change in the pattern of growth between
the early and the later part of the period: during the first half it was the
countries of northern and western Europe which grew most rapidly,
but (with the exception of Holland) their rate of growth began to
slacken towards the end of the nineteenth century, and they were overtaken by the countries of the east and the south.

Table 8. *Annual Rates of Population Growth in European Countries
during the 19th century*[a]

Annual rate of growth per 1000

	1801–20	1821–30	1831–40	1841–50	1851–60	1861–70	1871–80	1881–90	1891–1900
Sweden	4·8	11·2	8·4	10·8	10·3	7·7	9·1	4·7	7·1
Norway	5·1	14·7	9·7	11·7	14·0	7·9	10·0	4·1	11·3
Denmark	8·3	9·3	7·2	9·8	12·3	10·4	9·6	9·4	11·5
Finland	7·4	13·2	5·3	12·5	6·5	1·2	15·4	13·2	11·1
Great Britain and Ireland	13·0	13·7	10·4	2·5	5·5	8·3	10·2	7·8	9·6
Holland	5·5	9·6	9·3	6·7	7·2	8·4	11·7	11·8	12·7
Belgium	7·7	7·2	8·0	7·4	6·2	7·4	9·5	9·5	9·9
Germany	5·2	11·2	7·5	7·7	6·4	7·8	10·3	8·9	13·2
Austria-Hungary	5·3	9·8	5·3	3·6	6·8	7·5	4·4	9·1	9·6
Switzerland	4·6	9·0	6·0	7·4	4·4	6·3	6·5	3·9	11·4
France	5·5	6·2	4·6	4·4	2·4	2·8	2·0	2·2	1·6
Italy	2·4	9·3	6·8	7·0	4·9	6·0	6·0	7·6	6·2
Spain	4·2	6·2	5·1	3·5	7·8	5·1	3·7	3·8	4·9
Portugal	1·6	7·6	7·7	2·0	5·6	8·3	7·4	7·2	7·2
Russia	9·6	10·8	8·3	7·7	8·0	11·7	13·6	13·9	13·5
Balkans	4·2	3·3	6·3	6·3	5·2	6·2	4·6	11·0	10·5
Europe	6·5	9·4	7·1	5·8	6·2	7·7	8·3	9·0	9·9

[a] After Sundbärg, *Aperçus statistiques internationaux*, p. 31.

A word must be said about Russia. No figures relating to Russia
have been included in Table 7, because of the paucity of information.
'In Russia', writes Lorimer, 'information about the growth and distribution of population during the eighteenth and most of the nineteenth century, prior to the first and only complete census of the
Russian empire in 1897 is meagre and unreliable.'[1] The estimates for the

[1] F. Lorimer, *The Population of the Soviet Union* (Geneva, 1946), p. 8.

nineteenth century are based on tax lists, the so-called 'revisions' which are of doubtful comprehensiveness. For 1806 an estimate of 41 millions is given,[1] for 1811 the estimate is 44 millions[2] of whom 41 millions are in European Russia. Lorimer quotes a figure of 58·6 millions for 1859,[3] but Rashin gives 70·0 millions in 1863. The 1897 census showed 94·3 millions, and an estimate of 155·4 millions is quoted by Rashin for 1913. The discrepancies between the 1859 and the 1863 estimates are serious. The estimates given by Lorimer are substantially below those given by Urlanis[4] even for European Russia, and a reconciliation of his figures, which are based on Troynitski's estimates, with those given by the Russian writers could only be attempted on the basis of a thorough study of the tax lists. The discrepancy does, however, show that the figures given in Table 6 for Europe are subject to serious errors.

As regards the population of the U.S.S.R. after 1920, the United Nations estimates amount to 158 millions in 1920, 176 millions in 1930 and 192 millions in 1940. The official estimate given by the United Nations for 1956 is 200 millions.[5] This figure was considerably lower than had been expected and caused the United Nations to revise their previous estimates downwards. Originally the figures for 1920–40 were higher than those given above. But whatever figures are accepted, it is clear that the population of Russia grew more rapidly than that of Europe as a whole and that the rate of increase accelerated considerably in the second half of the nineteenth century.

II. *Asia*

A survey of basic demographic statistics available in 1947 suggested that reasonably adequate data on population size and growth were available for about 54 per cent of the estimated population of that

[1] B. Z. Urlanis, *Rosst Nasselenyia v Evrope* (Moscow, 1941), p. 194, quoting D. Herman, *Statisticheskiye Issledovaniye otnossitelno Rossiskoy Imperii* (St Petersburg, 1819).

[2] A. G. Rashin, *Nasseleniye Rossii za 100 lyet* (Moscow, 1956), p. 24. This is a very detailed study of Russian population history during the period 1811–1913.

[3] Lorimer, *op. cit.* p. 10.

[4] Urlanis, *op cit.* p. 414, gives an estimate of 66·7 millions for European Russia alone for 1860.

[5] The United Nations estimates relate to the population within the *present* boundaries of the Soviet Union and are not, therefore, comparable with pre-war figures. The census of 1926 yielded a figure of 147 millions, and the figure generally quoted for the population within the pre-war boundaries of the U.S.S.R. for 1939 was 170 millions. Cf. Lorimer, *op. cit.* p. 135, and also G. Frumkin, *Population Changes in Europe since 1939* (London, 1951), pp. 158 ff. The last census taken in the U.S.S.R. was that of 1959 and reported a total of just under 209 millions.

continent.[1] Even at that date, therefore, the estimates for almost half the population of Asia—including the population of mainland China—were based upon statistics which could not be regarded as 'reasonably adequate'; hence, it is not surprising that, going back in time, the coverage of relatively reliable estimates becomes still more limited. This may be seen by taking the three countries which at present contribute the largest components to the total population, namely India and Pakistan, China and Japan.

For the Indian peninsula, the first general census was taken between 1867 and 1872. Coverage was incomplete and methods of enumeration defective, and it is generally assumed that, out of the apparent growth of about 100 millions between 1871 and 1911—that is, from 203 to 303 millions—about half must be attributed to improved methods and additional areas covered.[2] For earlier points of time, the figures are estimates, the bases of which are scarcely very firm. Thus Davis's estimate of 120 millions in 1800 is based upon another estimate by William Playfair, published in 1801, of 41 millions for what was then regarded as 'British India', an area under one-third of the later, overall territory. Earlier computations are still more tenuous, being derived from mixed calculations of the size of the armed forces and the area of land under cultivation.[3]

As pointed out earlier, there is no shortage of what purport to be 'population statistics' for China. But the attempts which so far have been made to use them have been largely defeated by the lack of knowledge of the coverage or accuracy of the data. Although there are references to 'censuses' in terms which suggest that, at least on occasion, something approaching the present-day conception of an enumeration was envisaged,[4] there is no evidence that the statistics collected before 1953—when the present government took its first census—were obtained by methods which a modern demographer would regard as satisfactory. The well-known dynastic statistics were collected for fiscal and military purposes, and their scope and reliability have not so far been established.[5] And it is abundantly clear that the direct censuses of

[1] J. D. Durand, 'Adequacy of Existing Census Statistics for Basic Demographic Research', Pop. Studies, IV (1950), 179 ff. The survey related to countries with estimated total populations of one million or more in 1947.

[2] See, for example, K. Davis, The Population of India and Pakistan (Princeton, N.J., 1951), p. 27.

[3] Ibid. pp. 24–5.

[4] See, for example, the reference to a census of A.D. 1370 in A. J. Jaffe, 'A Review of the Censuses and Demographic Statistics of China', Pop. Studies, I (1947), 308 ff.

[5] Compilations of such statistics are given in Nanming Liu, Contribution à l'étude de la population chinoise (Geneva, 1935). This author also discusses in some detail the efforts at direct census-taking made in 1909–11, 1912 and 1928.

1909–11, 1912 and 1928 were incomplete and, even within the areas covered, inaccurate.[1] Thus all figures provided for China were estimates, and inevitably rather notional in character. The kind of margin of error involved may be illustrated by citing the figures published by the United Nations before and after the 1953 census. For 1950 the estimate given is 463·5 millions while the 1953 census purported to show a total of 582·6 millions.[2] If the latter figure is near reality, estimates for earlier points of time will require very substantial revision.

Somewhat similar difficulties arise in using the population statistics of Japan before 1920. As in the case of China, Japan has a long history of population statistics, provision for the establishment of population registers having been made by the Great Reform of A.D. 646, and fairly regular 'censuses' having been taken during the Tokugawa period. But the statistics are defective in various ways, and the statistical position was not improved under the Meiji restoration, for from 1872 onwards the population was estimated by adding natural increase (and making an allowance for migration) to the statistics of a somewhat defective household registration of 1872. It was not until 1920 that a modern census was first taken, and the results of this census were used in correcting the estimates for the period 1868–1919. Clearly, however, those revised estimates are subject to a margin of error, and this is still more the case with any revisions of the Tokugawa data. It is not unreasonable to assume that the population fluctuated around 30 millions in the Tokugawa period, but whether it was actually increasing by the time of the Meiji restoration is more uncertain. Similarly, it is very probable that the total population in 1872 was somewhat—perhaps 2 or 3 millions—above the 33 millions registered. And if that were so, then the subsequent rate of growth was correspondingly lower than would be inferred by a comparison of the uncorrected figures of 33 millions in 1872 and 56 millions in 1920. Considerations of this kind in turn affect the interpretation of the apparent levels of the birth and death rates in the period and indicate the difficulties involved in

[1] Ta Chen, *Population in Modern China* (Chicago, 1946), p. 7, does not even mention the censuses of 1912 or 1928, but refers to the 1911 attempt as 'the only one of its kind up to the present time'. On some of the problems involved in trying to collect demographic statistics in pre-war China, see C. M. Ch'iao, W. S. Thompson and D. T. Chen, *An Experiment in the Registration of Vital Statistics in China* (Oxford, Ohio, 1938), ch. 1, and S. D. Gamble, *Peking: A Social Survey* (London, 1921), pp. 93 and 104–10.

[2] U.N. *Demographic Yearbook* (1951), p. 97; (1956), p. 143. On the 1953 census, see I. B. Taeuber and L. A. Orleans, 'A Note on the Population Statistics of Communist China', *Population Index*, XXII (1956), 274; A. Sauvy, 'La population de la Chine', *Population*, XII (1957), 695; and J. S. Aird, *The Size, Composition and Growth of the Population of Mainland China*.

ascertaining exactly how a population responds to the early stages of industrialization.[1]

If the establishment of overall rates of growth is subject to such margins of indeterminacy, even larger margins must be expected in attempting to deal with the major components of growth, with rates of birth and death. It is usually easier to take an effective census than to ensure a comprehensive and reliable system of vital registration, the latter involving a persistent effort as compared with the periodic organization which may be sufficient for the former. In a country like Sweden, with a system of continuous registration supplying both population and vital statistics, the improvement of both types of data proceeded in parallel. But in many countries, ecclesiastical registration of marriages, baptisms and burials still obtained for some years after national censuses had been initiated. And when comprehensive civil registration was finally introduced, it by no means followed that the new registration system immediately achieved completeness. In England and Wales, civil registration began in 1837, by which time the censuses, initiated in 1801, were producing reasonably reliable statistics. Registration statistics were not reasonably complete, however, until after 1874.[2] And in the United States, where control of registration is vested in the individual states, it was not until the present century that comprehensive vital registration was aimed at, and not until 1935 that birth registration was 90 per cent complete.[3] There are still many parts of the world—in Africa and Asia, especially—where comprehensive registration systems have not yet been introduced, and others—especially in Latin America—where the existing systems show considerable defects. For such areas it is often necessary to collect information on births and deaths entirely through censuses or sample surveys, or to apply 'correcting' techniques which, while yielding reasonable approximations, may in

[1] On Japanese population statistics, see I. B. Taeuber and F. W. Notestein, 'The Changing Fertility of the Japanese', *Pop. Studies*, I (1947), 12–28; R. Ishii, *Population Pressure and Economic Life in Japan* (London, 1937), chs. I and IV; Y. S. Kuno, *Japanese Expansion on the Asiatic Continent* (Berkeley, 1940), II, appendix 13; M. Requien, *Le problème de la population au Japon* (Tokyo, 1934), chs. I–III.

[2] See D. V. Glass, 'A Note on the Under-registration of Births in Britain in the Nineteenth Century', *Pop. Studies*, V (1951), 70.

[3] See S. Shapiro, 'Development of Birth Registration and Birth Statistics in the United States', *Pop. Studies*, IV (1950), 86. There is no single study which discusses in sufficient detail the development of registration systems or provides consistent tests of the completeness of the various systems in successive periods. Useful material on registration history will, however, be found in the pre-war publications of the Health Organization of the League of Nations (Statistical Handbook Series—*The Official Vital Statistics of* [various countries]); in R. R. Kuczynski, *The Balance of Births and Deaths* (Washington, D.C., 1928 and 1931), vols. I and II, and in the studies of the demography of specific countries referred to in this chapter.

some cases preclude detailed analysis of trends.[1] Hence in the subsequent discussion of birth and death rates, and of the underlying levels of fertility and mortality, it will not be possible, even for the western world, to carry the account as far back as would be desirable. The early nineteenth century is a dim page for most countries, such illumination as is available deriving from investigations of special groups within the population. So far as the rest of the world is concerned, the discussion will be confined mainly to a number of 'sample' rates for those areas having usable data or for which not too unreliable approximations can be made.[2]

In surveys of the trends of fertility and mortality, the indices most widely used are crude birth and death rates, usually cited per 1000 total population. Because these rates are based upon total populations, they are influenced by the age and sex composition of the populations considered, as well as by the specific chances of bearing a child or of dying at any given age. This reduces the comparability of the rates for a particular country over time, and between countries (or between different areas in the same country) at a specified point of time, and if, for example, two countries have the same crude death rate, it does not necessarily mean that they have the same expectation of life at birth.[3] But in spite of these limitations, crude rates are a useful preliminary index, and accordingly the birth and death rates for a number of European countries have been listed in Table 9.[4] It will be convenient to consider the death rates first.

[1] It is, for example, possible to estimate birth and death rates on the assumption of a 'stable' population structure. But such an assumption also defines the general population trend, which is thus not susceptible to further analysis unless independent estimates are made.

[2] According to the United Nations, of the 214 countries covered by their international inquiries, only 149 had birth and death statistics for the whole or practically all of their national territories. Again, out of the total of 214 countries, birth and death statistics were virtually complete in fifty-eight; recognized as incomplete in fifty-six; with degree of completeness unknown in fifty-four; while for the remaining forty-six, no statistics were available to the United Nations. The figure of fifty-eight for 'complete' statistics includes countries in which the data do not cover all sections of the population (see U.N. *Demographic Yearbook* (1956), pp. 15–16).

[3] An extreme example of the influence of age and sex composition on the crude birth rate is given in R. R. Kuczynski, *Fertility and Reproduction* (New York, 1932), p. 4. In the state of Colorado, U.S.A., in 1860, women aged 15 to 50 years constituted only 3·2 per cent of the total population. Hence, even if half of the women had borne a child in 1860—a proportion higher than that found in Quebec in the seventeenth century—the crude birth rate would have been only 16 per 1000.

[4] The rates have been obtained from G. Sundbärg, *Aperçus statistiques internationaux*, for the period before 1900; for 1900 to 1935 from H. Bunle, *Le mouvement naturel de la population dans le monde, 1906 à 1936* (Paris, 1954); and for the period after 1935 from the various issues of the *Demographic Yearbook* of the United Nations. The three sets of rates are not always strictly comparable, but the differences in definition do not greatly affect the comparisons.

Table 9. *Crude Birth and Death Rates of European Countries*

(Rates per 1000 total population)

Country		1841–50	1851–60	1861–70	1876–80	1886–90	1896–1900	1906–10	1911–15	1916–20	1921–5	1926–30	1931–5	1936–40	1941–5	1946–50	1951–5
Austria[a]	BR	—	—	39.6	41.0	40.0	38.2	34.0	22.1	16.0	21.9	17.7	14.4	14.7	19.1	16.7	15.0
	DR	—	—	31.5	33.2	30.0	26.6	22.5	18.3	21.1	15.6	14.5	13.3	13.9	14.4	15.4	12.2
Belgium	BR	30.5	30.4	32.2	32.0	29.4	29.0	24.7	20.9	14.7	20.5	18.6	16.9	15.5	13.9	17.3	16.7
	DR	24.4	22.6	23.8	21.8	20.3	18.2	15.9	14.6	51.8	13.4	13.7	13.0	13.2	15.1	13.5	12.2
Bulgaria	BR	—	—	—	—	—	41.3	42.1	38.8	26.5	39.0	33.1	29.3	24.2	22.1	24.6[b]	20.7[c]
	DR	—	—	—	—	27.9	24.1	23.8	22.3	23.1	20.8	17.8	15.5	13.9	13.2	14.0[b]	10.1
Czechoslovakia	BR	—	—	—	—	—	—	—	—	24.6	27.1	23.2	19.6	17.1	20.8	22.4	22.0
	DR	—	—	—	—	—	—	—	—	18.6	16.1	15.3	13.3	13.2	14.3	13.4	10.9
Denmark	BR	30.5	32.5	30.8	32.1	31.4	29.9	28.2	25.7	24.0	22.2	19.4	17.8	17.9	20.3	21.6	17.9
	DR	20.5	20.5	19.9	19.4	18.7	16.4	13.7	12.8	13.1	11.2	11.1	10.9	10.6	10.0	9.6	9.0
Finland	BR	35.5	35.9	34.7	36.9	34.8	33.5	30.6	27.3	23.3	23.1	21.1	18.4	20.2	20.1	27.0	22.8
	DR	23.5	28.6	32.6	22.7	20.2	19.5	17.2	16.0	19.5	14.1	13.9	12.6	13.2	17.1	11.7	9.6
France	BR	27.3	26.1	26.1	25.3	23.0	21.9	20.2	17.4	13.2	19.3	18.2	16.5	15.1	14.7	20.7	19.5
	DR	23.2	23.7	23.6	22.5	22.0	20.6	19.1	21.5	22.1	17.2	16.8	15.7	13.2	17.9	13.8	12.8
Germany	BR	36.1	25.3	37.2	39.2	36.5	36.0	31.6	26.3	17.8	22.1	18.4	16.6	19.4	17.4[d]	16.6[ef]	15.8[e]
	DR	26.8	26.4	26.9	26.1	24.4	21.3	17.5	17.7	19.1	13.2	11.8	11.2	11.9	12.2[d]	11.2[ef]	10.5[e]
Greece	BR	—	—	—	—	—	—	—	—	—	21.0	29.9	29.5	26.8	19.6	25.5	19.4
	DR	—	—	—	—	—	—	—	—	—	15.1	16.4	16.5	14.5	17.3	10.8	7.1
Hungary	BR	—	—	—	—	—	—	36.7	32.8	16.0	29.4	26.0	22.5	20.1	19.3[d]	19.9	21.1
	DR	—	—	—	—	—	—	25.0	24.2	22.4	19.9	17.0	15.8	14.3	13.9[d]	14.8	11.4
Italy	BR	—	—	37.9	37.0	37.3	33.9	32.6	31.2	23.0	29.6	26.7	23.9	23.2	20.6	21.2	18.4
	DR	—	—	30.9	29.5	27.0	22.9	21.1	19.6	24.3	17.3	15.9	14.0	13.9	14.6	11.7	9.9

		1841–50	1851–60	1861–70	1876–80	1886–90	1896–1900	1906–10	1911–15	1916–20	1921–5	1926–30	1931–5	1936–40	1941–5	1946–50	1951–5
Netherlands	BR	33·0	33·3	35·7	36·4	33·6	32·2	29·6	27·8	26·1	25·6	23·2	21·1	20·3	21·8	25·9	22·2
	DR	26·2	25·6	25·4	22·9	20·5	17·2	14·3	12·8	13·7	10·3	9·9	8·9	8·7	10·2	9·5	7·5
Norway	BR	30·7	33·0	30·8	31·8	30·8	30·3	26·0	24·9	24·5	22·1	17·9	15·2	15·0	17·7	20·8	18·7
	DR	18·2	17·1	18·0	16·6	17·0	15·6	13·7	13·2	14·1	11·5	11·0	10·4	10·2	10·7	9·3	8·7
Poland	BR	—	—	—	—	—	—	39·8	—	—	34·7	32·3	27·6	25·4g	—	27·9f	30·1
	DR	—	—	—	—	—	—	22·8	—	—	18·5	16·7	14·6	14·0	—	11·4j	11·1
Portugal	BR	—	—	—	33·3	32·6	31·6	30·9	33·7	30·6	33·3	30·9	29·0	27·1	24·5	25·6	23·9
	DR	—	—	—	23·2	22·4	22·2	20·0	20·4	26·6	20·7	18·4	16·9	15·9	15·8	13·8	11·7
Roumania	BR	—	—	41·8	40·9	39·9	39·3	40·3	42·0	—	37·9	35·2	32·9	30·2	23·2	—	23·7h
	DR	—	—	26·6	28·7	30·2	26·8	26·0	24·5	—	23·0	21·2	20·6	19·6	19·1	—	11·5h
Spain	BR	—	—	37·8	—	36·1	34·5	33·2	30·8	28·8	29·8	28·5	27·0	22·0	22·0	22·3	20·3
	DR	—	—	30·6	—	31·1	29·0	24·0	22·1	24·6	20·2	17·9	16·3	17·9	15·3	11·9	10·2
Sweden	BR	31·1	32·8	31·4	30·3	28·8	26·9	25·4	23·1	21·2	19·1	15·9	14·1	14·5	17·7	19·0	15·5
	DR	20·6	21·7	20·2	18·3	16·4	16·1	14·3	14·1	14·5	12·1	11·8	11·6	11·7	10·8	10·4	9·8
Switzerland	BR	29·8	27·8	30·2	31·3	27·4	28·4	26·0	22·7	19·2	19·5	17·5	16·4	15·4	17·9	19·4	17·3
	DR	22·8	22·4	23·0	23·1	20·3	18·1	16·0	14·3	15·0	12·5	12·1	11·8	11·6	11·4	11·2	10·1
United Kingdom, England and Wales k	BR	32·6	34·1	35·2	35·3	31·4	29·3	26·3	23·6	20·1	19·9	16·7	15·0	14·7	15·9	18·0	15·2
	DR	22·4	22·2	22·5	20·8	18·9	17·7	14·7	14·3	14·4	12·1	12·1	12·0	12·5	12·8	11·8	11·7
Scotland	BR	—	34·1l	(35·0)	34·8	31·4	30·0	27·6	25·4	22·8	23·0	20·0	18·2	17·6	17·8	19·8	17·8
	DR	—	20·8l	(22·1)	20·6	18·8	17·9	16·1	15·7	15·0	13·9	13·6	13·2	13·5	13·8	—	12·1
Yugoslavia	BR	—	—	—	—	—	—	39·0	—	—	34·9	34·2	31·9	27·9	—	28·3	28·8
	DR	—	—	—	—	—	—	24·7	—	—	20·1	20·0	18·0	15·9	—	13·3i	12·5

a Austria-Hungary before 1906. b 1945–7. c 1951–4. d 1940–3. e West Germany. f 1946–9. g 1935–8.
h 1953. i 1948–50. j 1947–9. k Birth rates before 1876 not corrected for under-registration. l 1855–60.

III.   *Mortality Rates*

That the nineteenth century was one of falling mortality is well known, and the crude death rates in Table 9 confirm the trend. But the fall in the death rates before 1900 took place in western and north-western Europe, and it was not until the present century that the rest of the continent followed. 'Scandinavia achieved a death rate of under 20 per thousand in the 1860's; England, about 1880; the Netherlands, about 1890; Italy and Austria, about 1910; most of Eastern Europe and the Balkans, in the 1920's; and, finally, Roumania and probably the Soviet Union, in the 1930's.[1] By 1950–4 the death rate had fallen to below ten per thousand in a number of countries, and the highest rate shown for that period in Table 9 is 12·8 for France, with a population containing a larger proportion of old people than other European countries.[2]

Death rates which are as low as ten per thousand or under imply a very youthful population. Such rates must be transitory, for a constant death rate of ten per thousand would mean an expectation of life at birth of 100 years, very considerably higher than has been achieved so far by any country.[3] A measure of overall mortality—or rather, of its reverse—which is not affected by age composition is the expectation of life at birth, as derived from an appropriate life table. Such tables were constructed from the seventeenth century onwards, but many of the early life tables were based upon inaccurate or incomplete data, or computed by statistical techniques which would have yielded correct results only if the populations had been stationary.[4] Sweden, because of

---

[1] F. W. Notestein and others, *The Future Population of Europe and the Soviet Union, 1940–1970* (Geneva, 1944), p. 49.

[2] Indeed, out of a large, though selected, list of countries for which estimates or census data were available around 1950, France shows the highest proportion of persons aged 65 years and over—11·8 % (see U.N., *The Aging of Populations and its Economic and Social Implications* (New York), 1956, appendix, table II).

[3] The highest expectations of life at birth recorded in the 1956 U.N. *Demographic Yearbook* are (for females): United States 1954 (whites), 73·6 years; England and Wales, 1954, 73·05 years; the Netherlands, 1950–2, 72·9 years; and New Zealand, 1950–2 (excluding Maoris), 72·4 years. The lowest crude death rate shown in Table 9 is for Greece, which has almost the smallest proportion in Europe of persons aged 65 years and over—6·31 %. No current expectation of life is reported for Greece in the 1956 *Demographic Yearbook*, the most recent figure being 50·89 years for females in 1926–30. An estimate of 56·9 years for 1940 is given in U.N. *Age and Sex Patterns of Mortality* (New York, 1955), p. 34.

[4] For the history of life tables see H. Westergaard, *Contributions to the History of Statistics* (London, 1932), and L. I. Dublin, A. J. Lotka and M. Spiegelman, *Length of Life* (New York, 1949). The life tables referred to in this chapter are, unless otherwise described, current tables based upon the age-specific death rates observed in a given

its system of continuous registers introduced in the mid-eighteenth century, has a run of data allowing the construction of life tables from 1751-5 onwards. But few reliable national tables are available until the nineteenth century, and it is not until the middle of that century that a substantial number of such tables can be drawn upon. For England and Wales, the period covered is from the 1840's to the present day. Since the experience of that country is not untypical of the western world in the nineteenth and twentieth centuries, and since in general English mortality statistics—including statistics of deaths by cause and by socio-economic group—are more comprehensive than those of most other countries, it is those statistics which will be used here to illustrate the changes in the levels and pattern of mortality in the West during the past hundred years, though reference will also be made to other data.

The basic statistics of expectation of life in England and Wales are given in Table 10, which shows the number of years, according to the mortality observed in the specified period, an average male or female could expect to live from birth or from various subsequent ages.[1] The table records an uninterrupted increase in life expectation since the middle of the nineteenth century, as well as an acceleration of the rate of increase during the present century. How far, and in which periods, the expectation of life rose before the 1840's is not known in any precise way.[2] An examination of the statistics for the few countries with extensive historical records does not suggest that there was necessarily a single pattern of development before the mid-nineteenth century. In Denmark, for example, the expectation of life appeared to

calendar year or other short period—for example, a five-year period. Equally interesting—in some circumstances more interesting—are generation life tables, based upon the age-specific death rates of a given cohort of births—for example, the males born in England and Wales in 1846-50—followed through the successive years of their lives. A generation life table thus purports to show the number of years actually lived by a group of persons born in a particular period, in contrast to the number of years which a group would live if it were subject to the death rates observed in a particular short period of time. In an era of falling mortality, generation life tables will naturally show higher expectations of life than current life tables. The generation method has been very usefully applied in historical studies of special groups—for example, studies of the nobility—for whom there are records of the ages at death of all the members born in a given period. See, for example, S. Peller, 'Studies on Mortality since the Renaissance', *Bull. Hist. Med.* XIII (1943); XVI (1944); XXI (1947); and T. H. Hollingsworth, 'A Demographic Study of the British Ducal Families', *Pop. Studies,* XI (1957).

[1] The meaning of the statistics for the ages above 0 is that, for example, a man who had attained his twentieth birthday would, according to the mortality observed in 1838-54, expect to live another 39·48 years—that is, until the age of 59·48 years.

[2] Nor is it likely that reasonable estimates will be possible until new and much more extensive historico-demographic studies are undertaken.

Table 10. *Expectation of Life (in years) in England and Wales*

Age (years)	1838–54		1871–80		1881–90		1891–1900	
	M	W	M	W	M	W	M	W
0	39·91	41·85	41·35	44·62	43·66	47·18	44·13	47·77
10	47·05	47·67	47·60	49·76	49·00	51·10	49·63	51·97
20	39·48	40·29	39·40	41·66	40·27	42·42	41·02	43·44
40	29·06	27·34	25·30	27·46	25·42	27·60	25·64	27·82
60	13·53	14·34	13·14	14·24	12·88	14·10	12·93	14·10
70	8·45	9·02	8·27	8·95	8·04	8·77	8·05	8·78

Age (years)	1901–12		1930–2		1950–2		1957–9	
	M	W	M	W	M	W	M	W
0	51·50	55·35	58·74	62·88	66·42	71·54	68·0	73·7
10	53·08	55·91	55·79	58·87	59·24	63·87	60·1	65·5
20	44·21	47·10	46·81	49·88	49·64	54·17	50·5	55·7
40	27·74	30·30	29·62	32·55	30·98	35·32	31·6	36·5
60	13·78	15·48	14·43	16·50	14·79	18·07	15·1	19·0
70	8·53	9·58	8·62	10·02	9·00	10·97	9·4	11·8

Figures to 1900 from L. I. Dublin, A. J. Lotka and M. Spiegelman, *Length of Life*, p. 39; for 1910–52 from *The Registrar General's Decennial Supplement, England and Wales, 1951: Life Tables*, p. 12; for 1957–9 from *The Registrar General's Quarterly Return for England and Wales* (2nd qtr. 1960), appendix B.

fall somewhat in the 1840's, while in Norway and Sweden the analogous fall occurred in the 1830's.[1] For Sweden, whose data go back to the mid-eighteenth century, the statistics indicate a slightly higher overall level of expectation after 1790 than before, though the lowest expectation of life in the earlier period—that of 29·1 years for males in 1771–5—was almost matched at one point in the later period—30·7 years for males in 1806–10. There also appears to be something of a second watershed around 1820, in the sense that the general run of the figures is slightly higher thereafter than in the period 1790–1820. But the differences referred to here are all relatively small and, as in the case of England and Wales, a steady and clearly marked rise in expectation—a clear rise above forty years, that is—is not evident until the 1850's and

---

[1] The data for Norway and Denmark are from Dublin, Lotka and Spiegelman, *Length of Life*, appendix, table 87. The only other country for which a long run of reasonable statistics is given is the Netherlands. Here the expectations show a steady rise from 29·32 years for males in 1816–25, though it was not until 1880–9 that the figure rose above 40 years (42·5 years for that period). But the series is incomplete, with a gap between 1825 and 1840–51, so that evidence of a change in mortality in the 1830's is not given.

1860's.[1] For England the only realistic and relatively representative life table constructed before Farr initiated the series of national tables is that by Milne for Carlisle at the end of the eighteenth century, showing an expectation of life at birth (for males and females together) of 38·7 years.[2] This does not suggest any great difference in expectation between the beginning and the middle of the nineteenth century, though it is clearly impossible to draw any firm conclusions from a comparison of one town with the country as a whole. For the present, therefore, the movement of mortality before the 1840's must remain rather shadowy. Though a fall in the death rate between the mid-eighteenth and mid-nineteenth centuries is rather probable, it is as yet insufficiently documented. And whatever fall occurred is not likely—save as regards smallpox—to have been in any major degree the result of improvements in medical knowledge or practices[3] but rather of more general changes in the environment, changes which would in any case have applied to a large proportion of the population.

Turning again to Table 10, three features are clear. First, mortality changed very slowly until after the 1880's, suggesting that improvements in hygiene and medicine could scarcely do more than hold their

[1] The early data on expectation of life in Sweden are from unpublished calculations. Other evidence on the early nineteenth-century course of mortality is available—in the form of crude death rates—for Finland and France. For Finland these rates show a steady fall from 1801–10 to 1821–30, but marked fluctuations from that point until 1861–70 (see Statistique Générale de la France, *Statistique internationale du mouvement de la population* (Paris, 1907), p. 368). For France, on the other hand, the fall is somewhat more consistent, though there are upward fluctuations in 1826–35 and 1866–75 (see M. Huber, H. Bunle and F. Boverat, *La population de la France* (Paris, 1938), p. 79). The work of J. Bourgeois-Pichat (*Population*, Oct.–Dec. 1951) suggests that mortality may have been falling in France from the 1770's.

[2] The Carlisle table was based on the mortality of 1779–87 and was derived from enumeration and vital statistics collected by Dr John Heysham. See J. Milne, *A Treatise on the Valuation of Annuities and Assurances* (London, 1815), vol. II, ch. XI and pp. 564–5. On the correspondence between Milne and Heysham in relation to the data in the Carlisle table, see appendix to H. Lonsdale, *The Life of John Heysham, M.D.* (London, 1870).

[3] See R. G. Brown and T. McKeown, 'Medical Evidence related to English Population Changes in the Eighteenth Century', *Pop. Studies*, IX. Hollingsworth's study of the British ducal families (*op. cit.* p. 8) goes back to the fourteenth century in constructing estimates of the expectation of life. These are generation expectations, and show a major break as between the generation born 1680–1729 (that is, living on the average in the first half of the eighteenth century), with an expectation at birth of 33·0 years for males, and that born 1730–79 (living mainly in the second half of the century), with an expectation of 44·8 years. Thereafter the successive generations show a steady increase, but not one nearly so startling. It should be remembered, however, that these estimates relate to a small population and one which cannot be regarded as representative of the country as a whole. Hollingsworth's study is now being applied to the whole of the British peerage.

own against the environmental disadvantages of the growing urban population. Secondly, the statistics for the earlier years show a marked wastage of life in infancy and childhood. Thus, as a result, from 1838–54 to 1891–1900 the expectation of life was substantially higher at age 10 than at birth. Thirdly, the overall increase in life expectancy between the 1850's and the 1950's—66 per cent at birth for males and 71 per cent for females—has been due primarily to a reduction in the mortality of younger people and very little to an increase in the further lifetime of the relatively old. These two latter features are given more explicit expression in Table 11, which displays the relative fall of mortality in specific age groups. In addition, the table shows the accelerating rate of decline in the twentieth century of mortality at the younger ages. Infant mortality—mortality during the first year of life—did not indeed begin to fall consistently until the beginning of the present century.[1] At the end of the nineteenth century, out of every thousand live-born children, about 150 died before the first birthday, a rate not greatly different from that found in the 1840's.

The fall in mortality documented by the national statistics given above cannot be 'explained' in any detailed way—not, that is, in the sense of attributing a given proportion of it to a given set of measures or even to a broad segment of the environment. Apart from the investigation of direct occupational hazards, or the study of the efficacy of particular medical practices or forms of therapy, few surveys have attempted statistically to estimate the impact of, say, a particular paramedical service or to isolate the specific factors in the environment which would account for the continued differences in mortality between middle-class and working-class children.[2] Hence it is not possible to say which aspects of, for example, the maternity and child welfare services in Britain were responsible for what proportion of the fall in infant mortality in the twentieth century. At the same time, a somewhat general contribution to the problem of explanation can be made by an examination of the trend of mortality from various

---

[1] Again, although there are uniformities in the way in which mortality fell in the various western countries, there are also differences. Thus, in Sweden, infant mortality appears to have fallen consistently after 1815, and there was a similar, though rather less consistent, fall in Norway after 1840. In Denmark and France, however, the time pattern is more like that in England and Wales.

[2] On the questions involved in explaining such differences, there is a very extensive literature. See, for example, on infant mortality the papers by Heady, Morris *et al.* in *The Lancet*, 12, 19, and 26 February, and 5 and 12 March 1955; and on infant and early childhood morbidity, J. W. B. Douglas and J. M. Blomfield, *Children Under Five* (London, 1958), chs. IX and X. D. V. Glass, 'Some Aspects of the Development of Demography', *J. Roy. Soc. Arts*, CIV (1956), gives a very brief account of the development of mortality analysis in England.

Table 11. *Mortality Indices: England and Wales*[a]

(Mortality rates by age group expressed as a percentage of the corresponding mortality in 1846–50)

	Infant mortality	0–	5–	10–	15–	20–	25–	35–	45–	55–	65–	75–	85–
Males													
1846–50	100	100	100	100	100	100	100	100	100	100	100	100	100
1871–5	97	95	75	74	77	81	91	100	105	106	100	98	101
1896–1900	99	84	43	43	49	49	59	79	95	103	97	93	88
1921–5	50	36	27	31	36	35	37	46	63	76	83	89	85
1947	27	19	11	15	22	21	19	24	47	70	76	82	83
1955	16	9	5	8	12	12	12	19	40	66	78	84	80
Females													
1846–50	100	100	100	100	100	100	100	100	100	100	100	100	100
1871–5	97	94	72	70	73	77	84	86	94	97	97	96	99
1896–1900	99	83	46	42	42	43	51	65	82	90	94	91	87
1921–5	46	34	26	30	32	32	33	36	52	63	73	81	81
1947	25	17	9	11	15	19	17	19	34	43	56	69	74
1955	15	8	4	6	5	6	8	14	28	38	52	65	75

[a] Data for 1846–50 to 1947 from W. P. D. Logan, 'Mortality in England and Wales from 1848 to 1947', *Pop. Studies*, IV, no. 2; for 1955 from *The Registrar General's Statistical Review of England and Wales, 1955*, part I (London, 1956).

causes, as well as by a study of socio-economic differences in levels of mortality.

A broad picture of changes in cause mortality is given in Table 12, which shows the relative death rates (for all ages) after 1872 from the main groups of causes, expressed as percentages of the corresponding rates in 1848–72. If the rates for 1901–10 are taken as indicating what reductions in cause mortality had been achieved by the end of the nineteenth century, it will be seen that the primary fall by that point of time was in deaths from infectious diseases—especially from typhus and typhoid, smallpox, scarlet fever and cholera, as well as, though to a smaller extent, from tuberculosis, though the latter was so important a cause of death that even this smaller decline accounts for a major fraction of the total reduction in the nineteenth century. In the period 1848–72 there had been three severe outbreaks of cholera, but by the beginning of the twentieth century this disease and typhus had virtually disappeared. The great reduction in deaths from infectious diseases was in the main due to sanitary or public health action, and vital statistics of the kind presented by Farr in England and Shattuck in the United States were more important here than medical science. Indeed, medicine as such had to wait until after the work of Pasteur and Koch, from the 1870's onwards, had produced rapid advances in bacteriology, establishing the relationship between particular bacteria and particular diseases, and providing a rational basis for immunology. It was with such new knowledge, too, with the reorganization of hospitals and the application of antiseptic and aseptic procedures, that advantage could be taken of anaesthesia and of evolving surgical techniques which otherwise might simply have resulted in still higher mortality rates.[1] The impact of these changes was far more apparent in the twentieth than in the nineteenth century, and they were added to by the elaboration of new fields of medical and para-medical investigation, including nutrition[2] and chemotherapy. And it was in the twentieth century, therefore, that other causes of death than infectious diseases—for example, diseases of the respiratory system—began rapidly to respond to control. The reduction in maternal mortality is an example of the combined influence of various developments—of ante-natal services, of improvements in the nutrition of pregnant women, of more

[1] See, for example, R. H. Shryock, *The Development of Modern Medicine* (London, 1948), chs. XII–XIV. The consequences of surgery as such, in the absence of antiseptic procedures, are suggested by the report (Shryock, p. 229, citing Newsholme) that 'of the 13,000 amputations performed by French army surgeons during the Franco-Prussian war, no fewer than 10,000 proved fatal'.

[2] See J. C. Drummond and A. Wilbraham, *The Englishman's Food* (London, 1939), chs. XXII–XXV.

Table 12. Cause Mortality Indices: England and Wales

(Death rate at all ages by cause group, expressed as percentage of corresponding rate in 1848–72. Sources as in Table 11)

	1848–72		1901–10		1921		1931		1939		1947		1955	
	M	F	M	F	M	F	M	F	M	F	M	F	M	F
All causes	100	100	70	67	55	53	56	54	55	53	58	53	53	51
Infectious diseases	100	100	44	37	27	23	18	20	16	12	13	9	4	2
Cancer	100	100	351	214	519	266	659	315	758	349	920	377	1011	390
Diseases of the nervous system	100	100	63	68	43	49	34	40	32	40	34	46	37	55
Diseases of the circulatory system	100	100	128	117	147	130	253	230	345	296	418	328	437	360
Diseases of the respiratory system	100	100	84	84	64	60	52	50	34	30	36	27	33	24
Diseases of the digestive system	100	100	76	72	55	45	38	31	34	26	32	23	23	18
Diseases of the genito-urinary system	100	100	183	330	173	286	220	341	203	283	186	231	134	171
Diseases of pregnancy and child-birth	—	100	—	97	—	77	—	58	—	39	—	20	—	—
Suicide and violence	100	100	73	87	57	65	67	88	72	101	46	73	53	100

adequate obstetrical services, and of the new chemotherapy.[1] Analogous combined influences help to account for the reduction in infant mortality from 153 deaths per 1000 live births in 1891–1900 to twenty-seven in 1951–5. Nor should the importance of the general rise in levels of living, and of the improvement in living conditions, be underestimated; they must, indeed, explain the major part of the decline in mortality in the nineteenth century. In addition, one of the most significant developments in mortality analysis—that of the analysis of mortality differences between the different social classes—has, since 1911, provided a new basis for the development of social policy in the field of health by demonstrating the link between high mortality and low socio-economic status.[2]

Over the past century, therefore, the pattern of cause mortality has changed markedly. In the 1840's about a third of all deaths were due to infectious diseases, and almost a half to infectious and respiratory diseases taken together. In the 1940's infectious diseases had almost disappeared from the list; instead, over a third of all deaths were due to circulatory diseases—diseases of the heart and of the coronary arteries—and just over a half to circulatory diseases and cancer taken together. In part this shift is attributable to the factors already discussed. But there has also apparently been a genuine increase in cancer mortality, though it is difficult to estimate what proportion of the increased death rates is due to more accurate diagnosis and certification. These questions also apply to the apparent increase in deaths from circulatory diseases, though the major proportion of this increase is the result of changes in the age structure of the population.[3]

[1] Logan, 'Mortality in England and Wales, from 1848 to 1947', *Pop. Studies*, IV, pp. 132 ff; for 1955, from *The Registrar General's Statistical Review of England and Wales 1955*, part I (London, 1956), pp. 143–4.

[2] For a survey of these relationships, see *The Registrar General's Decennial Supplement, England and Wales, 1951, Occupational Mortality*, part I (London, 1954). By 1951 the previously consistent relationship between mortality and socio-economic group seemed to be breaking down to some extent for adult males and married women (though the data were not definitive). For infant mortality, however, the relationship remained unchanged, each socio-economic group appearing to have experienced the same proportionate fall in the death rate since 1911.

[3] Logan, *op. cit.* p. 167. The death rates for circulatory diseases have fallen at all ages below 45 years. For the higher ages they have risen, however, and it is the increased proportion of persons aged 45 years and over in the population which accounts for the overall rise in the death rate from this category of causes. It should be emphasized that, in the above discussion, only the major factors affecting mortality changes have been mentioned, and even those referred to very briefly. A full discussion would need to consider many additional factors. On the environmental side, for example, the ease of access to medical advice and care would have to be considered—a factor of great importance in differentiating between the position in developed and under-

Though the picture differs in detail, and though there have been variations in timing, the account given of changes in mortality in England and Wales would also apply fairly well to other countries in western Europe, as well as to the United States and to Australia and New Zealand. A recent and exhaustive study of a large number of life tables yielded the following generalizations regarding the course of mortality in the West:[1] (i) The increase in the expectation of life has probably been greater and more widespread during the past century than in the previous 2000 years. (ii) Modern increases became marked in the late nineteenth century, and in most countries the gains since the 1890's have probably been more than twice as great as the gains in the preceding fifty years. (iii) During the present century, in particular, there has been a substantial narrowing of the differences in mortality between the various countries of the West. (iv) What has happened during the past hundred years is in many respects unrepeatable. Any major increases in expectation of life in the future must, in the main, come about by a reduction in the mortality of persons aged 60 years or over.[2]

The general significance of these changes for western countries is

developed countries, and commented upon later in this chapter. And there are also demographic and genetic factors. For example, the reduction in family size may have helped to raise the average age of onset of infectious diseases among children and thus increased their chances of survival. On the genetic side, the spread of transport, the breakdown of local 'isolates' and the fall in family size have reduced the frequency of marriages between blood relatives and correspondingly lowered the probability of recessives coming together and resulting in children with inherited abnormalities (though this process will have increased the proportion of 'carriers' in the total population). Again, there is an extensive literature on these questions, but it is of a rather specialized kind. See, however, the general discussion in *Proc. World Pop. Conf. 1954*, Summary Report, pp. 111–15, and Papers, vol. VI.

[1] G. Stolnitz, 'A Century of International Mortality Trends', *Pop. Studies*, IX (1955); and X (1956). Stolnitz defines the West as including the United Kingdom and Ireland, Scandinavia, the Low Countries, France, Germany and Switzerland, the United States, Canada, Australia and New Zealand, the white populations of the Union of South Africa and Southern Rhodesia, and the Jewish population of Israel.

[2] The study undertaken by Stolnitz deliberately excludes any analysis of changes in urban–rural differences—understandably, for that would be a major undertaking in its own right. It would be complicated by the problem of comparability of definitions of urban communities between countries and over periods of time. And there would still be a basic question unsolved, namely, how far the urban environment as such would account for the differences found. It is, however, worth noting that in some of the western countries, at least, differences between urban and rural mortality appear to have been diminishing since the First World War. In England and Wales, 1950–2, the expectation of life at birth was slightly higher in Greater London than in the country as a whole. But in other large urban areas, mortality was above the national average, while in rural districts it was below that average. See *The Registrar General's Decennial Supplement, England and Wales, 1951, Life Tables* (London, 1957), pp. 17–21.

illustrated in Tables 13 and 14. Table 13 shows, for five European countries, the approximate quartile ages at death in the 1840's and in the 1940's, the first, second and third quartiles representing the ages by which 25 per cent, 50 per cent and 75 per cent respectively of a set of babies would have died given the mortality rates at the two points of time. The greatest difference is in the first quartile. A hundred years ago, a quarter of all the children would have died before their fifth birthday (with the exception of Sweden), whereas in the 1940's the corresponding age was above 50 years for males, and above 60 years for females in all the countries cited. The changes in the third quartile

Table 13. *Quartile Ages at Death in Selected European Countries*[1]

Country	1st quartile		2nd quartile		3rd quartile	
	M	W	M	W	M	W
				1840's		
Netherlands	2·5	2·5	37·5	37·5	62·5	67·5
Sweden	7·5	12·5	47·5	57·5	67·5	72·5
England and Wales	2·5	7·5	42·5	47·5	67·5	72·5
France	2·5	2·5	42·5	47·5	67·5	72·5
Belgium	2·5	2·5	42·5	42·5	67·5	67·5
				1940's		
Netherlands	62·5	67·5	72·5	77·5	82·5	82·5
Sweden	62·5	62·5	72·5	77·5	82·5	82·5
England and Wales	57·5	62·5	72·5	77·5	77·5	82·5
France	52·5	62·5	67·5	77·5	77·5	82·5
Belgium	72·5	62·5	67·5	72·5	77·5	82·5

have been far smaller. But if the expectation of life is to show a sizeable increase in the future, it is at the third quartile that the changes must occur, for further reductions in mortality at the younger ages, though they will no doubt be achieved, will not provide a comparable addition to the average length of life. Thus Stolnitz has shown, for sixteen western countries in the 1940's, that the elimination of all deaths before the 45th birthday would not increase the expectation of life at birth by more than ten years for males or females.[2] To reduce mortality at the older ages, however, is likely to involve different problems from those dealt with in the nineteenth or early twentieth cen-

[1] Data from Stolnitz, *op. cit.* The figures given are for the middle of the quinquennial age group within which the quartiles lie.
[2] Stolnitz, *op. cit.* p. 37. The single exception is Eire, for which the increase would amount to 11·0 years for males and 10·5 for females.

turies, since neither cancer nor the cardio-vascular complex of diseases appears to be related in any simple way to the kind of environmental factors so far distinguished.[1]

Changes since the late nineteenth century are shown in the form of expectations of life at birth in Table 14, which covers a wider range of western countries and which also includes a number of countries not coming within the definition applied by Stolnitz. For these countries— countries of eastern and southern Europe—the data are more limited. But the available statistics suggest that although high mortality prevailed for a longer period than in the West, a very substantial decline occurred after the First World War and again after the Second World War. At the present time, the expectations of life at birth are generally not more than five years below those in the western group and the differences are tending to become still narrower.

For Africa, Latin America and Asia, regions containing more than two-thirds of the estimated total world population, nothing approaching the above coverage of time or area can be given. Few of the countries have long series of data, and even present-day statistics are often subject to undetermined margins of error. Moreover, so far as mortality statistics are concerned, the possibilities of analysis are still further reduced because of the lack of medical attestation of causes of death. It is not, therefore, practicable to do more than indicate the present order of magnitude of the crude birth and death rates for the regions as units, and to supplement this with more detailed information for some of the component countries.

Estimates, prepared by the United Nations, of the crude birth and

---

[1] Really large increases in the expectation of life will also involve an extension in the 'span' of life, pushing upwards the extreme ages to which people live. So far, there is little evidence that this has risen in any serious way; developments during the past century or more have resulted in the main in an increasingly large proportion of the population living through a relatively unchanged 'span'. The possible effect of further reductions in mortality within the present 'span' may be seen from an hypothetical calculation. The expectation of life at birth for males in England and Wales, 1950–2, was 66·4 years. If it were assumed that mortality were halved at each age, but that there was no extension in the span of life, every male dying by the age of 104 years, the expectation of life at birth would rise to 75·1 years, an increase less than half of that already achieved since the 1840's. At the same time it is important not to underestimate the increased expectation of life at the older ages. How exactly that increase is regarded depends, of course, upon the perspective and upon the base line used in measuring the changes. For example, in England and Wales the expectation of life for men at the age of 60 years rose from 13·5 to 15 years between 1838–54 and the 1950's, an increase of 11 per cent, which is by no means inconsiderable. But on the other hand, this rise made a small contribution to the total increase in the expectation of life at birth for males between the two points of time, namely from 39·9 to 67·5 years, amounting to only about 5 per cent of that total increase.

6

Table 14. Expectation of Life at Birth (years) for Selected Countries, 1875–1950

Males and females shown separately

		1875	1895	1905	1925	1935	1945	1950	1955
Austria	M	31	37	39	—	55	—	62	—
	F	34	39	41	—	59	—	67	—
Belgium	M	—	45	—	56	—	—	62	—
	F	—	49	—	60	—	—	67	—
Finland	M	—	43	45	51	54	55	63	63[j]
	F	—	46	48	55	60	61	69	70[j]
Germany	M	36	41	45	56	60	—	65[a]	—
	F	38	44	48	59	63	—	68[a]	—
Greece	M	—	—	—	49	—	—	—	—
	F	—	—	—	51	—	—	—	—
Hungary	M	—	—	—	—	—	55	65[b]	—
	F	—	—	—	—	—	58	69[b]	—
Italy	M	(35)[c]	43	44	49	54	—	—	66[k]
	F	(36)[c]	43	45	51	56	—	—	70[k]
Poland	M	—	—	—	—	48	—	56	62
	F	—	—	—	—	51	—	63	67
Portugal	M	—	—	—	—	49	—	56	60
	F	—	—	—	—	53	—	61	65
Spain	M	—	—	(37)[i]	(44)[i]	49	—	60[d]	—
	F	—	—	(39)[i]	(47)[i]	52	—	64[d]	—
Switzerland	M	41	46	—	58	61	63	66	—
	F	43	49	—	61	65	67	71	—
U.S.S.R.[e]	M	—	31	—	42	—	—	—	63[l]
	F	—	33	—	47	—	—	—	69[l]
Australia	M	—	51	55	59	63	66	—	67
	F	—	55	59	63	67	71	—	73
New Zealand[f]	M	—	55	58	64	65	—	68	—
	F	—	58	61	68	68	—	72	—
U.S.A. (whites)	M	—	—	(49)[g]	(56)[g]	61	64	67[h]	—
	F	—	—	(53)[g]	(59)[g]	65	70	74[h]	—
U.S.A. (others)	M	—	—	(33)[g]	(43)[g]	49	56	61[h]	—
	F	—	—	(36)[g]	(46)[g]	52	60	66[h]	—

SOURCES. U.N., *The Determinants and Consequences of Population Trends*, p. 54; Dublin, Lotka and Spiegelman, *op. cit.* appendix tables; U.N. *Demographic Yearbook* (1948, 1956, 1959). The time points are approximate.

[a] Western Germany, corresponding figures for Eastern Germany are 65 and 69 years.
[b] 1955 figures. [c] Rough approximations. [d] From Instituto Nacional de Estadistica, *Tablas de Mortalidad de la Poblacion Española, Año 1950* (Madrid, 1960), pp. 82–3.
[e] European areas only.
[f] Europeans only. For Maoris, around 1950, 54 and 56 years for males and females respectively. [g] Original Registration States. [h] 1954 figures.
[i] Averages for 1900, 1918 and 1920, 1930, based on data in U.N. *Age and Sex Patterns of Mortality* (New York, 1955), p. 36.
[j] Figures for 1951–5. [k] Figures for 1954–7. [l] Figures for 1955–6.

death rates of the major regions of the world, are cited in Table 15. For Africa, the estimated death rates are similar to those prevailing in central Europe in the 1860's and 1870's, and this is also the case for much of Asia. But for Latin America and for East Asia the rates are more nearly the equivalent of those in western Europe at the beginning of the twentieth century, and in large part these lower levels have been attained in a short period, and particularly during the last ten or fifteen years. The contrast between these two types of level may be shown in greater detail for a number of countries.[1]

Table 15. *Crude Birth and Death Rates for the World and Major Regions, 1951–5*

(Rates per 1000 total population)

		Birth rate	Death rate	Natural increase
Africa	North	45	25	20
	Tropical and Southern	45	25	20
America	North	25	9	16
	Middle	45	19	26
	South	40	17	23
Asia	South-west	42	22	20
	South central	41	28	13
	South-east	45	28	17
	East	35	16	19
Europe	North and West	18	11	7
	Central	20	11	9
	Southern	21	10	11
Oceania		25	8	17
U.S.S.R.		26	9	17
The world		34	18	16

SOURCE. U.N. *Demographic Yearbook* (1956), p. 2. The rates for North America, Europe and the U.S.S.R. represent the recorded statistics. The remaining rates are estimates. (Adjustments presumably made to rates for North and South America, Europe, and Oceania to allow for migration.)

If, to begin with, Asia is looked at, a not untypical picture of much of the continent may be obtained from the material for India. The basic data are imperfect, but they have been studied in detail by Kingsley Davis and others, and there is thus a series of estimates which attempt to

[1] It is possible that both the birth and death rates are somewhat overstated for a substantial part of the population of Asia—that is, of the population of mainland China. In connection with the 1953 census of China, 'sample' studies covering 30 million people were undertaken, and information on births and deaths collected. These data appear to indicate a crude birth rate of 37 per 1000 and a death rate of 17 per 1000. See A. Sauvy, 'La Population de la Chine,' *Population*, XII (1957), 697.

overcome the deficiencies of past and present vital registration.[1] Some of the main indices are grouped together in Table 16, which, for the most part, shows death rates higher, and expectations of life lower, than in Europe at any time since the eighteenth century (though the birth rates are matched by those of eastern Europe in the middle and late nineteenth century). Nor, until very recently, was there any evident trend in the rates, the first fairly clear sign of a rise in the expectation of life appearing in 1921–31. Low expectations of the kind cited are the reflection of the heavy toll of infection and also of other diseases whose ravages are increased by malnutrition and extremely poor living conditions. Though the statistics of causes of death in India are far from

Table 16. *Estimated Vital Rates for India (including Pakistan)*

Period	Per 1000 of population		Expectation of life at birth (years)	
	Birth rate	Death rate	Males	Females
1881–91	49	41	24·6	25·5
1891–1901	46	44	23·6	24·0
1901–11	49	43	22·6	23·3
1911–21	48	47	19·4	20·9
1921–31	46	36	26·9	26·6
1931–41	45	31	32·1	31·4
1950–5	(40)	(25)	(35)	

SOURCE. 1881–1941, Kingsley Davis, *op. cit.* pp. 37, 62, 69, 86; 1950–5, estimates cited in United Nations, *Report on the World Social Situation* (New York, 1957), pp. 20 and 22. Ghosh, *op. cit.* p. 62, estimates the birth rate in 1941–50 at 39 per 1000 (for India only).

adequate, they confirm this situation. Until very recently plague, smallpox and cholera contributed significantly to the total death rate, though a much heavier toll was—and still is—taken by malaria. Some 60 per cent of registered deaths in India are ascribed to 'fevers', and perhaps a third of these would involve malaria, which thus probably causes more deaths than any other single disease. Tuberculosis would rank next to malaria, and the evidence suggests a steady increase in the incidence of the disease during the present century. Moreover, resistance to death from such causes can scarcely be increased by the widespread dietary deficiencies especially associated with rice as a

[1] Kingsley Davis, *The Population of India and Pakistan*, pp. 37, 62–3 and 69. See also the reprint of R. A. Gopalaswami, ch. v of the report on the 1951 census of India, Part I-A, in *Proc. World Pop. Conf. 1954*, III, 173–87; and A. Ghosh, 'The Trend of the Birth Rate in India 1911–1950', *Pop. Studies*, x, no. 1, p. 62.

main cereal. In such circumstances it is not difficult to understand why the influenza pandemic after the First World War should have had so devastating a result in India, causing perhaps as many as 20 million deaths, reducing the expectation of life to the lowest figures recorded and effectively eliminating population growth in the decade 1911–21.[1]

The statistics given in Table 16 suggested a significant though not very large fall in mortality in India from the 1930's onwards.[2] In some parts of Asia, and especially in island communities where malaria con-

Table 17. *Expectation of Life at Birth (years) in Ceylon and Taiwan*[a]

		1900	1910	1920	1945	1950–55
Ceylon	M	37·0	35·6	37·5	47·2⎫	
	F	37·6	36·4	39·0	48·7⎬	(61)
Taiwan	M	—	32·4	27·7	—⎫	
	F	—	35·6	29·6	—⎬	(55)

[a] Points of time approximate.

SOURCES. Ceylon, 1900–45, from N. Sarkar, *The Demography of Ceylon* (Colombo, 1957), ch. 6; Taiwan, 1910–20, from G. W. Barclay, *A Report on Taiwan's Population* (Princeton, 1954), p. 72; Ceylon and Taiwan, 1950–5, estimates in United Nations, *Report on the World Social Situation*, pp. 19–20.

trol through D.D.T. spraying has been more effective, the rates of change have been very marked since the Second World War. Two examples of such recent change are given in Table 17, namely Ceylon and Taiwan (Formosa). In Ceylon the expectation of life is now at a 'western level', and the pattern of mortality has shown the kind of

[1] On mortality in India, see Davis, *op. cit.* chs. 6 and 7; and Gyan Chand, *India's Teeming Millions* (London, 1939), pp. 116–30. The impact of the influenza pandemic on India also illuminates the process by which epidemics may have resulted in erratic population growth in European countries in the pre-industrial era. According to the life table for India, 1911–21, only about two-fifths of a group of babies would survive until their twentieth birthday. If, in such circumstances, the average number of live-born children per woman passing through the childbearing period were about five, a couple would just about replace themselves and there would be no inherent long-run population increase unless fertility were to rise or mortality to fall again. If epidemics and famine in Europe reduced the expectation of life at birth to a level equivalent to that in India in 1911–21, there would be consequential periods of no natural increase and, if death were age-selective, there might easily be substantial population decreases resulting from the warping of the age structure of the population.

[2] In more recent years—and especially since 1950—the rate of decline in mortality in India has increased substantially. Public health campaigns have become more widespread and more effective, in spite of the shortage of doctors and of their heavy concentration in the cities, and epidemics are being controlled by mass inoculation and vaccination. It is not unlikely that the expectation of life at birth is now (1961) above 40 years—still extremely low but nevertheless showing larger gains than in earlier periods.

change to be expected in consequence. Since 1939, when Ceylon obtained a greater degree of self-government, there has been a notable expansion in public health services, and this, together with the use of new insecticides and antibiotics, has brought down mortality rates from infective and parasitic diseases. During the past fifteen years there have been especially large reductions in the death rates from dysentery, malaria, ankylostomiasis (hookworm, producing debility analogous to bilharzia in Egypt),[1] typhoid and paratyphoid, while the estimated number of malaria cases fell from over three millions to under 40,000 between 1942 and 1954.[2]

Table 18. *Expectation of Life at Birth (years) in Japan*

Period	Males	Females
1921–5	42·1	43·2
1926–30	44·8	46·5
1931–5	45·9	48·3
1935–6	46·9	49·6
1947	51·8	55·6
1948–9	56·0	59·4
1949–50	56·2	59·6
1952	61·9	65·5
1953	61·9	65·7
1955	63·9	68·4
(1950–5)	(66)	

SOURCE. U.N. *Demographic Yearbook* (1948, 1955, 1956); H. Mizushima, *Archives Popn. Assn. Japan* (1952 and 1953).

Equally outstanding, though spread over a somewhat longer period, have been the changes in Japan, illustrated in Table 18. The data are reasonably satisfactory since the 1920's, and allow an analysis both of overall changes and of the regional and cause components of change. From the 1920's until the Second World War, mortality fell most in the north-east areas, where it had formerly been highest. Infant mortality fell very considerably and a definitely 'western' pattern of mortality emerged, with the expectation of life highest in the metropolitan districts. But though Japan had begun in the 1920's with an expectation of life above that of most other Asian countries at the time, the total increase by the Second World War was smaller than might have been expected, and the period of major change was that after the

[1] On the effects of bilharzia and ankylostomiasis on the Egyptian population, see W. Cleland, *The Population Problem in Egypt* (Lancaster, Pennsylvania, 1936), pp. 82–7.
[2] See N. H. Sarkar, *The Demography of Ceylon*, ch. 6, and D. M. de Silva, *Health Progress in Ceylon: A Survey* (Colombo, 1956), pp. 25–39.

war. A fall in mortality from tuberculosis, and a further decline in infant mortality were primary factors, and even the worst areas showed improvements. Altogether, between 1947 and 1955 Japan achieved an increase in the expectation of life which had taken from 1905 to 1947 to accomplish in England and Wales.[1]

Finally, a selection of statistics in Table 19 affords some indication of the trends and present levels of life expectation in Central and South America. The indication cannot be regarded as representative, both because large populations in South America are not covered, and because the estimates actually given are by no means free from error. In general, the countries included in the table are those in which mortality has fallen most. For the other countries the expectation of life at birth is not likely to be above 50 years, while for some—including Bolivia, Brazil as a whole, Colombia, Ecuador as a whole, Peru and Venezuela—it is more probably around 45 years.[2] This wide range of life expectancy is also reflected in the variation in the proportion of deaths attributed to infectious diseases, being as low as 3 per cent in Chile and as high as 55 per cent in Guatemala.[3] At the same time, the countries listed show, as did Ceylon and Japan, substantial gains in a relatively short period. Life expectancy increased by about eighteen to twenty-two years in a period of thirty years, and the fall in mortality became still more rapid in the 1950's. This is all the more noteworthy in that even in the 1920's many of the countries had levels of life expectation below those recorded for western Europe around the middle of the nineteenth century. In considering the future rate of decline in mortality in Latin America this sizeable change in a generation must be borne in mind, and it would be incorrect to assume a development analogous to that of Europe. Present techniques for reducing mortality are both less costly—especially in terms of capital equipment —and more effective than those available in Europe in the nineteenth and early twentieth centuries, and outside assistance, especially through the international agencies, can now more easily be drawn upon. As a

[1] See I. B. Taeuber and E. G. Beal, 'The Dynamics of Population in Japan', in Milbank Memorial Fund, *Demographic Studies of Selected Areas of Rapid Growth* (New York, 1944); T. Shimamura, *Japan. Inst. Popn. Problems, Research Data,* A-4 (1950).

[2] See U.N. *Report on the World Social Situation,* table 24. El Salvador and Guatemala are given as around 40 years. On the other hand, table 23 estimates Argentina, 1950–5 (both sexes), as around 64 years.

[3] For Chile, see Cabello, *Pop. Studies,* IX (1956). See also D. V. Glass (ed.), *Report of the United Nations Seminar on Population Problems in Latin America* (New York, 1958), part III. In Chile, tuberculosis accounts for 8 per cent of the deaths. It need hardly be said that the attribution is in many cases unreliable, since the proportion of deaths certified by medical practitioners is often low. Even in Chile, in 1950–2, only two-thirds of the deaths were so certified.

CENTRAL AND SOUTH AMERICA

88

Table 19. *Expectation of Life at Birth (years) in Selected Countries in Central and South America*

Country		1910	1920	1930	1940	1945	1950
Jamaica	M	39	36	—	—	51	56
	F	41	38	—	—	55	59
Trinidad	M	39	38	45	—	53	56
	F	41	40	47	—	56	58
Barbados	M	29	29	—	—	49	53
	F	33	32	—	—	53	58
El Salvador	M	—	—	—	—	—	50[e]
	F	—	—	—	—	—	52[e]
Mexico	M	—	—	32	38	—	—
	F	—	—	34	40	—	—
Argentina	M	—	45	—	—	57	—
	F	—	48	—	—	61	—
Brazil	M	—	37[a]	—	[b]	39	—
	F	—	—	—	—	46	—
British Guiana	M	30	34	40	—	49	53
	F	32	36	43	—	52	56
Chile[c]	M	—	31	40	—	41	50
	F	—	32	42	41	—	54
Ecuador[d]	M	—	—	—	—	—	50
	F	—	—	—	—	—	54

(Approximate points of time spans the year columns.)

SOURCES. U.N. *Demographic Yearbook* (1948 and 1956); U.N. *Age and Sex Patterns of Mortality* (New York, 1955); G. W. Roberts, *The Population of Jamaica* (Cambridge, 1957); O. Cabello, 'The Demography of Chile', *Pop. Studies*, IX (1956).

[a] Brazil: 1930 refers to Federal District and thirteen cities; for the Federal District only, around 1950, the expectation of life is given at 50 years for males and 56 for females.

[b] M. V. Da Rocha, 'La mortalité au Brésil', *Proc. World Pop. Conf. 1954*, Papers, vol. I, calculates the expectation of life at birth in 1939–41 in the state of São Paulo at 44 years for males and 46 years for females, and believes that this corresponds roughly to present-day mortality for Brazil as a whole. For 1949–51, as against this 'informed guess' for Brazil as a whole, the city of Rio de Janeiro had the life expectations shown in the table, amounting to 53 years for both sexes (compared with 41 years in 1920–1 and 42 in 1939–41), while the city of São Paulo had around 57 or 58 years in 1949–51 (compared with 43 years in 1920–1 and 49 in 1939–41). The figures for Brazil as a whole for 1940–50, given above, are cited from the *Anuario Estatistico do Brasil, 1957*, p. 51. A more recent official publication gives a slightly higher figure (41·5 years) for males (A. V. W. de Carvalho, *A População Brasileira* (Rio de Janeiro, 1960), p. 26).

[c] Chile: there are alternative life tables for Chile, 1930. That cited by the U.N. gives slightly lower results than the table given by Cabello, and cited here.

[d] Ecuador: refers to Quito only.

[e] U.N. *Report on the World Social Situation*, table 24, gives a rough estimate of around 40 years for 1950–5 for both El Salvador and Guatemala. But the U.N. *Demographic Yearbook* reports higher figures for El Salvador (as above) and Guatemala (44 years for both sexes, 1949–51). See also the estimates for Puerto Rico given by J. L. Janer, *Proc. World Pop. Conf. 1954*, Papers, vol. I: 38 years in 1920, 41 in 1930, 46 in 1940 and 61 in 1950 (both sexes).

result, substantial reductions in death rates, at least in the short run, have often been achieved without correspondingly large increases in material levels of living, though how long such reductions can be maintained without improving food intake and housing conditions is not known. The use of simpler and more effective techniques of death control also means that mortality reductions are not necessarily accompanied, or immediately followed by the massive social changes which characterized the West in the nineteenth century. Though social change takes place, it is necessarily both more explicit and external and less an aspect of the general context of change in which demographic and other phenomena became modified.[1]

[1] It is unfortunate that mortality levels and trends in Africa cannot be considered in this chapter, but the data for African populations (other than Europeans) are poorer and more scanty than for most other groups. Partial surveys of the data are given by A. Barkhuus, 'Non-European General and Infant Mortality in the Non-self-governing Territories in Africa, South of the Sahara', and M. Pascua, 'Brief Summary of Recent Mortality Trends in Areas of Higher Death Rates', both in *Proc. World Pop. Conf. 1954*, Papers, vol. I. See also U.N. *Report on the World Social Situation*, table 26, which estimates the 1950–5 level of the crude death rate at around 45 per 1000 for Egypt, for the indigenous populations of Tunisia and Uganda, and for the Moslem populations of Algeria and Morocco. The serial data for Egypt, though defective, suggest a decline in mortality during the past decade, but there was certainly room for decline, for the expectation of life at birth for males and females respectively was about 30 and 32 years in 1927–37 and 36 and 42 years in 1936–8 (see C. V. Kiser, 'The Demographic Position of Egypt', in Milbank Memorial Fund, *Demographic Studies of Selected Areas of Rapid Growth* (New York, 1944)). A similar, but much more marked, fall in death rates has taken place in Mauritius, especially following the campaign begun in 1945 to eradicate malaria. The expectation of life at birth has risen from 32 and 34 years for males and females in 1942–6 to 50 and 52 years in 1951–3, the latter excluding the Chinese population (see H. C. Brookfield, 'Mauritius: Demographic Upsurge and Prospect', *Pop. Studies*, XI (1957)). Expectations of life for other African populations include the following: Union of South Africa, 1945–57, Coloured population, 42 and 44 years for males and females; Asiatics, 51 and 50 years. Belgian Congo, 1950–2, 38 and 40 years (based on sample surveys). French Senegal, 1957 sample survey, both sexes, 37 years (see Ministère de la France d'Outre-Mer, Mission socio-économique de la Basse Vallée du Sénégal, *Enquête Démographique 1957* (Paris, 1957)). French Guinea, 1954–5 sample survey, 27 years, both sexes (Haut Commissariat Général de l'A.D.F., *Etude Démographique par Sondage en Guinée 1954–1955, Résultats Définitifs*, I (Paris, n.d.), p. 55). For references to recent demographic data for Tropical Africa, see F. Lorimer, *Demographic Information on Tropical Africa* (Boston, Mass., 1961). Some of the classic diseases formerly causing high mortality in Africa—for example, bubonic plague and relapsing fever—have decreased in importance in recent years, and others, like smallpox and cerebro-spinal meningitis, are being brought under control. But malaria is still an outstanding factor and so also, it is generally believed, is tuberculosis, while as background to the high death rates there is widespread malnutrition.

IV. *Fertility*

The discussion, in the previous section, of mortality levels and trends was relatively straightforward, and though there were major gaps in the account, the broad indications given are unlikely greatly to distort reality. But in attempting to provide a comparable outline of the history of fertility, more awkward problems are involved, reflecting differences not only in the availability of basic statistics, but also in the development of appropriate techniques of analysis. For individual and social reasons, effective interest in the study of mortality was evident at a relatively early period—indeed, well before national population and vital statistics had begun to be provided. In the seventeenth century Graunt had provided the outlines of the life table, and before the end of that century, Halley had elaborated the technique and applied it to the data for the city of Breslau. The eighteenth and early nineteenth centuries saw the construction of many similar tables, some based upon the experience of members of tontines, others incorrectly constructed from death statistics alone, and a few correctly derived from a combination of census and vital statistics. By the time of Farr, the life table approach was well known, and Farr himself introduced a new range of analysis, focused upon mortality differences between occupations and leading to the study of broader 'socio-economic' differences referred to earlier. Concern with the high level of nineteenth-century mortality, and the development of suitable methods of statistical analysis, combined to stimulate the supply of more reliable and more comprehensive death statistics, while from the 1850's onwards, meetings of official statisticians resulted in increasingly meaningful and comparable classifications of the causes of death. That there are still many gaps and defects in present-day materials is only too clear. But at least the main targets for improvement have been visible for many years. [1]

Fertility analysis, by contrast, has not shown so direct and consistent a path of development. The early bills of mortality essayed to list the specific causes of, and ages at death. But on the fertility side they gave only the numbers of baptisms and marriages, and Graunt's index of marital fertility was the ratio of baptisms to marriages. Gregory King,

[1] See H. Westergaard *op. cit.* and the introductory section of *Manual of the International List of Causes of Death* (London, 1940). The much earlier establishment of birth and death statistics in Sweden was in part, at least, a response to the population losses of the Great Northern War of 1700–21 and the subsequent epidemics. See H. Gille, 'The Demographic History of the Northern European Countries in the Eighteenth Century', *Pop. Studies*, III (1949). It was for Sweden that the first correctly based age-specific mortality rates were constructed—those prepared by Wargentin for the period 1755–63. From such rates a life table could easily have been derived, but Wargentin himself did not take that further step.

writing a generation later, was aware of the need for information on the distribution of marriages with various total numbers of live births, but such information was not collected on a national scale in Britain until 1911, and King's contribution to fertility analysis was the 'invention' of the crude birth rate. Even the Malthusian controversy did little to provoke new approaches, and Farr used the crude birth rate and the ratio of births to marriages as his main indices of fertility, though it was evident to him, as it had been to King, that far more detailed statistics were required. By the end of the nineteenth century, when the birth rates were falling in a number of western countries, direct censuses of fertility began to be taken, in which married women were asked to record the total number of live children they had borne, but those censuses were rarely analysed in full. Moreover, as an approach to the study of fertility levels and trends, they came to be overshadowed by the emergence of 'replacement rates'. Such rates, developed by Boeckh and Kuczynski in Germany and independently (and, from the mathematical point of view, much more profoundly) by Lotka in the United States, attempted to go beneath the current levels of births and deaths and to 'disengage' from them the inherent rate at which, given the persistence of existing probabilities of dying and of bearing children, a population would eventually grow in the future, and the age-composition which that population would ultimately exhibit.[1] The replacement rate was a most important addition to the techniques of demographic analysis, but the technique tended to be applied in a way which gave unrealistic results for western populations. The method of application, basing itself upon the approach of the current life table, involved splicing together the experience observed in a year or other relatively short period, rather than, as in a generation life table, taking the actual experience of, say, a group of women born or married in a given period. This is unrealistic because it assumes that the probability of a woman having a child when she is, say, in her thirties is independent of whether she has had a child or children in her twenties, an assumption which is only reasonably valid if fertility is largely uncontrolled and family size unchanging from generation to generation. In addition, when birth control is widespread and family size fairly small, births may be postponed—because of, say, economic depression—without affecting ultimate family size, for the postponed births may be made up later. But the conventional replacement rate, though supposed to measure inherent fertility and to abstract from temporary variation, would, like the crude birth rate, show a sharp fall when births are postponed and a sharp rise when they are made up, even though the ultimate size of the

[1] That is, the ultimate age composition is not a function of the present age composition but of the fertility and mortality rates which are assumed to persist.

families borne by a generation of women remains unchanged. Hence the conventional replacement rates understated fertility in the 1930's when births were postponed, and overstated it in the 1940's when births were being made up again.[1]

Since the mid-1940's there have been very considerable changes in the techniques of measuring fertility. The concept of the replacement rate is now being applied in a much more realistic and meaningful way, and is based upon a much wider range of statistics.[2] But just because these changes are recent, the more satisfactory indices now available do not apply to many countries or reach very far back in time. It is thus more difficult to give a consistent and meaningful picture of fertility trends during the past hundred years than it was to provide an equivalent outline of mortality trends. Equally, comparisons between countries at the present time have to call upon indices which are not always best suited for the purpose, and it is therefore necessary to bear in mind the limitations of such comparisons.[3]

[1] Moreover, the conventional replacement rate does not allow explicitly for the probability of marriage and, because of this, does not take into account changes in marriage probability which are in fact implicit in the assumption of the persistence of given levels of fertility and mortality. Thus, in the early 1930's the proportion of women marrying in western Europe was relatively low partly because of previous male war mortality and emigration. But if the then current levels of mortality had persisted and if there were no emigration (or an equal emigration of men and women) the sex-ratio of the adult population would have become more balanced and the chances of marriage would almost certainly have changed as a result. Taking marriage explicitly into account would in general allow the possibility of more realistic assumptions regarding prospective marriage frequency.

[2] Though the use of a more realistic approach means that the indices are less precise than they appeared to be previously.

[3] For a brief account of the development of techniques of fertility and mortality analysis, see D. V. Glass, 'Some Aspects of the Development of Demography', op. cit. The problems of fertility analysis over time are also dealt with fairly simply in N. B. Ryder, 'La mesure des variations de la fécondité au cours du temps', Population (January–March 1956); N. B. Ryder, 'Problems of Trend Determination during a Transition in Fertility', Milbank Memorial Fund Quarterly (January 1956); and in 'Introductory Memorandum by the Statistics Committee', Reports and Selected Papers of the Statistics Committee, Papers of the Royal Commission on Population, vol. II (London, 1950). There is a very extensive literature on fertility analysis, but much of it is somewhat technical. It should be noted that there are, of course, exceptions to the statement that fertility analysis made relatively little progress during the larger part of the nineteenth century. Thus one of the most interesting contributions is that of C. Ansell Jr. (On the Rate of Mortality at Early Periods of Life (London, 1874)), who, on the basis of an insurance company investigation among the middle classes in England, analysed differences in family size by date of marriage and by occupational group, and also examined the relation between birth-spacing and size of completed family. But Ansell's work appears to have had very little influence on his contemporaries. On Farr see W. A. Farr, Vital Statistics, ed. N. A. Humphreys (London, 1885),

Further, there are three general qualifications which apply to the various measures of fertility. First, however accurate or meaningful a particular rate may be, it does not follow that it will serve equally well for all the purposes the historian or the demographer has in mind. For some purposes, the crude birth rate, when compared with the crude death rate, may be more informative than a far more complex replacement rate. Secondly, different rates may give somewhat different pictures of trends, and each picture may be equally valid having regard to the perspective from which it is viewed. This qualification is especially relevant in discussing the so-called 'demographic transition'—that is, in attempting to see when fertility began to fall in various western societies, and how the fall was 'timed' in relation to other factors. Finally, and again important in relation to the nature and timing of the 'demographic transition', a given index, though purporting to measure fertility, may nevertheless also reflect the consequences of changing mortality. This needs to be taken into account in looking at the pre-industrial growth of population in the West and in examining the relative decline of fertility in western countries after the 1870's, and it may therefore be useful to give one or two illustrations of the way in which mortality changes may affect the level of fertility.

So far as the pre-industrial period is concerned, the illustrations must be necessarily mainly theoretical, for there are not sufficient serial records to show whether there was, say, a general rise in the crude birth rate.[1] Gille's study of the Scandinavian material, giving the most com-

pp. 31 and 105, and the references in R. R. Kuczynski, *The Measurement of Population Growth* (London, 1935), chs. II and IV. The reference by Gregory King is in his journal in the Public Records Office (T. 64/302), p. 8, 'Observations touching Marriages, Births and Burials and Persons Living at any one time', in which he posed the following questions: How many marriages annually; at what ages persons marry; how many widows and widowers; at what ages they become such; how many 2nd, 3rd, 4th, etc., marriages; how many barren marriages; how many teeming women; how many die in childbed; how many die in labour; how many marriages produce only 1 child, 2, 3, 4, 5, 6, etc., children? He also attempted to answer some of these questions, and his estimate of the incidence of marriages with various numbers of children was (reduced to percentages—King gave his distribution on a base of 200): 0, 5½; 1, 9; 2, 12½; 3, 15½; 4, 18; 5, 13½, etc. The total distribution yields an average of 4·1 children per marriage. There is no indication of the basis of this estimate. The average is similar to that for marriages in Great Britain, 1890–9 (continuing first marriages, brides under 45 years of age), namely 4·3 live births, though the distribution of family size is rather different, being 9·9, 9·5, 13·6, 13·6, 12·2 and 10% respectively for the sizes mentioned above (though not so wildly different as might perhaps have been expected).

[1] The cases of rising birth rates in the nineteenth century are more likely to be due to increasing completeness of birth registration than to any other factor. Thus the crude birth rate in England and Wales appeared to rise from 32·2 per 1000 in 1841–5 to 35·4 in 1871–5. But after allowing for the completeness of registration, this

prehensive picture so far available, suggests some rise in Finland, Norway and Sweden in the first half of the eighteenth century, a rise in Iceland at the end of the century, and more or less of a plateau during the period 1730–1800 in Denmark.[1] How far the apparent increase in the early eighteenth century is due to improving registration has not been estimated, though it is not unlikely that this is at least a partial explanation. But if there were a statistically validated rise in the birth rate, it would be necessary to look at three possible explanations, namely, an increase in the proportion of the population marrying; an increase in the fertility of marriage, defined in terms of the number of live births occurring to marriages of completed fertility; and an increase in the proportion of marriages which, because of falling mortality, continue unbroken until the wives have passed through the child-bearing period.[2] The last factor would raise the average marital fertility by increasing the proportion of marriages with completed fertility. Further, by raising the proportion of married persons in the population, such a fall in mortality, other things being equal, would produce a corresponding rise in the birth rate.[3] A recent study of generation fertility rates in Sweden—that is, of the average number of children born to a woman who was herself born in a given time-period—suggests that falling mortality may explain the apparent increase in the fertility of women born at the end, as compared with those born in the middle of the eighteenth century, the women born later—and their husbands, too—benefiting from the slightly lower mortality observed after the 1820's. If, instead of taking actual mortality into account, a constant level were assumed, fertility would appear to show very little variation until the end of the eighteenth century, after which it would fall consistently.[4] Similar implications follow from Hollingsworth's material on British

rising trend disappears, being replaced by a largely unsystematic variation of the rate within the range of 34·8 to 35·8 (see D. V. Glass, 'A Note on the Under-registration of Births in Britain in the Nineteenth Century', op. cit.). A very slight upward trend is still visible in the general fertility rate (number of births per 1000 women aged 15–44 years), but it is highly probable that this is due to an insufficient allowance for the under-registration of infant deaths in the early decades of civil registration.

[1] H. Gille, 'The Demographic History of the Northern European Countries in the Eighteenth Century', op. cit.

[2] The possible contribution of an increase in the incidence of illegitimate births would also need to be considered. This was an important factor in nineteenth-century Sweden.

[3] According to theoretical calculations by the United Nations, there would be a maximum increase of 10% in the crude birth rate if the expectation of life at birth rose from 30 to 60 years (see U.N. Report on the World Social Situation, p. 8).

[4] See N. B. Ryder, 'The Influence of Declining Mortality on Swedish Reproductivity', in Milbank Memorial Fund, Current Research in Human Fertility (New York, 1955), pp. 65 ff.

ducal families, the data suggesting that, for the particular group in question, the proportion of marriages with completed fertility increased very substantially both between the generations of 1680–1729 and 1730–79, and also between those of 1730–79 and 1780–1829.[1] It follows equally, of course, that when both fertility and mortality are declining, the decline in the birth rate will underestimate the fall in the fertility of marriages, because of the counteracting effect of falling mortality in increasing the proportion of marriages which continue unbroken through the childbearing period. Thus, taking mortality levels in Great Britain for the couples married in 1871, only 52 per cent of the marriages of women, aged 20–24 years when they married, would have continued unbroken (by the death of either partner) for 30 years, whereas with the mortality applying to couples married in 1911 the corresponding proportion would have been 71 per cent.[2] The increased average duration of married life would to some extent counterbalance the decline in the fertility of completed marriages as between the 1871 and 1911 cohorts.[3] A similar compensatory effect might also have occurred in France in the late eighteenth century, when, according to a recent study, both fertility and mortality were already beginning to fall.[4] Of course, both mortality and fertility are part of the complex obtaining in a given period and society, and to separate the two is artificial. From the analytical point of view, however, it is highly desirable that the contribution of falling mortality to family size be noted and, if possible, estimated. Otherwise, historical research, in seeking an explanation of demographic phenomena, may be focused on the irrelevant rather than on the relevant factors.[5]

Turning now to the data on fertility trends in the western world, a range of crude birth rates is given in Table 9. Before discussing them,

[1] For these generations the proportions were 35, 60 and 74% for dukes' sons, and 39, 58 and 71% for dukes' daughters. Over and above this, however, there appears to have been an increase in the fertility of completed marriages.

[2] D. V. Glass and E. Grebenik, *The Trend and Pattern of Fertility in Great Britain* (London, 1954), part I, pp. 89–90.

[3] The term 'cohort' as used here applies to a group of persons married in a given time period, and the term 'generation' to a group born in a given period. When, however, 'generation' is used as a measure of time in demography (for example, a reproduction rate indicating the inherent rate of population growth per generation), it means approximately the average ages of mothers (or fathers) at the birth of their children.

[4] J. Bourgeois-Pichat, 'Evolution générale de la population française depuis le XVIIIe siècle', *Population* (October–December 1951).

[5] This is especially important because it may often be possible to find what looks like suggestive evidence bearing upon both sets of factors and, as the late R. R. Kuczynski wrote in another connection, 'an explanation does not necessarily look less plausible if the event which is explained has not occurred'.

however, three further series should be referred to in order to extend
the range over which birth rate movements since the nineteenth
century may be considered. The series in question, relating to Ireland,
European Russia and the United States, has been put together in Table
20. The rates for Russia and the United States are estimates both for the
nineteenth and—though with considerably greater reliability for the
United States—for the twentieth century.[1] The birth rates for Ireland
have been added because they reflect a situation different from that in
other western countries, as will be shown later. Taking the whole
group of countries, the birth rates in the 1840's and the 1850's were
above 30 per 1000, France being the sole exception. And for some
countries, especially in eastern Europe, the rates must have been well
above that level. How the rates behaved in the late eighteenth or early
nineteenth centuries cannot be documented, except for a very few
countries and, save for Sweden, these countries show developments
which do not fit in any close way the customary generalizations
regarding the 'demographic transition'. In Sweden the rates move
very much in the expected way, exhibiting a general trendlessness before
the mid-nineteenth century, with fairly wide cyclical swings, the high
points occurring in the 1750's and 1820's. From the 1860's onwards,
the trend is definitely and consistently downwards. Before the mid-
century, it would seem that a major component in the movement of the
birth rate was the variation associated with economic conditions, and
especially with crop yields, the success of a harvest affecting both the
number of new marriages and, according to contemporary observers,
the fertility of existing marriages, and there is evidence suggesting that
contraception, probably in the form of *coitus interruptus*, was already of
some significance.[2] From the mid-nineteenth century, though cyclical

[1] For European Russia, the margins of error in the series as a whole are not known.
For the United States, as was pointed out earlier, birth registration was less than 90%
complete until about 1935. Estimates for the nineteenth and early twentieth centuries
were originally given in W. S. Thompson and P. K. Whelpton, *Population Trends in
the United States* (New York, 1933), p. 266, the estimates from 1909 onwards being
revised later in the light of the birth registration tests carried out in the U.S.A. (see
P. K. Whelpton, *Births and Birth Rates in the Entire United States*, 1909–48, Fed. Security
Agency, Vital Statistics—Special Reports, vol. XXXIII, no. 8, 29 September 1950).

[2] Gille, *op. cit.* p. 49 cites the first report (1761) of the Swedish *Tabellkommission*,
which discussed this question. Giving, as one example, the sharp fall in corn prices in
1749, the report stated: 'At once girls and boys were ready for the bridal bed, and for
married couples love began to burn more vigorously.' See also the references in
G. Utterström, 'Some Population Problems in pre-industrial Sweden', *Scand. Hist.
Rev.* p. 159. The relationship between economic cycles and demographic phenomena
was discussed at length in D. S. Thomas, *Social Aspects of the Business Cycle* (London,
1925). See also D. S. Thomas, *Social and Economic Aspects of Swedish Population
Movements 1750–1933* (New York, 1941), chs. 2 and 3.

Table 20. *Crude Birth Rates of Ireland, European Russia and the United States*

	Ireland	European Russia	United States
1801–10	—	(43·7)⎫	
1811–20	—	(40·0)⎭	54
1821–30	—	(42·7)⎫	
1831–40	—	(45·6)⎭	51
1841–50	—	(49·7)⎫	
1851–60	—	(52·4)⎭	44
1861–70	25·8	49·7⎫	
1871–80	26·3	50·4⎭	39
1881–90	22·9	50·5⎫	
1891–1900	22·2	49·2⎭	32
1901–10	22·5	46·8	29
1911–20	21·5		28
1921–30	20·2	(43·0)	23
1931–40	19·3		17
1941–5 ⎫			20
1946–50 ⎭	21·9	(26·6)	24

SOURCES

Ireland: (26 counties): Commission on Emigration and other Population Problems, *Reports*, Dublin (1955), p. 89. The first period is 1864–70.

Russia: Rates for 1801–10 to 1851–60 cited by Rashin, *op. cit.* p. 38, from the Russian edition of Brockhaus's encyclopaedic dictionary and purport to relate to the Greek-orthodox Population. Rates for 1861–70 to 1901–10 adapted from R. R. Kuczynski, *The Balance of Births and Deaths*, II, 14 and refer to the fifty provinces of European Russia. The rate for 1921–30 actually relates to the European part of the U.S.S.R., 1926–8 and is from F. Lorimer, *op. cit.* p. 87. The post-war rate, actually for 1950–2, is cited by the U.N. from Soviet sources (see *Report on the World Social Situation*, p. 11).

U.S.A.: The rates, which are estimates deriving from the work of P. K. Whelpton, are cited from the unpublished *Documentation for a Conference on Population Problems*, 1952 (prepared by the Princeton Office of Population Research).

variations can still be discerned, the downward secular trend was dominant. In European Russia, the break in the series during the nineteenth century—quite apart from the question of the reliability of the estimates—makes generalization impossible. Such as they are, however, the rates suggest a rise towards the mid-nineteenth century, the only case of movement in this direction among the countries covered. For the United States on one side of the Atlantic and France on the other, the rates show a consistent decline from the earliest period for which estimates are available. And for France, at least, the data are sufficiently well based from the beginning of the nineteenth century to ensure that the trend is not a mirage. Moreover, whereas the theory of demographic transition usually assumes that mortality began to fall well before fertility, this was not true of France and perhaps not of the United States either. Nor, so far as the nineteenth century is concerned, was it very clearly the case of England and Wales. At least, as was seen earlier, the expectation of life scarcely changed between the 1840's and the 1870's, and by the end of the latter period the birth rate was already beginning to fall. Indeed, by the 1880's a falling birth rate was common in western and north-west Europe. The rest of Europe experienced a later initiation of a consistent decline—not until the twentieth century in the eastern and south-eastern countries—and the different regions thus began to pull away from each other. As in the case of mortality, the twentieth century also saw a sharper fall in birth rates. Moreover, countries with a later initial fall tended to show a steeper one. In France, with the earliest decline, it took eighty years for the birth rate to fall from 30 to 20 per 1000; but the same cut was achieved in some forty years in Sweden and Switzerland, and in thirty years in Belgium, Denmark and Great Britain. And between the early 1920's and the early 1930's, the rate dropped 20 per cent in Poland and 25 per cent in Bulgaria.[1] By the eve of the Second World War some of the regional gaps were thus beginning to narrow again and this process continued after the war, for in formerly high birth-rate countries such as Bulgaria and Italy the fall persisted, while in some of the low birth-rate countries the rates either rose or appeared to become relatively stable. There were also substantial increases in the birth rate in the United States, Canada, Australia and New Zealand, major countries of immigration.

Though crude birth rates are less unsatisfactory than is sometimes believed as indicators of short-term trends in fertility, or for furnishing broad comparisons between countries,[2] they nevertheless suffer from two defects. Like conventional reproduction rates, as was explained earlier, they summarize the fertility behaviour, observed in a year or other short period, of a series of generations or cohorts of women, and

---

[1] There is a similar tendency between regions in some countries. Thus in England and Wales, between 1871 and 1911 fertility fell most in counties which had begun with the lowest fertility rates. After 1911, however, the fall was greatest in counties which had had the highest rates in 1911 (see D. V. Glass, 'Changes in Fertility in England and Wales, 1851 to 1931', in Political Arithmetic, ed. L. Hogben (London, 1938)).

[2] See the useful article by G. J. Stolnitz, 'Uses of crude vital rates in the analysis of reproductivity', Journ. Amer. Stats. Assn., Dec. 1955. It should be noted that Stolnitz only compares birth rates with conventional reproduction rates, the latter being equally subject to the limitations imposed upon any index which attempts to assess total fertility by summing the rates observed in a year or other short period of time, and which does not look separately at the behaviour of different cohorts or generations of women.

Table 21. *The Trend of Fertility in Sweden, 1751-1900*

Years of observation	Crude birth rate	Birth years of generation	Generation total fertility of women[a]
1751-5 ⎫ 1756-60 ⎭	35·7	1736-40 1741-5	4·64 4·47
1761-5 ⎫ 1766-70 ⎭	34·2	1746-50 1751-5	4·35 4·21
1771-5 ⎫ 1776-80 ⎭	33·0	1756-60 1761-5	4·22 4·32
1781-5 ⎫ 1786-90 ⎭	32·0	1766-70 1771-5	4·37 4·27
1791-5 ⎫ 1796-1800 ⎭	33·3	1776-80 1781-5	4·43 4·42
1801-5 ⎫ 1806-10 ⎭	30·9	1786-90 1791-5	4·49 4·61
1811-15 ⎫ 1816-20 ⎭	33·3	1796-1800 1801-5	4·66 4·68
1821-5 ⎫ 1826-30 ⎭	34·6	1806-10 1811-15	4·66 4·62
1831-5 ⎫ 1836-40 ⎭	31·5	1816-20 1821-5	4·51 4·48
1841-5 ⎫ 1846-50 ⎭	31·1	1826-30 1831-5	4·40 4·40
1851-5 ⎫ 1856-60 ⎭	32·8	1836-40 1841-5	4·37 4·38
1861-5 ⎫ 1866-70 ⎭	31·4	1846-50 1851-5	4·33 4·28
1871-5 ⎫ 1876-80 ⎭	30·5	1856-60 1861-5	4·12 3·96
1881-5 ⎫ 1886-90 ⎭	29·1	1866-70 1871-5	3·80 3·66
1891-5 ⎫ 1896-1900 ⎭	27·1	1876-80 1881-5	3·50 3·21

[a] No. of maternities per woman passing through the childbearing period.

SOURCES. Cited or calculated from: G. Sundbärg, *Bevölkerungsstatistik Schwedens*; R. R. Kuczynski, *The Measurement of Population Growth*; Sweden, *Statistisk Årsbok, 1945*; and Sweden, *Befolkningsrörelsen...1931-1940*, and *Befolkningsrörelsen...1954*.

they may therefore give an incorrect picture of the timing of a fall or a rise in family size.[1] In addition, birth rates are inexplicit. It is difficult

[1] See N. B. Ryder, 'Problems of trend determination during a transition in fertility', *Milbank Mem. Fd. Quart.* (Jan. 1956). The most comprehensive, but necessarily rather technical, analysis of the question of timing and of short-run variations is that by J. Hajnal, 'Births, marriages and reproductivity, England and Wales, 1938-47', in *Papers of the Royal Commission on Population*, II (London, 1950).

to grasp the implications for ultimate family size of a change of, say, five points in a crude birth rate. Yet to examine the process by which fertility changes, and to consider the factors associated with such changes, inevitably means looking at family size. Indeed, one of the difficulties in studying trends in fertility has been the separation between the formal demographer, dealing with rates which, even if not synthetic, are somewhat opaque to common observation, and the sociologist concerned with the changing pressures on the family but unable to link his work to formal demographic analysis. It is only recently, with the development of a more realistic approach to the measurement of replacement, that this gap has begun to narrow, with both demographers and sociologists working with similar concepts.

The question of the timing of a trend, and also in a considerable degree the question of an explicit and immediately meaningful index, are answered by the use of generation and cohort fertility indices—some examples are given in Tables 21–23 inclusive. In those tables, a generation is defined as comprising the women born in a specified period, and their total fertility is estimated by summing the actual fertility rates observed at the successive ages of their childbearing period, assuming that this begins at the age of 15. The total fertility of, say, the 1736 generation of Swedish women would thus be estimated from the appropriate age-specific fertility rates observed in the period from 1751 to 1786, the latter year being that in which the women attain their fiftieth birthday. The resultant index is intended to show the average number of maternities or live births occurring to a woman who survives throughout the childbearing period, and whose successive probabilities of bearing children are those actually observed for her generation.[1] In Table 21, the generation fertility averages are set in parallel with crude birth rates, so that the period of observation of the birth rate coincides with the period when the given generation of women reach the first childbearing age group (that is, 15–19 years).[2] A similar arrangement is followed in Table 22, save that generation gross reproduction rates (giving an estimate of the number of *female* children born to each woman) are substituted for total fertility rates, and are set in

[1] As was indicated earlier, it is not a 'pure' measure of fertility, for the age-specific fertility rates observed reflect in part the levels of mortality of men and women—that is, as influencing the probability of a marriage continuing unbroken through the childbearing period.

[2] There is no special virtue in this arrangement. It would be equally appropriate to set the birth rate period against the period corresponding to the mean age at which women bear their children, though this would be a varying quantity. But to put the birth rate period against the period of birth of the generation of women would be somewhat confusing, for the birth rate would not then be related in time to the generation rate.

Table 22. *The Trend of Fertility in France, 1750–1910*

Years of observation	Crude birth rate	Conventional G.R.R. of women	Generation birth years	Generation G.R.R. of women
c.1750	35–40	—	—	—
—	—	—	—	—
1771–5	38·6	2·4	—	—
1776–80	38·1	2·4	—	—
1781–5	37·5	2·3	—	—
1786–90	36·4	2·2	—	—
1791–5	35·9	2·2	—	—
1796–1800	34·8	2·2	—	—
1801–5	32·0	2·0	—	—
1806–10	31·6	2·0	—	—
1811–15	31·2	1·9	—	—
1816–20	31·3	1·9	—	—
1821–5	30·7	1·9	—	—
1826–30	29·9	1·9	—	—
1831–5	29·3	1·9	—	—
1836–40	28·2	1·8	—	—
1841–5	28·0	1·8	1826–30	1·66
1846–50	26·6	1·7	1831–5	1·66
1851–5	26·1	1·7	1836–40	1·66
1856–60	26·4	1·7	1841–5	1·65
1861–5	26·6	1·7	1846–50	1·63
1866–70	25·3	1·7	1851–5	1·60
1871–5	25·0	1·6	1856–60	1·54
1876–80	25·1	1·7	1861–5	1·49
1881–5	24·6	1·6	1866–70	1·40
1886–90	23·0	1·5	1871–5	1·31
1891–5	22·2	1·5	1876–80	1·28
1896–1900	22·0	1·4	1881–5	1·16
1901–5	21·6	1·4	1886–90	1·09
1906–10	20·2	1·3	1891–5	1·01

SOURCES. Birth rates and conventional G.R.R.'s from J. Bourgeois-Pichat, 'Note sur l'évolution générale de la population française depuis le XVIIIe siècle', *Population* (April-June, 1952), pp. 319–29 (the rates for the eighteenth and part of the nineteenth century are 'corrected' estimates). Generation G.R.R.'s are from (P. Depoid) *Réproduction nette en Europe* (Paris, 1941), p. 34. The estimated crude birth rate around 1750 is from Haut Comité Consultatif de la Population et de la Famille, *La Population Française* I (Paris, 1955), 16.

parallel with conventional gross reproduction rates as well as with crude birth rates. Finally, Table 23 brings together a collection of generation rates for a number of western countries and, as far as possible, shows the net as well as the gross rates. The net rate allows for the mortality to which a generation of women was subject, and thus

Table 23. *Generation Fertility and Replacement at Approximate Time Points*

Approx. year of birth of generations	Sweden		France		England and Wales		Norway		U.S.A.	
	TF	R	TF	R	TF	R	TF	R	(1) TF	(2) TF
1830	4·4	—	3·4	0·94	—	—	—	—	—	—
1840	4·4	—	3·4	0·97	4·7	1·42	—	—	—	5·0
1850	4·3	—	3·3	0·96	4·4	1·36	—	—	—	4·8
1860	4·0	—	3·1	0·92	3·9	1·22	—	—	—	4·4
1870	3·7	—	2·9	0·84	3·3	1·09	3·9	1·33	—	3·4
1880	3·2	1·10	2·6	0·81	2·8	0·96	3·4	1·21	—	3·1
1890	2·5	0·91	2·3	0·72	2·3	0·81	2·7	1·01	2·9	2·8
1900	1·9	(0·71)	2·3	0·73	1·9	0·71	2·3	0·91	2·4	2·4

TF = Total fertility (total number of maternities or live births per woman living until age 50).
R = net replacement rate—the generation equivalent of the net reproduction rate.

SOURCES

Sweden: Total fertility rates calculated from published maternity rates. Replacement rates—1880 and 1890 from H. Hyrenius, 'Reproduction and Replacement', *Pop. Studies*, IV (1951); 1900 (partly projected) from C. E. Quensel, 'Reproduktionstal för och storleksförhållandet mellan skilda generationer', *Ekonomisk Tidskrift* (March, 1950), pp. 15–31.

France: Adapted from (P. Depoid), *Réproduction nette en Europe depuis l'origine des statistiques de l'état civil* (Paris, 1941), pp. 31 ff.; and Haut Comité Consultatif de la Population et de la Famille, *La Population Française*, I, 18–19.

England and Wales: (Adapted from) *The Registrar General's Statistical Review of England and Wales...1946–1950, Text, Civil* (London, 1954), p. 220; and *1955, Part III, Commentary* (London, 1957), p. 28.

Norway: J. Vogt, 'En undersøkelse over generajonenes fruktbarhet i Norge', *Statsøkonomisk Tidskrift* (September, 1956), pp. 181 ff.

U.S.A.: (1) P. K. Whelpton, *Cohort Fertility* (Princeton, N.J., 1954), p. 134. The data refer to native white women. Whelpton uses the term 'cohort' for what most demographers refer to as 'generation'.

(2) These are numbers of live births per woman (all marital conditions) reported at the censuses of 1910, 1940 and 1950, the results being tabulated by the dates of birth of the women concerned. The data, given in C. Taeuber and I. B. Taeuber, *The Changing Population of the United States* (New York, 1958), p. 255, have been averaged to yield ten-year estimates centred on the time points listed above. The problem of the memory factor arises as regards these results especially for the 1910 census (which yields the estimates for the generations from 1835 to 1865). But for the more recent generations the results appear realistic.

attempts to estimate the number of girls born to a woman who experienced the fertility and mortality of a specified period, namely the period through which the woman actually passed.[1] As in the case of the conventional reproduction rate, a generation rate of 1·0 would mean that one girl of the original generation would be exactly replaced in the next generation. If such a situation were to persist, then, excluding migration as a factor, the total population would ultimately become stationary. Generation net rates above 1·0 would imply a persistently growing, and rates less than 1·0 an ultimately and persistently declining, population, provided always that the levels of fertility and mortality on which the rates are based continue to apply.[2]

A comparison of the generation rates with conventional indices (crude birth rates and conventional reproduction rates) throws light on some important features of the course of fertility. First, it shows that fertility began to decline, in a number of countries, somewhat earlier than is usually assumed to be the case. The birth rates of the 1870's were high not only because of the relatively favourable age structure of the populations, but also because earlier generations of women, with relatively large ultimate family sizes, were still bearing children. The newer generations, too, had not yet shown the full evidence of their reduced ultimate family sizes, because the decline in fertility began at the older ages and occurred both later and more slowly at the younger ages.[3] A conventional rate for the 1870's, based upon the splicing together of the fertility shown by all the various generations of women in the childbearing ages at the time, thus reflects the relatively high fertility of the older generations of women and the still fairly high childbearing rates of the early stages of married life of the newer generations. How this works out may be seen by citing a

---

[1] The concept may be somewhat easier to grasp if expressed as the number of girls born to 1000 women, taking into account the chances of death and the probabilities of childbirth in the period through which the women passed. Thus, if there were high infant and childhood mortality, many of the women would die before reaching the childbearing period, and additional numbers would die at each later stage. Even if fertility were high, deaths might be so numerous that, on balance, scarcely more than 1000 girls would be yielded by the original generation of 1000 women.

[2] Technically, a rate of 1·25 would imply an ultimate *increase* of 25 per cent, and a rate of 0·75 a *decrease* of 25 per cent per generation (using the latter term in the time-measuring sense referred to in footnote 3, p. 95, that is, about 28–30 years in western countries). But these rates of growth would obtain only if the given levels of fertility and mortality were to persist for a sufficiently long time—normally, after at least two generations. The rates are not predictive in any speculative sense: they merely draw the inferences for future growth from the given assumptions regarding fertility and mortality.

[3] That is, the decline occurred by a compression of the effective childbearing period, women ceasing to have, or to have so many, children at the later stages of married life.

few comparative rates for England and Wales and Sweden, given in Table 24, in which the two types of rates are shown. In both England and Wales and Sweden the 1850 generations of women show a fall in fertility and, indeed, in Sweden, Table 21 indicates a persistent fall in almost every generation after that of 1801–5. Further, if the generation rates are set at points of time roughly equivalent to those of the con-

Table 24. *England and Wales and Sweden; Conventional and Generation Total Fertility and Replacement Rates for Approximately Comparable Periods*

	Conventional rates					Generation rates			
	Total fertility		Replacement			Total fertility		Replacement	
Year of obser- vation	Eng- land and Wales	Sweden	Eng- land and Wales	Sweden	Year of birth of genera- tion	Eng- land and Wales	Sweden	Eng- land and Wales	Sweden
1840	—	4·5	—	1·44	1840	4·7	4·4	1·42	—
1850	4·5	4·3	1·33	1·33	1850	4·4	4·3	1·36	—
1860	4·6	4·6	1·41	1·45	1860	3·9	4·0	1·22	—
1870	4·8	4·5	1·46	1·48	1870	3·3	3·7	1·09	—
1880	4·6	4·3	1·53	1·44	1880	2·8	3·2	0·96	1·10
1890	4·2	4·1	1·39	1·44	1890	2·3	2·5	0·81	0·91
1900	3·5	3·9	1·24	1·43	1900	1·9	1·9	0·71	(0·71)
1910	2·9	3·3	1·13	1·28	1910	—	—	—	—
1920	2·8	2·6	1·11	1·06	1920	—	—	—	—
1930	1·9	1·8	0·81	0·75	1930	—	—	—	—
1940	1·9	2·4	0·84	1·05	1940	—	—	—	—

SOURCES. As in Table 23 and, in addition, conventional rates before 1940 for England and Wales from D. V. Glass, *Population Policies and Movements in Europe* (Oxford, 1940), p. 13.

The conventional rates for Sweden relate to quinquennia (1841–5, etc.); those for England and Wales are based on three-year averages centred on censuses (1840–2, etc.), save for 1940, which refer to 1940–4 (in order to include the upturn covered by the Swedish data). Similar differences of time apply to the generation rates. The conventional rates for England and Wales, 1940, are adapted from the single-year rates given in *The Registrar General's Statistical Review...1955, Part III, Commentary,* p. 16.

ventional rates—for example, setting the 1840 generation rates at 1870, at which point the women concerned would be at about the mean age at which they bore their children—they will be seen to be consistently lower than the conventional rates. In fact the forces responsible for the long-term reduction in fertility began to operate on relatively early generations of women, reducing the proportions marrying (and also the proportions of young marriages) and affecting the childbearing rates of the married women when they had reached the later part of the childbearing period. It was on such married women that the widespread discussion of birth control would have had a major impact in the 1870's and 1880's. In Sweden, for example, by the 1880's, married women aged 40–44 and 45–49 years had already experienced a reduction in fertility. Between 1871–80 and 1901–10, the fall in marital maternity rates for women aged 45–49 years was twice as great as for women aged 35–39 years and four times as great as for women aged 25–29 years. This timing of the decline also influenced the level of replacement, for the earlier generations of women were exposed to high mortality. Hence generation replacement rates fall below 1·0 well before the conventional replacement rates, which measure the impact of a lower mortality than that actually experienced by the women in question. It follows, too, that with a stabilization of fertility, such as occurred from the late 1930's onwards, generation replacement rates were bound to rise because of the continued decline in mortality.[1]

Though the changing level of total fertility and replacement cannot be shown in comparable detail for many countries, a not unreasonable indication of the fall in replacement levels since the late nineteenth century can be gained from the course of conventional net reproduction rates. Table 25 groups together a series of such rates—taken largely from the work of the late R. R. Kuczynski—deliberately arranged in rather broad bands in order to avoid emphasizing smaller differences which are more likely to reflect the limitations of the index than to show real variations in replacement levels. Similarly, rates after 1925 have not been shown, because the fluctuations over the years 1930–55 do not reflect equivalent movements in ultimate family size.[2] Even allowing for the fact that in a number of western countries current marriage and fertility levels imply a replacement rate of around 1·0 or higher—and considerably higher in some cases—the table shows a very heavy fall in replacement in just over fifty years, in spite of the marked reduction in mortality in that period. But it also shows a considerable range around 1925, with a substantial number of countries having rates well over 1·0.[3]

[1] Quite apart from an increase in average family size and in the proportions of women marrying, referred to later.
[2] The full significance of the 1930–55 movements will not be known until the women concerned have passed through the childbearing period.
[3] The position in a number of western countries in the 1950's is discussed by H. Gille, 'An International Survey of Recent Fertility Trends' (in National Bureau of Economic and Social Research, *Demographic and Economic Change in Developed Countries* (Princeton, N.J., 1960), pp. 17–34). For 1950–4 the gross reproduction rates for the countries of western and southern Europe, the United States, Canada, Australia and New Zealand ranged from 1·06 for England and Wales to 1·77 for Canada (with the continual fall in mortality, the gross reproduction rates of western countries are now very close to the net reproduction rates). The rates for the United States, Austra-

Table 25. *Conventional Net Reproduction Rates, 1895–1925*

Level	About 1895	About 1925
1·4 and over	Ukraine	Russia
	Russia	Ukraine
	Poland	Bulgaria
	Austria	Poland
	Denmark	S. Africa
	Finland	Japan
	Germany	
	Hungary	
	Norway	
	Sweden	
1·2–1·4	England	Italy
	Italy	Spain
		Greece
		Ireland
		Netherlands
		Norway
		Canada
		Australia
1·0–1·2		Denmark
		Finland
		Hungary
		U.S.A.
0·8–1·0	France	Austria
		England
		France
		Germany
		Sweden

SOURCES. R. R. Kuczynski, 'The International Decline of Fertility', *Political Arithmetic*, ed. L. Hogben (London, 1938), pp. 47–72; P. Depoid, *op. cit.* pp. 39–42; U.N. *Demographic Yearbook* (1948, 1954).

Although the generation approach provides a more realistic appraisal of the timing and significance of the fall in fertility, it does not reveal the actual process of decline unless it deals with the changing size of families as distinct from the changing total fertility of all women passing through the childbearing period. Since it is the children born in marriage who constitute by far the largest proportion of all children born in western countries,[1] to examine the way in which the fall in

lia and New Zealand were all above 1·5. Rates between 1·2 and 1·5 were shown by Denmark, Finland, France, Scotland, the Netherlands, Norway, Portugal and Switzerland. Lower rates—between 1·06 and 1·2—were shown by Belgium, England and Wales, Italy, and Sweden. Gille's conclusion, based upon these and other data, is that all the countries surveyed appeared to have replacement rates above 1·0.

[1] Even in the mid-nineteenth century, the proportion of illegitimate births to all live births was relatively low for most western countries, being less than 10 % save for

family size developed involves the study of marital fertility. Here there is an even greater shortage of data which would permit a generation or cohort approach. Apart, therefore, from citing examples of family sizes for a number of countries, which have had one or more fertility censuses, the discussion will be restricted mainly to material relating to Britain.[1] First, however, it is necessary to refer, if only very briefly, to changes in the extent of, and age at, marriage in the past hundred years.

Table 26. *Great Britain Proportions (per cent) of Women Ever-Married, 1851–1951*

	Census date				
Age (years)	1851	1911	1921	1931	1951
20–4	30·4	24·0	27·0	25·0	47·3
35–9	81·1	78·0	79·0	78·8	86·6
40–4	84·4	81·6	81·6	81·4	85·6
45–9	86·3	83·0	82·8	82·7	84·2

SOURCES. Basic data; 1851–1931, *Papers of the Royal Commission on Population* (London, 1950), II, 188 ff.; 1951, *Census 1951, Great Britain, One Per Cent Sample Tables*, part I (London, 1952), pp. 2–3.

One of the simplest ways of looking at such changes is by means of census data on the proportions of 'ever-married' persons in various age groups at different points of time—that is, of married, widowed and

Denmark, Austria and those German states in which 'Malthusian' marriage laws were in force—for example, Bavaria and Saxony. In the later nineteenth century, illegitimacy tended in general to decline, save notably in Sweden where—taking the form of concubinage rather than of promiscuousness—the proportion of illegitimate births rose until the early 1930's, since when it has fallen again. (On illegitimacy in Sweden, see A. Myrdal, *Nation and Family* (New York, 1941), pp. 39–47. The 'Malthusian' marriage legislation in nineteenth-century German states is discussed in D. V. Glass (ed.), *Introduction to Malthus* (London, 1953), pp. 39–47). At present Austria, Portugal and Sweden are the only countries in which illegitimate births constitute 10 % or more of all births.

[1] N. B. Ryder, in the papers referred to earlier, applies a generation approach to the study of marital fertility in Sweden. But this is based on age-specific marital fertility rates and provides no information on changing family size distributions. A more direct approach would be through a series of fertility censuses, in which the information on family size is tabulated by the date of birth of the married women. (A fertility census is one in which every married woman—or ever-married woman, or every married couple, etc.—is asked the total number of children she has borne. If the date of birth of each child is also asked, a more comprehensive analysis is possible—as in Britain, with the 1946 Sample Family Census.) There are, however, some advantages in studying marital fertility in terms of marriage cohorts rather than generations, notably that it is then easier to relate economic and social influences on the marriages to variations in family size.

divorced persons, who must have been married at least once. Table 26
gives such information for women in Great Britain at a few points of
time between 1851 and 1951, and shows a marked watershed in 1931.
Before that point and in fact from the 1870's onwards, the proportions
of ever-married women fell fairly consistently at most ages, and
especially in the youngest age group, thus reinforcing the influences
which affected fertility within marriage. After 1931, however, and
especially after the mid-1930's, the trend was sharply reversed. The
proportion ever-married rose markedly in the youngest age groups,
and to a level far in excess of that in 1851. Moreover, the proportions
in the age group 45–49 years were bound to rise still further—since they
were already exceeded in the two immediately younger age groups—
and also move above the 1851 level.[1] Even without any changes in
marital fertility, therefore, the change in marriage habits would tend to
raise overall replacement levels, while the younger age at marriage
might well raise marital fertility—and hence further increase the
replacement rate—if only by extending the length of exposure to the
risk of accidental pregnancies. Since these developments applied in
general to western countries, though not with uniform intensity, they
contributed to the birth rate 'boom' of the past fifteen years—by
drawing additional generations of women into marriage—and also to
the higher replacement rates of the period. How long the trend to
younger ages at marriage is likely to persist cannot be estimated unless
there are far more serious studies of marriage habits than have as yet
been undertaken. At present, however, in many countries, the proportions of young women marrying may well be higher than in any
other period since the beginning of the nineteenth century.[2]

[1] In England and Wales, in 1955, the estimated proportion ever-married among
women aged 45–49 years was 86·4% and 52·7% among women aged 20–24 years.
The rising trend had thus persisted (see *The Registrar General's Statistical Review*,
part III, 1955, p. 7).
[2] On recent changes in marriage frequency see in particular J. Hajnal, 'Age at
Marriage and Proportions Marrying', *Pop. Studies*, VII (1953). Hajnal has drawn
attention to the demographic background of the developments—the changing sex-
ratio of the marriageable population and the diminishing 'surplus' of women. But
the study of the more sociological aspects of the new trend is still to be done, historical
discussions of the kind found in J. A. Banks, *Prosperity and Parenthood* (London, 1954)
requiring to be supplemented by inquiries into current pressures and attractions.
Such inquiries are all the more relevant in view of the sharp contrast between present
and past proportions of young persons marrying. That the tendency to marry at a
very early age in the past has been overstressed may be seen, for example, from Gregory
King's census of Lichfield, 1695, which shows only 15% ever-married among women
aged 20–24 years, though 98% among women aged 45–49 years (the basic data are
from D. V. Glass, 'Gregory King's Estimate of the Population of England and Wales,
1695', *Pop. Studies*, III (1950), 364). On the 'myth' of universally early marriage in

Table 27. *Total Live Births per Marriage of Completed Fertility, for Marriages Existing at Census Date, as shown by Earlier Censuses*

Country	Census date	Live births per marriage	Marriage duration (years)
Australia	1911	6·7	30–4
France	1906	3·7	25 and over
Great Britain	1911	5·8	32–41
Ireland	1911	6·8	30–4
Norway	1920	6·4	33 and over
New Zealand	1911	6·8	30–4
South Africa	1921	8·0	30–4
Sweden	1930	5·3	30 and over

SOURCES AND NOTES

Australia: *1911 Census*, III, Melbourne (1914), excluding full-blooded aborigines. Number of live births per ever-married woman.

France: *1906 Census, Statistiques des Familles en 1906* (Paris, 1912), pp. 14–15. Number of live births per marriage existing at census date.

Great Britain: 1911 Census of England and Wales and Scotland, adjusted data from D. V. Glass and E. Grebenik, *The Trend and Pattern of Fertility in Great Britain*, part I (London, 1954), p. 135. Women married under 45 years of age and still married at census date or marriage not terminated until after forty-fifth birthday, total live births. The marriage years are 1870–9.

Ireland: *1911 Census*, 32 counties. *Commission on Emigration and other Population Problems, 1948–54, Reports* (Dublin [1955]), p. 94. Marriages existing at census date, women aged 15–44 years at marriage, total live births to existing marriage.

Norway: *1920 Census*, vol. VI (Kristiania, 1923), pp. 4–5 and 11. Existing marriages, women aged 16–45 years at marriage, total births to existing marriage.

New Zealand: *1911 Census* (Wellington, 1912), p. 383. Existing marriages, total births to existing marriage.

S. Africa: *1921 Census*, part IV (Pretoria, 1923), p. 20. Europeans only. Live-born children to existing marriages.

Sweden: *1930 Census*, part IX (Stockholm, 1939), p. 42. Total live births to existing marriages, women aged 15–44 years at marriage.

Within marriage itself, a comparison—though a rough one—of the average number of live children borne by women in different western countries and over a period stretching from the late nineteenth century to the very recent past is presented in Tables 27 and 28. An attempt is made in the first of these tables to provide a picture of family size—in

pre-industrial U.S.A., see T. P. Monahan, *The Pattern of Age at Marriage in the United States* (Philadelphia, 1951), I, 99–122. The available evidence, fragmentary though it is, makes it clear that, from at least the late seventeenth century, ages at marriage in western Europe were considerably higher, and proportions ultimately married considerably lower, than is the case in most of the less developed countries today.

Table 28. *Total Live Births per Marriage for Marriages Existing at Census Date, as shown by Recent Censuses*

Country	Census date	Duration of marriage (years)				
		15–19	20–4	25–9	30–4	45 and over
Australia	1947	2·71	2·97	3·26	3·61	5·24
Belgium	1957	2·46	—	—	—	—
Finland	1950	3·20	3·48	3·76	4·25	5·99
France	1946	2·31	2·31	—	—	—
Germany	1950	2·14	2·23	2·24	—	—
Great Britain	1946	2·09	2·34	2·59	2·88	—
Ireland	1946	4·09	4·44	4·73	4·91	6·30
Netherlands	1947	3·22	3·46	3·78	4·18	—
Norway	1950	2·40	2·59	2·96	—	—
Switzerland	1950	2·37	2·47	2·65	2·96	4·20
United States	1950	2·53	—	—	—	—

SOURCE. U.N. *Recent Trends in Fertility in Industrialized Countries* (New York, 1958); and Belgium, *1947 Census* (Bruxelles, 1951), VII, 19–20.

NOTES

Australia: Excluding marriage where the couple was permanently separated.

Belgium: Current marriage only. The duration given above is 15 years and over. The corresponding figure for 10–14 years is 1·82 live births per marriage.

France: First marriages only, including marriages where the woman was widowed or divorced at or above the age of 45 years. All children born alive to the woman are included. Durations 16–20 years, etc.

Germany: Federal Republic, excluding Berlin. Stillbirths included. Excluding marriages where the couple was separated.

Great Britain: First marriages only in which the woman was under 45 at marriage. Covers all children born alive to the woman. Includes marriages where the woman was divorced at or above the age of 45 years.

Netherlands: First marriages only.

Norway: Marriages where the woman was under 45 at marriage.

Switzerland: Covers all legitimate and legitimized children born alive.

United States: White women married once only (with husband present), 15–49 years of age at the date of the census.

the sense defined—in the late nineteenth century, or as near to that period as possible, and the dates of marriage covered vary from 1870–9 in the case of Great Britain, to 1900 and earlier years in the case of Norway. Apart from the extremes of South Africa and France, the range of family size differences is not much more than one child.

Whatever may have been the differences in the intensity and effectiveness of birth control practice at the time, they had not yet produced very wide discrepancies in fertility, though it would be unjustified to stress this too heavily because of the lack of full comparability of the statistics.[1]

Table 28, on the other hand, provides an indication of the reduction in family size in the present century. Since this reduction has been achieved by a compression of the effective childbearing period, the averages at 20–24 years' duration of marriage may be taken as fairly firm measures of completed fertility, and even the averages at 15–19 years' duration cannot be far short of the final levels. Thus the marriages of the 1920's and early 1930's will in most cases have produced families less than half the size of those produced by the marriages of around the 1880's or 1890's. The fall is less than this in France, where, with the very long historical decline, the speed of further reduction had slackened. It must also have been less in the Netherlands where, according to a recent study, the Catholic community applies religio-familial precepts with particular rigorousness,[2]

[1] Including, for example, differences in age at marriage. At the same time, if it is thought that the family sizes shown are well below what might be expected in populations with relatively little birth control practice—as was probably the case in most of the countries at the time, France being a notable exception—two points should be borne in mind. First, averages are lowered by the presence of physiologically infertile or relatively infertile marriages, and the *typical* sizes of family would be rather higher. (This will be referred to in the more detailed discussion of Great Britain.) Secondly, uncontrolled fertility does not mean that family size is necessarily constant or very large for a given age at marriage. Even if abstinence is excluded, the size of family in a situation of uncontrolled fertility will still depend upon such other variables as venereal infections (influencing ability to conceive or the probability of stillbirths); the level of nutrition; breast-feeding practices; genetic or physiological factors affecting the capacity to impregnate, to become pregnant, and to carry a viable foetus to term; as well as by the frequency of intercourse. An indication of the upper level of family size which might result when fertility is uncontrolled, when nutritional and other environmental factors are favourable, and when there are apparently no religious or social constraints on intercourse in marriage, may be obtained from the actual fertility of married women in the Hutterite community in North America. In that community, the average number of live births per married woman aged 45–54 years in 1950 was 10·6 (see J. W. Eaton and A. J. Mayer, *Man's Capacity to Reproduce* (Glencoe, Illinois, 1954), p. 20). This is higher than the fertility of married women in rural Ireland in the late nineteenth century (women marrying before the age of 20 years had an average completed fertility of 8·8 live births). Another community with very high fertility is that of French Canada in the early eighteenth century, when completed families in which the women married before their forty-fifth birthday averaged 8·4 live births. This figure was matched in 1941 by an average of 8·5 live births per married woman aged 45–54 years for Roman Catholic women in rural Quebec, born on farms, with French as their mother-tongue and having had not more than eight years of schooling (see E. Charles, *The Changing Size of the Family in Canada* (Census of Canada 1941, Census Monograph no. 1), Ottawa, 1948, p. 72; and J. Henripin, *La Population Canadienne au Début du XVIIIe Siècle* (Paris, 1954), p. 50).
[2] See T. van den Brink, *Eerste Resultaten van een statistische Analyse van de Loop der Geboortecijfers in Nederland* (Amsterdam, 1949), and F. van Heek, 'Roman Catholicism and Fertility in the Netherlands', *Pop. Studies*, x (1956).

and where, perhaps through fear of being outnumbered, Protestant groups also produce large families. And it was very considerably less in Ireland, the most deviant of western countries in respect of population trends in the nineteenth and early twentieth centuries. Ireland is the single country whose total population fell continuously from 1841 onwards,[1] substantial emigration being accompanied by a sharp reduction in the proportions of men and women marrying, so that although marital fertility was very stable until the present century, natural increase was controlled by more nearly 'Malthusian' practices than in any other country.[2] Marital fertility has fallen in the twentieth century, but it is still strikingly higher than in most other western countries and still relatively uncontrolled. Similarly, the proportions of men and women marrying at the younger ages have increased somewhat since the 1930's, but the voluntary restriction of marriage—and especially the linking of marriage in rural Ireland to a dowry and to the transfer of a farm to one child—still remains the primary means of controlling natural increase.[3]

[1] In the twenty-six counties (Eire), the population continued to fall until 1946, rising very slightly thereafter. In Northern Ireland, the population began to grow again from 1901.

[2] Using the term 'Malthusian' in the strict sense—namely, voluntary restriction of, and delay in, marriage, absence—at least to a considerable extent—of birth control in married life, and emigration acting as a complement to, and not as a substitute for, the control of natural increase. The common use—especially in France—of the term 'Malthusian' to imply the practice of birth control is in complete conflict with Malthus's views on the subject, for he was opposed to birth control on moral grounds and also social and economic grounds, believing that if couples could easily limit their families, a primary spur to social progress would be lost. The term 'neo-Malthusian' would be more appropriately used of birth control—it was coined for the Malthusian League, established in England in 1877 by individuals who accepted Malthus's theory of population but rejected his principle of 'moral restraint' as a solution.

[3] It is evident, from the differences in family size between the socio-economic groups, that birth control is now being practised in Eire, in spite of legal prohibitions and penalties (of a kind also found in France and Belgium). On demographic developments in Ireland, the major source is now *Commission on Emigration*, etc. See also D. V. Glass (ed.), *Introduction to Malthus*, pp. 30–8, and K. H. Connell, 'Peasant Marriage in Ireland after the Great Famine', *Past and Present*, no. 12 (November 1957). The fall in the incidence of marriage is shown by the change in the proportions of single persons (that is, never-married) in the age group 45–54 years between 1841 and 1951, namely from 10·0 to 31·0 % for men, and from 11·7 to 25·7 % for women (see *Commission*, etc., p. 72). The position of marriage in Ireland has also been influenced by the abnormally low ratio of females to males, due partly to the character of the emigration, but also partly to the fact that, relatively to males, females have experienced a less favourable mortality than in most other western countries. It should be added that some of the contributions to J. A. O'Brien (ed.), *The Vanishing Irish* (London, 1954), would join religious and cultural to economic and demographic factors in turning Eire into a 'nation of elderly bachelors'—for example, the Jansenist

For two of the countries covered by Tables 27 and 28—Norway and Great Britain—it is possible to show much more clearly the process of changes in family size since the nineteenth century.[1] Table 29 provides some of the main data for Norway, a marriage duration of twenty years having been taken to show completed fertility, while similar statistics for Great Britain are given in Table 30. Though the levels of fertility in the two countries are somewhat different, the process of decline is the same, namely an increase in childlessness and still more the virtual elimination of large families. In the nineteenth century, though the average family size was not astonishingly high, very large families were by no means uncommon. Thus in Great Britain, of the women married in 1870-9, almost 18 per cent had 10 or more live births. Among the marriages of 1925, however, the frequency of such families had fallen to 0·6 per cent. Thus time has produced a narrower range of family size in the community, even though differences between regions and social classes still persist. And for fertile women, the much lower final family size has tended to weaken the link, so evident in the late nineteenth century, between age at marriage and total number of live births. Moreover, the overall pattern of small families may itself help to explain the new stability of family size found in many countries among the marriages of the 1930's and later years, for a postponement of childbearing during economic depression need not now, as would have been probable in earlier decades, reduce the ultimate size of family. An average of 2·2 children can still be attained, even if a birth is postponed for a few years, and the data for Britain show just this kind of postponement and making up of births.

The previous discussion has implied—and at several points it has been stated categorically—that, save in the case of Ireland, it is through the spread of birth control, and of the more persistent use of birth control, that family size has been brought down in the West. There is ample evidence, both indirect and direct, to support this view, and some reference needs to be made to the timing of the development in different countries.

Among the major European countries, it is France for which there is the longest record of references to birth control as such, and also to

element in Irish Catholic teaching, and the dominant influence of mothers on their sons, denying them responsibility. That economic factors are not the whole explanation is fairly evident.

[1] In Norway there have been four fertility censuses and, in addition, a 'sample' study was undertaken in 1894. In Britain there have been two fertility censuses, and because the second—the sample Family Census of 1946—ascertained the date of birth of each live-born child, it is possible to go much farther back in the analysis than would otherwise have been the case.

Table 29. *Norway. Changes in Total Number of Live Births
per Marriage for Marriages of 20 Years' Duration
(Women under 45 Years of Age at Marriage)*

Date of census or sample survey	Approx. date of marriage	No. of live births per marriage	Percentage of marriages with following numbers of live births				
			0	1–3	4–5	6 and over	Total
1894	1874	(5·72)	5·5	21·4	17·7	55·4	100·0
1920	1900	5·09	7·1	26·0	23·0	43·9	100·0
1930	1910	4·17	9·4	36·4	24·6	29·6	100·0
1946	1926	2·66	11·6	60·9	18·8	8·7	100·0
1950	1930	2·49	12·0	64·1	16·7	7·2	100·0

SOURCE AND NOTES. The data are from G. Jahn, *Barnetallet i norske ekteskap* (in 1950 Census of Norway, vol. v, Oslo, 1957), especially pp. 12, 13, 24 and 25. For 1894 the marriage duration is 20–29 years. The full span of decline is greater than shown here, since the 1920 census estimated the fertility of marriages of 33 or more years' duration (marriages before 1888) at 6·39 live births.

Table 30. *Great Britain. Changes in Total Number of Live Births
per Woman for First Marriages of at Least 20 Years' Duration
(Women under 45 Years of Age at Marriage)*

Date of marriage	No. of live births per marriage	Percentage of marriages with following numbers of live births:				
		0	1–3	4–5	6 and over	Total
1870–9	5·8	8·3	21·1	19·0	51·6	100·0
1890–9	4·3	9·9	36·7	22·2	31·2	100·0
1900–9	3·4	11·3	49·2	20·4	19·1	100·0
1910	3·0	12·2	54·4	18·6	14·8	100·0
1915	2·5	15·0	60·6	15·4	9·0	100·0
1920	2·5	13·8	61·8	15·1	9·3	100·0
1925	2·2	16·1	65·0	12·2	6·7	100·0

SOURCE AND NOTES. The data are from D. V. Glass and E. Grebenik, *The Trend and Pattern of Fertility in Great Britain*, part I (London, 1954), pp. 85–7. The marriage durations range from over forty years for the earlier marriages, to just over twenty years for the latest marriages. The latter may nevertheless be regarded as having completed their fertility, in view of the compression of the effective childbearing period in the present century. The women covered are 'ever-married'—widowed and divorced (as well as married), provided that the first marriage was not terminated before the forty-fifth birthday of the woman. Marriages prior to 1870 may have had a still higher fertility, but it is difficult to tell because of the 'bias' introduced into the 1911 fertility census in respect of earlier cohorts of marriage—a 'bias' resulting from the way in which the universe of women was defined. This may be equally true of the early cohorts covered by the Norwegian census of 1920.

abortion as a means of birth prevention. Of the two forms of control, abortion has the longer record, the 1556 edict of Henri II being designed to combat what was already regarded as a fairly frequent practice.[1] Abortionists were among the prisoners in the Bastille in the eighteenth century,[2] and the practice spread until by the present century it was—and still is—widely believed that there were almost as many abortions as live births in the country as a whole. References to birth control as such—to contraception, that is—occur from the seventeenth century onwards. Initially the references were to the practice among *milieux galants*, with the object of saving women involved in 'high society' from the burden of too many pregnancies. But during the eighteenth century, many writers were convinced that birth control was already being extensively used in *bourgeois* circles and for more broadly economic and social reasons. During the early nineteenth century, with the acceptance of the Malthusian theory by influential economists, Academy awards and local officials encouraged 'prudence' in married life, and 'prudence' was not limited, as it was in Malthus's principles of conduct, to 'moral restraint'. *Coitus interruptus* and the use of the 'sponge'—one of the earliest mechanical contraceptives—were reported to be customary techniques for attaining, as Garnier urged, 'the day when the employed classes would realise that morality urged and welfare demanded the voluntary and preventive restriction of population, when blame would attach to those improvident individuals who brought forth into the world more children than they could feed'.[3] By the end of the nineteenth century, when the continued fall in the birth rate had, in reaction, stimulated the beginnings of a neo-mercantilist population policy, birth control, like abortion, had become deeply rooted in the community. In the 1920's it became part of pro-natalist policy to suppress birth control and abortion. But though the birth control movement as such was demolished—the movement had not become established in any effective sense, perhaps because it was not really needed—abortion and birth control practices persist with scarcely diminished intensity.[4]

[1] Cf. P. Le Ridant, *Code Matrimonial* (Paris, 1766), pp. 9 ff. See also E. Locard, *Le XVIIe Siècle Médico-Judiciaire* (Lyons and Paris, 1902), ch. XVI; and A. Corre and P. Aubry, *Documents de Criminologie Rétrospective* (Lyons and Paris, 1895), ch. XI.

[2] F. Funck–Brentano, *Les Lettres de Cachet à Paris* (Paris, 1903), *passim*. Ten abortionists were included in the lists covering the period 1659–1789.

[3] D. V. Glass, *The Background and Development of French Population Policy*, Memorandum to the Royal Commission on Population (mimeographed report).

[4] On the general history of birth control and abortion in France, see P. Aries, 'Sur les origines de la contraception en France', *Population* (July–September 1953); J. G. C. Blacker, *The Social and Economic Causes of the Decline in the French Birth Rate at the End of the Eighteenth Century*, Ph. D. Thesis (University of London, 1957) (of which one

In Britain, the history of birth limitation is shorter, but less chequered. There were occasional references to the practice of abortion from the late seventeenth century onwards,[1] but not of a kind which suggests an extensive practice, and it is unlikely that anything comparable to developments in France took place.[2] Birth control as such was scarcely discussed before the nineteenth century, though condoms were used— by Boswell among others—often as a protection against venereal disease, and though Bentham recommended the 'sponge' in 1797. The case for birth control was first presented to the public by Francis Place in 1822, and in 1823 he issued a series of leaflets in which he advocated, both to the working class and to the middle class, specific techniques of contraception. From the 1820's onwards there was a gradual increase in discussion and in the circulation of books and pamphlets recommending and describing birth control, some of this material certainly circulating fairly widely among the working-class population. Nevertheless, in spite of the attention given in the press at the end of the 1860's to Lord Amberley's espousal of the cause of birth control, it took the Bradlaugh–Besant trial of 1877 to bring the subject fully before the public—as the *Daily News* put it, to place it 'with the morning and evening newspapers on the breakfast table and the drawing-room table in thousands of homes'.

The Bradlaugh–Besant trial had a double consequence. First, though it was followed by other—and successful—prosecutions against publishers of birth control handbooks, no concerted attempt was made after 1877 to prevent the dissemination of, propaganda for, or know-

---

section is published in *Pop. Studies*, XI (1957)); D. V. Glass, *Population Policies and Movements in Europe*, ch. IV; C. Watson, 'Birth Control and Abortion in France since 1939', *Pop. Studies*, V (1952). There is an extensive literature on birth control policy and practice in other countries. On Sweden, a country with a pro-natalist but also a pro-birth-control policy, see H. Gille, 'Recent Developments in Swedish Population Policy', part I, *Pop. Studies*, II (1948). For a broad survey of the legal position in various countries, see H. T. Eldridge, *Population Policies: A Survey of Recent Developments* (Washington, D.C., 1954). The standard history of contraception as such is N. E. Himes, *Medical History of Contraception* (Baltimore, 1936), though it is unfortunately less satisfactory for the later nineteenth century onwards than for earlier periods.

[1] See R. R. Kuczynski, 'British Demographers' Opinions on Fertility, 1660 to 1760', in L. Hogben (ed.), *Political Arithmetic*, p. 292. Legal references to abortion occur from the thirteenth century onwards, and it was an offence under the common law, though not a statutory offence until 1803 (see L. A. Parry, *Criminal Abortion* (London, 1932), ch. XI).

[2] The Biological and Medical Committee of the Royal Commission on Population gave an 'informed guess' of 2–5 % of all pregnancies ending in induced abortion (see *Papers of the Royal Commission on Population* (London, 1950), IV, 4). Even if this were multiplied severalfold, the total would still be below what French writers believe to be the incidence in France.

ledge of, contraception. Nor was there any serious interference with the Malthusian League which, founded in 1877 expressly to spread neo-Malthusian ideas, was responsible for the initiation of similar movements in many other countries and, ultimately, for the establishment of modern birth control clinics in Britain and elsewhere. Secondly, the publicity attached to the trial came at a time when the society, or at least the middle class, was ready to be influenced by it. For middle-class families the late 1870's saw a new *malaise*, the emergence of a serious gap between aspirations and levels of living. On the side of consumption, the style of living was becoming more expensive, the opportunities for expenditure were multiplying. No less important, secondary and university education, formerly attributes or concomitants of social status, were coming to be regarded as means for achieving or maintaining status. The greater the provision of free education for the masses by the state, the more the middle class focused on costly education for their children, especially for their sons, and one of the unanticipated results of the 1902 Education Act, by which a ladder was provided from the primary to the grammar school, was, according to Norwood, to cause the professional middle class to aspire to send their sons to 'public' schools instead of to the local grammar schools which they had until then found reasonably adequate.[1] In response to such pressures, and in a period during which there emerged a wider rationality in the discussion of other aspects of life, the middle class began to limit the numbers of their children, and established a pattern which the rest of the community soon came to emulate, though the differences in family size between the black-coated and the manual sections of the population widened considerably, and only began to narrow slightly again in the marriages of the 1930's.[2] These differences in family size were a reflection both of the relative intensity of birth control practice

[1] Cf. C. Norwood, *The English Tradition of Education* (London, 1929), pp. 130–1. On the general background of the adoption of birth control, see J. A. Banks, *op. cit.*, and also J. A. and O. Banks, 'The Bradlaugh–Besant Trial and the English Newspapers', *Pop. Studies*, VIII (1954). On the early nineteenth-century history of birth control propaganda in England, see J. A. Field, *Essays on Population and Other Papers*, ed. H. F. Hohman (Chicago, 1931), ch. III.

[2] In the marriages from the 1900's to the 1920's, family size was 40 % larger among the manual sections. See Glass and Grebenik, *op. cit.* pp. 107–8 and 212. In the western world as a whole, fertility has, during the past fifty years, generally been rather higher among the manual workers than in middle-class families. But there are exceptions to this generalization, and it is not uncommon to find that the highest economic and social strata have larger families than the strata immediately below them. For discussions of recent trends in differential fertility in the West, see G. Z. Johnson, 'Differential Fertility in European Countries', and C. V. Kiser, 'Differential Fertility in the United States', both in National Bureau of Economic Research, *Demographic and Economic Change in Developed Countries* (Princeton, 1960).

and of the different conventions in respect of the numbers of children regarded as desirable or 'acceptable'. But on all groups, the small-family pattern had become firmly impressed, and by the eve of the Second World War, most groups in the population had adopted birth control, though modern appliance techniques were being used in only just over half of the marriages in which births were controlled.[1]

The brief case studies of Ireland, France and Britain will, it is hoped, serve to illustrate different ways in which the control of natural increase has emerged as a distinctive feature in western society during the past 150 years. The discussion may also help to forestall superficial generalizations, and to point to the need for a much more detailed analysis of

[1] Because of the research sponsored by the Royal Commission on Population, the spread of birth control during the present century is better documented for Great Britain than for any other western country. The sample survey directed by Lewis-Faning provides considerable evidence on incidence, techniques and effectiveness, and confirms the assumption that the role of the Bradlaugh–Besant trial was to publicize birth control as an acceptable means of limiting family size rather than to draw attention to new techniques, even though such techniques became increasingly available. Thus in the Lewis-Faning survey, of the women who were married before 1910 and who used birth control, only 16% used appliance methods; for the vast majority, the technique applied was *coitus interruptus*, known to, and used by, the rural population in Sweden and France in the late eighteenth and early nineteenth centuries. Even among the birth controllers married in 1940–7, only 57% used appliance methods. On the other hand, the total incidence of birth control in all forms amounted to only 16% among the marriages prior to 1910, whereas for the marriages of 1940–7 it was probably at least 72% (allowing for the short duration of the latter marriages at the time of the survey), and might well have been considerably higher. Exposure to birth control during married life also increased because of the rise in the proportion—from 25% to about 50%—of birth controllers who began practising birth control from the beginning of married life (see E. Lewis-Faning, *Report on an Enquiry into Family Limitation*, etc., *Papers of the Royal Commission on Population* (London, 1949), I, 6–12). The evidence on the effectiveness of birth control makes it unnecessary to search for physiological explanations of declining fertility. There may have been some change—though improvements in the environment, and in medical care, as well as the dissolution of territorial 'isolates', leading to a reduction in consanguineous mating and hence to a fall in the possibility of recessively inherited conditions lowering fecundity or fertility, would have tended to work in the opposite direction. Reduced frequency of coitus may also be a partial explanation, especially as, at present, that frequency appears to be lower for urban than rural populations, and for more, as compared with less, educated individuals. But the evidence for deliberate restriction of family size as the primary factor is overwhelming. For the most recent developments in the spread of birth control in Britain, see G. Rowntree and R. Pierce, 'Birth Control in Britain', part I, *Pop. Studies* (1961). Detailed analyses of the incidence and impact of birth control in the United States since the Second World War are given in R. Freedman, P. K. Whelpton and A. A. Campbell, *Family Planning, Sterility, and Population Growth* (New York, 1959). The most up-to-date research into the incidence of birth limitation in developed and less developed societies is surveyed in C. V. Kiser (ed.), *Research in Family Planning* (Princeton, N.J., 1962).

the background of control in the various societies. Even if a seemingly valid generalization were formulated—for example, that control is initiated when a gap between aspirations and levels of living exists and is recognized, and when individual control (whether of marriage or by birth prevention) appears both a possible and an acceptable means of closing that gap—detailed studies would still be required, for the origins of the gap will not necessarily be the same for all societies, nor will each society react in the same way to the conflict induced by rising aspirations. Land hunger, and the desire to guarantee the integrity of farm holdings in a peasant society, may inspire one kind of reaction; anxiety to assure a higher social status for one's children in a community with a firm but not entirely inflexible structure (as in eighteenth-century France) and with limited horizons of economic opportunity may produce another; continuing general opportunities but the sense of a shifting balance between the social classes may produce still a third. There is no substitute for the study of change in its particular historical context, even though that may not do more than facilitate an evaluation of relative probabilities. This also applies to the stabilization—and rise—of fertility levels in many western societies in the past fifteen or twenty years. There are certain uniformities in the situation, such as the changing sex ratio of marriageable persons—resulting from the ageing of the generation affected by the First World War; from the lessening and changing character of emigration; and from the smaller losses of men in some countries in the Second World War—and the achievement and maintenance of full employment. But there are also differences in the circumstances prior to the stability—positive population policies in some countries, for example, and not in others; an insecure middle class in one country, ravaged by unemployment during the 'thirties', while in another country suffering cuts in income but protected from the indignities of the 'dole'. In examining these differences and their significance in conditioning the size of family regarded as desirable or acceptable, the historian and the sociologist have at least as much to contribute as the demographer.

For the rest of the world the discussion must inevitably be more superficial and far less solidly grounded in reality. The inadequacy of the basic statistics has already been noted. Beyond this there are the problems associated with the study of fertility—and especially of the pressures upon and supports to high fertility—in societies with a wide span of familial arrangements. In some—as in India and Ceylon, and to a considerable degree in Japan as well, until quite recently—though the family is based upon marriage, marriage itself is scarcely an intervening variable, since the age at marriage is low and the ultimate probability of marriage not far short of 100 per cent. In such societies, it is widowhood, at a high level because of the low expectations of life, which acts to some extent as a control upon overall fertility. In other societies, as in the Caribbean and in parts of the mainland of Latin America, familial arrangements are by no means limited to legal marriage. In Jamaica, for example, over 60 per cent of all births are illegitimate—not the reflection of promiscuity in the western sense, but of the fact that familial relationships in the island comprise three types. Legal marriage is one, and in 1943 some 55 per cent of the women aged 45–54 years were or had been married. The second type, referred to in the census analysis as 'common law marriages', consists of fairly stable unions which have not been legitimated, though substantial numbers become converted into legal marriages later. About 11 per cent of the women aged 45–54 years were living in such unions in 1953. The rest of the female population is classified by the census as 'single'. But in fact many of the 'single' women are living in what are called 'keeper unions', unlegalized, like 'common law marriages', but looser and more subject to change of partners. Unless, therefore, the numbers in the three kinds of union are ascertained in censuses, it is impossible to estimate the exposure to risk of childbirth in the community. It is also important to distinguish the separate types as far as possible, for they have different social prestige and different levels of fertility, the legal marriages being both more highly regarded and more prolific than the consensual unions.[1] Finally, further complications are added in other parts of the world by the existence of polygamy, by the ramified kinship systems and associated definitions of the universe of possible mates, and also—as in some of the newly growing urban communities in Africa—by the temporary migration of men, which may separate the partners in a union for considerable periods.[2] Such complexities, coupled with the lack of reliable serial statistics, make it impossible to present any general account of fertility trends during even the present century. As in the case of mortality, the most that can be done is to indicate an order of magnitude for the main regions in this other two-thirds of the world, and to supplement this with the more detailed

---

[1] In Jamaica, the total numbers of children per woman over 45 years of age in 1943 were: married, 5·88; common law, 4·76; single, 3·32. See G. W. Roberts, *The Population of Jamaica* (Cambridge, 1957), ch. 8. Roberts's study is by far the most thorough available. On demographic developments and problems in the Caribbean area as a whole, see *Report of the Conference on the Demographic Problems of the Area served by the Caribbean Commission* (Trinidad, 1957). The several volumes of papers prepared for the conference contain a great deal of relevant material.

[2] Our knowledge of the levels and cultural context of fertility in such areas would be greatly increased if anthropologists were to include the study of fertility in their field investigations. But they rarely do so. See, however, some recent studies in F. Lorimer *et al.*, *Culture and Human Fertility* (UNESCO, 1954).

consideration of a number of 'sample' areas, illustrating something of the range of variability.

A rough idea of birth rate levels was given in Table 15, which indicated that the less developed regions in general have rates higher than were found in western Europe a century ago. The levels within the

Table 31. *Estimated Crude Birth Rates about 1950–5 for Countries in Asia, Africa and Latin America*

Continent	Country	Estimated rate per 1000
Asia	Burma	45
	Ceylon	39
	China (mainland)	(37)
	Cyprus	28
	India	40
	Pakistan	50
	Japan	20
	Philippines	50
	Thailand	50
Africa	Algeria (Moslems)	45
	Egypt	(45)
	Mauritius	46
Latin America	Argentina	25
	Chile	34
	Ecuador	
	Mexico	
	Venezuela	
	Bolivia	
	Brazil	45
	Colombia	
	Paraguay	
	Peru	
	Puerto Rico	36
	Jamaica	(35)

SOURCES. U.N. *Report on the World Social Situation*, pp. 6–9, except for China, A. Sauvy, *op. cit.*; and Puerto Rico and Jamaica, U.N. *Demographic Yearbook* (1956). The rate for Japan refers to 1953–5, since when the birth rate has fallen to just over 19 per 1000.

regions are shown in Table 31, which suggests that in two areas there is a considerable range of variation, though the number of countries with relatively low birth rates is very small. In most countries, too, there is little evidence of a downward trend in the birth rate. In Asia, Japan is a striking example of a fall, mainly in the very recent past, to such an extent that at present her crude birth rate (18·0 in 1958) is lower than

Table 32. *Total Number of Live Births per Woman for Women in Specified Age Groups*

Region	Country	Census date	Age (in years) of women 45–49	45 and over	
Africa	Egypt	1947	—	5·9	Births to current marriages
	Tanganyika	1948	—	4·4	
	Kenya	1948	—	5·3	
	Uganda	1948	—	4·8	
	Portuguese Guinea	1950	3·2	3·3	Married women only
	French Senegal	1957	4·8	5·0	
America	Barbados	1946	3·6	4·1	
	Bermuda	1950	2·7	3·0	
	Br. Honduras	1946	—	5·1	
	Puerto Rico	1950	—	5·7	
	Trinidad and Tobago	1946	—	4·0	
	U.S.A.	1950	2·5	2·7	Ever-married women upper age, 45–60 years
	British Guiana	1946	—	4·1	
	Venezuela	1950	4·9	4·8	
	Brazil	1940	6·4	6·4	
Asia	Ceylon	1946	4·7	4·7	
	Japan	1950	4·8	4·7	Married women only
	India (Madhya Pradesh)	1951	—	6·1–6·6	Married women only
	Malaya (Malaysians only)	1947	4·6	—	
Europe	Norway	1950	—	3·3	Live births to existing marriages
	Portugal	1950	—	3·6	
	England and Wales	1951	2·0	—	Married women only
	Scotland	1951	2·5	—	Married women only
Oceania	Australia	1947	2·8	3·2	Live births to existing marriages

SOURCES. U.N. *Demographic Yearbook* (1955), except for the following:

1. French Senegal. Ministère de la France d'Outre-Mer, Territoire du Sénégal, *Mission Socio-Economique de la Basse Vallée du Sénégal, Enquête démographique 1957* (Paris, 1957), p. 8. Some comparable material for French Guinea is given in another publication by the same Ministry, *Mission Démographique de Guinée. Etude démographique, Résultats provisoires*, Fasc. 2 (Paris, 1956), p. 38. For all women aged 45–54 years, the total number of live births per woman ranges from 4·9 in the urban centre of Conakry to 6·3 in High Guinea (rural). The data given above, as well as for Senegal and Portuguese Guinea, relate to the indigenous population.

2. Brazil. Adjusted figures, from G. Mortara, *Methods of Using Census Statistics... with Applications to the Population of Brazil* (U.N., New York, 1949), p. 47.

3. Egypt. M. A. El-Badry, 'Some Aspects of Fertility in Egypt', *Milbank Memor-*

ial Fund Quarterly (January, 1956). This is the unadjusted figure. El–Badry argues that, allowing for fertility in previous marriages, the total figure would be between 6·2 and 6·4 births.

4. Tanganyika. U.N. (in collaboration with C. J. Martin), *Additional Information on the Population of Tanganyika* (New York, 1953), p. 5. The figures relate to the African population, sampled in connection with the 1948 census; similar data were obtained for Indian women in Kenya, Tanganyika and Uganda. For women aged 45–49 years, the total number of live births per woman is around 5·8, though it appears to be slightly higher (6·0–6·4) for the age group 40–44 years (see C. J. Martin, 'A Demographic Study of an Immigrant Community: The Indian Population of British East Africa', *Pop. Studies*, VI (1953), 239). Data for Kenya and Uganda are from C. J. Martin, 'Some Estimates of the General Age Distribution...etc.', *Pop. Studies*, VII (1953), 194.

5. India. At the 1951 census, data on the number of children ever born to existing marriages were collected in some states and tabulated on a sample basis. The following statistics of total numbers of children per married woman aged 45 years and over are from S. P. Jain, 'Indian Fertility Trends and Pattern', *Proc. World Pop. Conf. 1954*, Papers, I, 909. Madhya Pradesh, East, 6·1; N.W., 6·3; S.W., 6·6; Travancore-Cochin, 6·6. The Mysore survey reports the following numbers of children born alive to married women aged 45 years and over (married once and remaining married until 45 years of age): Bangalore city, 5·9; rural districts, 5·8 (for ever-married women the figures would be 5·3 and 4·8). See C. Chandrasekaran, 'Fertility Trends in India', *Proc. World Pop. Conf. 1954*, Papers, I, 831. National sample studies carried out in 1951–2 give an estimate of 6·1 live children born to a marriage of completed fertility, a figure which, it is believed, is understated through faulty memory. The definition of completed fertility is in terms of marriage duration, but the results agree fairly well with the Madhya Pradesh results of the 1951 census. See A. D. Gupta and others, *The National Sample Survey, Number 7: Couple Fertility*, Government of India (Dept. of Economic Affairs) (December 1955), p. 47.

6. Malaya. From T. E Smith, *Population Growth in Malaya* (London, 1952), p. 38.

that in the United States, and very little higher than that in France. But Japan is the only example of a large population in Asia in which such a development has occurred. In India, it is true, the birth rates shown in Table 16 appear to have fallen somewhat since the late nineteenth century, but the total apparent decline in seventy years has only amounted to some 20 per cent (in contrast to an almost 40 per cent apparent fall in the death rate), while the deficiencies in registration, especially in the last 15 years, make it very difficult to judge how far the apparent fall is real. For Africa the estimates are too few to provide even a vague indication of a trend, but there is certainly no evidence of a persistent fall, not even in Egypt, which has a fairly long series of census and registration statistics (imperfect though those statistics may be). Latin America shows rather more variety. There are many countries with birth rates around or above 40 per 1000, and with no sign of a trend—including Brazil, Venezuela and Mexico. Chile, however, has shown some decline, and there has been a considerable fall in Argentina, probably from over 35 to around 25 per 1000 during the past thirty years (23 per 1000 in 1959). Puerto Rico has experienced some decline since 1940, in part because the heavy emigration to the United States has decreased the proportions of the population in the childbearing ages. The birth rate in Jamaica has also fallen, but less in seventy years than seems to have occurred in Puerto Rico in fifteen years. Moreover, the Jamaican rate appears to have risen again since the 1940's.

Table 33. *Comparative Estimates of the Proportions of Women 'Ever-Married'*

Region	Country	Census date	Proportion ever-married (%) in the following age groups (years) 20–24	45–49
America	Puerto Rico	1950[a]	63·2	91·4
	Bolivia	1950[a]	54·2	88·9
	U.S.A.	1950	67·7	92·1
Africa	Algeria (Moslems)	1948	77·0	97·6
	Egypt	1947	80·0	99·0
	Portuguese Guinea	1950	91·0	99·2
	Tunisia	1946	71·4	95·7
Asia	Ceylon	1946	70·7	96·6
	India	1951[b]	82·5	98·8
	Japan	1950	44·7	98·5
	Malaya	1947	86·7	97·5
Europe	England and Wales	1951	48·2	84·8

SOURCE. U.N. *Demographic Yearbook* (1955).

[a] It is not certain, especially in the case of Bolivia, that all types of consensual unions have been excluded from the category of 'single' women. If not, they would artificially lower the proportion of women 'ever-married' in the sociological sense.

[b] Age groups for India are 15–24 and 45–54 years.

Further information on the meaning of these birth rates is provided in Tables 32 and 33. The former table attempts to show how many live children are born to a woman, on the average, in the various countries, and some comparative data for a few Western nations have been included. Because the types of familial arrangements are not uniform, the averages generally relate to all women at the end of the childbearing period, save in the case of Western countries, where census tabulations are often restricted to married women. It is clear, however, that in these latter countries averages based on all women would be considerably lower, and thus increase the gap between developed and underdeveloped regions. But converting the averages per woman to averages per ever-married woman for the countries of Africa and Asia would not greatly raise their estimates of family size, for marriage in some form is nearly universal in those countries.[1] This is evident from the statistics on proportions 'ever-married', given in Table 33. Taking India and Ceylon as fairly typical of a large part of Asia, well over two-thirds of the women will have married by their twenty-fifth birthday, and over 95 per cent by their fiftieth birthday. It is not the particularly high fertility of marriage—as compared with the levels in nineteenth-century Europe—which accounts for the very high birth rates in many parts of the underdeveloped world—(though failure to remember all the children who died in infancy may well cause understatement in some of the averages in Table 33), but the particularly high proportions of persons marrying (or forming equivalent unions), and marrying at an early age—far above the proportions in western Europe a century ago.[2] Further, again taking India and Ceylon as type areas, relatively little conscious control of fertility appears to be taking place in marriage. There are differences in the fertility level between urban and rural areas, and between ethnic and religious groups, but the differences so far appear to be stationary, each sub-group maintaining about the same level in a general situation which itself has not changed significantly.[3] An analogous situation appears to apply in a number of Latin American countries. In Brazil, for example, fertility is higher in rural than in urban areas, and for European than for other ethnic groups,[4] but the levels of the different groups have so far shown very little sign of change, and the overall level of fertility in Brazil in 1940, as may be seen in Table 32, was one of the highest recorded for a large popula-

[1] Early marriage acts to some extent as a counterbalance to low expectation of life in maintaining the high average fertility of marriages.

[2] In respect of the proportions marrying by 25 and by 50 years of age, as also in respect of birth rate, the United States appears at present to be half-way between Western Europe and the underdeveloped areas. Part of this may be associated with the marriage and fertility patterns of the Catholic minority, amounting to perhaps 35 millions out of a total of about 162 millions. A recent study suggests both that the Catholics continue to have a higher birth rate than other groups, and also that Catholics have 'contributed disproportionately to the sustained high birth rate in the United States since the second world war' (see D. Kirk, in Milbank Memorial Fund, *Current Research in Human Fertility* (New York, 1955), p. 104). But that other groups are also more fertile than Western European populations is also clear.

[3] In 1931 the differences between castes in India appeared to be due primarily to the position of widows—that is, the taboos on the remarriage of widows were more strongly enforced among the upper castes. Marital fertility as such did not vary greatly (see K. Davis, *The Population of India and Pakistan*, p. 74).

[4] That is, as compared with half-caste, negro, or 'yellow'. A factor in all these differentials is the incidence of (and age at) marriage.

tion.[1] The question of urban–rural differences is of particular interest in South America. Urban growth in that region has been rather rapid, especially in recent years, and it is widely believed that South American cities—which contain a disproportionately large share of the total population—have outrun the industrial bases with which they should be linked. The shifting proportions of urban and rural population have not, however, so far contributed to a decline in fertility. This is perhaps understandable in that many of the rural migrants, driven from the countryside by poverty, find no greater economic opportunities in towns and swell the marginal groups which live in slum suburbs. It is, however, relevant to bear such a result in mind in speculating upon the possible contribution to a fall in fertility of future urbanization in underdeveloped areas.[2]

Taking the underdeveloped areas as a group—though this inevitably means placing together in one general category economic and social structures which have little in common with each other—western patterns of marriage and fertility have so far appeared only in special cases. And the cases are such as to give little indication of the probable spread of the new reproductive *mores*. In India, for example, one community, that of the Parsis, has experienced a radical change in its demographic situation in the past half-century. The expectation of life rose to near western levels, the proportions of women married at the younger ages in 1931 were well below those for Hindu or Moslem groups, and marital fertility also appears to have fallen substantially. But the community had a total population of only 115,000 in 1941, and its changed reproductive practices have produced no emulation by the larger society.[3] The persistence of high fertility in these areas is by no means explained simply in terms of lack of access to birth control knowledge. It is true that, until very recently, birth control clinics were generally very few in number and mainly found in the cities, though in some countries—in India, for example—there has been a marked ex-

[1] An extensive analysis of fertility levels in Brazil is given by G. Mortara, in F. Lorimer *et al.*, *op. cit.* pp. 407–501.

[2] Around 1950, South America contained about 4·6 % of the total population of the world, but 6·5% of the population living in cities of 100,000 or more. The attraction of the city in Latin America has been as much due to its association with the ruling groups and to its cultural eminence in the community as to the economic opportunities it provides (see U.N. *Report on the World Social Situation*, chs. vII and ix). A general discussion of fertility trends and levels in Latin America will be found in D. V. Glass, 'Gecimento y estructura, de la población: estudio sociodemográfico', in D. C. Villegas and E. de Vries (eds.), *Aspectos sociales del desarrollo económico en América Latina*, U.N.E.S.C.O. (1962).

[3] See C. Chandra Sekar, 'Some Aspects of Parsi Demography', *Human Biology*, xx (May 1948).

Table 34. *Conventional Gross and Net Reproduction Rates for Underdeveloped Countries*

Region	Country		1920	1940	1945	1950
Africa	Egypt	GRR	—	3·1	3·1	—
		NRR	—	1·4	1·5	—
	Mauritius	GRR	2·3	2·5	—	3·1
		NRR	—	—	—	2·4
Latin America	Jamaica	GRR	2·6	—	2·1	2·3
		NRR	1·5	—	1·6	1·9
	Brazil	GRR	3·2	3·2	—	—
		NRR	—	1·9	—	—
	Chile	GRR	—	2·1	—	—
		NRR	—	1·2	—	—
Asia	Ceylon	GRR	1·9	2·0	2·2	—
		NRR	1·2	—	1·6	—
	India	GRR	2·8	2·8	—	—
		NRR	1·0	1·3	—	—
	Japan	GRR	2·6	2·0	2·2	1·8
		NRR	1·6	1·4	1·7	1·5

(header: Approximate time points)

SOURCES AND NOTES (the gross (GRR) and net reproduction rates (NRR)):

Africa. Egypt: C. V. Kiser, 'The Demographic Position of Egypt', *loc. cit.* p.119, for rates around 1940; for rates around 1945 (1947), A. M. Farrag, *Demographic Development in Egypt in the Present Century* (Ph.D. thesis, University of London, 1957), p. 182.

Mauritius. Central Statistical Office, Mauritius, *Mortality and Fertility in Mauritius, 1825–1955* ([N.P.], 1956). The gross and net rates for 1955 were 2·8 and 2·2.

Other estimated rates for Africa. Approximate net rates for the Union of South Africa, around 1945, are: Asians, 2·4; Coloured, 1·6 (see L. T. Badenhorst, 'The Future Growth of the Population of South Africa', etc., *Pop. Studies*, IV (1950), 10–13. Rough approximations of net rates for other African populations around 1950 are: Gold Coast, 1·4; Mozambique, 1·1; N. Rhodesia, 2·0 (the two latter rates seem surprisingly high). See C. A. L. Myburgh, 'Estimating the Fertility and Mortality of African Populations...', *Pop. Studies*, x (1956), 206.

Latin America. Jamaica: Joint rates, to overcome temporary abnormalities in the adult sex ratio (from G. W. Roberts, *op. cit.* p. 278).

Brazil. Approximations from G. Mortara, *Methods...*, p. 55, and *ibid.* 'The Development of Brazil's Population', *Pop. Studies*, VIII (1954), 130.

Asia. Ceylon. N. K. Sarkar, *The Demography of Ceylon*, p. 99; U.N. *Demographic Yearbook* (1954) gives a peculiarly high net rate for 1952, 1·99, with a gross rate of 3·66. India. K. Davis, *op. cit.* p. 87.

Japan. Minoru Tachi, 'On a Replacement Index of Population', *Archives of the Population Association of Japan* (1953), pp. 43–50. As mentioned in the text, the net rate had probably fallen to about 1·1 in 1954. Estimates are given for Malaya, in T. E. Smith, *Population Growth in Malaya* (London, 1952), pp. 48, 73, 80, 87, 89. The gross and net rates around 1945 were: Malaysians, 2·7 and 1·7; Chinese, 3·3 and 2·6 respectively.

pansion in the past ten years. Equally, the contraceptive techniques now available are not the most suitable for use in societies in which education is scanty, illiteracy often high and privacy—in the sense visualized by married couples in the West—non-existent. But the spread of family limitation in the West was based upon very crude techniques, requiring neither expenditure nor access to technical information. And, at the same time, organized religion was generally strongly opposed to birth control in the West. In the less developed countries of Asia and Africa, local religions are not opposed—they play a relatively passive role in respect of family limitation, or (as in the case of Moslem groups) their doctrines are capable of reinterpretation in the light of present needs. Even in Latin America, though the Roman Catholic Church is opposed to any form of control other than by abstinence or the 'safe period', the behaviour of individuals does not appear to be strongly influenced by the official doctrine.[1] Moreover, recent surveys in urban and rural areas in India, the Caribbean, and in Latin America suggest that considerable proportions of the populations studied are in favour of family limitation by means of birth control. But interest of this kind has not yet been translated into action on an appreciable scale in many of the countries. Nor is this very surprising. A 'favourable' attitude to birth control and smaller families is not equivalent to positive involvement. In some of the surveys such involvement is found only among the small numbers of better educated and less traditionally oriented couples. Even then, the point at which birth control becomes adopted is influenced by traditional views of the desirable number of live-born or surviving children (or, perhaps still more important, of surviving sons). Thus, concrete interest in birth control—as distinct from a 'favourable attitude'—may not develop until a family already has four or more live-born children.[2]

[1] The main influence of the Roman Catholic Church has been on official policy—for example, in preventing U.N. agencies from associating birth control with international public health activities.

[2] Since the Second World War, many sample investigations of attitudes to family size and birth control have been undertaken in underdeveloped areas—in Puerto Rico, Jamaica, Mexico, and India, for example. See the papers by Hatt and Moore in Milbank Memorial Fund, *Approaches to Problems of High Fertility in Agrarian Societies* (New York, 1952); by Chandrasekaran, Blake and Hill *et al.* in Milbank Memorial Fund, *Current Research in Human Fertility* (New York, 1955); on Puerto Rico, R. Hill, J. M. Stycos and K. W. Back, *The Family and Population Control: A Puerto Rican Experiment in Social Change* (Chapel Hill, 1959); on Jamaica, J. M. Stycos, K. Back and D. O. Mills, *Prospects for Fertility Reduction* (The Conservation Foundation—mimeographed) (New York, 1957). Current research is collected in C. V. Kiser (ed.), *Research in Family Planning* (Princeton, N.J., 1962). For a general survey of the results of some of the recent studies, see D. V. Glass, 'Population Growth, Fertility and Population Policy', *Advancement of Science* (November 1960).

Japan has been referred to as a deviant case among Asian countries, and it is of interest to look somewhat more closely at her experience. Of the fall in fertility there is no doubt; the conventional gross reproduction rate, above 2·6 in the 1920's, was about 1·4 in 1952 and probably only about 1·2 in 1954. Even allowing for the continued decline in mortality, the net reproduction rate could not have been above 1·1 in the latter year and it was less than 1·0 in 1957. But in the early stages, the fall was associated largely with the shift of population from rural to urban areas, and with a rising age at marriage in both types of area. Between 1920 and 1950 there was some decline in the proportion of the labour force engaged in agriculture, and a very marked increase—from 23 per cent to 42 per cent—in the proportion of the population living in agglomerations with 20,000 or more inhabitants.[1] The increased urbanization might in itself, by transferring individuals to localities with smaller family patterns, have tended to bring down the national averages, and this fall was intensified by the changes in marriage. In addition, attempts were being made by various voluntary organizations to spread birth control, and there was a lowering of marital fertility at the older ages—that is, similar to the trend found in Sweden in the 1880's. But birth control campaigns as such could hardly be very effective or overt at the time, for they soon ran counter to the strongly pro-natalist attitudes associated with the new Japanese imperialism.[2]

The situation changed drastically after the Second World War. With the immediate impact of the war, and especially with the loss of empire and of supplementary sources of raw materials, the problem of levels of living presented itself in much sharper terms. Reluctantly at first, the government began to accept the view that, at least for the time being, the maintenance of even existing levels would be endangered by rapid population growth. The Eugenic Protection Law of 1948 which gave recognition to the new attitude—though formally the law was passed for eugenic and health reasons—not only allowed the manufacture and sale of contraceptives, but also permitted sterilization and legalized abortion on eugenic grounds and if the health of a pregnant woman were threatened by physical or economic factors. Official attitudes were still rather mixed, and it was not until 1954 that a policy of encouraging the widespread and effective use of birth control was clearly enunciated. But by that time the population had already chosen abortion as their major method of birth prevention, and it was partly

[1] It should be remembered that substantial numbers of Japanese are 'urban peasants', living in towns but working in agriculture nearby, this being part of the intensive system of cultivation.

[2] See I. B. Taeuber and F. W. Notestein, 'The Changing Fertility of the Japanese', *Pop. Studies*, 1 (1947), 2.

in reaction to the high incidence of abortions (and to the ill-health likely to be associated with repeated abortions) that governmental policy became clarified.[1] For the number of abortions reported increased from 246,000 in 1949 to 748,000 in 1952 and to 1,143,000 in 1954. It is commonly assumed that these numbers understate the incidence, and estimates of the probable total frequency have been made. One method of estimation would place the total figure for 1952 at about 1·7 millions, on which base the 1954 figure would be raised to considerably more than 2 millions, as compared with 1·77 million live births in that year.[2] It is to combat this rapid climb that the new policy aims to spread birth control information and contraceptives among all classes in society. But this involves further problems concerning the efficiency of birth control, for the incidence of abortion is heaviest among women who practise birth control, but who still have unwanted pregnancies.[3] At the same time it is probable that other factors also help to explain the wide recourse to abortion. In particular, the historical evidence suggests that in Tokugawa Japan, when the presence of a fairly large population in a closed economic system may have made population pressure rather evident, infanticide and abortion were not infrequently used to control natural increase. With the Meiji restoration, efforts were made to suppress both these practices, but in the less developed parts of the country infanticide was still taking place in the 1920's, though perhaps rather rarely, and the population had relatively little feeling of 'guilt' regarding abortion.[4] In a sense, therefore, the inter-war period of pro-

[1] See I. B. Taeuber and M. C. Balfour, 'The Control of Fertility in Japan', in Milbank Memorial Fund, *Approaches to Problems of High Fertility in Agrarian Societies* (New York, 1952). Maternal mortality—in contrast to morbidity—did not appear to rise.

[2] The reported figures are regarded as understatements both because there is a not inconsiderable reluctance to report abortions, even though they may be legal; and because abortions performed during the first four months of pregnancy are not reported as such but as stillbirths. See I. B. Taeuber 'Fertility and Research on Fertility in Japan', *Milbank Memorial Fund Quarterly* (April 1956); Y. Koya, 'A Study of Induced Abortion in Japan, and its Significance', *Milbank Memorial Fund Quarterly* (July 1954); M. Muramutsu and H. Ogino, 'Estimation of the Total Numbers of Induced Abortions...', *Bulletin of the Institute of Public Health* (Tokyo), IV (1954). See also M. Muramutsu, *Some Facts about Family Planning in Japan*, Population Problems Research Council, Mainichi newspapers (Tokyo, 1955).

[3] The practice of birth control has undoubtedly spread rapidly since the war, though its precise incidence at present is in doubt, different surveys yielding different proportions. The Mainichi newspapers have carried out several sample surveys between 1950 and 1955, the results indicating a rise from 19·5 to 33·6 % of married couples actually practising birth control, and from 29·1 to 52·5 % of couples who have ever practised it. By 1959 the proportion ever practising birth control (among couples in the childbearing ages) had increased to almost 63 %.

[4] See R. Ishii, *Population Pressure and Economic Life in Japan*, pp. 36 and 240; and R. P. Dore, 'Japanese Rural Fertility: Some Social and Economic Factors', *Pop. Studies*, VII,

natalism, associated—as in Italy from 1924 and Germany from 1933—with expansionist objectives, was the abnormal period, and it was practices for controlling natural increase which were more traditional to the society. Add to this the industrial transformation of the Japanese economy, the breaking down of earlier forms of social organization and the diminishing force, in consequence, of large-family ideals, and it would appear that at the end of the war Japan must have been more ready than other underdeveloped countries to accept the small-family pattern. The pressures on levels of living as a result of defeat, only too manifest to the population at large, were perhaps the final straws in the balance, and it may have been all the easier to adopt new targets of family size in that the methods of attaining them were old and imbedded in the society. There is no reason to believe that an analogous complex of circumstances obtains in other Asian societies or in underdeveloped societies in general. And in any case Japan is not an underdeveloped society. Though it displays many traditionalist elements, Japanese society also shows a high degree of literacy and a widespread secondary and technical education; an advanced industrial technology which contributed the main bulk of the net output of the country; high rates of saving and investment; and a substantial improvement in levels of living. The underpinning of demographic change in Japan has been economic transformation.[1]

81–2. In studies carried out shortly after the war, it became evident that, among the population at large, there was considerable misunderstanding regarding the term for 'birth control', many people believing that it also meant abortion.

[1] For the most comprehensive study of the demographic development of Japan, see I. B. Taeuber, *The Population of Japan* (Princeton, N.J., 1958). See also her paper, 'Japan's Demographic Transition Re-examined', *Pop. Studies* (1960). Current developments in population policy in India are reviewed periodically in the publications of the Directorate General of Health Services, Ministry of Health, New Delhi, including the journal *Family Planning News*. Reference should also be made to the pro-natalist or pro-family policies of various European countries. There were considerable variations in the demographic justification of these policies, as well as in the specific objectives and in the principles on which legislation has been based. In Sweden, positive population policy took 'voluntary parenthood' as its basic principle and thus, while attempting to improve the position of parents and children, also greatly increased the availability of birth control information and techniques. In France, Belgium, Germany and Italy, positive measures (before the Second World War) were accompanied by persistent attempts (through legislative and administrative action) to suppress birth control and abortion. Since the Second World War, the policies of Germany and Italy have not been revived. In the three other countries, the pro-family policy has continued and it has been greatly extended in France, the one country in which pro-natalist measures may have had some effect in raising fertility. The pre-war material on population policies is summarized in D. V. Glass, *Population Policies and Movements in Europe*. The most comprehensive post-war discussion will be found in a series of papers by C. Watson and by H. Gille in *Pop. Studies* (1948–53).

Looking back over the comparison of developed and less developed countries, it is relevant to point to some of the implications of the changes in mortality and fertility during the past 150 years. Discussion of the possible future is outside the scope of this chapter, and in any

Table 35. *Present and Projected World Population*
(Population in Millions)

Continent	Region	Esti-mated popula-tion 1955	Density: per-sons per sq. km.	1975 Medium assump-tion	2000 Medium assump-tion	2000 Low assump-tion
Africa	Total	216	7	303	517	420
America	North	182	9	240	312	274
	Central	58	21	99	198	147
	South	125	7	204	394	298
	Total	365	9	543	904	719
Asia	South-west	72	13	116	206	153
	South Central	499	97	737	1310	975
	South-east	186	41	280	498	371
	East	731	61	1075	1853	1395
	Total	1488	55	2210	3870	2890
Europe	North and West	137	61	154	180	157
	Central	134	132	156	183	160
	South	138	83	166	206	174
	Total	409	83	476	568	491
Oceania	—	15	2	21	29	27
U.S.S.R.	—	197	9	275	379	333
World	—	2690	20	3830	6280	4880

SOURCE. U.N. *The Future Growth of World Population* (New York, 1958), pp. 69–71; U.N. *Demographic Yearbook* (1956).
World totals are rounded.

case population projections have not hitherto had a distinguished record for anticipating reality. Nevertheless, it would be unnecessarily restrictive—even in an historical context—to avoid all reference to the balance of the present century. For unless there are fairly sharp breaks

There are also frequent references to French policy in *Population*, and an extensive account in Haut Comité Consultatif de la Population et de la Famille, *La Population Française*, 1 (Paris, 1955). For a further consideration of the bases and nature of population policy, see the collection of papers presented to Session 11 of the 1954 Population Conference, in *Proc. World Pop. Conf. 1954*, Papers, vol. 11 (New York, 1955).

in the course of development, certain consequences will follow from the present demographic situation. The kinds of consequences are illustrated in Table 35, which summarizes the results of two United Nations population projections, one assuming that fertility declines after 1975 (the medium assumption) and the other that fertility declines immediately (the low assumption). The latter indicates what might happen if underdeveloped countries adopted comprehensive policies for encouraging the spread of smaller families (as in the case of India) and if those policies were successful. The results of the two projections differ by over 1000 million people by the end of the century. But even the low assumption yields a very large increase in population during the next forty years. Short of catastrophe, populations are bound to grow considerably, and especially in less developed societies. For these latter societies have very young populations, so that even with a sharp fall in family size there would be high natural increase for the next generation. Mortality, too, may well decline much more quickly in the near future in those areas—and there are many—in which the expectation of life at birth is still less than fifty years, and thus add further to the rate of population increase. In considering the near future, therefore, economic and social policies must, to be realistic, assume continued population growth, and a growth especially marked in those countries which now have the lowest levels of living.

Whatever the particular rates at which various populations continue to grow during the next forty or fifty years, changes in fertility and mortality have already had—and are continuing to have—other consequences directly relevant to problems of economic and social development, the best-known being the shift in the age structure in western countries. All western countries—and some Asian countries, too—have seen considerable shifts in the proportions of young and old people in their populations. This transformation of the age structure is shown in Table 36, in which examples are given at four points of time, from the seventeenth or eighteenth centuries to the present day. Although there are differences between the countries, the general tendency is the same. Two hundred years ago, about one-third of the population consisted of children under 15 years of age, and old people of 65 years or more constituted only about 5 or 6 per cent. Today, old people constitute some 10 or 11 per cent while children comprise 22 or 23 per cent. When there are serious deviations from these proportions, they are accounted for either by the timing of the fall in fertility, as in the case of France, where the process of ageing was already clearly visible by the mid-nineteenth century; or, where, as in the United States, continued streams of immigrants maintained a relatively young structure until quite recently. Apart from immigration, important

Table 36. *The Age Composition of Western Populations at Various Points of Time (Percentage of Total Population in Age Groups 0–14, 15–64 and 65 Years and over)*

I Before 1800	Age group (years)	England and Wales 1695	France 1775	Sweden 1750	
	0–14	(38)	33·3	33·3	
	15–64	(57)	62·6	60·5	
	65 and over	(5)	4·4	6·2	
	Total	100	100·0	100·0	

II 1800	Age group (years)		France 1801	Sweden 1800	
	0–14	—	33·0	32·3	
	15–64	—	61·4	62·0	
	65 and over	—	5·6	5·7	
	Total	—	100·0	100·0	

III 1850	Age group (years)	Great Britain 1851	France 1851	Sweden 1850	U.S.A. 1850
	0–14	35·5	27·3	32·9	41·6
	15–64	59·9	66·2	62·3	55·5
	65 and over	4·6	6·5	4·8	2·9
	Total	100·0	100·0	100·0	100·0

IV 1900	Age group (years)	Great Britain 1901	France 1901	Sweden 1900	U.S.A. 1900
	0–14	32·6	26·1	32·4	34·4
	15–64	62·7	65·7	59·2	61·3
	65 and over	4·7	8·2	8·4	4·1
	Total	100·0	100·0	100·0	100·0

V 1950	Age group (years)	Great Britain 1951	France 1950	Sweden 1950	U.S.A. 1950
	0–14	22·5	21·7	23·4	27·0
	15–64	66·7	66·5	66·3	64·9
	65 and over	10·8	11·8	10·3	8·1
	Total	100·0	100·0	100·0	100·0

SOURCES AND NOTES

In general, from 1851 onwards, data from U.N. *The Aging of Populations and its Economic and Social Implications* (New York, 1956). In addition:

1. England and Wales, 1695. This is a very rough modification and interpolation of Gregory King's estimate, the obvious excess of people above 60 years of age having been reduced. Data from Glass, *op. cit.* Since King's data are in any case open to question, it would be unwise to stress the apparent differences between the proportions

derived from King's statistics, and those for Sweden, which have a much more solid basis. For what it is worth, however, King's material suggests a fertility level nearer to Finland than to Sweden. The 1821 census data for Great Britain—they are by no means perfect—suggest 38·9 % of the population under 15 years, 56·2 % aged 15–64, and 4·9 % aged 65 and over.

2. France, 1775 and 1801, from J. Bourgeois-Pichat, *op. cit.*

3. Sweden, 1750 and 1800, from Statistiska Centralbyrån, *Historisk Statistik för Sverige, I, Befölkning* (Stockholm, 1955), p. 22.

4. U.S.A. Estimate for 1850 derived by interpolation from data in U.S. Department of Commerce, *Historical Statistics of the United States 1789–1945* (Washington, D.C., 1949), p. 26. Remaining estimates from C. Taeuber and I. B. Taeuber, *op. cit.* p. 31. For 1800 a rough interpolation of the data on the white population would give 48 % under 15 years, 49·4 % aged 15–64, and 2·6 % aged 65 and over.

only when the volume is substantial,[1] the main factor in ageing has been the level of fertility. Mortality as such has had a far smaller effect. In the first place, reductions in infant and childhood death rates have increased the proportions of young people in the population. Secondly, death rates at the older ages have fallen much less—especially above the age of 60 years. Hence the proportion of people above 60 years of age has not been increased very greatly by the decline in mortality. It was emphasized earlier that attempts to deal separately with the factors of fertility and mortality are rather artificial. Nevertheless, applying this separation for the purpose of illustration, theoretical calculations show that given a gross reproduction rate of 2·5 and a rise in the expectation of life at birth from 40 to about 70 years, the proportion of persons aged 60 years and over in the stable population would remain constant at about 5·9 per cent; but with a fixed expectation of life at 40 years and a fall in the gross reproduction rate from 2·5 to 1·0, the percentage of people aged 60 years and over would rise from 5·9 to 20·4.[2]

Examples of the type of age distribution which obtains with high fertility are given in Table 37. The table includes four European countries with relatively high fertility and with high expectations of life, but most of the countries covered combine high fertility and high mortality. If in those countries mortality continues to fall during the next

[1] Emigration would tend to have the reverse effect, as in Sweden.
[2] These calculations are given in some detail in U.N. *The Aging of Populations*, pp. 26 ff., on which most of the present discussion is based. A stable population—the term derives from the work of A. J. Lotka—is one with a fixed age structure, resulting from the persistence of given levels of fertility and mortality. A stationary population is a special case in the general category of stable populations—one resulting from the persistent application of constant fertility and mortality at levels which yield a replacement rate of 1·0. Unless fertility rises, most western countries are likely to see a further increase in the proportion of old persons in their populations, for the full impact of the decline of family size is not yet visible. And, at the moment, the proportions of young people have been raised by the post-war 'baby boom'.

generation, the age structure will not change greatly unless fertility also falls. If fertility does not fall, the proportion of the population in the active age groups will continue to be smaller than is found in most industrialized countries. The possible consequences of this position may be shown more explicitly in the form of 'dependency ratios'—that is, the number of dependants (persons aged under 15 and over 64 years) per 100 persons aged 15–64 years. For a region like Latin America, with high fertility and fairly high mortality, the ratios are around 77 per

Table 37. *The Age Composition around 1950 of Populations with High Fertility (Percentage of Total Population in Age Groups 0–14, 15–64 and 65 years and over)*

I Europe	Age group (years)	Netherlands 1950	Spain 1950	Portugal 1950	Yugoslavia 1950
	0–14	29·3	26·2	29·5	30·8
	15–64	63·0	66·6	63·5	63·5
	65 and over	7·7	7·2	7·0	5·7
	Total	100·0	100·0	100·0	100·0

II Latin America	Age group (years)	Brazil 1950	Colombia 1950	Venezuela 1950	
	0–14	41·9	42·0	42·0	
	15–64	55·6	55·1	55·3	
	65 and over	2·5	2·9	2·7	
	Total	100·0	100·0	100·0	

III Asia	Age group (years)	Ceylon 1946	India 1951	Japan 1950	Mainland China, 1953
	0–14	37·2	37·5	35·4	35·9
	15–64	59·3	58·9	59·7	59·7
	65 and over	3·5	3·6	4·9	4·4
	Total	100·0	100·0	100·0	100·0

SOURCES. U.N. *The Aging of Populations*; and A. Sauvy, *op. cit.* (for China).

100, ranging from 90 per 100 for Paraguay to 53 per 100 for Argentina, where fertility and mortality have both fallen to general western levels. For India, Ceylon and China, the ratios are 70, 69 and 68 respectively, while for typically industrialized societies indices a good deal lower would be found—for example, 50 for Great Britain and 54 for the United States. The economic significance of the higher ratios in the less developed countries lies not so much in the present as in the near future. At the moment, so far as the labour force is concerned, high dependency ratios in underdeveloped societies are paralleled by a high degree of enrolment in the labour force of the very young and the

CONSEQUENCES OF POPULATION STRUCTURE 137

rather old; and it is customary to find between 70 and 80 per cent of the men aged 65 years and over actually at work, in contrast to only some 40 per cent in industrialized countries. Even so, because of the age structure, the ratio of dependants to employed males is generally higher in underdeveloped than in industrialized societies. Moreover, in some underdeveloped areas—and especially in Latin America—the proportions of women in active employment are relatively low. The problem may become much more acute if, without any marked fall in fertility, social change in, say, Latin America involves educational expansion and retirement provisions which reduce the degree of employment at both extremes of the age scale; for in that case, the dependency ratios will begin to rise and may thus add to the other difficulties with which social change is faced. In countries which have experienced declining fertility and mortality, on the other hand, the fall in family size has decreased the period during which mothers have very young children to care for. Such decreases, coupled with the extended provision of school-feeding, have helped to increase the proportions of married women able to continue in or return to the labour force, and may at least be one factor in the very marked rise in the employment of married women in, for example, Great Britain, during the past thirty years.

The above examples have been given to illustrate one aspect of the influence of particular levels of fertility and mortality and, at the same time, to show that this influence is not independent of the societies which are being considered. There are many other ways in which population growth and structure may have—or, historically, may have had—unanticipated consequences. Thus, in considering the question of family support to old people, it is not simply a question of the ratios of old to active persons, but also of the number of years the old are likely to live and the number of surviving children available to contribute assistance to surviving parents. The latter point, directly related to fertility levels, is of particular importance, and a 50 per cent fall in family size may double the burden per surviving child.[1] Housing demand, too, does not bear a simple ratio to population size or growth. Dwellings are demanded by households and though, in the main, households are created by marriages, there are various types of non-family household, the numbers of which reflect aspects of society not connected exclusively with demographic variables.[2] It would be

[1] In addition, if, in a society in which it has been customary for an unmarried daughter to look after her old parents, marriage probabilities increase considerably, a further problem arises in providing alternative assistance for the aged.
[2] For example, in Great Britain, 1951, 10·8% of all households were one-person households. See *Census 1951, Great Britain, One Per Cent Sample Tables, Part 1* (London,

superfluous to add to the examples. The point to be stressed here, as in the discussion of the timing of the fall in fertility, is that although there are uniformities in the relationship between demographic and other variables, the influence of population growth and structure requires to be examined in the context of a given society.[1]

1952), p. 114. For an analysis of the social and demographic aspects of household formation in Britain, see R. Glass and F. G. Davidson, 'Household Structure and Housing Needs', *Pop. Studies*, IV (1951).

[1] See, for example, D. C. Coleman, 'Labour in the English Economy of the Seventeenth Century', *Econ. Hist. Rev.* 2nd Ser. VIII, to cite a recent example. For a wide-ranging discussion of the demographic and social aspects of changing fertility and mortality, see, U.N. *The Aging of Populations*. Some of the aspects are also considered, with particular reference to Latin America, in D. V. Glass (ed.), *Report of the United Nations Seminar on Population Problems in Latin America* (New York, 1958), especially section III (v). On the economic and social problems associated with the ageing process, and particularly with the old as such, the literature is now vast. For a compact discussion of some of the problems in one society, namely Britain, see *Report of the Committee on the Economic and Financial Problems of the Provision for Old Age*, Cmd. 9333 (London, 1954).

CHAPTER III

The Opening up of New Territories

I. *The Growth of Knowledge*

IN the course of the nineteenth century much virgin land was occupied by people of European origin in America, Canada, Australia, New Zealand, Brazil and Argentina, to name only the most important countries concerned. These newly occupied territories provided an unexampled increase in the living space of the American and western European peoples who were chiefly concerned in this century-long expansionary movement. Thus the occupied areas of France, Great Britain, Germany, Italy, Holland, Belgium and the Scandinavian countries amounted in 1800—as with but little alteration they still do—to between 650,000 and 790,000 square miles, according to what meaning is attached to the word 'occupied'; whereas the overseas territories first entered and settled in the course of the nineteenth century added to this area a further area of not less than 8,000,000 square miles and not more than about 9,200,000 square miles. Or, to look at this matter in another way, the territory utilized overseas by people of European origin in 1800, which was already more extensive than the whole of western Europe, was multiplied in area approximately eight- or nine-fold between 1800 and 1900, while the degree of that utilization became, of course, in every sense, a very great deal more intense.

These newly occupied areas had all—except Australia and New Zealand—long histories of association with western Europe, stretching back, in some cases, far into the sixteenth century. But, geographically, they were not at all well known at the dawn of the nineteenth century, and formidable physical as well as economic obstacles delayed the growth of knowledge. The first two hundred years of occupation in North America, for example, provided settlers with little power, gave them scanty incentive, and left them with insufficient leisure to try to ascertain the nature and extent of the land lying beyond the immediate frontier of settlement, and these difficulties were again experienced, although they were overcome in a far shorter space of time, in nineteenth-century Australia. Thus the early American colonists were hemmed in by the Appalachian Mountains, one of the easiest passages round which—by the Hudson and Mohawk—was closed to the early settlers by the Iroquois, while a possible route round the south was closed by the Cherokees. The country inland of the mountains was accessible via the Great Lakes and the Mississippi in the eighteenth century, but this latter route, besides being long, was not under a single political control until 1803 and portage up the Mississippi was difficult and expensive until after about 1820 when the steamboats began to ply; so that the Cumberland Road (which was not half-way to the Mississippi from the coast even by 1840) represented the first route better than a mere track, along which settlers could move directly into the interior of America.

These early difficulties were not greater than those which awaited exploration and settlement (often closely allied) farther to the west. The first extensive exploration west of the Mississippi was carried out by Lewis and Clark, who reached the mouth of the Columbia river in 1805, eighteen months after setting out from Kansas. This expedition was promoted by Jefferson, who had purchased the whole central region of the United States from Napoleon in 1803 and wanted to know, naturally enough, what it was like. The information brought back by the early explorers was not favourable:

...from these immense prairies may arise one great advantage to the United States, i.e., the restriction of our population to some certain limits, and thereby, a continuation of our Union. Our citizens being so prone to rambling and extending themselves on the frontier will, through necessity, be constrained to limit their extent on the west to the borders of the Missouri and the Mississippi, while they leave the prairies, incapable of cultivation, to the wandering and uncivilized aborigines of the country.[1]

The immense prairie areas of the United States were accordingly marked down on the early maps as 'Desert'. This concept of a 'Great American desert'—'those barren wastes, the haunts of the buffalo and the Indian'[2]—was widely accepted after Long's expedition to Colorado in 1820. And not only was the prairie believed infertile; it was also most rightly seen as alien and lawless. The traveller who, like the youthful Francis Parkman in 1846, stood at Fort Leavenworth with 'the offscourings of the frontier'[3] and prepared to say 'a long adieu to bed and board, and the principles of Blackstone's Commentaries',[4] had already left behind 'the farthest outskirts of the great forest that once spread from the western plains to the shore of the Atlantic',[5] and which was the outstanding characteristic of the physical environment east of the Mississippi, and stood prepared to enter a strange land, treeless and, beyond the 98th meridian or thereabouts, semi-arid. 'Looking over an intervening belt of bushes, we saw the green, ocean-like expanse of prairie, stretching swell beyond swell to the horizon';[5] but most of it

[1] Z. M. Pike, Expeditions (1895), II, 524–5.
[2] Francis Parkman, The Oregon Trail (Oxford, 1944), p. 22.
[3] Ibid. p. 16.   [4] Ibid. p. 18.
[5] Ibid. p. 7.

Parkman thought 'a barren, trackless waste'.[1] Through this country, 'dreary and monotonous enough',[1] and peopled by buffalo, wolves, antelopes and prairie-dogs, besides Indians, settlers moved at a rate of from 50 to 150 miles per week. Beyond the prairies lay fresh obstacles, mountains and 'the very desert'. These former Parkman reached two months after setting out from Fort Leavenworth, and of them he has left a memorable description:

Wild as they were, these mountains were thickly peopled. As I climbed farther, I found the broad dusty paths made by the elk, as they filed across the mountain-side. The grass on all the terraces was trampled down by deer; there were numerous tracks of wolves, and in some of the rougher and more precipitous parts of the ascent I found footprints different from any that I had ever seen, and which I took to be those of the Rocky Mountain sheep. I sat down upon a rock; there was a perfect stillness. No wind was stirring, and not even an insect could be heard....I began again to move forward. A white wolf jumped up from among some bushes and leaped clumsily away...soon after I heard a rustling sound, with a cracking of twigs at a little distance, and I saw moving above the tall bushes the branching antlers of an elk. I was in the midst of a hunter's paradise.
Such were the Black Hills as I found them in July....[2]

Parkman passed through these hills in the company of a great party of Ogillallah Indians, who had originally set off on an expedition of vengeance against the Snakes. This was the year of the repeal of the Corn Laws.

Physical obstacles to the extension of settlement were no less severe as encountered on the other side of the world. The neighbourhood of Sydney had been peopled by the castaways of British society from 1788. Only ten miles west of Sydney were the Blue Mountains, and until they were crossed Sydney was 'a port without a hinterland';[3] yet at the end of a quarter of a century, 10,000 people remained hemmed in by these hills, condemned to a country which appeared nothing but forest, where trees grew so large 'that the removing them off the ground after they are cut is the greater part of the labour'.[4] Not until 1813 did three men succeed in traversing the cliffs and gorges, and in hacking a way through the luxuriant scrub and forest to reach the hundreds of miles of 'grazing country not divided by barren spaces as on the east side of the mountain', 'soil exceeding rich', 'hills green to the tops and country like a park and grounds laid out'.[5] In Tasmania similar difficulties appeared in an extreme form, and 'the roughest country

[1] Ibid. p. 45.　　　　　　　　　[2] Ibid. p. 184.
[3] Edward Shann, An Economic History of Australia (Cambridge, 1948), p. 1.
[4] Quoted ibid. p. 5.　　　　　　[5] Quoted ibid. p. 66.

imaginable'[1] was penetrated by the explorers Jorgensen (a convict) and Hellyer (surveyor to the Van Diemen's Land Company) in the 1820's when, in order to reach the Surrey Hills area, they made their way *over* 'an almost impenetrable espalier-grown scrub, that a dog could not get through below'.[1]

Much of Tasmania was, from the early settler's point of view, exceptionally rough and unfavourable country; but it is clear that almost everywhere the actual physical obstacles to the opening up and settling of new lands in the early nineteenth century were of an extremely formidable character, so that frontier settlements, even when located in territory which now looks very favourable for human enterprise, habitually bore the characteristics of the tiny and often poor communities dotted today along the Nova Scotian and Alaskan coasts, or half hidden in the African tropical jungle. The sometimes herculean task of subjugating virgin country could be carried out only by means of substantial doses of labour or capital; and as the latter was seldom to be had for tasks such as these in the nineteenth century, development depended chiefly upon human exertion extending sometimes, for a single piece of land, over several decades, the resulting farm, station or plantation representing the embodied sweat and toil of possibly several generations.

By 1850 or 1860 the actual task of exploration had been more or less completed, and the extent and physical configuration of the greater part of the new lands was tolerably well known; but their agricultural and mineral potentialities were for the most part still unappreciated. The principal gold deposits in most of these countries were located early enough. The discovery at Sutter's Creek was made early in 1848, and in 1849 the first gold rush was in progress, booming the American-reserved business of coastal shipping round the Horn, and persuading 40,000 people in 1849 alone to risk the long land route over the Oregon and California trails. Three years later gold was discovered in Oregon, and in 1858 in the Pike's Peak region where Parkman had travelled through a lonely wilderness only twelve years before. Australia was not far behind, and a squatter returned from California made public in 1851 the existence of gold in New South Wales; further discoveries were made in Victoria in the same year, in the Northern Territory in 1871, in Tasmania in 1877, in Western Australia in 1887. In New Zealand attention was first seriously turned to gold mining in 1858. In South Africa, likewise, important discoveries began to be made from 1884. In spite of the ephemeral and exaggerated boom which accompanied most new gold-mining enterprise, these discoveries were

[1] S. H. Roberts, *History of Australian Land Settlement* (Melbourne, 1924), p. 65.

in all cases most important in helping to open up the country. More stable and enduring ventures appeared with the discovery of the major deposits of copper, coal, iron, oil and tin. Of these, coal was found in considerable quantities in every expanding area of the nineteenth century except Argentina (although the Canadian deposits are extremely disadvantageously located); and copper likewise, except in Argentina, Brazil and New Zealand; neither oil nor iron ore, on the other hand, was found in significant quantities in any of these areas except America and Canada, and tin does not exist in any of them, although there are large bauxite deposits in Arkansas. The discoveries of these resources, and the technical developments which turned them into resources, took place all through the nineteenth century, but especially in the latter part of it. America mined iron ore in the seventeenth century, and coal in the eighteenth century; but the great iron-ore deposits of the Lake Superior region came into use only after 1853; and six years later the petroleum industry began its at first highly speculative career in Pennsylvania. Bauxite was, of course, of little commercial importance prior to about 1890.

The fundamental basis of the wealth of these newly developing territories—fundamental in the sense that it was first to provide an exportable surplus—was, as a rule, agriculture. But in scarcely any instance did agriculture provide a simple, easily foreseeable solution to the problems of economic development. Once again, the true value of new lands was hard to appreciate. In Australia, it is true, the breeding of sheep was energetically promoted from the end of the eighteenth century—largely through the remarkable vision of a single individual—and although the early attempts, in the forest country east of the Blue Mountains, were in conditions which were, for Australia, exceptionally unfavourable, even here success was achieved within two decades. But the problems of prairie settlement in America and Canada proved much harder. For example, widely conflicting accounts of the fertility of Rupert's Land, which became the North-west Territory in 1870, and of the whole of the Canadian North-west, were put about in the 1850's and 1860's. The great majority of these were intended to convince the most optimistic that the larger portion of this area was totally unfit for permanent settlement on account of climate, soil and absence of fuel. Those who knew the country best were most frequently wrong, and almost all early nineteenth-century accounts of little-known territory in North America were coloured by political prejudices and by the pre-conviction, fostered by innumerable explorers, geographers and meteorologists in the first half of the century, that 'the entire region west of the 98th degree of west longitude, with the exception of a small portion of western Texas and the narrow border along the Pacific, is a country of comparatively little value to the agriculturist'[1]—this chiefly because it was treeless, which was thought to argue infertility of soil, and because it undoubtedly was arid by comparison with the exceptionally heavy rainfall in the Red river region in 1855, which for years was used by influential writers as a standard of judgement for western Canada. The errors were certainly of a serious character and it was sometimes decades before they were exposed: of Palliser's so-called 'triangle', for example, marked off as an infertile area in 1853 and believed through several decades to be valueless country, a British Board of Trade Report in 1904 gave at least 20,000 square miles as 'areas in which wheat is a certain crop'.

Probably in no other part of the world were such misjudgements—simply mistakes—about the usefulness of the land made by men of comparable ability and authority. The economic importance of the prairies was seriously underestimated, as a general rule, until the 1870's; even in 1882 the evidence supplied to the Richmond Commission on this subject was, on the whole, seriously misleading. But similar though less remarkable mistakes were made in many other developing regions in the nineteenth century, and it is scarcely too much to say that when governments and settlers alike began to open up these great domains they first of all did not know exactly where they were, and when they had found that out they still knew nothing, almost, of the nature of the country which they had come to govern and to settle. To find this latter out was to prove a long and difficult task.

II. *The Controlling Factors*

What factors determined the rate and directions of movement into new lands in the nineteenth century? Why, for that matter, did movement take place at all? These are fundamental questions, and to the last of them no complete answer can be offered without trespassing far beyond the boundaries of economic history. The motives which drove people from their homes—and the homes which they left were often a reproach to the economies into which they had been born (there is a drawing by Ragnar Ljungman, reproduced in E. Heckscher's *Svenskt Arbete och Liv* depicting a Swedish crofter's family and home, with the caption 'The question is, which is better, Swedish flesh and blood in America or Swedish skin and bone in Sweden')—these motives were exceedingly complex, and the circumstances which chiefly moulded them had more to do, in an important sense, with the territories which emigrants left behind them than with those towards which they

[1] Professor Joseph Henry, quoted in W. A. Mackintosh, *Canadian Frontiers of Settlement* (Toronto, 1934), I, 36.

travelled. A discontent which was seldom divine but sometimes political, an adventurous spirit, ambition, poverty, sometimes even near-starvation—all these played their part, and were required probably to be powerful in proportion to the stability of the society which was to be abandoned and the magnitude of the task and of the changes which movement would involve. Francis Parkman, perhaps the best educated and most scholarly observer ever to set out on an emigrant trail, could find no answer to this elementary question:

The men, very sober-looking countrymen, stood about their oxen; and as I passed I noticed three old fellows, who, with their long whips in their hands, were zealously discussing the doctrine of regeneration. The emigrants, however, are not all of this stamp. Among them are some of the vilest outcasts in the country. I have often perplexed myself to divine the various motives that give impulse to this migration; but whatever they may be, whether an insane hope of a better condition in life, or a desire of shaking off restraints of law and society, or mere restlessness, certain it is, that multitudes bitterly repent the journey, and, after they have reached the land of promise, are happy enough to escape from it.[1]

Taking for granted, then, the willingness to move, generated by whatever forces may operate in more settled areas, the flow of people into new lands is determined, broadly speaking, by the knowledge of the presence of resources; but what the value of these resources is depends on the state of the industrial arts and—unless the new community is to be self-sufficing—on the relative prices of the newly available and other goods. The first of these propositions is self-evident: people will not attempt to settle new lands unless they have at least a reasonable expectation that they can support themselves there; although they may, of course, act on seriously erroneous expectations. It is equally obvious that most resources as such derive their utility from technical knowledge, and that as this develops—and it developed exceedingly rapidly, in exceedingly important directions, in the nineteenth century—a wider and wider range of material objects is likely to acquire economic importance, and fresh geographical areas are likely to become economically useful while the importance of old areas may change and develop. It need scarcely be added that transportation developments were, for the opening up of new lands in the nineteenth century, of fundamental importance, because these new lands were for the most part, at least at first, primary producing areas, serving other regions, and were therefore only indirectly or slowly affected by the development of industrial techniques which took place, up to about 1870 at least, first and foremost in Great Britain.

[1] Parkman, *The Oregon Trail*, p. 5.

Transportation developments, however, are of little if any significance to communities able and content to subsist on their own produce. Little isolated settlements and groups of settlements of this sort
were not unknown in the nineteenth century, but the standard of life
which they enjoyed was usually so meagre that their membership
characteristically increased slowly or not at all, most settlers showing
extreme eagerness to join in the main current of economic life. Thus a
witness before the Richmond Commission described how, in 1880, he
had spoken to a farmer near Dayton, Washington:

he had 50 acres in wheat, which he sold at 37 cents a bushel, and he had a
quantity of land in oats which yielded 100 bushels per acre, and he sold that at
a good price. He only made artizan's wages, i.e. two or three dollars a day,
ploughing it himself. He got a grant of 160 acres...and a man cannot get
more than his living from that with the present railway facilities...they
cannot, however, get rich, so that emigration is small there.[1]

In Tasmania likewise, for several decades before the discovery of gold
in 1875, poverty seemed to have marked the island for her own, and as a
result the population of Tasmania fell, while that of every other
Australian colony rose. Men did not emigrate to seek out and enjoy
the dreary indigence of Hobart or its like.

The growth of new settlements therefore depended as a rule on the
establishment of profitable economic relations with other territories,
that is, on fitting into the national or international pattern of the
division of labour; and this, besides depending on the development of
transportation, also depended on the existence of a competitive advantage in an old product or the development of a new one. As a rule, the
new nineteenth-century territories were well endowed to achieve progress along both these lines, although to begin with—that is, up to about
1870 in the case of America and 1900 in the case of Brazil—their progress was almost entirely a matter of competition in established lines,
cotton in the United States, wheat in America, Canada and Australia,
wool in Australia, mutton in New Zealand, coffee in Brazil. Now this
was a fact of extreme importance for the nineteenth century. First of
all, it produced large-scale alterations in the structure of the relative
profitability of different types of enterprise in the older economies—
alterations usually to the disadvantage of the European farmer, who
frequently sought to avoid the necessity of adaptation by having his
government check the flow of international trade. Secondly, it undoubtedly helped to produce the fall in prices which was so important
a feature of the last quarter of the nineteenth century in most countries,

[1] Royal Commission on Agriculture, evidence of S. Williamson, Minutes of
Evidence, Q 9564, 1881 (xv).

and which made the adjustment to the first set of changes more painful than might otherwise have been the case. Thus the last quarter of the nineteenth century was, for Europe, very largely an era of adjustment to new competition, and this adjustment was harder than it might have been because territorial expansion was producing economies in old lines of production so rapidly that it was exceedingly difficult to balance the contraction in some sectors of the European economy by expansion in other sectors. But this period did not in the least have this character for new territories. There, even falling prices were, in the long run (that is, over a period longer than the average trade cycle), not necessarily disadvantageous nor a hindrance to further expansion, because primary production was still taking place in conditions of increasing returns. Thus the prices of wheat at Liverpool were fairly steady for the 1870's as a whole and then showed a downward trend from 1880 to 1894, falling from around 150 cents a bushel to about 70 cents, and it is true that against this movement the settler had to contend; but it is illegitimate to argue that an upward trend is essential or nearly essential to expansion. While it is true that during the great period of settlement in the prairies of western Canada the trend of wheat prices was steeply upward (from 1895 to 1920), it is also true that settlement and expansion in the United States were rapid in the very years of falling prices— between 1875 and 1900 the acreage under wheat in the United States rose by 40 per cent, and by 1890 the frontier, in the classic pronouncement of the American census of that year, had disappeared. This is, of course, not to argue that rising prices do not as a rule favour territorial expansion while falling prices deter it; on the contrary, the history of Canadian prairie settlement, the check to the New Zealand mutton industry in the 1880's when mutton prices fell back to unremunerative levels, and to the Australian wool industry in the 1890's, for the same reason, show that rising prices were favourable to immigration—but merely because rising prices were likely to go with rising profits; the one was by no means essential to the other.

The economic prospects of new territories were, moreover, extremely obscure in their formative periods. This was so partly because their future depended on emergent transportation and technical improvements and also because the long-run average level of costs, even with a given level of technique, took years to determine. Thus there is no doubt that much early American farming was soil exhausting—millions of acres of eroded and wasted land are there to prove it—and American farmers were shouldering the true burden of the cost onto posterity. Contemporary observers knew this quite well. But they paid more attention to the fact that American wheat-yields per acre rose from 1875 to 1900; and Caird, in 1882, was looking at the short period only when he laid chief emphasis on the expectation (or hope) that America would yet experience many 'vicissitudes in the seasons'.[1]

This last was, nevertheless, a more important matter than was commonly realized at the time. Average annual rainfall in large and important areas of America, Canada and Australia is not only slight; much worse, it is extremely variable.

The only part of Australia where the rainfall is more reliable than the world normal is the winter-rain belt from south-west of Western Australia (Swanland) to Victoria (all with negative deviations), while over half of the continent is more than 10 per cent worse than places of the same average rainfall elsewhere in the world. Nowhere in the world is there such a huge area of pastoral land of such erratic rainfall as this pastoral country of Australia.[2]

Small wonder that agriculturalists, even when experienced in the ways of farming in the Old World, had much to learn in the Australian environment, and that such disasters as the drought of the 1890's—when flocks in New South Wales shrank from 57 million in 1894 to 26·56 million in 1902, in Queensland from 19·59 million to 7·21 million— took men unawares and made nonsense of their cost and profit expectations.

Similarly, wide rainfall variations are experienced in the short-grass, semi-arid country lying approximately between the 99th meridian and the Rocky Mountains; the so-called 'Great Plains' region. At Hays, in Kansas, the rainfall record from 1868 to 1934

reveals three periods of scanty rainfall and two intermediate periods of more abundant precipitation....The highest five-year average was 30·64 inches for the period 1874–78 and the lowest was 17·87 for 1891–95. The driest of the five-year periods received only 58 per cent as much rain as the more humid years....Evidence derived from tree-rings, lake levels, etc. indicates that in the Great Plains the period between 1825 and 1865 was a long drought with only occasional wet years. At that time the area may in truth have been the Great American Desert.[3]

Furthermore, these variations 'are neither uniform, similar nor synchronous in the various parts of the country', so that an excess of rainfall in one locality may co-exist with a decided deficiency in another only a few miles away.

[1] Royal Commission on Agriculture, evidence of J. Caird, Minutes of Evidence, Q 62658, 1882 (xiv).
[2] S. M. Wadham and G. L. Wood, *Land Utilization in Australia* (Melbourne, 1950), pp. 45–6.
[3] C. W. Thornthwaite in *Migration and Economic Opportunity*, Carter Goodrich (ed.) (Philadelphia, 1936), p. 219.

From the same causes emanate the same results; an ebb and flow of settlement and economic activity, the results of extreme uncertainty about costs and profits. Drought caused the abandonment of large tracts of sheep country in Australia in the late 1890's. An equally notable retreat in the face of drought took place in America in the 1890's also. Settlers from the humid north-eastern states ventured in the 1880's southward and westward into Kansas, Nebraska, New Mexico and Colorado. They established themselves during a humid period and were almost at once faced with the below-average rainfall of the early 1890's. As a result, the semi-arid lands of these four States almost immediately suffered a severe loss of population—fifty counties in the region had their combined population fall from 155,866 in 1890 to 108,529 in 1900. This emigration doubtless stimulated and was at the same time relieved by the contemporary opening up of Oklahoma territory. On the other hand, drought sometimes favoured expansion; the latter-day colonization of the Amazon basin was begun in 1877, when drought caused emigration westwards from Ceará.

But the economic consequences of such climatic conditions are obvious and inescapable. Farming becomes a gamble. Even if the farmer had perfect prescience of the weather, and planted no crops at all in unfavourable years, he would still incur certain fixed costs which he could not shed, although these might well be less than the further losses which he would incur by cultivating the land. The necessary information, however, is not available to him. Extreme uncertainty is then apt to cause his decisions as to what to raise and in what quantities to vary a good deal, and this increases the fluctuations in selling price and may, in the end, divert demand to other sources; his product becomes, in a peculiar sense, always marginal. Also, the transport system required to handle the produce of a good year is far in excess of normal requirements, so that either bumper crops do not reach the market or transport costs are always 'excessive'. Moreover, uncertainty makes capital hard to obtain, and shortage of capital is apt to drive farmers to rely on exploitative rather than on truly economic methods.

Another cause of uncertainty in farming new land is the difficulty of estimating the time and cost involved in breaking in the land to agricultural uses. This problem was seldom a grave one on the prairie; but in forest areas, such as were encountered in Australia and Brazil, it was extremely serious. For example, to clear the Australian mallee soils of the dense eucalypt scrub (or sometimes true tropical rain forest) which usually covered them was a task requiring at least four or five years, during which crops were usually poor, wear and tear on machinery was particularly high, and stock could not be carried. The cost of this operation per acre in the inter-war period was around 15s., but could rise (due to often unforeseeable difficulties) to 37s. a year. Obviously the farmer who started operations without considerable reserves of capital or credit might soon find himself in unexpected difficulties, the land absorbing capital at an immoderate pace while giving little or no return. And if he began operations in 1880, say, with wool at 10d. per lb., he would enter the market in 1885 with the price around 8d., and so on. In this sense the risks (at any rate in Australia) were always less after 1895, because after 1895 wool and wheat prices were rising *faster than costs*; but after 1895 there came the drought.

In short, profitability, viewed as an expectation, was in almost all cases an extremely hazardous one in cultivating new country in the nineteenth century, and the close connections between the activities of farming and land speculation in that period must be seen in the light of the even closer *similarity* between farming and pure commercial speculation. The fitting of great virgin lands into the world economy was thus a vexatious and costly enterprise for farmers both in the new lands and the old.

All these elements played a prominent part in determining the direction of movement; but besides the direction of movement there is the question of the rate at which it takes place. This also, of course, is influenced by factors on the borderline of economics and beyond; but as far as the strictly economic factors are concerned it depends on the above-mentioned techniques and profit prospects calling forth a sufficient supply of capital, on the multiplicity of the available resources, and on the readiness of their availability.

The necessity of capital is evident, although not always remembered. The land was there (although from the point of view of the individual settler it usually cost money—a point frequently overlooked); the settlers brought, in themselves, labour and enterprise; but capital also was needful—'It is difficult to make progress anywhere without capital, and nowhere is the need of money more keenly felt than in a new settlement'.[1] So wrote an official of the Burlington and Missouri River Railroad in 1873; but more precise advice was not given than to have 'a few hundred dollars to start with'.[1] Some more exact estimates of the money needed have survived. In 1861 the *Nebraska Farmer* reckoned that the cost of starting a farm totalled the sum given in Table 38. The *Scientific American* in 1857 declared that every farmer with 100 acres of land needed $400 to $700 worth of farm implements—and although it is certain that very few farms had equipment on anything approaching this scale, the need for such equipment was increasing and

[1] Quoted in Richard C. Overton, *Burlington West* (Cambridge, Mass., 1941), p. 549.

its cost high. The mere cost of clearing land might itself be very high, especially in rough country; some idea of the difficulty is given in the laconic comment, 'the root system must be dug out or blown up'.[1] In Australia in the early 1830's the cost of 'rapid clearing' varied from 28s. to 80s. per acre, and it is calculated that in mallee country a farm of only 200 acres would require an initial outlay in the neighbourhood of £150 per annum for—if all went well—five years, with scant return. But whatever the exact figures it is clear that even before 1860 a man or a family plus so many acres did not add up to make a farm.[2]

Table 38

	$
A house	250
Breaking 40 acres	120
500 walnut posts	25
500 post holes dug	5
12,500 feet of lumber	125
1½ kegs of 10d nails	6.37
	$531.37

It is also favourable for rapid economic development that a territory should have a variety of natural resources and that these should lie readily to hand—in the sense of being conveniently located, of requiring little capital for their development, and of demanding the use of only proven techniques. For, if a territory boasts only a single resource— the presence of oil, suitability of soil and climate for wool production and nothing else, and so on—it is liable to suffer a variety of ills. The most likely is that the solitary resource will be worked out—the soil mined, the trees cut down, the oil removed; this happened, of course, on a large scale in a great many areas in the nineteenth century, of which the 'dust bowl' of Oklahoma is merely the largest and best known. A severe price fall in the market due to fresh innovations and discoveries may have much the same effect, and price oscillations will severely upset a single-product locality (the Amazon basin, for example, after the price of rubber began its fall in 1910). Again, speculative development may produce the same results in an even more disastrous form, and speculation is all too likely in an area where serious investors are

[1] Wadham and Wood, *Land Utilization in Australia*, p. 64.
[2] Credit, of course, was usually freely given in 'good times', although it was expensive. In the Australian expansion of the 1830's 'any man that has £1000 in one of the Sydney banks will readily get credit for £3000 worth of stock'; but 10% was charged on three-month bills (see B. Fitzpatrick, *The British Empire in Australia, 1834-1939* (Melbourne, 1941), pp. 36-43).

apt to experience a kind of 'psychological loneliness' in putting money into a region barren of all profitable activity except their own.

In a territory where varied economic activity can exist, on the other hand, the situation is quite different. A decline in one line is not disastrous, for the specificity of capital tends to be lower where other opportunities are near at hand, and the local purchasing power is not likely to be suddenly destroyed by far-away happenings. There is a greater supply, and therefore choice of labour, and likewise there is a greater supply and choice of entrepreneurs and investors. Ability also is perhaps characteristically better directed in a mixed economy. Above all, mutual prosperity begets confidence, and investment begets further investment.

Nineteenth-century history affords at least one most illuminating example of the contrast between the development of a region with abundant and readily available resources and one possessing not only scantier resources but also having these far more widely dispersed. The discovery of gold in California in 1848 produced the first great gold rush: by 1850 the population of San Francisco was around 25,000. Within a few years, however, the first rich 'placer claims' on the western slopes of the Sierra Nevadas seemed stripped, and deeper mining, needing both capital and technical skill, became necessary. Thousands became unemployed; as early as 1853 a local newspaper commented: 'There has never been so deplorable an exhibition of mendicancy in our streets as may be witnessed daily at this time... hundreds of destitute men and scores of women...little girls are to be found in front of the city saloons at all hours of the day, going through their graceless performances.'[1] But scattered gold discoveries continued to be made, culminating with that of the Comstock Lode in 1859, only 100 miles or so from Sutter's Creek, in western Nevada; and all the time agricultural development in the nearby river valleys was proceeding, and a moderate local and coastal trade becoming established. By 1860 the gold rush was definitely over; the population of the State had increased from 92,000 in 1850 to 380,000 in 1860, and there was an established demand for locally grown food products. In 1869 the trans-continental railway was completed, and farming for distant eastern markets became possible. The marvellously fertile lands of the San Joaquin valley and the Sacramento delta were quickly occupied, and agriculture became a large-scale industry. The cultivation of wheat first attracted attention, and the State's wheat production rose from 6 million bushels in 1860 to 16 million in 1870 and 29 million in 1880. This wheat kept admirably on the long voyages to Britain. In the 1870's, however, wheat prices fell and transport costs rose. California

[1] Quoted in M. Josephson, *The Robber Barons* (New York, 1934), p. 26.

made a new start and escaped economic collapse, chiefly through the development of vineyards, orchards, seed-farms, and hop-yards. Fresh railroad connections with the east, plus the development of refrigeration, provided rapidly expanding markets. In 1886 the first full trainload of deciduous fruit was shipped eastward, and the fruit-growing area expanded rapidly until 1893. Checked then by overproduction, the growers turned to sugar-beet, with equal success. In the twentieth century Californian agriculture was further diversified, while the State added oil drilling and oil refining, not to mention aircraft manufacture, to its other activities. In short, this territory made at least four transitions from one form of economic activity to another in the course of little more than half a century, and effected these changes comparatively smoothly and quickly thanks to the clustering of manifold resources and to the small initial demands made on skill and capital.

In Western Australia the environment is not, superficially, very different. Gold was to be found there also, and while the area is not an agricultural paradise, it has, inland, considerable advantages of soil and climate. But the economic and historical differences are very great. Permanent settlers first went to Western Australia in 1829. They found, not fertile soil awaiting cultivation, but a sandy coastal plain, behind which stretched the sclerophyl forest of eucalypt and jarrah; they also found a complete lack of labour. They scattered over the coastal plain with its few acres of loam, and nineteen years later—still numbering fewer than 5000—petitioned the home government for convicts to be employed on public works, in the hope of thus stimulating a modicum of economic activity. This disastrous policy created new problems without solving any of the old ones, and Western Australia settled down to three further decades of near-stagnation, cut off from the world by the Indian Ocean and the Nullabor Plain. Then, between 1887 and 1889, widely scattered discoveries of alluvial gold were made, not, as in California, on the edge of wonderful agricultural land near the coast, but several hundred miles inland and in regions of intense heat and prolonged drought: Western Australia awoke from somnolence to the expectation of better things. But lack of water, poor transport facilities, disease, and the extreme 'patchiness' of early discoveries made the winning of gold in this region a peculiarly difficult proposition, requiring, almost from the start, considerable capital investment. Moreover, as luck—or history—would have it, gold prices began to fall after 1896, just when the new fields were achieving a fair degree of development. Once again, 'gold brought people but could not hold them',[1] and the immigrants turned to other pursuits. As in

[1] Shann, *An Economic History of Australia*, p. 355.

California, the readiest possibilities lay in wheat-growing; but Western Australian coastal soils favoured only high cost methods of wheat production, and only when the railways were extended into the inland wheat belts could the lower cost wheat areas be cultivated. Even then, difficulties greater than the Californian remained; a late summer rainfall deficiency made special varieties of wheat necessary if really good results were to be achieved, and a phosphate deficiency in the soil meant that yields were liable to fall off after a year or two. The skilled work of engineers, botanists and soil chemists was a prerequisite for the development of an area of considerable natural advantages, but of advantages which were geographically, climatically and geologically scattered and half obscured.

Lastly, production will not be carried on unless there is an available market. Britain in the first quarter of the nineteenth century created what was virtually a new type of economy when she began the large-scale production of cotton yarn and cloth for sale chiefly overseas: for this activity depended on the obtaining of raw materials wholly and the retention and extension of markets largely beyond the Continent of Europe. Her iron industry was developed on not altogether dissimilar lines; later, with the repeal of the Corn Laws, she began, although slowly, to commit herself to a similar position with regard to food supplies; her woollen industry, meanwhile, was developing like the cotton industry; and towards the close of the nineteenth century her coal industry also evolved to harmonize with a still-expanding international economic order. In the course of the nineteenth century more and more nations were affected by this type of development, and the newly developing territories were affected, perhaps, most decisively of all.

These territories had, from their very nature (by comparison with the more 'mature' economies of western Europe), far less formidable vested interests inclined to oppose a development of this sort. Australia, for example, had no economic group such as the British farmers in the 1840's, or the French iron manufacturers in the 1860's, who could conceive their interests as seriously threatened by policies favouring the extension of the international division of labour. To this extent circumstances favoured a rapid absorption of the new territories into the new international economic order. But geography, and the, so to speak, pre-industrial state of transportation in the first half of the nineteenth century, operated in the other direction. For as the extent, and, to a lesser degree, the superficial wealth of the new territories came slowly to be known, their economic possibilities remained largely unappreciated, because communications prior to about 1850 were too rudimentary to encourage or even allow any full development of new territories or any close integration of the economies of these new territories with those of the old. The improvements in transportation before about 1820, although considerable were largely the discovery, or rediscovery, of better ways of doing well-known things. Men, coaches, pack-horses travelled faster along better roads; stronger horses pulled larger loads in better-made barges down a multiplicity of new canals. The steam-engine, it is true, became a factor of economic significance on the Mississippi in the 1820's, on the new railroads of Britain and America in the 1840's and 1850's, on the Atlantic in the 1840's and the Pacific in the 1850's. But its influence, although strong, was limited. Canada had only 1800 miles of railroad in 1860, New Zealand only 46 miles in 1870. Railroads hardly penetrated the American prairie before 1860. In most and between most regions of the world transportation remained slow, expensive and its operation circumscribed, so that, although the day when long-distance transportation was confined to commodities both valuable and small in bulk had definitely passed away, the modern age, when commodities bulky, cheap and even perishable may be transported economically half round the world had equally definitely not yet dawned. In this twilight period between the old and the new, the extent of international specialization was therefore still severely limited by the efficiency or existence of the means of transport. This was well understood. Sir John Richardson, the Arctic explorer, said in 1857,

If, under the name of settlement, is meant the means of subsistence simply, I think that a considerable population might subsist as high as Peace River... but if it is to be a productive or progressive colony, I think that there are no means and that there are not likely to be any means of producing a flourishing colony without some market or some conveyance for the grain.[1]

Thus in the first quarter of the nineteenth century cotton from the United States, and in the second quarter wool from Australia came to Europe in considerable but not astounding quantities. Between 1821 and 1850 the value of United States raw cotton exports rose from $20·16 million to $71·98 million, and in the 1840's Australian wool exports to Great Britain rose from 12 million lb. to 39 million lb. This was an astonishing rate of growth which was not maintained in later years. But the subsequent volume of production and movement of these goods was comparatively enormous, especially having regard to the much slower rate of growth of population in the countries concerned. By 1880-5 American raw cotton exports were running at $218·76 million per annum, and by 1910-15 at $537·04 million, while Australian wool exports were £5 million in 1861 and (at 1861 prices) £39 million in 1890.

[1] Quoted in Mackintosh, *Canadian Frontiers of Settlement*, 1, 29.

Neither of these countries sent wheat in the earlier period, nor did Canada; weight for weight, wheat is a far less valuable commodity than either cotton or wool. Few if any observers in the period up to about 1850 foresaw the future of these overseas territories or the character of their twentieth-century relations with the older economies because these later developments were dependent upon enterprise building on the foundations of a system of communications only just in sight at the opening of the American Civil War.

The opening up of new land was thus an accelerating process through much of the nineteenth century. From a purely human point of view this is what one would expect. The roughest work of settlement is the earliest work; once this is completed, men and women move more readily into the new territories. And more than this; with the abolition of slavery in the United States in 1865 and in Brazil in 1888, and with the cessation of the transportation of convicts to all parts of Australia except Western Australia in 1853, and to Western Australia itself in 1867, serious social barriers to the immigration of individuals—especially those possessing some capital of their own—were removed, and further large areas opened up to an accelerated inflow of both men and capital. These factors—apart altogether from changes encouraging emigration in the countries from which emigration took place—all helped radically to alter the institutional social and economic background of settlement in the later decades of the nineteenth century, and make it easier to understand the truly astonishing pace at which the frontiers of settlement were pushed forward in this final period.

III.   The Extension of Settlement to 1850

On the basis of the pre-1850 system of communications, sufficient international trade existed to affect profoundly the development of virgin lands. There were two commodities, especially, which Europe craved and which, more and more after 1750, only the frontier was able to supply: timber and furs. It is the demand for these which chiefly links the expansion process of the eighteenth century with that of the nineteenth century.

The fur trade was one of the oldest trades in North America, and flourished in the early seventeenth century all the way from Virginia to Maine. It depended chiefly on the beaver, the fur of which was used to make hats in the wealthy metropolitan markets of Europe, although deerskins also were exported from the southern colonies and were substantially a part of the same trade. But the trade was self-destroying. Already by the commencement of the nineteenth century little fur was to be got east of the Appalachians and south of the 49th parallel. The beaver 'was not highly reproductive and it was not a migrant. Its destruction in any locality necessitated the movement of hunters to new areas.'[1] In 1793 a representative of the Canadian fur interests reached the Pacific overland, and in 1804 the North-west Company began to organize this western territory by building trading-posts. This expansion was stimulated by the Lewis and Clark expedition into the same area. In 1811 J. J. Astor founded Fort Astoria, but in 1814 sold this property to the North-west Company, and his own American Fur Company retired from the debatable lands of Oregon to dominate the region of the Great Plains and the Rocky Mountains. The international fur trade thus became a highly organized and thoroughly capitalistic business centred not near the Atlantic coast but in what is now Oregon, British Columbia and the North-west Territories.

In time, however, the European demand for furs slackened. This decline of demand in the main market, dating from about 1840, put an end to the fur trade as an enterprise of major economic importance. But its exploratory work was done. The first man to travel down the Fraser river to Vancouver in 1808 was a partner in the North-west Company, and the river bears his name; the Mackenzie river likewise commemorates a pioneer fur trader.

The great companies which carried on this trade ruled the regions of their choice with an absolute sway, and their servants were frequently also a law unto themselves. Some were Indian half-breeds, and many seemed to Parkman 'to aim at assimilating themselves to their red associates'[2] with whom they traded. Trappers were frequently murdered by Indians, and sometimes by one another. Two whom Parkman met at Fort Laramie in 1846 were about to set off for the country of the Arapahoe Indians—'ferocious savages'[3]—near Medicine Bow Mountain—an area 'perilous in the extreme'.[4] The lives of such men as these alternated between 'all the luxury of inaction'[5] and 'extreme privations and peril'[5] and they were continually returning from or losing their lives in areas which no other group of white men had ever penetrated, the ultimate or penultimate link between the fashionable markets of Europe and the animals whose skins were, weight for weight, among the most precious commodities of eighteenth-century trade.

Almost equally available in the virgin forests of North America was timber; as one pioneer himself wrote, 'The timber answers as a first crop, fully grown.'[6] This 'first crop', in stands of the highest quality,

---

[1] H. A. Innis, *The Fur Trade in Canada* (Toronto, 1956), p. 391.
[2] Parkman, *The Oregon Trail*, p. 51.   [3] *Ibid.* p. 175.
[4] *Ibid.* p. 176.   [5] *Ibid.* p. 177.
[6] Quoted in A. R. M. Lower, *Canadian Frontiers of Settlement*, ix, ed. W. A. Mackintosh and W. L. G. Joerg (eds.) (Toronto, 1935), 269.

was distributed all along the North American seaboard and far inland
as well. White oak, which was the most valuable as being the best shipbuilding timber, was found from southern Maine to Georgia, and
in abundance in the Ohio valley, Michigan, Wisconsin, Minnesota and
southern Quebec. Other hardwoods and softwoods grew all the way
from the coast to the Mississippi. The unexampled richness of the
country in this valuable resource had been in the minds of the earliest
'projectors' of settlement, and timber shipments had begun almost as
soon as the colonies were founded. Indeed, so rapid was the depletion
of the coastal forests—'the mast men are obliged to go a mile or two
farther into the country every year'[1]—that the industry was moving
out of the coastal areas by the middle of the eighteenth century. It went
northward then westward. First, 'The quest for lumber colonized
Maine.'[2] Then, after the American Revolution, the British turned to the
virtual wilderness of New Brunswick and to Upper Canada (Ontario),
and developed these regions, with the aid of the Loyalists who emigrated from the United States, during the Napoleonic Wars; while
American shipbuilders, after about 1835, found that the cheap coastal
supplies of suitable timber (a fraction of the whole) were exhausted,
and had to draw on the inland regions by road, canal and railroad.

International trade in timber was especially important in the development of Canada. There had been a 'Quebec trade' in timber in the
seventeenth century, but only after America was cut off from the
British market for political reasons did this trade achieve important
dimensions. The main work of development was carried out by three
great lumbering houses which risked their capital not to meet a temporary demand which, as soon as the Baltic was open again on the
conclusion of war, might soon vanish, but on the very satisfactory
inducement of an almost prohibitive British duty on Baltic timber—
from about 35 to 150 per cent, or more than twice what a House of
Commons Committee considered in 1821 to be 'effective Preference'.
On the basis of these and other timber duties—'those silent partners of
the Corn Laws',[3] which endured until 1860, thus converting a temporary expedient into a half-century long policy—great establishments
were developed at Quebec, rivalling those of Danzig and Riga in
extent, and lumbering 'suddenly became, and for some years remained,
the principal factor in the development of British North America'.[4]
In this trade the leading part was played by the Ottawa region, of

[1] J. G. B. Hutchins, The American Maritime Industries and Public Policy, 1789–1914
(Harvard, 1941).
[2] Ibid. p. 269.
[3] R. G. Albion, Forests and Sea Power (Harvard, 1926), p. 355.
[4] R. L. Schuyler, The Fall of the Old Colonial System (Oxford, 1945), p. 105.

which about seven-eighths is excellent timber country. The Ottawa river led nowhere except farther and farther into the forest, and from the first the lumberman was its representative figure. Hence its unique position in the economic life of Canada in the 1840's and 1850's, Lord Elgin remarking in 1853 that the Ottawa region 'is probably doing more at the present time than any other single section of the province to enable Canada to enter the markets of the world as a purchaser'.[1]

Lumbering for a local market was another, less speculative, less profitable, but more widespread form of forest activity. In a country where wood was widely available and iron and coal were apt to be expensive, wood was in general demand, and lumbering tended to become one of the by-occupations of general farming, to which a man could turn his hand during the winter months when more time was available and haulage might be facilitated by the presence of snow on the ground. Such a system might mean an early cash return for the settler; 'The woods furnish a sort of simple manufactory for the inhabitants, from which after attending to their farms in the summer they can draw returns during the winter.'[2] So the pioneer tended to see it. But the process was not as simple as it looked. The pioneer who devoted his wintertime to felling timber was liable to find that he was devoting his precious summertime to selling it, with results always bad for his farm and sometimes disastrous for his finances, for this was a trade in which annual price variations of 30 and 40 per cent were not uncommon. Consequently, it was soon found that those prospered most who stuck to farming or to lumbering exclusively, or who, at the farthest venture, cut the pine on their lands in wintertime to sell to the local mill or to 'trade' with neighbours.

Local utilization was not, of course, the simplest solution to the problem of what to do with standing timber; the simplest solution was to burn it. This was done very extensively; without it, settlement could not have proceeded. As a more profitable variant, where circumstances allowed, the woods were cut down and converted into potash and pearl ashes—products sufficiently valuable to bear the high transport costs even from inaccessible areas. When the day of the canals dawned —most notably with the completion of the Erie in 1825 and the Welland in 1829—and with the development of steam towing on the Lakes and larger rivers, this extreme localism of timber markets declined. The remaining timber resources within reach of the Lakes and of the St Lawrence began to be utilized, and a lumber industry sprang up on the Canadian shores of Lake Erie; while the forests of Michigan and Wisconsin began in the 1850's to supply the needs of settlers now venturing onto the treeless prairies.

[1] Despatch of 16 August 1853.　　[2] Quoted by Lower, *op. cit.* p. 32.

But while timber resources lured men into new regions, the effect which they might have on settlement was uncertain. In some cases, as on the Ottawa river until after 1855, lumbering and agriculture were mutually beneficial, the farmer raising provisions to sell to the lumberman, whose produce was sold in the Quebec market. But the story was different in New Brunswick: there, men tried to combine farming with lumbering and did both badly; or else lumbering, with its promise of large gains for a lucky few, turned the heads of the whole community and relegated agriculture to the level of a despised occupation. Thus in 1825 the province of New Brunswick committed the not uncommon folly of concentrating so much on its solitary export as to depend entirely on the outside world for the first necessaries of life; timber prices then collapsed—as they did again in 1842—and New Brunswick suffered a severe setback in its general economic development.

Much more serious than this competition between farming and lumbering for the pioneers' time and effort was the competition between the two for land. By 1850 the lumberman was beginning to be aware that the settler sometimes burned stands of timber which could have been cut, and the settler to realize that the lumberman wished to exclude him from some areas in which he might wish to settle. This conflict was inevitable as soon as it was realized that the timber resources of North America while enormous were not inexhaustible; but this fact, although stated (as an opinion) before a committee of the Canadian Legislative Assembly in 1835, attracted little notice before 1860, and was, for that matter, the concern of only a small minority in 1870 or 1880. The age when men in these new lands began to jostle one another for room and to be anxious for the future is decidedly of the second half of the nineteenth century, and scarcely in any sense at all of the first.

Settlement in North America was from the first associated with expectations that valuable products could be brought thence into the markets of Europe; and these expectations, although wildly optimistic about the *time* which would be taken to secure a return, were, by and large, justified by the event. The North American colonies were expected to find an exportable surplus along certain lines—notably furs and naval stores—and this they did. Indeed, they exceeded their founders' hopes in some respects, and returned to Europe some other commodities, most notably tobacco and cotton, the exportation of which was never originally allowed for.

The reluctance with which Europe at first received these goods is well known; it is equally well known that tobacco quickly proved the salvation of the Virginia enterprise, and was still the leading American export in 1800. From a few years before that date, however, it was declining in importance; embargo acts, war, competition from Cuba, Colombia and Sumatra, the gradual exhaustion of the land and, above all, the rise of cotton, all caused this industry to mark time until towards the middle of the century. Production areas shifted somewhat, moving westwards into western Kentucky and eastern and northern North Carolina, but the net gain in the area of cultivation was negligible or non-existent. It was, of course, quite otherwise with cotton, prodigy *par excellence* of nineteenth-century crops. The production of cotton in the United States was trifling until the later 1780's—and in 1793 fewer than three million pounds of upland cotton were raised. But in that year Whitney invented the cotton gin. This invention is a prime example of the importance to settlement of technological innovation, for by it the problem of the bottleneck in cotton production, namely, cleaning the bolls, was solved, and cotton, from being a relatively expensive textile fibre, soon became relatively cheap. The British manufacturers' demand could be satisfied, and at quite unexpectedly low prices; Britain and America together embarked on the enterprise of supplying the world with cheap cotton cloth, an enterprise which the American South was peculiarly ready for after the partial exhaustion of the tobacco lands and the withdrawal of the British bounties on indigo and rice. The production of cotton soared upwards. In the last quinquennium of the eighteenth century the average annual rate was 18·2 million lb.; in the first five years of peace after Waterloo it passed the hundred million mark; and in the late 1840's production first exceeded one thousand million pounds in a single year. On the whole, America was raising in this period about seven-eighths of the world's supply. Most of it she exported, and by 1821 her cotton exports exceeded in value all her other exports put together, a situation even more markedly in evidence in 1860 than in 1821; by the later date cotton was worth almost two thirds of American total exports.

This expansion, the dominating economic feature of the first half-century of American life, took settlement from the tidewater lands of Virginia and Carolina a thousand miles west into Texas. The spearhead of the advance was the small farmer, who broke in the virgin land to cultivation, and then, unable to refuse the high price which the cotton planter offered for the land, and outbidden by him in the competitive land sales, either retreated to the less fertile mountain areas to become yet another of the 'poor whites' of the South, or ventured on beyond the Ohio or Mississippi to conquer the wilderness in a non-cotton area. The cotton planters' demand for new land was continuous. To begin with, cotton was grown in Georgia and South Carolina; as late as 1820 more than half of the American cotton crop was raised in this area. Soon it spilled over into North Carolina, south-eastern Virginia and Tennessee. Then, when it was realized that the rich alluvial soils of Alabama and Mississippi were better suited to cotton than the uplands, Indians, Spaniards and cattle ranchers were pushed out of these regions to make a living farther west. Finally, in the 1850's, the invasion crossed the borders of Texas. This expansion was on so vast a scale that by 1860 Mississippi, Alabama and Louisiana, non-producers until after 1800, raised 76 per cent of the total crop, while Texas produced more than South Carolina. The periods of most rapid expansion were in the international boom years preceding 1837, and in the years immediately following the annexation of Texas.

But the rate of territorial expansion was not influenced solely by the demand for the product; it was also accelerated by the artless and exhausting nature of its cultivation. Soils in the South are, in the main, of medium to poor quality, but there is a long season, tempera-tures are mild, and rainfall is plentiful, well distributed seasonally, and fairly reliable. A balanced agriculture could have been developed; but the comparative advantage of the South lay in cotton, and with the 'excessive devotion to cotton the advantages for agriculture have not been adequately utilized.... Unlike the agriculture of grass lands and meadows, cotton culture is clean culture leaving the surface of the soil open to washing in summer and winter, with the result that over 50 per cent of all eroded areas mapped by the Soil Erosion Service are in the South.'[1] Consequently, the cotton planters wanted new land to keep pace with the ever-rising demand for their product, but they also wanted new land to replace that which they had partially destroyed, for virgin soil meant low or minimum costs. Their method, in fact, was to hold down costs by consuming the land-capital of the South. This method obviously favoured the rapid extension of settlement; but at the price of impoverishing the 'used' area; while the whole economic system, and especially the existence of slavery, which cotton cultivation fastened on the entire region, discouraged the flow of immigration.

North America, nevertheless, colonized as a region likely to send back staple exports to Europe, justified, and more than justified, men's hopes. It was otherwise with Australia. Of that continent no economic hopes at first were entertained whatsoever, the colony of New South Wales being established simply as a receptacle for convicts:

The Settlements in New Holland must clearly be considered as Receptacles for Offenders.... So long as they continue destined to these purposes... their growth as Colonies must be a Secondary Consideration, and the leading

---

[1] R. B. Vance in *Migration and Economic Opportunity*, Carter Goodrich (ed.) (Philadelphia, 1936), p. 125.

Duty of those to whom their Administration is entrusted will be to keep up in them such a system of just discipline as may render transportation an Object of Serious Apprehension.[1]

So wrote Lord Bathurst, four years after Waterloo; and the policy, if ill-conceived, was at least a straightforward one, so long as free colonists did not grow too many and the home government remained willing to subsidize the dependency for all time.

The free colonists, however, had views of their own. Among them, John Macarthur, as important here as Eli Whitney in the American South, had both the general conception of economic independence and the particular idea of how to utilize the Australian environment to achieve it. As early as 1792 he grasped the fact that

a petty population, established at so vast a distance from other civilized parts of the globe, could have no prospects of ultimately succeeding unless by raising as an export some raw material which would be produced with little labour, be in considerable demand, and be capable of bearing the expense of a long sea voyage; that, only by the production of some such commodity, whatever might be the natural fertility of the country, could it hope to escape the alternations of abundance and scarcity even of bread.[2]

The commodity which Macarthur considered capable of fulfilling these requirements was wool.

Sheep had been introduced into Australia in 1788, but with a view to meat production. Macarthur's first flock was of undistinguished and unsuitable parentage, but in 1797 he obtained some merinos from the Cape of Good Hope, and in 1804 reinforced his flock with fresh merinos from Britain, whither he had gone to interest British woollen manufacturers in his venture. The government made a grant to Macarthur of 5000 acres, and he set to work to convert Australia into 'John Bull's Greater Woolsack'. At first, the sheep did badly; they were not the best, and the coastal lands on which they were bred are not, in fact, favourable to Merinos, which do better on the drier Western Slopes. Of these slopes Macarthur, of course, knew nothing until after 1813, but he was never at a loss in his praises of the natural advantages of the country for sheep; he wrote, in October 1805, of 'tracts of land adapted for pastures so boundless that no assignable limits can be set to the number of fine-woolled sheep which can be raised...with little other expense than the wages and food of the shepherds'.[3] Australia, it is true, possessed such tracts; but neither Macarthur nor any other white man had at that time laid eyes upon them. He per-

---

[1] Quoted in Shann, *An Economic History of Australia*, p. 69.
[2] Quoted in Wadham and Wood, *Land Utilization in Australia*, p. 16.
[3] Quoted in Shann, *op. cit.* p. 81.

severed, however, although almost alone. In 1807 the first commercial export of fine wool from Australia took place—245 lb.—and up to 196*d*. per lb. was realized in London—a price not exceeded until September 1950. The times for wool export were propitious; British farmers were turning from wool to mutton, there was a colonial preference for wool from 1819 to 1825, the Spanish supply was contracting. From about 1813 sheep farming in Australia began to make progress. There were 50,000 sheep in Australia in 1813, 290,000 in 1821; in that year New South Wales and Tasmania exported twice as much wool as the average Australian export from 1814 to 1820, or just over 175,000 lb.; by 1831 the figure was just short of two and a half million lb.

This great pastoral industry, expanding even faster than the business of exporting American cotton, checked in its rise only temporarily by outbursts of land speculation in 1826 and 1838 (both ended when it 'pleased Divine Providence to visit the colony in the midst of these speculations with an afflictive drought of nearly three years continuance'[1]), derived its expansive power from four main sources: old settlers, new settlers, new land, and convict labour.

The population of New South Wales approximately doubled between 1813 and 1827, and doubled again between 1827 and 1837. This was not an increase of skilled workmen and enterprises, but the opportunities in this period were so novel that the benefit of experience was scarcely to be had. For the open, grassy plains beyond the Blue Mountains were a new country, and in the years after Waterloo stockmen were pioneering the occupation of the Bathurst plains, and extending settlement north of the Hunter river—'the nursery of sheep farming for the northern interior'[2]—and southward towards the Murrumbidgee; by 1840 the first station had been set out on the Darling Downs, and the country as far north as Armidale was thickly studded with outstations. Ten years later squatters were more than 450 miles from Sydney, and the settlement of Queensland had begun; and by the early 1860's the search for good and unrestricted pastures had extended settlement to the farthest extreme of Cape York Peninsula—a movement of a rather hectic nature which completed the conquest of Queensland.

In these same decades settlement was also pushing out from Sydney to the south west. Starting from the neighbourhood of Lake George in 1821, sheep farming spread down the Murrumbidgee to the west with extreme rapidity for a decade or so and then, after the trip had been made from Sydney to Portland and back in 1836, the flow of settlement followed this path—the Major's Line—to the sea. This turn

[1] Quoted in Shann, *op. cit.* p. 103.
[2] Roberts, *Cambridge History of the British Empire,* VII, 160.

southwards brought an intermingling of settlers. Tasmania had been occupied in 1803, and the expansion of its sheep industry was at first rapid, largely because Tasmania possessed extensive areas of suitable grazing land adjacent to the harbours. By 1836, however, emigrants from Tasmania (some of them escaped convicts) had settled the coastal lands near Melbourne and Portland, and these settlers, pushing north, met those coming down the Murrumbidgee, with the result that, between 1836 and 1844—when the first cattle were driven overland from Gippsland to Melbourne—the greater part of what is now Victoria came to be occupied through and through with sheep runs, until 1839 on no legal basis whatever.

In South and Western Australia, on the other hand, progress was rather slow. The attempt to settle South Australia did not begin until 1836, and ran into serious financial trouble at once. Land was taken up nevertheless, and by 1841 there were stations ninety miles from Adelaide. In Western Australia, where settlement began in 1829, speculation so outran agriculture that the farmers went 'almost mad with melancholy'[1] and the revenue was actually less in 1844 than in 1833. The essential trouble (apart from mistaken land policies) was the wide scattering of good pastoral land. The Murchison and Gascogne areas were not discovered until 1854 and 1858 respectively, and in the 1860's there was a rush to the north, but only the coastal fringe of Western Australia is—in places—well adapted to pastoral farming, and not until the advent of new discoveries and better international communications in the second half of the nineteenth century was Western Australia able to advance.

Throughout this period the price of wool in the London market remained, on the whole, encouraging. There was a temporary decline after the removal of the preferential duty in 1825, but prices rose in the 1830's, and were definitely low and discouraging only in the early and late 1840's. When prices fell wages might be cut and flocks increased in size, but the always rising wool-yield per sheep acted as a cushion against price setbacks. Land speculation, of course, its evil effects exacerbated by drought and deflation, ruined many, but this did not affect so calamitously the fortunes of those pioneering into new areas where land was probably, in effect, free, and it may even have encouraged such pioneering, which was a simple if hazardous business:

A man of small capital acquired a flock and simply set out....Each was a land-freebooter scanning the horizon for unoccupied or unclaimed land. He was an 'overlander', nursing his sore-footed flock, watching every pinch of flour in his bullock-dray of rations, and looking for his plains of

[1] Quoted in Roberts, *op. cit.* p. 50.

promise or his long-dreamt-of mountain-pastures. Over the desert and the mountains, over the sun-baked plains and the flooded marshlands he went, either seeking some vague landmark dimly hinted at by a previous explorer or one of his rivals or, more often, trusting to his destiny, and his bushman's sense to find virgin country in the general direction in which he was moving. ...He kept on despite distance and drought, starvation and disease, attacks by the blacks and desertions by his men. He was staking everything, often his life, on finding a suitable 'run' for his sheep, and until he reached this haven, nothing else counted.[1]

It is at first sight curious that convict labour was an asset in establishing this pastoral industry; but such was the fact, for the lonely routine labour involved in running a sheep station was within the competence of even the most degraded and unenterprising, whose labour thus cost little in reality as well as in appearance. These workers were 'found', and wages comparable to those of agricultural workers in Britain 'allowed'. Thus at a very low level of wages the supply of labour did not necessarily become too little for the demand. The situation, in fact, corresponded to that in the American South in the years before 1808. When Western Australia lamented the absence of convict labour it pointed to one—although only one—of the reasons for the colony's slow development in these early years. On the other hand, a settlement could have too much of a good thing: 4000 convicts a year poured into Tasmania between 1840 and 1853, by which date they comprised 50 per cent or so of the population, and the island had grown noted for its chain gangs, drunkenness, sheep-stealing, high murder rate, and the large number of desperate characters who were 'at large' in the secluded valleys and almost impenetrable forests. Like Western Australia, Tasmania lacked any natural comparative advantage over the mainland, and an adverse labour situation only made a natural inferiority more pronounced.

These difficulties underlined the achievement of the eastern mainland. By 1826 Australian wool was more popular in the British market than any other description; and a quarter of a century later the colonists had eclipsed the convicts, put an end to transportation, established flocks in most of the best sheep lands of the continent, and provided themselves with that staple which was needed to 'enable them altogether to provide for their own expenditure'.[2]

There is one other important commodity which nineteenth-century Europe often obtained from new lands, one raw material sure of acceptance on world markets, presenting only simple problems of technique, and scarcely any of marketing: and that is gold. Gold is pre-eminently

---

[1] Roberts, op. cit. VII, 191–2.
[2] John Macarthur, quoted in Shann, Economic History of Australia, p. 86.

saleable. And not only so; it is also cheap to transport; while experience shows that perhaps above all other commodities it has the power
(especially when newly discovered) to attract into the most neglected
places large and over-large supplies of men and capital, but especially of
men. It is this power which makes the discovery of gold so important
an event in the history of any developing territory.

Similarity of historical development is in few instances more con-
spicuous than in the case of the new nineteenth-century goldfields.
The Californian example has already been mentioned. About 77,000
persons entered California in 1849, and by 1850 the population was
greater than that of the 'original' State of Delaware; when gold-
mining developed to the point of requiring more 'round-about'
methods, an easy transition was made to agriculture. The development
of Colorado, Nevada, Arizona and Idaho was not dissimilar. Gold there
was not the first attraction; trappers of the Hudson's Bay Company and
the American Fur Company had worked in this region, and farmers
had followed them; but it was gold which drew men in such numbers as
to turn territories into States, although the mining centres themselves such
as Virginia City, to which ten thousand people came, it is said, in 1864,
often sank back, in a decade or two, into obscurity or even desolation.

The Californian experience was the first, and there is no doubt that it
'brought on', so to speak, the others. For it was a miner returned from
California who first publicised the existence of gold near Bathurst in
1851; there followed a rush to the goldfields of New South Wales.
Victoria, not to be outdone, offered a reward for the finding of gold
within 200 miles of Melbourne, and it was claimed almost at once.
During 1851 over one million pounds' worth of gold was found in
Victoria, and this State became the centre of a not yet international
attraction. The fields were peculiarly favourable to a quick, early
development, being all within 100 miles of Melbourne, across comparatively easy country, and endowed with unique surface wealth.
These diggings seemed 'the first real chance of independence that
Australia had offered the poor man'.[1] Little wonder that nearly a
quarter of the population (as it is said) was attracted into the goldfields at one time or another. Until September 1852 'pre-gold'
colonists had it all to themselves; then 'the first wave of a new type of
free immigration broke on the shore of Hobson's Bay'.[2] Nineteen
thousand people arrived in Melbourne in September 1852, and 94,664
in the course of the entire year, or seven times as many as the arrivals
in 1851. In 1854 the population of Victoria reached 236,798 (of whom
68,790 were mining for gold), and in 1857 410,766; New South Wales,
until 1855 the most populous colony, was quite eclipsed. In all, a

[1] Shann, *op. cit.* p. 170.   [2] *Ibid.* p. 173.

population of 190,000 in 1840 and 430,000 in 1850 had risen by 1860 to 1,146,000.

This development came when the woollen industry, recovering from the fall in the price of wool in the late 1840's, had just achieved a new although lower level of stability. This stability the gold discoveries upset. The exodus from the pastoral countryside was extensive and immediate; the abundance of cheap station labour on which the major industry of the country had come to rely vanished and was gone forever. The wages of station hands rose by 50–100 per cent, and even so the number of 'shepherds and persons engaged in the management of sheep' fell, it has been estimated, from 27,000 in 1851 to about 20,000 in 1856. As a result, the pastoral industry marked time for several years. Wool prices, like all Australian prices, rose rapidly; but the butcher's meat business received a prodigious stimulus, and a limiting factor throughout the decade continued to be labour. In Victoria in 1851 one person was employed per 650 sheep; in 1856 one per 950. In South Australia the ratio dropped to one per 2500 sheep. Wheat-growing in Victoria likewise suffered. Before gold-mining began, the colony had been nine-tenths self-sufficient in wheat; by 1855 only one-tenth of the demand was satisfied by home production, and food was being imported —from California.

By 1861 the stations were again employing as many men as 'before the gold', and flocks were again on the increase; but the technique of pastoral farming had changed. In the late 1850's, the practice of fencing had been introduced—especially where encouraged by security of tenure; and in doing this the pastoralists had discovered, almost by chance, Australia's greatest advantage in the raising of sheep and wool. Australia is the one really great area of the world where sheep can with advantage be left in the open for months on end. The resulting economies quickly repaid those who could face the heavy initial cost, including the wages of ex-diggers who, having refused to work as employees in the now essential gold-mining companies, took fencing contracts and emerged as a new type of migrant labour. The saving of man-power was considerable, and fencing spread from the highest-wage into the lower-wage areas, from Victoria in the 1850's into Queensland in the 1870's; in the middle 1880's it reached still stagnant Western Australia, where the stimulus of gold and phosphates had yet to come.

Thus the Australian gold discoveries, which temporarily impoverished the pastoral industry by raising labour costs, and which seemed for a time to threaten to eclipse it as the country's staple export industry, brought, in the end, new labour, new capital, new opportunities, and an enlarged domestic market for agricultural products.

The history of new territories cannot be written, of course, simply in terms of the discovery of overseas markets. Not even for those settlers whose aim it was, not merely to subsist, but 'to truck, barter, and exchange one thing for another' so that their standard of comfort might become greater than that to which they were used, was international trade essential. Homes could be made, and made comfortable, though perhaps scarcely any fortunes founded, in a purely domestic economy. It must be borne in mind that the great mass of settlers were traders, at most, with one another, and that the purposes for which new land was opened up were characteristically (when the opening up was not on a grand scale or at a spectacular speed) local in origin.

Thus there is ample evidence that most of the timber cut in the great forests of the New World in the eighteenth century was cut for local consumption at local mills, or else to be transported to nearby treeless areas or to growing cities; much, for example, was carried down the Mississippi to New Orleans and the rising Gulf ports in the 1850's and 1860's. The development of American agriculture in this period was likewise conditioned, outside the South, by chiefly American influences. Eastern farmers, to begin with, found a market for their crops in the great trading and industrial regions and cities near the Atlantic coast; then western competition in the great staple products of corn and wheat, flowing along first the Erie canal from 1825, and later the railways, compelled them to specialize in those lines which enjoyed natural protection or a natural advantage. It was on the basis of eastern, not foreign, markets that the Illinois Central Railroad successfully promoted the colonizing of Illinois in the 1850's; and when, by 1860, Illinois was the greatest corn-producing State in the Union, farmers as well as urban dwellers in New England had for twenty years been consuming flour made from western, not local, wheat. Competition in beef and pork was less easy, but shipments by rail of livestock and processed pork were growing in the 1840's; by 1850 it was reckoned that there were a hundred towns in Ohio, Indiana and Illinois engaged in meat-packing—and the canning industry also, on the east coast, was stimulated at this time by demand from the '49ers. It is significant that maize, a crop never exported, was in 1840 by far the most important of the staple crops, its value about twice that of the wheat or the cotton or the hay crops which ranked next in importance; and the meat products into which much of this corn was turned were also almost entirely for home consumption.

Possibly the most striking example in this early period of the dominance (in terms of size) of local demand is that of New Zealand. In this case an economy was developed in which local demand was for a time not merely the broad base of the profitable and expansionary activities of exporters, but was, very nearly, the whole driving force of the system. New Zealand possessed timber, coal, gold, and the conditions favourable to the production of immense quantities of perishable foodstuffs which Australia could not produce so cheaply, but which, in the absence of any artificial means of preservation, could not readily be sent abroad. There was an early but not extensive trade in timber with Great Britain, Australia and South Africa; the coal was not much worked to begin with and the richness of the gold deposits not realized until after 1861. High-quality hemp was an early export, but it slumped in the 1830's; only in 1844 was the first sheep station started in the Wairarapa, with sheep imported from Sydney; it was an immediate success, and by 1857 the New Zealand wool export was over two and a half million lb. But this was the solitary export upon which New Zealand could rely; her gold rush did not begin until 1861. The small area of land necessary to meet the local demand for meat and dairy products was easily taken into cultivation, and thereafter every further acre of land cultivated, beyond what was necessary to keep pace with the growth of population, merely tended to the general reduction of prices and profits. There was a regular but small demand for New Zealand dairy products in Australia, and wheat shipments overseas depended chiefly on failure of the Australian crop. In these circumstances the population grew to only 100,000 by 1861, the percentage of town dwellers increased, and the standard of living almost certainly did not rise. Settlement in the 1850's had been carried as far as local demand required, but the transition to production for a wider market was essential for further development. This transition New Zealand was for two decades painfully unable to make, and for this reason she entered the 1850's as an economy without an obvious future.

IV. International Trade after 1850

The international trading relations of the second half of the nineteenth century—or rather, of the period starting about the conclusion of the Crimean War—were of a considerably more intimate and much more complex nature than those which had preceded them. Between 1860 and 1900 the number of commodities entering into international trade on a large scale multiplied greatly; competition between many widely separated regions of the world first appeared or grew more intense; the standard of living—even the livelihood—of hundreds of thousands of industrial workers came to depend on the maintenance of overseas supplies, while that of millions of primary producers was determined by market fluctuations occurring sometimes on the other side of the world. The economic organization of a great number of countries thus became, in short, dependent upon the system of organization which embraced them all. This was a novel situation. It had applied, previously, only to a few industries, such as the cotton and wool manufactures; and when the American Civil War cut Britain off from the usual source of 70 per cent or so of her cotton supplies, the astonishment at the ensuing dislocation and distress showed how little prepared men were for the idea of an international economic order. Yet that order was already, by 1860, well established.

The reasons for the emergence of many products besides wool, cotton and timber as important in international trade were chiefly of a technical sort; and much the most important of these technical changes was the improvement in ocean transport. This depended, primarily, upon that 'synthesis of existing inventions',[1] the iron steamship. Steam-driven vessels were of little importance on ocean routes until after 1838, when regular and economic steamship services began between Europe and North America; and even then this method of transport, although rapid, was costly, and therefore suited chiefly to the carrying of passengers and mails. From about 1860, however, keen commercial competition existed between wooden vessels and iron vessels, between steam and sail, and this resulted in the driving down of freight rates in the course of the 1870's to unprecedentedly low levels; then, after about 1878, an entirely new range of cost economies was opened up by the use of metal-built steamships using steel hulls, steel boilers, twin screws, and compound engines. Freight rates for sailing ships on Atlantic passages fell from very remunerative to barely remunerative levels between 1874 and 1877–8, and then fell a further 40 per cent between 1877–8 and 1885–80; this eliminated the competition of sailing ships. In the East Indian trade they competed for rather longer. But by 1903 freight rates in general were down to about 20 per cent of the 1877–8 level, and the actual costs of ocean shipment had fallen by an even greater percentage due to reductions in the cost of insurance.

These developments were made still more important by the enormous extension of railway facilities which took place in the 1870's and 1880's. Caird, travelling in America just before the Civil War, 'found that the cost of transport, which I carefully enquired into, was 2d. per ton per mile for corn of any kind'; this meant that in 1000 miles 'a bushel of wheat exhausted itself' (that is, the cost of transport rose to equal its selling price); 'So long as anything like that cost of transport was likely to be maintained (and at that time there was no apparent probability of its being much reduced, for the railways in the east were paying badly);...the prospect of a competition...was a distant

[1] Hutchins, *The American Maritime Industries*, p. 327.

one.'[1] At that date total American mileage was approximately 29,000. But in the boom years between 1866 and 1872 America built another 33,000 miles, and in the 1880's a further 74,000 miles. The result was that whereas America emerged from the Civil War with about 32,500 miles of railroad, she entered the twentieth century with approximately 198,000 miles, and rail freights between the two dates were probably cut in half—certainly that on wheat between Chicago and New York fell from 33 cents to 13 cents per bushel between 1873 and 1884. Development in other parts of the world was similar. In the decade of the 1870's Australia built 2681 miles of railway, and thereby quadrupled the length of line open to traffic; by 1890 she had 10,800 miles of track. New Zealand, innocent of a single mile of open track in the 1860's, had over 2500 miles by the close of the century. Canada, with 1800 miles in 1860, increased this to almost 31,000 miles by 1914.

Almost as important as the provision of these greatly extended and cheapened facilities was the more intensive use which could be made of them as a result of the introduction of refrigeration. 'Natural' refrigeration, by means of stocks of ice, was introduced into American slaughter houses in the 1860's, and in the 1870's Swift was demonstrating the practicability of a refrigerator 'car' to be used on the railroads; by 1880 cars of this type were in regular use and the shipment of meat from Chicago westwards enormously facilitated. Almost simultaneously, on the other side of the world, experiments were being conducted to solve the problem of refrigeration at sea. In 1875 meat had reached England from New York chilled by means of natural ice and a hand-operated fan; but that was a voyage one quarter as long as the voyage from Australia, and the variation in latitude which it involved was negligible. Pastoralists in Australia and New Zealand, however, were very anxious for a solution to the problem, for wool continued to be the only part of the sheep for which there was an assured market, the animal itself being, so to speak, a mere by-product. In 1879 two successful shipments of frozen meat reached London from Australia, and freezing-works were immediately established in Queensland, Victoria, and New South Wales. But development of a frozen meat trade was even more important to New Zealand, and prices for wool continuing low (after the boom year of 1872–3), the New Zealand government in 1881 offered a prize of £500 for the first 100 tons of fresh meat landed in Europe in good condition; just over one year later the 'Dunedin's' cargo was landed in London, and meat which sold in New Zealand for 3*d*. a lb. fetched 6½*d*., the cost of transport having been only 2¼*d*. per lb. This was the 'prodigious fact' which was to revolutionize New Zea-

[1] Royal Commission on Agriculture, evidence of J. Caird, Minutes of Evidence, Q 62658, 1882 (XIV).

land's economy, increase the sheep population of Australia by nearly one-third between 1880 and 1890, and raise land values substantially in several parts of the world.

Apart from these transport improvements, other significant changes in the conditions of international trade took place. The unprecedentedly rapid increase of population in western Europe created at one and the same time an increased labour supply for industry and an increased demand for foodstuffs and consumer goods. Industrial production rose rapidly, entailing a greatly increased demand for raw materials. Also, technical changes enlarged the sphere of international trade by giving to new products a value in distant markets which exceeded their costs of production and transportation. The oil deposits of northern Pennsylvania, for example, only began to be exploited in 1859, but such was the demand in industrialized Europe that by the end of the Civil War America was exporting $16 million worth of oil, an item ranking sixth in the then list of American exports. Rubber, likewise, rose in value as Europe and America advanced in technical progress, and by 1890 about 19,000 tons of rubber was passing through the port of Pará for international markets. At the close of the century, Britain's 'bicycle boom' and, later and much more important, the rise of the automobile industry in Britain, France, Germany and America provided enormously expanded markets for this commodity. The great rise in the standard of comfort in America and western Europe in the latter part of the nineteenth century—due in part to the cheapening of basic foodstuffs by the means above outlined—also created new openings in international trade; to mention two conspicuous examples, the export of Brazilian coffee doubled between 1900 and 1907, while from the 1880's the export of fruit to western Europe, and especially Britain, made possible largely by refrigeration, gave new scope to farmers in America, Australia, Canada and South Africa.

Lastly, it is important to recognize that while technical experts, investors, business men and pioneers made possible these extensions of trade and the higher standard of life consequent upon them, politicians —guided by economists, consumers, and the interminable play of vested interest, innocent and otherwise—removed in this same period many of the barriers which might have prevented men from taking advantage of these novel opportunities. In this matter Britain led the way and her removal of any considerable restrictions on the import of corn in 1846 greatly accelerated, a couple of decades later, the movement westward into the new American, Australian and Canadian wheatlands. In 1860 France adopted this freer policy, so that her markets, also, were open to foreign imports when these began to cross the Atlantic in large volume in the late 1870's. France began to raise duties perceptibly on primary products from the mid-1880's, but not until after the Méline tariff of 1892 was wheat importation checked—it was Méline who spoke plaintively of the new countries

favoured by nature and by their financial situation with exceptional advantages, a virgin soil almost without value [i.e. selling price], for some, unbelievably cheap labour, the absence of military expenses and insignificant fiscal charges. In 1860 these peoples still slept....America was still so far! As for India and Australia, who for an instant could have thought of them? One hardly thought of Russia.

But suddenly there came the development of means of transportation and communication, the rapid decrease in freight costs, in a few years placing these great markets at our doors....[1]

Germany, similarly, reduced—was indeed without—corn duties from 1865; but they were re-imposed in 1880, although a really formidable tariff was not erected until 1903, and even that allowed in cotton and wool free of duty. America likewise, despite the McKinley tariff of 1891, placed only slight obstacles in the way of importation of those few primary commodities which she could not produce in ample quantities herself—with, of course, the notorious exception of wool. Thus the great markets of the world lay singularly open in the 1870's, and remained comparatively free of restrictions in the 1880's and even, to a lesser extent, in the 1890's, for the importation of those usually unprocessed commodities, novel or familiar, which the new countries were increasingly able in these decades to supply.

V. The Extension of Settlement after 1850

THE UNITED STATES

After 1850 it ceases to be possible to describe the American advance into virgin country by drawing a 'frontier line' southward from the Canadian border. The gold discoveries in California brought such a flood of people to the west in 1849 that California became an American State in 1850, and from that date occupation closes in on the intervening land from both east and west, facilitated by the passage of travellers and hence the establishment of trading posts through the uninhabited country. In 1850 this uninhabited region was still little known and understood, but this state of affairs was changing rapidly. From the mid-1840's pioneers were passing through the empty lands over the Oregon trail, mostly heading for the fertile and agreeable Willamette valley. The Mormon colony at Salt Lake was founded in 1847, with almost immediate success, demonstrating to America the

[1] Quoted in E. O. Golob, *The Méline Tariff* (New York, 1944), p. 182.

possibilities of irrigation farming; in 1853 Jefferson Davis initiated the survey of five possible transcontinental rail routes; and at the end of the decade, in 1859, another westward rush of gold-miners was precipitated by the discovery of gold in what was later to become the State of Colorado and also, farther south, in the neighbourhood of Lake Tahoe.

This double line of advance was not the only dichotomy in the situation by 1850, for in the east the clash between slave and non-slave was rapidly growing more serious, and this clash helped to accelerate the movement into the western lands. The decade before the Civil War saw the maximum extension of slavery, in territory as well as in numbers, and the use by the South of its political power to open to slavery all the debated territories and to prevent for a while the final passage of what became the Homestead Act. In spite of these manœuvres, or because of them, pioneers pushed westward to create the States of Iowa, Wisconsin, California, Oregon and Minnesota, all between 1840 and 1860, and to enter Kansas, Nebraska, South Dakota and, in the far north, Michigan: all States or territories hostile to slavery in the ensuing war.

Thus in 1861, when war broke out, there stood in the west the States of California and Oregon, thinly populated outside the mining regions and the fertile and easily cultivable valleys. In the east, another 'frontier line' ran westwards across the northern part of Wisconsin, turned southwards about the north-west tip of Minnesota, and from there, with a bulge westwards into Nebraska and Kansas, ran due south to the line of the Red river, which it followed westwards to take in approximately the eastern third of Texas. East of this line almost all territory had a population density of at least two inhabitants per square mile, but empty regions were southern Florida, northern Michigan and northern Maine, and there was an equally uninhabited pocket in northern New York State. Broadly speaking, however, there was this eastern area of occupation stretching well past the Mississippi, most of it settled to a density of from 6 to 45 persons per square mile, and then, 2000 miles to the west, separated by mountains and large regions of low rainfall, the western remainder.

This situation was produced by economic forces over which political pressures exercised, undoubtedly, some slight control; and the further extensions of the 1870's were likewise, in part, politically produced. For the Civil War was a by no means unmixed disaster for the American economy. The desirability of unifying the non-slave States and of linking the West to the North with economic as well as idealist ties persuaded the statesmen of that time to press on with the construction of transcontinental railroads and, in order to have them built in what seemed the most economical manner (as far, at any rate, as the public treasury was concerned), to finance them on the model of the Illinois Central Railroad, the charter for which, with the vital innovation of a large land grant, had been approved in 1851. Thus there came about the grant of the famous charter to the Union Pacific and Central Pacific Railroads in 1862, and the large-scale inauguration of the policy which ultimately transferred to the railroad corporations over 131 million acres of Federal land. This was a far greater innovation than was at the time generally realized, for it brought on the scene the great railroad corporations as entities not only with an interest in but with extensive power to affect the settlement of the public domain, at the same time that the Homestead Act, passed in the same year, appeared to give full freedom in this great task and opportunity to the small independent settler. Whichever party benefited most—small settler, railroad corporation, national treasury, or the country as a whole—the developments of this decade, particularly after the labour-consuming Civil War had been brought to an end, were even more rapid than those which had gone before.

The fall in American wholesale prices which occurred after the Civil War coincided with the British downturn in economic activity which followed the crisis of 1866, and for two years or so the rate of advance was not remarkable; but thereafter the greatest boom of the nineteenth century began to get under way. Men were free to take advantage of the provisions of the Homestead Act of 1862; the first trans-continental railroad was completed in 1869, and there was a wave of optimism concerning the profitability of building and investing in railroads; British iron prices for 1867-9 were below their average for the 1850's and the first half of the 1860's; and the device of paying for the necessary imports of capital goods by exporting food, made legally possible by the repeal of the British Corn Laws in 1846, was now an economic possibility also as a result of the low agricultural costs of the west and the already existing transport system with its falling shipping costs. But too much emphasis can be laid on the international trading aspect of the development, important as that was. For besides the European markets there were the markets of eastern America, emerging, by 1870, as one of the great manufacturing areas of the world. This development was based, fundamentally, on the linkage of the Bessemer process with the rich Lake Superior ore fields and the abundant supplies of excellent coking coal; and included also the oil discoveries in Pennsylvania, America's already established superiority in the manufacture of agricultural machinery, sewing machines, and some kinds of machine tools, and the growing competitive power of the cotton manufacturing industry. All in all, the number of wage earners in manufacturing rose from 1·3 million in 1859 to 2·7 million in 1879, an increase of over

107 per cent, while the population rose by 18·7 million or just under 60 per cent. Given such varied resources, and given an aggressive and industrious population continually augmented by natural increase and recruitment from overseas, internal reciprocal demand rapidly attained to very considerable importance, and industrial and tertiary developments in the east served to encourage settlement farther and farther west no less than did the expanding opportunities of international trade. What is so remarkable in the American development is the discovery of unsuspectedly—indeed unprecedentedly—abundant and varied resources along with both new techniques *and* the continual (till the end of the century) lowering of costs of production of agricultural articles *as well* as the costs of mining and manufacturing. For one hundred years improvements in organization and technique, but even more the extensive growth of the economy, maintained at a high level in America the marginal efficiency of both capital and labour in almost all branches of economic activity.

In the early 1870's, therefore, America reached her first pinnacle as the land of boundless opportunity. Two trans-continental railroads were building in the early 1870's, and 1870–1 saw the largest volume of railroad construction to that date. Settlement began to sweep across the prairies. 'In 1870 the farthest limit of Kansas settlement was Brook-ville, then a small railroad station; but two years later it had swept to the prairie uplands, 100 miles farther west.'[1] The population of Kansas almost trebled in the 1870's, while the numbers in Idaho, Wyoming, Texas, Minnesota and Montana all doubled or nearly doubled. But these rates of increase were left far behind by Nebraska, where the population more than trebled, Colorado, where it increased more than fourfold, and Dakota territory where it increased very nearly tenfold. Frontier towns, sometimes at the end of a railroad, with a handful of citizens and an unenviable reputation for lawlessness, were apt to grow into thriving and populous commercial centres in a few years. Dallas, Texas, for example, was a border town of 1500 inhabitants in 1872 and three years later a city of 15,000, served by the Texas and Pacific Railroad. Denver likewise grew from 5000 to 30,000 in the course of the 1870's, and changed from a wild frontier town into a seat of responsible government.

This surge into the hitherto neglected Great Plains region was part cause, part consequence of the construction of railroads, but was also linked with development of the range cattle industry. This industry, serving primarily the great cities east of the Mississippi, originated in Texas in the late 1860's, when Texas cattlemen first began to drive their

[1] C. C. Rister, *The Growth of the American Economy*, H. F. Williamson (ed.) (New York, 1944), p. 424.

cattle in large numbers through Indian territory into Kansas; in the early 1870's there were stock pens in such towns as Abilene, Wichita, and Dodge City. As the westward spread of settlement began to grow across the cattle trails the industry fanned out northward and westward into Montana, Wyoming, Idaho, Nevada, Utah, California and New Mexico.

Within a few years the cattle industry had invaded all parts of the Great Plains. The far-spreading bluestem, grama and mesquite grasslands were ideally suited for ranching and yearly expenses were nominal. Not uncommonly the rancher was a tenant-at-will, squatting on the public domain, or he leased his land at a nominal rental. In either case he built a sod house or dugout near a running stream, with appurtenant corrals and sheds, hired a cowboy to take care of his small herd, and bought a supply of groceries. At the end of the year he was able to sell enough cattle to meet all his expenses and to have a small sum left to purchase more cattle.[1]

The industry grew and spread at a tremendous pace, driven forward both by large-scale foreign investors and by individual immigrants of small means; to both, but especially to the former, it was, for a while, immensely profitable. By 1875 ranches were scattered all over the Great Prairie region, and cattlemen's associations were multiplying fast; and by 1880 the low-cost beef of the area was beginning to reach Britain, canned, most of it, in Chicago—and to aggravate still further the difficulties of the British farmer.

The chance to supply distant eastern and European industrial centres with cheap meat, produced on the extensive and unclaimed western lands, was thus the driving force behind the first general invasion of this area. But ranching did not mean *settlement*; it was, indeed, hostile to it— almost as hostile as fur trading. But even in its most prosperous days, around 1880, the range cattle industry could not withstand the advance of the 'true' pioneer and settler. The Homestead Act of 1862 and, later, the Timber Culture Act of 1875 and the Desert Land Act of 1877 all encouraged settlement for tillage. By 1877 the settler could, in extensive areas of North and South Dakota, Montana, New Mexico and Wyoming, obtain title to 1120 acres of free land with perfect legality; and men who wished to claim this right were not wanting. The advance of cultivation across the area was further speeded by technical innovation—would, indeed, have been impossible without it, the problems of farming west of the 98th meridian being radically different from those east of it. First of all, even the Deere all-steel plough was not entirely satisfactory for breaking the hard prairie soils, and Lane's soft-centre steel plough, introduced in 1868, was invaluable. The scarcity of

[1] C. C. Rister, *op. cit.* pp. 419–20.

wood in the area was also a serious matter, causing the first settlers to avoid the open prairie, although it was often the best land; when they were compelled to enter it they burned hay, corn or buffalo chips for fuel, went scores of miles to haul firewood of even the poorest quality, and could not be kept out of the timber lands on Indian reserves. This problem was solved only by the coming of the railroad. Absence of wood also meant absence of fencing. Here improvisation was almost impossible, and but for the invention of barbed wire in the mid-1870's the roaming herds of cattle might have possessed the Great Plains for decades longer than they did. Water, likewise, or rather the absence of it, was a problem at least as serious. The first settlers located in the valleys in order to be near running water as well as wood, or, at least, to be able to reach water at 20 or 30 ft. depth. On the rolling uplands, however, wells of one hundred or even two hundred feet in depth were required, and water barrels—which had to be taken into the houses in wintertime in order to prevent them from freezing solid—were a feature of every homestead. The manual labour of digging such wells and of hauling water considerable distances was of course immense, and it is surprising that 'the main use to which windmills in the Great Plains were put in the 'sixties and early 'seventies was pumping water for the railroad locomotives';[1] possibly the comparative poverty of the early settlers coupled with the large size and considerable expense of the first windmills (although manufactured as far west as Batavia, Illinois, in 1862) accounts for this. By the late 1870's, however, the windmill tower was 'the unmistakable and universal sign of human habitation throughout the Great Plains Area'.[2] Lastly, the techniques of dry-farming, experimented with in various early settlements in the semi-arid region, were developed and systematized; although even the best techniques could not redeem some of the submarginal lands into which settlers were reaching by 1885.

Thus equipped, farmers pressed upon and hemmed in the ranching industry. Cattlemen, by 1885 already embarrassed by an overstocked market and now facing adverse weather conditions, began to fence (not always legally) large areas of the public domain, and after a struggle, the industry became at last a more normal one of closed range ranching with stock grazing on—as a rule—leased land. Wheat production, the characteristic frontier activity, again moved west. Illinois had been the greatest wheat-producing State from 1859 to 1879; but following the greater diversification of economic activity on the prairies and the north-westward movement of spring wheat, Montana was in the lead in the returns of 1889 and 1899, superseded by North Dakota in 1909.

[1] E. Dick, *The Sod-House Frontier* (New York, 1937), p. 299.
[2] *Ibid.* p. 299.

Indiana, Illinois, Iowa and east Nebraska turned over largely to maize. Settlers who wished to 'keep in the wheat belt' moved west, the Red River Valley (for spring wheat) became 'settled up', while by 1890 the homestead entries in North and South Dakota, Nebraska, Kansas and Colorado reached their peak: in western Kansas and Nebraska, in fact, settlement was pushed too far, lured on by the succession of unusually wet seasons prior to 1887. Simultaneously wool growing, stimulated by the bounty of man (in the shape of the tariff of 1883) and not of nature, was attracting new settlers in Montana, Wyoming, Texas and the far west.

By 1889 Oklahoma was surrounded by this tide of white farmers. And when a section here was opened to settlement in April 1889 'thousands were waiting for the signal and a wild rush ensued. Some went in by rail, some on horseback, some in the old pioneer wagons, whole town outfits, portable houses and all, were shipped in and by nightfall Guthrie had become a city of 7000'.[1] When, in 1890, in mid-winter, a portion of a Dakota reservation was thrown open, troops were required to hold back the home-seekers till the legal time of entry. Such scenes suggest the ending of the abundance of free land, and by 1890 the frontier was declared to have disappeared. The rate of increase of the population west of the Mississippi had been, from 1860 to 1890, nearly four times as great as that in the east; from 1890 to 1920 it was only 50 per cent greater.

In this development, the idea of a 'line' of settlement is a gross over-simplification. Settlement was characteristically patchy, and groups of settlers were often scattered across virgin country to a depth of several score miles, with wide intervals of unpopulated territory lying between them. Also, the definition of frontier country as country with less than two inhabitants per square mile is largely arbitrary. The implication that genuine pioneering—in the sense of breaking in virgin soil to cultivation—did not take place *after* population had reached two per square mile is absurd. Moreover, the task of pioneering is not solely that of cultivating the soil for the first time; the first permanent farmer who builds a frame house and practises an economical system of rotation and planned agriculture is also a pioneer. Nor, for that matter, is there a clear distinction between the first homesteader and the first storekeeper, although the latter as a rule—but not always—follows the farmer. Storekeeping, indeed, was a well known and indispensable pioneer occupation.

In the flood tide of migration the business of a store increased by leaps and bounds in a single season in spite of a ten-fold increase in competition.

---

[1] C. W. Wright, *Economic History of the United States* (New York, 1949), p. 471.

Mr Joel Hull launched a merchandise business at Lowell, Nebraska, with the arrival of the railroad on July 3, 1874, when there were only 47 persons in the vicinity. Before August 1 the sales averaged over one hundred dollars a day and the demand was so great that in September he laid in a stock of thirty-three thousand dollars' worth of goods all bought on credit. At times he had barely enough to pay the freight bills.[1]

Small industrial enterprises, likewise, designed to serve a purely local market, quickly sprang up, and were as indispensable. There thus appeared in many areas a local 'frontier economy' with tenuous or negligible connections with distant markets, or else connections almost solely of the capital-importing variety. Almost all members of these communities might be, in a very real sense, pioneers, and many of them were pioneers in the stricter and more limited sense of engaging in the initiation of new modes of exploitation of the material environment. But to follow the process of more *intensive* exploitation is to enter imperceptibly into the general account of the development of the economy.

PROGRESS OF SETTLEMENT IN CANADA

The factor most powerfully influencing the history of the settlement of any territory is the nature of the country. The speed and complexity of the process of settlement in the United States is primarily a reflection of the exceptionally rich and varied resources which that country contained. In the case of Canada, on the other hand, we find a country less bountifully or variously endowed by nature, and as a result there takes place a process of development which is both slower and, in its essential outlines, considerably more simple.

The development of eastern Canada was dominated by the presence of the forest. The forest region was originally over one million square miles in extent, covering all of the three maritime provinces, all of Quebec almost to the Hudson Bay, all of Ontario, most of Manitoba, and parts of Saskatchewan, Alberta, and the North-west Territories. The forest did not extend into the true prairie regions, and its northward limit is set by climate and drainage. Merchantable timber grows in the river valleys as far north as 54° N., but at that latitude not outside them; while the extreme flatness of the land south of James Bay and along the west shore of Hudson Bay prevents drainage, leaves the land waterlogged, and makes the growth of trees impossible except along the rivers. This forest in its natural state is extremely dense and difficult to penetrate, growing in many places on rocky land totally unfit for cultivation; much of Nova Scotia and a large part of New Brunswick is

[1] Dick, *op. cit.* p. 411.

country of this type, and the most liberal estimate for Quebec gives that province about 60,000 square miles of good farm land out of a total of about 700,000 square miles. The ratio in Ontario is not dissimilar.

The timber which these regions grow consists chiefly of red and white pine and of spruce forest—the true 'northern forest'. The red and white pine, however, do not grow to any extent north of the 50th parallel, and as the forest industry of the early nineteenth century was based upon the broad axe and the saw mill, and upon transportation along natural waterways, it follows that the industry was then confined to the St Lawrence and Atlantic watersheds; only with the completion of the Canadian Pacific Railway in the 1880's was the lumbering industry able to penetrate west of the St Lawrence watershed, and only with the appearance of the pulp and paper industry as a great spruce-wood consumer did the more northerly Canadian forest areas acquire an economic significance.

In the second half of the nineteenth century, the development of the American west, with its demand for great quantities of building materials, was the real driving force behind the extension of the Canadian timber industry. Yet only those localities which enjoyed direct communication with the United States had any part in the trade. Simcoe county, for example, boasting magnificent stands of pine, exported none until the Northern Railway entered it in 1851. In 1853 the Northern Railway was completed, and lumbering spread generally into the Huron–Ottawa tract; in 1870 extension of this railway led to the erection of mills as far north as Parry Sound. A still greater extension came with the completion of the Canadian Pacific Railway, which finally took the timber industry clean out of the St Lawrence watershed and, furthermore, in opening the Canadian west, provided a new and nearby market. Exploitation reached into such far-away areas as Thunder Bay and Lake of the Woods. By the end of the century little good pine remained in the vast area tapped by the railways; north of the railway it was difficult to go, for there the rivers flowed not south but northward.

It should be made clear, however, that timber cutting is not, and is not necessarily followed by, settlement. The main line of the Canadian Pacific built north of the Lakes in 1884–5 passes through a country good for little but lumbering, and to this day 'there is no agricultural community of any importance from Sudbury on the east to Nipigon on the west, a distance of several hundred miles'.[1] Moreover, saw-mills themselves are neither large capital investments nor—like a steel mill—rigidly immobile; nor were the nineteenth-century mills by any stretch of the imagination non-inflammable. Thus a mill might easily provide local employment for a year or two and then cease to do so,

[1] Lower, *Canadian Frontiers of Settlement*, IX, 140.

either leaving 'a derelict and hopeless population marooned in the backwoods' or the country as unpeopled as it found it.

Fortunately, the history of Canada is not the history of a single predatory industry. Besides lumbering, exporting food on a small scale and practising very widely a peculiar native type of subsistence agriculture, Canadians entertained great hopes in the first half of the century of the future of their country as an artery of trade. British trade with the Mohawk as well as the St Lawrence valley passed, as a rule, through Quebec from the beginning of the nineteenth century, and as the American 'old North-west' developed, trade to the Detroit region did likewise. Thus Canadians formed the hope that the St Lawrence was to become the channel for all the trade of the Great Lakes region on both sides of the international boundary. This hope was particularly lively in the 1830's and early 1840's, and as a result of it several canals were constructed to improve the St Lawrence waterway, including the Ottawa, Welland and Rideau canals.

The commercial expectations which, in part, caused these canals to be built were doomed to disappointment. Faith in the future of the waterway continued till about 1848, but by then cyclical depression in the British market, the repeal of the Corn Laws, and the whittling away of imperial preference on timber all combined to check development in Canada. In the following decade, however, prosperity returned. It soon became evident that Canada did not require preference in corn, and while she did benefit from it in timber a new market was opened to her in the shape of the American north-eastern states—where the local supplies were failing—with the reduction of American timber duties in 1854. But as a grain port Montreal continued to fall behind New York, and in order to compete Canada embarked on railway building in the east. The Grand Trunk Railway was completed from Toronto to Montreal in 1856, with connections to Portland, New York and Boston, and lines were built throughout western Ontario and intensively in the neighbourhood of Montreal. By 1860 Canada had 1800 miles of railway, none west of Lake Huron. This construction secured the eclipse of the Canadian canals, but not the American carrying trade. This, however, was by no means a disaster. The timber industry was expanding and prosperous—in its cyclical manner—in these years; during the Crimean War especially timber prices in Britain were exceptionally high, and by 1867 America was taking as much wood and wood product as was Britain. Wheat prices also generally were high in the 1850's. Between 1852 and 1861 land under cultivation increased 36 per cent in Upper Canada and 30 per cent in Lower Canada, and then sales fell off sharply as it became evident that all good land was now either settled or in the hands of speculators; in

Lower Canada there was even talk of the 'redundant population of the old parishes', and in 1866 two-thirds of the British arrivals at Quebec were said to have gone on to the United States.

In these circumstances interest in the prairie area quickened. In 1856, the date of the last census before its purchase by Canada, the territory which now forms Manitoba, Saskatchewan and Alberta contained less than 7000 white inhabitants, of whom probably more than 5000 were half-breeds; agriculture, which was entirely subsidiary to the fur trade, had put less than one-thousandth of one per cent of the total area under cultivation. The Selkirk Settlement on the Red river had existed from 1812: but fifty years later it could boast no more than a few thousand inhabitants, and its ability merely to survive was doubted as late as the 1850's; in 1857 Sir John Richardson 'did not think any wise settler would go beyond that place, there being so much better land nearer the market to be had at very moderate rate'.[1] But ten years later this was ceasing to be true, and trade was developing between the Red river area and the United States. The interest of the United States in the region galvanized the British and Canadian authorities to action, and in 1869, after strenuous opposition, the Hudson Bay Company's land was sold to Canada. Anxiety about preservation of the fur-bearing animals of the region once removed, some 2,000,000 square miles of territory were open to settlement. Winnipeg saw its first saw-mill built in 1872, and by 1875 it had five, mostly engaged in cutting timber from Minnesota. In 1879 the railroad was completed from St Paul to Winnipeg, towns grew up along the route, and farming spread rapidly, homestead regulations being adopted which were similar to those of 'competing' areas in the United States. A boom in western land began, aided partly by such market factors as the exhaustion of the supply of good land farther east, the decline of the timber trade, and the increasing density of eastern population, and partly by such 'human' or 'supply' factors as the desire of wheat farmers to stay in their vocation, no matter where, and of railway agents and land speculators to 'capture' English and Canadian capitalists and farmers. The Canadian west was not only put up for sale, it was also widely advertised. As a result, farmers came from Ottawa and Ontario in bad years in the 1870's, while the early 1880's saw a boom in western land. The population of Manitoba grew from just over 25,000 in 1871 to over 152,000 in 1891. Wheat was exported from the province as early as 1876, but the interval between the appearance of grain in the local market and the close of navigation was at first too short to permit exportation on a large scale. This transport problem was solved by the construction of the Canadian Pacific Railroad which reached Regina in 1882, linked Winnipeg and eastern

[1] Quoted in Mackintosh, op. cit. p. 29.

Canada in 1883, and was completed from coast to coast in 1885. In that year the reputation of Manitoba no. 1 hard wheat was established in the British market, and by the close of the century just under 420,000 people were settled in the prairie provinces.[1]

This rate of growth—an almost sixfold increase from 1871 to 1901— was greatly facilitated by the use of techniques developed previously in the United States. The chilled steel plough, roller milling—which converted the hardness of the spring wheat of the northern plains from a blemish to a virtue—the twine binder, the grain elevator, even the humble sod-house and dug-out for storing water—all these were taken over from American experience. Dry-farming techniques also were important in the Canadian prairie; but while large areas have been brought into cultivation by this means there remains a rough correlation between rainfall deficiency and low population density—'scanty rainfall supports a scanty population because some land is not used at all: and because the remainder is used extensively rather than intensively'[2]—and in the north the spread of settlement is now limited not by lack of moisture but by the shortness of the growing season.

These developments form the solid core of Canadian settlement. There remain fringes of settlement, so to speak, in scattered and less accessible areas. The pulp and paper industry, for example, not significant until after about 1900, pushed into the spruce forest in the 1920's, and, generating power for its own needs and with some to spare, began to spread a diffuse industrialization over previously thinly peopled areas in eastern Canada. Simultaneously, farming settlement in the prairies spread away from the southern valleys, encroached upon and then thinly covered 'Palliser's Triangle' between 1906 and 1911, entered the Place river valley, and had created, by 1911, a pioneer fringe which was to prove the largest for the twentieth century. And lastly, gold discoveries had played a part in the slow development of British Columbia. Gold was worked in the lower Fraser valley in the 1850's, and on the upper Fraser in the 1860's and 1870's. Transportation costs, however, were very high, and it was only with the remarkable discoveries at Klondike in 1896 that a true gold-rush developed. Railway construction was undertaken, and the Crow's Nest Pass Railway was completed in 1898, destined greatly to stimulate both lumbering and fish canning in British Columbia; the raising of food in other regions (agriculture near the goldfields was all but hopeless) was encouraged; flour milling and pork packing in Edmonton and Calgary succeeded on the basis, largely, of the demand from Kootenay, while fruit-growing

[1] The rate of increase was at its maximum between 1900 and 1910.
[2] Mackintosh, *op. cit.* 1, 75.

in the Okanagan region and dairying in the Fraser valley received their first great stimulus.

It is idle to speak of the 'disappearance of the frontier' in the case of Canada, because in the north and north-west it is so visibly still in existence. But by the opening of the twentieth century—certainly by 1914—the bulk of the country was settled, and the frontier had ceased to be a primary interest of the nation.

PROGRESS OF SETTLEMENT IN AUSTRALIA

The opening up of the continent of Australia presented the nineteenth century with problems of a somewhat different order from those which confronted settlement in America or Canada. In the first place, enormous distances separated Australia from the industrialized markets of Europe; in the days before the Suez Canal, Melbourne was three times as far from London as is New York. This fact, coupled with the nature of much of the Australian soil and climate, compelled Australia to concentrate from the beginning and to a remarkable degree on a single staple export, namely wool; and from 1820 to 1850 Australian economic development may be summarized in a few words: 'The sheep greatly increased on the Downs and the price for wool was good.'[1] Thirdly—and this was largely the result of geographical isolation coupled with uniformity—the economy developed until after 1850 with little variation as between one district and another; all areas depended, to a greater or lesser degree, upon wool; and thus there was, so to speak, no diversified or industrialized base of economic operations on the continent (such as New England or Pennsylvania provided in the new world), the frontier type of economy existing all the way from the frontier itself back to the coast. Lastly, the areas suitable for settlement are seldom very far from the sea, so that settlement was not of a trans-continental but rather of a peripheral sort, originating in a number of small beginnings scattered along the coast and separated from one another by hundreds of miles (for distances are characteristically large) of virgin and unknown territory.

The discovery of gold in 1851 forced great changes upon the Australian economy. The food demand of a greatly increased population pressed severely upon the productive capacity of the country, while the volume of employment in gold-mining, after the early years, rapidly shrank; in Victoria the maximum was passed in 1858. The premier pastoral industry did not advance in the 1850's, although it was by then established as the chief supplier of the British market, and there were fewer sheep in Victoria and New South Wales in 1861 than in 1851.

[1] Quoted in Roberts, *Cambridge History of the British Empire*, VII, 201–2.

In the 1860's, nevertheless, the stage was set for a great forward movement of the whole Australian economy. In the first place, the American Civil War acted as a great stimulus to the British woollen industry; and in the second place, the increasing Australian and British demands for food encouraged the first intensive Australian movement to wheat cultivation.

Of these two changes the latter made, as a rule, an indirect rather than a direct contribution to the extension of settlement. Although wheat was through the entire nineteenth century the principal crop grown in the Australian colonies, Australians were scarcely able to meet their own requirements prior to the 1880's. When demand rose steeply as a result of the gold discoveries, South Australia emerged as the granary of the continent, with seven times as much land under crop in 1860 as in 1850, and the stream of farming settlement kept pace with the squatters in expanding north, south and east. In the other colonies, however, agriculture was slower to expand. This was principally because other occupations attracted too much of men's attentions; but everywhere inadequate transport facilities made wheat-growing away from the towns unattractive, while high labour cost and natural obstacles made it more unattractive still. Railways—built as a rule 'by pastoralists for pastoralists'[1]—overcame the first of these difficulties; agricultural inventions overcame the second—Ridley's stripper, in use in South Australia from 1843; the stump-jump plough, invented in 1876; and McKay's stripper-harvester of the middle 1880's. Of these inventions, the stump-jump plough most directly contributed to the extension of settlement; in South Australia and Victoria the fourteen million acres of mallee, covered with *Eucalyptus Dumosa*, and partly stocked from the 1840's, were conquered for agriculture in the 1880's thanks to the use of the stump-jump plough and the locally invented mallee roller. There was, indeed, a rush of farmers into this region in the late 1880's, for by then no other land remained unclaimed.

This movement to cultivation which is so prominent a feature of Australian development in the second half of the nineteenth century proceeded slowly, however (at least as compared with the United States), not only because of technical difficulties and the remoteness of the European market, but also because of the extensive 'impediment of pastoral priority'.[2] The Australian farmer usually pushed forward not into virgin territory but into lands already carrying stock—rather as the American farmer pushed into the already utilized Great Plains in the 1870's. Closer settlement, and settlement for tillage, thus drove the pastoralist into ever more remote country. The movement in Victoria

[1] Fitzpatrick, *The British Empire in Australia, 1834–1939*, p. 135.
[2] Fitzpatrick, *op. cit.* p. 145.

has already been remarked. In South Australia the gold discoveries initiated almost twenty years of progress, and the occupation of the north produced a strong body of squatters for the first time in that part of the continent. In New South Wales fresh legislation 'unlocked the land' in 1861, and by 1883 continued prosperity in the colony had led to the alienation of sixteen million acres of land, or thrice that of the entire period prior to 1861. But in these years the difference between alienation and occupation became painfully evident, a Royal Commission in 1883 reporting that ninety-six persons owned over eight million acres; and only in the 1890's did turmoil, dummying and open warfare in this area end in redistribution and final settlement of the land.

Probably the most considerable movement in this period into genuinely virgin lands took place in the Northern Territory and in Western Australia. The movement in the north was wildly erratic. There was failure in the 1860's. Ambitious schemes were afoot in the optimistic atmospheres of the 1870's, the first selection of Northern Territory lands taking place in 1870, and plans were laid for the importation of Japanese labour; these schemes collapsed in 1877, and were followed by 'settlement' by absentee speculators in the 1880's; this boom likewise was punctured by 1890, and not until the twentieth century was it appreciated that the Northern Territory is cattle country and little else. Progress in Western Australia was more solid. Expeditions to the extreme south-east and to the Gascogne region in the late 1850's made available at least two million acres of land, and a further six million acres were found near the Glenelg in 1863; genuine settlement ensued. In the 1870's the area under cultivation declined: but fresh discoveries, coupled with high prices for wool and meat, gave an impetus to pastoral extension, and by the mid-1880's the Eucla and Kimberley divisions were being widely utilized. Stocking, however, was not heavy, and agriculture, despite the York railway, languished. Then, at last, came the gold. The widely scattered discoveries made between 1887 and 1893 cleared the streets of Perth and Fremantle and brought from Melbourne, Adelaide and overseas 'unheard-of numbers...to be ready for the rush when the winter rains returned'.[1] Mining communities sprang up in a region of near-desert; and the government, unable to stand idly by while ten thousand or so people entered a district devoid equally of food and water, and finding itself newly emancipated from British restrictions on its capacity to borrow for public works, found money to build a railway, make a harbour at Fremantle, and construct the Goldfields Water Supply. Almost at once agriculture as well as mining benefited; lightly timbered areas of low but safe rainfall which had hitherto seemed useless were turned into scenes of agricultural

[1] Shann, *An Economic History of Australia*, p. 351.

settlement and, as far eastwards as Southern Cross, of light pastoral occupation.

These Western Australian developments of the 1890's and early twentieth century virtually marked the close of the period of expansion in Australia. Not all of it was successful. The expansion inland by South Australian squatters and farmers in the 1850's and early 1860's took place in what proved to be exceptionally favourable seasons; the drought from 1864 to 1869, especially to the north of Mount Remarkable, produced a 'fearful appearance of desolation'[1] and, in a single year, killed 235,000 out of 270,000 sheep. The experiences about the turn of the century were much worse. In 1902 New South Wales saw the culmination of eight years of subnormal rainfall, Queensland the culmination of four; these were the years when the sheep and cattle could be kept alive only by cutting 'the mulga': 'at the sound of an axe the poor skeletons would come running from every direction'.[2] Even so, the sheep population of Australia approximately halved between 1894 and 1902. These disasters inevitably turned men's thoughts to irrigation and improved farming techniques. Irrigation, begun in the 1880's, secured closer and more continuous rather than more extended settlement; but by its means the area under wheat was almost doubled in Victoria between 1890 and 1900; the extension in Western Australia has just been noticed; while the use of new wheats in New South Wales enabled that area to export breadstuffs for the first time in 1897, and the application of superphosphates (seldom abundant in Australian soils) from about the same date in South Australia ensured the continued success of wheat-growing in that region.

By 1900 little land that could be used without heavy capital investment remained to be alienated, and extension of settlement was more and more coming to depend on financial provision for irrigation and water conservation, and on world prices of wool, wheat and dairy products, rather than on the lure of new land and the 'original and indestructible powers of the soil'.

PROGRESS OF SETTLEMENT IN BRAZIL AND ARGENTINA

Unlike the English-speaking countries so far considered, Brazil and Argentina contained a good number of settlers as early as the sixteenth century, and had been extensively explored before the dawn of the nineteenth century. To some extent, these countries welcomed settlers. The plains of the Argentinian pampa, 250,000 square miles radiating in a semi-circle from Buenos Aires, are a farmer's and cattleman's paradise, with good soil, reasonable summer and winter temperatures, and

[1] Roberts, *op. cit.* p. 254.   [2] Shann, *op. cit.* p. 387.

adequate rainfall. Brazil, 'an empire in which the homeland and the colonies are housed under one geographic roof',[1] has the humid, tropical forest of Amazonia, the semi-arid cactus-infested scrubland of the Matto Grosso, but also the fine soil and climate of the tablelands reaching all the way from Bahia south to Rio Grande do Sul. This immense coastal area was conquered and after a fashion settled between 1550 and 1750, and all but the extreme northern, north-western and southern parts of the country were opened up, at least along the rivers, by farmers, missionaries, seekers after gold and 'bandeirantes'[2] in the first half of the eighteenth century. Some parts of the northern zone— the Amazon basin, extending almost to the foothills of the Andes— were fitfully penetrated by cattlemen from about 1750, while from the same period the south became, as it long remained, a quasi-militaristic region of stock-raising frontiersmen. Argentina likewise was, except for the most southerly parts of the country, completely if imperfectly known and to some degree settled before 1800. In a sense, therefore, comparatively little new land remained to be 'opened up' in these countries in the nineteenth century. But the actual settlement achieved up to that time was of a very scanty nature, often a few clearings in the wilderness, separated by miles of empty land, lying almost lost and out of touch with the rest of the world. Immense numbers of people were attracted into these countries in the second half of the nineteenth century. Immigration into Brazil, chiefly from Italy, Germany, Spain and Portugal, began on a really large scale in the later 1870's. Immigration into Argentina was free from the 1850's, and was on a very large scale from about 1870 or 1880. In the neighbourhood of five million immigrants arrived in these two countries in the second half of the nineteenth century, a far greater number than was absorbed by Canada and Australia in the same period. But this immigration did not result in an enormous expansion of settled territory. This was partly because most of the valuable land, despite some well-intended land laws, notably those passed in Argentina in 1824 and 1826, was engrossed as soon as available in the hands of a few individuals and corporations. The laws in Argentina were designed to encourage settlement and to delay or prevent the final alienation of public land. But politicians repeatedly used their power to seize land for themselves or to reward with land grants their friends and followers. Much of southern Argentina, opened to settlement by war against the Indians in 1879, was thus seized or given away. There were also large-scale land sales in the 1880's, a good part of them in Europe, by impecunious governments. Estates

[1] H. Herring, *A History of Latin America* (New York, 1955), p. 683.
[2] The *bandeirantes*, members of a *bandeira* or military company, were slave hunters whose raids did much to establish Portuguese authority in the uncharted 'backlands'.

of ten thousand acres were not uncommon in Latin America in the later nineteenth century. Also, immigrants to South America remained to an unusual degree in the already more densely settled regions. Before 1888, this was partly in order to avoid competing with slave labour in the Brazilian countryside. But it was also done in order to work in the commercial and industrial developments which were then going forward, as a rule, on or near the coast; 1885–1914 is sometimes described as the period when Brazilian industry was created, while the Argentinian boom of the 1880's—'prior to 1880 the modern Argentine can scarcely be said to have existed'[1]—depended on reckless borrowing in order to finance banks, railroads, and construction. On the other hand, many South American factories—creameries, freezing establishments, cotton mills—are entirely dependent on the local production of raw materials, so that industrial expansion on the coast is apt to have agricultural expansion up country as its direct corollary. For these reasons, a more intensive use of land appeared in Argentina and Brazil when these countries entered on their modern period of development; and this intensified use differed little in its problems and effects from simple extension.

The further development of South America required, in 1850, two conditions: political unification and improved means of transport. Both of these needs the second half of the century supplied. In Brazil, serious internal strife came to an end about 1850, and commercial activity at once began to grow. The first steamship service with Europe was established in 1850, the first line of steamships began to run on the Amazon in 1854, and the first railway line—only nine miles in length—was opened to traffic in the same year. Progress, however, was slow. In 1870 Brazil had a mere 470 miles of railway, and water, muleback and cart transportation remained so much the more common that it frequently took five months to travel from Matto Grosso to Rio de Janiero, a distance of 600 or 700 miles; by 1889, however, railroads had increased to over 6000 miles. The political conditions necessary for economic progress emerged more slowly in Argentina. The 'anarchical period' of her history ended only in 1868, when Sarmiento was elected to the Presidency; and it was eleven years later that an expedition led by the Minister for War totally destroyed the power of the frontier Indians in the south, who had been accustomed to raiding long distances northwards into the inhabited parts of the country. The land as far south as the Rio Negro was made safe, and millions of acres were opened for settlement. At the same time the central government, partly for politico-military reasons, pressed on with the construction

[1] J. H. Williams, *Argentine International Trade under Inconvertible Paper Money 1880–1900* (Cambridge, Mass., 1920), p. 27.

of roads and railways, so that when the political scene finally became favourable to economic development about 1880 (it deteriorated again after 1886), Argentina had some 1600 miles of railway line in service.

This development, however, in countries of such enormous area, albeit served also by water transport, was trifling. Great extensions of the railway had still to be made before the full possibilities of the inland areas could begin to be realized. The following table indicates the growth of lines under traffic:

Table 39. *Lengths of Railway Line (in miles)*

Argentina		Brazil	
1881	1,600	1880	2,100
1890	5,800	1890	6,100
1900	10,300	1900	9,500
1912	20,400	1910	13,400

These railways were easily and cheaply built, especially on the level, firm surface of the pampa. Their growth was partly cause, partly result of the novel possibility of exporting new commodities drawn primarily from the agricultural hinterland; it repeats yet again the story of the American, Canadian and Australian economies—but with marked differences. For these novel possibilities were various, and were opened to already old economies. In Argentina, efficient ranching had begun in 1844, when an Englishman ran a wire fence round his *estancia* and made possible the protection of crops, animal breeding, and, not least, the fixing of boundaries with a resultant rise in land values. But prior to 1880 agriculture (other than for subsistence) was largely confined to the western part of the province of Buenos Aires, the cost of transport in most other districts being prohibitive; as a result, Argentinian exports were chiefly made up of such items as wool, tallow, hides and horns, agricultural production was scarcely sufficient to meet the home demand, and in several years previous to 1880 wheat and flour had to be purchased abroad. In Brazil the situation appeared scarcely more promising. The working out of most gold deposits had led to the re-emergence of sugar-growing as the country's chief industry; but Brazilian sugar never dominated world markets in the nineteenth century as it had done in the seventeenth century. Tobacco production also faced severe international competition, and the revival of Brazil as a great cotton exporter during the American Civil War proved short-lived.

The more rapid period of development in modern Brazil began in connection with the expansion of the world market for coffee. First grown in Brazil in 1727, the coffee plant became acclimatized in the

Paraiba valley in the State of Rio de Janeiro, and thence spread through
the State into Minas Gerais (the old gold-mining region) and, above all,
São Paulo, the cool upland State where coffee began to be planted by
European immigrants in 1872. Great coffee plantations were built up
like the sugar plantations of earlier days, and as cultivation spread west
into the remoter woodlands, population in some of the older settled
parts of the State actually declined. By the last decade of the nineteenth
century, however, more than 60,000 coffee trees occupied over a
million hectares of land, while the spread of the industry in São Paulo
and Minas Gerais led to those areas becoming, for a time, the greatest
attractions to immigration. Brazil's share in the world production of
coffee, as well as the absolute volume of her production, increased continuously through the nineteenth century. By 1900 Brazil accounted
for over two-thirds of world coffee exports, and the Brazilian economy
came more and more to depend on this one product. In the early years
of the twentieth century high prices encouraged still more planting,
while new lines of railways traversed the uplands of São Paulo, Rio de
Janeiro and Minas Gerais, and immigrant workers supplied the needed
labour force. In 1906–7 prices collapsed. But meanwhile there had
occurred the spectacular rise of a market for Brazilian rubber. Rubber
was exported from Brazil in the 1820's, but forty years later the exportation was only about 3000 tons. From that point production rose rapidly,
and, as the following figures show, 1905–10 was the boom period:

Table 40

1877	9·22 m. kilograms
1887	13·93
1897	21·26
1907	38·9
1910	39·2
1922	19·2

The rise of this industry, therefore, partly diverted attention from the
coffee lands to the Amazon basin, a vast region of tropical jungle, which
even in 1940 boasted only 1200 miles of railway and 3400 motor
vehicles. Into this region a veritable rush took place at the beginning
of the twentieth century, and Manáus emerged as the 'rubber capital',
1000 miles up river and the sole town of any consequence in the region.
Rubber, like gold and timber, was a 'free gift of nature', and the cultivation of coffee, cotton, tobacco and other crops was neglected as
'pioneers' and seasonal expeditions financed in London, and manned
largely by Indians who were in effect enslaved by the rubber merchants,
pushed up the Amazon to gather the liquid gum from wild trees

already matured. There was an unusual migration from the north-east to Amazonia, and some of the immigrants remained; the population of Amazonas, Goiãz and Matto Grosso increased by 300 per cent between 1872 and 1920 (while the population of Brazil as a whole increased by 200 per cent) and food supply for the increased population had, for a time, to be brought from the south. But the day of Brazilian rubber was a brief one. In 1910 world rubber prices began to fall, and between 1912 and 1916 the highly capitalized rubber plantations of the Orient overtook Brazil in volume of production. The Amazon valley slipped back into the position of a region really beyond the economic frontier, and the wealth of Brazil came to be more instead of less concentrated in the agricultural states of São Paulo, Minas Gerais and Rio Grande do Sul.

In the Agentine, development depended more simply upon improved communications. Until 1904, wool formed the chief Argentinian export, thereafter exceeded by wheat or corn. The pampa, flat grassy plains, comparatively treeless, sloping gradually from the Andes to near the Atlantic coast, were long used for agricultural and pastoral purposes, but before the growth of railways it was impossible to market any but a tiny fraction of the produce of which this region was capable. But in the 1880's, when the railway building boom was under way, the production and exportation of wool, and in the 1890's that of wheat, rocketed upwards, extension of cultivation being especially noticeable in 'the great dry, windy plains of Patagonia';[1] on the pampa the railroads 'made the land easily accessible to immigrant settlers; the line of wheat culture advanced with the railroad and the immigrant farmer; and before them the sheep-raiser retired west and north, and to the southern part of the province of Buenos Aires'.[2] Meat exports began in 1876–7, and this trade too was established by the middle of the 1890's; this definitely put an end to the practice of killing the animals for their hides alone, increased the profitability of the cattle industry, encouraged farmers to import Lincolns and shorthorns and to breed for meat, and promoted the further extension of the industry. Thus the use of land in South America was improved out of all recognition by the opening up of new or enlarged markets (chiefly in Europe), by developments (mostly initiated elsewhere) in refrigeration and ocean transport, by improvements in South American flocks and herds, and, above all, by the construction of over 30,000 miles of railway in thirty years with the use of borrowed capital. As a result of these innovations, South American land values were, over thousands of square miles, raised for the first time from on or about zero.

[1] Williams, op. cit. p. 213.   [2] Ibid. pp. 226–7.

VI. *The Pioneers*

Of all the questions raised by the history of the first settlement of new lands, none is more difficult to answer with a fair degree of precision, and few are more interesting, than the problem as to the economic background and the motives of the pioneers. How unused was the average pioneer to the rigours and demands of a frontier life? How far was pioneering a means of escape for the urban wage earner? What were the economic motives, and were the economic motives the motives of major significance, which prompted men to travel into virgin territory and try to make a home there?

In trying to find an answer to these and similar questions, the one indisputable fact which must never be forgotten is that frontier life in every part of the world was hard and meagre, the standard of living low, the pioneer poor. No evidence casts doubt on the truth of this, and no sentiment should be permitted to obscure it. In every one of the great variety of types of frontier life the pioneer was poor; how poor, it is not always easy to realize.

The best known frontier, and that which drew to it the greatest number of pioneers, was on the American prairie—'The vast measureless prairie with nothing but unending grass, green in the spring, seared and brown in the early autumn, and burnt and black in winter. There were no trees, no rocks, not even a skyline, only the shimmering waves of blistering heat rising from the tropical prairie.'[1] Amid this setting the true pioneer lived in a sod-house or dugout—a room dug in the side of a hill or ravine, with a door and possibly a window, and a roof comprising brush-wood, prairie grass, and earth; the whole liable to cave in and bury the inhabitants after a heavy rain. Bedsteads were a rarity; a pioneer wrote in 1856; 'Sleeping on the ground is not confined to camping out but is extensively practised in all our cabins. Floors are a luxury rarely seen here. In our own dwelling part of the inmates rest on the earth while others sleep on sacking over our heads....I noticed yesterday a member of our family making up his bed with a hoe....'[2] The type of life is also indicated by Horace Greeley's description of a road ranch which he visited in Kansas, which was

a cabin some six by eight feet, and perhaps from 3 to 5 and a half feet high— large enough to contain two whisky barrels, two decanters, several glasses, three or four cans of pickled oysters and two or three boxes of sardines but

[1] Dick, *The Sod-House Frontier*, p. 233.
[2] Dick, *op. cit.* p. 243. This book contains excellent photographs of the primitive dwellings occupied by some American pioneers.

nothing of the bread kind whatever. The hotel-keeper probably understood his business better than we did, and had declined to dissipate his evidently moderate capital by investing any part of it in articles not of prime necessity.[1]

As for the frontier 'towns', they were notorious; insanitary and lawless. A Nebraska newspaper remarked at the end of the 1870's; 'During the past winter the report of guns and revolvers, and the whizzing of bullets sent on foolish errands became so common in the town that no-one thought of protesting against it',[2] while it is said that 'the gambler's cry of "keno" was the last thing heard at night and the first thing heard on waking in the morning'.[3] It was a hard world which gave birth to the saying 'plains travel and frontier life are peculiarly severe upon women and oxen'.

On the other side of the world, in Australia, shepherds and hut-keepers lived in comparable or even worse conditions. A traveller along the Lower Murrumbidgee in the late 1840's wrote: 'You can seldom lift a piece of food to your mouth without one hand driving away flies to make room for it. Anything like gravy in your plate is a sort of fly-trap. . . . Fleas are as abundant as may be expected from floors of dust and so many dogs about, cats, and parrots, and the thermometer indoors usually from 90° to 100°.'[4] This station employment was doubtless, in early days 'primarily a backwater of the tragic stream of transportation',[5] but the soul-destroying monotony of 'sheep-farming' affected others besides those sent to Australia for trying to live without working.

How long such primitive conditions had to be endured depended on a variety of factors—numbers of new immigrants, behaviour of market prices, appearance of a railroad, and so forth—most of which were outside the pioneer's control. One important consideration, however, was whether much clearing of land had to be undertaken. In this res-pect, the settler on prairie land was fortunate; oats and potatoes in Canada, for example, would yield well in the first year, while large quantities of wheat and oats might be sold off the farm in the third year of cropping.

On the prairie the homesteader of the previous summer might have 20 or 40 acres of land in crop. In addition, he might have some flax on spring 'breaking' i.e., land plowed for the first time. In addition to feed for his stock it was possible for him to have wheat and flax to sell for much needed cash. If luck was with him, and he believed it would be, he might harvest 30 or more bushels of wheat to the acre, and have as much as 600 bushels for sale.[6]

---

[1] Horace Greeley, *An Outward Journey from New York to San Francisco*, p. 74.
[2] Quoted in Dick, *op. cit.* p. 392.   [3] *Ibid.* p. 393.
[4] Quoted in Shann, *An Economic History of Australia*, p. 113.
[5] *Ibid.* p. 116.   [6] Mackintosh, *op. cit.* I, 136-7.

But to the settler in wooded country the real cost of settlement was the time which was required to clear the land. (Unless, of course, he had capital and could pay for clearance. But this was very costly. In Victoria in the 1870's land which sold for £1 an acre cost £4 an acre to clear.) In the Australian mallee, the method of clearance was to crush the scrub with heavy rollers, drawn by bullock teams, and then to burn it. In the autumn a wheat crop could be drilled, which— even if the 'burn' had been skilfully done—came up with innumerable suckers from the mallee roots. After four or more years of recurrent burning, aided by the damage done to the root systems by cultivating machinery, the ground became 'fairly clear' of shoots. 'During these years, when good cultivation was impossible, the crops were usually poor, wear and tear on machinery was particularly high, and stock could not be carried.'[1] In the wet sclerophyll forest, a rough pasture could more quickly be produced (once the arduous task of felling and ringing was completed) but life was made unpleasant and profit uncertain by the dingoes, eagles, poisonous snakes, gnats, mosquitoes and scorpions. But whatever the type of environment, hard physical toil with—certainly in the early years—a meagre return was the lot of the pioneer. Many an early settler survived only by working as a wage earner from time to time 'back home', on the railroad, or per- haps on a neighbour's farm.

If, then, back-breaking toil as farmer, lumberman or miner was the only immediate and certain return to pioneering, why were so many found who would willingly undertake it? The answer to this is three- fold: in brief, most pioneers left behind them a fairly low standard of living, most were accustomed to farming or similar pursuits, and the lure of the frontier can never be understood in terms of average economic achievement.

As a rule, those who farmed on or near the frontier had farmed somewhere else beforehand. Pioneering—true pioneering on a lonely frontier—was a specialized occupation. In America it was carried out chiefly by native-born Americans having the benefit of years—and behind them perhaps of generations—of frontier experience. Special- ized knowledge was also important even behind the primitive frontier. When the Canadian west was being opened up rapidly about 1900, American settlers were especially welcome as bringing with them not only suitable capital equipment but also appropriate experience of similar agricultural conditions in the United States. It was often remar- ked that immigrants took years to acquire the necessary knowledge. Of the British immigrant especially it was observed that, although proving himself 'on occasion an adventurous and successful pioneer,

[1] Wadham and Wood, *Land Utilization in Australia*, p. 61.

yet his invincible desire for a constantly increasing standard of comfort rather tends to diminish his chances of success in continuous cultivation on the frontier. He tends to come in or to drift into the town. The Continental emigrant has as a rule retained the capacity of producing everything that he requires for his own maintenance.'[1] In other words, it was the experienced settler, and the peasant farmer from Europe— Scandinavian, Swiss, Russo-German Mennonite—who was chiefly to be relied upon to establish more intensive settlement on a secondary frontier.

Secondly, the connection between immigration and pioneer settlement was at best a vague one. Some immigrants did, it is true, pass straight from their old homes in Europe to newly rising western States; but along with them came a large admixture of Americans from 'down the road'. Much westward expansion was the end phenomenon of a long succession of short moves. Thus of 2115 persons who purchased land in a part of south-eastern Nebraska in 1873, no less than 944 came from Nebraska itself or from the neighbouring States of Iowa, Missouri and Kansas in that order; roughly speaking, the farther distant the State, the fewer persons it sent—in this instance all of New England sent only 24. The same phenomenon appeared in Kansas in the 1870's and 1880's, while in 1900 Texas, then the State with the largest number of Americans not locally born, drew most of its immigrants from Arkansas and Louisiana. Likewise the Canadian west, in 1899, attracted 41,927 new settlers, of whom 11,724 came from eastern Canada, 9839 from the United States, the remainder from Europe. Imperfect as the statistics are, there can be no question that the opening up of truly virgin country was largely and perhaps preponderantly the work of men who were not newcomers to the country, although in the task of closer settlement foreign immigrants undoubtedly played a large part in this sense. (In the case of Australia, where pioneering tended to be a less highly skilled occupation, newcomers seem to have played a larger role.)

That these conclusions are justified seems the more likely when the probable motives and habits of mind of the pioneers are considered. Leaving aside the convicts, there were three types of consideration (barring the possibility—indeed the likelihood—of extreme poverty at home) which drew or drove the pioneer to the frontier. First of all, there was the speculative motive. Probably few pioneers remained settled upon the farm where they first located; they broke the soil, harvested a few crops, sold out at a profit and moved on. Partly, no doubt, this was no more than a customary and agreeable way of life; the tradition of moving was strong in the American mid-west in the

[1] Quoted Innis, *An Economic History of Canada*, pp. 241-2.

nineteenth century. But partly it was the result of economic calculation, for *some* lots, *somewhere*, were bound to rise steeply in value in a
few years. Hence the American passion in the middle decades of the
nineteenth century for town building; the 'great occupation of the few
citizens of Kansas and Nebraska' in the decades before and after the
Civil War was town-building—on paper. Towns brilliantly described and well illustrated,[1] which existed solely on paper, sold well
farther east, they also drew men to the west and in some cases even
ended by coming into existence. A good deal of money changed hands
as a result of this activity, and it would be gratuitous to suppose that
'genuine' settlers never had any part in it. For agriculture was itself
liable—as has already been remarked—to degenerate into a speculation. If the price of wheat is high and, in the Great Plains area, 'there
is adequate moisture and an abundant crop, the farmer will be able to
pay for his land and machinery in a single season. Farmers have actually
done this';[2] but the odds against success are overwhelming, although
they are seldom realistically considered.

Furthermore, some economic calculation which was not in the least
speculative was likely to result in movement. For the west was the
region of low costs, and as it was opened up farmers working on stony
and perhaps partly exhausted soil in Vermont, or even in good but
not as good conditions in the old North-west were liable to find prices
become unremunerative, and be faced with the choice of moving into
the town to work for wages or of moving west; many chose the latter
course, although making, perhaps, several steps between their old farm
and the true frontier. This threat to established security was at the back
of many decisions to preserve a type of occupation even at the cost of
movement across half a continent: 'Numbers of Ontario farmers seem
to be so wedded to wheat-raising, that rather than go extensively into
stock raising and fattening and the growth of various rotation crops
they prefer to sell out and go to Manitoba and the North-west, a
territory which is *par excellence* a wheat country.'[3]

Lastly, it is probably too easy to underrate the non-economic factors
which helped push back the boundaries of cultivation. The mere notion
of free land made a powerful appeal, especially to the peasant populations of Europe, while even some farmers 'well fixed in Iowa' moved
west because 'It seems a pity to waste all my rights.' Free land may
well turn out, when a man has it, to be one of the greatest of economic
disappointments; but there is no doubt of its appeal. In other cases,

[1] The illustrations in Dick, *The Sod-House Frontier*.
[2] C. W. Thornthwaite, *Migration and Economic Opportunity*, p. 235. The economic
feat referred to was probably accomplished in 1920.
[3] *Canadian Select Documents, 1783–1885*, H. A. Innis (ed.) (Toronto, 1933), p. 762.

groups of settlers moved into the wilderness because of discontent or frustration at home. And the Roman Catholic Church in Canada continues to press parishes of settlement into the backwoods of Quebec, spurred on by considerations which are certainly not predominantly economic: 'Conservons par tous les moyens possibles cette race qui sait encore se priver et souffrir sans révolter...[familles] pas riche [sic], mais plus heureuses et plus riches que certains ouvriers sans travail, des grands villes et les villages industriels sans industrie.'[1]

In short, few men set out to undergo the hardships of the frontier unless they hoped for quick gains, were already inured to heavy manual work and to a low standard of living, or saw on or near the frontier the only possibility of continuing their familiar way of life. Yet the 'few' which these generalizations account for were a formidable host. The towns and railroads which served the ever-moving and expanding frontier were built by men who came west with or without capital, as workmen, storekeepers, itinerant pedlars of the old European tradition, anything and nothing. Specialist businesses were started with no knowledge whatever, and the story told by a banker in one of the States east of the Missouri, when asked how he 'got started' in banking, is at least worth preserving:

Well, I didn't have much else to do and so I rented an empty store building and painted 'bank' on the window. The first day I was open for business a man came in and deposited one hundred dollars. The second day another deposited two hundred-fifty dollars, and so along about the third day I got confidence enough in the bank to put in a hundred myself.[2]

By such casual means, and often by such strangely functioning economic motives, the economy of the western world in the nineteenth century was shaken but preserved.

VII.   *Settlement and the Law*

The process of settlement outlined in this chapter was not an unregulated one; governments, indeed, sought to influence and even to control the manner and the rate of the opening up of new land, and it would be surprising, even in an age supposed to be devoted to *laissez faire*, had they not done so. It is, however, extremely difficult to give a brief and yet comprehensible account of the legislation which came into existence to deal with the problem, for it is scarcely an exaggeration

---

[1] A. R. M. Lower, *Settlement and the Forest Frontier in Eastern Canada* (Toronto, 1936), p. 89.
[2] Quoted in Dick, *op. cit.* p. 90.

to say that every conceivable form of land law was enacted in one country or another in the course of the nineteenth century, with results almost as hard to assess as the laws are, in some cases, hard to understand. Whether this quick march of land legislation across the various statute books was the result of ambiguity of intention, uncertainty as to the best means to secure well understood aims, the continual need to adapt legislation to changing circumstances, or a varying combination of all these three, is another question to which no easy answer can be returned.

The most important nineteenth-century land laws were those of the United States of America. Prior to 1816, most settlers in the west took up State land which at that time sold more cheaply than the public domain. But as the supply of good State land diminished while the number of settlers increased, the law concerning the disposal of the public domain assumed an increasing and very soon a dominating importance. It was early realized that there were two broad alternatives; if the aim was to be the encouragement of rapid settlement of the country, then it seemed likely that the more cheaply and easily land was disposed of the better the results would be; if, on the other hand, a good revenue was to be realized from the disposal of this great asset, a much higher selling price was indicated. In the early decades of the nineteenth century laws were passed which tended to make it progressively easier to acquire land: in 1800 the minimum unit was 320 acres and the minimum auction price per acre $2 (with, however, four years to pay); in 1804 this became 160 acres and $2; in 1820 80 acres and $1.25; in 1832 40 acres and $1.25. In other words, by 1832 it was possible to buy a farm for $50, though the terms had hardened to cash down. Thus the policy of facilitating settlement was gaining ground; it was, naturally, supported by the poorer sections of the population and by the west, and opposed by the commercial and industrial interests in the east—whose opposition diminished, however, as the receipts from customs duties (that most popular of all forms of taxation) began to grow. The choice of policy, unfortunately, very soon became a matter of prime political importance, and only after the secession of the Southern States was the opposition to the policy of the west—namely that land should be altogether free—finally overcome. The result was the passage of the Homestead Act of 1862, customarily eulogized as one of the greatest democratic pieces of legislation of all time. Under this law, citizens or intended citizens could obtain for a nominal fee a tract of 160 acres after they had improved it and resided upon it for five years. A commutation clause permitted the exercise of pre-emption rights to obtain title after six months' residence on payment of $1.25 an acre: this clause was in consonance with a series of preceding pre-emption Acts— important from 1830—which gave most settlers who had pressed beyond the limits of surveyed land the right of first option at $1.25 an acre, provided that they had effected an improvement.

It was with this promising and simple piece of legislation, enacted on the principle of free land in exchange for permanent settlement, that the United States entered the period of most rapid expansion. Within a few years, other Acts were passed to speed the disposal of the public domain. In 1866 mineral lands were thrown open to free occupation, although within a decade much of the land concerned was classified and kept for sale at prices ranging from $1.25 to $20 an acre. In 1873 the Timber Culture Act promised 160 acres to anyone eligible for a homestead, who maintained a stand of 40 acres of timber; in 1878 the necessary wooded area was reduced to 10 acres. Also in 1878 came the Timber Cutting Act and Stone Act. Little was left undone, it seemed, by which 'our democratic theory of equality would be put in practice, [and] closely associated communities could be established...'[1] all over the West.

Difficulties at once arose, however, first of all from the side of government legislation itself. For the Homestead Act never applied to all the public domain. The same Congressional session which approved the Homestead Act also approved the Morrill Act, which gave to each State for educational purposes 30,000 acres of land for each Senator and Representative then in Congress; this land was to be sold for what it would fetch. Under this law, over 200 million acres had been disposed of by 1930. Secondly, the policy of subsidizing railway construction by land grant was continued until 1871, 131 million acres (after forfeiture is allowed for) being given away in this manner, the land lying, as a rule, from six to sixteen miles on either side of the railroad track; in addition, the railroads received 49 million acres from the States. Much of the land obtained by treaty with the Indians was also sold rather than reserved for free occupation. In this way enormous stretches of land—and some of these the best—were removed from the operation of the Homestead Act.

In the second place, the Homestead Act came into operation just as settlement began to move into the semi-arid lands west of the 98th meridian. To give a man on these 'uplands of survival' a holding limited—at any rate in theory—to 160 acres was to invite him to destruction. The Homestead Act was technically well adapted to the east, of which Congressmen had some knowledge; but in the west—of which as a rule they had almost none—where a scanty rainfall moistens the soil only a few inches, survival can only be by means of irrigation, dry farming, or grazing. Irrigation plans were costly, and required a

[1] Quoted in L. H. Hacker, *The Triumph of American Capitalism* (New York, 1946), p. 368.

change in the methods of land survey in order to take into account the possible means of water supply; dry farming required, as experience was to show, a holding of nearer 1000 than 160 acres; while the most desirable subdivision for grazing varies from about 2500 to 4000 acres— a great area, yet economically no more than the equivalent of the 160-acre homestead in humid or irrigated areas. (The better watered valleys could, of course, be more intensively cultivated.) Thus the Homestead Act clashed with the technico-economic requirements of the area into which, as luck would have it, settlement was then reaching, and not until the Desert Land Act of 1877, permitting the purchase in certain circumstances of 640 acres at $1.25 an acre, was the law adapted to prairie needs.

Lastly, the Act was not difficult to evade. To some extent evasion was justified where the Act threatened to make holdings uneconomically small. But the commutation clause permitted speculators to acquire large holdings by means of entry under several names or through several persons, while small speculators also obtained land after a brief residence and without having effected any genuine improvements at all.[1] Criticism alleged that

Of all the motley crowd that helped themselves to public land during the boom of the 80s not one in three had the slightest intention of remaining upon it; not one in five remained more than long enough to prove up and sell out or 'mortgage out'; and not one in ten has left a permanent mark upon the landscape of Kansas, Nebraska or Dakota.[2]

In the semi-arid areas, moreover, a skilful location might enable the settler to control the water supply over a large area, and this led easily to the engrossing of large tracts of grazing land. And lastly, the administration of the law was never better than lax while corruption was by no means a rarity, so that even where legal provision was adequate the real intentions of the law would frequently not be realized.

That the Homestead Act was a partial failure is undeniable; Congress itself, to some extent, saw to that. Up to 1906 just under 100 million acres of land had been taken up under the Homestead Act and other Acts permitting free acquisition; but approximately 350 million acres, probably more, had been acquired or were available by purchase. Not all of the land sold for homesteads was used for that purpose, and the system also tended to make the fortunes of some individuals when land suitable for lumbering, mining or oil-well drilling was alienated on terms as easy as if that land had had no differential advantages. At

[1] See Dick, *op. cit.*, on the nature of the so-called 'improvements' which were often effected.
[2] Quoted in Wright, *Economic History of the United States*, p. 468.

the same time, an Act which permitted almost 100 million acres to be
acquired free in less than half a century, plus another 147 million acres
in the years 1906–40 inclusive, with the presumption that at any rate much
of this land went directly to the small settler, was a significant piece of
legislation, even though the aforesaid small settler very often found
that the choice which faced him when he reached the west was to buy
from a speculator, a railroad company, or a State, or else to go farther
afield into the less desirable areas. That the Act was a tremendous
stimulus to westward expansion and to European emigration and thus,
indirectly, to the growth of the wealth of the American nation there
cannot, of course, be the slightest doubt. It is to the statistical historian,
coolly calculating probabilities when all the facts are known, that the
land policy of the United States seems careless, contradictory and
misleading.

   In Canada, legislation was faced with two different problems—the
problem of settlement on the prairie, and of settlement in the timber
lands in the east. The former was met along lines little different from the
American practice; Canada, indeed, modelled her regulations fairly
closely on those of the 'competing' United States. With regard to the
timber lands, however, novel and interesting problems were involved.
The essential need was for the classification of land, in order both to
prevent settlement on uninhabitable land and to reserve for sale (and
therefore revenue) the timber assets of the eastern provinces. The land
policies of Ontario, Quebec and New Brunswick were, in general,
closely similar. No land was alienated for purposes other than settlement (the Canadian timber licence system, a legacy from the eighteenth
century, always allowed the sale of timber without the sale of the land
on which it stood), and improvements were required before the issue
of a patent. In Quebec, lands were sold, though for merely nominal
sums; in Ontario, the tendency was to sell the best land and to give
away the less attractive.

   The difficulty was to keep settlers off the timber lands. Sometimes
well-meaning attempts were made to cultivate these lands. This was
especially the case in Quebec, where, under the aegis of the Roman
Catholic Church, persistent attempts were made in all areas to extend
the territory settled by the French Canadian 'race'; the Canadian
Forestry Association reported in 1901 that cultivation in Pontiac
County, Quebec, was yielding a return of $4,036,773, whereas these
lands under good forestry management would have yielded permanently 2500 feet of merchantable timber per acre, which, turned
into pulpwood and thence paper, would have returned over $33
million. More frequently, timber land was 'settled' for less innocent
purposes. To begin with, the settler was free to locate on any surveyed

land he chose, and thus—especially before Confederation—the lumberman might reach the land on which he had a licence to cut

only to find that some 'pioneer' had 'bought' the lot which included his best
stand of pine, his camps, or his right of way to the water. 'Buying' meant
paying the first of several annual instalments. It can easily be imagined how
many more would be paid once the purchaser had cut off the merchantable
timber from rough and rocky land.[1]

It was largely the activity of these 'bogus settlers', whose 'farms' were
merely lumber camps under another name, which produced the great
discrepancy in eastern Canada between the amount of land alienated
and the amount of land actually improved.

The twin ideas of forest conservation and of the classification of land
made slow progress in Canada.[2] The concept of permanent forest
reserves was first put forward in Quebec in 1868, and in 1875 Quebec
passed the first forest reserve Act, but it was never effective, because
public opinion and the colonization societies would not accept the idea
that vast tracts of land should be withheld from 'the people', and
prevented the carrying out of its proposals. The offending Act was
repealed in 1888.

For some years the policy continued to be mainly one of expediency.
If settlers were insistent, lands were conceded. After all, there were many
settlers, and they had votes; the lumbermen, on the other hand, though
fewer, seem to have had little difficulty in securing land at prices which
gave the public treasury only a very small share in the gains which were
to be made from the sale of the timber. In 1893, however, Ontario
succeeded in setting aside the Algoncuin Park area, and about the same
time even 'practical men' became convinced of the fact that self-
regeneration of the forest was not a myth. This was of great importance,
for until the idea of the reproduction of pine was accepted, the 'universal point of view' was that the forest was merely a transitory
phenomenon and that the sensible thing to do was to get rid of it (on
behalf of the public, if possible) and encourage the settler in forwarding
the permanent business of the country—namely, agriculture. But once
the possible permanency of the forest was accepted, the motive to
conservation and classification was greatly strengthened. At about the
same time, unfortunately, the growth of the pulp and paper industry
stimulated the activities of bogus settlers, for small trees formerly
worthless began to command a good price. In 1904 an Act providing for the classification of all land before alienation, and retaining

[1] Lower, *Canadian Frontiers*, p. 63.
[2] In America they made no progress at all in the period in which it would really
have mattered.

permanently in the hands of the Crown all non-agricultural land, was passed in order to strengthen the policy of orderly and economical development. Figures available for Quebec, however, do not suggest that much success was achieved. Between about 1870 and the early 1920's, approximately 6·8 million acres of land were sold but only 2·3 million acres were added to the 'improved' area; 'Is it not a reasonable deduction that about two-thirds, or say, to be on the safe side, from 50 to 60 per cent of the Crown Lands alienated in these fifty years, have been alienated needlessly and that they have been probably [mainly?] sought for purposes other than settlement, mainly, that is, for the exploitation of their timber resources?'[1] Nevertheless, the almost total destruction of the forest is not the reality in Canada that it is in the United States, while the growth of land under cultivation in the prairie provinces, from less than 300,000 acres in 1881 to over 5·5 million acres in 1901, indicates a rate of growth of the economy with which any government, surely, could rest satisfied.

In Australia, the problem of settlement had peculiarities of its own, and the history of Australian land legislation is extraordinarily complex. In part, this is due to the fact that the transportation of convicts to New South Wales did not end until 1840, to Van Diemen's Land until 1853, and to Western Australia until 1867; it is also due to the fact that the different States—except in the years 1842–52—were free to enjoy considerable idiosyncracies in their land legislation, so that generalizations about 'Australian land policy' are almost bound to be meaningless. In these circumstances, it is possible to mention only three aspects of Australian policy: the influence of Wakefieldism; the squatting problem; and the important and long-lived land laws of the third quarter of the nineteenth century.

To Edward Gibbon Wakefield there must at least go the credit of giving systematic and original thought to a serious contemporary problem. In Van Diemen's Land, in the 1830's, less than 4 per cent of the alienated land was under cultivation, in New South Wales there was not even a survey of the whole of the 'nineteen Counties', and no attempt had been made to prevent aggregation. All told, the Australian colonies had attracted 10,498 emigrants by 1830. The consequence was, that settlers in Australia had millions of acres of land and could do nothing with them. Australia had work and no labourers; England had labourers and no work. Wakefield's idea was to bring systematic theory into colonial administration, and at the same time to relieve home distress by emigration. Primarily, it is true, Wakefield was a proponent of migration; but he also greatly influenced land policies, for his master-idea was to tie the price of land to the rate of immigration

[1] Lower, *op. cit.* p. 67.

and of investment; to secure, that is, 'a proper proportion' between the three factors of production—land, labour and capital. The trouble, according to Wakefield, was that if land were cheap or free there would be no labourers, for no one would work for a wage if he could achieve independence. Therefore, land should be sold at a 'sufficient price', a price, that is to say, just high enough to keep available a labour force, and yet not so high as to frighten off capitalists or to condemn the labourer to permanent wage-earning; the money received in this way was to foster immigration.[1] The theoretical beauty of the scheme was its 'automatic' nature: 'If there were more sales, more labour would be needed, and there would be a revenue to bring in this labour. On the other hand, if land sales were reduced, not so much fresh labour would be needed, but, since emigration was dependent on the land-fund, none would come.'[2] In practice, this bristled with difficulties. What *was* a sufficient price? And if a price were fixed sufficient to finance needed immigration, how (except by an accident) would this price also be right to attract capitalists, and, in due course, permit the labourer to become a landowner? Nevertheless, the theory attained great popularity; attempts were made to put it into operation in Western and South Australia, and as a result of it the need came to be accepted for some price at any rate higher than had previously ruled in Australian colonies. But the short-term results were uniformly disappointing. At Australind, a hundred miles south of the Swan river, land was sold at £1 an acre. There was an ample labour force at Australind by 1842—'combinable labour and landless proletariat after the best English model'[3]—but nothing happened, for the excellent reason that the value of the land, having regard to its fertility, distance from markets, etc., was nearer 2s. per acre than 20s.; earlier buyers, it was said, were willing to cut their losses and sell at a farthing an acre. In Victoria in 1839, faced with the opposite situation of a land boom—'On the wings of hope the reckless soared into the inane'[4]—the government tried raising the price of land from 5s. to 12s. This amounted to advancing the paper value of land by 140 per cent in a day. The result was a violent increase in the speculative fever. Lots that had been sold in 1837 were fetching up to eighty times their purchase price by 1839, and the Governor declared that around Melbourne the country was 'strewn for miles, almost hundreds of miles, with champagne bottles'. In 1840 the colony was racked by drought and panic, but the remedy of the Colonial Land and Emigration Commissioners was to raise the price of land from 12s. to £1, 'because in South Australia it has been found to answer well'. This was at best a doubtful statement, and the

---

[1] And in some later versions of the theory, to aid development in other ways.
[2] Roberts, *op. cit.* p. 80.   [3] Shann, *op. cit.* p. 141.   [4] *Ibid.* p. 104.

result in Victoria, not surprisingly, was 'an indisposition on the part of the public' to purchase land: only £370,000 worth of land was sold between 1839 and 1851 and labour was always seriously deficient.

The problem which Wakefieldism *completely* failed to deal with, however, was the essential Australian problem of these decades; that of the squatter. Nor was Wakefield alone in this: British and Australian politicians failed to understand the nature of squatting just as American Congressmen a decade or two later failed to understand the nature of the arid lands. The quiet in land matters which set in about 1850 and lasted for a decade was due chiefly to the temporary solving of this problem. Throughout the 1830's the search for pastoral country was taking flocks and herds in some untidy way into areas unsurveyed and sometimes almost unregulated, and the decision of 1842 to sell no land for less than £1 an acre was simply irrelevant to this movement. The aspiration of good Wakefieldians and the Colonial Office to restrain squatting—a 'systematic violation of the law'—was neither wise nor possible; the squatters could not be restrained, and even if they could, to do so would be a 'perverse rejection of the bounty of Providence', for 'the prosperity of the colony would be at an end'.[1] In New South Wales, where squatting was most prominent, its existence was recognized and legalized in 1836, but what the squatters sought was more than free tenancy from the Crown—they wanted security of tenure, a pre-emptive right, and compensation for improvements. The cautious regulations of 1844—'farsighted and just'—provided that the squatter's holding should be limited to 20 square miles, that he should be required to purchase 320 acres at the end of five years' occupation, and an additional 320 acres at the end of every eight years, and, if he would not buy, that any other purchaser would obtain the land by paying the retiring holder the value of the improvements. This plan aroused such bitter opposition that in 1847 Orders in Council instituted a system of leases of—in the area that mattered—eight to fourteen years, with a pre-emptive right. This gave the squatters all that they wanted—in effect, a firm hold on the land.

This era of squatter supremacy, with the squatters forming 'a class of privileged occupants', lasted in New South Wales until 1861, by which time the gold discoveries and the spread of cultivation had radically changed the Australian economy. In that year it became legal within certain areas to make free selection of holdings from 40 to 320 acres,[2] the price being 5s. an acre with three years to complete the purchase. This was Australia's most notable experiment in land policy, remaining substantially unaltered until 1884, and under its

---

[1] Sir George Gipps, quoted in Roberts, *op. cit.* p. 180.
[2] The limit was raised to 640 acres in 1875.

operation the most fertile agricultural lands in all the colonies were alienated. The operation of the Acts was unsatisfactory, chiefly because of fraudulent selection by 'dummies'. The topography of the country also made 'peacocking' easy, that is, selection of certain usually small areas of particular advantage (usually with watering facilities) without which much surrounding country was of little use; in one case, a pastoralist 'by scattering forty acre lots along the river frontage and by obtaining 27,000 acres, rendered the whole area of ten times that amount useless to anybody else'.[1] Thus the squatters fought the true home-steaders, and very often won. Sometimes, on the other hand, the Acts lured cultivators into areas into which they should never have gone; round Deniliquin in the Riverina only 244 selectors remained in 1882 out of 1426 who had applied for land after 1865.

That this legislation produced speedy alienation of the public lands is not to be denied. Between 1862 and 1883 almost 15·5 million acres of Crown lands were alienated by conditional purchase in New South Wales, more than twice the area alienated in all ways prior to 1862; so fast had alienation proceeded, indeed, that the original selections 'lay overlapping like a pack of cards thrown on a table'.[2] Yet in these years the area under crop increased by only 329,545 acres. What had become of the 129,571 selectors? A royal commission reported in 1883 that there appeared to be only 62,000 'residential selections', while selectors 'actually resident' probably numbered fewer than 20,000; and of these resident selectors one half were 'dummies', selecting for pastoral interests or in order to enlarge their own runs, one quarter were 'poor in money, education and intelligence, unable to compete in the ordinary occupations of life', and only one twentieth were men of the required capital and skill. Such were the results in New South Wales of 'unlocking the land to free selection' before survey. In Victoria, on the other hand, selection after survey was for long the rule; and when, in 1865, an Act was passed which gave the selector at first only a lease, convertible into freehold on easy terms *after three years of residence and the making of substantial improvements*, perhaps the most successful important land law of the nineteenth century came into operation. Up to 1869 three million acres were taken up under the Act, and when free selection before survey but with similar safeguards became the law in 1871, another eleven million acres were selected. Between 1861 and 1880 the cultivated area in Victoria grew from 410,000 acres to over 1·5 million acres, and although wheat growing led to soil exhaustion and hence 'nomadism' by the middle 1880's, the Victorian history was on the whole much happier than most.

The opening up of new lands helped to give the nineteenth century

[1] Roberts, *op. cit.* p. 227.   [2] *Ibid.* p. 231.

an economic background—consequently an economy—which was historically unique. The accelerated growth of European population from about 1750, which was the result of developments mainly within Europe itself, favoured territorial expansion, while the demands arising from the industrialization of Europe added to the need for more food the need for more of all sorts of primary products. The terms of exchange between industry and primary production moved in favour of the latter, and an expansion which would in any case have taken place was enormously encouraged.

The economic consequences of the movement can scarcely be exaggerated, and are, in a general way, obvious enough. It is much easier to overlook the economic problems raised by the process itself, unfamiliar problems with which nineteenth-century governments attempted to grapple. The task of government in this connection was not (except occasionally in the very early stages) to achieve territorial expansion—that, indeed, could not be prevented, so eager was the colonist in 'pursuing his own interest'—but to promote economical expansion; that is to say, to guide and assist the economy towards establishing that manner and rate of expansion which would maximize the utility of these new resources to the community through the present and the whole of the future. This could be and often was presented in an approximate fashion as a problem of justice as between present and succeeding generations. More often, settlement was viewed as a matter of political power: 'The settlement and opening up of our vacant lands and the consequent increase of our population constitutes our chief aim. All our energies are directed to that end, for from it comes the political influence which we now have and which we are to possess in the future.'[1] But the specifically economic problem emerged only fitfully, and when it did emerge was seldom if ever squarely faced. For the issue essentially involved the secular time preference of a community, and this is in principle insoluble; there are too many unknowns—future economic opportunities and relative prices, the tastes of future generations, the outcome of possibly unknowable population trends. 'Much sentiment is sometimes wasted', writes a Canadian economist, 'over the "magnificent forests of oak, walnut and chestnut" which were burned, without ceremony, by the pioneers.'[2] The wood might, when markets were opened up, have been sold at a good price; the forests might, left to today, provide even more utility as national parks. But against this there must be set the utility accruing through many decades of the farmlands which replaced them, and, in

[1] Report of Minister of Lands, Mines and Forests for 1902, *Sessional Reports of Quebec, 1903*, p. vii.
[2] Lower, *op. cit.* p. 42.

the framing of policy, the futility of trying to see more than a decade or two ahead. In these circumstances the sporadic attempts of the nineteenth century to prevent aggregation and to precede settlement by survey and classification must seem, little as was the success they achieved, the best practical measures which democratically elected, ill-informed and badly-served governments could reasonably seek to enforce. But the truly great economic issues which were involved were too big to be perceived, and government action did little to affect them until the control of immigration began after 1914. But by then the moving frontier, like the nineteenth century to which it had been so important, was a part of history.

CHAPTER IV

Transport

I. *The Evolution of Methods of Transport*

ON its first appearance, each new kind of transport is conceived as a way of complementing the particular method prevailing at the time. Thus steam was at the start a handmaid to the sail. The first railways helped to carry towards the estuaries of Great Britain cargoes that were destined for the coastal traffic, or conveyed freight towards its rivers and canals; and occasionally, because the nature of the land made the construction of locks a major and expensive undertaking, railways served to fill a gap between two networks of inland navigation. This first stage is a symbiosis between two systems of transport. 'Breaking bulk' was readily accepted, and the transhipment of cargoes was a normal routine.

The second stage is then reached. During this phase the new method of transport attains its typical form and develops its own capacities to the full: it is still able to find new fields of profitable employment, but its essential characteristics are fixed. The railways of the 1870's are a case in point. During this stage the new method of transport seeks to become predominant by asserting its complete independence. It refuses any co-ordination with the other means of transport and encourages competition with them. The railways, once the main network was set up, disregarded the waterways and took over types of freight for which they were not well suited, even if it meant carrying them at a loss. The same phenomenon was to be later repeated when the roads once again became a major form of transport and entered into vigorous competition with the railways.

At this point the new method of transport is being used for purposes in which it is less than economic. Thus round about 1830 steam was used to carry passengers on canals and rivers. Starting in 1880 France built railways which could not pay, and whose construction was an economic absurdity. In England and the U.S.A. private enterprise encouraged useless competition by building a number of lines over the same stretch of country.

When the need to renew equipment arouses hostility to the method of transport which has so far been predominant, this method reacts by trying to assume the characteristics of its more fortunate rival: thus waterways sought to acquire the rapidity and regularity of railway tracks; later, railways sought in turn to acquire something of the flexibility of the motor-car with experiments in forms of diesel transport. If the fight turns out to be decidedly unequal, the method of transport which has lost its preponderance relinquishes its independence and becomes one more auxiliary form. In this way road haulage abandoned the main lines of traffic to the railways, but learnt how to adapt itself to the new conditions; without disappearing, and indeed even managing to develop, it became a 'feeder' of the railway.

This evolution in methods of transport occurs at a given period of time in any particular geographical area. It is repeated progressively in the marginal areas which are situated farther and farther away from the place where the new method of transport first appeared. As early as 1855 the era of steamships on inland waterways had almost reached its close among the peoples of the North Atlantic; while it was still at its height on the Amazon, the Congo, and the Yangste-Kiang at the beginning of the twentieth century.

In those regions which are late in developing a transport system, a short-cut is sometimes possible, either because of the rapidity with which a new method of transport is diffused, or because it is capable of covering a very wide area. Thus many areas in the Far West of the U.S.A. changed from the trail of the bison and the Indian to the railway, without road haulage intervening as an intermediary stage. And, again, in a great number of marginal areas railways appeared too late, and an abrupt transition was made from beasts of burden to aeroplanes.

Even when reduced to the rank of a subsidiary, each form of transport still retains certain advantages, which prevent it from disappearing completely, and can even give it the chance to stage a come-back. It is possible for changes in equipment to restore the popularity of a sector that has long been overshadowed: thus the advent of the motor-car has revived long-distance traffic by road. This provides an element of stability in the otherwise unceasing evolution of the means of transport. Even in their hey-day railways never completely replaced inland navigation or road transport. The North Atlantic community, the first and best equipped in respect of transport, has always preserved, side by side, competing branches of the industry. The capacity of older forms of transport to survive carries with it the danger that the supply of transport facilities may become excessive when innovation outstrips the needs of traffic.

It is therefore necessary to consider the relation between the main stages of development in transport on the one hand and the requirements of the traffic on the other. The process of invention and innovation in transport has, as we have already seen, a rhythm and internal logic of its own. But much of this development consists of the combination of elements already in existence, for example, the adaptation of the railway and the locomotive to suit each other's needs (in contrast to the failure of the steam-engine on the road). The direction which development takes is therefore dominated by the needs of the economy. These partly account for the contrast between the use of steam in transport by sea and by land: steam was rapidly adapted to the railway, but the steamship was slow to establish its supremacy at sea, and this was due to some extent to the relatively high standard of perfection achieved by the sailing ship as a method of maritime transport and to the inefficiency of road transport on land. Technical innovation is subject to laws which apply to the whole field of transport, which in this respect possesses a structural unity.

The efficiency of the sailing ships as a means of sea transport made possible the growth of a North Atlantic economy, radiating out from Great Britain. But at the end of the eighteenth century the deficiencies of transport by land threatened to hinder the new developments within this economy—the 'industrial revolution' founded on the use of coal and iron, and characterized by the growth of large cities which presented inescapable problems of provisioning. In the event the railways provided the solution to the problems of internal transport, but this new means of transport, based as it was on iron and steam, itself depended on an already existing heavy industry. There was a vicious circle, which could only be resolved in England, where iron and coal existed within easy reach of the other, and at the same time in close proximity to the sea-routes. In this favourably endowed country, the railway could establish itself by playing, at the start, no more than the role of auxiliary to existing methods of transport. Similarly, all the big cities such as London and Amsterdam, with the outstanding exception of Paris, were also sea-ports. The creation of big cities and of great continental centres of industry was closely tied to the evolution of the new methods of transport.

Apart from these basic economic necessities, there were sometimes political reasons for the improvements in land transport. In France, for instance, the creation of the network of *routes royales* was undertaken, in most parts of the country, as a result of political and strategical considerations and in advance of the needs of the traffic born of economic conditions. When political causes precede economic requirements the economic situation can then be judged by the state of repair of the roads.

Thus the economic situation and political influences combine with more specific technical developments to determine the evolution of the means of transport. This evolution can be broken into broad chronological periods, and it is these periods that will now be examined.

II. *Highways and Waterways, 1800-30*

A first period can be discerned stretching from the turn of the century to the opening of the Liverpool–Manchester line. It is distinguished by improvements in both road transport and inland navigation in that part of the world undergoing an industrial revolution.

The year 1800 has no intrinsic significance of its own. As the century opened, sailing ships were at the height of their popularity as the method of maritime transport. By the end of the eighteenth century they had already attained a high degree of perfection, and the metallurgical industry was as yet far too small to allow contemporaries to envisage building ships of iron. The size and speed of sailing ships were increasing, foreshadowing the era of the clippers. The ratio of length to breadth increased from 4 to 5·5. The line of the ship became more slender and the mainmast shortened. The art of navigating also made great progress; better chronometers permitted navigators to establish their longitude far more precisely and thus reach their destination without useless detours. Even during the years of the great wars, and despite temporary shortages in tonnage, navigation by sea was able to meet the needs of the Anglo-Saxon powers. Great Britain could remain faithful to her stout but unwieldy East Indiamen; it was American shipbuilding on the whole that carried the day as regards quality and cost. There was no problem of timber supplies in New England and Nova Scotia. Moreover, the growth in the American cotton trade and in the West Indian trade in colonial products led to the creation of a North Atlantic maritime community. The Black Ball line provided services crossing the ocean from New York to Liverpool in 33 days, and taking 40 days over the return journey. As early as the end of the eighteenth century New Englanders crossed over to Canton. With the advent of the North Atlantic community a mainstream of maritime traffic flowed around the Cape.

Finally, sea transport was everywhere responsible for distributing both the products which today constitute the bulk of inland traffic, and those which form the cargoes of long distance trade. The affluence of maritime trade can be judged by the growth of such ports as London or Liverpool. Their importance astounded continental travellers after the Napoleonic wars. The French port of Le Havre, considered as quite outstanding in 1790, was completely outclassed thirty years later.

These developments must be underlined because they account for the relative silence which surrounds the first appearances of the steamship on the high seas. As early as 1808 Stevens had gone from Hoboken to Philadelphia by sea: this eccentricity on the part of an inventor had had no followers. The paddle steamer was expensive, because it consumed a fuel that was still scarce; it required a skilled crew; it was dangerous, being a prey to fire or explosion; and it smoked and shook. But it had one distinct advantage: it could guarantee regularity in the crossing of narrow seas. It was almost a ferry for estuaries and channels, thus effectively extending the area of inland navigation. From 1818 to 1823 steamships were introduced on the Irish Sea between Greenock and Belfast. In 1821 Calais was linked to Dover by steamer. About 1823 there were regular summer services between London and Leith and Rotterdam. Only two years later the steamer was already serving Hamburg and the Baltic ports, and had penetrated the Mediterranean with services between Naples, Leghorn and Marseilles. It took 12 hours to go from London to Calais by steamer, and 36 from Leghorn to Naples. Because of its comparative punctuality it was used for the transport of mail. Thus Portsmouth was only 64 hours from Corunna.

Long-distance journeys, however, did not seem to hold out much interest for this newcomer: its regularity, which was quite appreciable over short distances, became unimportant over longer journeys which sailing vessels could cover in the same time. Moreover, the amount of fuel that had to be carried, because of the low efficiency of the boiler, seemed an almost insuperable handicap. In 1819 the *Savannah*, a 300-ton vessel, linked the U.S.A. to Liverpool in 25 days. But sailing ships did the journey in the same time, and the *Savannah* was forced to rely on its sails for seven days, having taken only 80 tons of coal and wood. It is understandable why, until the *Royal Williams* in 1835, this exploit was not repeated. In the same way the voyage to India of the *Enterprise* assumed the character of an experiment in which steam was merely auxiliary to the sail. From all points of view the supremacy of the sail was still undisputed on the high seas in 1830.

It was on land, rather than on sea, that the revolution in transport made its first beginnings, by the improvement of roads and a more general use of steam vessels on inland waterways.

The organization of a road network became a reality at the end of the eighteenth century in France and Great Britain. At this time the French seem to have been technically superior, whether in the field of naval construction, that of ports and lighthouses, or in that of road building. Twenty-five years later the lead had definitely passed to the British as a result of their general economic superiority; in Britain, it was said, 'everything wears the face of dispatch'. Time was already valued in terms of money, to the great astonishment of French travellers such as Charles Dupin. About 1780 the journey from Manchester to London took 4–5 days; in 1820 36 hours were sufficient. Custom was plentiful; and a great many services competed to obtain it by undertaking races against each other (which often came to an unfortunate end), or from about 1827 by providing gas-light in their carriages. Round about 1820 England had nearly 21,000 miles of turnpike roads, as much as France, which is three and a half times its size.

Meanwhile the absence of any centralized organization presented special difficulties. The English did not want to have a government department in charge of their roads because it would have added considerably to the powers of the government as well as leading to an increase in taxation. Thus the turnpike trusts were local bodies managing a section of the road and charging tolls in return for their services. In fact there were so many exemptions and frauds that the tolls charged often proved insufficient to cover the cost of maintaining the road in a satisfactory condition. At the opening of the nineteenth century a great number of trusts were forced to devote the proceeds of their tolls to service loans rather than to the upkeep of the roads. Only some 6 per cent of the roads were in a good state of repair, and around the main centres of activity traffic literally wore the road away. In remote country districts the trustees decided to have the pot-holes filled with pebbles, and the traffic by-passed the road and cut across country.

Eventually the English network, the spontaneous product of local decisions, progressed out of this state of disorganization. Its isolated segments were linked up and ultimately provided a remarkably comprehensive network corresponding to basic national requirements. By trial and error and by comparing their processes, the trustees and their surveyors arrived at a general notion of what a road should be—'a moderately convex surface artificially constructed of small pebbles and gravels'. Nevertheless, it was clear that the volume of traffic far exceeded the capacity of the authorities to maintain the roads in a fit state. The trustees had influence in Parliament and by increasing without end the number of bye-laws they made every effort to see that traffic accommodated itself to the state of the road. It was of no avail; what was needed was something new.

It is particularly striking that this innovation should have emerged from Ireland and the Scottish Highlands, poverty-ridden areas in which government action was essential for political and financial reasons. Travellers returning from Ireland were ashamed at the state of the English roads. In 1802 the Commissioners for the Highlands began to complete and improve the network of military roads established in the previous century. The government contributed one-half of the estimated cost. Under the direction of Thomas Telford 900 miles of road were opened across the mountains.

From 1810 the need of a road from London to Holyhead and of one from the north to Edinburgh became increasingly urgent. John Macadam was able to secure the confidence of ministers and members of

Parliament. His 'surface making' technique was in no way better than that used in France or in Sweden, but he provided a measure of unity in the organization of road construction in place of the divided work of the trusts. His teams of professional road makers drove the amateurs, with their haphazard operations, out of the market.

Beginning in 1815 Henry Parnell put new life in the commission charged with the construction of the road to Ireland. He succeeded in bringing about the fusion of a number of small Welsh trusts, obtained government subsidies, and established Telford as General Surveyor. In 1826 Lord Lowther brought about the fusion of fourteen trusts in Middlesex, and thereby created the richest group in the kingdom.

But the different financial standing of the various trusts soon put an end to this movement of concentration. Parliament was cautious in the grant of subsidies and Telford was unable, in 1830, to repeat his success with the Holyhead road on that to Edinburgh. The organization of the Macadams, father and sons, guaranteed a better quality and a more uniform surface on the roads, but their design and their width turned out to be unsatisfactory for traffic which was already in 1829 travelling at 9 or 10 miles an hour. The stage-coach took 20 hours to reach Exeter and 40 to reach Edinburgh. This was the heyday of turnpike roads; but at this very moment the 'Rainhill trial' signalled the entrance of the locomotive on to the scene.

There was a marked contrast between the classical rationalism of the French *routes royales*, undertaken by the *Corps des Ponts et Chaussées*, and the anarchical yet powerful empiricism of the English. Arthur Young sang the praises of the technique of French road construction and was astounded at the small amount of traffic to be found on French roads. Tresaguet, Dausse—these were the worthy rivals of Telford as far as building roads across mountains was concerned. But, like the British, the French were not able to solve satisfactorily the problem of keeping the roads in a fit state of repair.

The cost of maintaining the roads was met by drawing on the funds provided by general taxation; an attempt in 1806 to introduce on the main roads the English system of tolls had been abandoned. But in 1800 after eight years of war, of financial penury, and of revolution, the state of the roads was abominable. The roads of the Napoleonic empire linked Paris to the various continental frontiers: the 'strategic' roads to the Vendée, the roads to the Alps in the direction of the Simplon or the Mont Cenis passes, the roads to Illyria, the road to the Rhine across the slaty mountains of the Rhineland—all these were the outstanding achievements of the Empire, but they were not able to sustain the wear imposed on them by the army and its baggage trains- They had, moreover, to carry a heavy haulage traffic, for this was the period of the continental blockade, and British mastery of the seas paralysed the ports and made coastal traffic somewhat risky. On top of all this came the two invasions of France in 1814 and 1815, followed by three years of occupation. At the Restoration the monarchy found a road network well conceived but falling into decay, at a time when it was still burdened with the financial consequence of the wars. This was serious for the country when it was just beginning its industrial revolution; large quantities of coal and iron had to be moved over a wide area, and the coal-mines and the industrial centres were far from the sea, and sometimes in hilly areas.

The *Corps des Ponts et Chaussées* employed small salaried teams of road makers, who by 1824 had repaired only 40 per cent of the 33,000 km. of royal roads. Because of the increasing volume of traffic, the layout of the roads had to be altered in quite a number of places. There was also an increase in the speed of traffic. The mail-coach with its four passengers linked Paris to Bordeaux in 86 hours in 1814 and in 46 hours in 1830; the journey between Paris and Brest was reduced from 87 to 62 hours, and that between Paris and Lyons from 68 to 55. By about 1830 the stage-coach covered 200 km. a day carrying 1400 kg. of goods, and 16 passengers with their luggage. The 'fly-wagon' carried 1500 kg. over 80 km. a day. In the best instances, therefore, the same speeds were achieved as on the English highways. The growth of road haulage was particularly outstanding: it was a peasant industry, especially practised by those who lived in the mountains during the long winter months. A succession of four-wheeled wagons each drawn by one horse moved along the roads in groups of four or six, delaying the swifter carriages (a fact that explains why traffic jams at English 'toll bars' appeared quite tolerable). Two-wheeled carriages were the dread of the *Ponts et Chaussées*: their wheels had narrow but hard rims to support the whole weight of the carriage. The result was the same as in England: bye-laws began to abound; the authorities attempted to strangle the traffic by a system of weigh-bridges that proved more vexatious than efficacious (in 1850 there were only 145), and by a system of fines that were seldom collected. In the meantime a search for something new was afoot. As early as 1822 the engineer Navier was sent over to England. He judged the English roads harshly, considering them no better than enlarged country lanes which had been badly laid out, but he was nevertheless won over by their surfacing: the *Ponts et Chaussées* adopted the Macadam system, but not more extensively than in its native land.

In retrospect what is particularly striking is the very small amount of traffic, although at the time it was considered excessive. The roads with the heaviest traffic, that from Gray, on the Saône, to the ironworks of

the Haute-Marne for instance, had about 650 tons of traffic a day, enough
to fill a very small goods train. As soon as one left the coast or some
navigable channel, the country was virtually in a state of permanent
blockade, being fenced in on either side by a small number of roads,
which were moreover unconnected with each other. But roads
were not the only problem; even where roads were available, road
haulage had to be fitted into the ordinary agricultural routines—for the
rural population it was an occupation for the dead-season—and the
number of draught animals that could be maintained depended on the
state of the harvests. Thus the activity of industrial establishments
was dependent on the fluctuations of agriculture, and the condition
of transport acted as a brake to the whole economic life of the
country.

On the Continent, France and the kingdom of the Netherlands were
the only States that possessed what could really be described as a road
network. In western Germany the regimes that had been under French
influence had achieved something fairly positive. The projects undertaken by governments with limited resources, such as Bavaria, had been
expanded. But if the French Empire undoubtedly provided an impetus,
it also wore out the roads and, what was more important still, exhausted
the finances of the small German states. Yet one fact stood out clearly:
the condition of the roads grew worse as one left the Rhine and
travelled eastward. In 1826 Prussia had 3340 miles of road: 2230 of
them in the Rhineland or in Westphalia. Government officials, such as
von Wincke, continued the work of Napoleon's administrators. In
1816 Westphalia had 450 miles of state roads and 790 in 1828. Beyond
the Elbe the State provided roads for the stage-coaches by levying a
special tax, but there were few of them and those that there were
turned out to be fairly mediocre. Despite the efforts made by Congress Poland, the Prussian and Polish districts that had bogged down the
Grande Armée changed very slowly. In Prussia 16–20 horses were
needed to drag the mail-coach over certain stretches of road. Between
Berlin and Breslau the fastest service took 40 hours. The Silesian metal
industry relied mainly on waterways. The Habsburg monarch gave
Austria and Northern Italy some good mountain roads which extended
the work of Napoleon's engineers. In contrast the Swiss cantons did
not as yet have any first-class roads.

In general, the road system was most satisfactory where industrialization had proceeded farthest; the road map of Europe corresponded
to that of the industrial revolution. The political ambitions of a
regime like the Napoleonic Empire might lead to a somewhat more
rational plan than that of the English network; but it was only economic
requirements that induced a high standard of maintenance, the 'solid

hard surface' of Macadam for instance, and kept the roads fit for wheeled traffic. And yet the wheeled traffic always proved to be tougher than the road. Napoleon failed because his attempt to establish an economic organization and a military empire founded on road communication turned out to be premature. Until the advent of the railway era the sea maintained its overwhelming superiority.

Another State, outside north-western Europe, was also envisaging the possibilities of setting out on the conquest of a whole continent, using its coastal regions as a base of departure. This was the United States. It had only the road to rely on for its undertaking, and the inadequacy of this means of transport was quickly apparent.

Despite the ruggedness of the climate, the vast distances, and its meagre population, the U.S.A. possessed, from about the middle of the eighteenth century, a network that was scanty but comparable in quality to that of England. As early as 1793 it was possible to travel from Boston to New York in four days. The first roads were built as 'feeders' to the rivers. Then the network began to take shape and the leading States established turnpike roads. In 1811 Connecticut had 800 miles of road and New York State 1400; New England had hard-surface roads at almost the same time as England and France. But a number of original features appeared in the New World. The youthful Union was poor both in money and in skilled craftsmen. On the other hand, the federal government owned a wealth of land which it was free to dispose of as it wanted, and in this way it helped to meet some of the needs of a network planned to embrace a whole continent. People were constantly crossing the 'gaps' in the Alleghanies to go and settle on the other side. At first they followed the 'trails'; then they took the 'pikes'. Pittsburgh was already an important road junction, with the Pennsylvania road linking it to Philadelphia. But the road joining Albany to Lake Erie was also proving important. After 1812 the frontier was pushed back to the banks of the Mississippi. In 1806 Congress allowed the sale of public land to finance highway construction. In 1808 Gallatin put forward a fairly bold plan. Finally in 1811 it was decided that the sale of federal land in the new States would be used to subsidize the construction of a federal highway linking all the states together. The Cumberland highway was started in 1811; it reached Wheeling in Ohio in 1817; by 1833 Columbus (Ohio) was the temporary terminal of this great 'highway of emigration'. But despite the encouragement provided by the example of the 'National Pike', the price of long-distance goods traffic by road remained exorbitant. The road could not give an effective east–west impetus to the member States of a federation that was oriented from north to south by both the rivers and the sea.

Until the twentieth century roads enjoyed no more than relative independence whenever inland waterways were in a position to compete with them. Waterways could transport heavy goods at low prices and naturally attracted this kind of traffic. During the first third of the nineteenth century roads captured the carriage of travellers, parcels and even manufactured goods; or to be more correct, they would have captured this traffic if the development of the steamship had not made it possible to make better use of rivers and to link them up by means of canals. The first thirty years of the century belonged to the roads, but perhaps even more to the steamer; for the steamer enabled waterways temporarily to recover passenger traffic in the old countries, and in the new ones acted as the great instrument of human settlement and transport. This was even more the case the farther inland one went. Thus the era of river steamers stands out particularly in the history of the United States and in that of central Europe, and to a lesser degree in the history of France during this period.

Strangely enough Great Britain, the founder of industrial civilization, and the first country to be provided with a large number of canals, was not really well endowed by geography for this method of transport. It is not large, and the sea makes numerous inroads into the heart of the country; moreover, the nature of the land is uneven, and the supply of water that feeds the streams is fairly limited, except at the estuaries. Thus if England, the first large consumer of coal, was also the first country to possess, as early as the end of the eighteenth century, an important network of canals, it was largely a result of historical factors rather than of natural endowment.

This network, the product of private ventures was, even more than the English road system, built by local initiative responding to local needs. It was consequently a heterogeneous system from the start, and it always maintained that character. On the same canal the cross-section of the water-way and that of the tunnels and locks varied considerably. Schemes were limited to immediate objectives which were within the bounds of financial possibilities. Nevertheless, these canals managed to transform the whole industrial order, as well as the markets for fuel and food. They enabled engineers to try out technical operations and to organize work yards. Finally, in contrast to the turnpikes, they made a profit, sometimes even a very substantial profit, and thereby revealed to capitalists the possibilities of gain opened up by the revolution in transport. The Caledonian canal formed part of the large projects undertaken in the Highlands after 1800 under Telford's supervision with government subsidies. The other ventures were the product of private enterprise. At the start of the century the whole Pennine Range was already crossed in a number of places. In 1805 the Grand

Junction canal linked the Midlands to London. It was, however, only in 1827, with the opening of the Birmingham and Liverpool Junction, that London and Lancashire were in direct contact. Besides, the interests of the coastal trade, and particularly of the Newcastle coal trade, delayed the development of inland routes across the island which were bound to draw off quite a large share of their traffic. Moreover, the traffic that really paid was the local Lancashire or Yorkshire trade. For these reasons canal users remained on the whole fairly indifferent to the transhipping of goods in transit; at the same time iron barges remained scarce while horses dragged barges at the maximum speed of 4–6 miles an hour. The steamer was tried out on the Forth and Clyde canal, but it damaged the banks. The steamships of John Laird of Birkenhead were in service on the Shannon and the Irish canals. But in England steamers were used mainly on estuaries.

The cost of carriage on canals was from a quarter to a half of the cost by road. At the same time many of them made substantial profits; in 1825 the Trent and Mersey canal yielded 75 per cent plus a bonus, the Mersey and Irwell 35 per cent, the Leeds and Liverpool 16 per cent. It is equally true, on the other hand, that out of a total capital of £13 million, 3 millions invested in the south brought in nothing at all. Canals were easier to build in the south, but they were located in an agricultural area. As the volume of traffic in industrial districts grew and the supplies of water available were exhausted the existing canals had no longer to fear the appearance of new competitors. As a result monopolies appeared which eventually forced the oppressed customers to risk everything—even the construction of a railway—in order to free themselves from the grip of the canal owners. Despite all these facts on their debit side, British canals were a model for people on the Continent. The very fact that they were among the earliest to be built made them well known.

There was no question of the Continent discovering inland navigation. For centuries past the northern plain of Europe, stretching from Flanders to Prussia, had had the advantage of a navigable network, even if it did not lend itself easily to the construction of good roads. The gradient was gentle and the rivers fairly shallow but suitable for long, large-bottomed boats. It was consequently more a question of adapting this traditional mode of navigation to the requirements of an industrial civilization.

France took up again the work of canal building begun at the end of the previous century and interrupted by the Revolution. In 1810 the completion of the St Quentin canal allowed coal from the northern mines to reach Paris. Of Napoleon's ambitious projects, such as the canal from Amiens to Düsseldorf, or the St Denis and St Martin canals which would have allowed the barges to get round the obstacle created by Paris, only the canal of the Ourcq (1808) linking the Marne to the Seine was completed. Both time and money were lacking for the others. At the Restoration therefore it was necessary to take up again plans that had remained in abeyance for more than a quarter of a century. In 1820 Becquey, director of the *Ponts et Chaussées*, proposed to establish 10,000 km. of entirely new canals. This systematic approach, which envisaged canals in the Massif Central, proved too ambitious. What was even more important, financial resources were limited. The laws of 1821 and 1822 made it necessary to associate groups of private financiers with the operation, and their participation turned out to be a very costly venture. The state lost its freedom to fix rates as soon as the canals were completed and in operation, while the technical qualities of the canals turned out to be far more limited than anticipated. They opened out onto rivers which were themselves in a very imperfect condition; like the English canals they were destined to serve local traffic only. As a result what canal building there was remained insufficient, though nearly 1000 km. were added to the 1200 already in existence.

The great undertaking of this period was the 'construction' of the Rhine under Prussian inspiration after 1815. The Congress of Vienna recognized the freedom of navigation on the river established by the Napoleonic Empire, though tolls remained frequent upstream from Mannheim.

It was in the United States, however, that waterways had their greatest success. They enabled heavy materials to travel long distances even better than by road. After the war of 1812 there began a burst of intensive canal building which crossed the Alleghanies and opened up the coal seams of the regions beyond. One project stood head and shoulders above the others in respect of its consequences: the Erie canal built between 1817 and 1825 from New York to Buffalo was undertaken by the State under the leadership of its Governor de Witt Clinton. Between 1820 and 1830 the population of New York doubled and the lakeside towns became the rivals of those bordering the Ohio and the Mississippi. In spite of all the work undertaken to make Montreal the outlet of the lakes (the Rideau and Welland canals), the principal port of exit of America had been found. It was true that the Erie Canal, only 30 feet wide and 4 feet deep, was still quite insignificant and it was soon congested with traffic; but passenger steamers now took $4\frac{1}{2}$ days to do the Albany–Buffalo run and the cost of carrying a ton from Buffalo to New York dropped from 100 dollars to 15, while the journey took 8 days instead of 3 weeks. As a result Pittsburgh was linked to Erie. The Union which had tended to develop along lines of communication running north and south was now re-orientated anew along lines running east and west.

What particularly added to the value of this work of inland navigation was the advent of the river steamer. It was due to the rapidity and regularity of these steamers that the inland States of the Union could manage without railways for a time. Along a river there was no problem as regards stocks of coal or wood, problems which proved so insoluble on the high seas. In particular, the steamer enabled use to be made of the long and powerful rivers of the U.S.A.

In 1807 the *Claremont* of Fulton travelled with its paddle-wheels 150 miles along the Hudson in 32 hours, an average rate of 4·3 miles an hour. As early as 1811 a steamboat sailed down the Ohio and the Mississippi, but it was not until 1815 that the steamer undertook the journey up-river from New Orleans to Louisville in 25 days. The cost of transport between Pittsburgh and the Gulf of Mexico was cut by a half. In 1825, 125 steamboats operated on this route. On Lake Erie sailing ships still predominated but as early as 1818 a steamer was built at Buffalo. Michel Chevalier, who travelled in the States between 1833 and 1835, described the 220 steamers of the Mississippi, comfortable and picturesque with their crowds of passengers who braved the possible dangers of fires and exploding boilers.

Europe adopted this invention at once. In 1812 the *Comet* appeared on the Clyde with its 3 horse-power motor. In 1814 the United Kingdom possessed two steamers drawing 456 tons; in 1830 315 with a total capacity of 33,444 tons. She carried the invention over to the rivers of the Continent. As early as 1816 English steamers sailed up the Seine. In 1822 Aaron Manby built an iron steamer and took it from London to Paris. His boat was already 29·30 m. by 5·20 m. He set up factories at Charenton, near Paris, and at Le Creusot, within reach of the Saône. In 1824 Sebastien Bourdon, who had worked in America, introduced a propeller-driven boat on the Rhone. By 1830 the big French rivers possessed their steamers. Crossing over from England via Holland steamers began to appear on the Rhine in 1824 after the voyage of the *Zeelander* from Rotterdam to Bacharach. Between the two towns the journey could now be done in 5 days instead of 10. After 1825 steam was used for towing between Rotterdam and Mannheim. The increase of steam navigation on the rivers, however, made the problem of their 'reconstruction' even more urgent. It was an enormous task, and the correct way of setting about it was only to be found empirically by trial and error. In the meantime steamers remained subject to changes in the water supply and were in fact a seasonal method of transport.

Railways were the product of the reciprocal adaptation of track and engine, both of which were closely linked to the revolution in metallurgy. From about 1800 many places already used rails made of cast or wrought iron which jutted out and could therefore grip the edges of wheels without blocking them. The appearance of these rails converted the track into a special way, for vehicles with flat-edged wheels could no longer make use of it. The railway had gained its independence. But the rail itself was still not very strong. It was not to be in a position to carry the locomotive until 1816, when the 'fish belly' rail presented a solid front able to offer the same resistance throughout its surface.

Before 1820 the Newcastle area had 600 km. of track and the county of Glamorgan nearly 400. Railways were still highly localized, and still mainly used in the service of mines, which had been responsible for their first development. They were the ideal method of carrying bulky goods over short distances at limited speeds towards coast or canal. The 1819 edition of *Ree's Encyclopaedia* dealt with railways in the article on canals, and regarded them merely as complementary to canals, where the land was too steep to make the task of canal building profitable. The usual instrument of traction on these limited runs consisted of a cable attached to a fixed engine, or of a horse. More-over, railways were cheaper to build and to run than canals: they could be used at all times of the year, and provided some relief for the overcrowded roads. They had their enthusiasts: the French engineer de Gallois on his return from Newcastle in 1818, and Thomas Gray who as early as 1821 was convinced that a railway network was a practical proposition. But there was still no effective instrument of traction; the locomotive had not yet been perfected and its possibilities were much debated.

On the Continent the first railways also linked mines to waterways. Examples of this were, in France, the railway from the mines of St Etienne to the Loire (1828) which was 18 km. long, or that in the basin of Charleroi. Harkort's propaganda in the Rhineland, or that of Thomas Gray in Belgium, and their dreams of a track from the Rhine to the Weser, or from Charleroi to Brussels, met with little encourage-ment. It was the same in America where the first miles of track, laid between 1828 and 1830, from Baltimore to the Ohio, made use of horse traction.

Without the locomotive the railway line would have remained only of local importance. But the steam-engine had already made its appearance on the road. Starting in 1800, and following in the foot-steps of the Frenchman Cugnot (1770), Oliver Evans ran his 'steamer on wheels' through the streets of Philadelphia, and Trevithick per-fected his 'steam road-carriage'. From 1822 to 1833 Griffith, Gurney and Hancock perfected steam-cars which carried fourteen passengers at 10 miles an hour—as fast as the mail-coach. Beginning in 1831 there were forty guaranteed services, and supporters supplied water free of charge to the new vehicles. But these latecomers were the terror of those responsible for the turnpike. Their vibrations wore the road out in no time, and their explosions terrified the other road users. It would have been better to provide them with roads of their own: but this would have meant imposing the same kind of limitation on their movement as a railway track and for a vehicle which was not capable of high speeds.

In contrast, on rails, the efficiency and speed of the locomotive went on increasing without end. As early as 1803 Trevithick's machine was capable of drawing 25 tons at 4 miles an hour. In 1813 Hedley solved the problem of travelling along a normally inclined plane. George Stephenson perfected his engine between 1814 and 1825. On 27 September 1825 his machine preceded by an outrider drew a few wagons filled with passengers at a speed of 4½ miles an hour. Finally in October 1829 the 'Rocket' won the Rainhill contest. It used the tubular boiler designed by Marc Seguin, weighed 4·3 tons, and carried 13 tons at 16 miles an hour. The day of horse traction or the fixed engine had passed. The locomotive appeared in France on the Loire line. In the U.S.A. in 1829 the English locomotive 'Stourbridge Lion' ran off the rails, but in 1830 the first American machine, 'Best Friend of Charleston', covered about 20 miles in an hour with four loaded wagons on the Charleston–Hamburg line.

From then on the locomotive was fully adapted to the track and it helped considerably to expand the possibilities of the railway. Moreover, Stephenson perfected his machine for a line that was not like other lines: for the Manchester–Liverpool, in the birth-place of the industrial revolution. It was no longer a question of using the railway to complete road systems or waterways; it was a question of replacing them and liberating trade from the insolent hold of the canal owners. Given the cost of the undertaking it was a leap in the dark, and Parliament doubtlessly authorized the project because it assumed that it would turn out to be an isolated venture. In fact, what was supposed to be a privileged exception proved the living demonstration that transport problems needed an original solution of this kind. Between 1824 and 1830 the estimated costs of construction more than quadrupled. Landed interests put up a stiff fight and defended their rights valiantly. Yet the size of the earnings showed that railways were as fruitful a source of gain as canals, if not more so. In 1830 passengers covered the distance from Manchester to Liverpool in an hour and a half, and goods in three hours. Michel Chevalier, going to Liverpool to sail for

America in 1833, set foot into a railway carriage for the first time at
Manchester and exclaimed: 'There are certain impressions that one
cannot put into words!' Man had just acquired a new sense—the
sense of speed.

III.   *Railways and Packet Boats, 1830–69*

With the opening of the Liverpool–Manchester line, rail prehistory
came to a close. The first dividends of this line were financed by means
of loans, but as early as 1833 a £100 share had more than doubled its
value. Thereupon the number of new lines began to multiply. In 1835
Parliament authorized the investment of £15 million, more than had
been spent on all the canals put together. The original movement was
sponsored by a fairly narrow circle of persons belonging to commerce
and industry rather than to the banking world. In 1833 an Act allowed
the construction of a line from London to Birmingham and one from
Birmingham to Manchester. In 1834 it was the London–Southampton
that was under construction, and in the following year the Great
Western. Landed interests took their share of the profits by accepting
bribes and claiming exorbitant expropriation indemnities. But the
capital involved was recovered as soon as the lines were opened and no
price seemed too high to attain this object: the London–Birmingham
line cost more than £50,000 a mile, and the Birmingham–Manchester
£23,000. The line from London to Brighton worked out at £60,000
per mile. And yet these trunk lines were goldmines, bringing in
6–10 per cent.

Henceforth, every industrial district had to have its line, whatever
the cost, for fear of losing its status. From 1836 the London Stock
Exchange played a part in this rising speculation. Parliament passed
one Act after another authorizing the construction of new lines:

Table 41. *Acts passed*

1825–35	54	1844	48	1847	190
1836–7	39	1845	120	1848	85
1838–9	6	1846	270	1849	34

Two great credit crises slowed down this tide of investments: from
1837 to 1841 and from 1847 to 1849. The causes of these crises were
complex, but credit inflation certainly contributed something to them.
Railways were already influencing the international economic situation
through the London money market.

Nevertheless, there was little hold-up in the work of construction:
the track reached Birmingham in 1838, Southampton and Bristol in

1840-1. From 1843 1900 miles were in operation and only the sparsely populated, and from the engineering point of view difficult, uplands of the Pennines, Wales, or the Scottish highlands remained isolated.

Table 42. *Miles in operation*

1843	1952	1847	3945
1844	2148	1848	5127
1845	2441	1849	6031
1846	3036	1850	6625

In twenty years the United Kingdom built its trunk lines, admittedly over a fairly limited area. Only the United States had a greater total mileage of track, but the railway lines there tended to be built as a speculation. Henceforth railway shares were put into circulation by new banks and backed by a specialist press, and the middle classes began to take an interest in them. Railway directors controlled from above a crowd of anonymous shareholders. The 'railway kings' organized a powerful group within Parliament which was quick to rise in the defence of their interests: even Sir Robert Peel treated them with indulgence.

The labour market was changed almost as much as the money market. In 1849 the railways had a permanent staff of over 50,000 men. From 1845 to 1850, 100,000 to 200,000 men were also employed on the construction of new lines. Railway engineers became public idols in place of canal and road engineers. The construction of the London–Birmingham line made the reputation of Lacke, and the Great Western that of Brunel, the champion of comfort and speed. After the engineers and the bankers it was the turn of the contractors to win fame. Mackenzie, trained in the Telford school, Samuel Morton Peto, Thomas Brassey—these were the great men. They had their assault groups, the well-fed, well-paid 'navvies', a rough bunch who specialized in difficult tasks. They had their own factories, their banks, their teams of workmen, their small sub-contractors to take over everyday jobs. Once the whole organization was set up, they maintained it in being permanently, and sought to find contracts that would provide constant employment even if it meant lower profits. Towards 1850 the business, at first middle-sized, became an end in itself. The 'contractor' built lines without being commissioned, and then tried to find someone to buy them. Henceforth he provided the banks and the metallurgical industry with a regular line of business. When the market became poor and unprofitable in England, he moved over to the Continent.

As soon as trains attained the speed of 50 miles per hour the companies had to begin thinking about organizing the traffic, for it could no

longer be confined to the limits of their individual lines. Railway
traffic could no longer be modelled on the traffic on the canals or
turnpikes. A question of central organization arose which had so far
been avoided by Britain's flair for decentralized empiricism. The need
to organize the traffic led to amalgamations.

Until about 1830 the permanent concessions granted to the railways
raised no problem. English law was, indeed, favourable to this kind of
arrangement, which avoided the need to redeem loans. Moreover, it
was commonly believed that the use of the rail, like that of the road and
the canal, would not be confined to the vehicles of those who owned it.
Besides, as long as speeds were limited, journeys involving several lines
and transhipments from one line to another proved in no way disturbing. It came as a surprise when the network, once it was established
in broad outline, sought to become entirely independent. In 1839 Carr
Glyn informed a parliamentary committee that locomotives not
belonging to his company could not count on being supplied with
water, fuel, or with the signal service. The locomotive made it impossible any longer to consider transport problems in the terms which
had been appropriate to the use of roads by horses.

Fusions began to take place from about 1840, and initially took the
limited form of the absorption by a main line of some of its 'feeders'.
But after 1844 Hudson created a genuine network in the Midlands.
From 1850 the war of the networks was in full swing in the north and
west over the question of the link with Scotland. One element assumed
an unforeseen importance: the 'broad gauge', commended by Brunel
as the best solution for high speeds, allowed the Great Western to
isolate and defend itself from the companies using the 'standard
gauge', the north's favourite gauge since the eighteenth century. The
'broad gauge' limited itself to the London, Birmingham, Swansea,
Dorchester area. But the growth of general traffic made it impossible
for one network to isolate itself completely from the others, given the
size of England. An Act of 1846 imposed the 'standard gauge' on all
future companies. Henceforth the 'break of gauge' at Gloucester was
doomed, and the Great Western and its subsidiaries had to adopt the
temporary solution of a 'mixed gauge' by the addition of a third rail.

The establishment of a national network led almost inevitably, if not
to nationalization, which was inconceivable at this period, at least to some
effective measure of government control. On the other hand, personal
and regional rivalries also played an important part in railway development. In 1847 the Great Northern had to defend itself against all its
neighbours. Two years later Hudson had to give up the direction of the
Midland Railway. The number of companies was still very large
(between 200 and 300), but in fact control rested in the hands of a few of

the big companies which had either acquired concessions, or bought or leased most of the smaller companies.

In 1850 George Carr Glyn crowned his patient work, started in 1842, to obtain some kind of central organization by the Railway Clearing Act. A copy of the bank clearing system, the new office pooled the accounts of a number of companies centrally and allowed an exchange of rolling stock at junctions. Formed by the successive adhesions of a number of companies to the London–Birmingham, it grouped together the standard gauge lines from Darlington to London and from Hull to Manchester.

From this time on, competition gave way to co-ordination and a sharing of the traffic. There were a number of important fusions between 1849 and 1854 and between 1860 and 1866. After the excitement of 1846, Watkin and Allport, the big railway strategists, merely sought to establish the virtual monopoly of a company over limited areas. Despite growing restlessness in public opinion and within Parliament, their efforts proved successful. Besides, the immense profits of the early days were over. The length of the network was increased: between 1850 and 1870, at which date 13,500 miles were in operation, it more than doubled. The maximum speeds of 1850 had become the average speeds of 1870. As early as 1841 a mile of single track needed 156 tons of rail, as against 53 when railways were first introduced. Trains had become part of the new economic pattern that they had helped to create. They were no longer speculative; they had become an institution.

The electric telegraph played an important part in this development. It alone could give the railways the security that was essential for their successful operation, and the telegraph network developed along the path of the railway track. Always in the lead, the Great Western was the first to introduce it in 1839. By 1848 half the railways possessed the telegraph. The link between railways and telegraph remained important, even though independent telegraph companies appeared after 1846. But these companies tended to establish their offices where there was a heavy demand for them and to ignore other areas. Public opinion assimilated the telegram to the letter, and demanded that the price be independent of the distance as was the case with the postal service, and in 1869 the Post Office bought up all the telegraph lines, a unique event in Victorian England. From being an uncertain speculation, the telegraph had become a public service, running at a loss.

Railways appeared in the United States almost at the same time as in England. They aroused tremendous enthusiasm, a 'passion' as Michel Chevalier described it on landing in the States in 1834. The Americans realized at once that only the railway could enable them to organize

their continent. Railways began to appear everywhere. In 1830 there
were only 32 miles of track, but by 1835 there were more than 1000,
almost 3000 ten years later, 9000 in 1850, and more than 30,000 in
1860. As early as 1840 the Americans had a network that was four
times the size of that of the United Kingdom. In 1865 they were still
ahead with 36,000 miles of railroad as against 13,000 in Great Britain.
The construction of canals was pursued simultaneously: the total
length rose from 1270 miles in 1830 to 3320 in 1840. Until about 1840
the canal was used in connection with the railway to break through the
crest of the Alleghanies. But in the ten years that followed less than 400
miles of new canals were opened. The era of the canal had come to a
close.

The American railroad was the product of improvisation, in contrast to the English track, which was built with great care. At first all
that was required was a fairly rough and ready line which could operate
with a minimum amount of equipment. Then as traffic increased and
profits began to be made, the whole enterprise was transformed to
take account of the requirements of increased traffic and of the greater
financial possibilities. The early rails were often made of wood protected by metal bands. There was little ballast and few drainage
trenches; the line was single-tracked and narrow; the bridges were of
wood; the stations provided few facilities: this covers fairly adequately
all that can be said about these American improvisations. Locomotives
sometimes ran on wood. Moreover, as land was not expensive and
often cost nothing at all, the cost of the railroad per kilometre did not
exceed 100,000 francs—at least in the early days, for as the rolling-stock
and rails became heavier the permanent way began to prove inadequate
and there were accidents. The timetable was haphazard, and it was not
until 1847 that a guide began to appear. But at the start an imperfect
line was preferred to no line at all.

Until 1844 metal rails were imported almost solely from England.
But this early situation soon improved. In the 1840's Philadelphia
firms began to sell locomotives to Europe. American trains aroused the
interest of the Old World, and it was in America that the Westinghouse
brake was perfected.

The American network was to a large extent financed by British
capital. In point of fact the companies took very limited risks in the
States. They obtained lavish subsidies in land and money from towns,
counties and States. The main object was to settle the population and to
increase land values by the advent of the locomotive. Thus the companies had entire freedom once they had managed to secure the co-
operation of a few influential persons and to bring together a fairly
small initial capital. Because of their permanent concessions they could

borrow money on the security of their land, entrust the whole of their projects to a 'contractor', and speculate in their shares. Every State was anxious to surpass its neighbours, and therefore constantly issued new bonds for the financing of internal improvements. By the end of 1835 more than 90 million dollars were invested in this way, more than half of which constituted a debt on the part of the States. The investments became less and less fruitful, and consequently the terms on which they were made more and more onerous. The States and the companies competed with each other in borrowing money in order to pay the interest on former issues. The result was a series of bankruptcies in 1839. Even the States withheld payment of interest on their debt: if they increased taxation the pioneers moved on to the next State. From 1840 to 1843 the uncompleted and unproductive projects passed from the hands of their creditors to those of speculators. It was not until the advent of gold from California and Australia that the London market resumed its investments in America. By then a new inflationary period had got under way, which was accentuated by the Civil War.

Both the federal structure of government and distances helped to make the network intensely heterogeneous. The future New York Central line, the only trunk line to be completed before 1850, was owned by sixteen different companies, and the gauge was nowhere the same. The fusion, or 'consolidation' as it was called, did not take place until 1853.

In Canada the construction of the Grand Trunk line, from Quebec to the St Claire river and to Portland, illustrated simultaneously the urgent need of a railway, if the country was to be opened up, and the cost of such an undertaking for a colony that was poor, without credit, and dependent on British capital, provided by the bankers Baring and Glyn Mills, and on British contractors, such as Peto, Betts and Jackson. The railway made little profit at first, and from 1851 to 1865 the contractors had to be paid out of taxes. To supply the needs of the Grand Trunk the race to the west was begun in 1858 against the Americans, a race from which the Dominion was to emerge.

Despite all their improvisations and wastage, the American railroads astonished Europe, which saw a whole continent come to life in the path of the lines. The railways opened up America for a second time. By 1850 the east–west link between western Europe and the Mississippi valley was already created by means of the States on the Atlantic seaboard. The supremacy of the Chicago–New York axis had become established, at the expense of the South and of Canada, which were taking more time to get organized. America swung away from a north–south to an east–west orientation. The northern railways allowed the Union to triumph in the Civil War, which was fought in part to determine the general direction to be taken by the future railways. But the victory of the North was also due to the influx of capital from the London market, and to the steady flow of immigrants from Ireland, Germany and Scandinavia. The bonds of the North Atlantic Anglo-Saxon community were strengthened in the course of this undertaking which has remained unparalleled in history. Furthermore, the railways placed the coal deposits of the Alleghanies at the disposal of the factories of the eastern States, and enabled them to establish an industrial and urban complex capable of satisfying the wants of the western States in return for agricultural products.

England was responsible for the early development of railways, but it was America that perfected the electric telegraph. The partnership of Samuel Morse and Ezra Cornell enabled the former to try out his new method of transmission. In 1846-7 New York was connected to Albany, Boston and Buffalo, along the path of the trunk road starting from Lake Erie, and from 1846 to Cleveland, Detroit and Chicago. In 1861 government subsidies enabled a telegraph connection to be established with the Pacific coast, and 50,000 miles of line were in operation. British capitalists reflected on the possibilities of a combined railway and telegraph system in Canada, 'from sea to sea'.

In spite, and perhaps because, of its limited size, Belgium was the first European country to possess railways. This was due in part to the proximity of England, which served as an encouraging example, but it was also a product of the desire of the young Belgian state to assert itself, and to make full use both of its situation as a European junction and its port of Antwerp. Until 1830 in fact Belgium treated the question of transport in terms of canals. In keeping with the plan conceived during the Napoleonic era, Antwerp sought to develop connections with Cologne and Charleroi by means of waterways, the very short and narrow railways being no more than their tributaries. The separation of Belgium from the kingdom of the Netherlands (which retained with Limburg and Luxembourg a great stretch of the valley of the Meuse) turned the attention of the new kingdom to railways.

After hesitating for many years between private and state enterprise, Belgium decided in 1833-4 to entrust its railway construction to the state. Straight away the purely economic concept of a line Antwerp-Liège-Cologne was replaced by a rational overall plan, which combined the ambition to take part in the European transit traffic with the needs of a truly national network, running in an east-west and north-south direction. State bonds were issued with the backing of British capital; and Belgium, without rejecting in principle the granting of concessions to private companies, decided first to try out on some of the earliest lines the possibilities of deliberately planned railway charges.

The limited extent of the network envisaged made such a project fairly simple. The opening of the Brussels–Malines line on 5 May 1835 (attended by Stephenson in a third-class carriage) had the character of a great European event; Belgium was taking the lead on the Continent. This line was as yet no more than a suburban connection which could not even be compared to the Liverpool–Manchester; but in the following year Antwerp was reached, and by 1842 Brussels was linked to the French frontier and to Ostend as well as to Antwerp. The sharp depression of the valley of the Meuse, however, which from 1838 had been provided with an inclined plane and a stationary traction engine, was really conquered only in 1843 when the Liège line reached the Prussian frontier. In 1844 the project begun ten years earlier was finally completed. The estimated cost had been exceeded because of intervening changes in technique, but even so, with an average of £16,500 a mile it remained far lower than that of the main English lines. Moreover, the charges were marked by their simplicity and moderation. As a result the network did not make any great profit at the start, especially as it was bound by law to redeem its debt as if it had been a short-term concession and not a state undertaking. The railway was considered a public utility rather than a profit-making venture. The first rails, as had been the case in America, came from Cardiff, and the first locomotives from Newcastle, but the later orders were placed in Belgium, especially at the Cockerill factories at Seraing. The swift growth of the Belgian industry removed any fear of economic vassalage.

Furthermore, from 1842 private companies were granted concessions to develop subsidiary lines at their own risk. In 1843 the state was operating 559 km. of line. In 1845 and 1846 855 km. were granted to private companies, which were for the most part English. England was at the height of its 'railway mania'; the minister Nothomb became alarmed: 'We are going to become a province of England'. But the 1847 crisis led to a loss of confidence in most of these companies which had overestimated, or at least pretended to overestimate, the importance of these secondary lines. The government was forced to agree to an extension of the accepted time limits for completion, and, moreover, to guarantee the interest payments. In 1870 the state operated nearly one quarter of the 3136 km. Given the small total length of the network, there was not much opportunity for fusions to take place, but from 1886, the scales of rates were combined so as to provide some measure of homogeneity. The state began to buy up the private lines; it was alarmed at the attempts made by the French Compagnie de l'Est to create a network in Luxembourg and the east of the country, while the Compagnie du Nord, also French, had leased a number of the lines in the south of the country from the English companies. In return, Belgian industry and Belgian capital played an important part outside the national frontiers. Belgian plant was sold as far away as Russia; Belgian contractors, such as Parent, Schaken, Philippart, undertook important projects in France. The Belgian network became the standard model for small countries with a large population and high technical capacities.

The Netherlands remained for a long time indifferent to the possibilities of railways, It was a small country in which maritime navigation and canals played a vital role, and which besides had a good road network and no heavy industries. In this amphibious land, the great number of waterways and the many inroads made by the sea raised complicated engineering problems. In 1839 a short line was opened between Haarlem and Amsterdam, but this was an isolated venture. In 1850 the Netherlands had only 179 km. of track. In 1852 Brassey built the 43 miles of the Dutch Rhenish Railway. Amsterdam was already connected to Antwerp via Rotterdam. By 1865 there were still only 865 km. in operation, built for the greater part by the state and farmed out to private companies. Holland knew that its future, just like its past, depended on water.

It was much the same in Scandinavia. Denmark opened its first line in 1847. It was 30 km. long and linked Copenhagen to Roskilde. In Sweden the era of the railway started as late as 1856.

In central Europe, where new territorial formations were in the making, the revolution in transport led to new economic conditions and made political changes indispensable. The changes in transport were later than in the Anglo-Saxon world. The industrial movement in the western parts of this area was curbed by governments distrustful of private initiative, although for a number of years they proved incapable of replacing it. In any case steam navigation on the Rhine made it possible to postpone the introduction of the rail, though Ruhrort did not become a centre of river steamer construction, independent of the English and the Dutch, until the end of the 1840's. On the Elbe and the Danube the bad condition of the river together with the number and level of the tolls meant the limited growth of navigation.

The possibility of a railway network took root slowly, despite the presence of persuasive advocates such as Baader, Harkort, and List. Before 1830 Rhenish industrialists and officials, anxious to avoid complete dependence on Holland for an exit, hoped to establish a connection with Aix-la-Chapelle and Antwerp and, in the east, with the Weser and Bremen. But it was only in December 1835 that the opening of the minute line from Nuremberg to Furth (6 km.) announced the era of the railway. It proved a profitable undertaking, carrying a great many Jews who worked in Nuremberg but were unable to live there. From then on companies began to be formed everywhere. In 1839 the heavily populated kingdom of Saxony opened the Leipzig–Dresden line. Twenty years later the bulk of the German network had been built: it consisted of two major lines from Berlin running westwards across the northern plain, followed later by a line from Vienna to the Rhine across the southern States, the completion of which was delayed by Prussia. Finally, cutting across these lines there were a series of other lines, which followed a pattern imposed by the geography of the region, and which duplicated the work of the rivers by linking the northern ports to the interior of the country. In 1847 the network had passed beyond the stage of suburban lines and of lines connecting one river to another. Two nebula of lines appeared: the Rhenish group, which emanated from Cologne in the direction of the Meuse and the Weser, and, through the gap in the Rhenish Massif, towards Frankfort and Basle; and the Prusso-Saxon group which ran in the direction of Cassel in the west, and Warsaw in the east, and was connected with the Austrian line coming from Prague. Only Wurtemberg and Bavaria remained with isolated lines. Prussian hegemony was asserting itself.

The first lines were built with private capital. The great number of territorial divisions meant that every centre aspired to become an important railway junction. As a result there were any amount of limited undertakings, resembling in some respects those in the United States. Just as in the U.S.A., land was cheap, though, in contrast to the situation in the New World, so was labour. Moreover, the German lines avoided costly foundation works and consequently did not provide much comfort: the fourth-class passenger carriages had neither seats nor roof. In 1850 the average cost per mile was £11,000 as against £16,500 in Belgium and £30,000 or £40,000 in England. As in Belgium a national industry soon developed and curtailed the need to use foreign materials. In 1840 Philadelphia, Newcastle and Manchester supplied plant to the German lines, but in 1843 there were already more locomotives from Borsig on the Berlin–Stettin line than from its English competitors.

At first governments remained aside, afraid of overloading their budgets. But, for military and political reasons, they had no intention of giving the companies an entirely free hand, even though the companies were not sufficiently strong to be really formidable. The Prussian state had to agree to advance them loans, or to guarantee interest payments on their capital; it used this opportunity to establish its control over the companies, a control that was instituted by the famous law of 1838. From 1842 to 1846 Germany, like the rest of the world, enjoyed an era of prosperity. The southern States took advantage of this to build themselves their trunk lines after the Belgian pattern. The economic and political crisis of 1847–50 brought down the value of the shares and enabled the state to buy them up. From 1850 to 1857 there was a considerable amount of foreign investment in German railway shares, but the crisis of 1857 caused foreign speculators to withdraw. As early as 1860 the Prussian state was already operating 55 per cent of its national network, and everywhere else the state took over the extension of its lines by means of public loans. In 1850 thirty-eight companies came to an agreement over methods of operation so that there should be some uniformity; and the creation of state networks, by state acquisition of the shares of the private companies, replaced fusions. In 1869, 17,330 km. of railway were in operation in Germany of which nearly 10,000 were in Prussia. France at this time had no more than 16,854 km., and in the whole of Europe only the United Kingdom with 24,768 km. surpassed Germany.

The role of the state in the Germanic world was striking. Railways seemed to be a civilian branch of the army. In a country where capital was sufficient but not over-abundant, wastages resulting from speculation, the scourge of Anglo-Saxon countries, were avoided. Moreover, lines of public utility, running at a loss but of vital importance from a national point of view, were undertaken in Bavaria and especially to the east of the Elbe (the Ostbahn was started in 1849), where the arrival of the locomotive was really a pioneering feat since roads were practically non-existent in those parts.

France had in 1840 427 km. of track, almost as much as Germany. Most of it consisted of mining lines, such as that from Alès to Beaucaire, or suburban lines, such as that from Paris to St Germain or Versailles. Between 1840 and 1850, however, the country lagged very much behind in comparison with its neighbours. In 1850 France had 3000 km. and Germany nearly 6000. In France the tradition of state paternalism had always been strong, and in this field it was incarnated in the *Corps des Ponts et Chaussées*. These officials were more concerned with the public utility aspect of railways than with their purely commercial side, and therefore drew up a general plan with lines radiating from Paris towards the frontiers and practically shadowing the roads. Besides they wanted to have from the start well-planned and long-lasting lines, which were very expensive to establish. Their plan was that the state should build and run the railways in the same way as the royal roads and the canals. They intended to go on with the plan drawn up at the Restoration for the canals at the same time as undertaking the construction of the railways. The whole venture turned out to be far beyond the resources of the state. Hence the idea arose of seeking the co-operation of private capital, though without the granting of permanent concessions. But many people feared the influence of capitalist interests under the July monarchy, and there were endless debates about railway policy in the Chamber, debates which, while appearing to deal with theoretical issues, were complicated by the pride and *amour propre* of individuals and localities. As a result a considerable amount of time was lost. Moreover, the companies which attempted to link Paris to Orleans and to Rouen for the first time were only able to complete their project in 1843 after great difficulties and with state help, although the lines had been excellently planned. This revealed quite clearly the timid approach of private capital to the whole field of railway construction. Even then almost half the capital of these companies came from England. It was believed in London that there was not much room left for large profits in Britain, and also that the French lines would be almost as heavily used as the English, so that they would be in a position to yield as much profit while costing only half the price to build. Once the English contractors had finished the line and the whole affair was well under way, it would then be possible to sell the shares back to the French at a profit. But this technical and financial colonization on the part of England aroused the suspicions of all those who opposed the July monarchy and were already much inclined to tax Louis-Philippe with being far too complaisant towards England. All this led logically enough to the state and private capital, whether English or French, joining forces. This was brought about by the law of 1842. The state undertook the most costly items, the road-bed and the bridges and tunnels; but the companies were given very short concessions so that the network was very soon back in the hands of the state. From 1842 to 1846 France got a touch of 'railway mania', most of it speculative, in which the English played a decisive part. Speculation was cut short by the economic crisis and then by the 1848 revolution. Shareholders were unable to meet calls on their shares; share prices fell; and the Republic considered buying up the lines. This possibility was vigorously opposed by French and English capitalists, and it was in any case set aside by the conservatives, who began to return to power in June 1848 and eventually supported the *coup d'état* of 1851 which established the dictatorial regime of Louis-Napoleon Bonaparte.

The new regime encouraged fusions, which led to the establishment of six large networks. It also backed the creation of the Crédit Mobilier by the Pereire brothers, which maintained a buoyant stock market and thus enabled new issues to be launched. In 1858 the state, which ever since 1851 had been granting long-term concessions, concluded agreements with the companies: the companies were to receive a share of the income equal to that which the operation of the 'trunk lines' had so far been yielding to shareholders, while all excess net income was to finance the deficit resulting from the running of the secondary lines which were to be opened. If there was no excess net income the state was to cover the difference by a guarantee of interest on the obligations of the railway companies. The companies, therefore, could proceed to the issue of new shares knowing that they would be backed by the state which had now become their partner. They had to some extent become official bodies. This arrangement led to railway shares permeating all sections of French society; and the shares made it possible to extend the network to the less productive parts of the country. In 1850 France had 3000 km. of railway lines, and in 1869 nearly 17,000. She was no longer far behind Germany, and only Great Britain could compete with her as regards the quality of her railways.

After 1855 and the end of the Crimean War, the Paris market played a vital, and sometimes indispensable, role in the financing of railways in Europe. The rivalry of the Pereires and the Rothschilds of Paris often went well beyond the frontiers of France, and had repercussions in the countries of the Mediterranean and the Danube. The financiers, with the backing of the French Empire, now at the height of its prestige, behind them helped to bring these areas out of the stage in which they had only stretches of suburban line. The Habsburg monarchy had already begun the creation of a state network out of public funds: the Prague–Dresden line was opened in 1850 and the Vienna–Breslau in 1847. The great minister, Bruck, would have liked to make Trieste an Austrian Hamburg, but the undertaking was too vast for the imperial finances and Austria had to appeal to foreign capital. The Pêreires took over the line from the state, and extended it from the Saxon frontier to the Turkish Empire via Prague, Vienna, and Pesth. In 1858 the Rothschilds, in partnership with London financiers such as Laing and Uzielli, bought up the Sudbahn which ran from Vienna towards Trieste— a 3000 km. line which extended to the heart of the kingdom of Lombardy and Venice. In 1867 the Brenner was pierced. The total network rose from under 3000 km. in 1855 to 8000 in 1869.

Anglo-French financial collaboration was also extended to Italy. Cavour's policy was conceived in terms of railways. Pius IX invited Mirès, a Frenchman, to come and build the network of the Papal State, which enabled pilgrims to come flocking to Rome. In 1855 Italy had under 1000 km. in operation; by 1869 it had 5772.

Spain also obtained her network by means of this blend of collaboration and intense rivalry. In 1855 there were under 500 km. of line; by 1869 it had 5400. Mirès, the Pereires, and the Rothschilds—all three were in the field. In fact these Spanish or Italian ventures did not yield very much, even to those who set them up. The same applied to the 700 km. of Portuguese railway. But the Paris market, the free partner of the London market, had now established itself.

Russia had already 1188 km. of track in 1855. As early as 1836 she possessed a suburban line from St Petersburg to Tsarkoe-Selo, and in 1851 St Petersburg was connected to Moscow. After losing the Crimean War, Russia realized the importance of developing her railways. In 1857 an Anglo-French company was established. The French engineers were struck by the cheapness of the land, but also by the low quality of the labour force supplied by the nobles. Moreover, the capital could not be raised very easily because exchange rates were unfavourable and because the Russian state was borrowing at the same time as the company. As a result the company very soon desired to have its contract revised, and the government made use of the opportunity to take over the lines which were being constructed. These lines were completed by the state, or else by small private companies, but in any case far too hurriedly. The trains were slow, and there were long stops for meals. The coaches were too large. In western eyes the whole network was ostentatious and improvised. It took one day to get from Moscow to St Petersburg. There was something about the trains that brought to mind those of the United States without of course their speed. Still, the railway had made its appearance in this vast empire. In 1869, 7685 km. were in operation.

Finally, from 1868 to 1870 the financier Hirsch, who was related to the Bischoffsheims of Brussels and had connections with the French and the English, began to construct a line right across the Turkish Empire from Sarajevo to Constantinople. The railway had pervaded the whole of Europe; the network had grown from 34,000 km. in 1855 to 75,000 in 1865. The Crimean and the Italian Wars had shown the military importance of railways. Foreign contractors had introduced the railway everywhere in return for subsidies of land and money. Brassey and Peto were in the process of building lines in Denmark and Sweden.

But henceforth there was too much competition for the British. Everywhere in Europe, London contractors were coming face to face with the financiers from Paris, Brussels, and Vienna. As a result they moved their centre of activity to the frontiers of economic civilization, and thereby helped to push these frontiers farther back. This meant, however, that the railways were to be built henceforth in countries that could not at this stage buy them back once completed or even undertake their administration. The railways had to be managed from London. South Africa and Australia both needed railways if the interior of the country was to be opened up, since neither possessed rivers with sufficient water supplies to make them navigable. The Australian network was started modestly in 1850; by 1859 the country still had no more than 170 miles. Work was also in progress at the Cape; but the prize area was India.

From as early as 1845, at the height of the 'railway mania', companies were set up to build lines from Calcutta to Raniganj (East India Railway), and from Bombay to the cotton-growing districts. But the crisis intervened and there were enough places nearer at hand in which to invest capital. Lord Dalhousie thereupon established a system of very long-term concessions, together with a guarantee of interest by the Indian government. The existence of such a guarantee implied that the higher authority, which was responsible both for the conception and the realization of the plan, was to have some measure of control over the railways. And though, at first, only the capital involved in the original estimates was guaranteed, the guarantee was later extended to cover the additional costs. The telegraph network was built at the same time along the path of the railways, and the value of this combined network was clearly revealed at the time of the Mutiny in 1857. After the Crown had taken over the government of India, and because of the shortage of cotton resulting from the American War, railways expanded at a rapid rate, giving the subcontinent the beginnings of political and economic unity. In 1870 £75 million were invested in some 5000 miles of Indian railway.

But the very speed at which the work was completed, the fact that both construction materials and coal had to be transported from Great Britain, and the low returns in the early years of operation (for the network was more strategic than commercial), meant that the cost of construction proved very high. The system whereby the state guaranteed interest, a delicate enough operation in France, became extremely dangerous when the persons involved were contractors who had behind them a whole section of British industry. In 1860 joint-stock finance companies in London began to take an interest in the Indian, as in the American, railways. The contractors kept the shares, and acquired the necessary funds by issuing bonds on the lines to be constructed. This was one of the causes of 'Black Friday', which in 1866 littered the London market with wreckage. As a result the idea of state construction began to gain ground in certain circles.

The Turkish Empire also attracted British contractors in search of outlets. But the Sultan's guarantee was not comparable with that of the Indian government, despite the fact that—like the Indian guarantee —it was revised to keep pace with rising costs. It was not until the creation of the Ottoman Bank in 1863, set up by Pereire, Baring, Glyn and Devaux, that western interests exercised control over the Turkish debt and the fiscal policy of the Ottoman Empire. Using rails that had already been used during the Crimean War, Peto and Betts between 1856 and 1866 built the line from Smyrna to Aydin. Another line was already in operation, between the Danube and the Black Sea, for the grain trade.

When the railway had achieved its independence by the creation of coherent networks, then the problem of its relations with roads and waterways faced the Atlantic community, which now possessed ample means of transport competing one with the other. At the death of McAdam (1836) and Telford (1834), railways were not much swifter than the mail-coach; but they were making steady progress; and the mail-coach was far more expensive. Three months after the opening of the London–Birmingham in 1838, regular coach services were reduced from twenty-two a day to four. There was indeed no real struggle. The owners of the coach services developed connections with the railways and, quite often, in France as well as in England, became their owners also. In England, between 1830 and 1850, revenue from tolls dropped by one-third, and it became almost impossible to farm out the roads running parallel to the railways.

But road traffic did not thereby disappear completely. It moved into other directions and concentrated itself in these other fields. The road became a 'feeder' for the railway. Tolls began to disappear from English roads at the moment that traffic was no longer generally dependent on road transport. Road haulage was changed into a short-distance service which ensured regular and frequent services. Even if horse breeding did not decline, transport ceased to be a rural occupation and became work of an industrial character, although it was still in the hands of country people who had now moved into the towns.

With internal navigation, on the other hand, a bitter struggle broke out; and it is not yet over today. The waterway abandoned without a fight the transport of passengers and mail, but, as a result, it was able to concentrate all the better on the rivalry over the transport of heavy goods. The early railways carried coal; then towards 1830 they began to devote themselves more especially to the transport of passengers. As a result the theorists, who had already forgotten the origin of the rail, concluded rather hastily that there was a natural division of labour in the transport world. In France and the United States, the state, which was responsible for the construction of an expensive canal network, did not welcome the advent of this newcomer, which threatened to make its canals redundant. State engineers in France, therefore, wanted stubbornly to press on with the opening of new canals planned long before the era of the rail. The State of New York allowed the construction of railways running parallel to the Erie canal on the express condition that they would not carry any goods; eventually the railways were granted this right, but only during such times as the canals could not operate because of ice, and it was only in 1851 that they received the freedom to organize their traffic as they wanted against payment to the treasury of a sum equal to the navigation dues. From that time on, the waterway retained the custom of very heavy and cumbersome goods only. In England the canals attempted to organize campaigns in Parliament. Their monopoly, however, had been oppressive and there was not much public sympathy for their cause. The Trent and Mersey saw its dividend drop from 75 to 32 per cent between 1825 and 1839. Beginning in 1846 the canals running parallel to railways were let out to the railway companies which could thereby control the strategic points of their networks. There were still 2750 miles of canal under independent administration, but the traffic on them, even though fairly heavy, remained purely local.

In France it was only in 1857 that the railway network was sufficiently advanced to allow it to carry a greater amount of traffic than the waterways. The state, which owned the canals, refused to farm them out to companies connected with the railways or the coal mines. It even began to buy back the shares of the capitalists whose help it had sought in 1821. This process, which continued until 1870, and proceeded at the same time as the lowering of navigation dues, proved extremely costly.

In Germany the result was also very clear. From 1850 to 1870 traffic on the lines in the Rhineland and Westphalia increased almost twenty-fold, while navigation on the Rhine was only three and a half times as great. As soon as the railway was opened (1847), the traffic between Hamburg and Berlin by water dropped by two-thirds. The transport of goods by rail from Cologne to Antwerp was, after 1847, twice as great as that by river from Cologne to Holland.

All in all the waterway everywhere found itself thrown back into a subsidiary role. The railway, which was more uniform, could reach larger areas than the waterway could ever hope to attain. And even in those areas where it did exist, the waterway consisted of heterogeneous stretches that did not lend themselves very easily to general traffic. Furthermore, it was slow, irregular and passive. It could not follow the example of the railway and adapt its charges to its cargoes: maintaining the full rate for the traffic that was forced to use it, and cutting its prices down to the minimum for all that might go elsewhere if it found better conditions. When inland navigation tried to streamline its organization and its equipment, as was the case for instance on the Rhine, by the creation of powerful steam-navigation companies whose customers were their principal shareholders, or, on the Seine, by the introduction of towing chains, then the members of the archaic guild of ferrymen raised a cry of monopoly. This was the case of the towers, or boatmen, of the Rhine who in 1848 attacked the steamers, and suggested to the Parliament at Frankfurt that an extremely reactionary programme be introduced.

In short, except in certain areas, such as the Rhineland or the Great Lakes, the railways were free, by means of the rates they charged, to draw up a new map of the economy in those countries which had been largely knit together by the building of the railways. There were first of all the differential rates: the greater the journey the less was the cost relative to distance. Places which were farthest away from the sources of raw materials or of fuel were thus artificially drawn nearer to them. Clearly enough, in order to attain maximum efficiency, the rail had to keep its freight for as long as possible: journeys which involved a break, and a change from rail to steamer, were not really approved of. The lowest rates were granted to large clients who could guarantee a regular volume of important and homogeneous freight. To these customers the railways meant speed and precision, and at a price that compared very favourably with the one charged by the waterways. Besides, the railway was closely tied to the coal mines and the establishments of the metallurgical industry, since it was their largest single client. Railways encouraged long journeys, killed the old entrepôt towns, where formerly goods used to be trans-shipped, and the areas which formerly possessed the monopoly of some particular product; and they substituted in their place new rivals not in a position to compete before because of their geographical situation. It is understandable that once it was established the railway, everywhere in demand, met with open hostility from many quarters: the former entrepôts; areas depending on a virtual monopoly for their existence or on their proximity to coal deposits or a navigable waterway; or even areas situated within reach of intermediate stations on one of the main lines and which the track could now afford to ignore; and finally the small ventures which were not capable of competing with their mighty rivals. As a result an accusation of monopoly was levied at them. At first governments set the maximum tariffs far too high. The railways could always operate well beneath them, and limited themselves to adjusting charges, with some measure of flexibility, when and as the need arose.

In the U.S.A., until 1869, there was such a demand for railways that the thought of restraining them did not arise. Besides, the country was so vast, and capital relatively limited, that fusions began to take place fairly late in the day. It was only between 1853 and 1858 that Vanderbilt built up his network around the Albany–Buffalo line.

In Great Britain, on the other hand, the question presented itself very early. The companies had permanent concessions, so that as soon as fusions removed the possibility of competition over a given stretch of line, the state had to intervene. The Railway Department of the Board of Trade was set up in 1842 at Gladstone's instigation, but it limited itself to issuing friendly warnings to the companies. The 1844 law merely established that concessions granted for future lines would be limited to the first fifteen years of operation, and that after that period the state could buy them back. Even the creation of 'parliamentary trains', running at reduced rates, could be imposed only on these future companies. The old ones remained in law completely free. Despite Dalhousie's zeal, the commission of the 'five railway kings' was practically abolished, for the railway interests, supported by Cobden's brand of liberalism, were dominant in Parliament.

On the Continent the state could apply more efficacious control, since it either owned the main lines, as in the case of Belgium, or else applied the repurchase clauses included in the temporary concessions, as in the case of Germany. In France the companies felt secure in view of their very long-term concessions, and the very large sums of money the Empire would have had to raise in order to buy them back, and also because of the system of state partnership instituted in 1858. But the Empire was a strong regime, and, if the need arose, could impose its will on the leading members of these capitalist groups that it had itself brought into existence. In all circles, moreover, especially among the republicans, the 1852 arrangement was always violently attacked, so that a political change could easily lead to a new agreement. Nevertheless, all told, until 1869 the companies enjoyed a great measure of freedom.

At a time when nearly all external trade was still done by sea, any new invention in sea transport was of incalculable importance. And it was between 1840 and 1869 that the iron steamship driven by a screw propeller definitely established itself.

The steamer left the estuaries and channels for the high seas, bringing with it in this new sphere greater regularity if not greater speed. In this way 'the ocean railways' built up a genuine passenger traffic. As regards freight, progress was slower: the paddle steamer of 1830 had a speed of 10 knots but a capacity of no more than 1500 tons. Its engine, moreover, was heavy, cumbersome, costly to install and to maintain, required a skilled and highly paid personnel, and used a fuel that was still fairly scarce. It was the screw propeller which allowed a progressive increase in the tonnage of ships, and thereby gave an advantage to construction in iron. As early as 1838–40 Smith, an Englishman, perfected the screw steamer *Archimedes* and sailed round the British Isles, and then on to Holland and Belgium. In 1839 Ericsson crossed the

Atlantic. In 1841 the *Corsica*, belonging to the Frenchman Sauvage, was a screw steamer. In 1850 Dupuy de Lome launched at Toulon the *Napoléon*, a screw vessel of 5000 tons which travelled from Toulon to Marseilles at a speed of 14 knots. But the *Napoléon* retained its three masts and 2800 sq. metres of sail. In 1847 Lloyd's was still not putting steamers in a special category. Out of a total tonnage of 3 million the British fleet had only 116,000 tons of steamers, and in that same year British yards were building almost the same tonnage of sailing ships as of all the steamers it possessed put together.

The construction of ships in iron was still in an imperfect stage. The parliamentary inquiries held in England between 1844 and 1848 on the subject of the repeal of the Navigation Acts hardly concerned themselves with steamers or with ships built of iron. The British Admiralty preferred wooden ships, and it was only in 1845 that it commissioned its first big iron ship at Birkenhead. Even then, all that was envisaged at this period was a metal lining over a wooden hull.

By 1869 steamers were being constructed solely of iron. Lighter, stouter, less subject to insects in hot climates, less liable to catch fire and, above all, with a greater carrying capacity, the iron ship proved more seaworthy and cost from 10 to 15 per cent less. After 1860 even some sailing ships were made of iron. But while the large steamer was hardly conceivable without the screw propeller sailing ships were well suited to wood. The years 1850 to 1860 marked the height of the glory of sailing ships, with the era of the 'clippers'. In 1858 clippers crossed the Atlantic in 12–14 days. American construction retained its lead, from the maritime provinces of Canada to Massachusetts. This was the golden age of the trade with China and California. The clippers used the nautical works of Maury on marine currents, and when the wind was with them exceeded 15 knots or 300 miles a day—and this with a cargo of 3000 to 5000 tons. After 1850 all records were broken: Liverpool–Melbourne in 83 days, Canton–New York in 84, San Francisco–New York in 80.

From 1837 British yards began to make some progress. But it was not until the economic crisis of 1857, and the Civil War, that the Americans sold a great proportion of their fleet and devoted themselves henceforth to their continent. After 1869 too many changes had taken place in the technique of construction of iron ships to allow American yards to rise again and compete with the English metal and mechanical industries which were in full expansion, employing an army of skilled workmen at wages which were lower than those in the U.S.A. In 1853 a quarter of the tonnage built in Great Britain was steam driven and more than 25 per cent of the steamers were of iron. In the same year 22 per cent of new construction in the U.S.A. consisted of steamers, but none of it was of iron. Between 1850 and 1860 the share of long-distance freight carried by steamer rose from 14 to 28 per cent. In 1875 wooden ships were built only in Canada, Norway, and Italy. The iron steamer had triumphed. But until 1850 its final victory was still in the balance.

The first *Royal William*, built at Trois-Rivières (Quebec) in 1831, still took more than forty days to go from Quebec to London in 1835; its younger brother, built at Liverpool, was the first true passenger steamer, but it very soon ended up as a coal store. Yet, between 1837 and 1840, the wooden paddle steamer started to cross the ocean using steam alone. At once it was adopted as the ideal instrument for the transport of mail and passengers. In 1837 France began to operate state passenger steamer services in the Mediterranean. But it could not compete with the P. and O., which ran a service between Falmouth and Alexandria in a maximum of fifteen days, introduced the first large passenger steamer of metal, and in 1851 adopted the screw. In 1840 Samuel Cunard's *Britannia* crossed the Atlantic in fourteen days, that is to say no faster than a clipper. It was soon rivalled by the Collins company on the New York–Bremen run. In 1856 Cunard commissioned the *Persia* to be built in iron; in 1862 his *Scotia* did the crossing in eight days; and in the same year the *China* was his first screw-propelled steamer. At this time paddle steamers achieved 15 knots, but their wheels were cumbersome and fairly fragile in rough weather. The compound engine, perfected by John Elder in 1854, achieved high pressures only in 1868. In 1869 the Inman line provided services between Queenstown and New York in a little under eight days using iron steamers with a screw.

The Anglo-Saxon powers—in point of fact that meant Great Britain—had a virtual monopoly. However, in France the Messageries Impériales replaced in 1851 the state lines in the Mediterranean, and they extended their services towards the Indian Ocean, the Far East and the South Atlantic. The Compagnie Transatlantique, founded in 1861 by the Pêreire brothers, was used at first to provide transport to Mexico, which Napoleon III wanted to transform into a satellite of France. In 1864 the company began to operate its service from Le Havre to New York, with two paddle steamers built at Greenock, and designed specially for passengers by the company's own engineers; but its services were slower than the Cunarders, and neither Saint Nazaire nor Le Havre could as yet accommodate comfortably the large transatlantic liners.

The Hamburg–Amerika line was founded in 1847, but it had its first screw-propelled steamer, built in England, only in 1856. In 1867 its steamers took 9–10 days to cross the ocean. The Lloyd line of Bremen was established in 1857. From as early as 1836 that of Trieste was successfully competing with the French packet boat services in the Mediterranean.

These steam packet boats gave the North Atlantic community a powerful and regular method of transport, an absolutely essential requirement if it was to achieve a really deep-seated unity at the moment when, on the continent, the railway age was beginning. Moreover, they ensured the transport of emigrants to the new worlds opening out before Europe. They established the triumph of the screw-propelled steamer. Every steamer was the precursor of a host of others. From 1865 the 900,000 tons of British steamers carried as much freight as the 4,900,000 tons of sailing ships. In 1855 the construction of a railway line across the isthmus of Panama, and more especially the opening of the Suez Canal in 1869, proved terrible blows for the clippers.

From the time of the first trials in 1831–5, it was clear that the companies which set up regular steamer services could survive only if they received large subsidies from their governments. Thus the Royal West India Mail Steam Packet Company, set up in 1838 by City merchants to ply between England and the West Indies and Central America, received a subsidy of £240,000 a year, while the sail packets obtained only £76,000. Despite a reduction in the distances covered, and in the number of ships employed, the Company could still only offer 6 per cent. Cunard in 1852 obtained a subsidy of £173,000. The mail subsidy was meant to be an encouragement to construction, and it gave the company tremendous prestige and a virtual monopoly.

The underwater electric telegraph was at first an achievement of English capital and technical skill, just like the steam-packet. The underwater cable crossed the 'narrow seas' in the 1850's: the Dover-Calais cable, for instance, was laid in 1851. But when an attempt was made to secure a connection with India or America it met with continuous difficulties. Eventually, the *Great Eastern* succeeded in linking Europe to America, and in 1870 England was in direct communication with India. There remained the Pacific to cross. Nevertheless, the civilized world had become a single market.

IV.   'From Sea to Sea': The Era of Transcontinentals

After 1869, in that part of the world which had undergone an industrial revolution, the important railway developments were over; the principal lines were operating, and the only further work that could be done was to increase the density of the networks. The stage had even been reached of 'parochializing' the railway, by transforming this means of mass transportation into a method of local traffic. But in 1869 the opening of the first American transcontinental marked the beginning of a new phase: the railway was to allow continental states to realize Napoleon's premature dream—the political domination of an entire continent. Until now the world had known only thalassocracies; but they were now to be confronted with an imperialism founded on railroads. The railways were one of the essential conditions of the American thrust westwards, the Russian thrust eastwards, and the domination of all the continents newly opened up by Europe from the sea.

First of all it is essential to point out that during this period Europeans were completing the final organization of their own continent by the great alpine passages. Until this time the barrier of the Alps could be breached only at its flanks, by way of Marseilles and Trieste. The railways which now pierced the Alps were undertaken by governments for political reasons. The Semmering (1854) and Brenner lines were part of Habsburg imperial policy. The origin of the Franco-Italian tunnel of Mont Cenis, built between 1858 and 1871, could be traced back to the Franco-Piedmontese policy of Cavour and Napoleon III; Anglo-French finance and technical skill were no more than the instruments of that policy. After 1871 the railway allowed Bismarck's Reich to set out in conquest of the Mediterranean by the domination of Italy and the Balkans. In 1882 the St Gothard was crossed, and the new state of Italy, financed until then by France and England, fell under German influence. From 1896 French political interests and French finance staged a return to the Italian scene; the Swiss lines, which had been nationalized, were no longer under German influence, and between 1898 and 1906 the Simplon line drew Milan towards Paris and London. The Arlberg, completed in 1884, connected Paris directly to Vienna via Switzerland, and thus enabled France to by-pass southern Germany in order to reach the Dual monarchy, where it still had important investments. These lines would have been constructed sooner or later; in actual fact they were undertaken by private capital which had now put itself in the service of the great rival powers.

Developments followed a similar pattern in America. The United States and Canada achieved their present-day proportions by means of the transcontinental railways. From 1860 the U.S.A. abandoned the Atlantic in order to organize the west of the continent. The dense network in the east, lying between the Atlantic and the Mississippi, served as a base of departure. In 1835 there were 1000 miles, 4600 in 1845, 18,000 in 1855 and 30,000 or over in 1860—that is to say nearly as much as the whole of Europe. In 1890 there were 167,000 miles in operation, a quarter more than in Europe, including Russia. Between

1867 and 1873, 33,000 miles were laid down, more than from the very beginning to 1860. The crises of 1873 and 1893 were largely due to overbuilding. It was in the U.S.A. that the cost of transport was lowest. In the larger cities horse-drawn trams were widely used: in New York people did not do much walking. In 1884 the first electric trolley line was brought into operation in Kansas City. From then on tramways replaced horses or steam for the 'street railways'. America led the world in the matter of these railways; in 1900 she had almost 200,000 miles.

French inquirers, such as Malezieux in 1872 or Louis-Paul Dubois in 1893, pointed out the essential features of this achievement. To begin with, little capital was involved, and what there was was raised by the contractors themselves, and more especially by mortgage of the lands granted by the towns. After 1850 the federal government itself began to offer subsidies in the form of land. Lack of traffic did not cause the work to be abandoned any more than it did in Europe: the line was administered by a 'receiver' in the name of the creditors until a rival company bought it over or took it on lease. In this way the extreme fragmentation of the network gave way to 'pools' and 'consolidations', the work of the railway kings, hungry for money and power. This was the epoch of outright competition and of the battle of the networks. From 1868 to 1873 Gould and Vanderbilt engaged in a truly epic struggle for the control of the traffic between New York and Lake Erie: railway tariffs were savagely manipulated, attempts were made to corner shares on Wall Street, attempts which were met by the watering of capital, fabulous fortunes were made and no less fabulous losses, both involving British and German capital. The struggles provide one of the sagas of capitalism. Everyone was in the pay of the presidents of the railways—municipalities, magistrates, senators. The market price of shares overdiscounted the prosperity; but it was America in the making, with its confusion and its dynamism. In the same way as in Europe, American railroads were largely the product of an influx of foreign capital and generous subsidies in land, the value of which was greatly increased by the advent of the railway. But with the fusions, giant monopolies were constituted, possessing permanent concessions and capable of determining the fate of the States whose authority they openly defied. Not even the federal government could control them. In 1891 there were 1785 companies in existence in the United States; but forty-one of them operated between them 56 per cent of the entire network. Vanderbilt controlled 16,000 miles, that is to say a great deal more than the leading French or English companies. But even the best networks did not yield more than 4–5 per cent. Over this vast continent the railway revealed the full extent of its capacities in transporting, over long distances, very great quantities of some commodities, and at lower rates than in Europe. The railroads allowed the U.S.A. to become the leading industrial nation.

Politically, the transcontinentals made America. To link up the two oceans it was necessary to cross vast steppe lands, which were of little economic value, and to surmount the Rockies. On top of all this the Indians had to be dealt with. In 1830 it took six months for a team of oxen to go from St Louis to San Francisco, assuming that they had fate on their side. In 1860 the relay system, called the Pony-express, took no more than 11 or 12 days, but it was more a sporting achievement than a journey. The only real way of reaching California was to cross the isthmus of Panama by the railway completed in 1855 and which preceded the canal linking up the oceans in the same way as at Suez.

The problem became of such urgency after the discovery of gold in California that America saw its future solely in terms of the transcontinental lines. In 1853-4 ten possible routes were explored, and the bulk of the knowledge acquired about the west summarized in thirteen large volumes. The war between the States was caused in part by the desire of each side to serve as the point of departure for the future railway, and the inferiority of its railway network really doomed the south to defeat from the start. On 1 July 1862 the federal government decided that the track was to start at Omaha on the Missouri, the farthest point to the west that the railway reached at the time, and that it was to extend to the Sacramento river. This secured, while the war was still at its height, the much-needed support of distant California. Two companies began constructing the line from either end, the Californian Central Pacific and, in the east, the Union Pacific. The exact point at which they were to meet had not been prearranged, so that the most active of the two companies could secure the greatest part of the State's subsidies. The government was lavish in money and land but, while the war was on, the companies found it difficult to raise the money they required. There was a great deal of unnecessary wastage. The subsidies granted by Congress could by themselves have covered the total cost of the operation. The Central Pacific had, at the start, a capital of 195,000 dollars; this was eventually swollen to 120 million dollars, while its share of the track cost no more than 58 million. The Union Pacific was by no means behindhand. With the help of the Crédit Mobilier, it amassed 109 million dollars to build a line costing 50 million. But for the rivalry of the line subsidized by the state, other transcontinentals would have been built without a doubt, and in less time, to the north and south. But the Central Pacific had to bring its materials to the scene of operations via Cape Horn, and the track advanced through wild country; besides, the speed at which the final work was completed in 1868 and 1869 involved heavy expenditure. The Chinese tracklayers, under Irish and German foremen, laid down 10 miles of track a day. Artesian wells and wind pumps were needed to obtain water. The workers had to carry guns: some of the men who came on ahead to prepare the ground were scalped by the Indians. Order was maintained by military discipline. Finally, in May 1869 San Francisco was no more than eight days distance from St Louis. It is easy to understand that, despite its defects, the opening of the line aroused lively enthusiasm; and the whole of the Union was able to participate in it by means of the telegraph.

Lincoln thought in political and in national terms. There were other possible paths for the railway, easier and across richer lands. As a result, other transcontinental lines were opened in the years following the 1873 crisis: the Northern-Atchison-Topeka-Santa Fe (1883), the Southern Pacific (1885), and finally the Great Northern in 1893. All these railroads raised the value of the land that was lavished on them (44 million acres, for instance, on the Northern Pacific, 24 million on the Southern). If the frontier was a thing of the past in 1890, or there-abouts, it was due to them. They allowed the resources of the lands they had created out of nothing, so to speak, to find their way to Europe, and thus enabled the Union to redeem its debt to the Old World and abandon once and for all its colonial status. The patronage exercised by the companies over the areas in which they had a transport monopoly led to abuses, but these abuses must be contrasted with the work of James Hill, president of the Great Northern, who undertook to people the States by bringing men without land to lands without men, and thus gave them the wherewithal to live. An agricultural and mining empire rapidly formed itself for which the Pacific appeared as the new western frontier of American civilization.

Europeans were particularly struck by the picturesque aspects of this feverish organization of the continent: the exceptional destinies of some adventurers, the battles of workers to make sure, by main force, of an indispensable stretch of the track, the 'snow-ploughs' and the 'cow-catchers' on the locomotives, the boldness of improvised wooden bridges over abysses, the mixed crowds in the smoking carriages, the colonial character of the stations where neighbouring shopkeepers issued tickets for the one and only train in the day over the one and only track. But Europeans were impressed by more than these picturesque features. In 1867 American locomotives created a sensation at the Paris international exhibition; the German States adopted American designs for their railway stock. The whole world imitated the sleepers and the saloon carriages of Pullman, as well as the variety of goods wagons (including the first tanker trucks for petroleum). In

1875 the trains of the Far West, and the 'feeders' of the east, might well be slower than in Europe, on account of their heavy plant and badly designed tracks, but, on the other hand, between New York and Chicago the trains ran as well as the very best in Europe.

The opening of the Canadian Pacific Railway was the product of a political objective: to realize and assert Canada's national existence in the face of the expansive dynamism of America. The dominion could only organize itself if a railway was built from one ocean to the other, and this was the wish of British Columbia. The history of the Canadian Pacific Railway is of particular interest because it shows how the dominion reacted, much more than did the U.S.A., against the excessive influence of railway magnates over the body politic. In fact the political campaign of the liberals against Sir John Macdonald and the business men who contributed to his electoral expenses merely delayed the opening of the Canadian transcontinental (1885) by about ten years. In this case too the speed at which it was built, five years, proved costly, despite the backing of the London money market: it took 25 million dollars and 25 million acres to construct the line from Winnipeg to the Rockies. But the 'all Canadian line' prevented the prairie from being absorbed into the United States.

Equally important was the construction of the Russian transcontinentals across Asia. Until 1860 European influence in India and other areas of the Asiatic coast was based on the sea. By contrast the Russians approached Asia via its steppe lands, alternately scorching and freezing, and thus consolidated an empire which could only be compared to that of America. Rail and telegraph were to be the life blood of this giant creation. Here again the railway was the product of a political objective. Between 1880 and 1888 the Trans-Caspian line was built by the army right up to the oases of Turkestan and the frontiers of India across deserts where the sand was alternately hard and dry or a shifting sea of quicksands, or even drenched with melted snow. At first an instrument of pacification, the railway soon became of economic importance for the carriage of cotton, and the insufficiencies of the line then became apparent: the transhipments necessary to cross the Caspian Sea, the insecurity of the wooden bridges over the Amu Darya, and the lack of both water and fuel. As a result the line, like the American lines, was progressively rebuilt, and was followed by the Trans-Aralian, whose path was better planned and determined more in relation to economic requirements.

The Trans-Siberian was begun in 1891 in order to tighten Russian supremacy over the province of Vladivostok. As in America, the desire to come into closer contact with a distant province by means of the railway hastened the realization of a project under discussion since 1858.

The Russian government had orginally hoped to make the contact by means of telegraph, road and waterway. But the canals built from 1883 onwards to link the catchments of the Ob and the Yenisey turned out to be highly impractical, with locks that were too few and too narrow. The English attempts to link the west of central Siberia to Europe by sea with steamers sailing up the Yenisey were not crowned with success either. By 1896 they succeeded in making a single voyage a year but this was certainly insufficient. At the same time traffic was overburdening the track. In 1880 it took two winter months to go from Kazan to Vladivostok. Ten years later it still took seven weeks, using steamers up to Tomsk and on the Amur. Going day and night the 'telega' did not exceed an average of 10 km. an hour. But for the construction of the future railway there was no money, and, as in America, local interests were at loggerheads over the place at which the junction was to be made between the Trans-Siberian and the rest of the Russian network. About 1890 the Tsarist government became alarmed at the extent of Chinese infiltration in the province of Transbaikalia, and also at the organization of Canadian and American steamer services across the Pacific. At that very moment the infusion of French capital into the Russian economy assumed a role similar to that played by English and German capital in the American economy. French capital allowed the line to be constructed without delay, and without the Russian state having to abandon any of its rights. Here labour was cheaper than in the New World: the legendary mobile muzhiks in search of work and land after bad harvests, military and prison labour, and in the east, as in California and British Columbia, Chinese coolies. The Russians had 6000 km. of track to lay as against much shorter stretches in the United States. But there was nothing in the lie of the land to compare with the Rockies or even the Western desert; bridges were costly but in no way out of the ordinary, and there was to be only one tunnel and that of the most common type. Besides, the American precedent was of some value: American excavators were used for the embankments, and the crossing of Lake Baikal by ferry boat was far less impressive than the crossing of the Great Lakes. The difficulties came rather from the constant flooding of the rivers of Transbaikalia, whose rate of flow was not well known, and also from the distances: wood had to be carried sometimes 500 km. and, as was the case with the Central Pacific, plant for the eastern section had to be brought by sea via Suez and Vladivostok. Without steamers the line could not have been built east of Lake Baikal. Nevertheless, the speed at which this rough and ready, but extremely long, line was built was an achievement.

Between 1891 and 1904 more than 600 km. a year were laid on the average, that is from 3 to 7 km. a day. The Americans had laid 10 to 17; but in general they had not been as fast as the Russians, not only because they were delayed by the war but also because they were dependent on the money market. The Russians, for their part, were less willing to take risks and avoided the mountains. They carried the line through low-lying areas where they became the prey of floods. Because it was a state venture the Russian line did not lead to much wastage or speculation, but it did involve, instead, corruption and technical incompetence, and these helped to inflate the cost. However approached, a major railway in a little-known area is always an expensive operation that can only pay in the long run. As Witte foresaw, the Trans-Siberian peopled Siberia and simultaneously confirmed the presence of Russia on the shores of the North Pacific, now promoted to the rank of a future Atlantic.

Conceived as part of imperial policy, the Trans-Siberian, which was completed in 1903, enabled Russian influence to penetrate farther into the Chinese world, but it was not the great international highway that it was originally intended to be. The war and Russian isolation were both in part responsible; but so was the strongly independent nature of maritime navigation, and, even more, the advent of the aeroplane to replace the steamer as a means of passenger transport. The railway played a decisive role in the setting up of vast territorial empires capable of confronting the empires born of the sea. Only the aeroplane could become a truly planetary means of transport.

After 1869 the railways began to invade every continent. But, outside North America and Russia, they were essentially the instruments of the expansion of that world economy whose motive power was centred in London. These foreign railways were financed from Europe, without very much local support; both the plant and technicians were supplied from Europe. The country involved paid for it all by the sale of some raw material, and hoped to provide only the manpower. The network was, therefore, merely a system of penetration, connected by way of the ports to Europe of which it remained a dependence. But after 1880 competition within industrial Europe led the great powers to fight over the control of these lines. The imperial ambitions of these powers took the form of each designing the network of the states under their influence. The imperial concept met that which had inspired the building of the transcontinentals. Eventually, when a dependence was duly peopled, it achieved independence of a kind, illustrated by the acquisition of a complex co-ordinated network clustering around the original line of penetration, which was promoted to the rank of the 'trunk line' of the national network.

Latin America is an excellent example of these states which were politically independent but economically subordinate. English and

French capital was responsible for the construction of the railway network of this continent, the Germans contributing to minor investments
after 1890. The railways were, and still are to a large extent, 'feeders' of
the river steamers or of the coastal trade. The supremacy of steam
navigation was shown by the precocious growth of Chile, whose
coast is very highly developed, and by the importance of steamers on
the Amazon, which was opened to international trade in 1866 although
the river led merely to equatorial forest. The railways were short and
not very efficient, connecting one of the important places on the high
plateaux to one of the ports on the low-lying coast: Lima–Callao,
Caracas–La Guara, São Paulo–Santos. For a long time these lines
remained isolated stretches which any company could control without
difficulty and without much expense.

Only one country held an immediate future for the railways,
Argentina. It has a temperate climate, and it possesses an inland sea in
the estuary of the River Plate, which is continued into the interior by
the other big rivers and could thus serve as a seaway fed by the railways
of the interior. Until 1852, in the case of Argentina, and 1875, in that
of Paraguay, the whims of dictators delayed the opening of navigation
much to the advantage of Montevideo. Between 1850 and 1860 the
railway network got under way in the pampas surrounding Rosario.
These lines were easy to lay since they were in a plain, and they led to
settlement and an increase in land values, just as in North America. The
pampas, like the Canadian prairie, was the creation of the steamer and
the railway. The City invested £250 million in the Argentine railways,
and the English companies encouraged exports from Argentina to
England by preferential rates. They used the 1·67 m. gauge, because at
first they employed equipment which had served in the Crimean War.
But after 1870 the very size of the penetration imposed some kind of
organization of the network. The railway followed the old trail from
La Plata to the Andes, along the length of which the state of Argentina
had established itself. The traffic on this trail had been intense, and yet
at the same time insufficient, absorbing large amounts of capital as in
pre-railway Europe; moreover, it took three months to go from
Buenos Aires to Salta. The railway era followed closely on that of the
steamer. The first Argentinian line which was opened in 1857 was
10 km. long and served the suburbs of Buenos Aires, but by 1870 the
train had reached Cordoba, Tucuman eight years later, Mendoza in
1885, and Salta in 1894. After 1875 the lines designed to colonize the
pampas were added to the big interprovincial lines and connected to
the estuaries. In 1910 the country opened international connections
with the establishment of the line across the Andes from Mendoza to
Chile via the tunnel of the Cumbre. In 1912 Argentina was linked to

Paraguay and after 1908 a connection with Bolivia was constructed. A 28,000 km. network was in operation and a former economic satellite of Europe had become a great nation. The differences of gauge remained, however, as a reminder of its colonial origins.

In Argentina land speculation played an important role, and the railway was at first a tributary of the steamer. In South Africa the railway was, at first, the outlet for the mines of the interior, for the continent is dry and cannot rely at all on inland navigation. The products of the mines were a very suitable freight for the railway and made them profitable from the start. In fact South Africa had half the network of the entire continent. From the 1850's the governments of the Cape and of Natal began the construction of their networks. The line from Beira, in Mozambique, reached Rhodesia in 1897 and Katanga in 1910. After a long struggle with Germany, England ended by gaining control of the three lines radiating from Lourenço-Marques, Beira and Lobito. As a result, the project of a Cape to Cairo line began to take shape. But this idea, which was inspired more by politics than economics, came to nothing as far as the railway was concerned. The lines of East Africa, those of Tanganyika or Uganda, like the French line which eventually reached Addis Harrar in 1904 despite many financial ups and downs, all followed the immemorial trails which led to the Red Sea rather than the lines of longitude. In the equatorial basin of the Congo 'which, without a railway, is not worth a penny', steam navigation was still more important than the narrow gauge railway, which merely served to replace those stretches of the river that could not be used, such as the Matadi–Leopoldville line opened in 1897. But from 1914 the Belgians had to supplement their waterway policy with a railway policy in order to avoid being at the mercy of their Anglo-Saxon carriers. In contrast, the Algerian and the Egyptian networks were still quite small—although the existence of phosphates in Tunisia had led to the construction of a narrow-gauge line. In French West Africa the equatorial forest separated the coast from the steppe lands, and furthermore very few mineral resources were to be found in this vast country without any continuous stretch of navigable waterway. Pacification took a long time, but it would have come sooner and faster if the military narrow gauge lines had been undertaken more actively. In 1903 by means of loans backed by the state, lines began to penetrate the country and to connect the coast with the inland rivers. The project of a Trans-Sahara line was abandoned in 1881 after the massacre of the Flatters' mission—an astonishing act of renunciation on the part of a nation that was rich enough to lavish milliards on foreign investments.

Private capital and initiative are naturally attracted to projects that are immediately remunerative. Much more than Africa, which was still fairly 'marginal', outside the mining areas, the Far East appeared to be a paying proposition with its very heavy population. In fact the Japanese state reserved the construction of its lines for its own nationals. Plant came from England, which in 1870 agreed to the first railway loan bearing an interest of 9 per cent. Japanese railways charged lower rates than the European colonial railways, and in 1895 they yielded 10 per cent on the capital spent on construction, despite a fair amount of carelessness in the way they were run. In 1906 the private network was nationalized. In 1896 the Union of Indo-China, created by France, imitated the Indian Empire, and abandoned its policy of developing navigable waterways to launch out on the execution of a plan of railway construction. The Trans-Indochina and a line going up the Red river to Yunnan, opened in 1910 to forestall the English line coming from Burma, were the main achievements of this project realized without the backing of the French state but with loans bearing a very high interest rate.

China, therefore, was the principal sphere of competition. After the opium war, Europe began to take an interest in communications to China by way of the sea. The Chinese were most eager to obtain steamers along their coastline or up the Yangtze Kiang. At the time of the first spring crossing from Shanghai to Tientsin the steamers of rival companies undertook a race that was a most successful form of publicity. But the governments distrusted the ambitions of the Europeans. The small railway of 17 km. from Shanghai to Woosung was opened in 1876, after negotiations lasting thirteen years, and was dismantled in the following year by order of the Chinese authorities. The 'break up' of China started after her defeat by Japan in 1895. It came late in the day; at a time when private capital was seeking government protection in view of the bitter competition between the industrial nations, and when governments, for their part, used private capital for political ends. Chinese governments were, therefore, in a position to play one company against another, each of them in this age of imperialism trying to outbid the other. The concessions granted after 1895 were on the whole discretionary: the construction companies placed the Chinese loans through the intermediary of financial groups to which they were closely tied; then they kept the line as security until the loan was redeemed, claiming 20 per cent of the income. But with the help of competition, and also of the Boxer rebellion, the Chinese succeeded in obtaining representation on the boards of commissioners. From 1908 the Chinese government took advantage of the surprising standing it enjoyed among the industries of Europe in search of markets, and successfully secured the removal of all foreign financial control, in return for a guarantee on the part of the Chinese state. The lines under Russian control were built with French capital, so that it can truly be said that the English and French played the leading roles in the financing of these lines. In 1911 China operated a few trunk lines but had no 'feeders'; in all, there were 11,500 km., even less than Japan. As a result of foreign initiative these lines were in part already owned by the Chinese government, but two-thirds of the network was in foreign hands. One-third of the network was in Manchuria: 1722 km. under Russian control and 1150 km. taken over by the Japanese after their victory in 1905. These lines were controlled by companies belonging to the state and financed by loans placed in Paris, in the case of the Russians, and in London, in that of the Japanese. This foreign network faced the national network of northern China which was centred around Peking. The Peking–Hankow line, opened by a Franco-Belgian consortium in 1905, was bought back by the Chinese state in 1909. South of the Yangtze Kiang, the Shanghai–Nanking line was completed in 1908, and the Canton–Hankow line was still under construction. China, like Japan, had proved a field for some profitable financial operations, and had also provided the metallurgical industry with orders. But maritime Europe had in this way helped to finance Japanese and Russian imperialism, which was to eliminate it from this part of the Far East. This area was to assimilate itself, by means of the railways, to European civilization, but only to put it into serious danger, all too soon, both politically and economically.

In the vast area that stretches from the lower Danube to the Persian Gulf, neither the technical character nor the economic results of railway development were of much interest; but it does supply striking examples of the way in which railway investments served the politics of imperialism in the decaying Turkish Empire and in the new Balkan states. The line undertaken by Hirsch after 1869, from Sarajevo to Constantinople, with Austro-French capital and a subsidy from the Ottoman government for every kilometre laid, was at first a purely financial operation. Turkish government bonds were bought by Hirsch at 128 francs and sold at 170 francs. But very soon this line became an instrument of Austro-German policy, which contemplated the colonization of the Middle East by the railway and the drawing of this part of the world away from the Anglo-French, who approached it by sea, into the community of *Mittel Europa*, with which it would be attached by rail. Turkey distrusted the plan and authorized the company to build no more than 1274 km. of isolated sections and it was only in 1888 that Vienna was linked to Constantinople. At this very moment, however, Serbia and Bulgaria ceased to be economic satellites of the central powers, and became bitterly hostile to the Austrian thrust to Salonica. In 1908 Serbia began to appeal to the Paris market to bar the path of the Austrians by the construction of a line from the Adriatic to the Danube and linked to the Roumanian and Russian lines. But the Austrian army provided Bosnia with 1400 km. of narrow-gauge railway. In 1914 Serbia had 1000 km. of normal track and the Croatian areas of the Habsburg Empire more than 5000. A formidable German penetration towards Baghdad was under way, since Salonica was still temporarily outside its reach. From the 1850's onwards the English and French had made sure of the control of a regular patchwork of stretches of railway from the coast of Asia Minor or of Syria to the interior steppe plateaux. From there two big lines of penetration were launched across the desert. One was the line from Damascus to Medina (1908), which did not reach Mecca and which was built by German engineers with funds drawn from the whole muslim world. The other was the line from Constantinople to Baghdad, a project the Germans had presented to the vizirs as early as 1872, and which was to be the axis of a future Turco-German imperialism, and the transcontinental of Abdul Hamid's empire. This short cut to India was a challenge to the maritime powers. In 1904 the Baghdad Railway Company was set up; in 1911 the track was within 600 km. of Baghdad. But the Germans were short of funds, and so had to come to terms with the English and French, for this line led to the oil-bearing countries. The war hindered the completion of the project; the same thing happened in Iran. It was the logical conclusion of imperial rivalries. After 1919 the Turkish Empire had disappeared. The line of the three B's had disintegrated, and different stretches went into creating the national networks of the new states. Baghdad was not to be a railway crossroads after all. The aeroplane, the car and the pipeline brought the era of railway expansion to a close.

In the early years of the twentieth century the railway system was reaching its completion, at least in that part of the world in which it had originated, the North Atlantic world. There were railway lines for all who wanted to use them, and full advantage was in fact taken of this new mode of transport. But the element of monopoly, economic and financial, which it involved needed to be modified. To achieve some measure of protection consumers called in the help of their governments. In Anglo-Saxon countries this took the form of some kind of government control, whereas on the European continent it led to nationalization. Finally, after 1880, public opinion and governments encouraged almost everywhere a revival of inland navigation, not merely as a subsidiary, but more especially as a kind of counterweight to the monopolistic nature of the railway. In all parts of the world the same accusations were made against the railways: they favoured long journeys by means of differential tariffs, and big clients by means of preferential tariffs. Moreover, the railways favoured imports that travelled a long way from the sea-ports. They also made up for the sacrifices accepted at 'competitive points' by increasing the charges at points where there was no competition to fear.

In America, moreover, the rivalry between the railway kings led to tremendous instability in rates. It is understandable that from as early as 1869 the Grangers should have organized themselves so as to put pressure on the authorities of the agricultural States in the west and force them to regulate railroad charges. The movement started in Illinois in 1869, and reached Iowa, Minnesota and Wisconsin by 1874. Its principal demands were for rates that were proportional to the distance covered and maintained stable by State authorities, the encouragement of competition by parallel lines, since concessions were permanent but not exclusive, and finally the end of the system of free travel for influential persons. But these States stabilized the charges at a level which made it impossible for the railroads to meet any crisis (their management was seldom very far-sighted). And in any case differential tariffs were essential for any successful railway undertaking. Without them the farmers of the west could not sell their products to the east of the Union and to Europe. Things went from one extreme to the other, but the Grangers' revolt did show the railway kings the danger of flouting public opinion. In the east, moreover, public opinion, more considered than that of the mid-west, also demanded some measure of control. In 1869 Massachusetts set up a commission which acted as the companies' moderate, but respected, adviser. The other States of the east followed suit. But the activities of the railroads extended beyond the frontiers of each State; the national government was forced to intervene. The campaign launched, in 1878, by Senator Reagan led to the passing of the Interstate Commerce Act in 1887, which extended the process inaugurated in Massachusetts to the whole Union. Railways remained private concerns but the principle was laid down that they were public utilities and that as such their complete freedom of action had to be limited in some ways. The Interstate Commerce Commission, a tribunal resting on the support of public opinion, regulated the operation of the railways in the public interest. It avoided excessively severe measures which would hinder the growth of the American economy, and took care not to attempt to take the place of the management in the running of the railways. But it attempted to ensure that rates were just and reasonable and that companies did not discriminate between individuals or charge more for short than for long distances. Though, in the earlier years of its existence, it experienced difficulty in enforcing its decisions, its control was progressively strengthened. The Sherman Anti-Trust Act (1890) helped it enormously. The Hepburn Act (1906) granted it the power to fix rates, after inquiry, and to insist on their being made public. Nevertheless, the small pioneering venture no longer stood a chance now that it was confronted with the giant networks. Only the federal government was in a position to arbitrate in case of conflicts between these powers that shared after all some responsibility for the making of the nation.

In Great Britain commercial interests invested in railway shares, especially in the Midlands, but objected vigorously to the complete freedom of the companies. It was commonly said that either the state would run the railways or else the railways would run the state. The freedom of the companies became greater as one moved inwards from the coast and the coastal trade. After the establishment of the Railway and Canal Commission in 1873, parliamentary control of rates became increasingly effective and was encouraged by the spread of socialist ideas in some sections of public opinion. Partisans of nationalization, however, remained a minority. The state had never owned the railways or been responsible for their management, and the public authorities showed no desire to take them over.

The Continent, on the other hand, had long been familiar with control by public officials, and in several countries there was an extension of nationalization. The Tsars had never willingly accepted private companies, of which there were but a limited number in Russia. Liberal Belgium had always kept the main lines in the hands of the state. After 1873, furthermore, anxious to preserve its national independence and to avoid unnecessary competition with the state network, the state took over several private lines; this was not done in a spirit of hostility to private enterprise, since the government paid very handsomely for the lines it took over; thus Belgium was able to have in this way the lowest charges in the whole of Europe, and its cheap workmen's trains were a social innovation of the greatest importance in a country where capitalist initiative still had a large part to play.

Germany followed Belgium's example. Without completely suppressing the private sector, it allowed the state network to become increasingly predominant. In Prussia the state network increased from 5300 km. in 1879 to 37,400 in 1909. In 1909, out of the 60,000 km. in the whole Reich, private companies operated only 3600 km. and these were of minor importance. Every state retained its own network out of fear of Prussian domination, and because none was particularly eager to cover the losses on the lines of its neighbours. The Imperial Railway Office, set up in 1873, was responsible for co-ordinating the various networks. But if it helped to simplify the structure of rates, it did not in any way help to bring them down, except in the case of goods designed for export, and also of imports which had a long way to travel inside Germany. The railways proved most remunerative for public finances, especially in Prussia. Like the post office and the telegraphs, they provided a substantial proportion of the income of the various states (nearly one-fifth in Prussia from 1887 to 1906); this meant that there was no need to ask Parliament for taxes. Finally, railways were under military discipline and no labour movement was tolerated. In contrast with Belgium, the control of railways by the state in Germany did not lead to the reduction and equalization of rates.

In France, ever since 1858, the state and the companies had shared financial responsibilities jointly, and no government desired to take over the lines completely—though this did not mean that control was not as, or even more, efficient than in the Anglo-Saxon countries, though somewhat more meddlesome. But the lines which had to be built after 1860 were secondary lines which were bound to run at a loss, and the companies undertook to construct them only in exchange for better financial terms from the state. The state tried to grant its concessions to new companies, but the lines in question were very diverse in character and of secondary importance, and only interested the construction firms which did not want to be responsible for their management once completed. The state was thus forced in 1877 to take over 2600 km. of track from the Compagnie de l'Ouest which the influential Compagnie de l'Orleans was unwilling to accept. The new state network had a rough beginning. After 1879 the state planned to build new lines right into the last bastions of conservatism, the mountain and country districts. This was one of the essential objects of the Freycinet plan. But the state did not want to overburden its budget with costly loans, and so fell back on the big companies, which finally, by the conventions of 1883, undertook to build and incorporate these expensive lines into their own networks. Railway shares financed the construction, but the state had to back them, just as it had done in 1858, by a guarantee of interest. The companies were in this way completely covered in case of trouble. But the profits they were to make enabled them to repay the state the money it had advanced, without in any way lowering the high dividends paid to the shareholders. The state became more than ever the partner of the companies. It could hope to buy back only the companies which manifestly proved unable to repay it. This was doubtless the case with the Compagnie de l'Ouest which was bought up in 1908, at great cost. The other companies were doing very good business, and repaying their debt, when the world war broke out and frustrated all their hopes. Only the Compagnie du Nord and the P.L.M. had cleared their debt to the state. Railway shares, guaranteed by the state, were very widely diffused and constituted almost a second national debt, but without depressing the price of government bonds. Technically, the solution provided by the Third Republic to the problem of railway financing was in many ways a skilful one. Moreover, the companies guaranteed to the Republic the political backing of the big concerns, and this may well have allowed the regime to settle down more quickly; though in return for this support, the companies were led to put pressure on Parliament—as the companies had often done in Anglo-Saxon countries—in order to defend their interests from economic and political opponents who supported nationalization.

Railways always roused the fear of monopoly, whether they were in the hands of the state, or in those of private companies enjoying permanent or short-term concessions. The inland waterway seemed to be in the process of disappearing under the pressure of the railways. In every country large sections of public opinion, and notably the owners of the mines, tried, with some success after 1880, to put new life into inland navigation, by modernizing it in such a way as to obtain concessions on rates and charges from the railways which were faced with a possible competitor.

Great Britain was the only country in which waterways, although running at a loss, received no contribution from the state in order to remain as a competitor of the rail, and the waterways were unable to hold their own, except on some small localized stretches. A certain counterbalance to the railways was, it is true, provided by coastal trade; its tonnage was much reduced, but it drew new vigour from the adoption of steamers.

In the U.S.A. the waterway lost its status in twentieth-century America because it was too slow, involved transhipments, and stopped functioning in winter. In 1833 the New York State canal carried 80 per cent of the total traffic in the State; in 1908 this had dropped to 4 per cent and the traffic was made up of heavy goods carried at very low rates. By 1909 more than half of the 4633 miles of canals had been abandoned. There was even a fall in traffic on the Mississippi. The authorities tried to remedy matters, but without achieving very much: in 1882 tolls were abolished on the Erie canal; from 1903 on, a number of canals were improved at the expense of the Treasury, for example, the New York Barge canal (1903), which could take barges of up to 1000 tons. Inland navigation had only one success in this land of great distances, and that was on the Great Lakes. But here, despite the obstacle of ice in winter, conditions resembled more closely those of maritime navigation, and the railway fitted in naturally with the pattern of traffic. In 1900 the carriage of a bushel of wheat between Chicago and New York cost 4·42 cents by the Lakes and 9·98 by train; the American economy was in some respects determined by the existence of this vast inland sea, but it is particularly striking that inland navigation did not extend its activities to any extent beyond the shores of the Great Lakes.

One thing seemed to be certain: government intervention could not put a stop to the decline of the waterways. Everything spent on them was either no more than a reminder of their former greatness or else a waste of valuable funds. Nevertheless, France took up again in 1860 the task of canalization and of river improvements that had been interrupted by the advent of the railway in 1846. This was the basis of the Imperial Plan of 1860, completed and extended under the Republic by the Freycinet Plan of 1879. This effort at modernization and improvement had been urgently requested by the chambers of commerce and by the left-wing political groups who were the progressive elements of the regime—in other words by all those who feared the monopolies held by the big railway companies which had been in such close association with the state ever since the conventions of 1859. To threaten them with a competitive waterway was, in certain districts, a method of obtaining a reduction in railway charges, that the state might well have been unable to obtain in any other way. In fact with the exception of the canals parallel to the lines of the Compagnie du Midi, which were leased to this company until the beginning of the twentieth century, the state was after 1850 sole owner of the canals. The railways were never able to gain control, in contrast to the situation in Anglo-Saxon countries. Navigation dues were lowered in 1860, and completely abolished in 1880. The state tried to put pressure on the railway companies, its independent partners, by setting up a competitor at its own expense and paying its inevitable losses. A part of the Freycinet Plan was abandoned; the navigable network remained fairly separate in its functions, and its trade stayed in the hands of small artisans. Its renovation was only effective in the north-east of the country, the most heavily industrialized area. Without a doubt the waterway was saved from complete disappearance. Trade increased from 322 million kilometric tons in 1890 to 618 in 1913. But during the same period rail traffic rose from 1170 to 2590 million kilometric tons. The mines gave three quarters of their trade to the railways.

In Europe inland navigation enjoyed one positive success, that of the Rhine. Even in this rather exceptional case, where conditions were favourable to river transport, railways increased their trade by 183 per cent between 1865 and 1879, while even the most prosperous navigation companies increased theirs by no more than 35 per cent. Moreover, it was the industrial development resulting from the railways that allowed river navigation to prosper, as a counterpoise and a complement to the railways. Bismarck believed that the control and management of railway charges would by itself secure for Germany economic safeguards equivalent to those provided by a waterway. It was the abundance of freight, and also the influence of the Ruhr magnates, that led to the realization of the Maybach Plan of 1879, a scheme comparable to the Freycinet Plan. The German States were forced to foster the competition of waterways against their own railways. This had some success. From 1880 to 1898 the tonnage carried on the Westphalian railway network doubled, while that of the Rhine at Emmerich trebled. But in 1910 the rail carried nearly seven times more coal than the waterway. Besides, the state networks waged a merciless war against the waterways, and the governments could not, or did not want to, arbitrate between them. Moreover, the Agrarian party was sufficiently powerful to hinder the construction of the *Mittelland Kanal* which would have connected the Ruhr to the German coast. The success of the Rhine, which in 1900 carried a greater volume of trade than all the French inland waterways together, was to a large extent illusory. It showed, however, that a well-equipped waterway capable of carrying barges of 1000 tons could complement the railways and compete successfully with them in a highly industrialized area, where there was an abundance of freight. Such waterways could not be found everywhere. In all other cases waterways tended to vegetate, making their way by carrying particularly cumbersome types of freight at low rates.

On the seas, after 1869, it was the steamer that carried the day. In 1875 the British had 1·9 million tons of steamers as against 4·2 million tons of sailing ships. Ten years later steamers accounted for 4 million tons against 3·4 million tons of sailing ships. And the steamer did six times as much work as the sailing ship. A steamer of wood was something which belonged to the past. There were even iron sailing vessels. About 1885 it was steel construction that began to make progress. In 1890 the 5 million tons of British steamers were mostly of steel. Germany in 1900 had 1·3 million tons in steel out of a total tonnage of 1·94 million tons. By contrast, out of a million and a half tons, Norway had two-thirds in sailing ships. But from the start of the twentieth century the decline of the sailing ship was under way; it was maintained for special journeys and for special kinds of cargoes. It had sunk to the status of a subsidiary.

The screw and the compound engine enabled the tonnage of vessels to be increased. In 1873 the average tonnage for the world as a whole of a vessel was 841 tons; in 1898 it reached 1587 tons. To increase the speed at which the North Atlantic crossing could be made the companies launched giant liners. The average statistics for the twenty largest steamers in the world between 1873 and 1898 are interesting:

the length increased from 119 metres to 165; the keel from 7·30 metres to 9·40; the tonnage from 4413 to 10,717. The North Atlantic liners did 18–22 knots; in 1905 the fastest German liners exceeded 23 knots and the best Cunarders attained 25. In that year Great Britain had 35 ships of over 10,000 tons and Germany 25. As early as 1884 the English vessel *Umbria*, of 8000 tons, crossed the North Atlantic in 6 days. This ocean, around which the new industrial civilization had risen, shrank to the proportions of the Mediterranean of the ancient world. Besides, the steamers awakened echoes of the ancient 'Mare nostrum'. The opening of the Suez canal made them masters of the route to India.

Despite the increasing efficiency of the steam-engine, the speed attained by the liners turned out to be costly. In order to pass from 21 to 24 knots it was almost necessary to double the horse-power, and to go from 21 to 26 it had to be tripled. The speed which corresponded to the maximum commercial use of a vessel of 8000 tons was no more than 12 knots. Cargo steamers were, therefore, slower than liners; but the amount of freight which had to be transported increased all the time. It rose from 27 million tons in 1873 to 63 million in 1898 for the world as a whole. Competition led to lower charges. The rate on the boats of the Messagerie Maritime for 1000 kg. was in 1873 260 French francs; in 1883, 143; in 1893, 81. Round about 1900 passenger steamers obtained very large subsidies from the state. In the case of cargo boats construction outstripped the demands of freight. Regular services had increased without number, and the 'tramps', not tied to particular routes, competed with them. In 1854 Cunard yielded almost 10 per cent; in 1900 the average dividend of twenty-four English companies was 4·8 per cent. From 1895 'rings' and 'pools' began to be set up to organize the market. Members pooled the incomes derived from their lines, and divided it in proportion to the tonnage they possessed. To eliminate the tramps, special tariffs were offered to clients who gave all their freight to the pool. Rate wars between rival groups were the natural consequence, and exceptionally low charges were offered to foreign customers. From 1900 on, the rates for maritime transport followed the general level of prices and ceased to fall.

On the high seas national rivalries were sharp. Until 1890 the British merchant marine was supreme. In 1895 73 per cent of the global high seas tonnage belonged to it. Its shipbuilding yards dominated the world market for ships. In 1900 60 per cent of the ships launched in the course of the year came from them. In the shelter of their system of protection, Americans took no interest in the ocean. In 1860, 66 per cent of the foreign trade of the States was carried under the American flag; in 1900 only 7 per cent.

But at the turn of the century competition reappeared. France could not reintroduce taxes on a ship's flag or tonnage dues, and so she embarked in 1881 on a system of bounties. After 1885 German competition began to increase rapidly. The Germans did not use the bounty system, but they used railway rates so as to encourage exports. About 1900 the Hamburg-Amerika and the Norddeutscher Lloyd increased their services and improved their performances with ships built in the Stettin yards. The following table compares the advances made by British, German and French marines measured in tonnages of their shipping

Table 43

	(In millions of tons)	
	1870	1910–12
U.K.	5·69	11·7
Germany	0·98	3
France	1	1·46

Finally, Japan began to play a part in the carriage of freight, while Norway and the Netherlands continued their progress. The share carried by the English dropped between 1890 and 1902 from 63 per cent to 53 per cent, and that of Germany rose from 7·2 per cent to 10·2 per cent of the world trade. Foreign coastal traffic was gradually closed to the English. The U.S.A. decided to keep the New York–San Francisco run by way of Cape Horn, and the San Francisco–Honolulu run, for its nationals. Russia included in the trade reserved for her nationals, all traffic between her Black Sea and her Baltic ports, and that between her European and Pacific ports. There was no more room for liberalism. In 1902 Pierpont Morgan, who planned a mercantile trust which would dominate the Atlantic, bought up a part of the English fleet of liners and came to an agreement with the Germans about sharing traffic on the North Atlantic. Great Britain was disturbed by this American intrusion which was the prelude to the return of the stars and stripes on the ocean.

Nevertheless, even if England was no longer alone on the ocean, she still maintained an indisputable supremacy. In 1912 her total tonnage was almost one-third greater than that of Germany, the U.S.A., Norway, France, Italy and the Netherlands, all put together. Nineteenth-century Europe had developed under the aegis of free trade and of the Pax Britannica. Steamers played the part of ocean 'railways'. The sea was not liable to 'traffic jams'. A 5000-ton cargo boat was the equivalent of ten goods trains in 1913. Men and goods could bridge the seas in large quantities and at low rates. In 1800 the organization of overseas trade took the form principally of isolated ventures, limited in duration and involving considerable risks and high profits, embarked upon to take advantage of some very specific possibility of gain. A century later this ancient form of organization still existed occasionally in the tramp trades; but there were now also shipping lines which plied regularly on given routes, and which not only served existing demands but, even more, stimulated traffic. As on land, transport had become an end in itself, because its cheapness had immeasurably increased the volume of freight. The sea had lost its quasi-monopoly of external trade; but it still remained the main means of such trade. National rivalries did not have, on the seas, the power to curb the flow of trade which they had within territorial frontiers. Born of the sea, the world market continued to depend on it.

But the world market could become a reality only when the telegraph ceased to be confined to the continents. The country which was able to centralize the network of underwater cables would automatically become the main business centre, and at the same time an essential factor in world politics. In this field also Great Britain paved the way; the work was left to private enterprise despite the fact that since 1869 the telegraph system of the United Kingdom had belonged to the state.

In 1866 the unity of the North Atlantic community was achieved when the deep-sea cable was finally laid between Britain and the U.S.A. In 1872 Hong Kong was connected to San Francisco via London. After 1874 Latin America was linked by cable. Only the Pacific had still to be crossed. In 1902 the cable linking Vancouver to Auckland and Brisbane closed the circle of the 'all-British' underwater cables around the globe in what was a truly imperial operation.

Despite the creation of the German and French networks after 1900, and the opening of the American cables from San Francisco to Manila (1903) and to South America, the English were still as supreme in 1914 in this sphere as in that of shipping. Of a total of 516,000 km. of submarine cables 94,000 were in the hands of states (and a third of this in those of the British Empire). Out of 422,000 km. of underwater cables belonging to private companies 250,000 were the property of companies registered in London.

V.   Conclusion

A number of points stand out in clear relief at the outbreak of the war in 1914, which shattered the world economy: an economy which was to such a large extent a consequence of the technical revolution in transport based on the joint use of iron and steam.

If inland navigation had become localized and confined to limited areas, roads had been reduced to the role of feeders, and, even in this field, the narrow-gauge railway sometimes intruded on territory that should have belonged to the road. But in the new countries the railway track had preceded the road and was effectively responsible for the existence of roads. Because of the railway era travel was no longer a troublesome venture, but much rather a pleasure essential to life. Man no longer remained in his place of birth. With the railway, the notion developed that time was money. Human psychology was changed as a result.

Large urban agglomerations had been brought into being by the railway. Railway junctions now enjoyed the privileges formerly reserved for great ports. It was the railway once again that allowed the organization of transport within large cities: from 1863 on, London had an underground railway. New York followed suit in 1878, Berlin in 1885, and finally Paris in 1900 began to work on the construction of the subterranean town without whose existence the city above-ground would have been paralysed.

In respect of transport facilities the world in 1914 can be divided into three main sections.

The first included the east of the U.S.A., up to the 100 meridian west, and those parts of Europe, within an ellipse circumscribed by Lancashire, Copenhagen, Warsaw and Genoa. These two nuclei were connected by an extremely active maritime traffic, and the economic structure of the whole area was based on the rapid and regular transportation of men, coal and iron in large quantities. In this sector, the problem in 1914 was already one of an excess of transport. The stage of over-equipment was approaching—and, with it, movements for nationalization and protection.

In the second sector, transport facilities were still not adequate to the needs of traffic. They consisted mainly of lines into the interior designed to serve the ports which connected this sector to the first. But already a number of these dependencies were developing the capacity to become independent and acquire a coherent transport system.

Finally, there was a third sector as yet untouched by the revolution in transport. Here, time had conserved some of its ancient value or rather was not considered of importance. Transport remained the means of effecting an occasional transaction.

Except in this last section, a system of transport, with uniform technical characteristics, originating in the North Atlantic, had replaced indigenous methods of transport. Distance had lost its meaning and taken the shape of a scale of charges, and physical obstacles had been overcome by technical skills. The sector that was as yet untouched by this revolution occupied a large part of the map of the world, but it was sparsely inhabited. The interior of China remained the only heavily populated area where traffic was still at the mercy of pre-industrial methods of transportation. There, overpopulation gave rise to opposition to technical progress, resistance which only a powerful state could hope to overcome.

Henceforth, maritime and land transport were in a state of equilibrium. The possibility of a continental autarchy was no longer a Utopian dream, and the Atlantic phase of world civilization was drawing to its conclusion. The opening of the Panama canal in 1914 acquired symbolic significance as the sign of the rising importance of the Pacific. The vast South Pacific remained the last gap in the network of maritime links henceforth connecting all the shores of the world.

In future the problem of improving transport was to be purely a financial question; all technical obstacles had been removed. The psychological shock and the material effects of railways and steamers had been assimilated. They had become part of a way of life which they had brought about, and which they could no longer alter to any great extent. Their services were to become more and more costly; they could no longer stimulate the growth of an economy by freeing capital.

But a second technical revolution was in progress which was to give the railway and the steamer a somewhat antiquated appearance. The development of electricity, it is true, gave the railway new life by enabling it to conquer the capital cities and the mountains. But more important, technical developments allowed the internal combustion engine to be used for transport purposes. From 1891 onwards the tyre made both the bicycle and the motor-car practical methods of transport. Their appearance on the roads, which at that time had been abandoned to country folk, opened in the twentieth century 'a new turnpike era'. And from 1910 London buses were already competing with the tramways. Finally, between 1901 and 1907, when Blériot crossed the channel, aviation made its appearance.

There were also other technical changes. Oil began to be used to drive ships; in 1914, 2 per cent of the world's shipping was oil driven. In 1879 Graham Bell took out the first patent for a telephone, and by 1910 the Emperor Francis-Joseph appeared to be a man from another generation because of his attachment to the telegraph. Lastly, Marconi in 1896 built his first wireless set. In 1908 transmissions from the Eiffel Tower were received in Morocco. Politics, business, strategy, all were to be faced with a totally new set of circumstances, although the mass of the people at the time did not seem to realize it, any more than the men of 1815 had appreciated the possibilities of steamers and railways. These forms of transport which had dominated the nineteenth century were to lose, in the century to come, their independence and their sovereignty.

It was their turn to dream of 'sharing the traffic', and of securing government intervention to freeze the precarious balance between the different sections of the transport industry. It was only by following the example of inland navigation, and concentrating on the field which was most characteristically theirs—cheap mass transportation—that they could successfully adjust themselves to these changing conditions.

Whatever the course of future history, the century of the railway and the steamer marks a decisive period in the history of transport, and that of the world. Particular events in political history often tend to assume less and less importance as time goes on. But the prophecies of Saint-Simon on the unification of the planet, and the meeting of the races for better or for worse, remain excitingly topical. Man has changed the world, and the world has changed man—in a very short time indeed. It is more than likely that new inventions will appear to make the men of the nineteenth century look like rather unimportant precursors. But what will remain as the essential achievement of their transport revolution is that they were able by lowering the cost of transport to make the masses mobile, and thus to establish a truly democratic civilization. The technical innovations of the twentieth century, quite as amazing as those of the previous century, have not yet led, to any similar extent, to a comparable result. This is the reason why the century of steam, even though it has passed into history, continues to strike the imagination of men as well as that of children.

C E H VI

CHAPTER V

Technological Change and Industrial Development in Western Europe, 1750-1914

I. *The Industrial Revolution in Britain*

IN the eighteenth century, a series of inventions transformed the manufacture of cotton in England and gave rise to a new mode of production —the factory system. During these years, other branches of industry effected comparable advances, and all these together, mutually reinforcing one another, made possible further gains on an ever-widening front. The abundance and variety of these innovations almost defy compilation, but they may be subsumed under three principles: the substitution of machines—rapid, regular, precise, tireless—for human skill and effort; the substitution of inanimate for animate sources of power, in particular, the introduction of engines for converting heat into work, thereby opening to man a new and almost unlimited supply of energy; the use of new and far more abundant raw materials, in particular, the substitution of mineral for vegetable or animal substances.

These improvements constitute the Industrial Revolution. They yielded an unprecedented increase in man's productivity and, with it, a substantial rise in income per head. Moreover, this rapid growth was self-sustaining. Where previously, an amelioration of the conditions of existence, hence of survival, and an increase in economic opportunity had always been followed by a rise in population that eventually consumed the gains achieved, now for the first time in history, both the economy and knowledge were growing fast enough to generate a continuing flow of investment and technological innovation, a flow that lifted beyond visible limits the ceiling of Malthus's positive checks. The Industrial Revolution thereby opened a new age of promise. It also transformed the balance of political power, within nations, between nations, and between civilizations; revolutionized the social order; and as much changed man's way of thinking as his way of doing.

In 1760 Britain imported some $2\frac{1}{2}$ million pounds of raw cotton to feed an industry dispersed for the most part through the countryside of Lancashire and existing in conjunction with the linen manufacture, which supplied it with the tough warp yarn it had not yet learned to produce. All of its work was done by hand, usually (excluding dyeing and finishing) in the homes of the workers, occasionally in the small shops of the master weavers. A generation later, in 1787, the consumption of raw cotton was up to 22 million pounds; the cotton manufacture was second only to wool in numbers employed and value of product; most of the fibre consumed was being cleaned, carded, and spun on machines, some driven by water in large mills, some by hand in smaller shops or even in cottages. A half-century later, consumption had increased to 366 million pounds; the cotton manufacture was the most important in the kingdom in value of product, capital invested, and numbers employed; almost all of its employees, except for the still large number of hand-loom weavers, worked in mills under factory discipline. The price of yarn had fallen to perhaps one twentieth of what it had been, and the cheapest Hindu labour could not compete in either quality or quantity with Lancashire's mules and throstles. British cotton goods sold everywhere in the world: exports, a third larger than home consumption, were worth four times those of woollens and worsteds. The cotton mill was the symbol of Britain's industrial greatness; the cotton hand, of her greatest social problem—the rise of an industrial proletariat.

Why did this revolution in the techniques and organization of manufacture occur first in Britain? A few theoretical considerations may help us to organize the argument. Technological change is never automatic. It means the displacement of established methods, damage to vested interests, often serious human dislocations. Under the circumstances, there usually must be a combination of considerations to call forth such a departure and make it possible: (1) a need or opportunity for improvement due to inadequacy, present or potential, of prevailing techniques;[1] and (2) a degree of superiority such that the new methods pay sufficiently to warrant the costs of the change. Implicit in the latter is the assumption that, however much the users of older, less efficient methods may attempt to survive by compressing the costs of the human factors of production, entrepreneurial or labour, the new techniques are enough of an improvement to enable progressive producers to outprice them and displace them.

The technological changes that we denote as the 'Industrial Revolution' implied a far more drastic break with the past than anything since the invention of the wheel. On the entrepreneurial side, they necessitated a sharp redistribution of investment and a concomitant revision of the concept of risk. Where before, almost all the costs of manufacture had been variable—raw materials and labour primarily—more and more would now have to be sunk in fixed plant. The flexibility of the older system had been very advantageous to the entrepreneur: in

---

[1] The criterion of adequacy would, for my purposes, be marginal costs. Steeply rising costs per unit under conditions of growing demand would imply a need for and incentive to technological improvement.

time of depression, he was able to halt production at little cost, resuming work only when and in so far as conditions made advisable. Now he was to be a prisoner of his investment, a situation that many of the traditional merchant-manufacturers found very hard, even impossible, to accept.

For the worker, the transformation was even more fundamental, for not only his occupational role, but his very way of life was at stake. For many—though by no means for all—the introduction of machinery implied for the first time a complete separation from the means of production; the worker became a 'hand'. On almost all, however, the machine imposed a new discipline. No longer could the spinner turn her wheel and the weaver throw his shuttle at home, free of supervision, both in their own good time. Now the work had to be done in a factory, at a pace set by tireless, inanimate equipment, as part of a large team that had to begin, pause, and stop in unison—all under the close eye of overseers, enforcing assiduity by moral, pecuniary, occasionally even physical means of compulsion. The factory was a new kind of prison; the clock a new kind of jailer.

In short, only the strongest incentives could have persuaded entrepreneurs to undertake and accept these changes; and only major advances could have overcome the dogged resistance of labour to the very principle of mechanization.

The origins of the entrepreneurial interest in machines and factory production must be sought in the growing inadequacy of the older modes of production, an inadequacy rooted in internal contradictions, themselves aggravated by external forces.

Of these pre-factory forms of organization, the oldest was the independent craft shop, with master often assisted by one or more journeymen or apprentices. Fairly early, however—as far back as the thirteenth century—this independence broke down in many areas, and the artisan found himself bound to the merchant who supplied his raw materials and sold his finished work. This subordination of the producer to the intermediary (or, less often, of weak producers to strong ones) was a consequence of the growth of the market. Where once the artisan worked for a local clientele, a small but fairly stable group that was bound to him personally as well as by pecuniary interest, he now came to depend on sales through a middleman in distant, competitive markets. He was ill-equipped to cope with the fluctuations inherent in this arrangement. In bad times he might be completely idle, with no one to sell to; and when business improved, he usually had to borrow from his merchant the materials needed to get started again. Once caught on a treadmill of debt—his finished work mortgaged in advance to his creditor—the craftsman rarely regained his independence; his work sufficed to support him—no more—and he was in fact if not in principle a proletarian, selling not a commodity, but labour.

Aside from his pecuniary difficulties, the local artisan was in no position to know and exploit the needs of distant consumers. Only the merchant could respond to the ebb and flow of demand, calling for changes in the nature of the final product to meet consumer tastes, recruiting additional labour when necessary, supplying tools as well as materials to potential artisans. It was largely in this way that the rural population was drawn into the productive circuit. Very early, urban merchants came to realize that the countryside was a reservoir of cheap labour: peasants eager to eke out the meagre income of the land by working in the off-season, wives and children with free time to prepare the man's work and assist him in his task. And though the country weaver, nail-maker, or cutler was less skilled than the guildsman or journeyman of the town, he was less expensive, for the marginal utility of his free time was, initially at least, low, and his agricultural resources, however modest, enabled him to get by on that much less additional income. Furthermore, rural putting-out was free of guild restrictions on the nature of the product, the techniques of manufacture, and the size of enterprise.

The above description of a long and complex historical process inevitably oversimplifies. If it seems reasonable to assert that, taking Europe as a whole, most putters-out came from the mercantile side, it is important to note the many exceptions: the weavers who became clothiers by hiring their less enterprising neighbours; the fullers and dyers who had accumulated capital in the finishing processes and integrated backwards by contracting directly for yarn and cloth. In some areas, most notably the region around Leeds in the West Riding of Yorkshire, rural artisans organized their own small weaving sheds, joined when necessary to create common facilities, and sold their pieces as independent clothiers in the weekly cloth halls. But even in Yorkshire, this fragmentation of enterprise was characteristic primarily of the woollen trade; in the worsted manufacture, where capital requirements were greater, the productive unit was larger and the merchant putter-out more important.[1]

The English textile industry built its fortune in the late medieval and

---

[1] In his discussion of the shift from urban to rural industry, P. Mantoux, *The Industrial Revolution in the Eighteenth Century* (London, 1928), pp. 64–6, conveys the impression that the putting-out system was the result of the decay of what he describes as 'domestic manufacture', that is, dispersed independent cottage industry of the kind found in Yorkshire. Often, as we noted, this was true, but even more often, probably, putting out was the product of mercantile initiative seeking new sources of labour and drawing the rural population into the commercial circuit.

early modern periods on rural manufacture. No centre of production, except perhaps Flanders, was so quick to turn from the towns to the countryside; it is estimated that as early as 1500 over half the output of wool cloth was accounted for in this manner. The trend continued: by the mid-eighteenth century, the great preponderance of the British wool manufacture was cottage industry; of all the towns immemorially associated with the wool trade, only Norwich remained as an important urban centre, and it was rapidly declining in relative importance. Allowing for such regional variations, moreover, and for occasional pauses, the industry as a whole had prospered impressively. In the late seventeenth and early eighteenth centuries, at a time when the Italian manufacture was a shadow of its former self, when Dutch cloth output was shrinking steadily, and when France was in the throes of a prolonged depression, British consumption of raw wool was growing at the rate of about 8 per cent a decade; and from about 1740 to 1770, the decennial increase was 13 or 14 per cent.[1]

This growth merits detailed attention, for it was the principal precipitant of the changes we denote by the Industrial Revolution, and understanding it may help us understand the reasons for British precedence in technological and economic development. In part the wool industry grew because of favourable conditions of production. Thus no country had so abundant a supply of raw wool, particularly the long wool required for the lighter, harder, worsted fabrics. And rural manufacture, largely unhampered by guild restrictions or government regulation, was in a position to make the most of this resource advantage by suiting its product to demand and changes in demand. In particular, it was free to develop cheaper fabrics, perhaps less sturdy than the traditional broadcloths and stuffs, but usable and often more comfortable. This freedom to adjust and innovate is particularly important in light industry, where resources and similar material considerations often are less important as locational factors than entrepreneurship. A good example from within the British wool industry is the rapid growth of the Yorkshire worsted trade, to the point where it passed the older centre of East Anglia in the course of the eighteenth century; compare Clapham's explanation: 'the ordinary case of a pushing, hard-

---

[1] P. Deane, 'The Output of the British Woollen Industry in the Eighteenth Century', *J. Econ. Hist.* XVII (1957), 220. These figures are derived from informed contemporary guesses and are therefore gross approximations. But it is the trend that interests us here. On this, compare the much slower growth of the Verviers-Hodimont area near Liège, one of the most enterprising centres of wool manufacture on the Continent. P. Lebrun, *L'industrie de la laine à Verviers pendant le XVIIIe et le début du XIXe siècle* (Liège, 1948), pp. 518–19. Note also the difference in size of output between Yorkshire alone (aulnage returns in T. S. Ashton, *An Economic History of England: the Eighteenth Century* (London, 1955), pp. 249–50) and the Verviers area.

working locality with certain slight advantages, attacking the lower grades of an expanding industry'.[1] We shall have occasion to remark comparable examples of the advantages of entrepreneurial freedom when we turn to the continental countries. In the meantime, we may note that the British wool manufacture profited the more from its liberty because some of its most dangerous competitors across the Channel were being subjected in the seventeenth and early eighteenth centuries to increasing regulation and control.

Finally, one should cite the relative freedom of British industry from the disturbance and destruction of war, the uneven but long and often rich inflow of skilled foreign artisans, and the access of the producing centres to water transport, hence distant markets—all factors conducive to lower costs of manufacture and distribution.

On the demand side, the British wool manufacture was comparably favoured. The population of the kingdom was not large, but it was growing, faster probably by the middle of the eighteenth century than that of any of the countries across the Channel. From not quite 6 millions around 1700, it rose to almost 9 millions in 1800; 70–90 per cent of the gain came in the second half of the period.[2] What is more, the absence of internal customs barriers or feudal tolls created in Britain the largest coherent market in Europe. This political unity was confirmed by the geography of the island: the land mass was small; the topography, easy; the coastline, deeply indented. By contrast, a country like France, with more than three times as many people, was cut up by internal customs barriers into three major trade areas, and by informal custom, obsolete tolls and charges, and, above all, poor communications into a mosaic of semi-autarkic cells.

Moreover, what nature bestowed, man improved. From the mid-seventeenth century on, there was a continuous and growing investment of both public and private resources in the extension of the river system and the construction of new roads and bridges. By 1750 there were over a thousand miles of navigable streams in Britain; and Parliament had been passing turnpike acts at the rate of eight a year for half a century. Impressive as this development was, it was inadequate to the needs of the economy, and the pace of investment increased markedly

[1] J. H. Clapham, 'The Transference of the Worsted Industry from Norfolk to the West Riding', *Econ. J.* xx (1910), 203. Eric M. Sigsworth, *Black Dyke Mills: a History: with Introductory Chapters on the Development of the Worsted Industry in the Nineteenth Century* (Liverpool: University Press, 1958), p. 17, subscribes to this point of view.

[2] For different but roughly concordant estimates of this increase, see Phyllis Deane and W. A. Cole, *British Economic Growth 1688–1959: Trends and Structure* (Cambridge, 1962), p. 5, n. 3. In the same period, the population of France went from about 20 to 27½ millions. E. Levasseur, *La population française* (3 vols.; Paris, 1889), I, 201–6, 215–18.

in the fifties and sixties. These years saw the first canals (Sankey Navigation, 1755–9; Duke of Bridgewater's canal, 1759–61) and turnpike acts at the rate of forty a year. In two decades (1760–80), navigable water and solid roads linked the major industrial centres of the North to those of the Midlands, the Midlands to London, and London to the Severn basin and the Atlantic.

Within the market of Britain, purchasing power per head and standard of living were significantly higher than on the Continent. We have no precise measures of national income for the eighteenth century,[1] but there is an abundance of impressionistic testimony by travellers from both sides of the Channel to the greater equality of wealth, higher wages, and greater abundance to be found in Britain. Thus one of the best signs of comfort in Europe is the consumption of white bread; in the nineteenth century, one can almost follow the rise in *per capita* income and the diffusion of higher living standards among the poorer sections of the population, into rural areas, and into central and eastern Europe by the wheat frontier. In the eighteenth century England was known as the country of the wheaten loaf. This was an exaggeration: in large areas, particularly in the Midlands and North, rye and barley were the staple grains, especially in the early part of the century. Even there, however, the bread grew whiter over the years, and nowhere was there anything like the reliance one found across the Channel on coarser cereals like buckwheat and oats. Similarly, there was much myth in the image of John Bull, beefeater. Yet when Arthur Young sat down to soup in the Pays Basque—'what we should call the farmer's ordinary'— he received 'ample provision of cabbage, grease, and water, and about as much meat for some scores of people, as half a dozen English farmers would have eaten, and grumbled at their host for short commons'.[2] Even workhouse menus, hardly designed to make life agreeable for the residents, provided for meat daily or at least several times a week.[3]

The English labourer not only ate better; he spent less of his income on food than his continental counterpart, and in most areas this portion was shrinking, whereas across the Channel it may well have risen during much of the eighteenth century.[4] As a result, he had more to spare for other things, including manufactures. The Englishman was

[1] See, however, the article of P. Deane, 'The Implications of Early National Income Estimates for the Measurement of Long-Term Economic Growth in the United Kingdom', *Economic Development and Cultural Change*, IV (1955), 3–38.

[2] Young, *Travels during the Years 1787, 1788 and 1789* (2 vols.; Dublin, 1793), I, 87 f., 93.

[3] Cf. Dorothy Marshall, *The English Poor in the Eighteenth Century* (London, 1926), p. 268.

[4] This is the position of C. E. Labrousse, *Origines et aspects économiques et sociaux de la Révolution française (1774–1791)* ['Les Cours de Sorbonne'] (Paris, n.d.), pp. 54–8.

reputed for wearing leather shoes where the Fleming or Frenchman wore clogs. He was dressed in wool where the French or German peasant often shivered in linen, a noble fabric for table or bed, but a poor shield against the European winter. Defoe vividly and proudly described the importance of this demand for British manufactures in his *Plan of the English Commerce* in 1728:[1]

...for the rest, we see their Houses and Lodgings tolerably furnished, at least stuff'd well with useful and necessary household Goods: Even those we call poor People, Journey-men, working and Pains-taking People do thus; they lye warm, live in Plenty, work hard, and [need] know no Want.

These are the People that carry off the Gross of your Consumption; 'tis for these your Markets are kept open late on *Saturday* nights; because they usually receive their Week's Wages late...in a Word, these are the Life of our whole Commerce, and all by their Multitude: Their Numbers are not Hundreds or Thousands, or Hundreds of Thousands, but Millions; 'tis by their Multitude, I say, that all the Wheels of Trade are set on Foot, the Manufacture and Produce of the Land and Sea, finished, cur'd, and fitted for the Markets Abroad; 'tis by the Largeness of their Gettings, that they are supported, and by the Largeness of their Number the whole Country is supported; by their Wages they are able to live plentifully, and it is by their expensive, generous, free way of living, that the Home Consumption is rais'd to such a Bulk, as well of our own, as of foreign Production....

Defoe's reference to the Englishman's 'expensive, generous, free way of living' calls to mind a final aspect of the British domestic market: a consumption pattern favourable to the growth of manufactures. More than any other in Europe, probably, British society was open. Not only was income more evenly distributed than across the Channel, but the barriers to mobility were lower, the definitions of status looser. Nothing is more revealing in this regard than a comparison of contemporary images of society in the different countries of western Europe. For Britain, we have schemes like those of Gregory King or Joseph Massie—congeries of occupational groups ranked according to wealth and so intermingled as to preclude the drawing of horizontal status lines across the whole of the social pyramid. For France, we have a neater tripartite structure: aristocracy, bourgeoisie, *peuple*; within these, to be sure, there are fine distinctions, and it is not always easy to rank people of different occupations or to place borderline groups like artisans and retail shopkeepers; nevertheless, the arrangement is orderly, traditionally logical. For most of west Germany, we have the French system, but more rigid and carefully defined, to the point

---

[1] [Daniel Defoe], *A Plan of the English Commerce* (Oxford: Blackwell, 1928), pp. 76–7.

where status, even of sub-groups, is often written into law. And east of the Elbe, society was simpler yet: a small landholding aristocracy; the large mass of personally dependent peasants; in between, a thin layer of commercial bourgeois, spiritually and often ethnically alien to the body social within which they lived and moved encapsulated.

So far as the rate of consumption is concerned, the implications of greater equality of income are a matter of some debate.[1] Similarly, mobility is ambiguous in its effects: some people will save to climb; others will consume to announce their arrival. The net result will depend on circumstances.

Quality and direction of consumption, however, are something else again. In non-primitive societies, where skills are fairly advanced and there has been some accumulation of wealth, inequality fosters a taste for extravagant luxuries and services among the few, whereas equality encourages a demand for more sober, solid comforts among the many. Great riches amid a sea of poverty are generally the product of a low capital–labour ratio (or of misinvestment of capital). They give rise to a prodigal expenditure of labour on pleasure and elegance: an over-abundance of domestics—to the point where the mistress of the house spends more time supervising her staff than more modest wives spend doing their own chores; ornamental garments of great price; lavish decoration of residences; the production of exquisitely difficult works of art.

A more even diffusion of wealth, however, is the result of costly labour. This was indeed the case in Britain, where wages—allowing for the uncertainty and partial incomparability of the estimates—ran about twice as high as in France and higher yet than east of the Rhine. In such an economy, production functions are more capital-intensive, while the rich consumer caters less to whim and satisfies himself with a greater abundance of those goods that are available on a smaller scale and in lower quality to his poorer fellows. On the other hand, the relatively high purchasing power of the poorer elements of the population implies a correspondingly greater demand for the things they need

---

[1] The traditional assumption is that inequality does increase the savings ratio. But there is some question whether this is justified for a pre-industrial society, especially one in which a small privileged group commands the levers of power and can draw a kind of tributary income from the rest of the nation. It seems quite probable, for example, that the court aristocracy of eighteenth-century France lived beyond its income, consuming freely in the knowledge that there would always be ways of obtaining more from the crown. Cf. Milton Friedman, *A Theory of the Consumption Function* (Princeton, 1957), pp. 235 f., who argues that inequality of 'permanent' (as against measured) income *per se* does not affect the consumption–savings ratio; that it is uncertainty about future income that promotes savings, against a rainy day as it were.

and can afford—the cheaper, plainer articles most susceptible of mass production.[1]

Mobility in such a society is a force for standardization. For mobility implies emulation, and emulation promotes the diffusion of patterns of expenditure throughout the population. Where there is no movement between status groups, clear, inviolate distinctions of dress and way of life mark the gradations of hierarchy. Where there begins to be movement, as in the late Middle Ages, sumptuary laws are often needed to keep people in their place. And where mobility has become so commonplace as to seem to many a virtue, discriminatory controls over expenditure are unenforceable.

In England, sumptuary laws were dead letters by the end of the sixteenth century; they were repealed by James I in 1604. Over the next two centuries, the trend toward homogeneity of expenditure— the effacement of vertical regional differences as well as horizontal social distinctions—continued. Contemporaries complained of the luxury of the lower classes, who dressed so as to be indistinguishable from their betters. This was an exaggeration; social lament as a literary genre is invariably hyperbolic. Besides, much of the elegance of the populace was meretricious, the result of an active trade in second-hand clothes. Even so, the very demand for cast-offs was evidence of the absence or decay of customary distinctions: the poor man could and did wear the same kind of coat as the rich. Similarly, contemporaries complained of the farmer's imitation of city ways, his abandonment of the rustic simplicity of yore. Again an exaggeration—yet the truth was that in no economy was the countryside so closely integrated into the commercial circuit; nowhere were the local pockets of self-sufficiency so broken down.

All of this was part of a general process of urbanization, itself a reflection of advanced commercialization and industrialization. London alone was a monster: Defoe estimated in 1725 that it contained a million and a half inhabitants, almost a quarter of the people in the

---

[1] On the implication of inequality of income, or, more precisely, inequality of consumption, for the nature and composition of industrial output, see the suggestive article of W. Paul Strassman, 'Economic Growth and Income Distribution', *Quarterly J. of Economics*, LXX (1956), 425–40; also S. Kuznets, 'Economic Growth and Income Inequality', *Amer. Econ. Rev.* XLV (1955), 1–28, which is more concerned with the reverse relation.

The best single index to relative factor costs and the pattern of consumption is the extent and character of domestic service: the twentieth century, sometimes called the era of the common man, is also the age of the disappearing maid. And while the British merchant of the eighteenth century had less cause for frustration than his present-day descendants, he had his servant problem. Cf. Defoe, *Everybody's Business Is Nobody's Business*, in *The Novels and Miscellaneous Works of Daniel Defoe* ('Bohm's Standard Library'; 7 vols.; London, 1889), II, 499–500. See also J. Jean Hecht, *The Domestic Servant Class in Eighteenth-century England* (London, 1956), esp. chs. I and VI.

kingdom. This figure is testimony, not to Defoe's accuracy, but to the impression the 'great wen' made on contemporaries; yet even conservative estimates put the population of the metropolitan area at about half that number. In the provinces, the cities and towns developed steadily after the Civil War; among the most rapidly expanding were unincorporated 'villages' like Manchester, which had perhaps 12,500 inhabitants in 1717 and 20,000 by 1758. An estimate of 15 per cent of the population in cities of 5000 and over by mid-century and 25 per cent by 1800 is probably close to the truth. By contrast, the French figure on the eve of the Revolution was something over 10 per cent; and Germany was even more rural.

But it was not only that England had more people living in cities than any other European country except perhaps Holland;[1] it was the character of British urban life that made the pattern of settlement particularly significant. On the Continent, many of the cities were essentially administrative, judicial, ecclesiastical in function. Their populations consisted essentially of bureaucrats, professionals, soldiers, and the shopkeepers, artisans, and domestics to serve them. The city was not so much a node of economic activity, trading manufactures and mercantile services for the products of the countryside, as a political and cultural centre drawing tax revenues and rents from the rural population in return for government and by traditional right. Madrid is the classic example of this kind of agglomeration; but Paris was much like this, and perhaps a majority of the larger French provincial cities—including places like Arras, Douai, Caen, Versailles, Nancy, Tours, Poitiers, Aix, and Toulouse—were little else. In Germany, of course, the very fragmentation of political power was an incitement to the multiplication of semi-rural capitals, each with its court, bureaucracy, and garrison.

By contrast, the relatively smaller size of Britain's political apparatus and its concentration in London left the older provincial centres to somnolence and decay. Nothing is more striking about the map of Britain in the eighteenth century than the modernity of the urban pattern. The medieval county seats—Lancaster, York, Chester, Stafford —were overshadowed by younger places like Liverpool, Manchester, Leeds, and Birmingham, and there was already a substantial shift of population in favour of the North and Midlands. Much of the increase, moreover, did not take place within the cities proper, but took the form of a thickening of the countryside. Numerous overgrown industrial villages sprang up—concentrations of hundreds of spinners and

---

[1] And Holland's urban population was declining sharply, both relatively and absolutely. Cf. William Petersen, *Planned Migration: the Social Determinants of the Dutch-Canadian Movement* [University of California Publications in Sociology and Social Institutions, vol. II] (Berkeley and Los Angeles, 1955), p. 20.

weavers in the manufacturing districts of Lancashire and Yorkshire, similar in many ways to the earlier rural agglomerations of East Anglia.

The pattern throughout was one of close contact and frequent exchange between city and land. Trade and shops went to the customers: the late A. P. Wadsworth noted the numerous advertisements of cottages-to-let for tradesmen in the villages around Manchester, reflecting on both sides the keen response to economic opportunity.[1] In spite of the sparseness of the data, it seems clear that British commerce of the eighteenth century was, by comparison with that of the Continent, impressively energetic, pushful, and open to innovation. Part of the explanation is institutional: British shopkeepers were relatively free of customary or legal restrictions on the objects or character of their activity. They could sell what and where they would; and could and did compete freely on the basis of price, advertising, and credit. If most shopkeepers continued to haggle, many followed the lead of the Quakers in selling at fixed, marked prices. In so far as such methods prevailed, they conduced to a more efficient allocation of economic resources and lower costs of distribution.

In sum, the home market for manufactures was growing, thanks to improving communication, increase in population, high and rising average income, a buying pattern favourable to solid, standardized, moderately priced products, and unhampered commercial enterprise. How much it grew, however, one cannot say precisely; we have no statistics on domestic consumption.

We are better informed about foreign trade, if only because most of the commodities that came in or went out of the country had to pass under the eyes of the customs officers. Admittedly, the trade statistics are incomplete, inaccurate, and biased by the use of fixed values in a world of fluctuating prices. But they do furnish an order of comparison, showing for example a three- or fourfold gain in British exports (including re-exports) in the century from 1660 to 1760.

We have seen that the growth of Britain's sales abroad, as at home, reflected in large part her natural endowment; to this should be added some institutional and historical advantages. She had a strong maritime tradition, and, unlike most of her continental rivals, did not divert her energies into the maintenance of costly armies and territorial aggrandizement. Rather she concentrated her efforts on securing trading privileges and a colonial empire, in large part at the expense of her leading continental rivals, France and Holland. This kind of thing cost less than European territory and in the long run paid better. No state was more responsive to the desires of its mercantile classes; no country more alert

[1] A. P. Wadsworth and Julia de L. Mann, *The Cotton Trade and Industrial Lancashire, 1600–1790* (Manchester, 1931), p. 276, n. 2.

to the commercial implications of war. Mr Ramsey perceptively notes the role of London in promoting this harmony of trade and diplomacy, contrasting in this regard the isolation of Bordeaux, Marseilles, and Nantes from Paris and Versailles.[1]

At the same time, Britain developed a large, aggressive merchant marine and the financial institutions to sustain it. Of all the Continental countries, only Holland again could rival her in this regard, and the comparative advantage of Holland lay in trade, not industry. Between Dutch mercantile power and Britain's combination of mercantile and industrial strength, the issue was never in doubt; the greatest asset of a port is a productive hinterland.

In the long run, this was Britain's forte: the ability to manufacture cheaply precisely those articles for which foreign demand was most elastic. The most promising markets for Britain in the seventeenth and eighteenth centuries lay not in Europe, whose own industries were growing and whose mercantilist rulers were increasingly hostile to the importation of manufactures, but rather overseas: in the New World, Africa, the Orient. These areas were very different in needs and tastes. The tribesmen of Africa and the plantation hand of the Antilles wanted thin, cool fabrics, bright colours, flashy metal—light woollens, the cotton-linen checks of Manchester, the cheap stampings of Birmingham. The requirements of the Indian or Chinese peasant were similar (excluding most cotton goods) though more sober. The New England farmer or Philadelphia merchant, confronted by a harsher, more variable climate and more sophisticated technologically, bought heavier cloth and sturdier hardware. For all, however, there was one common denominator, and that a negative one: they were not especially interested in costly, highly finished luxuries.

The effect of increased export, then, was to reinforce the pressures toward standardization as against differentiation, quantity as against quality. The sacrifice of quality to quantity was an old story in English manufacture. By this I do not mean adulteration or the sale of inferior goods as first quality—this was an international evil, as the iteration of government and guild regulations on the Continent evidences. Rather I mean the adoption of new methods of production that save costs at the expense of solidity or appearance; the use of coal in place of wood in glass-making or brewing is the best example.[2]

[1] G. D. Ramsay, *English Overseas Trade during the Centuries of Emergence* (London, 1957), pp. 247 f.

[2] J. U. Nef has argued in a number of works that the adoption of mineral fuel itself gave strong impetus to the production of 'quantity and utility rather than quality and elegance'. See, *inter alia*, his *Cultural Foundations of Industrial Civilization* (Cambridge, 1958), pp. 52–3. Yet it is clear that the readiness to accept coal was itself indicative of a deeper rationality; such nations as France, confronted with the same choice, obdurately

This readiness to abandon old ways for new, to place profit above craft pride and even the appearances of pride, implies a certain separation of the producer from production, an orientation to the market instead of to the shop. To some extent it reflected the early domination of British manufacture by mercantile interests and the reduction of the rural artisan to a mere employee of the putter-out. Clearly, however, this is not enough to account for the phenomenon; in the wool industry, for example, the most enterprising centre of manufacture was in Yorkshire, a stronghold of the small independent clothier; and in metallurgy, glass-making, brewing, and chemicals—the industries most affected by the introduction of mineral fuel—the organization of production had nothing to do with putting-out.

Instead, this cost-mindedness must be seen as part of a larger rationality, itself in some measure the result of material circumstances— above all, the greater cohesiveness of the British market and the effectiveness of competitive pressures—but also as an ideological force of its own, whose sources still remain to be explored. In no country in the eighteenth century, with the possible exception of Holland, was society so sophisticated commercially. Nowhere was the response to profit and loss so rapid; nowhere did entrepreneurial decisions less reflect non-rational considerations of prestige and habit. We shall have occasion to consider this again when we speak of investment and the supply of capital for industrialization. At the moment, my only concern is to explain where market pressures were pushing the producers and why the producers responded.

How much of the increase in demand and the trend toward mass production of cheaper articles is to be attributed to the expansion of home as against foreign markets is probably impossible to say. We have only the grossest, global estimates of the proportion of domestic to overseas sales, and these presumably comprise everything, including agricultural products. What interests us here, however, is the demand for manufactures, and only certain manufactures at that. One may perhaps attempt this kind of comparison for the wool industry: at the end of the seventeenth century English exports of wool cloth probably accounted for upwards of 30 per cent of the output of the industry; by 1740, the proportion had apparently risen, possibly to over half, and in 1771-2, something under a half.[1] In this important branch, then, the

---

rejected coal—even where there were strong pecuniary incentives to switch over to the cheaper fuel.

[1] These figures are based on Phyllis Deane, 'The Output of the British Woollen Industry in the Eighteenth Century', *J. Econ. Hist.* XVII (1957), 209-10, 211-13, 215-16, 220. The article itself makes clear the limitations of these figures, which are essentially informed inferences from informed guesses.

major impetus seems to have come from the export trade, and the most active exporting area in the industry, Yorkshire, was also the most rapidly growing centre of manufacture. It has indeed been argued that not only was the minimum critical market required to induce a technological breakthrough too big for any one country to provide, but that only a large fraction of the growing world demand could supply the necessary push; and that it was that peculiar combination of economic and political circumstances that permitted Britain to win for herself in the eighteenth century so large a share of the trade in manufactures that accounts for the successful leap to the 'higher' mode of production.[1]

Yet the answer is not so simple. Such figures as we have on British exports (overwhelmingly manufactures) show a distinct levelling off in the third quarter of the century. The volume of woollen shipments falls from the late fifties; cottons falter in the late sixties and seventies; the break comes later in iron and steel—in the late sixties—but it is sharp and the drop persists until the nineties.[2] David Eversley argues cogently against the easy acceptance of exports as the leading sector of the economy in process of revolution: noting the weight and relative stability of home demand, he reasons that only the existence of this kind of dependable market justified and permitted the accumulation of capital in manufacture.[3] On the other hand (as in many historical questions, one can fairly shuttle back and forth between pros and cons), this very variability of exports was surely a stimulant to industrial change and growth. It is not only that the marginal increment of sales often spells the difference between profit and loss; the bursts of overseas demand placed abrupt and severe burdens on the productive system, pushed enterprise into a position of rapidly increasing costs, and enhanced the incentive for technological change. Certainly, from the late eighteenth century on, the waves of investment seem to follow on increases in sales abroad.[4]

In any event, this rising demand contained the seeds of difficulty. Every mode of industrial organization has, built into it, opportunities for conflict between employer and employed. These are particularly

[1] Cf. Kenneth Berrill, 'International Trade and the Rate of Economic Growth', *Econ. Hist. Rev.* 2nd ser. XII (1960), 351–9; also P.A., 'The Origins of the Industrial Revolution' [summary of a symposium], *Past and Present*, no. 17 (1960), pp. 71–81.

[2] Deane and Cole, *British Economic Growth*, pp. 46, 59.

[3] D. E. C. Eversley, 'In Pudding Time: the Early Stages of Industrialization in England, 1730–1780' [Faculty of Commerce and Social Science, University of Birmingham, Discussion Papers, Series D, 'Economic and Social History', no. 1 (May 1962)].

[4] Cf. François Crouzet, 'La formation du capital en Grande-Bretagne pendant la Révolution Industrielle' (paper presented to the World Congress of Economic Historians, Aix-en-Provence, 28 August to 4 September 1962; to be published).

serious in putting-out because the system furnishes the arms as well as the causes of hostility: the worker has custody of the materials of the employer and transforms them in his own good time, in his own home, free of supervision. The only resource of the merchant is his limited control over the income of his employees: if he pays them little enough, they are compelled to work for fear of hunger; and if he abates their pay for any departure from standards of quality, they are compelled to maintain a minimum level of performance. To be sure, the exercise of such constraints is contingent on the establishment of some kind of monopsonistic bond between employer and worker; otherwise the employer can do no more than accept the prevailing market price for labour. That such a nexus did in fact often exist—because of actual monopsony in some areas, or personal ties, or debt—and that it led to abuses, seems incontrovertible.[1] There is a substantial body of folklore built around the figure of the grasping clothier and his even greedier minion, Jimmy Squeezum.

On the other hand, it is equally clear that these controls were at best spotty and limited in effect; that the worker early learned to eke out his income by setting aside for his own use or for resale some of the raw materials furnished by the merchant. Such embezzlement was usually effected at the expense of the finished product: the yarn was sized to give it false weight; the cloth was stretched up to and beyond the point of transparency. Nor was there any feeling of moral compunction about such abstraction; it was looked upon as a normal perquisite of the trade, more than justified by the exploitation of the manufacturer.

The employer's control over labour was strongest in a declining market. At such times, the menace of unemployment hung heavy over the domestic workers, and indeed, from the manufacturer's point of view, one of the greatest advantages of the putting-out system was the ease of laying off labour; overhead costs were minimal. (Later on, when the alternative of concentrated factory production became available, many an entrepreneur, in the continental countries especially, delayed shifting over because of the flexibility of the older arrangements.) In the eighteenth century, however, the British putter-out was confronted with a secularly expanding market, which sapped industrial discipline while aggravating the conflicts endemic in the system. Thus the worker's predilection for embezzlement, sharpened in depression by the desire to compensate for increased abatements and lack of work, was nowise dulled in prosperity; on the contrary, the reward for theft was greater.

[1] For one example of the role of debt in holding a worker to his employer, cf. T. S. Ashton, 'The Domestic System in the Early Lancashire Tool Trade', *Econ. Hist. Rev.* 1 (1926), 136.

What is more, though the system was flexible downwards, expansion of output was difficult. Up to a point, rural manufacture expanded easily by opening new areas—moving from the environs of the manufacturing towns into nearby valleys, invading less accessible mountain regions, spreading like a liquid seeking its level, in this case the lowest possible wage level. It was in this way that the woollen industry filled the dales of Wiltshire and Somerset and came to thrive all along the Welsh marches by the end of the sixteenth century; on the Continent, the growing woollen *fabriques* of Verviers and Monschau were seeking their weavers in the Limburg by the mid-eighteenth century, while the cotton manufacture of Normandy, after covering the Pays de Caux, was spilling over into Picardy.

But in eighteenth-century Britain, the possibilities of geographical expansion had been largely exhausted. The most accessible areas had been explored and drawn into the system. The worsted weavers of the West Riding were buying yarn in the northern dales and as far afield as East Anglia. In Lancashire, by mid-century, weavers were walking miles to collect the weft needed to keep their looms busy the rest of the day and buying the spinsters with ribbons and other vanities. Much of the difficulty was due to the difference in labour requirements for spinning and weaving: it took at least five wheels to supply one loom, a proportion ordinarily at variance with the composition of the population. So long as it was merely a question of finding rural spinsters—whose husbands worked in the fields—to furnish yarn to urban weavers, there was no problem. But once weaving spread to the countryside and the men gave up cultivation for industry, the imbalance was bound to become an obstacle to expansion. There is evidence that some spinners had begun to specialize in particular types of yarn by the middle of the eighteenth century, that a division of labour had come about, in parts of Lancashire at least, in response to the pressure of demand. But this was hardly enough, given the state of technology, and the price of yarn rose sharply from the late seventeenth to the mid-eighteenth century.

Essentially the increase was due to the ever-wider dispersion of the labour force, for nominal spinning wages changed little. The cost of transport was high to begin with; even more serious, in a world of poor communications, the price of moving goods is not a smooth function of distance; costs jump sharply each time one has to cross a natural barrier or bridge gaps in the network of roads and waterways. Barring sharp increases in the price of the finished product, the expanding manufacturer was thus caught in a cost cage and compelled to seek higher output from within his zone of operations.

In the long run, to be sure, he could expect immigration and natural increase to augment his labour force. Thus there was considerable movement of population in spite of restrictions due to the laws of settlement; Lancashire in particular was a kind of internal frontier, attracting thousands from the adjacent counties as well as from Ireland and Scotland well before the coming of machinery and the factory. And industrial activity, by providing new resources, made possible extensive division of the land, encouraged early marriage, and gave rise to densities of settlement that would otherwise have been inconceivable. Professor Habakkuk and others have called attention to the attraction of industry for overpopulated areas;[1] but here, as so often in history, the process is one of reciprocal reinforcement: rural industry frequently laid the basis of what was eventually to become overpopulation.

Yet migration and natural increase are slow-acting palliatives. In the short run, the manufacturer who wanted to increase output had to get more work out of the labour already engaged. Here, however, he again ran into the internal contradictions of the system. He had no way of compelling his workers to do a given number of hours of labour; the domestic weaver or craftsman was master of his time, starting and stopping when he desired. And while the employer could raise the piece rates with a view to encouraging diligence, he usually found that this actually reduced output. The worker, who had a fairly rigid conception of what he felt to be a decent standard of living, preferred leisure to income after a certain point; and the higher his wages, the less he had to do to reach that point. In moments of affluence, the peasant lived for the day; gave no thought to the morrow; spent much of his meagre pittance in the local inn or alehouse; caroused the Saturday of pay, the sabbath Sunday, and 'Holy Monday' as well; dragged himself reluctantly back to work Tuesday, warmed to the task Wednesday, and laboured furiously Thursday and Friday to finish in time for another long weekend.[2]

---

[1] Cf. H. J. Habakkuk, 'Family Structure and Economic Change in Nineteenth-Century Europe', *J. Econ. Hist.* xv (1955), 1–12; Joan Thirsk, 'Industries in the Countryside', in F. J. Fisher, ed., *Essays in the Economic and Social History of Tudor and Stuart England in Honour of R. H. Tawney* (Cambridge, 1961), pp. 70–88.

[2] Adam Smith (*Wealth of Nations*, Book I, ch. viii) perceptively noted the connection between intense application and prolonged relaxation, and argued that the former gave rise to the latter. Cf. T. S. Ashton, *An Economic History of England: the Eighteenth Century* (London, 1955), p. 205. This interpretation seems to put the cart before the horse. It was because the worker preferred this kind of leisure and could achieve it by working at full speed for two or three days that he adopted this sporadic pattern; not because he enjoyed working himself to the limit for a few days and needed a long weekend to rest. The latter position is equivalent to arguing that students rest the first three months of the term because of the heavy 'cramming' they do for final examinations.

Thus precisely at those times when profit opportunities were greatest, the manufacturer found himself frustrated by this unreasonable inversion of the laws of sensible economic behaviour: the supply of labour decreased as the price rose. Nor was the other tack more effective. Outright wage cuts were not feasible in the face of increasing demand, for there was a limit to the employer's hold over his workers. More common were surreptitious increases in the worker's task: he was given longer warps or less credit for waste; or procedures of measuring and weighing were altered in the employer's favour. This kind of cleverness, however, brought with it its own penalties. The resentful workers were incited thereby to embezzle the more, and frictions built into the system were correspondingly aggravated. The eighteenth century saw a persistent effort to halt the theft of materials by making embezzlement a criminal offence, providing employers and law officers with special rights of search and seizure, placing the burden of proof on any person holding materials he could not account for, and repeatedly increasing the penalties for violation. These last included corporal punishment, for fines were of no effect on penniless spinners and weavers. The very iteration of these acts is the best evidence of their ineffectiveness; by the last quarter of the century the black market in wool and yarn had become an organized business and many a cotton manufacturer was said to have begun his career by buying materials from this source.[1] Similarly the laws to compel workers to finish their tasks promptly and to fulfil their obligations to one employer before hiring out to another—a problem that apparently grew with the demand for labour—were little more than admissions of difficulty and expressions of intent. The discipline of the industrial system was breaking down.

The shift in attitude toward the labouring poor in the late seventeenth and early eighteenth centuries reflects in part the employer's frustration and vexation. Where once poverty had been looked on as an unavoidable evil and the poor man as an object of pity and a responsibility to his neighbour, now poverty was a sin and the poor man a victim of his own iniquity. Defoe is only the clearest and most effective spokesman for this viewpoint, which castigated the worker for the sloth that made him waste his time in idleness and low diversion, and the vice that led him to squander his scanty resources on alcohol and debauchery. This virtuous indignation seems to have softened from the middle of the century; at least writers on economic matters were beginning to argue that labour was not incorrigibly lazy and would in fact respond to higher wages. Mr Coats has suggested that this shift owed much to

---

[1] Travis, *Notes...of Todmorden and District* (1896), p. 56, cited by Wadsworth and Mann, *Cotton Trade*, p. 399.

the introduction of machinery and the promise of a definitive solution to the problem.[1] Perhaps; in the meantime, the businessman continued sceptical, and in places like Manchester people were still told in 1769 that the 'best friend' of the manufacturer was high provisions.[2] One can understand why the thoughts of employers turned to workshops where the men would be brought together to labour under watchful overseers, and to machines that would solve the shortage of manpower while curbing the insolence and dishonesty of the men.

Yet if the presence of this growing need for a change in the mode of production clarifies the demand side of technological innovation, it will not suffice to explain the supply side: the conditions that made possible the devising of new methods and their adoption by industry. One thing seems clear: if Britain was the country that felt most keenly the inadequacy of the prevailing system, she was not the only one. The major continental centres were also disturbed by shortages of labour and the abuses of domestic manufacture. As noted above, the weavers and merchant-manufacturers of Normandy and Verviers, of the Rhineland and Saxony, were obliged to find their yarn over an ever wider radius, often in the face of laws in the country of origin forbidding its export to competitors. Nor was this the first time in history that demand had pressed hard on the capacity of craft and domestic manufacture: in medieval Italy and Flanders analogous difficulties arose without calling forth an industrial revolution.

The problem may be broken down into two aspects: the conditions governing the invention of labour-saving devices; and those determining the adoption of these devices and their diffusion in industry.

On the first, it would seem clear, though by no means easy to demonstrate, that there existed in Britain in the eighteenth century a higher level of technical skill and a greater interest in machines and 'gymcracks' than in any of the other countries of Europe. This should not be confused with scientific knowledge; in spite of some efforts to tie the Industrial Revolution to the Scientific Revolution of the sixteenth and seventeenth centuries, the link would seem to have been an extremely diffuse one: both reflected a heightened interest in natural and material phenomena and a more systematic application of empirical searching. Indeed, if anything, the growth of scientific knowledge owed much to the concerns and achievements of technology; there was far less flow of

---

[1] A. W. Coats, 'Changing Attitudes to Labour in the Mid-Eighteenth Century', *Econ. Hist. Rev.* 2nd ser. XI (1958), 46–8.

[2] Arthur Young's famous testimony, from his *Six Months Tour Through the North of England* (4 vols.; London, 1770), III, 248–9. Cf. Edgar S. Furniss, *The Position of the Laborer in a System of Nationalism* (New Haven, 1920), pp. 98–105.

ideas or methods the other way; and this was to continue to be the case well into the nineteenth century.[1]

All of which makes the question of British mechanical skill the more mysterious. The testimony of contemporary observers on this point is mixed: some found the British creative as well as highly gifted craftsmen; others looked upon them as simply clever imitators; there is no evidence before the great innovations of the eighteenth century of any exceptional reservoir of talent in this sphere. To be sure, there were the millwrights, clock-makers, joiners, and other craftsmen whose experience in construction and contriving trained them in effect to be the mechanics of a new age. But England was not the only country with such artisans, and nowhere else do we find this harvest of inventions.

Yet if there is no positive evidence of a superior level of technical skill in Britain, there is a strong indirect argument for this assumption: even after the introduction of the textile machines (and the new metallurgical and chemical techniques, as well), the continental countries were not prepared to imitate them. The most effective of the early copies were almost all the work of British emigrant mechanics, and it was a matter of decades before the rest of Europe freed itself from dependence on British skills. Nor was this long apprenticeship drawn out simply because of a desire to employ more productive workers. The English artisans who came to the Continent were costly, homesick, insubordinate. Their employers could hardly wait to be rid of them.

Why the British developed these skills earlier and faster than others is another matter. Was it because corporate controls of production and apprenticeship had largely broken down by the end of the seventeenth century, whereas the continued influence of guild organization and the active supervision of mercantilistic governments on the Continent tended to fix techniques in a mould and stifle imagination?[2] Is the *Encyclopédie*, with its careful descriptions of the proper way to do things, a symbol of this rigidity? Or was it because the avenues of social advancement were different in Britain than in the aristocratic monarchies of the Continent, that talent was readier to go into business,

---

[1] This was true even of the steam-engine, which is often put forward as the prime example of science-spawned innovation. See below, p. 333.

[2] See Gabriel Jars's comparison of Sheffield, where industry was still fettered by the guild system in 1764–5 (though the growth of certain enterprises had burst these bonds), and Birmingham, where any man could engage in any business and at most 20 per cent of the workers had properly served their apprenticeships. 'The multiplicity of trades has given rise to emulation such that each manufacturer is ceaselessly occupied in inventing new means of cutting down labour costs and thereby increasing his profits. This has been pushed to such an extent that it seems unthinkable that ironmongery can be produced anywhere so cheaply as in Birmingham.' Chevalier, 'La mission de Gabriel Jars', *Trans. Newcomen Soc.* XXVI (1947/8 and 1948/9), 63.

projecting, and invention than in more traditionalistic societies? One is struck by the middle-class origins of most of the creators of the first textile machines. John Kay was the son of a 'substantial yeoman'; Lewis Paul, the son of a physician. John Wyatt's background is vague, but he had attended grammar school and was presumably from the kind of family that felt schooling was desirable. Samuel Crompton's father was a farmer who produced cloth on the side and was apparently comfortably situated. Edmund Cartwright was the son of a gentleman and a graduate of Oxford. It was not discreditable in the eighteenth century for children of good families to be apprenticed out to weavers or joiners.[1] Manual labour and dexterity were not stigmata of the *peuple*, as opposed to the *bourgeoisie*.

A further consideration suggests itself. Was it not only that the English atmosphere was more favourable to change, but also that special experience in certain areas provided unique facilities for training? What, for example, was the role of the Newcomen engine in shaping English metallurgy and machine construction? Or does the explanation lie simply in the *greater* need for innovation on the island (a matter of degree, to be sure, but questions of degree can often be decisive): need for labour-saving devices in a textile manufacture whose products lent themselves to mass production; for effective pumping equipment in mines; for ways to make use of mineral fuel in a country with the largest appetite for iron in the world?

The fresh and important researches of A. E. Musson and Eric Robinson offer an impressive picture of the energy with which Lancashire mobilized and trained technological skill in the second half of the eighteenth century—importing craftsmen from as far away as London and Scotland and capitalizing on its own strong traditions of skilled labour to turn joiners into millwrights and turners, smiths into foundry-

---

[1] Thus Peter Ewart, son of a Scots clergyman, one of whose brothers became minister to the Prussian court, another a physician, a third, partner to John Gladstone in the Liverpool trade: because of his talent for mechanical matters, he was apprenticed as a millwright to John Rennie. W. C. Henry, 'A Biographical Notice of the Late Peter Ewart, Esq.', *Memoirs of the Literary and Philosophical Society of Manchester*, 2nd ser. vii (1846). Or James Watt, father of the famous inventor: son of a mathematics teacher who was an Elder of the presbytery and Kirk Treasurer at Cartsdyke (Scotland), he was apprenticed to a carpenter-shipwright. His brother was trained in mathematics and surveying. S. Smiles, *Lives of Boulton and Watt* (London, 1865), pp. 81–3. Or Charles Tennant, son of a farmer and 'factor to the Earl of Glencairn', who was apprenticed to a weaver. E. W. D. Tennant, 'The Early History of the St Rollox Chemical Works', *Chemistry and Industry*, 1 November 1947, p. 667. Similarly, there was no derogation in marrying a craftsman. See the pedigree of the Pilkington family in the eighteenth and early nineteenth centuries. T. C. Barker, *Pilkington Brothers and the Glass Industry* (London, 1960), pp. 20–30.

men, clock-makers into tool and die cutters.[1] Even more striking is
the theoretical knowledge of these men. They were not, on the whole,
the unlettered tinkerers of historical mythology. Even the ordinary
millwright, as Fairbairn notes, was usually 'a fair arithmetician, knew
something of geometry, levelling, and mensuration, and in some
cases possessed a very competent knowledge of practical mathematics.
He could calculate the velocities, strength, and power of machines:
could draw in plan and section....'[2] Much of these 'superior attainments and intellectual power' reflected the abundant facilities for
technical education in 'villages' like Manchester during this period,
ranging from Dissenters' academies and learned societies to local and
visiting lecturers, 'mathematical and commercial' private schools with
evening classes, and a wide circulation of practical manuals, periodicals,
and encyclopaedias.

Whatever the reasons for British precocity in this domain, the results
are clear; and equally clear is the relative ease with which inventors
found financing for their projects and the rapidity with which the products of their ingenuity found favour with the manufacturing community—if anything, too much favour, for many of the earlier
inventors spent more time enforcing their patent rights than earning
them.[3] Some have accounted for this swift diffusion of change by the
relatively greater accumulation of capital in Britain than anywhere else
in Europe except Holland (which was kind enough to send some of its
surplus funds to England, rather than invest them in its own industry).
They argue that the greater supply of capital was reflected in lower
interest rates, which tended to decline in the course of the eighteenth
century, and that this in turn made change that much less costly and,
pari passu, that much more profitable and attractive.[4]

---

[1] A. E. Musson and Eric Robinson, 'The Origins of Engineering in Lancashire',
J. Econ. Hist. xx (1960); 'Science and Industry in the Later Eighteenth Century',
Econ. Hist. Rev. 2nd ser. xii (1960). Also G. H. Tupling, 'The Early Metal Trades and
the Beginnings of Engineering in Lancashire', *Trans. Lancashire and Cheshire Anti-
quarian Soc.* LXI (1949), 25 f.

[2] Wm. Fairbairn, *Treatise on Mills and Millwork* (2nd ed.; 2 vols.; London, 1864),
i, vi.

[3] A number of writers have laid stress on the incentive effect of patent legislation.
I am inclined to doubt its significance. This kind of protection was not new; the basis
of the system was laid by the Statute of Monopolies of 1624. In our period, the cost
and difficulty of obtaining a patent was rising steadily. Cf. Witt Bowden, *Industrial
Society in England Towards the End of the Eighteenth Century* (New York), 1925, pp.
26–30. At the same time, there was good reason to doubt the efficacy of patents
against determined competitors, as numerous inventors learned to their sorrow, and
many an entrepreneur placed his reliance on secrecy, rather than the law.

[4] This was the position of Prof. T. S. Ashton in his *Industrial Revolution, 1760–1830*
('Home University Library', London, New York, and Toronto, 1949), pp. 9–11,

The argument is persuasive, but the historical facts tend to modify it at a number of points, diminish its import at others. On the one hand, it is most unlikely that differences in the rate of interest of the order of two, three, even half-a-dozen points are a decisive consideration where the mechanical advantage of innovation is as great as it was for the early textile machines. One can understand that the timing of canal and road construction, or similar costly projects of slow gestation, was affected by shifts in the rate of interest, in part because the very possibility of flotation was frequently dependent on an easy money market. But for the prospective textile entrepreneur, the problem was not whether his profits would cover 6 per cent or 12 per cent on borrowed capital, but whether he could raise the capital at all.

In this regard, the cotton manufacturer of the eighteenth century was favoured by the very newness of the Industrial Revolution. The early machines, complicated though they were to contemporaries, were nevertheless modest, rudimentary, wooden contrivances, which could be built for surprisingly small sums. A forty-spindle jenny cost perhaps £6 in 1792; scribbling and carding machines cost £1 for each inch of roller width; a slubbing billy with thirty spindles cost £10. 10s.[1] And these were new. Similar equipment was frequently advertised in used condition at much lower prices. The only really costly items of fixed investment in this period were buildings and power, but here the historian must remember that the large, many-storeyed mill that awed contemporaries was the exception. Most so-called factories were no more than glorified workshops: a dozen workers or less; one or two jennies, perhaps, or mules; and a carding machine to prepare the rovings. These early devices were powered by the men and women who worked them.[2] Attics and cottages were reconverted for the

90–1, but he has since modified it considerably, emphasizing, not cost of capital but its availability. The rate of return on government securities was important, he argues, because of the 5 per cent ceiling on the rate of interest: when the funds fell and the return (including the prospect of capital gains) rose, capital would shift in that direction, diminishing the supply to industry and trade. *An Economic History of England: the Eighteenth Century*, pp. 26–9. There is an excellent discussion in L. S. Pressnell, 'The Rate of Interest in the Eighteenth Century', in Pressnell (ed.), *Studies in the Industrial Revolution* (London, 1960), pp. 190–7.

[1] W. B. Crump (ed.), *The Leeds Woollen Industry, 1780–1820* (Leeds: The Thoresby Society, 1931), pp. 212–13, 293; also Herbert Heaton, 'Benjamin Gott and the Industrial Revolution in Yorkshire', *Econ. Hist. Rev.* III (1931), 52. For purposes of comparison, a cotton weaver earned perhaps 7s. 6d. a week in 1770, a hand spinner between 2s. and 3s. Thus the 40-spindle jenny cost about two weeks wages of the forty women it replaced. Wage figures from Wadsworth and Mann, *Cotton Trade*, pp. 402–3. A traditional hand-loom cost more than a jenny; anywhere from £7 to £10.

[2] The first application of water power to the mule was apparently in 1790 at the New Lanark mills. The increased drive made possible 'double mules' of 400 spindles;

purpose; later on a steam-engine might be added to this kind of improvised structure. Moreover, there were premises to rent—here we have
another example of the responsiveness of English capital to economic
opportunity. Not only were complete buildings offered to prospective
tenants, but larger mills were subdivided and let in small units. So
that an industrialist could in fact start with a minimal outlay—renting his
plant, borrowing for equipment and raw materials, even raising funds
for payment of wages by contracting in advance for the finished product.
Some no doubt began with nothing more than the capital accumulated
by petty local trading in yarn and cloth; others, as noted above, apparently built their fortunes in the black market for embezzled materials.

On the other hand, a good many of the early mill owners were men
of substance—merchants whose experience in selling finished commodities had alerted them to the possibilities of large-scale, mechanized
production; putters-out, who had had direct experience in manufacture;
even independent small producers with enough set by to change their
methods and expand. And here, of course, the direct accumulation of
capital within the textile manufacture itself and the trades allied with it
was a major factor in the rapid adoption of technological innovation—as
it was in industries like iron and chemicals. We are now come full circle:
the inventions came in part because the growth and prosperity of the
industry made them imperative; and the growth and prosperity of the
industry helped make their early and widespread utilization possible.

All of which serves to emphasize an important caution: it was not
capital by itself that made possible Britain's swift advance. Money
alone could have done nothing; indeed, in this regard, the entrepreneurs
of the Continent, who could often count on direct subsidies or monopoly privileges from the state, were better off than their British counterparts. What distinguished the British economy, as we have already had
several occasions to remark, was an exceptional sensitivity and responsiveness to pecuniary opportunity. This was a people fascinated
by wealth and commerce, collectively and individually.

Why this was so is a question worthy of investigation. Certainly the

thus capital bred capital. George W. Daniels, *The Early English Cotton Industry*
(Manchester, 1920), p. 125. It is not clear when the steam-engine was first so used—
perhaps in the late 1780's, certainly in the early 1790's. A large proportion of these
early engines were employed, not to drive the machinery directly, but to raise water
upon a wheel; some of them, indeed, were Savery-type steam pumps (see below,
p. 331), which were preferred to more efficient machines because of their lower initial
cost. An engine delivering 2–4 h.p. could be had new for between £150 and £200.
A larger Boulton and Watt rotative engine (15–20 h.p.) cost four or five times as much.
Steam came earlier to frame spinning: Arkwright's atmospheric engine at Shudehill
(Lancs.), to raise water for a wheel, was installed in 1783. A. E. Musson and E. Robinson, 'The Early Growth of Steam Power', *Econ. Hist. Rev.* 2nd ser. XI (1959), 418–39.

phenomenon was closely related, as both cause and effect, to the already noted openness of society; and this was linked in turn to the peculiar position and character of the aristocracy.

Britain had no nobility in the sense of the other European countries. She had a peerage, composed of a small number of titled persons, whose essential and almost unique perquisite was the possibility of sitting in the House of Lords. Their children were commoners, who often received, to be sure, courtesy titles in token of their high birth, but were no different in civil status from other Britons. Even the peers had only the most modest privileges: trial by their fellow noblemen in criminal proceedings, for example, or the right of direct access to the sovereign. They did not enjoy fiscal immunities.

Below the nobility stood the gentry or so-called squirearchy, an amorphous group, without legal definition or status, that had no equivalent on the Continent. Its edges were blurred, its ranks loosely and heterogeneously constituted. Some gentry were of noble ante-cedents; others had made their fortunes in trade or the professions or government service and had purchased estates as much for their social prestige as for their income; others were scions of old country families; still others were farmers or yeomen grown wealthy. They had two things in common: land ownership and a way of life that was a vestige of medieval seignorialism. These were the local notabilities—lords of the manor, justices of the peace, county sheriffs. With the peers, they were the true rulers of provincial Britain.

Both nobility and gentry generally practised primogeniture: the oldest male child inherited both title (where pertinent) and land. This had two large consequences: it increased the economic burden of the head of the family; and it compelled most of the children to earn their living, in whole or part.

Thus it was no easy task to preserve and if possible increase the family estate for transmission to one's heir while finding places for younger sons and dowries for daughters. Daniel Finch, Earl of Nottingham, put the point well in a letter of 1695 to his executors; he favoured primo-genitary strict settlement, he wrote,

not so much out of a vain affectation of continuing a great estate in my family, as because [my son] will thereby be under a necessity of observing some good economy that he may be able to provide for his younger children, and consequently will not run into that foolish or extravagant way of living which debauches and corrupts the manners of many families, as well as ruins their fortunes....[1]

[1] Quoted by H. J. Habakkuk, 'Daniel Finch, 2nd Earl of Nottingham: His House and Estate', in J. H. Plumb (ed.), *Studies in Social History: A Tribute to G. M. Trevelyan* (London, New York, Toronto, 1955), p. 156.

To be sure, British society had provided careers for cadets of good family: remunerative offices in government; Church livings; commissions in the armed forces; a growing number of potentially lucrative situations in the colonies (not really important until the second half of the eighteenth century). Yet excessive and otiose as many of these places appeared to contemporary reformers, they were not enough to satisfy the demand, as the competition for patronage testifies, and they had to be shared with such other groups as the legal profession and the mercantile interest. Sinecures and offices came high, and it was a rare father who could place more than two or three sons well. To quote Nottingham again: 'no estate can provide so fully for younger children, but that they must in great degree help themselves'. The fourth and fifth sons, of gentry and even noble families, would have to be apprenticed to trade—not the trade of the shop, to be sure, but the international commerce that was at once the pride of the English economy and the seed-bed of new houses.[1]

Admittedly, there were rarely as many as four or five sons that survived to manhood, and the flow of gentle talent into business was presumably small.[2] Certainly it was less important in the eighteenth century than it had been in earlier periods, partly perhaps because the royal house brought with it from Hanover strong German prejudices against this kind of mobility, partly because the proliferation of office and the extension of British dominion were opening up alternative opportunities that were more attractive and preferentially accessible.[3] Yet it was not so much the substantive contribution to enterprise that counted, as the symbolism of the example, the sanction that this legiti-

[1] Much depended, however, on necessity and opportunity. In Scotland, the gentry were poor and had few claims to preferment. The Established Church was closed to them; the prospect of fighting the battles of England, unattractive; foreign commerce and colonial enterprise offered few employments until the century was well advanced. The more intellectual could prepare for the Bar, but these were necessarily few. Many sought their livelihood, therefore, as shopkeepers, alias 'merchants'. As Henry G. Graham puts it in his classic study, '...in those days, a gentleman's son felt it as natural to fall into trade as for a rich tradesman to rise out of it'. *The Social Life of Scotland in the Eighteenth Century* (4th ed.; London, 1950), p. 33.

[2] We really do not know how important, absolutely or relatively, was the participation of these younger sons of noble or gentry families in business. A systematic survey of the entrepreneurs of the Industrial Revolution would be immensely valuable, though difficulties of definition (what is active participation?) would confuse the issue, especially as regards the aristocratic contribution. In the meantime, we are reduced to discrete impressions. Cf. Walter E. Minchinton, 'The Merchants in England in the Eighteenth Century', *Explorations in Entrepreneurial History* [henceforth *Explorations*], x (1957), 62.

[3] For the earlier period, see Lawrence Stone, 'The Nobility in Business', *ibid.* pp. 54–61.

mate participation, however small, conferred on trade as a respectable activity and on pecuniary rationality as a way of life.

In the meantime, the head of the family had to build the patrimony and make it work for him and his children. Not all landowners did well in the contest for fortune or even tried, but at their best they formed a class of 'spirited proprietors' that warmed the hearts of improvers like Arthur Young. Noble or gentle, they lived on their estates (and not at the court), rode their lands and noted their yield, sought improvements to enhance traditional revenues, conceived new ways to produce income. They rarely cultivated or operated directly— though one can cite contrary instances like Thomas Fitzmaurice, brother of the Earl of Shelburne, who, among other enterprises, bleached and sold the linens woven by his Irish tenants.[1] (Even if they had made their fortune in trade and continued in the firm, they inevitably gave less time to mercantile concerns.) Rather they leased their land to tenants—peasants, commercial farmers, or industrial contractors. When they financed business ventures, it was as creditors more than as partners; or they bought shares in joint-stock companies and trusts. Their interests were generally handled by stewards, agents, and solicitors, and this exposed them to abuses of confidence. Yet that was all the more reason to supervise their affairs closely, and many of them made the decisions that are the hallmark of active entrepreneurship. A significant few opened mines, built iron works and mills, dug canals, developed ports, and leased their urban properties for building. What is more, they anticipated demand, undertook investments on speculation, advertised if necessary for tenants, and stood ready to operate their installations through agents or partners if no lessees were forthcoming.

They also enclosed the land, concentrated their holdings, introduced or found tenants who would introduce better crop rotations and techniques of cultivation, helped spread new ideas about the country. This is not the place to discuss the so-called 'agricultural revolution' of the eighteenth century, or to assess the benefits or injustices that accompanied it. My aim here is to underline the generality of this spirit of innovation and its effects; and also to recall the well-known fact that this was a society that interposed relatively few institutional barriers to a fundamental change of this kind. The Tudor monarchy may have been concerned about enclosures; the parliamentary regime of the eighteenth century was less paternalistic. For good or evil, Britain's countryside was being kneaded like dough; and the improving landlords were a powerful leaven.

[1] A. H. Dodd, *The Industrial Revolution in North Wales* (Cardiff, 1933), pp. 32–3.

It is probable that such industrial ventures as people 'of name' under-took were on the whole less remunerative than competitive efforts by 'professional' businessmen; or for that matter, that the great estates could not bear comparison with the lands of the small proprietors in their neighbourhood.[1] It is also true that the nobility and gentry tended over time to change from active entrepreneurs into rentiers; this was the experience, for example, of areas like Wales and Northumberland, where large coal and ore deposits had initially provided a favourable base for industrial activity by landowners. Yet the significance of these efforts lay in the efforts themselves, not in their return. Once again it lay in the legitimacy conferred on innovation and the pursuit of wealth as a way of life.

A comparison will illuminate the argument. Thus far I have treated this permeation of country life by the spirit of enterprise and calculation as a consequence of social structure and the system of inheritance. There was undoubtedly more to it. In part, it reflected the quickening pace of the economy: new men kept moving up and the older families had to move faster to hold their own. In part, it was probably a response to new opportunities, in particular, to the increasing demand for resources that lay in the hands of the landed proprietors. Yet this response was neither necessary nor inevitable. It would have been just as easy for the nobility and gentry to turn their backs on their new rivals and break off competition by defining the means of their ascension as intrinsically ignoble. This is what the aristocracy of Europe had done in the Renais-sance, when it had developed the very idea of the gentleman as a weapon against the pretensions of the bourgeoisie.[2] And this was to be the reaction of much of Europe's aristocracy in the nineteenth century in the face of industrial revolution and a corresponding shift in the balance of political power. The British nobility and gentry chose to meet the newcomers on middle ground: they affirmed their distinction of blood or breeding; but they buttressed it with an active and produc-tive cultivation of gain.

This momentous decision was self-reinforcing. The concern of the British gentleman for the accretion of his fortune made him a partici-pant in society rather than a parasite upon it—whatever judgement one may pass on the character of this participation. Business interests promoted a degree of intercourse between people of different stations and walks of life that had no parallel on the Continent. 'We used to sit down to dinner,' wrote Lord Hervey in 1731, 'a little snug party of

[1] Cf. Adam Smith, *Wealth of Nations*, Book III, ch. II; Arthur Young, *Travels during the Years 1787, 1788 and 1789*, I, 90, 99, 108, and especially 198.

[2] See the article by Arthur Livingston on 'Gentleman, Theory of the' in the *Encyclopaedia of the Social Sciences* and the references given there.

about thirty odd, up to the chin in beef, venison, geese, turkeys, etc.; and generally over the chin in claret, strong beer and punch. We had Lords Spiritual and Temporal, besides commoners, parsons and free-holders innumerable.'[1] Compare Arthur Young's reflections on a visit with the Duc de la Rochefoucauld:[2]

At an English nobleman's, there would have been three or four farmers asked to meet me, who would have dined with the family amongst the ladies of the first rank. I do not exaggerate, when I say, that I have had this at least an hundred times in the first houses of our islands. It is however, a thing that in the present state of manners in France, would not be met with from Calais to Bayonne, except by chance in the house of some great lord that had been much in England, and then not unless it was asked for.

Or, to return to Britain, consider the friendship of Robert Hewer, successful supercargo and trader turned landowner and lord of the manor of Manadon (near Plymouth), with the Duke and Duchess of Bedford: he spent weeks as their guest at Woburn Abbey, where he was 'of all their parties of pleasure!'; and the visit was repeated several times.[3] Such a continuing relationship is more significant of true society than a dozen marriages between noble blood and bourgeois gold *pour redorer le blason*.[4]

   Below the level of the gentry, there was no barrier between land and trade—not even a permeable membrane. Given the rural character of most industry and the intermittent claims of agriculture, many cultiva-tors were at the same time manufacturers or middlemen or both. This was true not only of textiles, but of branches like metallurgy where one might think the nature of the manufacturing process would have im-posed a more rigorous division of labour: witness Isaac Wilkinson, Aaron Walker, Jedediah Strutt and others. Note that where similar conditions prevailed on the Continent, one found the same combina-tion of activities: the land brought forth industrial enterprise and enterprisers. Yet again, what sets Britain apart is a question of degree. Nowhere else, as we have seen, was the countryside so infused with manufacture; nowhere else, the pressures and incentives to change greater, the force of tradition weaker. It was all of a piece: improving

---

[1] A. Goodwin (ed.), *The European Nobility in the Eighteenth Century* (London, 1953), p. 4.

[2] Young, *Travels*, I, 207.

[3] Conrad Gill, *Merchants and Mariners of the Eighteenth Century* (London, 1961), p. 138.

[4] There was much of that too—on the Continent as well as Britain. But inter-class alliances are to be found in all but rigid caste societies. The real test is not the union; it is what follows: how many great families in such circumstances are willing to know their new relations after the wedding?

landlords, enclosures, commercial farming, village shops, putting-out, mines and forges, the active mortgage market—all combined to break the shackles of place and habit, assimilate country and city, and promote a far wider recruitment of talent than would have otherwise occurred. In a society of which four of five people lived on the land, this was a powerful stimulus to overall development.

By the same token, the flow of entrepreneurship within business was freer, the allocation of resources more responsive than in other econo-mies. Where the traditional sacrosanctity of occupational exclusiveness continued to prevail across the Channel, enforced sometimes by law but in any case by habit and moral prohibitions, the British cobbler would not stick to his last nor the merchant to his trade. It was not merely a kind of negative phenomenon—that is, the absence of confining regula-tions or opprobrious strictures; rather it was a positive drive, an ambitious versatility that was always alive to the main chance. One cannot but be impressed by a man like this Thomas Griggs, grocer and clothier of Essex in the mid-eighteenth century, who invested and speculated in real estate, fattened cattle for market, malted barley, lent money on pawn.[1] Or like Thomas Fox, Quaker clothier of Wellington, who was moved by hard times in the wool trade to look into the possibilities of lead, calamine, or copper mining—or all three.[2]

One could extend the list considerably, but one final example will have to suffice: Samuel Garbett of Birmingham, originally brassworker, then merchant and chemist, partner in spinning, chemical (Birmingham and Prestonpans, near Edinburgh), iron-smelting (Carron works, Scotland), and flour-milling (Albion Mills, London) enterprises, and shareholder in the Cornish Metal Co. (copper mines). To appreciate the force of this drive for wealth, one must remember that these men were risking their fortunes at each throw of the entrepreneurial dice. With rare exceptions, there was no haven of limited liability. Garbett went bankrupt in 1772 because of the failure of one of his partners.

Similarly, the structure of the firm was more open and rational in Britain than in the continental countries. Everywhere, the fundamental business unit was the individual proprietorship or the family partner-ship, but where, in a country like France, the family firm was almost always closed to outsiders, British entrepreneurs were far more willing to enter into association with friends or friends of friends. Indeed, this seems to have been the preferred way of raising capital to expand or of attracting and attaching special skills to the enterprise. In textiles, a capitalist like George Philips would seek out and take as partner an

[1] K. H. Burley, 'An Essex Clothier of the Eighteenth Century', *Econ. Hist. Rev.* 2nd ser. XI (1958), 289–301.
[2] Herbert Fox, *Quaker Homespun* (London, 1938), pp. 46 f.

experienced manager like George Lee, late employee of Peter Drink-water; or an already hardened flax spinner like John Marshall, faced with a crisis in the trade, could throw out his partners ('As they could neither of them be of any further use, I released them from the firm and took the whole upon myself'); and when, shortly after, though mortgaged to the hilt, he determined to expand, would bring in new ones for much larger amounts.[1] In brewing, where the need for capital was so great and urgent 'that it could not be produced fast enough from the profits of the firms', 'established concerns welcomed into their partnerships bankers and merchants, who of necessity brought in the social and political consequences of vast wealth made in other fields'.[2] In machine building, it was probably skill more than capital that was the scarce factor, though it took thousands of pounds to turn a repair shop into an engineering plant. Boulton and Watt are perhaps the best model of this alliance of money and talent, but one could cite many similar associations, with varying division of contributions and responsibilities.[3] The pattern was probably most widespread in metal-lurgy; there the requirements of both capital and talent were heavy, and the partnership was the normal business form.[4] Even where a firm was essentially a family affair—the Crawshay smelting mill at Cyfarthfa or ironmongery in London, for example—outsiders were brought in as needed; bought out later if advisable; and new partners found. Professor Ashton has pointed out the importance in this con-nection of interfamilial associations of Dissenters: the bonds of a common, persecuted religion proved almost as effective a business tie as blood itself.[5]

The cohesiveness and mutual support of the nonconformist business community was only one element in their commercial success. They

[1] These were the Benyons, woollen merchants of Shrewsbury. W. Gordon Rimmer, *Marshall's of Leeds, Flax-Spinners 1788–1886* (Cambridge, 1960), pp. 40–4.

[2] Peter Mathias, 'The Entrepreneur in Brewing, 1700–1830', *Explorations*, x (1957), 73–6.

[3] Thus Bateman and Sherratt of Salford: Fenton, Murray and Wood of Leeds; Hazeldine, Rastrick and Co. of Bridgnorth (Salop); and somewhat later, Maudslay, Son and Field of London; Nasmyth, Gaskell and Co. of Manchester; Sharp, Roberts and Co. of the same city; *et al.*

[4] To be sure, some of the facilities available in textiles were present in metallurgy as well. Thus landowners, desirous of increasing their incomes, were often ready to let mineral rights on favourable terms and otherwise promote enterprise on their estates; sometimes, as at Cyfarthfa and Dowlais, leases fixed at absurdly low rates ran for a century. Also, it was often possible to rent plants already built for a moderate sum. Nevertheless, it took a thousand pounds or more to launch even a modest furnace or forge.

[5] Ashton, *Iron and Steel in the Industrial Revolution* (2nd ed.; Manchester, 1951), ch. IX: 'The Ironmasters'.

suffered numerous disabilities because of their religion, and business was in many ways the most convenient outlet for their energy and ambition; their faith itself, with its stress on diligence, thrift, and rationality as a way of life, was often a competitive advantage. It is surely no coincidence that they were most numerous in the North and the Midlands, the centres of most rapid industrial development. On the other hand, Britain was not alone in having Calvinists, who played the role of an entrepreneurial leaven throughout Europe. What distinguished Britain was the extent to which her religious nonconformists conformed to a wider social pattern; the entrepreneurial differences were differences of degree, and not of kind.

The same observations are relevant to the oft-cited thesis that price inflation brought bigger profits, and that bigger profits made possible industrial change.[1]   Even if it could be shown that profits did increase over the century and that it was higher prices that were responsible— and the usual demonstration proves nothing of the sort—the fact remains that Britain was not the only nation to have price inflation in this period; that the best enterprises on the Continent made just as high rates of profit and relied more, if anything, on self-financing.[2] The point again is not so much the rate of return as the manner of its use: where British firms ploughed profits back into the business, their competitors abroad too often transferred them from trade to more honorific callings, or held them as a reserve in the form of land, mortgage loans, and similar non-industrial placements.

Finally, a word should be said about the role of banks and bank credit. In no country in Europe in the eighteenth century was the financial structure so advanced and the public so habituated to paper

---

[1] The *locus classicus* is Earl J. Hamilton, 'Profit Inflation and the Industrial Revolution', *Quart. J. Econ.* LVI (1941–42), 257–70. See also his earlier article, 'American Treasure and the Rise of Capitalism, 1500–1700', *Economica*, IX (1929), 338–57, and his reply to the criticisms of John U. Nef, 'Prices and Progress', *J. Econ. Hist.* XII (1952), 325–49.

[2] See the excellent analysis of the problem in David Felix, 'Profit Inflation and Industrial Growth: the Historic Record and Contemporary Analogies', *Quart. J. Econ.* LXX (1956), 441–63. One should note that most of the price increase in the second half of the eighteenth century occurred in the 1790's. Felix argues that such expansion of profits as did take place was the result of greater productivity rather than a combination of price inflation and wage lag. This is clearly so: the very industries that were making the most rapid technological advances were the ones whose prices were falling and the nominal wages of whose workers (or real wages, for that matter) were rising through most of this period (1760–1830). The mule spinners were a privileged group. What is more, there is considerable direct evidence that rates of profit in these industries were not increasing over the long run, but rather reached a peak with the introduction of the critical mechanical innovations (Schumpeter's entrepreneurial profits) and then declined as new firms were attracted into the field.

instruments as in Britain.[1] Nominally, the credit offered by the growing multitude of private banks was for short periods—up to ninety days—to cover commercial transactions; in fact, much of it was in the form of revolving and open credits, or even of standing overdrafts, which served as quasi-capital.[2] What is more, the development of a national network of discount and payment enabled the capital-hungry industrial areas to draw for this purpose on the capital-rich agricultural districts. The system was just developing in the last quarter of the eighteenth century. By the 1820's and 1830's, however, when the problem of disposing of the products of British factories had become more difficult than that of financing technological change, bank credit was a pillar of the industrial edifice.

Yet while these institutional developments clearly promoted an easier, more abundant flow of resources from land to industry, the nature and direction of the balance of payments between these two sectors are less obvious. It is a commonplace of economic literature that one of the major aspects or criteria of development is the shift of resources from agriculture to manufacturing; and that a condition of rapid development is an increase of productivity in husbandry that will generate the savings to finance industrial expansion. The best example of such a sequence is Japan, where output per head in agriculture almost doubled in the space of a generation (1878/82–1903/7) at little expense of capital; and where, especially in the early years, the land tax drained a substantial fraction of farm income for investment in development.[3] The British case, however, differs sharply. For one thing, gains in farm productivity were assuredly far lower. The statistics available are in no way comparable to the Japanese, but, such as they are, they have led one authority to speculate that 'output per head in agriculture increased by about 25 per cent in the eighteenth century, and that the whole of this advance was achieved before 1750'.[4] The same source

[1] Note, in this regard, the experience of Robert Owen, who found in 1797 that the toll collectors of the Glasgow–New Lanark turnpike preferred the notes of the local banks to gold coin. *The Life of Robert Owen by Himself*, ed. M. Beer (New York, 1920), p. 71.
[2] Not to speak of accommodation paper, which was a means of obtaining credit, if only for short periods, with or without the co-operation of the banks. With the connivance of banks or discount houses, accommodation paper could be the basis for generous medium- and long-term credit. On all this, see W. T. C. King, *History of the London Discount Market* (London, 1936); L. S. Pressnell, *Country Banking in the Industrial Revolution* (New York, 1956); D. S. Landes, *Bankers and Pashas: International Finance and Economic Imperialism in Egypt* (London, 1958).
[3] Kazushi Ohkawa and Henry Rosovsky, 'The Role of Agriculture in Modern Japanese Economic Development', *Econ. Devel. and Cult. Change*, IX, no. 1, part II (October 1960), 43–67; also G. Ranis, 'The Financing of Japanese Economic Development', *Econ. Hist. Rev.* 2nd ser. XI (1959), 440–54.
[4] Deane and Cole, *British Economic Growth*, p. 75.

suggests that the real output of the farm sectors rose about 43 per cent in the course of the century, 24 per cent during the critical decades from 1760 to 1800;[1] by contrast, Japanese agricultural product about doubled from the late 1870's to the early 1900's.

Moreover, the increase in British farm output was due in large measure to enclosures and the improvements they made possible: concentration of holdings, elimination of fallow, more productive choice and rotation of crops, selective breeding of livestock, better drainage and fertilization, more intensive cultivation. It is still a matter of dispute how rapidly these new techniques spread or how quickly they followed on enclosure itself. What is clear is that both the division of the land and the subsequent improvements in its use cost money: for legal expenses, roads, ditches, and fences, to begin with; and eventually for buildings, equipment, drains, and materials. Unfortunately, we have no figures of the area affected, but such partial statistics as are available—enclosure of commons and waste, for example, by parliamentary act—suggest that from 1760 to 1815 Britain enclosed millions of acres at an initial cost of redistribution of upwards of £1 per acre, and at an eventual cost of anywhere from £5 to £25 per acre, depending on the original condition of the soil and the nature of its use.[2] Such investments paid, as the higher yields and rents on consolidated land show. But it may well be that in the early decades of heavy enclosure, that is, the very years that also saw the birth of modern industry, British husbandry was taking as much capital as it was giving; while in the period from 1790 to 1814, when food prices rose to record levels, the net flow of resources was probably toward the land. The great contribution of agriculture to industrialization came after 1815, when both enclosure and the breaking of marginal soil slowed and proprietors and tenants reaped the fruits of earlier efforts. Yet even then, these returns depended on protection against foreign corn and were therefore not a net addition to the savings generated by the economy. Rather, they were bought at the price of a certain misallocation of resources, and abundant and responsive though they may have been, they were probably less than what the land would have provided under more competitive conditions. Still, it was thanks to enclosures and what is sometimes called the 'Agricultural Revolution' that Britain fended off as well as she did Ricardo's 'stationary state'—that end of growth and accumulation wherein the pressure of population on the

---

[1] Deane and Cole, op. cit. p. 78.

[2] On the cost of enclosure, cf. Great Britain, Board of Agriculture, General Report on Enclosures (London, 1808), p. 97. On subsequent expenses of improvement, Albert Pell, 'The Making of the Land in England: A Retrospect', Journal of the Royal Agricultural Society of England, 2nd ser. XXIII (1887), 355-74.

supply of food has so raised the cost of subsistence and hence wages, that manufacturers can no longer make a profit and the wealth of the nation flows as rent to the owners of the land.

To sum up: it was in large measure the pressure of demand on the mode of production that called forth the new techniques in Britain, and the abundant, responsive supply of the factors that made possible their rapid exploitation and diffusion. The point will bear stressing, the more so as economists, particularly theorists, are inclined to concentrate almost exclusively on the supply side. The student of economic development, impressed on the one hand by the high cost of industrialization, on the other by the low level of savings in underdeveloped countries, has devoted most of his attention to the problem of capital formation: on ways to raise the rate of net investment from, say, 5 per cent to 12 or more; and on devices to prevent increased income from dissipating itself on increased consumption.[1] His approach is essentially analogous to that of an economic historian like Hamilton, with his thesis of industrial revolution born of and fed by profit inflation. And indeed, many a planner has seriously contemplated the deliberate use of inflation, which tends to shift resources from consumers to savers, to promote industrialization.

Yet however justified this concern with saving and capital may be in this age of costly equipment and facilities and abysmally poor would-be industrial economies, it is less relevant to the British experience. For one thing, eighteenth-century Britain enjoyed far more wealth and income per head than the backward nations of today; it started, in other words, from a higher base. For another, the capital requirements of these early innovations were, as we have seen, small—within the reach of a single person or family. Moreover, they were concentrated at first in a small sector of the economy, and their effects—and thus their appetite for capital—spread from this narrow base by a process of derived demand that fed on earlier success.[2] In Britain, starting from scratch, the investment of one period was built on the productivity gains of the one before, plus the injection of new labour from popula-

---

[1] One could cite numerous examples. For some idea of the wide spectrum of thought along this one line, cf. W. A. Lewis, *The Theory of Economic Growth* (London, 1955), pp. 201 f.; W. W. Rostow, 'The Take-off into Self-Sustained Growth', *Econ. J.* LXVI (1956), 25–48; and a review by O. Ehrlich of Gerald M. Meier and Robert Baldwin, *Economic Development: Theory, History, Policy* (New York, 1957), in *J. Econ. Hist.* XVIII (1958), 74.

[2] So much for hypotheses of balanced growth; the historical experience, under conditions of relatively unplanned development, followed other lines. See below, pp. 314 ff., 321, 338. Also John Hughes, 'Foreign Trade and Balanced Growth: the Historical Framework', *Amer. Econ. Rev.* XLIX, no. 2 (May 1959), 330–37; and Goran Ohlin, 'Balanced Economic Growth in History', *ibid.* pp. 338–53.

tion increase and immigration. It was the flow of capital, more than the stock, that counted in the last analysis; so much for the Marxist preoccupation with primitive accumulation.

Technological innovations are only part of the story. The question remains why they had the effect they did. An institutional order is a remarkably complex and elastic system; not everything can turn it upside down. Only changes of a certain quality and scope could have transformed the mode of production and initiated a self-sustaining process of economic development.

In order to understand the nature and impact of the advances in cotton manufacture, a few words are needed on the technology of the industry. The manufacture of almost any textile may be analysed into four main steps: preparation, in which the raw material is sorted, cleaned, and combed out so that the fibres lie alongside one another; spinning, in which the loose fibres are drawn and twisted to form a yarn; weaving, in which some yarn is laid lengthwise (the warp) and other yarn (the weft) is run across over and under the longitudinal lines to form a fabric; finally, finishing, which varies considerably with the nature of the cloth, but may comprise fulling or sizing (to give the cloth body), cleaning, shearing, dyeing, printing, or bleaching.

At the beginning of the eighteenth century, only a handful of these processes had as yet been mechanized. In the wool manufacture, the fulling mill, its heavy hammers driven by water, was known on the Continent as early as the eleventh century and by the thirteenth had spread widely over the English countryside. The gig mill, which raised the nap on the cloth preparatory to shearing, dated from the sixteenth century; and though legal prohibition and the opposition of the shear-men delayed its diffusion, the repeated clamour against the device is the best evidence of its gains. There had also been two major improvements on the immemorial loom: the knitting frame, a complex, hand-run contrivance for weaving hosiery (invented by William Lee in 1598); and the Dutch or small-wares loom, invented at about the same time, and designed to weave as many as twenty-four narrow tapes or ribbons simultaneously.

Another precocious mechanical innovation was the silk-throwing machine, which twisted the filaments to form a thread. It was invented in the seventeenth century in Italy, where the secret was jealously guarded. But the plans were smuggled out by an Englishman named John Lombe in 1716–17, and within a few years John's brother Thomas built a huge throwing mill at Derby, a 500-foot power-driven factory of five or six stories and some 460 windows that was one of the wonders of the age. By the middle of the century, similar plants had been established in London and the provinces, some of them even larger than Lombe's monster.

In addition to these complex devices, which anticipate in their ingenuity and relative efficiency the better-known inventions of the mid-eighteenth century, a number of less spectacular advances had occurred, gradually and almost unnoticed. Over the centuries, the spinning wheel, large or small, had replaced the distaff, and the wheel itself had been altered to work faster and turn out a more even yarn. At the same time, those processes that required the use of fuel— dyeing, for example—had from the sixteenth century on learned to use coal instead of the more expensive wood. Finally, a variety of small improvements had been made in preparing the fibre for spinning, weaving the yarn in more complex patterns, and finishing it with the sheen and smoothness that betokened quality.

None of these advances, however, was sufficient in itself to trigger a process of cumulative, self-sustaining change. For it took a marriage to make the Industrial Revolution. On the one hand, it required machines which not only replaced hand labour but compelled the con- centration of production in factories—in other words, machines whose appetite for energy was too large for domestic sources of power and whose mechanical superiority was sufficient to break down the resis- tance of the older forms of hand production. On the other hand, it required a big industry producing a commodity of wide and elastic demand, such that (1) the mechanization of any one of its processes of manufacture would create serious strains in the others, and (2) the impact of improvements in this industry would be felt throughout the economy.

Neither the knitting frame nor the Dutch loom nor the throwing mill could satisfy these conditions. The first two, hand driven, were quite suited to domestic manufacture; and all three were employed in the production of goods whose actual market was small and potential demand limited. It was not until the techniques of spinning and weaving cheap textiles were transformed that the threshold of revolu- tion was crossed.

It was crossed first in the cotton manufacture. Why in cotton? One would have expected the passage to occur in wool, which was far and away the most important industry of the day, whether in terms of numbers employed, capital invested, or value of product. In England, imports of raw cotton (net of re-exports) in the first decade of the century averaged a little over a million pounds a year, worth perhaps £30,000 or £35,000; at that time, if we are to rely on available estimates, the woollen industry was consuming about 40 million pounds of material, valued at some £2 million. Even some decades later, in 1741, when both cotton consumption and prices were up and the price of wool had fallen, the disparity was still enormous: something over 1½ million pounds of raw cotton worth around £55,000, as against almost 60 million pounds of wool valued at perhaps £1,500,000.[1] In the other countries of Europe, the comparison was equally in favour of the older industry.

It has long been customary to explain this apparent paradox by denying it, that is, by asserting that it was just because the cotton industry was new, hence free of traditional restrictions on the scale and character of production, that it was able to adopt new techniques. The argument will not stand scrutiny. In England—which is the country that counts for our purposes—the extensive development of putting-out in the West Country and East Anglia and the rise of independent clothiers in Yorkshire had long freed the bulk of the wool manufacture from guild controls; indeed, in so far as legal restrictions entered into account, they favoured the older industry, on which the economic prosperity of the nation had been built.

On the other hand, the smallness of the cotton manufacture on the eve of the Industrial Revolution should not deceive us. For so young a creation, it was a spectacularly lusty child, and so rapid were its gains that almost from the beginning the older wool and linen trades were impelled to demand succour from the state. In England, a whole series of laws and decrees were passed from the late seventeenth century on to stimulate the consumption of domestic wool cloth: sumptuary laws like the Act requiring that all dead be buried in wool shrouds; prohibitions on the import of competitive fabrics; restrictions on the output of calicoes at home (1721). To no avail. The closing of England to East Indian cottons simply encouraged the domestic producers, whose fustians and linen-cottons (they were not yet able to turn out pure cottons) did not come under the interdiction. By the middle of the century, gains at home and abroad had made the cotton manufacturers a vested interest too powerful for even the still pre-eminent wool trade to overcome.

Still more important, cotton lent itself technologically to mechanization far more readily than wool. It is a plant fibre, tough and relatively homogeneous in its characteristics, where wool is organic, fickle, and subtly varied in its behaviour. In the early years of rudimentary machines, awkward and jerky in their movements, the resistance of cotton was a decisive advantage. Well into the nineteenth century, long after the techniques of mechanical engineering had much im-

[1] Cotton figures from Wadsworth and Mann, Cotton Trade, pp. 520–2; wool from P. Deane, 'The Output of the British Woollen Industry in the Eighteenth Century', J. Econ. Hist. XVII (1957), 220.

proved, there continued to be a substantial lag between the introduction of innovations into the cotton industry and their adaptation to wool. And even so, there has remained an element of art—of touch—in wool manufacture that the cleverest and most automatic contrivances have not been able to eliminate.

Once mechanization did come to cotton, of course, it was successful far beyond what it could have hoped to be in wool. On the one hand, the elasticity of supply of the raw material was substantially greater: one can increase acreage sown far more rapidly than the number of sheep. Thus cotton prices rose by about half in the 1770's and 1780's under the pressure of demand from the new spinning machines, while imports increased more than sixfold. Once the North American plantations entered the market, moreover, and the cotton gin made slave labour profitable, imports kept rising spectacularly while prices fell. In the peak year of 1860, Britain purchased over 1·4 milliard pounds of cotton at about the same 7½ pence it cost at the start of the eighteenth century.

On the other hand, the market for cotton goods was more elastic than for wool. Not only was the trend of taste in favour of the new fibre—for centuries, there had been an irregular but almost uninterrupted shift in the direction of lighter fabrics—but the availability of a cheap, washable textile gave rise to new patterns of dress of unforeseen potential. No longer was it the wealthy alone who could enjoy the comfort and hygiene of body *linen;* cotton made it possible for millions to wear drawers and chemises where before there had been nothing but the coarse, dirty outer-garments. A new kind of work-clothing was born—tough, yet comfortable to the skin and easy to clean and maintain. Even the rich, impressed with the colour and elegance of cotton prints, learned to distinguish more and more between the seasons and dress for the summer in muslins and calicoes.

At the same time, the bulk of the untapped markets in the pre-industrial areas of the world lay in the warmer climes or in temperate areas with hot summers. Already in the sixteenth and seventeenth centuries, a good part of Britain's gains as an exporter of wool cloth had been in the countries bordering the Mediterranean, the western plantations, and India; similarly, the spurt in re-exports of Indian calicoes that marked the late seventeenth century was due to the new demand of semi-tropical lands enriched by sugar, tobacco, and other 'colonial wares'. The story was no different in the eighteenth and nineteenth centuries: the commercial frontier of Britain lay overseas— in America, Africa, south and east Asia. The first was by far the most important: the West Indies and mainland colonies together bought 10 per cent of English domestic exports in 1700-1, 37 per cent in 1772-3, about 57 per cent in 1797–8.[1] Wool had played a big part in these gains: the sale of cloth in the new Atlantic market (America and Africa) grew sixfold from the beginning of the century to the eve of the American Revolution.[2] Now it was cotton's turn.

And so, although the first of the famous series of inventions that transformed the textile industry—both the fly-shuttle of Kay (1733) and the spinning frame of Wyatt and Paul (1738)—were designed for the manufacture of wool, the requirements of technology and the logic of the economic situation willed otherwise.

There is neither time nor space to review at this point the history of these inventions, which will be familiar to most readers. A number of summary observations, however, are indispensable.

(i) They came in a sequence of challenge and response, in which the speed-up of one stage of the manufacturing process placed a heavy strain on the factors of production of one or more other stages and called forth innovations to correct the imbalance. We have already noted the difficulty of supplying weavers with yarn. Kay's fly-shuttle, which did not really catch on until the 1750's and 1760's, only aggravated an already serious disequilibrium. The problem was solved by a family of spinning devices: carding machines by Paul and others (in use from the 1750's); Hargreaves's jenny (c. 1765; patent 1770); Arkwright's water frame (1769); Crompton's mule (1779)—so called because it combined some of the features of the frame and the jenny.[3]

[1] Deane and Cole, *British Economic Growth*, p. 34. These figures show a somewhat more rapid increase to the 1770's than those of Ralph Davis, 'English Foreign Trade, 1700–1774', *Econ. Hist. Rev.* 2nd ser. xv (1962), 292.

[2] *Ibid.* p. 291. The sale of 'other manufactures'—nails, tools, metal wares, leather goods, cordage, other textiles, and the like—grew even faster, to almost nine times its volume at the beginning of the period. As a consequence, the share of wool manufactures in total exports shrank from more than two-thirds to perhaps 27 per cent over the course of the century. Even at the end, however, they were still worth twice as much as cotton exports. Deane and Cole, *British Economic Growth*, pp. 30–1. Cottons followed a deviant geographical pattern: major expansion in overseas areas to about 1770, that is, the eve of technological revolution; then the most rapid gains, in Europe. Wadsworth and Mann, *Cotton Trade*, p. 146.

[3] Technically the family was composed of two branches. On one side were the throstles (beginning with the water frame and continuing through various avatars down to the cap and ring machines of the present day), which drew the roving out first and then imparted twist. On the other were the jenny and mule, which imitated the action of the human spinner by drawing and twisting simultaneously. Because the weakness of the untwisted thread limited the length of the draw, the throstle could not produce fine counts and was used primarily for the production of warps. In the early period, this was extremely important since the jenny—and later the mule—spun too loose a thread for this purpose. On the other hand, because the long draw gave more play to the twist, which concentrated in the thinner spots and built them up, the

The mechanical advantage of even the earliest jennies and water frames over hand spinning was enormous: anywhere from six up to twenty-four to one for the jenny; several hundred to one for the frame. The spinning wheel, which had taken some centuries to displace the rock, became an antique in the space of a decade. Moreover, the victorious jenny scarcely outlived its victim; even the later models, with eighty and more spindles, could not compete in productivity—to say nothing of quality—with power-driven mules of two and three hundred. By the end of the century, the jenny was obsolete.

What is more, the quality of the machine-spun yarn was better than anything the distaff or wheel had been able to produce. A thread spun by hand is necessarily uneven in thickness and strength; and no two hanks are ever the same. One of the most difficult tasks of the manufacturer of the eighteenth century was to assemble suitable assortments of yarn. On occasion, he paid a premium for the work of an especially gifted spinster. The machine changed all this. Not only was its work more regular and stronger in proportion to weight, but the mule, which drew and twisted the roving simultaneously and continued to draw even after the twisting stopped, could spin higher counts than man had ever known: where the most skilful Indian spinner working with the wheel, or Swiss spinster using a distaff, could barely surpass 150 hanks to the pound, the better mule operatives were able to approach 300 by the start of the nineteenth century.

The tremendous increase of the supply of yarn that resulted from these inventions—reflected in a more than twelve-fold increase in cotton consumption from 1770 to 1800[1]—made improvements in weaving imperative. This was the golden age of the hand-weaver, whose unprecedented prosperity was a shock to all, a scandal to some. The answer was the power loom, invented by Cartwright in 1787. It caught on with difficulty owing to mechanical shortcomings (the main problem was how to achieve speed without excessive breakage of the

mule made a more regular thread than the frame; moreover, later improvements enabled the mule to produce a harder twist, and from 1800 the throstle tended to fade from use. There was a renewal of favour in the 1820's and 1830's, however, with the development of the ring principle and the growing use of power looms, which especially at first needed the strongest possible warps. Nevertheless, the British cotton industry, with its steady shift to finer yarn and cloth, has never made so much use of the throstle as the continental countries. Cf. Daniels, *The Early English Cotton Industry*, p. 164; also Julia de L. Mann, 'The Textile Industry: Machinery for Cotton, Flax, Wool, 1760-1850', in Ch. Singer *et al.*, *A History of Technology*, vol. IV: *The Industrial Revolution* (Oxford: Clarendon, 1958), pp. 283-91 and the sources cited there; and F. Nasmith, 'Fathers of the Machine Cotton Industry', *Trans. Newcomen Soc.* VI (1925-6), 167-8 (letter of E. J. Welffens).

[1] Average net imports, 1768-72; 3,703,000 lb.; 1798-1802, 47,233,000 lb.

threads), and its diffusion can be linked directly to fluctuations in the demand for cloth and hence the cost of hand labour. Thus its adoption was slow during the first two decades of the century, when war and, later on, tariff barriers cut Britain off from important markets. In the meantime, performance was improved, and where, in the first decade of the century, the machine worked hardly faster than the traditional hand loom, the technical advantage had risen by the mid-1820's to as much as $7\frac{1}{2}$ to 1, and one boy on two looms could do up to fifteen times as much as the cottage artisan.[1] At that point, the aim seems to have been not so much to speed the machine as to simplify its operation so that one person could handle more units at the same time: in 1833, a young man with a twelve-year old assistant could run four looms and turn out as much as twenty times the output of a hand worker.[2]

Such figures are clearly impressionistic and unstandardized. Yet they convey a general picture of the growing gap between machine and man, a gap reflected in the statistics, themselves approximate, of power looms in operation in Great Britain: 2400 in 1813, 14,150 in 1820, 55,500 in 1829, 100,000 in 1833, 250,000 by mid-century.[3] By contrast, the number of hand-loom weavers declined, although at a rate that testified to the obstinacy and tenacity of men who were unwilling to trade their independence for the better-paid discipline of the sheds. In the teens, their number actually rose to about a quarter of a million, and hung steadily there for another decade, though wages had fallen by over a half; by 1830 these reached an apparently irreducible minimum of about 6s. a week. The next two decades saw attrition shrink the weavers—in spite of recruitment of Irish immigrants whose subsistence level was even lower than that of the English artisans—to a remnant of 40,000. It is likely that many, if not most of these, were employed only part time—a reserve supply of labour in the event of unusual demand. A dozen more years, and there were perhaps 3000 left.

One point remains to be made about the pattern of challenge and response. The prominence of the inventions in spinning and weaving has tended to obscure the importance of this principle for all stages of textile manufacture. In particular, the mechanization of spinning

[1] Cf. Edward Baines, *A History of the Cotton Manufacture in Great Britain* (London, 1835), p. 240, citing R. Guest, *A Compendious History of the Cotton Manufacture* (Manchester, 1823).

[2] It is not clear how common this practice was. The impression one gets from comparisons between British and Continental practice is that the usual work load in a British cotton shed remained two looms until the 1870's, when conflicts arose over the effort to double the assignment.

[3] The figures up to 1833 are from Baines, *History of the Cotton Manufacture*, pp. 235-7. The 1850 number is from the factory reports, cited by T. Ellison, *The Cotton Trade of Great Britain* (London, 1886), pp. 76-7.

would have been unthinkable without a corresponding speed-up of the preliminary processes of cleaning, carding, and preparation of the roving. The eighteenth century saw, therefore, the development of an entire complex of pre-spinning machines, linked in rationally calculated combinations to the frame and the mule; the early machine builders often sold their products in sets or 'assortments' covering the various stages of manufacture from raw fibre to yarn. Similarly, the finishing processes were transformed: it was no longer feasible to bleach cloth in open meadows when more of it was being turned out than there was ground available. The answer lay in the use of chemical agents: often sulphuric acid at first; from the 1790's on, chlorine. In the same way, cylinder printing was introduced in place of the block press in London in 1783; it had been known for some time before; but by then the need was ripe, and it spread quickly to the rest of the country.

(ii) The many small gains were just as important as the more spectacular initial advances. None of the inventions came to industry in full-blown perfection. Aside from the trial and error of creation, there were innumerable adjustments and improvements—in articulation of parts, transmission of power, and the materials employed—before these primitive contrivances would work commercially. The first decades of industrialization saw a ceaseless war against breakdowns. By the turn of the century, however, not only the heavy motionless frame of the machine could be built of iron, but also the moving parts; leather belts had replaced pulley-ropes of cotton-mill waste. In subsequent decades, improvements in the steam-engine produced a smoother stroke; gearing and shafting were rationalized; and increasing automaticity achieved its consummation in Roberts's self-acting mule (1825).

(iii) Nothing illustrates better the continued importance of purely technological considerations than the persistent lag of mechanization in the woollen industry. It was not until the 1780's that the jenny came into general use in the Leeds area, and the mule was not really a success until the 1830's. In worsted, where the combed fibres will take more strain, machines came in faster: in the 1780's and 1790's, Yorkshire mills and shops were using jennies, hand- or animal-powered mules, and modified water frames. The first use of the steam-engine dates from before the turn of the century, and by 1820 there were perhaps two dozen steam-powered factories in the West Riding. By then hand spinning was almost a curiosity.[1]

Even when mechanized, the wool industry was compelled to work more slowly than cotton. William Fairbairn, probably the greatest

[1] The best source is Eric Sigsworth, *Black Dyke Mills: A History* (Liverpool, 1958), chs. I–II; see also J. James, *A History of the Wool Manufacture in England from the Earliest Times* (London, 1857).

authority of the period on factory design, has the mules of his sample cotton plant running at 232 r.p.m., those of his hypothetical woollen mill at 152.[1] Limitations of speed were still more serious in weaving, where the power loom offered nothing like the gains in productivity characteristic of the new spinning equipment. Thus Fairbairn's cotton looms were working at from 140 to 160 picks per minute, while his woollen equipment was doing 46. To be sure, it was harder to weave woollen yarn than the tougher worsted, but even in worsted the power loom came in slowly. The transition in the West Riding came in the late 1830's and 1840's: 2768 power looms in 1836, 11,458 in 1841, 19,121 in 1845, 35,298 in 1856.[2] The woollen manufacture was about a decade behind (6275 power looms in Yorkshire in 1856, 5733 in Lancashire, 14,391 in the whole of Great Britain); and even after the hand loom had been driven from the sheds of larger enterprises, it survived in the Yorkshire countryside—a fortiori in the West Country, the home of the old-fashioned broadcloth trade.

Because of its subsequent importance, the iron industry has some-times received more attention than it deserves in histories of the Industrial Revolution. Looking back from the vantage of one hundred years and more, living in a world in which heavy industry is the basis of the economy, writers have tended to overemphasize the immediate significance for the eighteenth century of the technological advances in smelting and refining. Not in number of men employed, nor capital invested, nor value of output, nor rate of growth could iron be compared with cotton in this period. If the unit of production, larger at the start than in other industries, grew under the stimulus of technical change, the social impact of this growth was nowise com-parable to that of the transition from putting-out to factory in textiles. On the other hand, the growing supply of ever-cheaper metal did facilitate enormously the mechanization of other industries, the shift from water to steam power and, eventually, the transformation of the means of transportation. In the process, the units of manufacture in metallurgy grew until they overshadowed in their vastness and Vulcanian energy the largest cotton mills in the kingdom.

To understand the history of the iron and steel industry, a knowledge of the purely technological determinants is indispensable. In this regard, three points must be kept in mind:

(1) Metallurgy is a chemical process: the problem is to reduce the

---

[1] *Treatise on Mills and Millwork* (2nd ed.; 2 vols.; London, 1864–5), II, 187, 195.

[2] H. Heaton, *The Yorkshire Woollen and Worsted Industries* (Oxford: Clarendon, 1920), p. 357; *Parl. Papers*, 1857 Sess. I, XIV, 180. The last is for the county of York-shire as a whole; the vast majority, however, were in the West Riding.

ore, which is iron in compound form, to a suitably pure metal. The reaction requires large quantities of carbon as well as heat, and the fuel, which serves a double purpose, is necessarily placed in direct contact with the ore. This in turn poses special difficulties. All fuel, whether vegetable or mineral, contains substances other than carbon—oils, as well as minerals like sulphur and phosphorus—that are harmful to the final product. Charring will get rid of the volatile impurities; already in ancient times, smelters and smiths were using charcoal rather than wood, and the introduction of coal as a fuel in the late Middle Ages was soon followed by the development of the analogous coked form. But charring or coking will not get rid of mineral impurities, which are far more serious in coal than in wood. So that although techniques were developed by the seventeenth century for using coke in glass-making, malting, dyeing, and other heavy energy-consuming industries where fuel and raw material can be kept separate, efforts to employ it in iron smelting failed.[1] Not until a semi-adventitious mix of fairly clean ore and coal was achieved by Darby at Coalbrookdale in 1709 did coke-blast iron become a commercial reality.[2] Even then, the process did not spread until half a century later, after decades of empiricism had achieved a knowledge of mix and finished product that made it possible to make use of less favourable materials and improvements in the blast had yielded the higher temperatures required. Moreover, another generation had to pass before innovations in refining made it possible to convert coke-blast iron into competitive wrought iron, comparable in tenacity and malleability to metal made with charcoal.[3] Britain was only the first country to face the problem: the late adoption of coke smelting on the Continent was in large measure due to the same chemical difficulties. Similar considerations were to prove decisive in the second half of the nineteenth century in the application of new techniques for the mass production of steel.

(2) The charcoal or coke used in the blast furnace must be at once porous enough to provide as large a surface as possible to combustion and passage to heat and flames, yet at the same time strong and rigid enough to withstand the weight of the charge. This is one reason why there have always been limits—especially before the coming of the

[1] A simple point, but generally overlooked. Thus J. W. Nef, 'Coal Mining and Utilization', in C. Singer et al., A History of Technology, III, 79.

[2] There is some question about the exact date. See M. W. Flinn, 'Abraham Darby and the Coke-smelting Process', Economica, n.s. XXVI (1959), 54–9; and R. A. Mott, '"Coles": Weights and Measures, with Special Reference to Abraham Darby and the Coke-smelting Process', ibid. pp. 256–9.

[3] In 1765 Jars wrote: 'the production of good wrought iron from pit-coal pig iron is considered impossible.' Gabriel Jars, Voyages métallurgiques (3 vols.; Lyons, 1774–81), I, 250.

railway—to the transport of either fuel; once crumbled by jolting and handling, they are useless. This also explains why not all coal is suitable for metallurgical coke: if it is very oily, the end product of carbonization is too hollow, hence friable; and if it has little or no oil, like anthracite, the result is too solid for combustion. To be sure, there is a certain amount of leeway, and indeed modern metallurgy has made major advances in mixing otherwise unsuitable qualities of coal to produce a satisfactory coke. Nevertheless, differences in quality impose differences in costs, and in the nineteenth century especially, the distribution of coking coal—which was particularly favourable to Britain and western Germany—was a critical factor in the location and competitive position of metallurgical enterprise.

(3) Efficient combustion in the blast furnace requires a powerful, forced draught; the larger the furnace, the more powerful the draught. The substitution of coke for charcoal required and encouraged the use of ever bigger furnaces. Efforts to increase the blast of traditional water-powered leather bellows were on the whole unsatisfactory. Not until the cast-iron blowing cylinder (c. 1760 at Carron) was combined with the rotative steam-engine (1776 at John Wilkinson's furnace at Willey in Shropshire) was the problem solved.[1] Even then, furnace technique fell far short of the chemical possibilities of the combustion process. To exploit these, one had to alter the character of the blast itself. The first and most rewarding step on this path was to preheat the air (Neilson in 1829; see below, p. 322). The next, not taken until after the Second World War, was to modify the wind by maintaining humidity constant and/or by enriching it with oxygen.

(4) The product of the blast furnace is pig iron, a hard metal too brittle to work. The only way to shape it is to cast it in moulds; even then, the resulting pieces will not stand up to pressure, strain, or blows. To change this form of iron into one that can be worked and will support stress (what is called wrought or malleable iron), one must refine it by removing most of the remaining carbon and such other chemical impurities as diminish its malleability, tensile strength, ductility, and other virtues. In the early eighteenth century, this was done by heating and reheating the metal in charcoal fires and pounding out the dross with hammers—a long, costly process that yielded a product of high, though uneven, quality and irregular shape.

From the 1730's on, British forgemasters devoted great effort and expense to finding a shorter, surer technique that would use mineral rather than vegetable fuel. The search took half a century. The first advance provided only a partial solution: by introducing a refinery

[1] H. R. Schubert, *History of the British Iron and Steel Industry* (London, 1957), pp. 332–3; cf. Gabriel Jars, *Voyages*, I, 277.

hearth and sometimes also a reverberatory fire (one in which the flames did not play on the metal directly) between the furnace and the forge, it was possible to use coal or coke rather than charcoal for some and eventually all of the fining process. The operation was still slow and the resulting product was not so good as charcoal bar, but it was cheaper, and by 1788 according to one estimate, about half the wrought iron in the kingdom was being made with mineral fuel.[1] By this time, however, the definitive triumph of coal was assured by the invention of a quite different technique—Henry Cort's combination of puddling and rolling (patents of 1784 and 1783). The former process made use of a reverberatory furnace to decarburize the pig in one step, alternately heating and cooling the metal until the wrought iron could be separated out by reason of its higher melting-point. After some preliminary hammering, the rolling mill—long used for such light work as slitting rods—then squeezed rather than beat out the dross, shaping the iron the while. This application of the rotative principle (see below, p. 536, n. 1, offered two great advantages over the reciprocating action of the tilt-hammer: it worked perhaps fifteen times as fast; and by grooving or otherwise preforming the rolls, one could now turn out an almost unlimited range of those standardized crude shapes—beams, bars, rails and the like—that have come to constitute the framework of industry, construction, and transport.

The course of technological change in metallurgy suggests the following generalizations:

(1) There is in iron-making, as in textile manufacture, a see-saw of challenge and response. Thus the diffusion of coke-smelting put new pressure on refining, in spite of the ingenuity of ironmasters in developing new applications for cast iron. Cort's combination of puddling and rolling temporarily eased the difficulty, but the construction of new and larger furnaces gave rise in the course of the nineteenth century to a new imbalance. The fundamental difficulty was the physical hardship of puddling, which called for exceptional strength and endurance. There was simply a limit to what flesh could stand, and after a while the only way to increase output was to train more men and build more hearths. Much money and effort was expended on finding a way to mechanize the process. In vain: the imbalance was not corrected until Bessemer and his successors learned to make cheap steel.

(2) Again, in iron as in textiles, small anonymous gains were probably more important in the long run than the major inventions that have been remembered in the history books. And again, as in textiles, the reason is to be found in part in the empirical approximateness of these early advances. Patents were a beginning as well as an end, and

[1] Ashton, *Iron and Steel*, p. 88. No source given.

ironmasters found that each combination of ore and fuel or metal and fuel required its own recipe. The word is used advisedly. Iron manufacture was essentially a kind of cookery—requiring a feel for the ingredients, an acute sense of proportion, an 'instinct' about the time the pot should be left on the stove. The ironmasters had no idea why some things worked and others did not; nor did they care. It was not until the middle of the nineteenth century that scientists learned enough about the process of converting ore to metal to provide a guide to rational technique and measures for testing performance. As late as 1860, Bessemer was baffled by the failure of his converter on phosphoric ores.

Aside from the adaptation of the processes of smelting and refining to ores and fuel of different characteristics, the lesser improvements in iron technology were concentrated for the most part in three areas:

(a) *Fuel economy.* The gains are hard to measure because of statistical incomparability. In South Wales, changes in the blast and in the shape and size of the furnace cut coal consumption (including engines and lime and ore kilns) per ton of pig from perhaps 8 tons in 1791 to $3\frac{1}{2}$ in 1830. The most important single advance was Neilson's hot blast, introduced in Scotland in 1829: with some materials, it yielded a fuel saving of over a third if coke was employed, more than two-thirds if coal, the while increasing output per furnace markedly. The hot blast was the beginning of a surge of Scottish iron production: the make of pig rose from 29,000 tons in 1829 to 825,000 in 1855. Results were impressive but less spectacular south of the Tweed, and certain areas, like the Black Country and South Wales, were decades in switching to the new technique. In general, British interest in fuel economy was limited by the cheapness of coal; much of what improvement there was, was simply a by-product of growth—larger, more efficient furnaces tended to burn less coke per unit of output.

In refining, the traditional techniques had consumed $2\frac{1}{2}$–3 tons of charcoal per ton of crude iron produced. The use of mixed fuel (part coke, part charcoal) reduced the ratio to about 2 to 1. Puddling then brought it down to $1\frac{1}{2}$ to 1, and with further improvement, to about $\frac{3}{4}$ to 1 by the middle of the nineteenth century.[1] The gains were thus substantial, though less important than in smelting. One should keep in mind, however, that every technique that permitted the substitution of mineral for vegetable fuel added that much to man's energy resources.

(b) *Economy of metal.* The problem was especially serious in refining:

[1] Over the same period, the producers of charcoal-wrought iron fought hard to hold their market. Among other things, they succeeded in cutting their own fuel consumption to less than $1\frac{1}{2}$ tons of charcoal per ton of crude bar. On this phenomenon of the technological stimulus of obsolescence, see below, p. 488.

in the early puddling furnaces, half the pig was drawn off in the slag. A series of changes, culminating in the late 1830's in Joseph Hall's furnace bed of roasted tap cinder (instead of iron-hungry sand), cut waste to 8 per cent while speeding the conversion process. Hall's innovation pushed iron economy almost to its limit; at the end of the nineteenth century, waste still amounted to about 5 per cent.[1]

(c) *Adaptation to growth.* The constant enlargement of the blast furnace was aimed, not so much at saving raw materials as at raising output and, if possible, the productivity of labour; it brought with it a great increase in the number of puddling furnaces. At the same time, greater familiarity with the uses of iron brought a demand for ever-larger pieces of metal. With this growth of both output and size of product came difficulties in moving the raw materials and in handling and shaping the work. These were solved by a variety of devices: elevated platforms for loading the blast furnace, rails for transportation within the plant and even within the forge sheds, overhead chain pulleys and cranes to lift the blooms and finished pieces. The steam hammer, conceived in 1839 by Nasmyth and first applied by Bourdon of Le Creusot (the debate over priority has assumed the character of a national quarrel), was in effect a way of placing in the hands of the forge worker unprecedented power and strength, subject to precise control; large boring machines were an analogous advance.

The development of the British iron industry was directly linked to these technological considerations. Up to the middle of the eighteenth century, the pecuniary and material limitations on the transport of charcoal or wood restricted growth and often compelled the ironmaster to halt work for as much as several months while sufficient fuel was collected for another run; the effect was to raise overhead charges enormously. The irregularity of the supply of water for power, due to drought in the summer and, less often, frost in winter, imposed similar interruptions. Both difficulties combined on occasion to push the furnaces and forges into lonely rural areas, where abundance of fuel and water was largely offset by isolation from the market.

It has long been customary to argue that the excessive appetite of the British iron manufacture had by the eighteenth century so exhausted its supply of wood that numerous furnaces and forges were forced to shut down, that overall output fell or at least stood still from about 1660 to 1760, and that only the introduction of mineral fuel saved the industry from slow starvation. Recent studies, however, have modified the picture, noting that the wood employed by the furnacemaster was

[1] David Mushet, *Papers on Iron and Steel* (London, 1840), p. 32; W. K. V. Gale, 'A Technological History of the Black Country—Iron Trade' (typewritten MS.), p. 58. I am grateful to Mr Gale for allowing me to consult his extremely informative study.

coppice rather than construction timber; that much of this was systematically cultivated for the iron industry, so that in some areas, at least,
the supply increased; and that a substantial number of new furnaces
and forges were fired after 1660, more than compensating for those
that had to be abandoned.[1] The fact remains that charcoal was getting
ever costlier in some of the traditional iron-making areas; far more of
the new furnaces were founded before 1700 than after; much of the
industry survived in the face of Swedish and Russian competition only
thanks to customs duties; and production, though rising, was rising
far more slowly than imports or the output of more prosperous
industries. Mr Flinn has suggested an increase of 'upwards of 10,000
tons' from 1660 to 1760; this would imply at most a gain of 75 per
cent. By comparison, purchases of iron from Sweden and Russia more
than doubled from 1711–15 to 1751–5.[2]

As early as 1740, Great Britain was using perhaps 10 or 11 pounds of
wrought iron per person a year. In the next fifty years, consumption
about doubled. By comparison, the French were using around 5 pounds
per head at the later date, and the average for the Continent as a whole
was far lower. These gross estimates are confirmed by the qualitative
impressions of observers: thus Arthur Young, who notes with surprise
that 'the wheels of these [French] waggons are all shod with wood
instead of iron'.[3] Whatever the sources of this ferruginous temper—
which Alfred Marshall attributed to 'that sturdy, resolute Norse
character' of his ancestors[4]—it is the more impressive for having
developed in the face of the growing scarcity of fuel; until well into the
eighteenth century, Britain used iron because she wanted to, not
because it was abundant or cheap. (To be sure, the most likely substitute, wood, was perhaps even dearer.) Even so, one can but wonder
what would have happened, had she had to go on depending on costly
and inelastic foreign sources for much, if not most, of the principal
structural material of modern technology.[5]

[1] See especially M. W. Flinn, 'The Growth of the English Iron Industry, 1660–
1760', *Econ. Hist. Rev.* 2nd ser. XI (1958), 144–53; G. Hammersley, 'The Crown
Woods and Their Exploitation in the Sixteenth and Seventeenth centuries', *Bull. of the
Institute of Historical Research*, XXX (1957), 136–61.

[2] H. Scrivenor, *History of the Iron Trade* (London, 1854), p. 58; K. G. Hildebrand,
'Foreign Markets for Swedish Iron in the 18th Century', *Scandinavian Econ. Hist. Rev.*
VI (1958), 4–15.

[3] Young, *Travels*, I, 46.   [4] *Industry and Trade* (London, 1919), p. 60.

[5] On the rigidity of the Swedish supply after 1750, cf. Eli F. Heckscher, *An Eco-
nomic History of Sweden* (Cambridge, Massachusetts: Harvard, 1954), p. 178. On
Russia, cf. M. Goldman, 'The Relocation and Growth of the Pre-Revolutionary
Russian Ferrous Metal Industry', *Explorations in Entrepreneurial History*, IX (1956–7),
20; R. Portal, *L'Oural au XVIIIe siècle* (Paris, 1950); R. Portal, 'Une route du fer au
XVIIIe siècle', *Revue historique*, CCXI (1954), 19–29.

In any event, the problem was solved by the substitution of coal for wood, which, thanks to Britain's exceptional resource endowment and favourable transport conditions, changed a high-cost industry into the most efficient in the world. The make of pig iron rose sharply (the 1780's seem to mark a definite break in the curve), and where, in 1750, Britain imported twice as much iron as she made, by 1814 her exports alone amounted to five times her purchases. Some of this rapid increase in output reflected the special needs of the war years. But the coming of peace simply brought other sources of demand to the fore: engineering; the construction of factory plant and equipment; the manufacture of agricultural implements, hardware, piping for water and gas, and, especially after 1830, rails. Most important, exports of iron rose almost twentyfold by the middle of the century (57,000 tons in 1814; 1,036,000 in 1852). In the 1780's Britain's output of iron was smaller than that of France; by 1848 she was smelting almost two million tons, more than the rest of the world put together.

Table 43 a. *Pig-Iron Output of Great Britain (in long tons)*

1740	17,350	1830	678,417
1788	68,300	1835	940,000
1796	125,079	1839	1,248,781
1806	258,206	1848	1,998,568
1825	581,367	1852	2,701,000

SOURCES. For the years 1740–1830 and 1852, Scrivenor, *History of the Iron Trade*, pp. 136, 302; for 1835, M. Meisner, *Die Versorgung der Weltwirtschaft mit Bergwerkserzeugnissen, I, 1860–1926* [in *Weltmontanstatistik*, pub. by the Preussische Geologische Landesanstalt] (Stuttgart, 1929), p. 84; for 1839, Mushet, *Papers on Iron and Steel*, p. 421; for 1848, Ludwig Beck, *Geschichte des Eisens in technischer und kulturgeschichtlicher Beziehung* (5 vols.; Braunschweig, 1894–1903), IV, 665. Note that all of these are informed guesses. The first official returns of iron production do not come until 1854. Cf. R. Hunt, 'The Present State of the Mining Industries of the United Kingdom', *J. Royal Statistical Soc.* XIX (1856), 317; Howard G. Roepke, 'Movements of the British Iron and Steel Industry—1720 to 1951' [*Illinois Studies in the Social Sciences*, vol. XXXVI] (Urbana, 1956), p. 24.

The development of mechanized industry concentrated in large units of production would have been impossible without a source of power greater than what human and animal strength could provide and independent of the vagaries of nature. The answer was found in a new converter of energy—the steam-engine; and in the exploitation on a tremendous scale of an old fuel—coal.

Each of these called the other forth. The strongest source of demand for increased power was mining, especially coal mining. From the sixteenth century on, as we have noted, the need for new sources of thermal energy in a country almost denuded of its forests led Britons to substitute mineral for vegetable fuel in a wide variety of heat-absorbing industrial operations. At the same time, the consumption of coal for domestic purposes rose steadily: there was perhaps a time, in the sixteenth century, when the Englishman recoiled at the acrid, sulphurous fumes of burning coal; but by the modern period, such scruples were laid by familiarity and necessity.

The more coal man used, the deeper he dug; until, by the end of the seventeenth century, the pits in many areas had penetrated beneath the water table and flooding threatened to put an end to further extraction. (The same difficulties were beginning to afflict the tin, lead, and copper mines of Cornwall.) Ingenious systems were devised to lead off the water, when possible, or to pump or raise it out of the pits by animal power. But the task was fast getting out of hand: in one colliery in Warwickshire, five hundred horses were employed to hoist the water, bucket by bucket.

The use of five hundred horses is evidence of a simple but sometimes neglected fact: there is in principle no limit but numbers to the amount of work that can be accomplished or power that can be generated by human or animal labour. One thinks, for example, of the construction of the pyramids or of such comparable tasks as the removal of a 327-ton obelisk in Rome in 1586 by the massed efforts of 800 men and 140 horses working forty capstans in the presence of the official executioner.[1]

Yet the use of gangs or of veritable herds of animals poses logistical difficulties that increase sharply with the number of labour units: there is the problem of co-ordination, first, and linked to it, the sheer limitations of space and the high cost of a complex system for the transmission of power. Moreover, man and beast are subject to fatigue; they must be relieved, and the more there are, the more difficult the passage from one team to the next. Mass labour of this kind is reasonably effective— if certain precautions are observed and discipline is maintained—in the performance of sporadic work demanding intense effort for short periods. It is ill suited to providing the steady, concentrated power required by industry.

Here lay the great advantage of the steam-engine. It was tireless, and one could direct its tens of horsepower far more effectively than one could combine the efforts of five hundred horses. Moreover—and in the long run, this was the key to the steam-engine's revolutionary effects on the pace of economic growth—it consumed mineral fuel and

---

[1] See the contemporary pictorial representation of this operation in T. K. Derry and Trevor I. Williams, *A Short History of Technology from the Earliest Times to A.D. 1900* (Oxford, 1960), frontispiece; also pp. 180, 245.

thereby made available to industry, for the provision of motive power as against pure heat, a new and apparently boundless source of energy. The early steam-engines were grossly inefficient, delivering less than 1 per cent of the work represented by their thermal inputs. This was a far cry from the performance of organic converters: both animals and man can deliver from 10 to 20 per cent of inputs, depending on conditions. But neither man nor beast can eat coal. And since the supply of organic nourishment was and is limited—as the Malthusian checks of famine and disease abundantly testify—it is this increment of fuel made available by the steam-engine, however wastefully used, that counted.

To make the point clear, compare man's consumption of coal with its hypothetical alimentary equivalent. By 1800 the United Kingdom was using perhaps 11 million tons of coal a year; by 1830, the amount had doubled; fifteen years later it had doubled again; and by 1870 it was crossing the 100-million-ton mark. This last was equivalent to 800 million million Calories of energy, enough to feed a population of 850 million adult males for a year (actual population was then about 31 million); or to supply one-fourth as many people with the complete energy requirements of a pre-industrial society.[1]

Or—to approach the subject from a different angle—in 1870 the capacity of Great Britain's steam-engines was about 4 million horse-power, equivalent to the power that could be generated by 6 million horses or 40 million men.[2] If we assume the same patterns of food consumption as prevailed in the eighteenth century, this many men would have eaten some 320 million bushels of wheat a year—more than three times the annual output of the entire United Kingdom in 1867–71. And this does not take into account the even larger number of workers required for activities other than furnishing power, or the young, old, and other unemployed members of our hypothetical coal-innocent society.

It would be easy, by selecting a later date and a higher consumption of energy, to conjure up more awful pictures. From 1870 to 1907, the capacity of prime movers in British industry alone more than doubled,

[1] That is, the energy required for heat and manufacture, as well as for the internal nourishment of the biological organism. C. Cipolla, 'Sources d'énergie et histoire de l'humanité', *Annales: E.S.C.* XVI (1961), 528.
[2] This is a conservative estimate, for the equivalency is between capacities over brief periods of time, a working day, for example. And while many of these steam-engines undoubtedly operated only part of the time and then often at less than full load, it seems reasonable to assume that animal generators would deliver an even smaller fraction of capacity. Thus men, and the beasts they use, rest most of each day and a substantial portion of the days in each year; whereas many steam-engines worked around the clock, day in and day out, year after year. On balance, double the number of men or animals would seem a more accurate equivalent.

and from 1907 to 1930, doubled again; to this would have to be added the even greater increase of engines in land transport and shipping. Or, to shift to a larger scene, world consumption of commercial sources of energy multiplied six times in the fifty years from 1860 to 1900 and more than tripled in the next half-century. One can imagine an industrial world compelled to depend exclusively on animal engines for work, a world swarming with so many men and beasts that every inch of the earth's surface, including mountain, desert, and icy tundra, would not suffice to feed them. But one need not persist in these fantasies. The point is obvious: no such industrial world could come into being. It is precisely the availability of inanimate sources of power that has enabled man to transcend the limitations of biology and increase his productivity a hundred times over. It is no accident that the world's industry has tended to localize itself on and near the earth's coal measures; or that the growth of capital has been proportional to the consumption of mineral fuel. Coal, in short, has been the bread of industry.[1]

At this point, some words of caution are advisable. Like food, coal has been a necessary but not a sufficient cause of industrial performance. One cannot work without eating; yet the availability of food will not make one work. We shall have several occasions in the course of this survey to consider feats of industrial accomplishment by localities or countries poor in energy resources. Some of these have benefited from compensating advantages; others have transcended their handicaps by acts of creative entrepreneurship. Usually, however, these triumphs have occurred in light industry, where energy requirements are a relatively small portion of total cost. It is (or was) hard to make bricks without straw; or iron and heavy chemicals without cheap fuel.

It should be remembered, moreover, that the coal-steam combination was not the only source of inanimate power available to the European economies of the eighteenth century. The force of the wind had been harnessed for millennia, first by means of sail for navigation, then from the Middle Ages on, through mills for pumping and grinding. Even more important was water power. Already known in antiquity, the water mill first came into wide use in the Middle Ages, perhaps as an answer to the growing scarcity of slave labour. Its introduction into British wool manufacture to drive the fuller's hammers gave rise to that rapid expansion of rural production that Professor Carus-Wilson has described as 'an industrial revolution of the thirteenth

---

[1] The above discussion owes much to conversations with Professor Carlo Cipolla. See his *Economic History of Population* (London, 1962), ch. II. Also Fred Cottrell, *Energy and Society* (New York, 1955); E. A. Wrigley, *Industrial Growth and Population Change* (Cambridge, 1961); and idem, 'The Supply of Raw Materials in the Industrial Revolution', *Econ. Hist. Rev.* 2nd ser. xv (1962), 1–16.

century'. In the eighteenth century and the first decades of the nine-teenth, the water wheel accounted for the greater, though a diminishing, share of the power used by British industry; and there is no doubt that, had Britain been better endowed by nature with hydraulic energy, or had she been poorer in coal, the dominance of the wheel would have continued much longer than it did. This was the case in the United States, where the great coal deposits lay in what were at first the rela-tively inaccessible lands west of the Appalachians and where the eastern slopes of the same range offered superb sites for the erection of water-driven mills. The same was true of comparable areas in Europe, the whole Alpine region, for example—Dauphiné, Switzerland, Baden, Bavaria, northern Italy.

Coal and steam, therefore, did not make the Industrial Revolution; but they permitted its extraordinary development and diffusion. Their use, as against that of substitutable power sources, was a consideration of costs and convenience. The advantage of wind and water power was that the energy employed was free; their great disadvantage was that it was often not abundant enough and in any event was subject to variations beyond human control. The wind might not blow; the stream might dry up or freeze. By contrast, the steam-engine could be relied on in all seasons; but the initial outlay was higher and it was costly to operate. As one writer of 1778 put it, 'the vast consumption of fuel in these engines is an immense drawback on the profit of our mines, for every fire-engine of magnitude consumes £3,000 worth of coals per annum. This heavy tax amounts almost to a prohibition.'[1] This was clearly an exaggeration, for the use of steam was growing. Still, it cost only £900 a year to feed those five hundred horses in Warwickshire. Small wonder that the early engines were generally employed only where coal was extremely cheap—as in collieries; or in mines too deep for other techniques, as in Cornwall; or in those occasional circum-stances—the naval drydock at Saint Petersburg for example—where cost was no object.

As a consequence, the leitmotif of steam technology was the effort to increase efficiency, that is, the amount of work performed per input of energy. By comparison, the goal of greater power, that is, work per-formed per unit of time, took second place, although the two objectives were linked and what made for the one, permitted or yielded the other.

This pursuit of fuel economy and power, like other movements of technological advance, had its multitude of small and often anonymous gains: better materials, closer tolerances, the introduction of safety

[1] Price, in the Appendix to *Mineralogia Cornubiensis*, cited by Robert A. Thurston, *A History of the Growth of the Steam Engine* (Centennial edition; Ithaca, New York, 1939), p. 71.

valves and gauges, the recognition and adoption of coal specially suited
to the production of steam, the collection of accurate information on
the performance of engines under different conditions. But it was also
punctuated by some great leaps forward, each marked by a critical innovation that widened substantially the commercial applicability of steam.

The first practicable device for the conversion of thermal energy into
work was Thomas Savery's 'fire-engine' of 1698. It was in effect
steam-engine and pump combined. There was no piston, no transmission of power to other machinery. Steam was heated in a boiler, then
passed into a 'receiver', where it was condensed to create a partial
vacuum. This drew in water from below (more accurately, the water
was driven up into it by air pressure), which was then expelled upwards
by the next injection of steam, and the cycle began again. The waste of
energy was enormous, not only because of the alternate heating and
cooling of the receiver, but also because, in the absence of a piston, the
steam came into direct contact with the cold water. The system had
one other serious drawback: one could increase the power only by
raising the pressure, and some of the Savery engines were worked at as
much as three atmospheres. That was about the limit of safety. Given
the quality of the materials employed and of the metal work of the day,
anything higher was almost certain to result in an explosion, as a
number of operatives learned too late. The only alternative, in deep
mining, for example, was to use two or more engines in tandem, a
costly procedure and one especially vulnerable to breakdowns.

What Thurston calls the first true engine, that is, a device for
generating power and transmitting it to a machine performing the work
desired, was the contribution of Thomas Newcomen, ironmonger and
blacksmith of Dartmouth, England, in 1705. Here the pump was
separate from the cylinder that received the steam. The vacuum produced by condensation was used, not to draw in water, but to work a
piston connected to one end of a see-sawing cross-beam, the other end
of which rose and fell and thereby operated the rod of the water pump.
Note that the steam was not used to drive the piston, but only to
create a vacuum; ordinary air pressure provided the force that pushed
the piston downward against the weight of the pump at the other end
of the beam. Hence the name, 'atmospheric engine'.

Newcomen's method offered two advantages over Savery's conception. First, it eliminated the loss of heat due to contact with the water
being pumped. The saving was not large and was almost dissipated in
the transmission of force from engine to pump. Years later, when construction of both types had much improved, tests of the two engines
showed duties generally ranging between five and six million foot-pounds
per bushel of coal, a yield of less than 1 per cent. Still, every bit helped.

Far more important, the use of a piston made it possible to obtain more force without increasing the steam pressure; all that was required was a larger surface on which the atmosphere could push, that is, a larger piston. As a result, the Newcomen engines were at once more powerful, safer, and more dependable. Indeed, some of them were to remain at work for five decades and more, well into the nineteenth century.

Not that the Savery steam pump disappeared. Builders like John Wrigley in Lancashire were manufacturing improved versions of it to the very end of the eighteenth century, and so enterprising a cotton spinner as John Kennedy used 'Savary's' machine to drive his improved mules in Manchester in 1793. One would like to know how many of these there were, where they were used, and for what purposes. Those we know of were small, generating a few horsepower, and were used to raise water to drive the wheels of light industrial plants.

By contrast, the Newcomen engine dominated the market for large prime movers. Thurston writes that within a few years of its invention, 'it had been introduced into nearly all large mines in Great Britain'; and that many new mines were dug that could not have been exploited before. The statement may be exaggerated; we do not have statistics on this point. But we do know that the engineer Smeaton found 57 of these machines, totalling 1200 horse-power, in the Newcastle basin alone in 1767, and 18 large engines in the Cornish mines in 1780. In the Midlands, the Coalbrookdale foundry, better known for its pioneering of coke smelting, was the major supplier of Newcomen engines to the collieries of the region; and even after the introduction of the Watt engine, the older type continued in demand, for coal at pithead was cheap or even a free good (many boilers burned unsaleable slack), and the lower initial cost of the Newcomen engine, its simplicity of maintenance, and its remarkable durability gave it the preference.[1]

Yet the persistence of the Newcomen engine should not lead us to underestimate the crucial significance of Watt's contribution. By building a separate condenser (patent of 1769; first commercial application, 1776), he saved the energy that had previously been dissipated in reheating the cylinder at each stroke. This was the decisive breakthrough to an 'age of steam', not only because of the immediate economy of fuel (consumption per output was about a fourth that of the Newcomen machine), but even more because this improvement opened the way to continuing advances in efficiency that eventually brought the steam-engine within reach of all branches of the economy

---

[1] On the continued use of the Savery and Newcomen engines, see A. E. Musson and E. Robinson, 'The Early Growth of Steam Power', *Econ. Hist. Rev.* 2nd ser. XI (1959), 418–39; Thurston, *History of the Growth*, pp. 68 ff.

and made of it a universal prime mover. Watt himself effected some of the most important of these further gains (patents of 1782 and 1784): the double-acting engine, with the steam working alternately on each side of the piston; the use of steam to drive the piston as well as to create a vacuum; the cut-off stroke, which took advantage of the expansive force of the steam to obtain a substantial saving of energy; above all, the sun-and-planet gear, which converted the reciprocating stroke of the piston into rotary motion and made it possible to drive the wheels of industry.

Watt believed firmly in the low-pressure engine; and, indeed, most of the power of his machine derived, not from the force of the steam, which rarely went above $1\frac{1}{2}$ atmospheres, but from the vacuum on the other side of the piston. Other men were less dogmatic. Around the turn of the century, William Bull, Richard Trevithick, the American Oliver Evans, and others evolved the high-pressure engine (two or more atmospheres), which eventually yielded fuel economies of $1:1\frac{1}{2}$ and better. In the beginning, however, its main advantage lay in its simplicity and its ability to deliver the same work with a smaller piston; it was thus lighter and cheaper than the low-pressure engine and used far less water. This saving of space and materials was of primary importance in the construction of movable engines. The locomotive and steamboat would have been sharply restricted commercially had only low pressure been available.

Moreover it was high pressure that made possible the effective application of compounding, which made use of the energy that remained in the steam after it had driven the piston, by leading it into a second cylinder (eventually a third and even a fourth) of larger dimensions. The principle was the same as that which made possible the cut-off stroke: theoretically there is no difference between the expansion of the steam in one cylinder or more than one. Practically, there is a significant gain in efficiency: the sum of the forces exerted by more than one piston varies less throughout the action than that of a single piston; more important, the temperature of each cylinder varies less if the range of expansion of the steam is divided than if it is confined to one vessel. The result was a major saving of fuel: by the middle of the nineteenth century, an average compound engine used slightly over $2\frac{1}{2}$ pounds of coal per horsepower-hour; Watt's machine needed about $7\frac{1}{2}$, and the Newcomen engine of 1769 used 30.[1] Jonathan Hornblower built a two-cylinder engine on these lines as early as 1781, but he used steam of low pressure, and his machine was found to be no more

---

[1] For figures on coal consumption and a discussion of the statistical difficulties involved, see W. Stanley Jevons, *The Coal Question* (London, 1906), pp. 145–9; also Conrad Matschoss, *Die Entwicklung der Dampfmaschine* (2 vols.; Berlin, 1908), 1, 506–7.

efficient than that of Watt; moreover the latter sued him for infringement of patent, and when Hornblower was unable to pay royalties and fine, he was clapped into prison. It was Arthur Woolf who, in 1804, produced the first commercially successful compound engine. He used high pressure and a separate condenser—by this time Watt's patent had expired. In the long run, compounding found its widest application in shipping, where the saving on fuel was multiplied by the space released thereby for cargo and passengers.

Unlike the wooden machines for spinning and weaving cotton or wool, the steam-engine required from the start a corresponding revolution in the relevant fields of metallurgy and construction. Smeaton predicted that Watt would not be able to build his engine because it required more accuracy than the techniques of the day permitted; and indeed some seven years elapsed between the patent and the first commercial realization. The difficulty was solved in part through the ingenious efforts of John Wilkinson, who learned to bore cylinders with some precision; as Watt put it, he could 'promise upon a seventy-two inch cylinder being not farther distant from absolute truth than the thickness of a thin sixpence [say 0·05 in.] at the worst part'. Even this was hardly close enough for an effective vacuum, and Watt and engineers after him continued to use packed rope or hemp and tallow to plug the gaps between piston and cylinder. Not until well into the nineteenth century had materials and machine construction advanced to the point where full advantage could be taken of the intelligence of Watt's conception.

This raises the related but larger issue of the connection between science and technology. It is often stated that the Newcomen machine and its forerunners would have been unthinkable without the theoretical ideas of Boyle, Torricelli, and others; and that Watt derived much of his technical competence and imagination from his work with scientists and scientific instruments at Glasgow. There is no doubt some truth in this, though how much is impossible to say. One thing is clear, however: once the principle of the separate condenser was established, subsequent advances owed little or nothing to theory. On the contrary, an entire branch of physics, thermodynamics, developed in part as a result of empirical observations of engineering methods and performance.[1] Nor is it an accident that this theoretical work was begun in France, where a school like the Polytechnique devoted its efforts explicitly to the reduction of technique to mathematical generalization. All of which did not prevent England from continuing to lead the world in engineering practice and invention.

[1] T. S. Kuhn, 'Energy Conservation as an Example of Simultaneous Discovery', in M. Clagett, ed., *Critical Problems in the History of Science* (Madison, Wisc., 1959).

Because of the steam-engine's early shortcomings, it was less suited than the gently turning water wheel for work requiring a certain smoothness and regularity of motion. This, together with purely economic considerations like relative size of firm, goes far to explain the slower adoption of steam in wool than in cotton. As late as 1850, more than a third of the power available to the wool manufacture of England and Wales came from water (12,600 h.p. steam; 6800 water); for the cotton industry of all of Great Britain, the corresponding figure was about one-eighth (71,000 steam; 11,000 water). The biggest users of steam power among the other industries were mining and metallurgy; unfortunately, overall figures are not available. We are thus reduced to crude estimates for the kingdom as a whole. Thus it has been suggested that there were no more than one thousand engines in use in 1800; guessing at an average size of 10 h.p. (it would not matter to the argument if one chose a multiplier twice as large), one arrives at an aggregate capacity of perhaps 10,000 h.p. Fifteen years later, according to the French observer Baron Dupin, this total had risen, for Great Britain alone, to 210,000 h.p.; and by the middle of the century it had further increased more than sixfold. For the United Kingdom in 1850, Mulhall estimates 500,000 h.p. of stationary engines, 790,000 h.p. of mobile engines, mostly in the form of railway locomotives. The latter had constituted an insignificant category a generation earlier.

One of the cherished myths of economic history is the image of a swift and drastic shift from rudimentary hand tools to machines. According to this, we begin with carpenters and millwrights with chisels and files, cutting and scraping by eye and feel; and then, within two generations, we have machinists and engineers operating precision power tools and working to specifications and blueprints. In fact, as is so often the case with revolutions, the old and new were not that far apart, and the change was slower than usually pictured.

The craftsman of the mid-eighteenth century, particularly in fields like clock-making, was familiar with an impressive variety of machines, including lathes, punches, drills, and screw- and wheel-cutting engines. These were slow and only moderately accurate; yet they were adequate to the industry of the day—both pre- and post-innovations—and indeed have survived in some out-of-the-way places to the present.[1] Of the great mechanical inventions of this period, only the Watt steam-engine

[1] On the technical competence of wood and metalworkers before the Industrial Revolution, see especially Musson and Robinson, 'The Origins of Engineering in Lancashire', *J. Econ. Hist.* xx (1960), 209–33. Also M. Daumas, 'Precision Mechanics', and K. R. Gilbert, 'Machine Tools', in C. Singer *et al., A History of Technology,* iv: *The Industrial Revolution, c. 1750–c. 1850* (Oxford, 1958), 379–441.

required, as noted above, an immediate advance in metal-working technique.

In the long run, however, the diffusion of mechanized manufacture called forth major improvements in tool design. For one thing, the productivity of the new machines for making consumers' goods was directly related to speed of operation and efficient utilization of power; both of these in turn demanded precise, smoothly working parts. For another, the scarcity of skilled wood and metal workers created a need for the kind of equipment that would enable a mechanic to do more in less time and with as little training as possible. And both these considerations were reinforced by the growth of an autonomous, specialized machine-construction industry in which imaginative artisans had an opportunity to modify old tools and devise new ones; the same process of gradual, cumulative technological advance by anonymous increments that characterized the consumers'-goods industries was equally important in the manufacture of capital goods.

Because of the anonymity of many of these improvements and the great diversity of practice, it is impossible to convey more than an approximate notion of the overall pace of advance. In the cotton industry we can at least count spindles and categorize them under rubrics like 'mules' or 'water frames', which, though embracing equipment of different efficiencies, are homogeneous enough to be meaningful. In machine construction, we have no counts, and even if we had, the range of variation between tools of the same name is so great as to render classification illusory and even the timing of innovation uncertain. Two examples will suffice. We know that gauges were being employed by machine builders as early as the 1770's and 1780's; indeed, the use of the word to designate an instrument for measuring dimensions dates to the late seventeenth century. Yet it hardly seems likely that men were 'working to gauge' in this early period, that is, using these devices, not only to measure size or scribe lines, but to assure standardization. Where and when the latter technique was introduced, and how fast it spread, is impossible to say. Similarly, we know that the slide rest was in wide use in the eighteenth century. Yet the invention of this basic instrument of precision work, which took the cutting tool out of the fallible hands of the artisan and made possible control of the direction and depth of its action, was attributed by Nasmyth and others to Maudslay. A myth? Perhaps. More likely, however, contemporaries who credited him with it had in mind some change in its character or innovation in its use, perhaps simply insistence on its use where others were content to work by hand.

But if we cannot measure the state of technique at a given point in time we can speak of the trend. In the space of two generations, in large part owing to a handful of gifted figures who learned from each other and formed as it were a family of toolmakers, wood- and metal-working techniques were transformed, at least at the margin.[1] Tools became heavier and more rigid (Maudslay's all-metal lathe), more automatic and precise (Clement's self-regulating lathe and double-driving centre chuck, Nasmyth's self-acting nut-milling machine and shaper, a whole succession of improvements in planing), more versatile and easier to operate (the turret-lathe and milling machines). By the middle of the nineteenth century 'the majority of the machine tools now in use...had been brought into existence',[2] and men like Nasmyth were toolmakers to machine builders, stocking standard models and selling from catalogue descriptions.[3]

The means of performance came first; the standards of accuracy after. The invention of power tools did not change the personal character of the work. Each craftsman remained judge of his own performance, working to approximate specifications that were not always uniform even within the shop. The assembling of any piece of machinery required a costly and time-consuming adjustment of all the parts, which were individually filed down to fit the whole. Reproduction or replacement was similarly approximate. Every screw had its individual thread.

Maudslay and Clement made an effort to correct some of these shortcomings by insisting on the use of true plane surfaces and standardizing the screws produced in their shops. But the major work in this area was done by one of their pupils, Joseph Whitworth, who, building on the work of his masters, worked out standard threads for bolts and screws of all sizes and developed the gauges that bear his name. Diffusion of these principles and techniques was another matter. Whitworth's contributions go back to the 1830's and his methods were made public in 1840, yet in 1856 he was still pleading for accuracy.

Generally speaking, standardized precision work, which made

---

[1] For the family tree of innovations and innovators in machine-tool manufacture, see John W. Roe, *English and American Tool Builders* (New Haven, 1916), p. 7; Gilbert, 'Machine Tools', p. 418. This pattern of direct employer–employee contact as a source of technical training and seed-bed for entrepreneurship characterized the continental industry as well. On Germany, see F. Redlich, 'The Leaders of the German Steam-engine Industry during the First Hundred Years', *J. Econ. Hist.* IV (1944), 146.

[2] Gilbert, 'Machine Tools', p. 441.

[3] See A. E. Musson, 'James Nasmyth and the Early Growth of Mechanical Engineering', *Econ. Hist. Rev.* 2nd ser. X (1957). Nasmyth expressed his intention of operating on this principle as early as 1836 in letters to his future partner Gaskell. Cited in R. Dickinson, 'James Nasmyth and the Liverpool Iron Trade', *Trans. of the Historical Society of Lancashire and Cheshire*, CVIII (1956), 99.

possible interchangeable parts, preceded the adoption of common, industry-wide norms. Thus if working to gauge was still the exception before 1850, it was spreading rapidly, and a number of machine makers, like Roberts of the self-acting mule, had long made use of templets and jigs to facilitate the performance of repetitious operations. Uniformity of standards of screw and bolt manufacture, on the other hand, came only in the second half of the century (common within the enterprise by 1860) and for a long time stood alone; all the weaknesses of human vanity combined with habit and the cost of change to deter acceptance of general patterns by particular producers.

One field in which standardization of product was achieved early was stampings. The principle went back to antiquity, when dies were used to mint coins of uniform design. In the early modern period, the punch was introduced, and made possible regularity of shape and size. In industry proper, the technique was obviously appropriate to the manufacture of buttons, gewgaws, buckles, and similar small objects. Birmingham, if not the first to use it, was the city that made the most of it while limitations of power restricted its application to the light metal trades; in the nineteenth century, a number of minor industries—pen nib manufacture, for example—were revolutionized by adaptations of this process.

Such products are clearly not to be compared to interchangeable parts, which must be exact enough to fit and interact with others in a larger mechanism. Nor are they—and the less so in this early period—so strong as pieces wrought, forged, and milled in the traditional sequence. (Even today a drop-forged blade commands a premium over a stamped one.) Nevertheless, the principle was as promising as that of precision machining, which would always be more expensive, and the application was enormously broadened by the introduction of power presses and similar big equipment. By the middle of the century, the steam hammer was beginning to be used in the manufacture of railway wheels. This was only a beginning, but it was the herald of a new kind of machine construction that was eventually to make possible the streamlined, inexpensive hard goods of the twentieth century—automobiles, refrigerators, bicycles, television sets.

Like the machine-building and engineering trades, the chemical industry has tended to be neglected in textbook histories of the Industrial Revolution, in part for the same reasons: the complexity and many-sidedness of its development, and the need for technical knowledge that the historian rarely possesses. Probably even more important, however, in promoting this oversight have been (1) the unrevolutionary character of this development—the organization of labour remained essentially unaltered while gains in productivity were usually smaller in chemicals than in those areas where mechanization was feasible; and (2) the secondary position of the industry in this early period—its growth was largely a response to the needs of other branches of manufacture, in particular, textiles, soap, and glass. We are accustomed today to look on the chemical manufacture as a giant, partly because of its success in creating wondrous new materials like nylon or plastics, partly because of the 'miracle' drugs that pour out of its laboratories in an endless stream; we are less aware of the enormous output of what is generally known as the heavy chemical industry, which is concerned with those inorganic agents, acid and alkali, used in the production of other commodities.

Yet the derivative character of this growth in our period in no way diminishes its importance. The transformation of the textile manufacture, whose requirements of detergents, bleaches, and mordants were growing at the same pace as output, would have been impossible without a corresponding transformation of chemical technology. There was not enough cheap meadowland or sour milk in all the British Isles to whiten the cloth of Lancashire once the water frame and mule replaced the spinning wheel; and it would have taken undreamed-of quantities of human urine to cut the grease of the raw wool consumed by the mills of the West Riding.

The solution was found in a simultaneous advance along several lines: (1) by substituting where possible vegetable for animal sources of raw material; (2) by substituting inorganic for organic raw materials; (3) by making use of the by-products of each reaction to produce other reactions yielding useful compounds; and (4) by improving the tools and equipment of the industry—furnaces, vats, mixers, piping, and the like—so as to permit the more rapid processing of larger quantities with greater safety. The first two were analogous in significance to the substitution of coal for wood in metallurgy: they freed the industry from the bondage of inelastic supplies. The third is particularly characteristic of the chemical manufacture and largely accounts for the conditions of increasing return that prevailed in the heroic age of early innovation. The fourth yielded perhaps the smallest gains in our period, but was to grow increasingly important as innovations in the other areas were absorbed and the increasing scale of production shifted attention to the physical plant and the logistical problems of work flow.

The course and character of this advance are best conveyed by examining the changes in the production of those key compounds that are the basis of the heavy chemical manufacture and the industrial commodities derived from them. The most important of these, even then, was sulphuric acid, a substance of such versatility (oxidizing agent, dehydrating agent, acid, electrolyte) that its use has come to serve as a rough index of industrial development. In the first half of the eighteenth century, sulphuric acid was employed chiefly as a nostrum, occasionally as a bleach. The method of preparation was slow, constrained, inefficient; the price, 1s. 6d. to 2s. 6d. an *ounce*, prohibitive for most industrial use. Within the space of a few decades, however, the introduction from the Continent of the bell process (first successful application by Joshua Ward and John White at Twickenham in 1736) and then the substitution of large lead-lined vats for the much smaller glass 'bells' (John Roebuck and Samuel Garbett at Birmingham in 1746) increased the scale of operation a thousand-fold and pushed the cost down to $3\frac{1}{2}d$. a *pound*. By the end of the century Britain, which had once eked out the home supply with purchases from Holland, was exporting up to two thousand tons a year.[1]

In industrial chemistry, one compound leads to another. Sulphuric acid, in combination with salt, yielded as one product hydrochloric acid, from which chlorine could be freed for use as a bleaching agent. The method of accomplishing this was wasteful, and chlorine in its pure form was dangerous and so corrosive that it tended to rot the fabric being treated. Yet it offered important advantages over such older bleaches as sunshine, buttermilk, and even dilute sulphuric acid, and the search began for chlorine compounds or mixtures that would handle more easily. The first of these were liquors, the most important of which, potassium hypochlorite or Javel water, was invented in France in 1796 and has remained a household cleaning agent ever since. For the textile manufacture, however, the major advance was Charles Tennant's invention of bleaching powder (patents of 1797 and 1799), made by absorbing chlorine in slaked lime. Tennant's output of the powder rose from 57 tons the first year, to 239 tons in 1810, 910 tons in 1825, 5719 tons in 1850; in 1852, production for Great Britain as a whole was 13,100 tons. In the meantime, the price fell to one-tenth its original level—from £140 to £14 per ton.[2]

Alkalis too were indispensable to the manufacture of textiles; and of a wide variety of other commodities as well. Two types were employed: potassium carbonate (commonly in the form of potash or the purer pearl ash) and sodium carbonate (generally called *soda*), along with compounds related to one or the other. Potassium alkalis were com-

---

[1] A. and N. Clow, *The Chemical Revolution: a Contribution to Social Technology* (London, 1952), pp. 132–9; Pub. Record Office, T. 64/241: 'An Account of the Exports of British Manufacturers from Scotland to Holland....' I am indebted to Dr T. C. Barker for this material.

[2] These and other details of this discussion are taken from L. F. Haber, *The Chemical Industry during the Nineteenth Century* (Oxford, 1958), ch. II.

bined with tallow or other animal fat to make soft soap, used especially by the woollen industry for scouring and fulling; were mixed with sand to produce one of the silicates that we call glass; went into the manufacture of gunpowder and alum; and were employed in bleaching and cleaning cloth and in the softening of leather. For all their versatility, however, they had the disadvantage of deriving from raw materials in scarce and inelastic supply. Potassium carbonate was obtained from prepared wood ash in a ratio of perhaps 1 part of pure compound to 600 parts of wood, necessitating a rate of consumption that was out of the question in timber-starved Britain. Europe and America were combed for supplies, and from the middle to the end of the century imports grew from about 1500 to 9000 tons. Moreover England was not the only country in the market; as demand outstripped supply, the price went up substantially, doubling in the period from 1780 to 1815. Not until the 1860's, when the Germans began to exploit the rich deposits of mineral potash in the Stassfurt area, did this bottleneck ease. By that time, a revolution in the manufacture of sodium carbonate had altered drastically the relative importance of the two alkalis.

Sodium alkali is as versatile as the potassium variety; indeed, the two are substitutable for each other in many of their applications. The main difference industrially is that soda is used in the manufacture of hard soaps and curd soaps—hence, of a household staple as well as of a production good. In the eighteenth century, sodium alkali also was obtained from the ashes of plants: the saltwort, which grew chiefly in Spain and the Canary Islands and yielded barilla, containing 20–35 per cent by weight of soda; and dried seaweed from western Scotland and Ireland, from which was derived kelp, with a soda content of from 5 to 10 per cent. The latter was able to compete because barilla, though richer, paid duty; moreover imports were just about cut off during the Napoleonic wars.

The supply of sodium alkali was more elastic than that of potash but could not possibly keep pace with increasing demand. Once again, the answer was found in the substitution of mineral for vegetable raw materials—in this instance, an especially abundant mineral, common salt. The actual technique was worked out in France in the 1780's by Nicolas Leblanc: conversion of salt to saltcake (sodium sulphate) by means of sulphuric acid (whose usefulness was multiplied thereby many times); and burning the saltcake in mixture with coal and calcium carbonate (usually in the form of limestone) to yield sodium carbonate and wastes.

British producers, who were certainly aware of the Leblanc process by the end of the eighteenth century, were slow to adopt it; large-scale manufacture began only in 1823. Scholars have usually attributed this delay to the effects of the tax on salt; more important, probably, was Britain's continued access to the traditional vegetable sources, combined with the conservatism of alkali users, who were reluctant to change over to the synthetic product even after James Muspratt made it available at a favourable price.[1] By contrast, France, which was cut off from Spanish barilla during the Napoleonic wars, had begun commercial manufacture in 1808 and within a decade was producing between ten and fifteen thousand tons of Leblanc soda a year.[2] Once the initial resistance was overcome, however, British output of synthetic alkali increased spectacularly, from the few hundred tons of 1820 to almost 140,000 tons in 1852. (French output at the latter date was perhaps 45,000 tons.) This rise was accompanied by a sharp fall in the price of soda; crystals, for example, went from a wartime peak of £59 a ton, to £36. 10s. on the eve of Leblanc, to £5. 10s. by mid-century.

Owing to the importance of bulky raw materials in chemical manufacture—it took ten to twelve tons of ingredients to make one ton of soda—the industry was sharply localized almost from the start. The three main centres were the Glasgow area, Merseyside and Tyneside. The first was oriented originally to the local textile industry. Its resource position was not so strong as that of the other two, and its continued importance was a tribute to the technical creativeness and commercial energy of the Tennant firm. This enterprise built its fortune on bleaching powder and branched out from there into the manufacture of acids, alkalis, fertilizer and related commodities. Overall, it was the biggest chemical producer in the world in the thirties and forties, and its giant works at St Rollox, with its skyscraper chimney of $455\frac{1}{2}$ feet to dissipate the noxious fumes high above the countryside, was the world's largest chemical factory.

Merseyside was favoured by the availability of coal on one side and salt on the other, a network of excellent waterways, and proximity to the biggest textile market in the world. Its major product was soda ash, whose availability promoted the related soap manufacture: by 1835, the output of hard soap along the Mersey was 47,750,000 lb., as against 32,650,000 in London; output had tripled since 1820, as against a 75 per cent increase for the nation as a whole. Cheap soda and saltcake (sodium sulphate) were also factors in the rapid growth of glass-making in Lancashire—though less important than in soap; where in 1832 the factories

---

[1] Cf. T. C. Barker, R. Dickinson and D. W. F. Hardie, 'The Origins of the Synthetic Alkali Industry in Britain', *Economica*, n.s. XXIII (1956), 158–71.

[2] Based on J. A. Chaptal, *De l'industrie françoise* (2 vols.; Paris, 1819), II, 70, 173, which gives the price as 10 frs. per quintal and output as 2–3 million francs.

in the Liverpool area paid less than an eighth of the excise on glass, by 1870, this region was probably making half the glass manufactured in England.[1]

The greatest centre of chemical manufacture was the Tyne basin, again an area with easy access to water transport and an abundant supply of cheap coal. Salt, on the other hand, had to come across the island from Cheshire; and the local market for chemical products was small, for there was no textile industry in the area and little manufacture of soap and glass. Yet the Tyneside firms found ample compensation in London and abroad, especially in northern Europe. From a late start— output of alkalis and acids was negligible in 1820—the north-east came by mid-century to account for half of the chemical plant, labour force and output of the entire kingdom.[2]

The encouragement given by the mass production of heavy chemicals to other branches of manufacture was only in part a function of the supply and price of the chemicals themselves. On the one hand, the availability of relatively pure compounds made possible the adoption of new raw materials that would otherwise not have been susceptible of treatment. Thus the development of purer soda ash made it feasible to use palm oil instead of animal fat in soap manufacture. The importance of this is apparent: the demand for fats was growing even faster than population and the traditional sources of supply were relatively inelastic; by mid-century, vegetable oils were being used in food, candles, and lubricants as well as soap.

On the other hand, the manufacture of synthetic compounds gave rise to enormous quantities of waste, which, by a kind of paradox not uncommon in technology, were a powerful stimulus to innovation. There was the positive lure of profit: waste turned to use had value; and the negative goad of expense: unexploited waste had to be disposed of. There were two tons of 'galligu' for every ton of soda made, and land for dumping cost a small fortune. Moreover, much of the waste was noxious and brought down on the chemical manufactures a hail of lawsuits, the attention of Parliament, and eventually official inspection and controls.

It would be impossible here to follow in detail the various solutions to this problem, or the interaction of these new techniques with one another and with outside processes to open new possibilities for growth. The story of chemicals in the first two-thirds of the nineteenth century is in large part this effort to use up all the materials, an effort which

[1] T. C. Barker and J. R. Harriss, *A Merseyside Town in the Industrial Revolution, St Helens, 1750–1900* (Liverpool, 1954), pp. 202, 363. Unfortunately for our statistical evidence, the excise duty on glass was removed in 1845.

[2] For a partial census in 1852, see Haber, *The Chemical Industry*, p. 18.

stemmed largely from soda manufacture but in specific instances originated elsewhere, in the production of chlorine for bleaching, for example. Every operation undertaken led to others, and the size of the productive unit grew with the proliferation of commodities. Yet this was not an industry that employed large numbers of men; as in metallurgy, plant and materials were the most important factors of production. In 1851 the industrial census gave 9172 adult workers in chemical manufacture, as against 292,340 in cotton, 152,205 in woollen and worsted, some 390,000 in the building trades.[1] The importance of chemicals, however, was clearly out of proportion to its numbers, or even its capital investment.

One aspect of the industry is worthy of special note. More than in any other, development derived from scientific research. This is not to say that the research itself was always conducted along correct theoretical lines—there was much empirical trial and error in the laboratories of this period—or that the industry made as much use of scientific knowledge or scientists as it might have. On the contrary, many of the advances were the work of self-taught 'chemists' and the more successful enterprises were characterized not so much by innovations in chemical process as by the effective organization of the factors of production within the prevailing scientific and technological framework. The fact remains, however, that the laboratory was indispensable, at least to the invention of new procedures, whereas it was to all intents and purposes unknown in other fields. In this regard, the really important research in theoretical and applied chemistry was being done abroad, where the education of chemists was already more systematic and thorough than in Britain. For the moment, however, the abundance of cheap raw materials and economies of scale gave Britain a tremendous competitive advantage: soda exports, for example, went from 75,704 cwt. valued at £44,575 in 1840 to 2,049,582 cwt. worth nearly £1 million in 1860.[2] Not until the last quarter of the century did new techniques in both light and heavy chemicals threaten this hegemony.

Machines and new techniques alone are not the Industrial Revolution. They meant gains in productivity, a shift in the relative importance of the factors of production from labour to capital. But by revolution we mean a transformation of the organization as well as the means of production. In particular, we mean the assemblage of large bodies of workers in one place, there to accomplish their tasks under supervision

---

[1] *Parliamentary Papers*, 1852–3, LXXXVIII, Part I, Table XXVIII, pp. ccxl–cclxii (males and females, twenty years of age and over).

[2] *Hansard's Parliamentary Debates*, 3rd ser., vol. CLXVI, col. 1455.

and discipline; we mean, in short, what has come to be known as the factory system.

In this regard, two important questions call for consideration. The first is the relationship between the supply of labour and the extension of the new mode of production; the second, the place of the factory system in the overall pattern of economic change.

The first—the recruitment of a factory labour force—has been the subject of much debate. The facts are reasonably clear. By 1830 there were hundreds of thousands of men, women, and children employed in factory industry.[1] They had entered the mills in spite of a strong fear of the unknown, an aversion to supervision and discipline, and resentment of the unremitting demands of the machine. The rules of the early factories are our best indication of the importance of these issues: the heaviest fines were reserved for absence (the cardinal sin, often worth several days' pay), lateness, and distraction from the job.

The interpretation of these facts is something else again. For a long time, the most accepted view has been that propounded by Marx and repeated and embellished by generations of socialist and even non-socialist historians. This position explains the accomplishment of so enormous a social change—the creation of an industrial proletariat in the face of tenacious resistance—by postulating an act of forcible expropriation: the enclosures uprooted the cottager and small peasant and drove them into the mills. Recent empirical research has invalidated this hypothesis; the data indicate that the agricultural revolution associated with the enclosures increased the demand for farm labour, that indeed those rural areas that saw the most enclosure saw the largest increase in resident population.[2] From 1750 to 1830, Britain's agricultural counties doubled their inhabitants. Whether objective evidence of this kind will suffice, however, to do away with what has become something of an article of faith is doubtful.

A more recent interpretation takes the opposite tack and argues that, since the factories were manned in the long run, there was never any problem of recruitment; that in the deceptive language of common sense, there was no labour shortage.

The proposition is non-refutable, hence meaningless. From the hindsight of any given level of resource utilization, the resource in

[1] Even after passage of the Act of 1833 and the institution of regular inspection, we have no full count of the factory labour force at a given point of time. For one thing, the official definition of factory limited the term to power-driven textile mills; for another, employment varied constantly, and the different inspectors collected their statistics over a period of some months. See the data for 1835 in A. Ure, *Philosophy of Manufactures* (London, 1835), Appendix.

[2] See the important article of J. D. Chambers, 'Enclosure and the Labour Supply in the Industrial Revolution', *Econ. Hist. Rev.* 2nd ser. v (1953), 318–43.

question has proved adequate to that level. Besides, the economist knows no shortage; he knows only relative prices. The meaningful question is the influence of labour supply on the choice of techniques and rate of investment.[1]

Here, unfortunately, we are confronted by the apparent contradictoriness of the relationship. On the one hand, as we have seen, the high and rising cost of English labour was an encouragement to mechanization, hence growth, in the eighteenth century. Even after the initial period of industrialization, the rate of substitution of machines for men reflected fluctuations in wages or wage demands; thus the textile manufacturers introduced automatic spinning equipment and the power loom spasmodically, responding in large part to strikes, threats of strikes, and other threats to managerial authority. That famous apologist for the factory system, Andrew Ure, wrote a happy chapter on the capacity of the machine for taming labour.[2] In sum, high wages were a stimulus to innovation and technological advance.

On the other hand, one can have too much of a good thing. British industry could not have grown much if factory labour had been so much more costly than, say, agricultural labour, or so much more costly than labour in other countries that it no longer paid to invest in manufacturing. Something of the kind was happening in the late eighteenth century when, with the power loom not yet practicable and English weavers enjoying the unprecedented demand consequent on the introduction of machine spinning, it began to pay to ship British yarn to central Europe, there to be woven by peasants accustomed to a far lower standard of living than Englishmen.[3] The difficulty that certain isolated country mills found in obtaining workers at commercially feasible wages, to the point of being compelled on occasion to leave new equipment idle, is another example.[4]

[1] Cf. Morris Morris, 'Some Comments on the Supply of Labour to the Bombay Cotton Textile Industry, 1854–1951', *Indian Economic Journal*, I (1953), 138–52; and his 'Recruitment of an Industrial Labor Force in India, with British and American Comparisons', *Comparative Studies in Society and History*, II (1960), 305–28. This position derives in part from the experience of industrialization in India, where the pressure of an almost unlimited labour reserve and the development of a kind of symbiotic relationship between factory employment and village subsistence facilitated recruitment. Similar forces eased the transition in Japan as well. Characteristic of both economies has been the extreme paternalism of the industrial employer: 'A job with Tata's is like a piece of land.' It would be most dangerous, however, to infer from the Asian to the British experience.

[2] Ure, *The Philosophy of Manufactures*, pp. 364–70.

[3] It was this yarn trade that brought Nathan Rothschild to Manchester in 1797, to lay the foundations of the British dynasty. It was this also that inspired Wm. Radcliffe to write his *Origins of Power Loom Weaving* (London, 1828).

[4] Cf. A. Redford, *Labour Migration in England, 1800–1850* (Manchester, 1926), p. 88.

Fortunately, the supply of labour increased substantially in Britain from the mid-eighteenth century on, almost as much, indeed, as the demand. In the first place, the rapid growth of population created a surplus of labour in the countryside, much of which found its way into the new urban centres of the North and Midlands. Secondly, while eighteenth-century England does not fit the economists' model of the pre-industrial society with unlimited supplies of labour,[1]—there were two societies nearby which do fit it and were in a position to send some of their surplus humanity to England—Scotland and, even more, Ireland. And finally, though least important, the same highly developed rural textile industry that had absorbed the free labour of the English countryside released an increasing number of workers as mechanization of weaving advanced and immigrant Irish labour began to compete for employment. The hand-loom weavers went into the mills reluctantly, but they went.

Even so, the task would have been immeasurably more difficult had the technological requirements of manufacture, especially in the early years of the jenny and water-frame, not allowed the employment of marginal elements—children, women, vagrants when necessary; and had social and political institutions not permitted a certain amount of explicit and concealed conscription, especially of parish apprentices. With the coming of the power mule, however, grown men were required in increasing numbers and the employer was compelled to turn to the free labour market. This time it was the familial organization of factory labour that eased the change: the employer could hire parents and children together, which not only increased the financial incentive but also, by preserving the parents in their tutorial role, reconciled them the more easily to the undesirable features of factory work. By the time further technological advances—the introduction of long mules and the self-actor in the twenties and thirties—and limitations on child employment once again changed the composition of the labour force, a new generation had grown up, inured to the discipline and precision of the mill.[2]

---

[1] The excellent analysis of W. Arthur Lewis, 'Economic Development with Unlimited Supplies of Labour', *The Manchester School*, XXI (1953), 139–91, is applicable to Britain only with major modifications.

[2] On the recruitment of the factory labour force in cotton, see, in addition to Redford's classic study of *Labour Migration*, George Unwin, *Samuel Oldknow and the Arkwrights* (Manchester, 1924); R. S. Fitton and A. P. Wadsworth, *The Strutts and the Arkwrights, 1758–1830* (Manchester, 1958); F. Collier, 'An Early Factory Community', *Econ. Hist.* II (1930), 117–24; F. Collier, 'The Family Economy of the Working Classes in the Cotton Industry, 1784–1833' (Univ. of Manchester dissertation, 1921); Neil Smelser, *Social Change in the Industrial Revolution: An Application of Theory to the Lancashire Cotton Industry, 1770–1840* (London, 1959). For comparable problems in

How, now, does one reconcile the advantages of scarce labour and abundant labour in explaining Britain's economic development? It is not possible yet to give a definitive answer; we need to know a lot more of the facts before generalizing from them. At the moment, one can only advance the tentative hypothesis that the factor cost pattern required for a technological breakthrough is different from that needed for exploiting the possibilities of that breakthrough. Scarce labour seems to have encouraged a deepening of capital in eighteenth-century Britain; while a more abundant supply facilitated widening in the following decades.

Our second question is the place of the factory in the economy as a whole. There was a time when the coming of the factory system was pictured as a cataclysm, overwhelming the old order and transforming British industry within a generation. This was certainly the impression of contemporaries who, engaged in a fierce polemic over the social consequences of technological change, inevitably starkened the issues and saw everything in black and white. Some of the early economic historians accepted this view, though largely for different reasons. Among other things, the tendency to see the factory system as the last of a sequence of ascending stages of industrial organization, beginning with the craft shop and passing through putting-out, implied the mutual exclusiveness of these forms and obscured those peculiar competitive advantages of each that have made possible their co-existence to the present day. Only in this century have scholars reversed the interpretation by stressing continuity rather than change. Clapham's classic *Economic History of Modern Britain* is a monument to this new point of view; it is, in Herbert Heaton's words, 'a study in slow motion'.[1]

The economic basis for the survival of the older modes of production is to be found partly within them, partly in the demands of the factory system and the general growth attending its development. Thus both craft shop and factory make possible the control of the work process from above (in the shop, the employer is usually worker as well); and while the factory is able to turn out more goods cheaper, the shop can work far more economically to special order. So that although factory production meant the end of many shops, it meant the beginning of many more. Machine building and maintenance, in particular, called forth a swarm of small artisanal enterprises; but large-scale industry in

---

other industries, see D. C. Coleman, *The British Paper Industry 1495–1860: a Study in Industrial Growth* (Oxford, 1958), ch. XI; A. H. John, *The Industrial Development of South Wales, 1750–1850* (Cardiff, 1950), ch. III. Also D. F. Macdonald, *Scotland's Shifting Population, 1770–1850* (Glasgow, 1937), chs. III and IV; and J. E. Handley, *The Irish in Scotland, 1798–1854* (Cork, 1945), ch. IV.

[1] Heaton, 'Industrial Revolution', *Encyclopedia of the Social Sciences*, s.v.

general found it desirable, for rational pecuniary reasons, to subcontract for much of its work.

The putting-out system is weak on both scores: the domestic artisan is rarely skilled enough to make individual finished products of the highest quality; nor can he compete with the factory in mass production of standardized items. Yet the weakness of putting-out is in many ways deceptive. For one thing, the capacity of dispersed manufacture for improvements in productivity should not be underestimated. Thus the division of labour made possible remarkable levels of output in certain trades—the metal-working ones in particular—well before the coming of machinery. Moreover, while the simplification of the work process implicit in such specialization is an invitation to mechanization, the devices that result often reinforce at first the position of the home worker; the early punching, cutting, and stamping machines were eminently suited to the cottage or the cellar. It is only when a higher stage of machine construction is reached, with the building of large, power-driven devices, that factory manufacture wins out.

Even where specialization and simplification cannot be pushed very far, in textiles for example, the home worker has one great advantage: he is cheap. He is usually able to draw some of his sustenance from the soil, if only from a garden plot; and his affection for the freedom of home work is such as to reconcile him to wages that a mill hand would not tolerate. For the manufacturer, moreover, he is dispensable; the immobilization of capital in plant and equipment is minimal, and in time of difficulty work may be halted without fear of heavy, uncompensated fixed costs.[1]

For these reasons, the putting-out system proved hardier than might have been expected. It dragged on unconscionably in those trades where the technological advantage of power machinery was still small (as in weaving) or where the home artisan could build himself a rudimentary power device (as in nail-making and other light metalwork). And it often survived in symbiosis with the factory; many manufacturers found it profitable to install only so much machinery as would supply a conservatively estimated normal demand, relying on a reserve pool of dispersed labour for additional output in time of prosperity.

At the same time, much of the ground that the craft shop and putting-out lost in the newly mechanized industries was made up in other fields. On the one hand, the gains in productivity in certain stages of manufacture, with resultant reduction in price and rise in demand for the

[1] For a theoretical analysis of some of the competitive advantages of putting-out, see A. Hirschman, 'Investment Policies in Underdeveloped Countries', *Amer. Econ. Rev.* XLVII (1957), 557–60.

finished product, increased the labour requirements of the other, traditionally organized stages. Thus the clothing trades profited from the transformation of spinning and weaving, and lace-making and embroidery from the availability of cheap yarn. On the other hand, certain kinds of technological advance created craft and domestic industry where they had not existed before or extended them far beyond their traditional boundaries. The sewing-machine is an excellent example: it made ordinary women seamstresses and seamstresses tailors, and so doing hastened the transformation of what had once been the task of every woman into a professional activity.

In general, the whole tendency of industrialization and urbanization was to specialize labour ever farther and break down the versatility of the household. A whole range of occupations—baking, butchering, the manufacture of things as diverse as candles, soap, and polish—expanded or appeared in response. Along with this, the growth of population and *per capita* real income—as a result of productivity gains in agriculture as well as industry—augmented consumption and increased the portion devoted to manufactures and services, with consequent stimulation of the traditionally organized trades as well as the newly mechanized ones. Housing alone required an army of carpenters, masons, plumbers, plasterers, glaziers, tilers, and plain labourers.

All of this is clearly brought out by the occupational statistics. The British census of 1851—for all its inaccuracies—shows a country in which agriculture and domestic service were far and away the most important occupations; in which most of the labour force was engaged in industries of the old type: building trades, tailoring, shoemaking, unskilled work of all sorts. Even in the cotton manufacture, with over three-fifths of its working force of over half a million (of a total of almost sixteen millions) in mills,[1] almost two-thirds of the units making returns employed less than fifty men;[2] the average mill in England employed less than 200; and tens of thousands of hand looms were still at work in rural cottages.

Yet just as it would be wrong to picture the factory system as a tidal wave, so we would be deceiving ourselves to see it as a gentle erosion of the traditional order. For one thing, there was the trend: in the period from 1834, when the factory inspectors sent in their first returns, to mid-century, the number of cotton mill operatives in Britain increased from 220,825 to 330,924—and this in spite of substantial

[1] The figures are of population and working force ten years of age and older.

[2] This is a guess based on the assumption that most of those employers who did not give the number of their men employed less than fifty. J. H. Clapham, *An Economic History of Modern Britain* (3 vols.; Cambridge, 1932–9), II, 35.

gains in productivity. In other industries—leather, paper, the metal
trades—factory employment was growing even more rapidly; they
were where cotton had been two generations earlier. Moreover the
speed of the shift from old to new was increasing *pari passu* with the
rate of technological change. In particular, the improvements in the
technique of machine construction meant the rapid translation of concepts and devices developed in one industry to analogous operations in
others; it is a short jump from cutting cloth to cutting leather or
metal. They also meant larger and faster equipment that demanded
power and was incompatible with domestic manufacture.

In a class by themselves, but following a similar path to factory
organization, were those industries in which work had always been
separated from the home and dispersion of labour was impossible.
Iron, chemicals, machine work, shipbuilding all fall into this category.
Long before the coming of the cotton mill, these branches of manufacture had been characterized by large units of production. A charcoal
iron furnace of the early eighteenth century might employ eight or
ten men, plus as many as a hundred digging ore, cutting and charking
wood, transporting materials, and generally servicing the smelters.
In the same period, the naval arsenal at Chatham employed upwards of a
thousand men, all of them carefully assigned and supervised, so that
'tho' you see the whole Place as it were in the utmost Hurry, yet you
see no Confusion, every Man knows his own Business...'.[1]

Should such units be designated as factories? From the standpoint
of the two critical criteria—concentration of production and maintenance of discipline—the term certainly fits. At the same time, they
differed in one important regard from the textile mills that were in fact
the prototype of the factory as we know it: however thoroughly the
work in these forges and yards was supervised, the pace was set by men
and not machines. It was spasmodic rather than regular. There were
moments that required a burst of concentration and effort: when the
furnace was tapped or the vat poured; the mast hoisted or keel launched;
the hot blooms moved or turned. And there were quiet moments,
while the mix boiled or the men waited for the next piece to be ready.
At their loosest (disregarding the question of mobility), these production units were very much like the assemblage of craftsmen and
assistants on a building job; or the construction gang on a canal or
railway project.

Such enterprises multiplied and grew considerably in average size as
a result of industrial expansion. In 1849 Dowlais, probably the largest
iron plant in the kingdom, employed 7000 men to work its eighteen

[1] Daniel Defoe, *Tour thro' the Whole Island of Great Britain*, ed. G. D. H. Cole;
2 vols. (London, 1927), p. 108.

blast furnaces, its puddling ovens, rolling mills, mines, and the rest.[1] Yet the difference from the foundries and forges of the eighteenth century was more one of degree than of kind, and the social impact of this development was not so great as that of the rise of a disciplined proletariat in the textile mills.

On the other hand, the effect of improved technology was to push the man-paced industries toward the precision and regularity of spinning and weaving. In iron and steel, the rolling mill, steam hammer, and more effective handling equipment all led in this direction; and throughout the metal trades, the development of special-purpose machine tools and more precise parts was a portent of the assembly lines of the twentieth century.

Secondly, the contribution of factory industry to the economy was out of proportion to its share of total production. Thus the factory promoted a higher rate of investment, hence of growth, than other forms of manufacture. Partly this was simply a consequence of capital intensity: the man who lived by the machine was more likely to be interested in and save for mechanical improvements than the merchant who relied on cheap cottage labour.[2] Even more, it reflected the technological orientation implicit in concentrated production. In contrast to putting-out, where the entrepreneur was primarily a seller, a merchandiser of goods turned out by others by methods inattentive to market needs and opportunities, the factory placed the emphasis on making: the mill owner was first and foremost a production man, able within fairly wide limits to alter the techniques and conditions of work at will. As a result, technique was responsive to economic opportunity as never before. The pressures for change already inherent in the new technology—with its calculus of efficiency, its systematization of empirical investigation, its implicit and growing ties to a growing body of scientific theory—were thereby enormously reinforced. The factory was a new bridge between invention and innovation.

In sum, one must not mistake the appearance for the reality. The census returns and other numbers to be found between the covers of dusty parliamentary papers are the economic historian's butterfly under glass or frog in formaldehyde—without the virtue of wholeness to compensate for their lifelessness. As described by occupational data,

---

[1] Beck, *Geschichte des Eisens*, IV, 663.

[2] Cf. A. O. Hirschman and G. Serkin, 'Investment Criteria and Capital Intensity Once Again', *Quarterly Journal of Economics*, LXXII (1958), 470, who cite the contrast in this regard between the owner of the land-intensive hacienda and the operator of the capital-intensive plantation. On this point, see also E. R. Wolf and S. W. Mintz, 'Haciendas and Plantations in Middle America and the Antilles', *Social and Economic Studies*, VI (1957), 380–412.

the British economy of 1851 may not seem very different from that of 1800. But these numbers merely describe the surface of the society— and even then in terms that define away change by using categories of unchanging nomenclature. Beneath this surface, the vital organs were transformed; and though they weighed but a fraction of the total— whether measured by people or wealth—it was they that determined the metabolism of the entire system. We have seen that, in so far as small-scale enterprise continued to flourish, it did so largely because of demand derived from the growth of concentrated manufacture: the demand of the large producers themselves; of their employees; and of the urban agglomerations that grew up around them. But not only small industry was tied in this way to the modern sector. Agriculture, trade, banking—all came increasingly to depend on the needs, the products, the bills of exchange, the investments of Lancashire, the Midlands, and the other nodes of British factory industry. The people of the day were not deceived by the pristine air of much of Britain's landscape. They knew they had passed through a revolution.

It was, moreover, a revolution like nothing ever experienced. Previous transformations, political or economic, had always finished by stabilizing at a new position of equilibrium. This one was clearly continuing and bid fair to go on indefinitely. Many Britons would have stopped it in its course, or even turned it back. For good reasons or bad, they were distressed, inconvenienced, or outraged by its consequences. They mourned a merrie England that never was; deplored the soot and ugliness of the new factory towns; bemoaned the growing political power of crass *parvenus*; cried out against the precarious poverty of a rootless proletariat. This is not the place to assess these judgements, which have remained a matter of controversy to the present day. But it is worth noting that these pessimists, vociferous though they were, were a small minority of that part of British society that expressed an opinion on the subject. The middle and upper classes were convinced by the marvellous inventions of science and technology, the increasing mass and variety of material goods, the growing speed of movement and convenience of everyday activities, that they were living in the best of all possible worlds and what is more, a world getting better all the time. For these Britons, science was the new revelation; and the Industrial Revolution was the proof and justification of the religion of progress.

The 'labouring poor', especially those groups by-passed or squeezed by machine industry, said little but were undoubtedly of another mind.

II. *Continental Emulation*

It is something of a commonplace that the Crystal Palace Exposition in 1851 marked the apogee of Britain's career as the 'workshop of the world'. True, the historian can detect premonitory indications of successful emulation by other nations, even evidence of foreign superiority in special areas of manufacture. But then, there is little the historian cannot detect if he sets his mind to it, and such harbingers of trouble hardly alter the general picture. This little island, with a population half that of France, was turning out about two-thirds of the world's coal, more than half of its iron and cotton cloth. (The figures are approximate, but they furnish orders of proportion.) Her income *per capita*, which cannot be compared precisely with that of the continental countries, all ingenious efforts to the contrary, was correspondingly higher than that of her neighbours.[1] Her merchandise dominated in all the markets of the world; her manufacturers feared no competition; she had even—in a move that marked a break with hundreds of years of economic nationalism—removed almost all the artificial protections of her industrialists, farmers, and shippers against foreign rivals. What other country could follow suit? She was, in short, the very model of industrial excellence and achievement—for some, a pace-setter to be copied and surpassed; for others, a superior economic power whose achievements rested on the special bounty of an uneven Providence, hence a rival to be envied and feared. But all watched and visited and tried to learn.

Actually the learning process had started long before. By the middle of the eighteenth century, it was already obvious that British industrial technique had advanced significantly beyond that of the rest of the world. Government representatives and private businessmen came from the Continent on tours of inspection; their reports, often published, are

[1] An impressionistic estimate of 1832, by the Baron de Morogues, *De la misère des ouvriers et de la marche à suivre pour y remédier* (Paris, 1832), gave French *per capita* income as 198 fr. 30; English at 800 fr. Cited by E. Buret, *De la misère des classes laborieuses en Angleterre et en France* (2 vols.; Paris, 1840), I, 126. The gap would seem too large. More recent calculations, presumably more accurate (but *caveat lector!*), indicate that *per capita* income was about £32·6 for the United Kingdom in 1860, £21·1 for France (1859), and £13·3 for Germany (1860–9 average, 1913 area). Francs and marks have been converted to £s at 25·18 and 20·42 to 1, respectively. Sources: for the United Kingdom, Mulhall estimate, as given in P. Deane, 'Contemporary Estimates of National Income in the Second Half of the Nineteenth Century', *Econ. Hist. Rev.* 2nd ser. IX (1957), 459; for France, F. Perroux, 'Prise de vues sur la croissance de l'économie française, 1780–1950', in S. Kuznets, ed., *Income and Wealth*, Series V (London, 1955), p. 61; for Germany, P. Jostock, 'The Long-term Growth of National Income in Germany', *ibid.* p. 82.

among our best sources for the industrial history of the period. The heyday of these visits was roughly the third quarter of the century, before the British became aware of the competitive advantage afforded by their methods and began, in the best historical tradition, to erect barriers to their diffusion.

In this effort to study and emulate British techniques, the nations of western Europe were favoured by a number of advantages. To begin with, they had behind them an experience of organized and increasingly effective political behaviour. In one decisive respect, their 'age of troubles' was over: the issue of central *versus* fragmented authority had been largely settled in favour of the former, and the remnants of feudal jurisdiction and provincial autonomy were being steadily eroded by the limitless pretensions of the *Beamtenstaat*. Here, indeed, lay the basis and justification of monarchical supremacy: the creation of a standing bureaucracy administering a known corpus of law and separating the function and prerogative of office from personal interest. This it was that made possible the elaboration of coherent policy and the pursuit of continuing objectives; this, that insured the victory of the crown over insubordinate vassals who could fight better than they could govern. And if, in this struggle, the rising commercial and industrial interest generally found itself on the side of the king, it was in part because the bureaucratic state offered that definition and stability of the political environment that is propitious, if not indispensable, to business.

Similarly, their supply of capital and standard of living were substantially higher than in the 'backward' lands of today. And with this went a level of technical skill that, if not immediately adequate to the task of sustaining an industrial revolution, was right at the margin. Culturally, of course, the outlook was even brighter. The continental countries were part of the same larger civilization as Britain; and they were certainly her equals, in some respects her superiors, in science and education for the elite. In short, if they were in their day 'underdeveloped', the word must be understood quite differently from the way it is today.

Nevertheless, their Industrial Revolution was substantially slower than the British. Although they were able to study the new machines and engines almost from the start and indeed acquire them in spite of prohibitions on their export, they were generations in absorbing them and even longer in catching up to British practice.

Why the delay? Surely, the hardest task would seem to have been the original creative acts that produced coke smelting, the mule, and the steam-engine. In view of the enormous economic superiority of these innovations, one would expect the rest to have followed automatically. To understand why it did not—why even the quickest nations marked time until the third and fourth decades of the nineteenth century—is to understand not only a good part of the history of these countries but also something of the problem of economic development in general.

The industrialization of continental Europe may be broken down analytically into two aspects: (1) the response to endogenous pressures toward change, of the kind that precipitated an economic revolution in Britain; and (2) the reaction to the new methods developed across the Channel.

In order to clarify the first, one must examine briefly the character of continental industry in the pre-factory period. For one thing, nature had not been so kind to the lands across the Channel as to Britain. The key consideration was space: these countries were larger in proportion to population; and size, combined with difficulties of terrain, made for higher transport costs and fragmentation of markets. Roads were bad everywhere in the eighteenth century, but the British roads were possibly a little better and certainly shorter. And Britain had the sea. On the Continent, only Holland was so well served by water transport. The rivers of western Europe were used as much as possible for the movement of goods, but their usefulness was often vitiated by natural shortcomings—they were too shallow in the dry season, too rapid and treacherous at the full—and by poor communication between the different basins.

On the supply side, the contrast between Britain and the Continent was less sharp. Yet the resources of the mainland countries were in fact less favourable to industrial expansion than those of Britain even before the change in raw materials requirements consequent on the Industrial Revolution. The cloth industries of France, the Low Countries, and Germany, for example, had to import the bulk of their fine wool from abroad. And the lack of concentrated, easily accessible known deposits of coal led to a neglect of the possibilities of mineral fuel; here, indeed, even nature's bounty hurt, for the *relative* abundance of timber seems to have encouraged retention of the traditional technique.

Too often, moreover, man aggravated the handicaps that nature had set in his way. Thus the very best roads and waterways were dotted along their length by toll stations, whose exactions were so outrageous and formalities so tedious as to drive shippers miles out of their way and compel them on occasion to break and remake cargoes in an effort at evasion. Political boundaries were a further obstacle. Germany especially—and what are now Belgium and Italy somewhat less—was a patchwork of kingdoms, archduchies, duchies, bishoprics, principalities, free cities, and other forms of sovereignty, each with its own laws, courts, coinage and, above all, customs barriers. Even France, a unified polity by the end of the seventeenth century, continued to be divided economically into trade zones reflecting the gradual accretion that had built the nation-state. And these formal barriers were complicated by a network of informal boundaries defining markets and zones of supply for goods, like grain or wood or salt, that were vital to local survival. Finally, there were instances of the deliberate use of power to cripple trade. What is now Belgium was the worst victim: the natural access of the southern Low Countries to the sea via the Scheldt had been interrupted by the Dutch in the early seventeenth century and was to remain blocked until the annexation of the area by France during the revolutionary period. Efforts to make Ostend another Antwerp were only partly successful. The manufacturers of Wallonia, the industrial heart of the country, were compelled to turn to central Europe for markets.

These direct obstacles to the flow of goods were compounded by social and institutional limitations on demand. We have already had occasion to note that income and wealth were more unequally distributed on the Continent than in Britain, that indeed the societies of the mainland were cleft by deep horizontal fissures that discouraged emulative consumption of standardized products. The contemporary thesis linking luxury and prosperity—which Sombart picks up, with a wealth of illustrative detail, in his *Luxus und Kapitalismus*—makes some sense in this context. Some of the most important industrial enterprises were largely dependent on the orders of the wealthy few: the numerous courts, large and small, ranging from Versailles to the *Hof* of some German princeling; the Catholic Church; the socially aspiring *haute bourgeoisie*. By contrast, the great mass of near-subsistence consumers operated in an entirely different market. They could afford only the shoddiest articles, requiring a minimum of craft skill. What they could, they made at home; the poor of the eighteenth century entered the market as little as possible. Nor was what they bought standardized or mass-produced—in spite of its coarseness and simplicity. It was almost always the work of local artisans, turning out textiles and even tools in accordance with local tradition rather than some regional or national standard. Thus provincial patterns of dress lingered much longer on the Continent than in Britain, and longest in those semi-isolated rural areas where status and home were most firmly fixed.

Moreover, the poor of Europe were, as already noted, far worse off than those of Britain. The diaries of travellers offer abundant testimony to the contrast: one finds repeated references to bare feet, meatless tables, glassless windows, and the absence of iron where one would expect to find it—on the wheels of wagons, for example. Listen to Arthur Young's indignant reflections on the poverty of the Dordogne:[1]

Pass Payrac, and meet many beggars, which we had not done before. All the country girls and women are without shoes or stockings; and the ploughmen at their work have neither sabots nor feet to their stockings. This is a poverty, that strikes at the root of national prosperity; a large consumption among the poor being of more consequence than among the rich: the wealth of a nation lies in its circulation and consumption; and the case of poor people abstaining from the use of manufactures of leather and wool ought to be considered as an evil of the first magnitude.

Of the large number of similar comments, I shall confine myself to one, chosen to convey the progressive diminution in the demand for manufactures as one proceeds eastward. In 1835 a young German officer named Moltke travelled down the Danube on his way to an assignment in Turkey. Seeking means of land transport in Wallachia, he observed that the common vehicle of the country was 'like a child's wagon... so short and narrow that one man could hardly sit in it, if he brought along even so little baggage as we. On the whole waggon, there is not the smallest piece of iron: hub, axle, everything of wood. Nor is there any more point in looking for any kind of metal in the horse's harness'.[2] Nothing conveys better the circular link between poverty, the absence of industry, and a pattern of consumption that reconciles need with means and confines means to need.

Continental producers were similarly handicapped in foreign markets. Aside from higher costs due in large part to the material difficulties discussed above, they paid more for all the accessory commercial and financial services—insurance, bank credit, shipping. To be sure, the assistance of the most efficient middleman of the day, Holland, was available in principle to all. In fact, however, the nation that stood most to gain from this, France, systematically discouraged recourse to Dutch intermediaries in an effort to build up her own merchant marine— in spite of the cost and occasional impracticability of this challenge to the rules of comparative advantage.[3]

On the supply side, we have the same combination of political and social considerations compounding natural handicaps. Thus, far more

[1] *Travels* (2 vols.; Dublin, 1793), I, 38.
[2] Cited in Karl Braun-Wiesbaden, *Eine türkische Reise* (2 vols.; Stuttgart, 1876), I, 339.
[3] On this form of self-impoverishment, cf. Adam Smith, *Wealth of Nations*, Book IV, ch. ii. Navigation Acts were a far more serious handicap to the French than to the British, and Paris had to make numerous exceptions to insure the flow of goods to and from the colonies. E. Levasseur, *Histoire du commerce de la France* (2 vols.; Paris, 1911), I, 489–90.

than in Britain, continental business enterprise was a class activity, recruiting practitioners from a group limited by custom and law. In France, commercial enterprise had traditionally entailed derogation from noble status; and although the monarchy made repeated efforts from Louis XIII on to make trade, especially international trade, and large-scale manufacture compatible with aristocracy, it found social values more powerful than decrees. In much of Germany, the cleavage was even wider, for there class prejudice was reinforced by law, and lines were carefully drawn between noble, burgher, and peasant enjoining each from trespassing on those areas reserved to the others. Indeed, the farther east one goes in Europe, the more the bourgeoisie takes on the appearance of a foreign excrescence on manorial society, a group apart scorned by the nobility and feared or hated by (or unknown to) a peasantry still personally bound to the local *seigneur*.[1]

This is not to say that European aristocrats did not engage in industrial activity, especially in those fields, like mining and metallurgy, that depend heavily on the ownership of land; or that they did not on occasion invest in manufacturing at the behest of a mercantilist sovereign intent on promoting economic development. Even there, however, their entrepreneurship was more often than not vicarious, and the few aristocratic industrialists who have caught the attention of scholars are not enough to alter significantly the picture of a class deriving its material strength at best from agriculture and estate management, at worst from rents, feudal dues, state offices, royal favours, and other perquisites of gentle birth. Here, as always, attitude is more decisive than law or fiat; and the attitude of most continental noblemen was summed up in the sententious quip of one Austrian magnate: 'Geschäfte macht kein Windischgrätz'.

The effect of this invidious social segregation of business enterprise was to discourage outside talent and capital from entering the field and to draw out the most successful of those already engaged. If the aristocrat was too high to stoop to trade, the ambitious, capable *novus homo* preferred to by-pass it and seek eminence via the professions and government service. Those who, for want of instruction, because of religious discrimination, through personal opportunity, or for other reason, sought their fortunes in manufacturing or commerce found financial assistance hard to obtain. Free capital flowed to the land, whose price was bid up to a point where a substantial and persistent gap developed between the rate of return in agriculture and industry. One

---

[1] Foreign often in the literal sense: it is precisely in these traditionalistic agricultural societies, with their strong suspicion of trade and the trader, that commerce was left almost entirely to the metic, the stranger in the midst—Jew, Greek, or western European.

does not find on the Continent the opportunities that offered themselves in Britain to the small man with more skill and ambition than money. The owners of non-business wealth, of land and buildings, were not awakened to the possibilities of gain that lay in converting such property and renting it for industrial use. Contrast, for example, the facilities offered in South Wales and the royalty policy of a firm like Boulton and Watt with the Draconian terms imposed on mining firms leasing Newcomen steam-engines in the Hainaut in the mid-eighteenth century: the machines had to be worked at minimum force (thereby multiplying fuel consumption per horsepower many times) for fear of straining them; and royalties ran as high as 10 per cent of gross output.[1] Mineral resources usually belonged to the state and were conceded on terms that made them inaccessible to thin purses. Loan funds, even at short term, were scarce and expensive; in those rural areas where industry would ordinarily be expected to locate, interest rates of 15 per cent and more were not uncommon. In effect, capital was limited to those who had received it from their ancestors or accumulated it by their own efforts.

At the same time, capital accumulated in business was continually draining off into more honorific channels: land, office, aristocratic status. So seriously were industry and trade weakened by this chase after prestige that the state intervened. In France, patents of nobility began to stipulate that the new rank was conditional on continuance of the family enterprise. On the whole such efforts to keep the bourgeois a bourgeois were no more successful than those to turn the gentleman into one. A majority of the descendants took their capital into the country to finance a life of gentility, while a handful carried on the business, at least for a while.

Turning from the supply of talent and capital to industry and trade to the actual conduct of business affairs, one is again struck by the contrast between continental confinement and inhibition and British freedom. The effect of mercantilist and guild controls on the scale and techniques of production is too well known perhaps to require discussion here. Suffice it to say, simply, that almost to the end of the eighteenth century the tendency of continental governments was to extend and reinforce these restrictions, partly from a conviction that this was the only way to maintain quality of production and hence sales (particularly sales abroad), partly because both the enforcement of regulation and derogations therefrom were excellent sources of revenue. A country like France actually reversed the decay of this medieval institution, bolstering the guilds where they were declining, establishing

---

[1] A. Toilliez, 'Mémoire sur l'introduction et l'établissement des machines à vapeur dans le Hainaut', in Société des Sciences, des Arts, et des Lettres du Hainaut, *3e anniversaire de la fondation de la Société* (Mons, 1836), pp. 57–8.

them where they never had been. Even when the state accorded rural
craftsmen in 1762 the right to weave cloth for market, it did so not in
belated recognition of a sphere of free enterprise, but in order to bring
this growing volume of unregulated output under inspection and
control.

Yet enterprise, like love, usually finds ways to laugh at locksmiths,
and institutional restrictions will explain only a small part of the
shortcomings of continental industry. More important, probably,
were social and psychological attitudes unfavourable to effective
entrepreneurship.

We have already had occasion to allude in passing to some of the
differences between Britain and the Continent in this regard. To begin
with, the business firm in France, the Low Countries, or Germany was
far more likely to be exclusively familial, indeed to be so closely identi-
fied with the family as to be almost indistinguishable from it. The
British entrepreneur had come a long way toward seeing a given
industrial venture as a means to an end, as a device to be rationally
utilized for making money. For his competitors across the Channel,
however, the firm, *in conjunction with* the family whose reputation it
contributed to and whose way of life it made possible, was an end in
itself. This in turn had important consequences for the conduct of the
enterprise. It made it difficult to view techniques and products imper-
sonally, to sacrifice when necessary quality to quantity, to abandon
traditional ways when more efficient and profitable tools and methods
became available. It placed a premium on security and led to an over-
estimation of risk in investment decisions. It discouraged the use of
outside capital, whether in the form of long-term loans or share investment, and, by throwing the firm on its own resources, drastically
limited its opportunities for expansion while encouraging a policy of
pricing that maximized unit rather than total profit.[1]

This pattern of behaviour was reinforced by the dominant values of
the society as a whole. Thus the identification of the producer with his

[1] This reluctance of family firms to borrow, except *in extremis*, goes far to explain
the paradox of the large and persistent gap between the interest paid by state funds and
other 'safe' investments and that charged industrial enterprise. For an analysis of
this entrepreneurial pattern and its implications for growth, see D. S. Landes, 'French
Entrepreneurship and Industrial Growth in the Nineteenth Century', *J. Econ. Hist.*
IX (1949), 45–61; and *idem*, 'French Business and the Businessman: a Social and
Cultural Analysis', in E. M. Earle, ed., *Modern France: Problems of the Third and Fourth
Republics* (Princeton, 1951), pp. 334–53. Also A. Gerschenkron, 'Social Attitudes,
Entrepreneurship, and Economic Development', *Explorations in Entrepreneurial
History*, VI (1953–4), 1–19; Landes, 'Social Attitudes, Entrepreneurship, and Economic
Development: a Comment', *ibid.* VI (1953–4), 245–72; Gerschenkron, 'Some Further
Notes...', *ibid.* VII (1954–5), 111–19; Landes, 'Further Comment', *ibid.* VII (1954–5),
119–20.

tools and methods and his reluctance to scrap old ways for new was closely related to a worship of thrift that characterized the bourgeoisie as well as the peasantry to a degree unknown in Britain. I use the word 'degree' advisedly, for we are not dealing here with differences of kind. Yet it seems clear that along the wide spectrum of attitudes on this issue, ranging from the prodigality of an American family trained to look on a three-year-old automobile as unfashionable, even unpatriotic, to the parsimony of Maupassant's peasant bending to pick up a piece of string, the Englishman of the eighteenth century was substantially closer to a psychology of abundance than the Frenchman or the German. The reason lay partly in the fact of abundance: the English entrepreneur, as noted above, simply had more and cheaper resources at his disposal. But it also reflected greater security. The British farmer or burgher did not know war as did the Walloon or Bavarian; it was generations since his land had last been wasted by armies, his home pillaged; and no one in Europe could afford to be so confident of freedom from arbitrary exactions and confiscation. He had, in short, less fear of a 'rainy day'.

Similarly, the entrepreneur's preference for the greatest possible profit per unit of sale, as against higher total profit at some larger output, accorded with a general condemnation of competition, particularly price competition, as unfair and even socially subversive. The societies of the Continent and the local communities of which they were composed tended to see the total product of the group, as well as the aggregate demand for that product, as more or less fixed, growing only slowly over time with population. Under the circumstances, a man could become rich only at the expense of his neighbours, who, however inefficient they might be, had a right to sustenance appropriate to their station so long as they performed work of acceptable quality and satisfied thereby the needs of the community. The rich man who built his fortune on the ruins of less productive or talented competitors was not a model of achievement, a culture hero; he was a *mangeur d'hommes.*[1]

These generally accepted sanctions go far to explain why those continental enterprises that stood out above their fellows in size and

---

[1] This attitude, like the obsession with thrift, once again derives originally from the conditions of the rural community. Given a limited supply of land for cultivation, the peasant does in fact add to his holdings at the expense of his neighbour, who may well finish as his tenant or—in other times and societies—his debt bondsman. With the rise of towns and cities in the Middle Ages, this fear of the impoverishment and dependency consequent on inequality was transferred to the urban community, where it inspired much of the guild regulation of production and competition. The guilds have long since disappeared, but in countries like France and Germany, the reprobation of judgment by the market place prevails to this day.

efficiency did not take advantage of their superiority to wipe out smaller competitors and impose their technology on industry as a whole. For one thing, there were serious social penalties for inconsiderate behaviour, penalties that should not be underestimated in societies that place so much emphasis on 'connections'—in all matters, from profitable business transactions to honorific marriages. For another, social attitudes were translated into political institutions, and local authorities in countries like France and Prussia could on occasion interpose real obstacles to free-wheeling enterprise. Finally, there was a serious material deterrent: in a market dominated by a few large units amid a swarm of small, aggressive price competition by one giant is sure to invite painful reprisal from the others.

This is not to say that there was no competition or that there was no elimination of inefficient firms. The contrary is clearly true. The point is that these patterns of behaviour diminished the effectiveness of the price mechanism as a force for rationalization and slowed the diffusion of technological change. The effect varied from industry to industry. In one sense it was most significant—that is, it made the most difference—where it was *not* reinforced by and inextricably bound up with contributory factors—in textiles and other light manufactures, for example, where transport costs were not high enough to cut down competition regardless of entrepreneurial policy.

As a result of this combination of natural and human limitations on the demand for manufactured products and the supply of effective industrial enterprise, pre-industrial, pre-Revolutionary Europe was a conglomeration of small, semi-autarkic markets, each with its own fairly complete array of trades. The scale of operations of the individual enterprise was small enough to make locational resource and supply considerations almost irrelevant. Textiles were produced everywhere, most often with local flax or wool; small out-croppings of iron fed the local furnaces and forges, placed along streams in wooded areas to insure a provision of fuel. Only a few industries were compelled by special requirements to concentrate in suitable localities: porcelain manufacture, certain branches of the chemical industry, non-ferrous metallurgy.

To be sure, even in those industries that were most dispersed, there were centres of exceptional activity catering to more than local needs: French Flanders, Verviers, Saxony, Normandy, Languedoc in woollen cloth; Switzerland, south Germany, Normandy in cottons and fustians; Wallonia, the Nivernais and upper Marne valley, the Siegerland, Silesia, and Styria in iron. Some of this localization reflected a specially favourable resource position: large flocks of sheep in Saxony; easy access to overseas cotton sources in Normandy; generous iron deposits in the Liégeois, Nivernais, or Siegerland; rapid streams in the Sauerland for the refining and working of the crude pig. Sometimes it rested on long tradition and a consequent inheritance of special skills: thus weaving in Flanders or the cutlery manufacture at Solingen and Thiers. Sometimes it was largely a product of entrepreneurial initiative, as in the textile centres created by Calvinist refugees at Krefeld, Elberfeld, and other points in the Rhine valley; and sometimes a *fabrique* was created by the state, as the fine-cloth manufacture at Sedan. Usually, as in the metal industries of Liège, it is a combination of two or more of these that accounts for growth. Finally, the localization of industry, particularly in textiles, was a function of the availability of cheap rural labour; spinning and weaving were most active in areas where the parsimony of the soil or the excessive fragmentation of the land compelled the peasant to eke out his living with the wages of industry. All the better if he was engaged in livestock raising or mixed husbandry rather than simple cultivation; his hands would be the smoother for handling yarn and fabric.

It is hardly surprising that the most successful of these centres— those growing most rapidly if not always the largest in absolute output —were almost invariably those unhampered by guild regulation. In France, where most industry was in principle subject to control, a city like Lille waged a long, vain struggle against the overgrown textile villages of the *plat pays*, which were stimulated by competition 'to by-pass the regulations, seek new processes, and vary their fabrics continually'.[1] In the Low Countries, the woollen trade of Liège declined steadily, while a few miles away, the free *fabrique* of Verviers throve; what is more, freedom raised a rival to Verviers itself, as from the middle of the eighteenth century the weavers of Dison pushed iconoclasm almost to the limit and built their prosperity on the use of waste yarn, the so-called *queues et pennes*.[2] In Aachen, the introduction of regulation merely served to drive the most enterprising producers to the suburb of Burtscheid.[3]

What *is* in some ways surprising is the superior performance of free industry to that of state-supported enterprise. The seventeenth and eighteenth centuries saw most of the governments of continental

[1] A. de Saint-Léger, in a review of J. Crombé, *L'organisation du travail à Roubaix avant la Révolution* (Lille, 1905), in *Annales de l'Est et du Nord*, II (1906), 414.

[2] Pierre Lebrun, *L'industrie de la laine à Verviers pendant le XVIIIᵉ et le début du XIXᵉ siècle* (Liège, 1948), part III, section I, ch. iii.

[3] C. Bruckner, *Aachen und seine Tuchindustrie* (Horb am Neckar, 1949); cf. the failure of similar efforts to contain enterprise in the wire industry of western Germany. R. Sommer, 'Die Industrie im mittleren Lennetal', in *Spieker: Landeskundliche Beiträge und Berichte* (Münster), no. 7 (1956), p. 37.

Europe—foremost among them France, Prussia, and the Austria of Maria Theresa—engage in extensive and costly programmes of industrial development. Their objectives were more or less the same: political aggrandizement through wealth and employment; but their methods, which were essentially empirical and dependent on uncertain resources, varied with place and time. In the beginning, the emphasis was usually on direct participation in economic life: almost every nation had its state enterprises producing the staples of royal consumption—armaments first, and then decorative furnishings like mirrors, tapestries, and porcelain. In Prussia the monarchy, with its large Silesian properties, was the largest producer of iron and coal in the kingdom.

Yet the economic ambitions of the state surpassed its resources in men and money, and compelled it from the start to rely heavily on private industry. Assistance sometimes took the form of direct investment, but more often of fiscal favours, assignment of labour, patents on techniques or exclusive sales privileges, guaranties of supplies, technological advice, loans at low interest or no interest, outright subsidies, or some combination thereof. From 1740 to 1789 the French monarchy lent without interest some 1·3 million *livres* and gave away 5 million more; to this, certain regional authorities like those of Brittany and Languedoc added their own subventions. All of these did not add up to much; but they were intended as 'seed money', planted in pilot enterprises in the hope that it would bring forth a crop of imitators. The state also designated numerous *manufactures royales* and *privilégiées*, and when necessary gilded the honour with monopoloy rights as an inducement to the foundation of new industries or importation of new techniques. Finally, it sent observers abroad on technical missions; engaged inventors and manufacturers, for the most part Britons like Kay and Wilkinson, to teach their methods to French industry; and encouraged foreigners like Holker and Milne to settle in France and set up their own enterprises.

In Germany, Prussia was most active in this campaign of forced industrialization. Businessmen, even noblemen and local governments, were urged to set up 'factories' for the production of textiles, glass, chemicals, nonferrous and ferrous metals. This royal invitation was usually equivalent to a command, particularly to those Jewish merchants and court purveyors whose situation in a virulently anti-Semitic country was utterly dependent on the pleasure of the ruler. Hundreds of enterprises were brought into existence in this manner, many in the newly conquered province of Silesia, which was an object of special solicitude.[1] The other governments of central Europe were

---

[1] The standard work remains H. Fechner, *Wirtschaftsgeschichte der preussischen Provinz Schlesien in der Zeit ihrer provinziellen Selbstständigkeit, 1741–1806* (Breslau, 1907).

less energetic only by comparison: witness Maria Theresa and her con-
sort Francis, whom Frederick the Great called 'the greatest manufacturer of his time'; or the successive Kurfürsten of Saxony; or on a
modest scale, the rulers of such lesser states as Württemberg, Hesse and
Nassau-Saarbrücken.

In the long run, however, these efforts were only moderately
successful. The state of the seventeenth and eighteenth centuries was
incapable of planning development nationally or allocating resources
efficiently. It lacked the conceptual tools, even the empirical statistical data, required; it had a strong affection for the wrong products,
for labour-intensive luxuries like Gobelins tapestries and Dresden fig-
urines; it promoted monopoly, when nothing could have been more
harmful to long-run development; and it was not even sure of its own
purposes in the face of resistance from conservative interests—corporate
industry, landed proprietors, military leaders with their own ideas
how to spend the nation's money.

In the particular, state assistance was more often than not an encouragement to laxity and a cover for incompetence. With some notable
exceptions, privileged manufactories were sloppily managed and
required repeated transfusions of royal capital. Often they turned out
an inferior product that could be disposed of only to captive customers
—army regiments or, in Germany and Austria, Jewish and foreign
merchants. As the elder Trudaine put it, 'the money of the king brings
bad luck to those who receive loans or advances'.[1] Many of these enterprises failed the moment a change in government personnel or an
ideological shift toward *laissez-faire* cut them off from state largesse.
Within his own lifetime, Frederick the Great saw dozens of his creations
fold; most of the rest followed soon after his death.

This is not to say that this effort to promote industrial development
from above was a complete waste of energy and money. It clearly was
not. If it did nothing else, mercantilism did prepare many of the
bearers of economic change. Thus these abortive manufactories and
factories were often training grounds for the next generation; the
fine-cloth 'factory' at Brno in Moravia was a stumbling undertaking
that eventually collapsed, but its alumni helped to make the city the
centre of textile manufacture in what is now Czechoslovakia.[2] Similarly, there were few British technicians who emigrated to the
Continent to set up shops and mills who did not teach, sometimes in-

[1] Cited in Ch. Schmidt, 'Les débuts de l'industrie cotonnière en France, 1760–1806,
II. De 1786 à 1806', *Revue d'histoire économique et sociale*, VII (1914), 30 n. 2.

[2] See the unpublished dissertation of Herman Freudenberger, 'A Case Study of the
Government's Role in Economic Development in the Eighteenth Century: The
Brno Fine-Cloth Factory' (Columbia University, 1957).

advertently, some of their eventual competitors. Finally, one must not underrate the long-run importance of the technological civil service—with men like Trudaine and Jars in France, Heinitz, Stein and Reden in Prussia—which continued to influence economic development on the Continent after the other aspects of mercantilistic policy had been discarded. The zeal of these officials was no substitute for a high general level of skill and empirical ingenuity; but they were a force for the rational study and promotion of change, and once the initial steps had been taken on the path of industrial revolution, once the process of cumulative advance had begun, they did channel innovation effectively.

In striking contrast, the industrial centres of west Germany—Krefeld, Monschau, the Wuppertal in textiles, Solingen and Remscheid in metalwork—grew rapidly without assistance and gave rise to large firms of international reputation. It was these and similar areas like Verviers-Hodimont that were the potential sources of technological revolution, for it is here that we find those bottlenecks in the supply of the factors which triggered change in Britain. The shortage of water power was already compelling a costly dispersion of iron-working in the Sauerland and Siegerland.[1] And the growing demand for labour led the merchant clothiers to seek spinners and even weavers, first in the nearby countryside, and then far afield in heavily populated agricultural areas like the Limburg, which lay at the centre of the triangle marked off by Verviers, Monschau and Aachen. Spinning was the worst bottleneck: sometimes the state intervened and prohibited the export of yarn in an effort to protect the supply of its own nationals. In the meantime, embezzlement seems to have increased, in spite of repressive measures comparable to those imposed in England.[2]

How heavy was this growing pressure on supply? Clearly much less than in Britain. Such evidence as we have indicates that up to the last decade of the century, the flow of cheap labour on the Continent continued to be abundant; the marginal cost of this factor was not rising. On the contrary, the growth of population was outstripping that of industry and giving rise in some areas to the kind of pauperized rural proletariat that is a signpost of economic backwardness. Some of the strongest opponents of mechanization in the late eighteenth century were officials and peasants who feared that increased produc-

---

[1] Max Barkhausen, 'Staatliche Wirtschaftslenkung und freies Unternehmertum im westdeutschen und in nord und südniederländischen Raum bei der Entstehung der neuzeitlichen Industrie im 18. Jahrhundert', *Vierteljahrschrift für Sozial- und Wirtschaftsgeschichte*, XLV (1958), 234, 239. An important article.

[2] Cf. C. Schmidt, 'Une enquête sur la draperie à Sedan en 1803', *Revue d'histoire des doctrines économiques et sociales*, V (1912), 100, 103; A. Crapet, 'L'industrie dans la Flandre wallonne à la fin de l'Ancien Régime', *Revue d'histoire moderne*, XII (1909), 28.

tivity would reduce thousands to unemployment and starvation. There was still room to expand industry in the burgeoning villages of Flanders, the Limburg, Saxony, and Bohemia-Moravia. In the last-named area, to take one example, the number of wool weavers rose from 12,700 to 24,800 between 1775 and 1788/9, while spinners more than doubled, increasing from 26,400 to 59,000; taken together, they represented 1 in every 90 persons at the earlier date, 1 in 50 at the later.[1] Similarly, the very slowness of certain technological changes is negative evidence of abundant labour: in France, the spinning wheel did not widely displace the distaff until the middle of the eighteenth century;[2] in Flanders, it was only in the early years of the nineteenth century that Liévin Bauwens introduced the fly-shuttle into the cotton industry of Ghent.

How long growth could have continued without necessitating a change in technique is another matter. Yet the issue is an idle one, for the continental countries did not have the opportunity to work out their own destinies. The changes across the Channel drastically changed their economic and political situation. For private enterprise, the immediate effects were frightening: traditional domestic industries, wherever they were unprotected, began to smother under the weight of cheap British goods. By the same token, exporters found their competitive position in international trade gravely undermined; and while most were reconciled by this time to seeing English manufactures win a privileged position in overseas markets, they were not prepared to abandon the struggle entirely. Moreover change had its positive attractions; the British had opened a mine of profit for all the world to see.

For the state, British progress was a direct, unavoidable challenge. The governments of Europe had long come to look upon economic development as the key to a favourable balance of trade—hence wealth;

[1] H. Freudenberger, 'The Woollen-Goods Industry of the Habsburg Monarchy in the Eighteenth Century: a Case Study in Development', *J. Econ. Hist.* xx (1960). This increase gave rise, however, to institutional bottlenecks. In spite of the readiness of individual lords to allow manufacturers to hire serfs on their estates, the inability of the rural population to move toward work made impossible the swollen villages that had characterized East Anglia and Lancashire. Manufacturers began to compete for labour, wages went up, and the state attempted to ease the pressure by allotting regions to each establishment. So long as serfdom prevailed, however, concentrated factory production was unfeasible. In 1781 the state recognized the nature of the problem and declared that the abolition of serfdom would 'usefully influence the improvement of agriculture and industry'. A Klima, 'Industrial Development in Bohemia, 1648–1781', *Past and Present*, no. 11 (1957), 96–7.

[2] Cf. P. Leuilliot, 'Commerce et industrie en Europe du XVIe au XVIIIe siècle; les industries textiles; problèmes généraux et orientation des recherches', in Comitato Internazionale di Scienze Storiche, X Congresso Internazionale di Scienze Storiche, *Relazioni*, vol. IV: *Storia Moderna* (Florence, n.d. [1955]), 287.

to large tax revenues—hence power; and to stable employment—
hence public order. They had traditionally encouraged enterprise as
best they knew, cherishing especially those trades that furnish the
means of war. Now they found the entire balance of economic forces
upset. Industrialization was, from the start, a political imperative.

Admiration of British performance was one thing, however; emulation, another. The same objective obstacles to industrial expansion
and technological change remained, aggravated in some respects by the
nature of the innovations across the Channel. Thus Britain's advantage
in industrial resources was greater than ever, now that cotton, a material
of overseas origin, replaced wool as the chief textile fibre, and coal
replaced wood as the main source of fuel. The continental countries
not only had too little coal. What they had was widely dispersed, usually
at a distance from associated raw materials like iron and, more often
than not, of the wrong kind. France, for example, had little coking
coal to begin with and has discovered little since. The rich deposits of
the Ruhr were as yet unsuspected. Only in Belgium and Silesia was
there known to be substantial, accessible coal measures, and in both
places, particularly in Silesia, oil content was too high; the coke
obtained was friable and not suited to furnaces above a certain size.

More than ever, therefore, the producers of the Continent found
themselves confined by cost disadvantages to home consumers; and
now the problem of scale was more acute as a result of the higher
productive capacity of the new equipment. The old geographical and
social limitations on demand were still there, and the same abundance
of untapped rural labour that had made possible the expansion of the
pre-factory period now acted as a deterrent to mechanization and
concentration. Moreover, the lack of requisite technical skills posed an
obstacle to innovation that only time could overcome.

Actually, time seemed to work at first against the continental
economies. In France, a bare handful of cotton mills were built in the
1770's and 1780's, using jennies and water frames; one official estimated at 900 the total number of jennies in the entire country in 1790.
Clearly mechanization was proceeding far more slowly than in
Britain. The pace may have quickened, however, as a result of the Eden
treaty of 1786, which opened the French market to British cottons and
made modernization a matter of survival.

In metallurgy, the government promoted efforts to learn and apply
the technique of coke smelting. William Wilkinson, ironmaster of
Bersham, was brought over to act as technical adviser; it was he who
suggested Le Creusot as a promising site, and it was there in 1785, in a
furnace apparently built to his specifications, that Ignace de Wendel
produced the first coke-blast iron on the Continent. For the moment,

however, he had no imitators. Nor did anyone attempt to introduce Cort's puddling and rolling processes for another generation. French metallurgy was growing in scale but changing little in technique.

Le Creusot was also the first place in France to use the rotative steam-engine—one in 1784 to drive the hammers of the forge, in addition to four other Watt-type machines for pumping the mines and blowing the furnaces.[1] But in this too it was exceptional. Elsewhere the steam-engine, particularly the separate-condenser type, was a curiosity. On the other hand, it was in large measure a French-built curiosity (beginning in 1780-1, the brothers Perier were constructing *pompes à feu* at their works at Chaillot just outside of Paris), and this was in itself a major technological advance.

The other continental countries were even slower to change. The first German cotton-spinning mill, using Arkwright's water frame, was established in 1794 in a village appropriately named Kromford, east of Düsseldorf. In Saxony, the frame and mule came in just before the turn of the century; in the Low Countries (Verviers and Ghent) slightly later. In metallurgy, it was Silesia that took the lead, thanks to the pertinacity of Reden and the financial support of the Prussian government; the resemblance to the French experience is striking. The first coke-blast iron was tapped in 1791-2 from a charcoal furnace in the royal works at Malapane, and in 1794-6 a true coke-blast furnace was built at Gleiwitz by a Scots engineer named John Baildon (formerly employed at Carron) and two gifted German technicians, Bogatsch and Wedding. Similar attempts in western Germany, beginning in the 1760's in the Saar, were unsuccessful.[2] The Low Countries, by contrast, seem to have done little in this sphere before the 1820's.[3]

In engineering the story was reversed: here the long experience of the Walloons in metal work enabled them to become machine builders to Europe. The first Newcomen engine on the Continent was erected in Liège in 1720-1, and by the middle of the century the ironworks of the vicinity were making copies for the Hainaut and other nearby mining

---

[1] The first atmospheric engine to be used in France had been installed at the Fresnes coal-mine near Condé (Nord) in 1732. The second came at Anzin in 1737; the third at Littry in Normandy in 1749. For purposes of comparison, around 1765 there were 127 atmospheric engines in the Newcastle district alone. Jean Chevalier, 'La mission de Gabriel Jars dans les mines et les usines britanniques en 1764', *Trans. Newcomen Soc.* XXVI (1947/8 and 1948/9), 59, 67.

[2] These were financed by Prince Wilhelm Heinrich of Nassau-Saarbrücken. The ore smelted well, but the iron produced was of poor quality, and the death of the Prince in 1768 put an end to the experiment. Beck, *Geschichte des Eisens*, III, 985-6.

[3] Pierre Lebrun, 'La rivoluzione industriale in Belgio: Strutturazione e destrutturazione delle economie regionali', *Studi storici*, II (1961) [special number: Studi sulla rivoluzione industriale], 610, mentions one brief attempt in the Liégeois.

districts. No area in Europe took so quickly to steam: in the period to 1790, thirty-nine atmospheric engines were installed in the Mons basin, and twenty of these were still operating at that date.[1] As these figures show, the adoption of steam power in the Low Countries was closely linked to the needs of mining. Thus the Liégeois, where the nature of the coal deposits permitted drainage by adit, exported its engines and made use of only a few in its own pits. As for other industries, neither the techniques employed nor the scale of manufacture called for more power than the water wheel could provide. Hence the slow adoption of the Watt engine: the first, a single-acting model, seems to have been introduced in the late 1780's, and the first rotative machine may well be the one imported by Bauwens around 1801 for his mule-spinning mill in Ghent.[2]

We know something of one of the peripatetic mechanics of Liège, Jean Wasseige, whose career in the 'Austrasian coal field' (that complex of deposits which extends from the Pas-de-Calais in northern France through Belgium to the Ruhr) covered almost the entire second half of the eighteenth century:[3] in 1751 he built what may well have been Germany's first steam-engine, for a lead mine near Düsseldorf; thirty-five years later, he is mentioned as installing a machine at Eschweiler (near Aachen).[4] He and others like him were carrying on the old tradition of an international community of skilled craftsmen and technicians and anticipating the heavy contribution that Belgium was to make to the industrialization of Germany in the nineteenth century.

In spite of Belgian and British assistance, however, Germany made relatively little use of steam in this period. By the turn of the century,

---

[1] Pierre Lebrun, *ibid.* pp. 625 f., 637.

[2] On a Watt machine installed in a mine at Produits 'fifty years ago', see N. Briavoinne, *De l'industrie en Belgique* (Brussels, 1839), p. 240. On the first rotative engine, Jan Dhondt, 'L'industrie cotonnière gantoise à l'époque française', *Revue d'histoire moderne et contemporaine*, II (1955), 241 and n. 2. This seems to correct Briavoinne, *Sur les inventions et perfectionnemens dans l'industrie, depuis la fin du XVIIIe siècle jusqu'à nos jours* [Mémoires couronnés par l'Académie Royale des Sciences et Belle-Lettres de Bruxelles, Série in-4°, vol. XIII] (Brussels, 1838), pp. 35–6. Toilliez, 'Mémoire' [see p. 359, n. 1, above], pp. 52 f., shows that for an area specializing in coal-mining like the Hainaut, the wasteful but simple Newcomen engine was preferred to the Watt machine well into the nineteenth century.

[3] For the definition and concept of the Austrasian field, see E. A. Wrigley, *Industrial Growth and Population Change* (Cambridge, 1961); also the older, but still valuable, book by Guy Greer, *The Ruhr-Lorraine Industrial Problem* (New York, 1925).

[4] Beck, *Geschichte des Eisens*, III, 984, is in error when he calls the steam-engine at Griesborn (1773) the first steam mine pump in what was later Germany. (Griesborn was then in Lorraine.) On the Düsseldorf engine, see Irmgard Lange-Kothe, 'Die Einführung der Dampfmaschine in die Eisenindustrie des rheinisch-westfälischen Industriegebietes', *Stahl und Eisen*, LXXXII (1962), 1669.

'a few' Newcomen machines were operating and even fewer Watt engines. The first of these was erected by order of that extraordinary technocrat Reden, at Tarnowitz (Silesia) in 1788; and after an initial failure in 1785, a second was set to work near Mansfeld (Province of Saxony) in 1789.[1] Both used cylinders and other parts of English manufacture. Not until 1791 did German engineers succeed in building a machine in its entirety. It was a Newcomen engine, ordered in 1788 by the Freiherr von Stein from Silesia for use in the Ruhr and completed in 1791. By the time the parts made their way down the Oder, through the Baltic and North seas to Amsterdam, and up the Rhine to Ruhrort in 1792, the mine they were destined for no longer wanted them. They lay in storage eight years, until the Freiherr von Romberg decided to buy them and erect the engine at the Vollmond mine, near Bochum. This was the pre-Homeric age of industrial Germany, when steam-engines made odysseys and became subjects of fable to subsequent generations.[2]

At this point, the course of technological advance on the Continent encountered a political roadblock—the series of upheavals and wars that began with the French Revolution and ended with Waterloo. They brought with them capital destruction and losses of manpower; political instability and a widespread social anxiety; the decimation of the wealthier entrepreneurial groups;[3] all manner of interruptions to trade; violent inflations and alterations of currency. Above all, they cut continental Europe off, sometimes by formal restrictions, from active intercourse with Britain and did more than anything else, certainly more than the British embargo on the emigration of artisans and export of machinery, to hinder the diffusion of the new techniques across the Channel.

[1] On Reden, see W. O. Henderson, *The State and the Industrial Revolution in Prussia, 1740–1870* (Liverpool, 1958), ch. 1; on the Mansfeld engine, Lange-Kothe, 'Die Einführung', p. 1671.
[2] Lange-Kothe, 'Die Odyssee der ältesten Dampfmaschine des Ruhrgebietes', *Der Ausschnitt*, VII (1955), 24–6. The new and important researches of Miss Lange-Kothe have turned up a whole array of myths and misconceptions about the pre-history of German steam power. See her article on 'Johann Dinnendahl', *Tradition*, VII (1962), 32–46, 175–96.
[3] Pecuniarily, as a result of business fluctuations, interruptions of trade, and destruction of capital: and sometimes physically, for political reasons. Cf. P. Masson, ed., *Les Bouches-du-Rhône: encyclopédie départementale* (16 vols.; Marseilles, 1913–38), IX, 7–21, for the effects of the Terror in Marseilles; Schmidt, 'Une enquête sur la draperie à Sedan en 1803', *Revue d'histoire des doctrines économiques et sociales*, V (1913), 99, for the purge at Sedan. Or consider the disruptive effects of proscription and exile on such enterprises as the Wendel iron-works in Lorraine. Arch. Hayange, *passim*.

Some areas were more seriously affected than others. In the beginning, it was France who suffered the most. Her economy, already weakened by the commercial treaty of 1786 with England and by the financial disorder of the monarchy, was racked between the requirements of a revolutionary government at war with enemies without and within and a general withdrawal of confidence by producers in all sectors. Internally, the demand for quality manufactures fell precipitately; abroad, she was deprived of almost all her foreign and colonial markets. In the decade following 1789, the output of some of her major textile centres fell by a half and more; only cotton seems to have held up, in part no doubt as an inferior good. Even metallurgy, which benefited from the increased demand for arms, seems to have declined: the make of pig iron was probably not much greater in 1815 than in 1789, in spite of a distinct rise during the Empire. Some parts of France, notably the west and south-west, underwent during these years what François Crouzet has called a process of pastoralization, from which they have never recovered.[1]

From the late 1790's on, the fortunes of politics changed. Now the states of northern Italy and central Europe bore the brunt of the fighting; they were the scene of combat, the source of much loot and continuing levies; the French discriminated against their economies in favour of the Empire; their governments were disrupted and too demoralized to continue their programmes of development. Yet even France, profiting from the spoils of war and the commercial advantages of 'imperial preference' and beneficiary of the most solicitous economic paternalism, lost ground in the long run. Commerce was naturally hardest hit: the Atlantic trade was never to be the same again. But industry also suffered: the cotton manufacture, which had expanded with spectacular rapidity, collapsed in the depression of 1810–12; wool advanced, but no more and probably less than it would have under conditions of peace; ironmaking grew in capacity but changed little in technique—there was no coke smelting or puddling, and only some isolated uses of rolling for the production of special shapes; the steam-engine was neglected.

With government assistance, a few industrial giants arose—Richard Lenoir and Liévin Bauwens in cotton, Douglas in machine construction—but like the hothouse creations of the *ancien régime*, they shrivelled in the first winds of adversity. In general, the tendency to rely on state aid and protection, already excessive, was aggravated by this experience. The last five years of the Empire were years of spasmodic

[1] See his informative article, 'Les conséquences économiques de la Révolution: à propos d'un inédit de Sir Francis d'Ivernois', *Annales historiques de la Révolution française*, XXXIV (1962), 182–217.

crisis that left the economy much enfeebled and momentarily helpless to meet the rush of cheap British products that came with peace.

To be sure, war and isolation had some favourable effects, at least prima facie. Technology, for example, was stimulated by the need to create substitutes for overseas imports; thus the invention of beet sugar and the spread of the Leblanc soda process. Similarly, the need and opportunity to increase rapidly the output of certain commodities encouraged mechanization, as in the woollen manufacture of Verviers and the cotton industry of Saxony. Here indeed were the greatest beneficiaries of the 'new order'—those small industrial states long locked in a tight tariff cage and now released into the huge spaces of Napoleon's Europe.

Yet it would be fallacious to assume that even these advances were a contribution to long-run development. They were the products of economic distortion, and if some, like the Leblanc technique, were fundamentally sound, others were unviable in normal circumstances. The trouble was that not all of these wartime anomalies were ready to disappear once peace returned. For every substitute that died quietly, like the woad of Languedoc, another remained as a vested interest and a burden on the consumer or taxpayer. Thus mechanized textile manufacture in central Europe, essentially a product of wartime shortages, made a strong effort to convert momentary advantage into permanent privilege, with some success; and one may reasonably attribute much of the persistent backwardness of the cotton industry in a region like Saxony to the legacy of small-scale primitive plant inherited from the period of the continental blockade.

More helpful in the long run were certain changes in the institutional climate of enterprise. In particular, traditional restraints on the mobility of capital and labour were removed or so undermined as to be incapable of blocking innovation further. Admittedly these restraints, as embodied in the corporate organization of production or, in central Europe, in the formal attribution to the various classes of society of functions and of legitimate objects of investment and expenditure, were already moribund before the Revolution. They were incompatible with the leading trends in economic life: the rise of a new industry like cotton, the spread of production into rural areas, the growing interest of the aristocracy in the possibilities of business investment, the shift toward freer enterprise and *laissez-faire*. The Revolution, however, hastened this movement, and in some areas consummated it. In France the Loi Le Chapelier of 1791 abolished the guilds, and the subsequent triumphs of the revolutionary and imperial armies brought these principles of free enterprise into the Low Countries, western Germany, and northern Italy. Where the French did not impose their institutions directly, the state was sometimes moved by French influence or success to take independent action: thus the reforms of Stein in Prussia, which were aimed not only at freeing the peasant from corporal and pecuniary servitudes (with obvious implications for the supply of industrial labour), but at opening the great mass of occupations to all comers and removing restraints on the movement of capital.

However introduced, freedom was contagious. In subsequent decades, all the lesser states of western and central Europe succeeded in eliminating this political expression of medieval economic and social values—despite tenacious opposition from craftsmen whose numbers and prosperity were often increasing as a result of overall economic growth.

So much for the direct consequences of the Revolutionary upheaval. More important in the long run were the secondary effects of the delay. In particular, the gap between continental and British industrial equipment had increased, and while such a spread may mean in theory a greater incentive to modernization, it constituted in fact an obstacle.

Already under the Empire, best practice had long passed the stage of the jenny shop or garret factory. The few technicians, mostly British, who were capable of constructing textile machinery, were asking anywhere from 7500 to 12,000 francs for an 'assortment' of the equipment required for yarn manufacture, including four spinning devices (probably mules of 80 spindles each, operable by animal power, of the type used in Britain in the 1780's).[1] By the 1820's, however, the mule had become a long machine of up to a thousand spindles, workable only by steam or water power and costing more than a thousand pounds. Blast furnace, puddling furnace, rolling mill, and coke oven had all grown in size; the story was the same in chemicals. Even where important capital-saving improvements had occurred—as in the case of the steam-engine, thanks to changes in design and the techniques of metal working—the increased scale of the other stages of the industrial process more than compensated by pushing up the size of the minimal effective unit. The early factory steam-engines were often of 6 and 8 h.p.; by the 1820's, machines of 50 h.p. and more were not uncommon.[2]

[1] Of the three cotton mills founded in Ghent in 1805, one cost 80,000 fr. (about 550 spindles), another 90,000 fr. (about 600 spindles), and the third 400,000 fr. (about 2000 spindles). Dhondt, 'L'industrie cotonnière', Revue d'histoire Moderne, II (1955), 244–5. It is not clear that some of this did not in fact pay for post-spinning (weaving, finishing) equipment.

[2] It seems likely that as a result of improvements in the techniques of machine-building and economies of scale in the engineering trades, the ratio of capital to real

There are two points to note here. First, increased capacity meant that the latest equipment was sometimes less suitable to the post-Waterloo continental market than the rudimentary pre-Revolutionary machinery. After all, although legislation and decree had removed many of the man-made barriers to trade, central Europe still remained in 1815 a patchwork, and the fundamental topographical obstacles were yet to be overcome. Nor was the consumption pattern significantly different, though effective domestic demand was certainly larger.[1] As for outlets abroad, not only was the higher cost of materials on the Continent a continued bar to export, but Britain had made use of the war years, as noted above, to enter the preserves of her blockaded continental rivals (France and Holland, primarily), destroy their shipping, and ruin their merchants—all the while building up her own connections in South America, Africa, and the Orient. As a result, markets remained small. The potential yield of the most efficient production methods was thus lower on the mainland, and the marginal gain over less capital-intensive techniques correspondingly smaller.[2]

Second—rate of return aside—the size of the initial lump of investment now required was itself an obstacle to change. Not only was it often beyond the reach of the small, prudent, self-financed family enterprise, but even those that could raise the money were reluctant to sink so much of their capital at one stroke. What we have here in effect is the well-known phenomenon of the differential evaluation of deprivation and incremental income: it was usually far more painful

output in textile manufacture fell rapidly from the Napoleonic period to the 1830's and then tended to level off. Witnesses before the tariff inquiry of 1834 estimated the initial cost of spinning plant at 32 francs per spindle; in 1860, at from 40 to 55 francs. (Of course, output per spindle had increased in the meantime.) The English experience was probably similar. Mark Blaug, 'The Productivity of Capital in the Lancashire Cotton Industry during the Nineteenth Century', *Econ. Hist. Rev.* 2nd ser. XIII (1961), 359, has the ratio of total capital to net output rising from 2·0 in 1834 to 3·3 in 1860. The important point for us, however, is not so much the efficiency of capital as the minimal competitive investment required. And this depended, not only on the production function and relative factor costs, but also on the schedule of returns to scale and the size of competitive units of production—both machines and plant as a whole. From this point of view, best practice became far more costly as time passed.

[1] If only as a result of the increase in population, which grew in a country like France, in spite of the losses and dislocation of revolution and war, from about 26 to over 29 millions. For what they are worth, estimates of French national product indicate an even faster rate of growth, from 6,100,000,000 to 8,290,000,000 francs at current prices. Perroux, 'Prise de vues sur la croissance de l'économie française, 1780-1950', *Income and Wealth*, Series V, p. 61. The reader should treat such figures as gross indicators of direction.

[2] The more so because the newer as well as the older models of industrial equipment were essentially labour-saving rather than capital-saving; the later steam-engines were a notable exception.

to contemplate the loss of a large fraction of the family's wealth than it was agreeable to envisage increasing the firm's income by some conjectural amount.

As a result, the mechanization of continental industry in the post-Napoleonic period did not follow the usual model that correlates newness and modernity. The bulk of the entrepreneurs of France, Belgium, and Germany did not take advantage of their opportunity to install the latest equipment and surpass the British in productivity. Rather they chose to invest in plants less efficient and *often less remunerative* than the best available. Many made do with used machines, and indeed there came to be a regular flow of used equipment from the richer, more advanced centres of manufacture to the more backward areas, with many pieces passing through several avatars on the way to the scrap heap. This voluntary obsolescence, in so far as it exceeded the dictates of the production functions and relative factor costs, helped maintain Britain's competitive advantage in third markets, confirmed many continental industrialists in their sense of inferiority, and reinforced the pressure for those artificial devices, such as prohibitive tariffs, which solved the immediate problem of economic survival at the expense of long-run growth.

On balance, then, emulation of Britain was probably harder after Waterloo than before. The gap in technique had widened, while most of the fundamental educational, economic, and social obstacles to imitation remained. The story of the generation after 1815 is in large measure the elimination or diminution of these, in part by state action, even more by private entrepreneurial effort.

The most immediate difficulty was technological ignorance: continental industry needed mechanics as much as machines. In the early years, while a native cadre of technicians was being formed and a machine-construction industry developed, the continental countries imported skills and equipment from abroad, at first from Britain, with time, from secondary centres like Belgium and France as well. Indeed, the Industrial Revolution is an excellent case study—one of the best documented on record—of the larger phenomenon of cultural diffusion.

The transfer of techniques was not easy. Aside from the alleged shortcomings of the pupils (and the sources have an abundance of references to the awkwardness and incompetence of continental labour), the teachers were not always free to move or bring their paraphernalia with them. The emigration of British artisans was forbidden until 1825; the export of what appeared to be the most valuable types of machinery —in particular, the major textile inventions and parts and plans thereof

—until 1842.[1] Yet there were so many loopholes and the ingenuity of smugglers and industrial spies was such, that these efforts were in the long run unavailing. By 1825 there must have been two thousand—and perhaps more—skilled British workers on the Continent. Similarly, while we will never know precisely how much machinery crossed the Channel illicitly, legitimate exports (by special licence of the Treasury) amounted to £600,000 (official value) in 1840 alone; the sources on the continental countries are full of evidence of the successful purchase and installation of British equipment.

The best of the British technicians to go abroad were usually entrepreneurs in their own right, or eventually became industrialists with the assistance of continental associates or government subventions. Many of them came to be leaders of their respective trades: one thinks of the Waddingtons (cotton), Job Dixon (machine-building), and James Jackson (steel) in France; James Cockerill (machine construction) and William Mulvany (mining) in Germany; Thomas Wilson (cotton) in Holland; Norman Douglas (cotton) and Edward Thomas (iron and engineering) in the Austrian empire; above all, John Cockerill in Belgium, an aggressive, shrewd businessman of supple ethical standards, who took all manufacturing as his province and with the assistance of first the Dutch and then the Belgian governments made a career of exploiting the innovations of others.[2]

Some of these immigrants were early examples of what we today would call business executives, combining managerial and technical skills: thus John Maberley, who in 1838 became director of a joint-stock company to build flax-spinning machinery at Amiens; or in a later period, Charles Brown, who directed the machine shops of the Sulzer firm at Winterthur. Most, however, were simply foremen or skilled craftsmen. They were a costly investment, especially since many were not at all prepared to stay long enough for the employer to amor-

---

[1] Paradoxically, steam-engines and machine tools were permitted to be exported by special licence—the former, because they were considered 'only a moving power', and not machines; the latter because it was felt to be impracticable to discriminate between tools used for the manufacture of machines and those used for other purposes. See the testimony of J. D. Hume in the 'First Report of the Select Committee ...Exportation of Machinery', *Parl. Papers*, 1841, VII, p. 5. Q. 17. The export of otherwise prohibited machinery by licence of the Board of Trade began some time before 1825—the parliamentary inquiry of that year could not ascertain the origin of the practice, its basis in law, or the extent to which it had been carried. *Ibid.* Second Report, p. iv.

[2] The most convenient source is W. O. Henderson, *Britain and Industrial Europe*, 1750–1870 (Liverpool, 1954). Of the many specialized articles, see the interesting case study of Paul Leuilliot, 'Contribution à l'histoire de l'introduction du machinisme en France: la "Biographie industrielle" de F. C. L. Albert (1764–1831)', *Annales historiques de la Révolution française*, XXIX (1952), 3–22.

tize the initial expense of bringing them over. In view of the size of this original outlay, manufacturers had a strong incentive to hire such workers away from competitors; the sources are full of complaints about such 'dishonest' practices. In this way, the high salaries originally promised were pushed higher, to the intense discomfort of employers, who not only found this a heavy levy on their purses but also learned that better pay often meant less rather than more work. Most of these technicians were used on jobs where they set their own pace; often they were paid by time rather than output; and many placed a high premium on leisure—the more so since they were generally homesick, unhappy, and prone to drown their sorrows in alcohol. They had a keen sense of their indispensability, and this combined with national pride to make them arrogant and fractious.

Thus in 1824 François de Wendel, ironmaster at Hayange and Moyeuvre in Lorraine, sent the chief of his English workmen back to Britain to bring back some technical information, two more of his countrymen, and the wives of those who were already employed. When his return was delayed, Wendel wrote him a letter, the rough copy of which has come down to us: 'I have received you letter from febr your absence me nuit beaucoup je paye your worckmans [?] and they do not worck the carpentar is an ivrogne, one can not employe him. I believe it is better for you to kom and to remaine her;...'[1] Small wonder that industrialists like Fritz Harkort, pioneer of the German engineering industry, could not wait for the day when German moulders were trained, 'so that the Englishmen could all be whipped out [herausgepeitscht]: we must even now tread softly with them, for they're only too quick to speak of quitting if one does so little as not look at them in a friendly fashion'.[2]

The day came. Perhaps the greatest contribution of these immigrants was not what they did but what they taught. Employers or employees, they trained a generation of skilled workers, many of whom became entrepreneurs in their own right. Thus the Cockerill firm sold its machines as far east as Poland, and every assortiment brought with it a mechanic, to install the equipment and live on the job while instructing the customer in its operation and maintenance. Needless to say, some of these never returned to the home office. As continental technology improved and the stirrings of industrial revolution moved eastward and

---

[1] Archives. Les Petits-Fils de François de Wendel et Cie, Hayange, Carton 856.
[2] Cited in Franz Schnabel, *Deutsche Geschichte im neunzehnten Jahrhundert* (4 vols.; Freiburg, various editions and dates), II (2nd ed.; 1954), 287. In later years, Harkort used to say: 'I had at that time to cut several of my Englishmen down from the gallows, so to speak, if only in order to get some of them.' L. Berger, *Der alte Harkort* (Leipzig, 1890), p. 153.

southward, the countries on the western edge of the land mass—
Belgium and France in particular—served increasingly as reservoirs of
capital and skills. This secondary flow was especially important from
the 1840's on, not so much in manufacturing industry, however, as in
the construction of railways, roads, canals, and bridges.[1]

The growing technological independence of the Continent resulted
largely from man-to-man transmission of skills on the job. Of less
immediate importance, though of greater consequence in the long run,
was the formal training of mechanics and engineers in technical schools.
France and Germany in particular created a veritable hierarchy of such
institutions: on the highest level, the *Ecole Polytechnique* (and its
graduate affiliates of *Mines* and *Ponts-et-Chaussées*), the Berliner *Ge-
werbe-Institut*, the Prussian *Hauptbergwerks-Institut*; a middle range of
mechanical training schools, the *écoles des arts et métiers* in France and
provincial *Gewerbeschulen* in Prussia; and at the bottom a heterogeneous group of local courses, sometimes private, sometimes public,
in manual arts, design, and the rudiments of calculation.

Here the state made the major contribution. Initial costs were too
high and pecuniary rewards too distant for private enterprise to do
more than offer its benediction and support to those lower-level schools
whose short courses were aimed at training people to go directly into
the mills. Only the government could afford to send officials on costly
tours of inspection as far away as the United States; provide the
necessary buildings and equipment; feed, clothe, house, and in some
cases pay students for a period of years. Moreover, these pedagogical
institutions were only part—though the most important part—of a
larger educational system designed to introduce the new techniques and
diffuse them through the economy; there were also non-teaching
academies, museums, and, most important perhaps, expositions. The
importance of the last is hard to realize in this age of world fairs for
tourism and propaganda. There were no midways or aquacades in these
early industrial competitions. All was business, and the medals awarded
were a source of profit as well as pride to the victorious firms. They
were, in a way, a kind of advertising before the age of the penny paper
and mass publicity. As a result, the expositions did much to stimulate
technological emulation and diffuse knowledge. In this, their influence

[1] On the contribution of the Belgians and French to German industry, particularly
in the Rhineland, see B. Kuske, in H. Aubin, Th. Frings, *et al.*, *Geschichte des
Rheinlandes von der ältesten Zeit bis zur Gegenwart* (2 vols.; Essen: Baedeker, 1922),
II, 198–9; Jean R. Maréchal, 'La contribution des Belges et des Français à l'essor de la
grande industrie allemande', *Rev. universelle des mines*, 8e ser. XIII (1937), 517–31;
Rondo Cameron, 'Some French Contributions to the Industrial Development of
Germany, 1840–1870', *J. Econ. Hist.* XVI (1956), 281–321.

ran counter to a deep-rooted tradition of secrecy, the stronger for the ineffectiveness of patent protection and the depth of technological ignorance. The rarer the skills, the greater their value. There were clashes on this score, but the juries made clear by their awards that they did not like secretive firms.

Finally, the government provided technical advice and assistance, awarded subventions to inventors and immigrant entrepreneurs, bestowed gifts of machinery, allowed rebates and exemptions of duties on imports of industrial equipment. Some of this was simply a continuation of the past—a heritage of the strong tradition of direct state interest in economic development. Much of it, in Germany particularly, was symptomatic of a passionate desire to organize and hasten the process of catching up.

In so far as this promotional effort stressed the establishment of rational standards of research and industrial performance, it was of the greatest significance for the future. At the middle of the century, technology was still essentially empirical and on-the-job training was in most cases the most effective method of communicating skills. But once science began to anticipate technique—and it was already doing so to some extent in the 1850's—formal education became a major industrial resource and the continental countries saw what had once been compensation for a handicap turned into a significant differential asset.[1]

It was not enough, of course, to bring techniques and technicians over from Britain; they would have remained curiosities had there not been a growing demand for them. Indeed this marked the main point of contrast between the eighteenth and nineteenth centuries: where before the government had been preaching in a kind of wilderness and had been obliged to take upon itself the task of implanting some of the new methods, it now faced a sympathetic business community moving ahead in its own right, to the point of anticipating the state and exploiting its resources.

In explaining this change, it is useful to distinguish between those factors that were essentially a continuation of eighteenth-century forces—though writ larger—and those that were new. Thus, as noted earlier,

---

[1] The cultivation of systematic instruction as a cure for technological backwardness fits well into Professor Gerschenkron's model, which postulates the establishment of private financial institutions or—under circumstances of severe retardation—the intervention of the state to mobilize capital for economic development. See his 'Economic Backwardness in Historical Perspective', in B. Hoselitz, ed., *The Progress of Underdeveloped Areas* (Chicago, 1951), recently reprinted in A. Gerschenkron, *Economic Backwardness in Historical Perspective* (Cambridge, Mass., 1962), pp. 5-30. A school system is in this sense simply a device for mobilizing and developing productive skills and knowledge.

much of this heightened entrepreneurial interest in industrial development was part of a general process of growth: of accumulation of capital, of increasing demand, of the imbalances consequent on growth, of the contact with the British example. The rise in population was an important part of this story: it seems clear, in spite of the lack of census figures, that numbers were already mounting steadily in the eighteenth century; in the nineteenth they rose even more sharply—in France, from about 27·5 million in 1801 to 34 million in 1850; in Germany, from about 23·5 million in 1810 to 33·5 million in 1850; in Belgium from perhaps 3 million to 4·3 million in the same period.

On the other hand, changes in the economic and institutional environment after 1815 gave a strong push to this long-term rise in demand for manufactures and supply of the factors of production. On the demand side, the internal unification of national markets was substantially completed in western Europe by the formation of the German *Zollverein*: the long lines of wagons waiting through the cold night for the toll gates to open on the New Year of 1834 were eloquent testimony to the new opportunities that opened with them.[1]   Analogous, and less important only by comparison, was the opening of the Rhine mouth to German shipping after centuries of mercantilistic restrictions. These changes probably more than compensated for such tariff increases as occurred in the areas affected.[2]

All of western Europe, moreover, profited by improvements in transportation. These took the form, first, of better channels for movement—this was a period of active road building, river work, and a certain amount of canal construction; and second, of faster, more capacious vehicles. To some extent, the two went hand in hand: it was impossible to shift from pack animals (the main method of transport in most areas of the Continent) to wagons until roads were better; and the use of steamboats and steam barges required waterways of greater depth and dependability.

The railroad was a special case. Except in Belgium, whose major lines were completed by mid-century, and to a much smaller degree, Germany, which built an important part of its network by that time, the railroad did not significantly affect the structure of the market in

---

[1] For France and what was to become Belgium, the task had been achieved before 1815. Indeed, for both of these, the end of the Empire was a step backward, a return to a smaller sphere. This was far more serious for Belgium, which was cut off from the bulk of its potential market; the injury was aggravated by the secession from Holland in 1830.

[2] The trend was more complicated than might appear at first glance. On the one hand, Prussian tariff rates tended effectively to rise through most of this period; on the other hand, all states joining the *Zollverein* were compelled to accept the Prussian tariff, which was usually lower than their own.

this period. The economic gains from a transport system increase in a kinked line, with steep jumps in results when certain junctions are made; the key connections for western Europe were not made until the 1850's and 1860's.

In other respects, however, the impact of the railway on industry is not to be underestimated. In the short run, it created an unprecedented demand for iron (as well as wood, glass, leather, stone, and other substances used in the manufacture of cars and construction of fixed facilities); moreover, it wanted these materials in a wide variety of finished forms, ranging from relatively simple items like rails and wheels to complicated engines and machines, all of which gave a special push to the metalworking and engineering trades. If to this we add the general effect of this huge investment on the demand for consumers' goods, it seems fair to say that by the 1840's railroad construction was the most important single stimulus to industrial growth in western Europe.

It is doubtful, however, whether the influence of railway demand on technology was as consistently favourable as on output. In so far as the railroad required new products, it promoted innovation; witness the growing ability to mould and manipulate large masses of metal. On the other hand, the increase in demand for traditional products like pig iron in markets sheltered from outside competition was often an invitation to easy expansion along old lines. The 1840's saw in both France and Germany an increase in the output of charcoal pig iron and wrought iron.[1]

One can hardly imagine a major technological or institutional change in the economic environment affecting demand and not supply. Thus cheaper, faster transport meant cheaper materials and more mobile labour, as well as wider markets. It also was the equivalent of a substantial increase in entrepreneurial capital: funds once sunk in stocks of raw cotton or buried for months in warehouses until bulky iron products could move on thawed or flowing streams were now freed for investment in plant and equipment.[2] By the same token, the growth of

---

[1] The increase was smaller in Germany, which imported large amounts of Belgian and British coke-blast pig. From 1837 to 1850 output of charcoal pig in Prussia went from 87,449 to 98,521 metric tons (up 12·66%); charcoal wrought iron went during the decade 1837–47 from 39,092 tons to 45,841 (up 17·26%). Beck, *Geschichte des Eisens*, IV, 714–16. In France, the make of charcoal pig went from 246,000 metric tons in 1835 to 339,000 in 1847 (up 37·8%). During the same period, however, output of charcoal wrought iron remained about the same. France, Min. des Travaux Publics, *Statistique de l'industrie minérale* (1893), pl. 10; idem, *Résumé des travaux statistiques de l'Administration des Mines en 1847*, p. 13.

[2] For a good case study of the effects of transport difficulties on capital requirements, see some of the material in G. Thuillier, 'Fourchambault et la sidérurgie nivernaise de 1789 à 1900' (thesis: Institut d'Etudes Politiques, Paris [Th 1081], n.d.).

population yielded more abundant manpower as well as a larger outlet for manufactures.

On the other hand, more people needed more food, and this rising demand for nourishment might well have necessitated in the long run a diversion of productive factors to agriculture and higher costs for industry. Fortunately, on the Continent as in Britain, new methods of cultivation and a revolution in land tenure increased the surface culti- vated, the yield per unit area, and the productivity of the agricultural worker.[1] As a result, it was possible to feed a growing industrial force at constant or diminishing prices while releasing the surplus farm population for industrial employment.[2]

Finally, the provision of capital for industrial ventures increased sub- stantially in this period. Part of this was simply an aspect of the rise in overall income; part was the fruit of rapid accumulation in industry— as in Britain, the enterprises of these early years financed themselves as much as possible out of earnings.

Changes in the credit structure, however, by easing the flow of capital, accounted for much of the gain. To begin with, the countries of the Continent began in this period—long after Britain—to develop national capital markets, that is, markets that bound together the major business centres and the provinces and allowed funds to flow from local industry and even agriculture into other areas of activity. Clearly, little of this investment went into manufacturing proper; the favourite placement was government bonds. Yet had it not been for this new source of mobile capital, *rentes* would have siphoned off much of the liquid capital potentially available to industry and trade. This is what happened in Austria, where the incessant demands and disorderly finances of an impecunious government made loan contracting and speculation in the funds so profitable that the merchant bankers of Vienna had no eyes for anything else. It took the railway, with its large appetite for metal and fuel, to win their attention and some of their resources from imperial finance to industry.

All of this, as the reader will have already remarked, implies that the

---

[1] Thus for a country like France wheat crops averaged 51,719,000 hectoliters (10·78 per hectare) from 1815 to 1824; 79,590,000 (13·68 per hectare) from 1841 to 1850—a rise of over 50%. Average potato crops over the same period went from 28,755,000 hectoliters to 71,329,000, a rise of 150%. Population, by contrast, went from 29,380,000 in 1815 to 35,630,000 in 1850. *Annuaire statistique*, xxv (1905), Résumé rétrospectif, pp. 10*, 32*–33*.

[2] Here, too, as in the case of railway demand, the effects were clearly more favour- able to output than to technological change as such. It is interesting to speculate on what a sustained demand for manpower in agriculture would have done to relative factor costs in industry and thus to the rate of substitution of capital for labour. Compare the American experience and the implications of the frontier.

supply of capital was limited. For all the controversy that still attends this point, this was certainly the case in the aggregate, as the heavy demands of railroad building made clear.[1] In France, the boom of the forties immobilized enormous sums—spasmodically, as syndicates assembled hundreds of millions of francs to bid against one another for concessions, then released the greater part of these monies once the award was made; and progressively, through these ups and downs, as one company after another began work. Both the money and capital markets were squeezed dry, and the anticipatory scare of 1845 became the collapse of 1846-7. Many of France's most solid enterprises found themselves on the brink of disaster because of funds frozen in railway shares—not only coal and iron firms, which stood to win sales by promoting construction, but textile mills and merchant banks as well. Bertrand Gille has even speculated that the poor harvest of 1846 owed something to the diversion of disposable funds from agriculture to railways.[2]

The hypothesis is worth careful investigation; at least this is what seems to have happened in Germany. There, Prussia and other states had established Landschaften as far back as the 1760's, to finance agricultural development by issuing mortgage bonds to the general public and lending the proceeds to landowners at low rates of interest.[3] Over the years, tens of millions of thalers had been drawn in this way from the savings of the industrial and commercial sectors. In 1835, however, the volume of Pfandbriefe in circulation, which had more than doubled since the beginning of the century, stopped growing and remained about the same for a decade.[4]

It is obvious that, despite increased mobility of capital, the continental

[1] On Germany, see the important article by Knut Borchardt, 'Zur Frage des Kapitalmangels in der ersten Hälfte des 19. Jahrhunderts in Deutschland', *Jahrbücher für Nationalökonomie und Statistik*, CLXXIII (1961), 401-21, which argues, in large part from the low rate of interest on funds and best commercial paper, that capital was relatively abundant.

[2] See the analysis in his *La banque et le crédit en France de 1815 à 1848* [Mémoires et documents publiés par la Société de l'Ecole des Chartes, vol. XIV] (Paris, 1959), pp. 349 ff., especially p. 358.

[3] Note, however, that some of the funds lent by Landschaften went to manufacturing enterprises borrowing on their land; and that some were invested by landowners in industry. Cf. Bergenroth, 'Ueber deutsche Anstalten zur Förderung des Kredits', *Zeitschrift des Vereins für deutsche Statistik*, I (1847), 753-4.

[4] Value of Pfandbriefe of Prussian Landschaften in circulation:

1805	53,891,638 thaler	1835	100,915,598 thaler
1815	62,677,898 thaler	1845	103,339,223 thaler
1825	83,141,365 thaler	1855	118,353,373 thaler

C. F. W. Dieterici, *Handbuch der Statistik des preussischen Staats* (Berlin, 1861), pp. 574-5. I am indebted to Prof. Hans Rosenberg for this reference.

countries had less to work with than Britain. On the other hand, their very weaknesses in this area led them to an innovation that was to give them eventually a real advantage over their precursor: the joint-stock investment bank. The effectiveness of this institution lay in its combination of capital resources, larger by far than those of merchant or private banks, and great freedom of action. The pioneer here was Belgium, with its Société Générale and Banque de Belgique, both investors on a large scale in mining and heavy industry. The precocious development of the Belgian coal industry—in the 1840's the biggest on the Continent—and the efficiency of its iron and machine industries—the only ones able to compete to some extent with the British—owed much to this injection of outside capital.[1]

France and Germany accomplished less in this area, the former largely because of official hostility, the latter partly for that reason, partly because the very shortage of capital that called for such institutions was still too serious to permit their establishment. The French brought forth a number of substitutes in the form of joint-stock partnerships (the so-called *caisses*). Visionaries and businessmen of both countries talked excitedly of the need for credit banks to finance industrial development: propagandists like the Saint-Simonians and bankers like Jacques Laffitte in France; Mevissen, Camphausen, Hansemann, and the rest of their Rhenish circle in Germany. By the 1840's, the stage was set in both places for a financial revolution; owing to depression and political upset, however, it was not to come until the following decade.[2]

In the meantime, the scarcity of capital in France and Germany was eased by flows from two sources. There was, to begin with, a certain amount of government investment and subvention of the traditional variety. This was much diminished, however, especially in France, where the budget-balancing governments of the Monarchie Censitaire concentrated almost all of their development expenditures on public works. In Germany, the state gave more generously to industry. The most active agency in this regard was the Prussian Seehandlung, which, under the direction of Christian von Rother, invested not only in the seaborne trade covered by its nomenclature, but also in roads, railways, and a variety of manufacturing enterprises. It was the Seehandlung, for example, that financed in 1842 Prussia's first mill to weave worsted by power, at Wüste Giersdorf. By the 1840's this

[1] P. Schöller, 'La transformation économique de la Belgique de 1832 à 1844', *Bull. de l'Institut de Recherches Economiques et Sociales* (Louvain), XIV (1958), 525–96.
[2] See D. Landes, 'Vieille banque et banque nouvelle: la révolution financière du dix-neuvième siècle', *Revue d'histoire moderne et contemporaine*, III (1956), 204–22.

policy of industrial promotion was under sharp attack, on the grounds
that it was prejudicial to unsubsidized private enterprise and that it did
not pay. The last reproach was true enough, although Rother argued
that an official institute of this kind, whose primary aim was national
development, should not be judged by ordinary criteria of profit and
loss. Nevertheless, under pecuniary and political pressures, the Seehandlung divested itself of almost all its industrial holdings by the
mid-1850's.[1]

The Belgian pattern was closer to the German than to the French.
In the Dutch period especially, the government gave generously to
private industry, partly through a special Industrial Fund, partly through
such corporate organisms as the Société Générale, already mentioned,
and the Société de Commerce. In the years from 1824 to 1830, the
Fund lent 5,821,052 florins to shipbuilding. About four-fifths of the
money went to the Belgian provinces.[2] This solicitude was motivated
largely by political considerations: the government was anxious to
placate the south, whose nationalistic resentment of Dutch rule was
exacerbated by commercial policies more favourable to the trade of
Holland than to the industry of Wallonia and Flanders.

After 1830 the flow of direct subsidies and investments continued,
though less abundant than before. The new government made a special
effort to assist the cotton and linen industries, both suffering from the
competition of cheap British textiles. In general, however, the regime
reacted sharply against the irregularities that had marked the management of the Industrial Fund and preferred to let private institutions
like the Société Générale and the Banque de Belgique assume the
burden of industrial finance.

It is always difficult to assess the contribution of such aids and subventions. Where they furthered the growth of demonstrably successful
enterprises—as with Cockerill in Belgium, Jackson in France, or the
Egells machine shops in Berlin—they may well have hastened technological change by freeing talented entrepreneurs from the limitations
of impecuniosity. But too often, the state seems to have chosen the
wrong enterprises or the wrong entrepreneurs and to have permitted by
its assistance sloppy performance. And sometimes it was clearly on the
side of reaction, as in Belgium, where hundreds of thousands of francs
went to sustain an antiquated, unviable linen manufacture in the
Flemish countryside.[3]

[1] Henderson, *The State and the Industrial Revolution in Prussia*, ch. vii.
[2] R. Demoulin, *Guillaume Ier et la transformation économique des provinces Belges,
1815–1830* (Liège and Paris, 1938), p. 179.
[3] Cf. G. Jacquemyns, *Histoire de la crise économique des Flandres, 1845–1850* (Brussels,
1929), pp. 173–93.

More useful, perhaps, in the long run, was the flow of funds from Britain to the Continent, which grew steadily as capital accumulated in the United Kingdom and reached a high point during the railway boom of the 1840's. Most of this went into government securities and public works, in France more than any other country. But substantial amounts went farther east, and these were augmented after a while by French and Belgian capital, attracted not only by higher returns but also by the abundant mineral resources of countries less experienced in the ways of industrial capitalism—witness the development of non-ferrous metallurgy in the Rhineland.

Unfortunately, we know relatively little as yet about these early capital movements. It seems clear, however, that they were more complex than one might think, and that there was a substantial amount of return investment from Germany and eastern Europe, particularly in the funds of western governments. Moreover, the criss-cross of flows, in so far as we can follow it, leaves the distinct impression that it was enterprise and opportunity that drew the capital rather than the reverse. Thus this same movement of German investment into British, French, and Belgian funds slowed down markedly once railway promotion and industrial development began competing for capital; whereas French investors and financiers—who early found it difficult to place their money in home enterprise owing to institutional and material limitations on growth and the repugnance of family entrepreneurs for outside assistance—were among the first and most active in financing the development of poorer nations to the east and south.

We may now turn to the technological evolution of the major industries on the Continent. Here, as before, we shall begin with the textile manufacture, although for reasons to be examined later, its place in the overall transition to a factory system was less important on the mainland than in Britain.

Two preliminary remarks are in order. First, the sequence of technological change was different on the two sides of the Channel. Where in Britain the new machines spread in cotton far more rapidly than in wool, on the Continent the interruption of the supply of raw cotton during the Napoleonic period and the sharp increase in the military demand for woollen cloth temporarily reversed the order. It was two clothiers of Verviers who brought John Cockerill to the Low Countries to build spinning machinery; and it was the wool manufacturers of France, Spain, and the Germanies who bought the bulk of the equipment produced under the Empire by Cockerill and rivals like Douglas in Paris or Spineux in Liège. Within a decade after Waterloo, however, the return to peaceful trade relations and the natural susceptibility of the vegetable fibre to mechanical manipulation restored the cotton industry to its earlier technological pre-eminence. It was never to lose its lead again.

Second, there was nothing on the Continent comparable to the rapidity of British localization of manufacture in one, perhaps two, naturally advantaged centres: Lancashire and the Glasgow area in cotton; the West Riding of Yorkshire in woollen and worsted. In countries like France and Germany, the textile manufacture was highly dispersed to begin with. In the course of the nineteenth century, the transformation of technique and the triumph of factory manufacture were accompanied in each by a steady but slow localization of production in a handful of centres—not one, but three or four. The less efficient, smaller *fabriques*, moreover, proved surprisingly tenacious; it took a cotton famine, tariff changes, and the Great Depression of 1873–96 to kill even the weakest of them off. Finally, in so far as manufacture did thrive more in certain regions than in others, material advantages seem to have been a less important determinant of success than in Britain; human factors, especially entrepreneurship, played a decisive role.

In France the great bulk of the cotton industry lay north of the Loire. In 1815 there was still a major concentration of spindles and looms in Paris itself, but these firms faded quickly—the capital, with its high costs of land, labour, and raw materials, was no place for cotton mills.[1] By 1830 the map of the industry had taken on the appearance it was to keep for the rest of the century: heavy patches of enterprise in Normandy (centre Rouen), the North (Lille and Roubaix-Tourcoing), and the East (Alsace and the Vosges); and scattered dots throughout the rest of the country, with occasional clusters in places like Dauphiné or the Cholet area where cheap labour compensated somewhat for poor location and poor entrepreneurship.

Of the big three, the most progressive was Alsace, in particular the region around Mulhouse. There the industry grew out of cotton printing; the finished product was of high quality, competitive in foreign markets; the fortunes accumulated in this field, plus funds advanced by capitalists of Basel, enabled the entrepreneurs of the area to build large spinning and weaving mills almost from the start. Moreover, the Mulhousian industrialist, usually a dedicated Calvinist of the Weberian type, early evinced considerable initiative in improving technique, especially the chemistry of dyes; this interest in rationalizing the finishing process carried over to the other stages of manufacture when the industry integrated backwards.

[1] See David Pinkey, 'Paris, capitale du coton sous le Premier Empire', *Annales: E.S.C.*, v (1950), 56–60.

The Mulhousians began comparatively late—the first mill using mules and throstles was built apparently in 1802; the fly shuttle was unknown before 1805. Growth was rapid, however:

Table 44. *Cotton Manufacture: Department of the Haut-Rhin*

	Spindles	Hand looms	Power looms
1786	—	c. 1,900	—
1806	—	1,900	—
1809	24,000	—	—
1811	—	3,600	—
1812	48,000	—	—
1822	—	18–20,000	—
1826	—	30,000	—
1827	—	—	426
1828	466,000	—	—
1831	—	—	2,123
1834	—	31,000	3,090
1839	—	—	6,000
1844	—	19,000	12,000
1849	786,000	—	—
1856	—	8,657	18,139

SOURCES. Ch. Ballot, *L'introduction du machinisme dans l'industrie française* (Paris, 1923), pp. 150–2; A. Penot, 'Notes pour servir à l'histoire de l'industrie cotonnière dans le Haut-Rhin', *Bull. Soc. Indust. de Mulhouse*, XLIV (1874), 167–8.

As can be seen from the figures on hand and power looms, expansion and technological advance went hand in hand. In spinning the most rapid gains in productivity occurred between 1815 and 1830 (replacement of water frames and hand mules by power-driven mules), and from 1855 to 1870 (adoption of the self-actor); in weaving, it was the period in between that saw the decisive shift from hand looms to power. The timing reminds one of the alternating imbalance between spinning and weaving in the British cotton industry. The readiness of the Alsatian manufacturer to invest in up-to-date equipment owed much to the development of a creative local machine-construction industry. By the 1840's Mulhouse had become a centre of mechanical invention and was exporting mules and looms in competition with Britain throughout Europe.

In some ways, the pattern of development in the North was similar to that of Alsace: growth was impressively rapid; technology, well above average; entrepreneurship, dedicated and yet supple. Like his counterpart in the East, the northerner was a production man.

There were, however, important differences. The northerner was not so rich as the Alsatian: he had less wealth of his own, less access to the wealth of others, and was less willing to introduce foreign capital into the enterprise. The result was a smaller scale of production: where the average cotton mill in the Haut-Rhin counted 14,375 spindles in 1845, the figure for Lille in 1848 was 7,040; for Tourcoing in 1844, 4,000. Capacity for the department as a whole rose from about 112,000 spindles in 1818 to some 550,000 in 1849, of which 128,000 were in Roubaix and 60,000 in Tourcoing.

Technologically, the North was in some ways ahead of Alsace. Owing to the shortage of water, it was never able to use hydraulic power; there was hardly enough water even for the steam-engine, which did not come in until 1819. Nevertheless, there was clearly no alternative, and steam capacity rose faster than in the East. Similarly, the self-actor was introduced in Roubaix on a large scale in 1843—18,000 spindles in the plant of Motte-Bossut—and was starting to spread by mid-century. On the other hand, the weaving of cotton was somewhat neglected in the North, which exported most of its yarn to other parts of the country or twisted it into thread; as a result, the power loom was adopted quite late—there is evidence of a few around 1845, but they did not really come in until the mid-1850's.

The largest, yet most backward, of the major cotton centres was Normandy. It was the oldest and best located: convenient to the Paris market and overseas; rich in water power; close to the point of entry of the raw material. Rural labour was almost as cheap as in the North. As might be expected, however, these very advantages were a deterrent to technological change, the more so as they compensated, hence encouraged, a kind of inbred entrepreneurial conservatism. The *cotonniers* of the area were notorious for their penny-pinching and short-sighted avidity; the Alsatians looked down upon them as merchants and speculators rather than as industrialists. They were among the first groups to try the mule, yet were the slowest to improve their machines and replace them by later models. They were late in adopting steam power, primarily because water was so cheap, but also because steam-engines cost a lot of money and the Norman was reluctant to sink so much into his business. In 1847 there were still eighty-three mills in the area driven by hand or animal power; eighteen of these contained over ten thousand spindles each.[1] The use of such techniques had, so far as we know, disappeared in Alsace and the North. The availability of cheap water power was also a deterrent to innovation in other equipment; one of the reasons the self-actor was adopted so late—it was first coming in around 1860—was that it called for more power than water wheels could provide, and thus imposed a shift to steam.

[1] Claude Fohlen, *L'industrie textile au temps du Second Empire* (Paris, 1956), p. 193.

In the meantime, cheap cotton and power helped the industry expand in these early decades before the self-actor. The last years of the Empire and the first of the Restoration were wretched: continental blockade, commercial crisis and, finally, the inundation of long-pent-up British cottons reduced the number of active spindles from a high of almost 400,000 in 1808 in the Seine-Inférieure to 98,000 in 1818. In the next decade and a half, however, years of prohibition of foreign yarn and cloth, the number decupled; in 1834 there were 960,000. And by 1847 there were 1,200,000, plus several hundred thousand in the Eure.

As fast as spinning capacity grew in this area, weaving outstripped it. Around 1860 tens of thousands of full-time rural workers (estimated at from 30,000 to 50,000) in Normandy itself, as well as an almost equal number of part-time weavers in Picardy and Artois, processed all the local yarn and more.[1] Wages were extremely low; workers were easily hired and fired with fluctuations in trade, and the availability of a reserve pool of labour in other regions was an enormous convenience to the manufacturer. Little wonder that the power loom did not make serious inroads until the 1850's and 1860's.[2]

There are a number of general points to be made about French cotton technology in this first half of the century. First, the range of efficiency from one region to another, or even within regions, was very wide; as backward as Normandy was, it was far ahead of the small centres of the West and South. There are instances of northern firms selling their discarded equipment to silk enterprises of Lyon, which, after getting all possible use out of them, sold them in turn to mills in places like Nîmes, where the cotton manufacture was a generation behind the times. 'Everyone remembers,' wrote Jules Simon, 'the obsolete mules of M. Jean Dolfus [Dollfus, one of the leading manufacturers of Mulhouse], which he wanted to sell as scrap and which, to his great astonishment, were bought as mules and functioned for a long time in the Vosges.'[3]

Second, this range of technique, which was explained above by divers market and entrepreneurial considerations, does not follow the usual pattern. One would expect those enterprises specializing in cheaper goods of standard quality to be the first to mechanize. Yet in

---

[1] A. Corneille, *La Seine-Inférieure commerciale et industrielle* (Rouen, 1873), pp. 185, 195 ff., gives 60,000 hand looms for this department alone in the late 1860's. Some of these, however, were used for linen manufacture.

[2] About ten thousand in 1859. Alphonse Cordier, *Exposé de la situation du coton et des produits chimiques dans la Seine-Inférieure et l'Eure, 1859–1869* (Rouen, 1869), pp. 116–23.

[3] J. Simon, *L'ouvrière* (4th ed., Paris, 1862), p. 101. Cf. Claude Fohlen, *Une affaire de famille au XIXe siècle*: Méquillet-Noblot (Paris, n.d. [1955]), pp. 30, 45–6.

France such firms were usually the most backward. It was Normandy that was known for coarse cottons, much of it used in the manufacture of working clothes; places like Flers and Laval turned out ticking; Cholet specialized in cotton handkerchiefs and fustians for domestic use.[1] By contrast, Alsace and the North not only turned out the finer fabrics, but early devoted much of their effort to what the French call *tissus de fantaisie*. In both regions, the enterprise aimed at diversification and flexibility rather than specialization; the result was short runs that helped raise unit costs substantially above those of comparable mills in Britain. This was especially true of the northern firms and no doubt explains in part their delay in adopting the power loom.

Why this inversion of the usual relationship between price of good and mechanization? The answer would seem to be partly historical, partly social. For one thing, under the conditions of hand manufacture—in the eighteenth century, for example—there was no doubt more profit in the manufacture of more costly products. Not only was the margin per unit greater, but only the fabric that was somewhat better than the home-made article could compete in more than a local market. It was the merchant-manufacturers of the better cloth who accumulated the wealth that built the mills of the industrial revolution. For another, and partly as a result of the first, there was traditionally much more prestige attached to the production of quality products—prestige reinforced by government policy from Colbert on. The exact importance of this consideration is hard to assess, but it was not negligible: we have instances of northern firms making their fortunes in cheap cloth and then abandoning it to turn to fashion fabrics. Finally, and paradoxically, technological considerations often made it inadvisable to mechanize the production of cheaper articles. One must distinguish here between coarseness and standardization; where the latter was always a spur to mechanization, the former sometimes had the opposite effect. Thus in the early days of power weaving, when machine looms were not much quicker than skilled craftsmen, it cost less to turn out a coarse fabric by hand: the thicker the yarn, the smaller the proportion of labour required for weaving proper, as against that employed in still unmechanized processes like dressing the warp.

In general, the French cotton industry continued to lag far behind that of Britain. Plants were smaller; machines were older, less efficient;[2]

---

[1] On the analogous pattern in Germany, F. O. Dilthey, *Die Geschichte der niederrheinischen Baumwollindustrie* (Jena, 1908), pp. 18–19.

[2] In 1848 the effort of the spinners of the North to introduce spinning machines of 480–600 spindles aroused sharp labour resistance. The British manufacturers had fought and won the battle to install the so-called long mules of 1000 spindles in the 1820's.

even allowing for differences in equipment, labour was less productive. It was a high-cost industry, unable except for certain enterprises in Mulhouse to compete outside the country. It profited in the first half of the century from growing wealth and population at home and the opening of overseas markets like Algeria. (See Table 44 a.) But its expansion, which rested on the exclusion of competition, was paid for in slower overall economic growth; and with few exceptions, enterprise was inordinately cautious, even sluggish.

Nevertheless, France was the most important manufacturer of cotton goods on the Continent. The Belgian industry, active early in Napoleon's reign, was hard hit by the continental blockade and the inrush of British goods at the end of the Empire, then suffered from low protection under Dutch rule. The producers complained bitterly, and indeed output fluctuated widely from boom to crisis and back again; thus the make of yarn in eastern Flanders, including the main centre of Ghent, went from 443 tons in 1806, to 693 in 1810, down to 374 in 1817, then up to 1720 in 1826. For all these uncertainties, capacity more than doubled—from 129,000 mule spindles in 1810 to 300,000 in 1829. Separation from Holland brought new difficulties: the colonial market, such as it was, disappeared, and home demand was cut almost in half. From 1829 to 1839, spindlage in the Ghent area actually dropped from 300,000 to 250,000. Yet this purge seems only to have strengthened the industry by eliminating the least efficient enterprises. During the same years, output of yarn in eastern Flanders rose to 4500 tons, and this trend continued into the forties. By 1846 there were perhaps 360,000 spindles in the kingdom, producing about 6500 tons of yarn, or 18 kg. per spindle. Compare this with the 5·4 kg. per spindle of 1810 and remember that owing to the increasing fineness of the product, the machines had to work that much faster to turn out a given weight of yarn.

The weaving sector seems to have done even better than spinning, largely because British yarn was available at low cost and the producers were ready to shift over to power. Machine looms, first adopted around 1825, numbered 700 in 1830, 2900 in 1839, 3500 in 1845-6. By that time hand weaving had disappeared entirely in Ghent, though it persisted in the countryside. In part the completeness of this transition was due to the usual difficulty of compelling performance by cottage workers; in part, interestingly enough, it was a reaction to the poor quality of hand work, itself no doubt a consequence of the frictions inherent in putting-out.

Weaving was only one of several areas in which the Belgian cotton manufacture was more modern than the French. North of the border, with coal cheap and water dear, the steam-engine rapidly displaced all

Table 44 a. *Consumption of Raw Cotton in Western Europe, 1815–1850*
(in metric tons)

	Great Britain	France	Belgium	Zollverein
1815	36,932	—	—	—
1816	40,245	—	1,349	—
1817	48,956	—	811	—
1818	49,864	—	1,788	—
1819	49,684	—	2,198	—
1820	54,582	—	1,100	—
1821	58,530	—	1,970	—
1822	66,011	—	2,245	—
1823	69,918	—	2,054	—
1824	74,955	—	1,175	—
1825	75,680	—	2,372	—
1826	68,149	—	3,213	—
1827	89,473	—	3,115	—
1828	98,866	—	2,311	—
1829	99,455	—	4,804	—
1830	112,341	—	3,016	—
1831	119,192	28,217	971	—
1832	125,634	33,623	2,435	2,422
1833	130,217	35,534	3,071	1,814
1834	137,657	36,881	2,032	7,536
1835	144,327	38,712	4,784	4,498
1836	157,620	44,294	6,673	7,618
1837	165,923	43,789	6,978	10,219
1838	189,062	51,173	6,853	8,996
1839	173,182	40,301	4,053	6,823
1840	208,208	52,812	9,049	12,835
1841	198,771	55,689	7,508	11,148
1842	197,410	57,141	6,107	12,145
1843	235,294	59,584	7,482	15,336
1844	247,181	58,506	6,680	13,310
1845	275,582	60,377	8,452	17,048
1846	279,076	63,952	4,823	16,008
1847	200,631	45,191	6,807	13,830
1848	262,153	44,760	6,924	15,427
1849	286,335	63,903	10,709	19,815
1850	222,046	59,273	7,222	17,117

SOURCES. United Kingdom: Ellison, *Cotton Trade*, table no. 1; France: *Annuaire statistique*, LVII (1946), résumé rétrospectif, p. 241*; Belgium: 1816–1830, from Robert Demoulin, *Guillaume Ier et la transformation économique des provinces belges*, p. 423 (I am indebted to Prof. L. Dupriez for calling my attention to this source); for the years after 1830, from Min. des Finances, *Tableau général du commerce de la Belgique avec les pays étrangers pendant les années 1831, 1832, 1833 et 1834*, and subsequent volumes (Brussels, 1835–); Zollverein: K. F. W. Dieterici, *Statistische Uebersicht der wichtigsten Gegenstände des Verkehrs und Verbrauchs im preussischen und im deutschen Zollverbande* [title varies] (6 vols.; Berlin, 1838–57), *passim*.

other sources of power; by the mid-1840's the process was complete. The self-actor came in about the same time: in 1845–6, there were three mills (of fifty-three) in the Ghent area using the new machines, which cut labour requirements by a half or more, markedly diminished the physical demands on the spinners, and by eliminating the rapidly swinging hand cranks of the old mules, removed a prolific source of accidents.[1]

In many ways, the German industry was comparable to that of Belgium in this period. Tariff protection was relatively low, though higher on the coarser yarns and fabrics. As a result, there was a substantial import from Britain; indeed, large numbers of rural weavers, traditionally occupied with linen, shifted over to cotton manufacture and rested their survival on cheap yarn from abroad. Nevertheless, domestic spinning took hold, particularly after the establishment of the *Zollverein* in 1833: in 1844 there were 815,000 'factory' spindles; in 1849, some 900,000. Consumption of raw cotton increased eightfold from the early 1830's to the late 1840's. Even so, the German industry was no more than a third, perhaps only a quarter as large as the French at the end of our period.

Structurally and technologically, however, the German industry was close to the French. It was dispersed, with concentrations in the Rhine valley, Saxony (the most important in the period before 1850), Silesia, and Bavaria. The typical enterprise was small, family-run; in Prussia, for example, the average spindlage was 828 in 1837, 1126 in 1846; in Saxony it fell from 4300 in 1830 to 4100 in 1845. As contemporaries put it, 'when a peasant or a miller was feeling too good, he built a cotton mill'.[2] Finally, the older centres gave evidence in this period of an extreme conservatism; Saxony in particular, endowed like Normandy with cheap water power, lost ground as it clung to outdated equipment and methods. The manufacturers of the Gladbach-Rheydt area (Rhineland) did not build their first up-to-date spinning mills

[1] On the Belgian cotton industry, see particularly Belgium, Ministère de l'Intérieur, *Enquête sur la condition des classes ouvrières et sur le travail des enfants* (3 vols.; Brussels, 1846–8), vol. III: Société de Médicine de Gand, *Enquête sur le travail et la condition physique et morale des ouvriers employés dans les manufactures de coton à Gand*; also L. Varlez, *Les salaires dans l'industrie gantoise*, I. *L'industrie cotonnière* (Brussels, 1901). Figures on output of yarn are from Demoulin, *Guillaume Ier*, p. 329; and Belgium, Min. de l'Intérieur, *Exposé de la situation du Royaume...de 1851 à 1860*, vol. III (Brussels, 1865), p. 148. The great bulk of the Belgian factory cotton industry was concentrated at Ghent.

[2] 'Wenn ein Bauer oder ein Müller sich zu wohl fühlte, baute er eine Spinnerei.' G. Schmoller, *Zur Geschichte der deutschen Kleingewerbe im 19. Jahrhundert* (Halle, 1870), p. 455. The spindlage figures are taken from the same work, p. 162. For the Zollverein as a whole, the average was 2740 spindles in 1844. Germany, *Amtlicher Bericht über die Industrie-Ausstellung aller Völker zu London im Jahre 1851*, II, 21.

until the 1840's. Up to then, such mills as were founded operated on the so-called 'French' system, based on the British machinery of the 1780's as adapted and diffused on the Continent under the Empire. Only the preparatory cleaning and carding engines were power driven, sometimes by water, sometimes by animals; the final spinning was accomplished by hand mules. Some plants did no more than prepare the raw cotton for the traditional wheel; as late as 1858 there were still eight roving machines supplying cottage spinners.

In the 1840's a new generation of entrepreneurs founded joint-stock companies to build and operate large factories of the British type. These were not very successful; few survived the depression that marked the last part of the decade. For a while it seemed as though their unhappy example would serve to discourage others. In fact, however, they were accurate harbingers: the trend toward concentrated manufacture by corporate enterprise resumed in the 1850's, beginning in south-west Germany, where Swiss capital found a fertile soil. Thus in Baden, the average mill increased in size from 73 to 110 employees from 1849 to 1861. Where there were only two steam-engines (130 h.p.) in the cotton industry of the Grand Duchy in 1847, in 1861, the occasion of the first industrial census of the *Zollverein*, there were 46 (1160 h.p.). At the same time, spindlage doubled, from 155,000 to 296,000; power looms increased from 1960 to 5190 (22 per cent of the *Zollverein* total); while hand looms in mills fell off from 2535 to 391 (3 per cent of the *Zollverein*).[1]

It is instructive to contrast the Swiss and German cotton manufactures in this period. Until 1850 the Swiss had no tariff on foreign yarn or cloth, their only protection being the cost of transport from Lancashire or closer centres like Alsace. For British goods, this was already a substantial obstacle, though probably not so great as the combined barrier of freight charges and customs duties that shielded the German and Belgian manufacturers.

In spite—or more correctly, because—of this, the Swiss cotton industry thrived and stood at mid-century as one of the most modern on the Continent, comparable in equipment and method to those of Alsace and Belgium. Manufacturers were compelled to turn out a competitive product. Fortunately they had the means to do so. On the one hand, Switzerland was unusually well endowed for light industry. She possessed in her rapid streams a cheap source of power that enabled a small entrepreneur to undertake machine spinning with a minimum of capital. Most of her mills began, as in Britain, as small carding and mule shops, the work of putters-out or of weavers who had managed to set a small

[1] Franz Kistler, *Die wirtschaftlichen und sozialen Verhältnisse in Baden 1849–1870* (Freiburg i. Br., 1954), p. 92.

sum aside over years of hand labour. And as in Britain, those with larger ambitions or insufficient resources could get support from a prosperous, active merchant class—Switzerland had long been the middleman between central Europe and the Mediterranean.

Many of these merchants were Calvinists, of native origin or descendants of refugees from the wars and persecutions of the lands to the west. Their membership in a cohesive, yet dispersed 'in-group' was a major commercial advantage: the Swiss merchant-banker had access to a wide-flung network of trustworthy correspondents, commanded in other words rapid, accurate intelligence on business conditions and opportunities.[1] Capital was abundant, so much so that by the end of the eighteenth century the bankers of Basel were financing some of the Alsatian cotton printers. (Switzerland was probably the first country on the Continent to invest substantial sums directly in foreign industry.)

As a result, the tiny spinning mills spawned by the continental blockade, with their handful of hand-operated mule jennies and their two or three dozen employees, had just about disappeared by the late 1830's. They had been sustained for a while by their easy access to rural weavers, but this advantage faded quickly before the competition of large, semi-automatic mules. As the number of firms diminished, spindlage increased from around 400,000 in 1830 to about a million in 1851; from 1827 to 1842, the average per firm in the canton of Zurich went from about 1900 to 4800. At the same time, the spinners learned to turn out ever-finer counts: by the early 1840's, about a third of the output was no. 60 and higher. At that point, Swiss mills were supplying all home requirements of coarse and medium yarn and beginning to look elsewhere for markets.

Mechanization was slower in weaving. Rural labour was cheap and it was hard to import good British equipment before 1842. As in Alsace, the weaving shed followed on the development of domestic machine manufacture. Thus, although the first power looms came in 1825 and the first weaving factory was established in 1830, the new technique did not catch on until the 1840's, when Caspar Honegger developed an improved loom and thereby founded an industry. At mid-century, there were an estimated three thousand power looms in operation.[2]

At the end of our period, therefore, the cotton manufacture on the

---

[1] On the advantages and success of Calvinist merchant-bankers, see D. S. Landes, *Bankers and Pashas: International Finance and Economic Imperialism in Egypt* (London, 1958), pp. 20–4, and the references cited there.

[2] Oscar Haegi, *Die Entwicklung der zürcheroberländischen Baumwollindustrie* (Weinfelden, 1925), p. 57; A. Jenny-Trümpy, art. 'Textilindustrie: a, Baumwollindustrie', in *Handwörterbuch der schweizerischen Volkswirtschaft, Sozialpolitik und Verwaltung*, ed. N. Reichesberg, vol. 3, II (1) (Bern, 1911), p. 889.

Continent was still strongly characterized by the dispersion and provincialism of the beginning. There were great international and interregional differences in productivity and skill, but these had not yet compelled the kind of concentration and rationalization that they implied. Technology was a generation or more behind that of Britain. For the moment, natural and artificial barriers protected local markets, and the general growth of population and wealth left room for all.

The woollen manufacture was, of course, even slower to mechanize, and this in spite of its early start. Here too, we find a pattern of dispersion and provincialism, and here too, the growing gap between progressive and backward centres.

In France, the leading firms were to be found in Roubaix (an impressive entrepreneurial achievement that involved shifting from cotton to wool), Reims, and, to a much smaller degree, Saint-Quentin and Elbeuf. There were also a few plants in Alsace, as usual among the most modern in the country. At the other end of the scale were the small residual centres of the south—Lodève, Carcassonne, Castres—and the specialists in luxury cloth—Sedan, Louviers, Paris. In general, the industry suffered from all the obstacles to technological advance inherent in the fibre, heightened in this case by special circumstances: the uneven and inferior quality of the raw wool employed, and the effort to turn out a great variety of fabrics and stimulate rapid shifts in fashion. This effort was, it should be noted, successful, and the manufacturers of the finer, softer fabrics earned international reputations; the British tried vainly for decades to imitate the French merino worsteds.

Historically, the first process mechanized was the spinning of woollen yarn; by the early 1820's, only the more backward regions spun carded wool on the wheel or jenny. Yet in the long run, the worsted spinners were to move far ahead, partly because of the greater resistance of combed wool to mechanical treatment, partly because the demand for the harder, lighter cloths was more elastic. There are isolated instances of machines in worsted spinning before 1820, but they did not really spread until the late 1820's and early 1830's; by the mid-1840's, over half a million spindles were in operation. As early as 1844, there were a few self-actors at Reims.

Weaving was another matter. The mechanical advantage of the power loom over the hand loom was even smaller than in cotton, and the variety of the finished product precluded long runs, increasing considerably labour cost per unit of output. Once again, it was Reims that seems to have introduced the new technique, in the 1840's; but power looms remained a rarity and their diffusion dates from the end of the next decade.

In what is now Belgium, wool manufacture was concentrated in and around Verviers, which we have already noted as a vigorous, forward-looking centre, well able to compete in distant markets and alert to changes in technique and fashion. Verviers had prospered enormously under Napoleon, thanks to the widening of the market and the heavy government demand for woollen cloth. The dissolution of the Empire, however, hurt all the more, and the injury was compounded, as it was for the cotton industry of Ghent, by the pro-commercial tariff policy of the Netherlands. Nevertheless, capacity and output rose, to the point where a number of firms over-extended themselves; the crisis of 1830 brought the greatest harvest of failures in history. In the mid-1830's, the expansion resumed, owing in large part to a shift from standard cloth [drap] to novelty stuffs and mixed fabrics; this was the path that Roubaix-Tourcoing, Reims, and the other French centres were taking. All in all, an impressive achievement; yet growth was not so rapid as in Roubaix or even Elbeuf: statistics indicate an increase from 35,000 to 64,000 pieces between 1809 and 1852. Woollen yarn output seems to have grown faster—from 11,300 to 25,000 kg. between 1842 and 1849 alone.[1]

Although Verviers was the first wool centre on the Continent to use machines, it did not maintain its technological advance. Not until 1818 was the mule introduced—hand-driven, wooden devices of 120–180 spindles each—and it was not until the 1860's that the self-actor came in; further, it would seem that the true throstle [continu saxon] was not adopted until around 1840. Worsted spinning was even slower to develop, in part perhaps because there was no local market for the yarn. In 1822 Mme Biolley, one of those legendary woman entrepreneurs who seem to be a by-product of the continental family firm, founded the first mill for the working of combed wool. It was a commercial success, but was slow to develop technically—the mules employed in 1840 had only 40 spindles each—and did not mark the beginning of a trend. When, in 1870, Verviers began to weave worsteds, it was compelled at first to import the yarn from Roubaix. As in the cotton industry of Ghent, the quickest gains came in the use of steam power; the river Vesdre was already inadequate for the fulling mills of the area by the late eighteenth century. The first engine was installed in 1816, and by 1845, of 214 in the province of Liège, 99 were used in the woollen manufacture, and 68 of these were at Verviers.

The wool industry had never been strong in Germany. As in

---

[1] Apparently these figures refer to the city alone, and not the area. J. S. Renier, *Histoire de l'industrie drapière au pays de Liège et particulièrement dans l'arrondissement de Verviers* (Liège, 1881), p. 108; Lebrun, 'La rivoluzione industriale', *Studi storici*, II (1961), 606 n. 51.

Belgium, linen was the popular fabric: it was far cheaper than wool, and flax was cultivated everywhere. The statistician Dieterici, who estimated *per capita* consumption of wool around 1800 as half an ell a year, wrote: 'It is notorious how poor in woollen clothing the rural populace, in other words, the mass of the nation, were before 1806. The woollen coat of the peasant had to hold out many years, and servants and day labourers often appeared before the landlords and on court days in the coldest winter in linen blouses.'[1]

In such a situation, the introduction of mechanical spinning and weaving profited primarily the cotton industry, which—aside from its technical affinity for machinery—produced the poor man's substitute for linen cloth. Two of Germany's outstanding statisticians estimated consumption per head of the three principal fabrics in 1849 as follows: wool, 1 ell; linen, 5 ells; cotton, 16 ells.[2] With the supply of the raw material inelastic and demand weak, the wool industry grew slowly, clinging the while to antiquated techniques.

The jenny came in toward the beginning of the century and spread easily among the more well-to-do drapers, who found this a fairly cheap way to secure the bulk of their yarn requirements within the shop. The usual enterprise could and did get along with only two or three of these devices. Mechanization did not constitute therefore an immediate threat to the hand spinners in rural areas; where the peasant wove, he spun, and some of the knitting and hosiery yarn continued to be made on the wheel right past the middle of the century.

There were, to be sure, a few centres of factory manufacture— Aachen, Monschau, Reichenbach and other towns of the Saxon Vogtland, Augsburg, Kottbus. But the word 'factory' is probably too grandiose. Most plants were no more than large shops attached to a putting-out weaving operation. The equipment comprised some preparatory machinery and a jenny or two; average spindlage in Prussia in 1837 was only 103. The largest firms were in the Aachen area (around 1000 spindles in 1843), Saxony (570 in 1837), and Silesia.

The major deterrents to the development of large-scale machine industry were the extraordinary cheapness of labour and the pressure of British competition. Most small firms rested their survival on the development of a speciality not produced abroad; the effect was to place a ceiling on demand and constrict the opportunities for growth. The official German commission at the Crystal Palace Exposition criticized their countrymen for their lack of imagination, their persistence in making a given style of cloth. And yet the 1840's had seen sundry new factories, large by German standards, very modest by British.

[1] Cited by Schmoller, *Deutschen Kleingewerbe*, p. 473.
[2] *Amtlicher Bericht* (cited above, p. 395, n. 2), II, 86–7.

Alongside these the small, shop-like mills found themselves in difficulty. Their rough product looked poor by comparison with the highly finished fabrics of the larger, more experienced centres, and with improvements in transport, the local market was no longer an isolated preserve. Confronted with falling sales, the small manufacturer tried the traditional remedy—adulteration. He cut prices, but gave thinner, poorly fulled and shorn cloth for the money—which only increased his difficulties. Long before the machine loom sealed his fate, he was on his way out, and with him his tiny spinning shop. Between 1837 and 1849 average spindlage in Prussia more than doubled, from 103 to 235; by 1861 it was up to 592. The largest mills were still in Silesia (average 784), the kingdom of Saxony (914), and the Rhineland (1246). For the *Zollverein* as a whole, with 1,117,870 spindles, the mean was 629, representing perhaps half-a-dozen machines; the average work force was 15—a far cry from the West Riding.

By contrast with the woollen manufacture, which drew on a supply of domestic wool more than sufficient to its needs, the German worsted industry suffered from a lack of long-fibre wool suitable for combing. Moreover the reverse of these circumstances, that is, the availability of home-grown long wool, made British yarn almost unbeatable and seriously discouraged German ambitions of competition. In 1840 there were 56,258 worsted spindles in Prussia, as against 380,839 woollen. By 1846 the number had actually shrunk to 32,470, distributed among 253 enterprises; the average of 128 per firm was equal to the capacity of three jennies or a pair of small hand mules. Saxony did better: she had 14 mills in 1836–7, averaging 1400 spindles; a quarter-century later, there were 39 and the mean size had almost doubled, to 2680. For Germany as a whole, Viebahn estimates worsted spindlage in 1845 at about 300,000. This presumably includes cottage wheels and jennies; otherwise one is confronted with a serious overall decline to the 252,000 factory spindles of 1861.[1] Yet such a contraction is not inconceivable. Increasingly in these years, the German wool manufacture relied on foreign yarn, imports of which rose from an insignificant amount in 1836, to 53,000 cwt. in 1850, and 213,000 cwt. in 1864. Most of this was English combed yarn; and if we generously estimate the consumption of worsted yarn at one-half that of woollen yarn, these imports already accounted for about a quarter of the supply of the weavers of worsted and mixed cloths by the middle of the century. By the early 1860's, when the domestic output of worsted yarn ran about 110,000 cwt.

---

[1] [G. W. von Viebahn], *Amtlicher Bericht über die allgemeine deutsche Gewerbe-Ausstellung zu Berlin im Jahre 1844* (3 vols.; Berlin, 1845), I, 174–93, especially p. 185; Idem, *Statistik des zollvereinten und nördlichen Deutschlands* (3 vols.; pagin. cont.; Berlin, 1858–68), pp. 885–8.

a year, imports probably supplied over half the requirements of the industry.

The stagnation or decay of much of the German worsted yarn manufacture and the small scale of production betray the technological backwardness of the industry. Which was cause and which effect, would be hard to say. Probably the influences worked both ways. In any event, hand spinning, which seemed on its way out in the thirties, got a new lease on life when English yarn prices rose in the forties, and survived in the countryside past the middle of the century on the cheap labour of old men, women and children. Weaving, as might be expected, was even slower to change. The power loom, which came in woollens in the early 1830's, in worsted at Wüste Giersdorf (Silesia) under semi-official auspices in 1843, remained a rarity until the 1850's. Prussia had some 1200 of them in woollen and worsted in 1849, as against 26,700 hand looms.[1] For a long time they offered little pecuniary advantage, though they did weave a tighter, more regular cloth and found use in the manufacture of simple, solid fabrics.

Because of this relatively small margin between new and old techniques, the penalties of obsolescence were far lighter in weaving than spinning. More important than equipment were the style and finish of the fabric, and these depended on the skills and taste of labour and management. Whereas the Germans imported an increasing share of their yarn from abroad, their exports of cloth throve: that of woollens tripled from 1836 to 1864, when it represented perhaps two-thirds of total output; in an even shorter period, from 1843 to 1864, that of worsteds rocketed from 313 to 108,082 cwt. Viebahn was anxious for the spinning branch, which clearly was one of the weak points of German industry. But he could be well pleased with the cloth manufacture: 'Even if the English still have an advantage in many strong and solid articles, or the French in a few very fine and patterned fabrics, the German wool industry still stands in its specialities at the head of this branch of civilization.'[2]

As in textiles, so in heavy industry the first half of the century saw, not a transformation of techniques as in Britain, but a slow, spasmodic diffusion of new methods alongside the old. There were, however,

[1] A. Wache, *Die volkswirtschaftliche Bedeutung der technischen Entwicklung der deutschen Wollindustrie* (Leipzig, 1909), p. 81; Schmoller, *Deutschen Kleingewerbe*, p. 523. For the *Zollverein* as a whole, there were 2592 power looms in woollen mills in 1861, as against 11,818 hand looms; 3655 power looms in worsted mills, as against 9068; plus 67,343 hand looms in cottages and shops. O. Schwarz, 'Die Betriebsformen der modernen Grossindustrie', *Zeitschrift für die gesamte Staatswissenschaft*, xxv (1869), 580.
[2] Viebahn, *Statistik*, pp. 917–18, 921, 923.

major differences. In metallurgy as against light manufactures, material factors—availability and quality of resources, costs of transportation—were of critical importance. Good entrepreneurship often seems to have been a decisive advantage in textiles: how else explain the success of such centres as Mulhouse, the Roubaix-Tourcoing area, or Krefeld—or, for that matter, Brno or Lodz—which were not significantly favoured by nature or were even worse situated than less prosperous competitors? In iron-making, however, cheap ore and coal could cover a multitude of sins, and all the ingenuity in the world could not compensate for their absence.

Furthermore, the shift in the continental iron industry from old to new techniques took place under special external stimulation. Thus the improvement of transportation did much more to promote industries producing commodities of great weight and volume in proportion to value than light manufactures. At the same time, demand grew more rapidly (that is, the demand curve shifted farther to the right) for industries whose market grew not only with the increase in population and wealth but also with the general change in technology: the substitution of mineral for plant fuel, of metal for wooden machinery; the use of iron pipe for gas, water, and sewage; the diffusion of the steam-engine; the coming of the railroad. In Britain, the Industrial Revolution had been built on the cotton manufacture, which grew more rapidly than other branches of industry before 1800 and drew them with it. On the Continent, it was heavy industry—coal and iron —that was the leading sector. This reversal, it should be emphasized, was essentially the consequence of the timing of growth—not of some structural law of economic development. The clustering and interaction of technological changes made this an age of metal, and even in Britain, where the cotton trade sold most of its goods abroad and continued to enjoy a highly elastic demand curve, the make of iron grew faster in these years than that of yarn or cloth.

The effect of this strong and growing demand for metallurgical products on technique was something else again. On the one hand, by pressing on the capacities of the old plant and promising substantial rewards to innovation, demand encouraged change. On the other, the very security of outlets permitted many an ironmaster to sit back and rake in substantial profits with obsolete equipment, especially where—as was often the case—his market was naturally or artificially protected from outside competition. To be fair, his location did not always permit him to convert to mineral fuel; and even where there was coal, conversion was expensive; modernization required a larger initial outlay than in the textile manufacture.

As a result, the development of the continental iron industry in this period, unlike that in Britain, was two-pronged. On the one side, there was the introduction and considerable diffusion of the new mineral-using techniques; on the other, there was an expansion of old-type plant, improved to some degree, but obsolescent.

The process varied, of course, from one country to another. In France, iron-making, like textile manufacture, was hard hit by the flood of British imports before and after Waterloo. At that point, the only plant to make coke-blast iron was Le Creusot, and Le Creusot made it poorly; the firm failed in 1818. Around the turn of the decade, however, a number of ironmasters succeeded in overcoming the technical difficulties (the biggest of which was the unsuitability of the coal, the ore, or both to the coke-smelting process) and established the new method on a firm basis: Gallois at Terrenoire, Dufaud at Four-chambault, Wendel at Hayange in particular. In the mid-1820's, the national output of coke-blast pig was perhaps four or five thousand tons; within a decade it had increased eightfold, and by 1846 amounted to 187,411 tons. During this interval, however, the number of char-coal blast furnaces increased by about two-thirds—there were some 375 in 1825 and 623 in 1846—and output rose slightly faster, from 194,000 to 335,000 tons.[1] Indeed, not only did the old smelting tech-nique thrive, but even the so-called Catalan forge, a descendant of the antique oven that antedated the blast furnace, dragged out a stubborn existence on the slopes of the Pyrenees and in the Massif Central.

In contrast to Britain, where puddling came more than half a century after coke smelting, the continental countries learned to refine with coal first. This is the normal sequence technologically: the fuel and ore economies are greater in refining; the absence of direct contact between fuel and metal excludes some of the most serious difficulties associated with the chemical composition of the materials employed; and the initial cost of the shift to coal in refining is much less than in smelting.

In France, the period of innovation was the later 'teens and early 1820's; the innovators, again men like Wendel, Dufaud, Gallois, and somewhat later, Frèrejean at Vienne and Manby and Wilson at Charenton and Le Creusot. This is just what one would expect: the greatest economy lay in combining coke smelting with puddling and rolling, and the pioneers in one area were bound to be pioneers in the other. Within a few years, the new technique had spread throughout the country: at the beginning of 1826 there were probably well over 150 puddling furnaces in activity (only about a third of which were operated in conjunction with rolling mills), and some 40 per cent of the total output of malleable iron was being made with coal. Two decades

---

[1] The second figure includes production by a mixture of wood and coal. Within this mixed category, more than two tons of wood or charcoal were used for every ton of coal or coke. *Résumé des travaux statistiques de l'Administration des Mines en 1847*, p. 11.

later, in 1845, there were some 437 puddling furnaces (of which 382 employed according to the *méthode anglaise*, that is, in combination with rolling mills) turning out 226,788 tons of wrought iron and rails, or two-thirds of a total make of 335,267 tons.

Along with the shift from vegetable to mineral fuel went various improvements in the construction and operation of plant and equipment. As in Britain, the blast furnace grew. In 1825 a 15-metre furnace at Le Creusot was exceptional; the average French unit turned out some 1325 metric tons of pig a year. In 1846 this was a characteristic height for coke-blast furnaces, and output averaged 3400 tons. Similarly, the make of wrought iron per puddling furnace doubled, going from 300 tons at most, to almost 600 in the same period.

The Belgian iron industry changed over to mineral fuel faster than the French, for a number of reasons: the relative abundance of coal and its proximity to the ore—in the 1830's and 1840's, Belgium was the largest coal producer on the Continent; the lower tariff barrier and consequent pressure of British competition; the unity of the national market and resulting inter-regional competition; and the availability of substantial venture capital from such institutions as the Société Générale.

The first blast furnace to use coke was that of Haudires, near Couillet—a small affair originally intended to burn charcoal. The first built for coke was that of Cockerill at Seraing in 1823. The years thereafter were, as in France, a period of trial and error; most of the early coke furnaces—there were ten in 1830—were small and uneconomical. Then came an alternation of boom and stagnation. The early 1830's saw a rapid advance (there were twenty-three coke furnaces in 1836), which was followed by a severe setback in 1837–9. Cockerill was forced to liquidate; the Société Générale momentarily suspended payment; numerous iron firms failed; the number of active coke-blast furnaces fell to seventeen. Expansion resumed in the 1840's, however, and by 1847, forty-six coke furnaces were in operation. During the same period, from 1830 to 1847, the number of active charcoal units fell from ninety-one to twenty-five.[1]

[1] These figures are from Beck, *Geschichte des Eisens*, IV, 688. They do not accord with the figures cited on p. 687, and the inconsistencies probably reflect the diversity of sources. The official *Exposé de la situation du Royaume, 1840–1850*, part IV, p. 118, gives the following statistics:

Blast Furnaces in Belgium

	Active		Idle	
	Coke	Charcoal	Coke	Charcoal
1845	33	23	19	52
1846	44	33	13	37
1847	50	35	12	34

This expansion and rationalization reflected in part the opening of the German market to Belgian iron. As in textiles, the main difficulty of the Belgian ironmasters was the inadequacy of local demand and the consequent inability to achieve the economies of scale implicit in the new techniques. In the 1830's, the Belgian government tried to solve the problem by forming a customs union with France, but the opposition of French manufacturers, for obvious reasons, and of the British government for reasons of state, killed the project. A similar effort to join the *Zollverein* in the 1840's (as did Luxembourg in 1842) failed because of French political opposition, but the Belgian government did succeed in obtaining a 50 per cent reduction in the German duty on iron. At a time when German consumption of iron was breaking records owing to the railway boom, this advantage gave the Belgian industry a tremendous push: where Belgium had accounted for a sixth of German iron imports in 1842–3, it provided over two-thirds in 1850; shipments of pig to the *Zollverein* jumped from 9500 to 76,000 tons.

In Germany, by contrast, these were decades of extremely slow progress. The greatest advances came in the manufacture of those finished goods—steel and steel objects, for example—that demanded special skills and high inputs of labour, as against the initial, mass-production processes. This preference reflected in part the craft traditions of the people and relative factor costs; but it was also the result of a tariff policy that treated pig and even wrought iron as a raw material and exposed the antiquated German furnaces and forges to the competition of Belgium and Britain.

The bulk of the German iron manufacture, like that of France, was based throughout this period on ore, wood, and water. The largest centre was in the Rhineland: in the hills around Siegen, where high-quality iron was easily accessible in small, dispersed outcroppings; and on the Sauerland plateau to the North-West, heavily forested and cut deeply by numerous rivers driving dozens of forge and mill wheels. The Siegerland concentrated on smelting; the Sauerland, on refining and finishing. Here lay the internationally known centres of Solingen, its coat of arms flaunting an anchor on crossed swords; Remscheid, with its sickle under a lion rampant; Iserlohn, home of a pin and needle industry whose division of labour recalls the famous chapter of Adam Smith.

The effect of growing demand on these districts was essentially to intensify output along traditional lines; more mines, more water wheels, more forges. Coal came in slowly, and then in those works that lay close to the Rhine and could import it by water from the Ruhr. It was used at first in refining only; indeed, the Sauerland developed a flourishing forge and shaping industry to process Belgian and British pig, or convert *Spiegeleisen* from the Siegerland into steel. Not until the 1840's was coke-blast pig manufactured in the Rhineland.

By comparison, the Ruhr was insignificant. No one realized as yet the extent and quality of the coal that lay beneath its still-green fields. As late as 1852 the official German commissioners to the Crystal Palace Exposition were able to write: 'It is clearly not to be expected that Germany will ever be able to reach the level of production of coal and iron currently attained in England. This is implicit in our far more limited resource endowment.'[1] Besides, in the 1830's and 1840's, Belgian and British pig iron was, or at least seemed, too cheap to compete with. Almost all of such pig as the Ruhr did turn out went into castings, and the first coke-blast furnace in the area was not blown in until 1851.[2] Here, too, puddling and finishing developed on the basis of imported iron and local fuel: in 1844, of some 35,000 tons converted into various forms of merchant iron, tinplate, and steel, less than 5 per cent came from Westphalian furnaces.

Several of the newer forges of the Ruhr and Sauerland were among the most modern on the Continent. And in one field, steel, Germany was in the van of technical progress. In 1849 Lohage and Bremme founded a company to exploit their process for producing steel by puddling, the first major advance on the road to cheap steel since the invention of the crucible process in the eighteenth century. Two years later Krupp startled the Crystal Palace Exposition by exhibiting a huge two-ton block of cast steel, the result of a marvellous co-ordination of labour and supervision in the pouring of dozens of crucibles simultaneously.

Silesia was the only area whose output in this period was comparable to that of the Rhineland. It would be difficult, however, to find two districts so different in vocation and in the character of their development. Where the one was thickly settled, western in social structure and political tradition, located near the heart of what for centuries had been one of the main thoroughfares of European civilization and commerce, the other was heavily forested, thinly populated, parcelled into large estates of privileged aristocratic landowners, a frontier march won in war and therefore closely administered by the Prussian government.

[1] *Amtlicher Bericht* (cited above, p. 395, n. 2), I, 238.
[2] According to Dr Irmgard Lange-Kothe, the Friedrich-Wilhelms-Hütte in Mülheim, which is usually credited with having blown in the first coke-blast furnace in the Ruhr (1849), ran in fact into technical difficulties and had to extinguish the fires shortly thereafter; not until 1853 did the furnace work successfully. In the meantime, coke smelting had been introduced by the Eintrachthütte at Hochdahl (near Düsseldorf) in 1851 and by Detillieux at Bergeborbeck (near Essen) in 1852.

Silesia did not compare with the Rhineland in markets, capital, or enterprise; but she had minerals, including valuable deposits of non-ferrous metals and apparently inexhaustible coal measures; she also had the solicitous patronage of the state. The earliest of the great Silesian iron-works and coal-mines were royal establishments; the names often announced the fact: Königshütte, Königshuld, Königsgrube. As noted earlier, these state enterprises were among the first in continental Europe to smelt with coke successfully, thanks to the assistance of British technicians and the work of civil servants like Reden.

By contrast, the private sector remained backward. Most of the mineral and forest wealth was held by noblemen whose entrepreneurial ambitions were limited to a diffuse appetite for gain and whose horizon was restricted to the traditional agrarian vocation of the domain. For most of them, coal and iron were a kind of treasure trove, an unexpected addition to wealth yielded by cultivation and husbandry; it took decades before a few pioneers realized that there was more to iron-making than the small forge or smithy that serviced the estate and that industry was a greater potential source of income than agriculture. Their fellows were slow to follow suit, partly no doubt because of inertia, partly because wood was so cheap that, given the differences in quality, charcoal blast iron could compete with the coke-smelted pig; for many, indeed, wood seems to have been almost a free good (save for cost of labour)—if it was not used in the furnaces, it simply went to waste. As a result, the share of coke-blast pig in the total output of Upper Silesia rose from 28 per cent in 1838 (9108 out of 32,426 tons by eleven out of eighty furnaces) to only 35 per cent in 1847 (13,050 out of 37,550 tons, by eighteen out of sixty-three furnaces.)

Germany was thus the slowest of the west European countries to develop a modern iron industry, in spite of the early start in Silesia; and Belgium the fastest. In all, however, the scale of enterprise was smaller than in Britain. No company on the Continent was capable of turning out 80,000 tons of pig a year, as the fifteen furnaces of Dowlais did in 1845. The Wendel firm of Lorraine, probably the largest in France, produced 22,000 tons in 1850; the Forges de Decazeville, some 16,000 tons at the height of the boom of the 1840's. As late as the end of the 1850's, the six furnaces of the S. A. John Cockerill were producing 11,000–12,000 tons. The German enterprises were on average even smaller; the Laurahütte, newly created in 1838 and a giant of the Silesian industry, had four blast furnaces and a capacity of about 16,000 tons.

Similarly, British equipment was larger. The biggest Welsh furnaces were smelting 120 tons a week in the late 1840's; the average was 90; for Britain as a whole, the mean was 89. On the Continent, only

Belgium was comparable, with a general average of 60 tons. By contrast, the make of French coke-blast furnaces in 1846 was 66 tons a week; of all furnaces, less than 18. And in Germany, where the coke-blast furnaces of Silesia were restricted in size by the friability of the fuel, even these averaged only 14 tons a week in 1847.[1]

The same differences in scale of output and size of equipment characterized the refining processes. Only in certain special cases—Seraing's rail-rolling mills or Krupp's steel-pouring shed—were continental plants comparable to those of the United Kingdom. Nor was it coincidence that both of these installations were developed to supply the state. Private demand seemed too limited and fickle to justify investment on the British scale.

In one respect, however, the best practice on the Continent was moving ahead of that of Britain. The higher cost of fuel, otherwise a serious disadvantage, was an incentive to technological innovation. Where British ironmasters continued to allow the flames and gases of their furnaces to illuminate the night, the best continental producers took steps to use this once waste energy for refining the pig, heating the blast, or driving the steam-engines. Similarly, Neilson's hot blast spread fairly rapidly among French manufacturers of coke-blast pig: in 1846 some forty-three out of fifty-five active furnaces were so equipped. Belgium was slower in this regard, perhaps because cost conditions were closer to those of Britain; but Belgium was the leader in putting to use the waste gases of carbonization.

To be sure, these savings were not large enough to offset the British cost advantage; until the systematic exploitation of Lorraine ore and Ruhr coal in the second half of the century or, indeed, the application of the Thomas process in the 1880's and 1890's, no iron was cheaper than British iron. The fact remains, however, that continental ironmasters were making more of their resources than their competitors across the Channel; and since fuel economy was the key to efficiency in almost every stage of manufacture, these tentative advances of the 1830's and 1840's were the starting-point of a scientific metallurgy that was to pay off in major improvements a generation later. For the moment, however, nothing could compare with the wealth of British resources or the ingenuity of such inventors as Neilson, Mushet, and Hall.

On the Continent, even more than in the United Kingdom, the steam-engine was linked to mining and metallurgy. For where it was still possible in the second third of the century to use water to drive the smaller, obsolescent types of textile machinery (which, as we have

---

[1] Beck, *Geschichte des Eisens*, IV, 700. This figure does not accord with statistics for the same year cited on p. 699, which indicate an average of 21 tons a week.

noted, were competitive under continental conditions), the coke-blast furnace and rolling mill usually required far more power than the water wheels could provide and were less compatible than the equipment of other industries with a fluctuating supply of energy. Once again, we do not have adequate statistical evidence for the United Kingdom, but the data, such as they are, give the impression of a relatively high concentration of steam power in the cotton industry. France seems to have occupied an intermediate position, with 42·2 per cent of her rated steam horsepower in mining and metallurgy (including engineering) and 29·5 per cent in textiles. Belgium was at the other extreme: in 1851 over 55 per cent of her steam power stationary engines were in coal-mining, another 15 per cent in iron-making, only 11 per cent in textiles. Here, as in heavy metallurgy, the Belgian achievement was by far the most impressive of the period. In 1846 she had some 38,000 h.p. for 4,337,000 people (8·76 per thousand), as compared with 50,000 h.p. for France (1·5 per thousand).[1] Germany was slow by comparison: 26,400 h.p. in 1846 (approximately 0·76 per thousand).

Technologically, steam power on the Continent followed the same path as metallurgy; that is, far more emphasis was placed on fuel economy than in Britain. From the very start, the Woolf compound engine (patents of 1803 and 1804; commercial realization c. 1812), which made use of high pressure to operate two cylinders alternately and offered a fuel economy over the Watt machine of about 50 per cent, found its greatest market in France. Unfortunately the compound engine was costly to build and difficult to maintain, handicaps particularly serious in capital- and skill-poor countries, and for some time it was confined primarily to marine and river shipping. Instead, the continental industrialists preferred simple engines working at medium or high pressure; as pointed out earlier, these were cheaper to build as well as more economical of fuel than the Watt-type machine.[2] They were also more dangerous, however, and it was some years before metal-

---

[1] These are stationary engines only. Briavoinne, *Sur les inventions*, p. 38, remarks wryly: 'If it is correct to say with M. Chaptal that the extent of the industry of a country is measured today less by its population than by the machines it possesses, the disproportion between France and Belgium would not seem to be very great.'

[2] As of the end of 1836, of a total steam-engine capacity of 38,173 h.p. in France, 35,440 was so-called 'high-pressure' (that is, high and medium), and 2733 low. The corresponding figures for 1846 were 103,739 and 5196. France, Ministère des Travaux Publics, *Compte rendu des travaux des ingénieurs des mines, pendant l'année 1847* (Paris, 1848), p. 88. The figures are necessarily approximate, since they rest in large part on declarations made for the purpose of securing authorization for the machines in question. Also, they probably include machines authorized but not installed as yet; this is no doubt compensated, however, by machines installed in anticipation of authorization.

workers learned to build reliable boilers and even more years before the public would put any faith in them. Acceptance did not come until the 1830's, in large part as a result of improvements in marine engines and the development of the steam locomotive.

Whenever possible, the continental manufacturer used water power. In the textile districts of Normandy, steam was used only as a *pis aller*: where the streams were so crowded there was no room for another wheel; or where energy was required over and beyond what water already furnished. Even in heavy industry, water continued to play a far greater role than is usually thought: as late as 1844, the French iron manufacture was using hydraulic engines of 21,710 h.p., as against steam-engines of only 5982 h.p. (3213 fuelled by coal, 2769 by gas from the furnaces).[1] In general, it was the coal-short French who were most active in developing the technology of water power. The key figures are J. V. Poncelet, whose undershot wheel with curved vanes achieved efficiencies about three times as great as the ordinary wheel; and Fourneyron, whose turbine (1827) holds a place in hydraulics comparable to that of Watt's engine in the field of steam power.

In the eighteenth century, almost all of the continental steam-engines came from England: if it was hard for British metal-workers to achieve the precision required, it was almost impossible for French or German craftsmen. Not only did they lack the manipulative skills, but their materials were inadequate to the task—too soft or brittle and uneven in quality.

By the 1820's, however, the combination of imported British labour, continental determination, and, in some countries, high tariff barriers and similar constraints on foreign competition led to the development of a home machine industry. At first, the mainland producers were essentially copyists, reproducing British models with negligible alteration—and then largely in the direction of economy of material, even at the expense of solidity. The French and Belgians were the first to break away and conceive their own machines, increasingly on the basis of theoretical speculation; observers contrasted them with the practical British in this regard. At mid-century, Germany was just beginning to enter this 'independent' stage. Some of her engineers still had difficulty in obtaining proper materials locally, and many firms continued to import accessory machine tools from abroad.

Few continental machine construction firms worked for export, and the industry as a whole was much smaller than the British. The division of labour within the trade reflected these limitations of scale. Thus while the industry tended, as in Britain, to split into light and heavy

[1] *Ibid.* 1845, pp. 26–43.

sectors, there were not on the Continent such pure machine-tool firms as Maudslays and Nasmyths.[1] Instead, most of the engineering houses —Schneider, Gouin, or Calla in France; Cockerill in Belgium; Harkort, Borsig, Egells in Germany—were ready to undertake anything ordered, from locomotives and marine engines to distilling apparatus and lathes. Some even tried their hand at textile equipment, although it was soon recognized that this was the kind of product best left to specialists.[2]

In these circumstances, the industry made little attempt at standardization, except in the manufacture of spinning machinery and similar apparatus, where the volume of demand permitted and encouraged the appearance of types and models. Even here, however, the manufacturer made everything to order, and every order was in some way different from the one before. There was no production on speculation of the kind that Nasmyth attempted.[3] Interchangeable parts were unknown; there was little or no working to gauges; and the file was still the machinist's most important tool.

There was far more improvisation than in Britain. Engineering shops made their own equipment, and the larger manufacturing firms— in textiles, for example—often maintained machine departments large enough to stand on their own. Some of these did in time split off and become independent enterprises. Smaller factories depended on local mechanics and repair men, ready to put their hands to anything. This was an expensive way of doing things: 'home-made' machines cost a lot more than the products of the large national firms. But local production meant immediate attention and easier maintenance, and most manufacturers were agreed that these versatile, on-the-spot artisans were indispensable. Besides, repair shops were factories in embryo, and

[1] The witnesses before the Select Committee on Machinery of 1841 asserted that while continental machine shops were able to make special-purpose machine tools for themselves, they did not ordinarily manufacture them for sale, that industrialists needing tools imported them from Britain. According to one machine maker, William Jenkinson of Manchester, three-fourths, if not four-fifths of the machine tools made in England were intended for export. The figure seems very high. *Parliamentary Papers*, 1841, VII, QQ. 1312–29, esp. 1326, 3182, 4459–62.

[2] Even in Britain, however, most machine shops in the 1840's and 1850's were general shops. The producers of textile equipment were the major exception. A more advanced division of labour did not come until the 1870's, and it was another decade or two before specialization became the mark of the modern efficient enterprise. J. B. Jefferys, *The Story of the Engineers 1800–1945* (n.p., n.d.), p. 53.

[3] See above, p. 336 and note 3. To be sure, Nasmyth was an exception even in England. The German commissioners at the Exposition of 1851 noted that many British firms did not have price lists, preferring, 'in view of the great diversity of requirement', to quote on order. *Amtlicher Bericht* (cited above, p. 395, n. 2), I, 589.

many a small mechanic became an industrialist by ploughing back profits and borrowing from sympathetic and dependent manufacturers. In few trades was entrepreneurial advancement so rapid.[1]

Much more than in Britain, machine-building on the Continent grew with heavy industry. Not only was textile manufacture relatively less important but, as noted above, much light manufacturing continued to rely on water power. It was mining and metallurgy at first, the railroad later, that provided the major market for engines and complex metal shapes. Railway construction was particularly important. It called forth a large number of machine shops, encouraged as in Britain the diffusion of major innovations in the working and handling of heavy forms—among them the steam hammer and overhead cranes—and provided for the first time so large a demand for machine tools that specialization in their manufacture became feasible. But this was not to come until after mid-century.[2]

The chemical industry encountered the same problem in more serious form; the effects of weak demand were aggravated by the dispersion of the critical raw materials. The market was limited to begin with: the textile industry was, as we have seen, nowise comparable to that across the Channel, and this was the most important single customer for chemical products. Moreover the market was cut up: chemicals were cheap in proportion to volume, sometimes hard to handle, and liable to spoilage and breakage of containers; no industry suffered so much from the high cost of transport. Finally, these geographical handicaps hurt on the supply side as well: there was nothing like the Merseyside concentration of coal and salt in combination with water carriage. All of which limited the scale of operations, raised costs above the British level, and led producers to stress versatility rather than volume. Most chemical manufacturers were kitchen cooks on a large scale.

Their equipment and techniques were consonant with this kind of industrial cuisine. On the one hand, the thriftiness of the small producer

[1] To choose but two areas where this kind of promotion from shop to factory took place on a large scale: on St-Etienne, cf. L. J. Gras, *Histoire de la métallurgie dans la Loire* (St Etienne, 1908), pp. 223f., 267–9, 220, 265f., 393f.; L. Thiollier, *Notices industrielles* (St Etienne, 1894), pp. 41–50; on central Germany, G. Aubin, *Die wirtschaftliche Einheit Mitteldeutschlands* (Merseburg, 1927), pp. 17–19.

[2] Switzerland was an exception. There, lack of coal and iron and an abundance of cheap water power made metallurgy and engineering relatively less important. As a result, machine building grew, not so much out of the independent metal trades, as out of the young factory textile industry. Cf. Bruno Lincke, *Die schweizerische Maschinenindustrie und ihre Entwicklung* (Frauenfeld, 1910), pp. 9–12; Walter Bodmer, *Die Entwicklung der schweizerischen Textilwirtschaft im Rahmen der übrigen Industrien und Wirtschaftszweige* (Zurich, 1960), pp. 328–39.

and official regulations on the capture and disposal of noxious wastes encouraged rationalization, which meant in effect the recuperation and exploitation of by-products. On the other hand, proper recuperation cost money and sometimes made other processes more difficult; thus the apparatus for the recovery of hydrochloric acid in the manufacture of sodium sulphate (Glauber's salt) cut down on furnace draught and made it that much harder to effect the initial reaction. The result was often a compromise between rationality and compliance on the one hand, and penny-pinching shortcuts on the other. In Belgium, where the chemical industry was comparatively well endowed by nature, government inspectors noted in 1854 the poor condition of the equipment, the sloppiness of the work: the glass bells for hydrochloric acid installed outdoors, where changes in temperature cracked them; the dosage of materials, approximate and variable; little effort made to maintain the purity of the reagents. Most of the firms producing sulphuric acid counted themselves fortunate to obtain 75 per cent of the theoretical yield.

Rationality of techniques would seem to have advanced further in France. At least this is the impression one gets from the report of a Belgian inspector, J. S. Stas, who visited the Kuhlmann plant at Lille in the same year: 'I had a great deal of trouble convincing myself that I was dealing with furnaces for the manufacture of sodium sulphate.' In Belgium, he notes, such furnaces 'sweat hydrochloric acid and remind one constantly, by their state of disrepair, more of ruins that are painful to look at, than of active equipment belonging for the most part to wealthy industrialists'.[1]

Yet one must not confuse Kuhlmann with the run of French firms. As in Belgium, the large, rationalizing establishment was the exception; the small pot boiler, the rule. At mid-century Kuhlmann's Madeleine plant was recovering 158 kg. of hydrochloric acid per 100 kg. of salt, a loss of perhaps 2 per cent in view of the impurity of the salt; at Aniche (Nord) results of up to 183/100 had been achieved under better conditions. Yet a decade later, the plants in southern France were still losing two-thirds of their by-product acid, and even in Britain there were losses of as much as a half.

The main difficulty was lack of apparent financial incentive. As one Belgian manufacturer, whose recovery ratio of hydrochloric acid was 70/100, put it, there was no profit in doing any better. Yet the argument should not be taken at face value. For one thing, there were a number of producers in both countries who did better and sold their acid at a profit. For another, few if any of the manufacturers of the

[1] Belgium, Chambre des Représentants, 1854, *Fabriques de produits chimiques*, Annexes, p. iv.

period could really say in a precise way what paid and what did not. Scientific standards of performance were still confined to laboratories, and there was as yet no clear-cut choice of technique that imposed itself on the investing entrepreneur. As a result, each firm had its own procedures or combinations thereof.

In Germany the chemical industry of this early period gave little hint of the great things to come. The textile manufacture was far weaker than that of France; the standard of living, lower; and soap and glass consumption, that much smaller. On the supply side, as we have noted, the mineral wealth of Westphalia was as yet unsuspected. Not until 1840 was soda produced by the Leblanc method, and as late as the 1870's, when the Solvay process was beginning to transform the industry, German output was less than that of France a generation earlier.[1] Indeed, demand far outstripped supply, and soda imports rose in a decade (1836–45) from 634 to 6913 metric tons, almost all of this from Britain;[2] not until the 1880's did Germany become a net exporter of soda. Similarly, the make of sulphuric acid long remained low, amounting in 1878 to about half of that of France.[3] Here, however, supply early passed demand and by the mid-1840's Germany was selling more acid abroad than she imported.

Yet if the German chemical industry was productively weak at mid-century, it had important technological assets. It was more scientific than that of other nations, to the point of what might appear superficially as economic inefficiency. The typical German firm outdid those of the other continental countries in diversity of output; the largest producers of sulphuric acid and soda also turned out the rarest pharmaceuticals, alkaloids, and organic acids. The experts attributed this versatility to the skill and training of the young technicians—not the *savants*, but the production men:

...most of our chemical manufacturers are in a position, because of a much stronger scientific education, and because of the ease with which they [can draw], partly on our array of pharmacists, whose scientific knowledge goes

---

[1] Output did not pass the 40,000 metric ton mark until 1872. The plants in the Marseilles area alone were turning out this amount by the 1840's. L. F. Haber, *The Chemical Industry in the Nineteenth Century* (London, 1958), pp. 47, 41. According to R. Hasenclever, 'Über die deutsche Soda-Fabrikation', *Chemische Industrie*, VII (1884), 280 ff., soda output was 58,000 tons in 1872, shrinking to 42,000 by 1878 under the pressure of British competition. The higher figure, however, does not alter the significance of the comparison.

[2] Gustav Miller, *Die chemische Industrie in der deutschen Zoll- und Handelsgesetzgebung* (1902), cited in H. Schultze, *Die Entwicklung der chemischen Industrie in Deutschland seit dem Jahre 1875* (Halle, 1908), p. 7.

[3] An estimated 112,000 against 200,000 tons. *Ibid.* p. 71.

so far beyond that of the apothecaries of other countries, partly on the large number of other young chemists, to obtain at any time the kind of help that is only rarely to be had elsewhere and then only with great expenditure. These circumstances enable them to compose, alongside the most extensively active products of the trade, a great many preparations that can be entrusted only to educated and experienced men.[1]

Wissenschaftliche Bildung was to pay handsomely in the second half of the century.

At mid-century, then, continental Europe was still about a generation behind Britain in industrial development. The relative disparity showed clearly in the population figures. Where in 1851 about half of the people of England and Wales lived in towns, in France and Germany the proportion was about a quarter; not until the last years of the century did urban population pass rural in Germany, and in France the even point did not come until after the First World War. The occupational distribution tells a similar story. At mid-century, only a quarter of the British male working force (twenty years and older) was engaged in agriculture. For Belgium, the most industrialized nation on the Continent, the figure was about 50 per cent.[2] Germany took another twenty-five years to reach this point; indeed, as late as 1895, there were more people engaged in agriculture than in industry.[3] And in France industry was outnumbered until the Second World War and the economic recovery that followed.

By the same token, the continental proletariat was very different from the British. The concentration of large numbers of workers in huge factories was only just beginning, and then more in heavy industry than in textiles. There was nothing yet like the new slums of Manchester and Leeds, filled with pallid mill hands crowding into a smokestack jungle. Continental slums were different. They were usually the run-down older quarters, comparable to the wynds of Edinburgh, and were inhabited primarily by artisans and domestic workers—handloom weavers in the damp cellars of Lille or the tenements of Liège; woodworkers in the Faubourg Saint-Antoine. Here and there were

---

[1] *Amtlicher Bericht* (above, p. 395, n. 2), I, 262. The original is grammatically incomplete.

[2] According to the Belgian census of 1846, 1,075,000 were engaged in agriculture, 660,000 in industry. Counting dependants, agriculture supported 2,220,000, industry 1,400,000, and commerce 290,000 of a population of 4,340,000. B. S. Chlepner, *Cent ans d'histoire sociale en Belgique* (Brussels, 1956), p. 13.

[3] Of a working force (including unemployed) of 22,913,683, 8,292,692 were engaged in agriculture, forestry, and fishing, as against 8,281,220 in mining and industry. *Statistisches Jahrbuch für das deutsche Reich*, XIX (1898), 7 (Table I, 9).

new mill towns on the British pattern; but Roubaix, Mulhouse, and the cities of the Wuppertal were so much smaller than their counterparts in Lancashire and the West Riding that they were really a different species.

Much more than in Britain, industry was dispersed through the countryside. The continued reliance on water power was one factor; the greater place of metallurgy and mining, which were bound to locate at the sources of raw materials, was another. As late as 1858, 19 of 49 spinning mills, 49 of 57 blast furnaces, 75 of 152 wire mills, 158 of 167 steel plants, and 15 of 28 machine factories in Westphalia were *auf dem platten Lande*.[1] To be sure, this was a legalistic definition, and many of these plants were in fact situated in communities that deserved to be called urban. Many, however, were located in what were in effect swollen villages, essentially rural in character. There was, as in Lancashire in the eighteenth century, a thickening of the countryside; it had not yet thickened enough, however, to form a continuous industrial conurbation.

There was, moreover, a great expansion of rural putting-out, a continuation of the trend of the eighteenth century, paradoxically accelerated by the mechanization of some—but not all—of the stages of manufacture. Thus the availability of cheaper semi-processed materials—yarn, rough metal shapes, tanned leather—increased the demand for the corresponding finished goods and stimulated the trades that made them. Here differentiation of product was often pushed to the extreme, and the importance of skill or painstaking labour gave the shop and cottage an advantage over the factory. Even the march of the machine did not always favour power-driven, concentrated manufacture. When the embroidery loom was finally improved in Switzerland to the point of commercial effectiveness in the 1850's, it was installed at first in large weaving sheds; a device of this complexity was beyond the means of most home workers. But before long the manufacturers found that it paid to place these machines in cottages, as the stockingers of Nottingham had done with their frames two hundred years before; and in subsequent decades the loom found its way into the most isolated villages of the Voralberg.[2]

The extension of putting-out on the Continent owed much to the pattern of land tenure. In Britain, the enclosures had promoted the absorption of small holdings into large, commercial exploitations. In east-Elbian Europe, the emancipation of the serfs had similar consequences: the debts imposed on the peasants as the price of their freedom

[1] Peter Quante, *Die Flucht aus der Landwirtschaft* (Berlin-Grünewald, 1933), p. 5.
[2] Lincke, *Die schweizerische Maschinenindustrie*, pp. 46-7.

and property so burdened them that many had no choice but to sell their land and either hire out as labourers or leave. Much of western Europe north of the Alps and Pyrenees, however, lay in the hands of independent proprietors; moreover, the prevalence of partible inheritance (written into the Code Civil in France) led to a progressive fragmentation of their already small holdings. The system held an ever larger population on the land, for the children of each generation tended to stay on to work their shares of a diminishing patrimony. On the other hand, even with improved techniques, these small plots were less and less adequate to nourish their occupants. Increasingly, the peasant had to eke out his income with earnings as a farm labourer or cottage worker. Poor soil and division of holdings were the parents of rural industry.

This persistence of the old social framework was a source of great satisfaction to many continental statesmen and writers. In France particularly, where the traditional structure was most tenacious and British industrial success least palatable, society was wont to congratulate itself on being spared the penalties of unbalanced and immoderate growth: the white slavery of the factories; the filth and misery of the cities; the godlessness and radicalism of a rootless proletariat.

In fact, the Continent had its poverty, as conscientious observers were quick to perceive, but much of it was dispersed and, as one investigator put it, latent.[1] In societies where population was increasing more rapidly than the demand for factory labour, there was a heavy flow into cottage industry, depressing wages in the short run and creating in the long run huge pools of depressed humanity, barely subsisting until the day when even the wages of hunger would not be low enough. The same thing happened in Britain, but to a much smaller degree. For one thing, there was more alternative opportunity: industry drew people; people did not press into industry. The Irish hand-loom weaver was an exception, but, little as he earned, he was probably better off in Lancashire than in Mayo. At least he survived. For another, as we have already noted, it was the Continent that supplied much of the hand labour required to process the semi-finished manufactures of Britain. The weavers of Silesia, Saxony, and central France (the tulle trade of Tarare) were in one sense beneficiaries of British industrial progress; they were also its victims. In effect, they were taking part of the burden of adjustment to the new economic order from Britain's shoulders. The reckoning came in the 1840's, both for those processing British exports and those—in linen, for example— working up home materials. Technological advance, trade depression,

---

[1] Buret, De la misère des classes laborieuses, I, 209, 249.

and famine combined to produce misery and death on a scale that Britain never knew. Only in Ireland was there anything comparable to the tragedy of the Silesian woollen weavers or the flax spinners of Flanders.[1]

The principal reason for the long survival of putting-out on the Continent was undoubtedly the low cost of rural labour. Linked to this, however, was the docility that normally accompanied dispersion: the entrepreneur found the cottage worker easier to deal with. Again and again, businessmen and officials note the dissipation and indiscipline of the urban proletariat, whether employed in mills or at home. The British hardly discuss the issue—and this in spite of the greater militancy and effectiveness of their labour movement.

The contrast is significant. It reflects, first of all, the difference in entrepreneurial response to factor costs. For the British employer, the best remedy for insubordination was technological unemployment. It hardly occurred to him to allow social considerations to modify the rational organization of his enterprise. Secondly, it reveals the insecurity of the continental bourgeoisie, the deep-rooted fear of another political and social upheaval like 1789. To be sure, England could have and did have her scares: witness Peterloo, or the emergency constabulary of 1848. But these passed, cured by good sense, humour, or both. Generally speaking, Britain took social order for granted. The industrialist had no illusions about the hostility of the working class or the possibility of violence; but he never doubted that the law would prevail. His French counterpart—and to a lesser extent, the German or Belgian manufacturer—was never sure when labour unrest or unemployment would turn into political revolution. Hence his readiness to equate working-class poverty and criminality—*les classes laborieuses* and *les classes dangereuses*.

Finally, the continental entrepreneur had a different conception of his role from the British. In societies with a strong feudal and manorial tradition, the successful factory owner tended to see himself as master as well as employer, with the duties as well as the privileges that such a position entails. He placed himself *in loco parentis*, treated his workers as minors in need of a firm tutorial hand, and felt a certain responsibility for their job security and welfare—always, of course, at the very modest level suitable to their station. This paternalistic sentiment varied considerably from person to person and place to place; just as Britain had her benevolent manufacturers, especially among the

---

[1] On Silesia, see, in addition to Hauptmann's classic, *The Weavers*, the study by S. B. Kan, *Dva vosstaniia silezskikh Tkachei (1793–1844)* [Two uprisings of Silesian weavers] (Moscow, 1948). On Flanders, the standard work is the above-cited (p. 386, n. 3) Jacquemyns, *Histoire de la crise économique des Flandres (1845–1850)*.

owners of the country mills, so the Continent had its 'exploiters'.[1] On the whole, however, the continental industrialist never achieved that freedom of manœuvre and conscience that comes from looking on labour as just another factor of production, to be hired and fired as needed.

To be sure, even his paternalism was not entirely idealistic. Some of it was a response to the danger and inconvenience of losing a working force collected with difficulty and only too easily dispersed. This was one reason why, in contrast to what Marxist doctrine might lead us to expect, he often encouraged and assisted his men to become pro- prietors; or why he kept his working force on part time in moments of crisis, even at some sacrifice.[2] Moreover, there was the pressure of public and official opinion. In these early decades of industrialization, both the traditional elites and the governments they dominated had serious qualms about the implications of a concentrated proletariat. There were many who felt that economic strength was not worth the price of social subversion. If many of these doubtful elements were won over in the long run to industrial capitalism, it was partly because they accepted the image of the paternalistic entrepreneur and saw in the maintenance of traditional personal bonds between employer and employed a powerful instrument of social control. And when the employer forgot his obligations, the state was prepared to remind him of them. In France, the government was sensitive to factory unemploy- ment as to nothing else, keeping close watch on hiring and firing and utilizing political pressure when necessary to limit the number of jobless, even in—or rather, especially in—severe crises.

What we have, in short, is the usual phenomenon of legitimation by means of assumption of a role acceptable to the society as a whole. In the process, these attitudes, whatever their original motivation, tended to become an integral part of the entrepreneurial personality. The paternalistic manufacturer of the Continent believed that he was

---

[1] Michelet's generalization, impressionistic as it was, probably sums up the situa- tion as well as anything short of a detailed empirical study. The paternalistic employers, he argued (Le peuple, ed. L. Refort (Paris, 1946), p. 87), were the very large factory owners and the very small; those in between were hungry, hard, indifferent to every- thing but their own material interests. Even if they began with some feeling for their men, he noted, they lost it on the battlefield of trade. He might also have noted the opposite phenomenon—the assumption, with prosperity, of the 'enlightened' role expected of the responsible employer. For an analogous phenomenon of assimilation to responsibility with success, this time in banking, cf. Landes, Bankers and Pashas, p. 40 and n. 3.

[2] For an analysis of paternalism as a means of training and fixing the industrial labour force, cf. Carl Jantke, Der Vierte Stand: die gestaltenden Kräfte der deutschen Arbeiterbewegung im XIX. Jahrhundert (Freiburg, 1955), pp. 175-8.

father to his men. And it was the very sincerity of this belief that often made him inflexible in his dealings with organized labour. For the British employer, a union may have been an adversary, a strike vexing and costly, the effort of labour to raise wages chimerical. He did not like these things, but he was prepared to face up to them. For the continental employer, however, a union was a conspiracy against public order and morals; a strike, an act of ingratitude; the effort of labour to raise wages, the indiscipline of an impatient son. All of this was evil. And there is no negotiating with evil.[1]

Similarly with the efforts of the state to dictate hours or conditions of work: any such move was an intolerable intrusion that could only undermine the authority of the master. To the requirements of the factory act of 1841, the family enterprises of France, of northern France especially, opposed a deep, indignant immobility that discouraged examination and disarmed enforcement. The law called for voluntary inspectors from among the manufacturers themselves, active and retired. It was a fiasco: few volunteered and many of these soon resigned in despair or under pressure of friends and colleagues. There is no collaborating with evil.

III. *Closing the Gap*

The period from 1850 to 1873 was continental industry's coming-of-age. It was a period of unprecedentedly rapid growth, which may be best conveyed—in the absence of year-by-year calculations of national income or product—by certain critical time series:[2] railroad mileage,

---

[1] This paternalism will seem to some incompatible with that deep-rooted fear of the people discussed above. On the contrary: the paternalistic businessman rarely feared his own men; presumably he knew them and they trusted him. But they were children, even savage children, and could be led astray. See the reaction of Gaston Motte to a strike in his great-grandfather's plant in 1847: it was probably the work of outside agitators, as was not infrequently the case. L. Machu, 'La crise de l'industrie textile à Roubaix au milieu du XIXe siècle', *Revue du Nord*, XXXVIII (1956), 72, n. 1.

[2] We have annual estimates of the national income of Great Britain from 1870 on. There are several series at the historian's disposal; they differ in detail, but are essentially congruent. See the brief discussion and the literature cited in William Ashworth, *An Economic History of England 1870–1939* (London and New York, 1960), pp. 186–9. For the earlier period, we have occasional contemporary estimates, critically analysed by Phyllis Deane (see above, p. 280, n. 1), and the decennial figures (1801 on) calculated by Deane and Cole, *British Economic Growth* (1962), pp. 166–7. The nearest thing we possess to an *annual* estimate of national product is Walter Hoffman's series of industrial output. See his *British Industry 1700–1950* (Liverpool, 1955).

We now have decennial averages of French national product (goods, not services) going back to the late eighteenth century. These have been calculated at the Institut de Science Economique Appliquée by a group headed by Jean Marczewski. He offers a

coal consumption or output, steam-power capacity, make of pig iron, consumption of raw cotton. In all these areas (with the exception of cotton, whose manufacture suffered a grievous setback in the 1860's), whether for France, Belgium, or Germany, the *compound* rate of increase runs between 5 and 10 per cent a year (see Table 45).

These were also years of technological maturation. They were marked in essence by the working-out on the Continent of those innovations that constitute the heart of the Industrial Revolution and had been developed and diffused in Britain a generation or more earlier. In textiles the self-actor and power loom replaced the mule and hand loom. The iron industry consummated the shift from vegetable to mineral fuel. The steam-engine sealed its triumph over the water wheel. The heavy chemical industry was firmly established and the technical possibilities of the salt-soda-acid complex exploited along the lines implicit in the Leblanc process. Finally, the machine spread ever more widely—into nail-making and the cutlery trade, the stamping of heavy metal forms, tailoring, the manufacture of paper, and other fields too numerous to list.

This description of the middle decades of the century as a period of technical maturation, of the working-out and diffusion of earlier developments, is not meant to imply that invention had ceased and that the gains of productivity were all made behind a stable technological frontier. On the contrary, these were years of sustained creativity which saw some of the most important innovations of the century. But these innovations were either complementary to the original bundle of changes that constituted, as we noted, the heart of the Industrial Revolution; or they anticipated the future and did not come to fruition until the last third of the century. The machine comber, steam hammer, and the compound steam-engine—all of them actually introduced in the 1840's—fall in the former category. The Bessemer converter and Siemens-Martin hearth, the industrial use of electricity, the gas motor, artificial coal tar dyes, and the Solvay ammonia process

preliminary statement of the results, which represent the first step in a long-range programme to develop an annual series, in 'Some Aspects of the Economic Growth of France, 1660–1958', *Economic Development and Cultural Change*, IX (1961), 369–86; see also W.W. Rostow (ed.), *The Economics of Take-off into Sustained Growth* [papers of a Conference of the International Economic Association at Konstanz, 2–11 September 1960] (London, 1963).

German figures of national income, in the form of decennial averages, have been worked out by W. G. Hoffmann, J. H. Müller, F. Knoll and associates back to 1850. It is hoped to develop an annual series and to push the data farther back in time. Cf. the chapter by Hoffman, *ibid.*, pp. 95–118. See also Hoffmann and Müller, *Das deutsche Volkseinkommen 1851–1957* (Tübingen, 1959); and Wagenführ's estimates of industrial output cited below, p. 556, n. 1.

Table 45. *Economic Development in the Third Quarter of the Nineteenth Century*

	Railroad mileage (statute miles)	Coal production or consumption (1000 metric tons)[b]	Steam-power capacity[e] (1000 h.p.)	Pig iron output (1000 metric tons)	Raw cotton consumption (1000 metric tons)
Germany					
1850	3,639	5,100[c]	260	212	17·1
1869	10,834	26,774	2,480	1,413	64·1
1873[a]	14,842	36,392	—	2,241	117·8
France					
1850	1,869	7,225	370	406	59·3
1869	10,518	21,432	1,850	1,381	93·7
1873[a]	11,500	24,702	—	1,382	55·4[g]
United Kingdom					
1850	6,621	37,500[d]	1,290[f]	2,249	266·8[f]
1869	15,145	97,066	4,040[f]	5,446	425·8[f]
1873	16,082	112,604	—	6,566	565·1[f]
Belgium					
1850	531	3,481	70	145	10·0
1869	1,800	7,822	350	535	16·3
1873	2,335	10,219	—	607	18·0

SOURCES AND NOTES

Railroad mileage. G. Stürmer, *Geschichte der Eisenbahnen* (Bromberg, 1872), pp. 90–1, 54–61, 137, 149, 154–8; William Page, *Commerce and Industry* (2 vols.; London, 1919), II, 170–1; *Statistisches Jahrbuch für das deutsche Reich*, XII (1891), 90; *Annu. statistique de la France*, VII (1884), 456; *Annu. statistique de la Belgique*, XXI (1890), 326, 328.

Coal. We have no official estimates for Britain before 1854. The unofficial guesses before that date all proved to be serious underestimates when complete returns came in. For this early period, see the 'Report of the Commissioners Appointed to Inquire into

[a] All German figures for 1873 are swollen by the annexation of Alsace-Lorraine; conversely the French achievements are diminished.

[b] For Germany, production; for the U.K., France, and Belgium, consumption. (The one country for which consumption figures are indispensable is France, which was importing almost 40 per cent of its coal requirements in 1850, almost 30 per cent in 1869.) For Germany, production of ordinary coal only; to this would have to be added lignite (7,569,000 tons in 1869, 9,752,900 tons in 1873), with a calorific content roughly equal to two-ninths that of regular coal.

[c] An estimate based on extrapolation of a ratio of Prussian to German output of 82 to 100 (the ratio of 1860). Prussian coal output in 1850 is given as 4,153,000 tons.

[d] By extrapolation from post-1854 figures.

[e] Estimates for 1850 and 1870 (on 1869 lines) only.

[f] Great Britain, rather than United Kingdom.

[g] A bad year; consumption in 1872 was 80,257 tons.

the Several Matters Relating to Coal in the United Kingdom, Report of Committee
E', in *Parliamentary Papers*, 1871, XVIII (C. 435–II). These have been reprinted in such
other sources as J. R. McCulloch's *Commercial Dictionary*, and A. J. Mundella, 'What
Are the Conditions on Which the Commercial and Manufacturing Supremacy of
Great Britain Depend, and Is There Any Reason to Think They May Have Been or
May Be Endangered?' *J. Roy. Statistical Soc.* XLI (1878), 109. For the period after
1854, there are the annual volumes of Robert Hunt's *Mineral Statistics*: or the 'Final
Report of the Royal Commission...Coal Resources' (Cd. 2363), in *Parliamentary
Papers*, 1905, XVI, 24–5. For Germany, official figures for the entire *Zollverein*
go back to 1860; cf. the *Statistisches Jahrbuch*, I (1880), 30; XIV (1893), 128. For
earlier years, we have figures of output in Prussia in A. Bienengräber, *Statistik des
Verkehrs und Verbrauchs im Zollverein* (Berlin, 1868), p. 260; and K. F. Dieterici,
*Statistische Uebersicht der wichtigsten Gegenstände des Verkehrs und Verbrauchs im preuss-
ischen Staate und im deutschen Zollverbande* (6 vols.; Berlin, 1838–1857), *passim*. For
France, *Annu. statistique*, rés. rétro. LVII (1946), 230*–1*. For Belgium, Amé Wibail,
'L'évolution économique de l'industrie charbonnière belge depuis 1831', *Bull. de
l'Inst. des Sciences Economiques* (Louvain), VI, no. 1 (1934), 21–2.

Steam power. From Mulhall, *Dictionary of Statistics* (4th ed.; London, 1899),
p. 545.

Pig iron. As with coal, official British iron statistics begin in 1854; the subsequent
returns are given in Hunt, *Mineral Statistics*. See also the *Iron and Coal Trades Review*,
Diamond Jubilee Number (December 1927), p. 133. For the years before 1854, see
British Iron and Steel Federation, *Statistics of the Iron and Steel Industries* (London,
1934), p. 4; H. Scrivenor, *History of the Iron Trade* (London, 1854); and W. Oechel-
häuser, *Vergleichende Statistik der Eisen-Industrie aller Länder* (Berlin, 1852), p. 144. For
Germany, see Beck, *Geschichte des Eisens*, IV, 731–2, 982; *Statistisches Jahrbuch*, III (1883),
34. For France, *Annu. statistique*, rés. rétro. LVIII (1951), 134–5. For Belgium, A.
Wibail, 'L'évolution économique de la sidérurgie belge de 1830 à 1913', *Bull. de l'Inst.
des Sciences Economiques*, V, no. 1 (1933), 50–1, 60.

Raw Cotton. For Britain, T. Ellison, *The Cotton Trade of Great Britain* (London,
1886), appendix, table 1. For Germany, Bienengräber, *Statistik*, pp. 202–3; *Statistisches Jahrbuch*, III (1882), 134. For France, *Annu. statistique*, LVII (1946), 241*–2*. For
Belgium, *Annu. statistique de la Belgique*, II (1871), 226–7; VI (1875), 236–7.

belong in the latter; with their ramification and elaboration in later
decades, they laid the basis for a new long wave of expansion that some
writers have come to call the Second Industrial Revolution.

The quickening of the pace of development in the 1850's can be
understood only in terms of a remarkable conjuncture of endogenous
and exogenous stimuli to growth. Negative, first: the nations of
western and central Europe had lifted the mortgage of pre-capitalist
institutions, broken the strongest of the bonds of tradition, and, thanks
to the railroad, were well on the way to eliminating those natural
obstacles to the movement of the factors of production and to the
exchange of goods that had fragmented and straitened economic
activity since time past memory. We noted above that the productivity of a transportation facility is discontinuous, jumping sharply
with each of the connections that turn isolated lines into a coherent

network. Belgium had her north–south, east–west cross by 1844. For Germany, the critical gains came in the late 1840's: by 1850 goods and passengers could move by rail—with numerous changes, to be sure—from Aachen to Breslau and from Kiel to Munich. France was the slowest of the three: as of the middle of the century, she still had only the beginnings of a radial network out of Paris, plus some scattered pieces in the provinces. But the early 1850's were years of rapid construction, and by the end of 1854 lines were open from Lille to Bordeaux and Marseilles and from Le Havre to Strasbourg.

The economic implications of cheaper transport have already been discussed; the effect on the market and competition, however, deserves to be stressed again. Rapid growth and technological advance do not necessarily go hand in hand. On the contrary, an increase in demand may so raise prices as to make obsolescent methods profitable and encourage producers to retain, or return to using equipment that would otherwise be abandoned. If the decades of the 1850's and 1860's were characterized by both major gains in output and a drastic purge of industrial enterprise, it was in large measure because certain of the changes in the technological and commercial climate were at once excitant and cathartic. The railroad was basic here: it provided the means by which competitive pressures could be applied and marginally inefficient units, once protected by distance and topography, squeezed out.

On the other hand, rail transport by itself was simply a means. In societies like those of the Continent, where human values, habit, and law joined to deprecate and diminish price competition, an incentive or compulsion to struggle was needed if the market mechanism was to be effective in diffusing technological change. Periodic crises, with their abrupt contractions of credit and deflation of demand and prices, served in their times as 'moments of truth'; that of 1857 was especially purgative. At the same time, however, a conjuncture of institutional changes exercised over these decades a persistent pressure toward rationalization—(1) within the individual national economies, by facilitating the entry of new firms and the expansion of the more efficient and ambitious; and (2) between economies, by opening them to foreign enterprise and manufactures.

Thus, already before 1850, the limitations on *Gewerbefreiheit* that persisted in some parts of central Europe were essentially confined to the traditional handicrafts and had little effect on the development of a factory labour force. But in the early 1860's even these vestiges of control disappeared in all but a few areas, and freedom of enterprise was incorporated in the *Gewerbeordnung für den Norddeutscher Bund* adopted by the North German Confederation in 1869 and introduced into the southern states from 1870 to 1872.[1] Similarly, restrictions on the establishment of joint-stock corporations—a form of enterprise indispensable in economies poor in capital and yet compelled to create much of their industry *de novo*—were mitigated by increasing complaisance of the state or evaded by recourse to substitute forms not requiring official authorization, in particular, the *société en commandite par actions* (*Kommanditgesellschaft auf Aktien*). In Germany, moreover, the very multiplicity of jurisdictions proved an advantage. In fields like banking and insurance, where location was not rigidly dictated by material considerations, it was often possible to obtain from the smaller states the authorization refused by Prussia or Frankfurt.

In the meantime, the growing demand by projectors, industrialists, and investors for easier conditions of company formation overcame the suspicions and hostility of the governing bureaucracy and the general resentment and fear of free speculation and secured the right to limited liability by simple registration. The first country to take this step was Britain, in 1856 (generalized by Act of 1862). In 1863 France created the *société à responsabilité limité*, a true limited-liability corporation, but restricted in size; the complete abolition of controls did not come until 1867. Germany was somewhat slower. A number of jurisdictions, Hamburg and Lübeck for example, had always permitted free incorporation. The vast majority, however, including Prussia, required authorization, and while the state proved tolerant in certain areas— insurance, transportation, public utilities—it tended to be difficult about manufacturing ventures and intolerant of banking projects. Nothing illustrates more clearly the dampening effect of these controls than the increase in company formation in Prussia after the establishment of automatic registration in June 1870: 123 firms capitalized at 225 million taler in all the years before 1850; 295 firms capitalized at 802 million taler from 1851 to 1870; 833 firms at 843 million taler from 1870 to 1874.[2] Even allowing for the stimulating boom conditions of

[1] The most convenient introduction to the history of *Gewerbefreiheit* is the articles on 'Handwerk' and 'Zunftwesen' by Wilhelm Stieda in the *Handwörterbuch der Staatswissenschaften* (3rd ed., Jena 1911). The classic study of the subject is Kurt von Rohrscheidt, *Vom Zunftzwang zur Gewerbefreiheit* (Berlin, 1898). See also T. Hamerow, *Restoration and Reaction* (Princeton, 1958), ch. II and bibliographical notes, pp. 295–6, and Wolfram Fischer, *Handwerksrecht und Handwerkswirtschaft um 1800* (Berlin, 1955), ch. III, which in spite of the title deals with later developments.

[2] *Jahrbuch für die amtliche Statistik des Preussischen Staates*, IV, 1 (1876), 134. See also Ernst Engel, *Die erwerbsthätigen juristischen Personen, insbesondere die Actiengesellschaften, im preussischen Staate* (Berlin, 1876). On the general question of legal structure, company formation, and economic development, see D. S. Landes, 'The Structure of Enterprise in the Nineteenth Century: the Cases of Britain and Germany', in Comité International des Sciences Historiques, XIe Congrès International des Sciences His-

the last years, the power of this release from constraint is impressive. A similar explosion took place in Britain in the early 1860's and another, though much weaker, in France after 1867.[1]

There were other legal changes in the direction of freer, easier enterprise. The prohibition of usury was dropped in Britain (1854), Holland (1857), Belgium (1865), Prussia and the North German Confederation (1867).[2] Increasingly, foreign corporations were permitted to cross boundary lines and operate on a basis of equality with home firms without special authorization (thus agreements by France and Belgium, 1857, and France and Britain, 1862). New commercial instruments like the cheque were legalized and domesticated; the penalties for debt and bankruptcy were eased; patent law was amended to include trademarks and other intangible forms of business property; and commercial relations in general were simplified by the codification of the congeries of statutes and decrees accumulated over the years (French law of 13 June 1866; *Allgemeines Deutsche Handelsgesetzbuch*, 1861 [Prussia] *et seq.*).

In all these and other areas, the gains of the middle decades were simply a continuation of trends that went back to the eighteenth century and beyond. The history of commercial and civil law in the West is in large measure the story of the progressive adaptation of the usages of an agrarian, community-centred, tradition-bound society to the requirements of an industrial, individualistic, and rational—hence mobile—capitalism. The full story remains to be told; unfortunately, this is an area that economic historians have tended to ignore or leave to legists.[3] Yet one should not confuse indifference or dismissal with a considered judgment, and it would be a mistake to construe the paucity of material as evidence of the triviality of the subject.

On the other hand, lack of data and analysis does make it difficult to integrate legal considerations into the complex of factors shaping economic growth. Clearly, many of these changes are simply surface manifestations of a deeper transformation; the law is the reflection—frequently a belated reflection—of man's values and material needs. But the fact that it is often belated is evidence that it is not simply a dependent variable in the service of economic development. Not only do economic interests conflict and pull both legislation and administra-

toriques, Stockholm, 21–28 août 1960, *Rapports*, vol. v: *Histoire contemporaine* (Uppsala, 1960), pp. 107–28, and the sources cited there.

[1] On the British boom of the 1860's, see Landes, *Bankers and Pashas*, ch. 11.

[2] By law of 9 June 1857, the Bank of France was permitted to set its rate of discount at more than 6 per cent; this privilege was extended by judicial interpretation to all banking houses.

[3] One of the few books that have attempted to deal with the problem is Georges Ripert, *Aspects juridiques du capitalisme moderne* (2nd ed.; Paris, 1951).

tion in different directions; non-economic considerations have their say, and questions of morality and social prejudices intervene. Finally the law has a rationale of its own—a conservatism built on precedent and the niggling complexity of institutionalized justice.

As a result, the timing of changes in legal institutions can and does materially affect the pace and character of economic development. The impact on short-run growth—on the rhythm and amplitude of the cycle, for example—is most obvious. The long-run effect is less easily discernible, and indeed the nature of the relationship between short and long run is still a subject of debate among economic theorists and historians. Suffice it to note here that this reciprocal adjustment of law and industrial capitalism did take place over a period of more than a century; that one of the periods of most rapid change in both areas was the middle decades of the last century; and that the legal changes of that period, especially those establishing the charter of modern corporate enterprise, contributed substantially to continental Europe's new-found ability to compete with Britain.

One modification of the politico-legal climate of enterprise deserves special mention: the general lowering of barriers to international trade. This took three forms: (1) the elimination or reduction of restrictions and levies on the traffic of such international waterways as the Danube (1857), the Rhine (1861), the Scheldt (1863), the lower Elbe (1861), upper Elbe (1863 and 1870), the Danish Sound and the channels between the Baltic and North Seas (1857); (2) the simplification of the confusion of currencies that was the monetary counterpart of Europe's political fragmentation (German union thaler of 1857; uniform Austrian florin, 1858; Latin monetary agreement among France, Belgium, Switzerland, and Italy, 1865); and most important (3) a series of commercial treaties providing for a substantial diminution of tariff rates between the leading industrial nations of Europe (Britain–France, 1860; France–Belgium, 1861; France–Prussia, 1862; by extension, France–Zollverein, 1866; Prussia–Belgium, 1863 and 1865; Prussia–Britain, 1865; Prussia–Italy, 1865; and numerous others).

This cluster of trade agreements is unique in economic history. It would be impossible here to examine in detail the particular reasons why each of the signatories decided to sacrifice traditional protections of home industry and trade for the benefits of increased exchange and the risks of competition. We may note in passing, however, that aside from the usual pressure of selected business groups for lower tariffs and the special political considerations that motivated, first, Napoleon III and then the government of Prussia to seek freer trade by treaty, these accords reflected a general mood of optimism and of doctrinal acceptance, in political and intellectual if not in business circles, of the pacific as well as economic virtues of international exchange. *Aperire terram gentibus* was the slogan of the day. Here we rejoin in effect the legal liberalization discussed above. It was as though the very expansiveness of the economy, the general euphoria of growth and prosperity, had persuaded nations and people to let their guard down, to trade control for freedom, parochialism for universalism, tradition for change, the safety of exclusiveness for the danger yet potential profit of the open world.

Freedom was, as we shall see, a fleeting mood, an aberration. The period from the late 1870's on was one of steady closure and constriction, reversed—and then for how long?—only after the Second World War. While the mood lasted, however, it gave a powerful impetus to specialization along lines of comparative advantage, with concomitant economies of scale and increases in return. To the surprise of adamant protectionists—if not to their discomfiture—all nations saw their volume of exports grow. Home industries did not collapse before British competition, but rather changed and grew stronger in the process. Marginally inefficient firms, vegetating in the shelter of protective duties, were compelled to re-tool or close. In France especially, where the high tariff had long been a fetish, the effect of the commercial treaties, coming as they did on the heels of a severe commercial crisis (1857–9), was to purge manufacturing enterprise and hasten its relocation along rational lines.[1] In Germany and Belgium, where customs rates had been lower, the impact was necessarily weaker.

Even more important than these negative stimuli in shaping the conjuncture of the 1850's and 1860's were the positive forces for expansion: (1) improvements in transport, (2) new sources of energy and raw materials, (3) a sharp increase in the supply of money, and above all (4) a creative entrepreneurial response to this combination of long-run opportunity and short-run facility.

1. Transportation first: the most important advance was the continued ramification of the railroad system.[2] Fifty thousand miles of new line were laid in Europe between 1850 and 1870, as against 15,000 in all the years before, at a cost of 30 milliard francs. Of these, the French built 9300, at an outlay of over 7 milliard francs, while the Germans, profiting from lower land costs and economizing on the

---

[1] Cf. A. L. Dunham, *The Anglo-French Treaty of Commerce of 1860 and the Progress of the Industrial Revolution in France* (Ann Arbor, 1930); and C. Fohlen, *L'industrie textile au temps du Second Empire* (Paris, 1956). The archives of individual firms—for example, De Wendel and Le Creusot in iron and steel manufacture—offer eloquent evidence of the retooling undertaken in response to the new conditions of international competition.

[2] On the contribution of the railway to economic growth, see above, p. 382.

roadbed, built 7500 miles for about 4 milliards. Even so, almost three quarters of the share capital invested in Prussian joint-stock companies from 1850 to 1870 went to railway firms. And these expenditures do not take into account investment in and production of rails and rolling stock for lines in other countries. Already in the 1840's, Britain had played an important role in the construction of the early continental railways, exporting labour and skills as well as capital and material. In the 1850's Britain turned her attention increasingly to areas outside of Europe—Egypt, India, North America—while France became the most active promoter and builder of European roads—in Spain, Switzerland, Italy, the Danube valley, and Russia. Exact figures are not available, but it would seem that France was placing more than half as much money in foreign railways in this period as she put into her own.[1] From mid-century on, the railroad, by its demand for capital goods and labour and the cumulative effect of these expenditures as they worked and reworked their way through the economy, had displaced textiles as the drummer of industrial activity, setting the beat for short cycles and long trends alike.

2. Manufacturing industry is from one point of view the use of energy to transform raw materials into finished products. With the growth of industry, the appetite of European economies for both these ingredients grew enormously; one can follow the hunt for new sources of supply from the Middle Ages on. And clearly, if this search had not been successful or if substitutes for commodities in short supply had not been found, the Industrial Revolution as we have known it would have been impossible. The reader will recall in this connection the importance of coke smelting to the British iron manufacture, of the replacement of vegetable by mineral sources of alkali to the chemical industry, of Eli Whitney's gin and American cultivation to the cotton trade.

The discovery or creation of new sources of energy and raw materials is in part responsive to need, in part fortuitous. Both factors give rise

---

[1] On Britain, the best treatment remains Leland Jenks's classic *Migration of British Capital to 1875* (New York, 1927). On France, see Rondo Cameron, *France and the Economic Development of Europe, 1800–1914: Conquests of Peace and Seeds of War* (Princeton, 1961), who estimates French investment in foreign transport at 5250 million francs from 1852 to 1881 (see table 3, p. 88). A team at the Centre de Recherches sur l'Histoire des Entreprises (which is in turn part of the Centre de Recherches Historiques) in Paris is currently preparing, under the direction of Bertrand Gille, a series of studies on the export of French capital. A number of preliminary articles on the subject have already appeared in the *Bulletin* of the Centre. Germany, poorer to begin with and investing more heavily in home industry, was slow to join the competition for concessions and contracts; even then, her role was never comparable to that of Britain or France.

to irregularity in the growth of the stock of resources at the disposal of the economy: there are fat periods and lean. The middle decades of the nineteenth century were bonanza years in both respects. Bird droppings (guano) were collected from islands in the Pacific and brought as fertilizer to the fields of Europe. Wool and hides from Australia, South Africa, and South America began to pour into the European market and submerge domestic sources of supply; the wool was the more welcome for the cotton famine of the 1860's, which cut severely into the output of cotton cloth and clothing.[1] Vegetable oils, mainly from Africa, became increasingly important as a substitute for traditional animal fats in the production of soap and candles.[2] The effort of a French syndicate of the 1830's to exploit a monopoly of Sicilian sulphur and squeeze the European chemical trade led to the perfecting of processes using sulphides as the raw material for the manufacture of sulphuric acid and to the discovery of new deposits of pyrites in the United Kingdom, Norway and, above all, Spain. By the 1870's, well over 90 per cent of Britain's acid was prepared in this manner.[3] The world was indeed opening up.

More important, however, and second only to the railroad as a focus of investment and stimulus to entrepreneurial activity, was the availability of newly found or exploited energy resources, above all, coal. The existence of deeper beds beneath the marl of Westphalia was known as early as the 1830's, but the first efforts at extraction were handi-

[1] Imports of raw wool into the United Kingdom by source (annual averages in millions of pounds weight):

	South Africa	Australia and New Zealand	South America
1840–4	1·4	14·0	5·0
1850–4	6·7	43·7	6·5
1860–4	18·9	75·0	14·3
1870–4	37·1	188·6	18·2

SOURCE. Statistical Abstract for the United Kingdom.

[2] Annual averages of imports of vegetable oils into the United Kingdom:

	Palm oil (thousand cwt.)	Coconut oil (thousand cwt.)	Olive oil (thousand tuns)
1840–4	395·0	57·2	10·9
1850–4	593·9	125·8	12·8
1860–4	773·4	267·0	19·1
1870–4	1001·7	244·8	28·7

SOURCE. Statistical Abstract for the United Kingdom.

[3] In the period from 1840 to, say, 1880, Britain's annual consumption of pyrites increased from a negligible amount to perhaps 700,000 or 800,000 tons. Cf. Haber Chemical Industry, p. 103.

capped by lack of capital, and a precise apprehension of the nature of the deposits took decades. The discovery and prospection of the Pas-de Calais extension of the Northern field in France came later, in 1845–7. In both cases the real harvest came in the 1850's. Coal output in the Ruhr went from 1,640,000 tons in 1850 to 11,812,500 in 1869; the gains in the Pas-de-Calais were equally spectacular: 4672 tons in 1851 to 2,188,247 in 1871. At the same time, as noted earlier, overall extraction rose substantially in both countries—in Germany, from 4,192,000 to 23,761,000 tons; in France, from 4,434,000 to 13,330,000.[1]

The Germans were doubly favoured in their exploitation of the deeper Ruhr beds. Not only did the coal extracted provide energy; it produced a coke ideally suited to the blast furnace; and iron ore was found interspersed with some of the measures, yielding a *Kohleneisenstein* comparable to the blackband that had made possible the great expansion of Scottish metallurgy in the 1830's. From 1852 to 1860 ore extraction in the Ruhr jumped from 5000 to 227,000 tons. Once the Westphalian industrialists realized the potentiality of this providential combination, they went over to coke-blast iron with a vigour that not only redeemed the technological retardation of the first half of the century but has tended to obscure the very memory of this earlier lag.

3. The contribution of new gold to European industrial development in the 1850's is only partially measurable in terms of the direct increase in the supply of money. This was impressive enough: even allowing for a responsively swelling export of silver to the East, the net gain was a substantial fraction of the pre-existing metallic circulation, especially important in countries like France and Germany where popular mistrust and the conservatism of financial and official circles inhibited the use of paper money. At the same time, issue of paper money increased on the strength of the growing stock of bullion: note circulation of the Bank of France more than tripled, rising from 450 million francs in 1850 to 1550 million in 1870;[2] while that of the Preussische Bank, desirous of replacing with its own paper the notes of other German institutions, shot upward at a dizzy pace—from 18,370 million taler in 1850 to 163,260 millions in 1870.[3]

---

[1] For statistics of the output of coal in the Ruhr, see Prussia, Königliches Statistisches Bureau, *Jahrbuch für die amtliche Statistik des Preussischen Staates*, IV, 1 (1876), 235.

[2] *Annuaire statistique*, LVII (1946), rés. rétro. pp. 140*–1*.

[3] H. von Poschinger, *Bankwesen und Bankpolitik in Preussen* (3 vols.; Berlin, 1879), II, 373. Some of this increase is explained by laws of 1855 and 1857 that forbade the circulation of banknotes of other German States within the Prussian monarchy. But Poschinger seems to have underestimated the increase. According to the *Jahrbuch für die amtliche Statistik des Preussischen Staats*, IV, 1 (1876), 469, the note circulation of the Preussische Bank in 1870 was 586,437,000 marks (equal to 195,479,000 taler).

More significant, however, were the indirect consequences of easy money. The rate of interest fell, momentarily to as little as 2 per cent on short-term paper in Britain, 3 per cent in France, slightly higher in Germany (always hungrier for capital). Concomitantly, the volume of credit expanded. This was the critical consideration, for—as mentioned earlier—it is not so much the price of capital that counts as its availability. Supply and demand curves may be smooth and continuous in theory; they may even be so in practice for certain commodities in certain markets at certain times. But the short-run supply curve of bank credit—as against that of all credit, usurious and otherwise—is truncated by the banker's values, by his sanctification of prudence, security, liquidity. Up to a point, the institutional lender tries to ration funds by price; beyond that point, he fixes quotas, or simply waits for the outlook to improve. And while there are other lenders, these are often limited in resources or set conditions so onerous as to make borrowing irrational—without choking it off, however: desperation is notoriously deaf to reason.

Moreover, this increase in the volume of credit was far out of proportion to that of the money supply. The critical consideration was the rediscount policy of the central banks, and this was essentially a function of bullion reserves. These jumped for the Bank of England from £8·3 millions in October 1847, to an average of £21·8 million in the third quarter of 1852; for the Bank of France, from one of 122·6 million francs in 1847 to 584·8 million in 1852.[1] And when the central banks were ready to take paper, everybody was ready to take paper. The great pyramid of debt could be built higher, fostering speculation in commodities and securities, facilitating the formation of new companies and the operation of old. Like the merchants of the Medina del Campo and the Antwerp *bourse* in the sixteenth century, the traders and bankers of nineteenth-century London and Paris waited eagerly for the first word of sails off Land's End or l'Ouessant bringing golden cargoes from the Pacific. The amounts involved were a tiny fraction of debts outstanding in the money and securities markets; but they made all the difference between easy and hard liquidation at month's end.

To be sure, the stimulus afforded by such an injection of money weakened rapidly as inflation vitiated the incremental advantages of investment and the exponential demand for credit pushed the rate of interest upward. Nevertheless, one must not underestimate the long-

[1] For the Bank of England, T. Tooke and Newmarch, *A History of Prices and of the State of the Circulation from 1792 to 1856* (5 vols.; New York [reprinted], n.d.), p. 566; see also J. R. T. Hughes, *Fluctuations in Trade, Industry and Finance: A Study of British Economic Development 1850–1860* (Oxford, 1960), p. 290. For the Bank of France, *Ann. statistique*, LCII (1946), *rés. rétro.* p. 140*.

run significance of such periodic excitants. For one thing, they can change the pattern and significance of the business cycle, making upswings more buoyant and downturns milder, with obviously favourable consequences for the rate of growth.[1] Thus the industrial as well as commercial development of this period is in large measure the story of three great credit booms: 1852–7 (Britain, Germany, France); 1861–6 (more Britain than Germany or France); and 1869–73 (primarily Germany). The last, like the others, was built on easy money, derived, however, not from an influx of gold, but from a transfusion of five milliard francs—Bismarck's unprecedented war indemnity after the triumph of 1870. For another, they facilitate the accomplishment of technological and institutional changes of continuing importance.

4. These bring us to what may be called the 'financial revolution' of the nineteenth century. This was closely associated with the credit inflation of these years, both as cause and effect, and was the counterpart and companion piece in the banking sphere to the technological transformation of industry.

The revolution had two aspects. One was a drastic widening of the clientele for banking services and credit. Here, as in industrial mass production, Britain pioneered. Her early 'vulgarization' of the money market was, as we have seen, a source of great economic strength, and the rise of the great discount houses and the joint-stock commercial banks (London and Westminster Bank, 1834) continued the process.[2] If one sets aside certain early efforts, generally abortive, the diffusion of these principles to the Continent dates from the 1850's. There were, first, the joint-stock discount banks established to ease commercial credit during and after the crisis of 1848: the French and Belgian *comptoirs d'escompte*; the *Union du Crédit* in Brussels (1848); the *Schaffhausen'sche Bankverein* in Cologne (1848); the *Discontogesellschaft* in Berlin (1851); the *Frankfurter Bank* (1853). These were followed by such institutions as the *Crédit Industriel et Commercial* in Paris (1859), explicitly intended to introduce English commercial banking practice to France and a pioneer on the Continent in the use of the cheque as an instrument of payment. Finally, the great branch banks rounded out the system, some resulting from the proliferation of the institutions in the great financial centres (including central banks like the *Banque de France*), others developing out of local enterprises like the *Crédit Lyonnais* (1863). The result was a vastly more efficient sweep of financial

---

[1] Cf. the analysis of I. Svennilson, *Growth and Stagnation in the European Economy* (Geneva: United Nations Economic Commission for Europe, 1954), pp. 12–13.

[2] The best source is W. T. C. King, *History of the London Discount Market* (London, 1936); see also S. Evelyn Thomas, *The Rise and Growth of Joint-Stock Banking*, vol. 1: (*Britain to 1860*) (London, 1934).

resources: the new banking networks were able to draw in the rapidly growing savings and working capital of myriads of small and middling tradesmen and producers; for the first time, they brought country as well as city into the money market. Thus the Continent began to approach that mobility of capital that Britain had achieved half a century before.[1]

More important, however, for industrial development was the second half of this revolution: the rise of the joint-stock investment bank. This was a continental innovation and went back at least as far as those years after the Congress of Vienna when Europe set out once again on the path to a modern economy. As early as 1819 a plan for a Bavarian National Bank included a provision for mortgage loans to industrial enterprise; the Estates tabled the proposal.[2] A more specific project by a group of French bankers and manufacturers to found a *Société Commanditaire de l'Industrie* failed in 1825 owing to opposition from the defenders of the power of landed wealth. It was in Belgium that the institution got its start. There the *Société Générale* (founded 1822; began with mortgage loans to industrial enterprise in the 1820's; turned to intensive investment banking in 1835) and the *Banque de Belgique* (1835) promoted a company boom in mining and metallurgy in the years 1835–8 that accounts for the precocity of Belgian industrialization.[3] In the 1840's the French returned to the charge and established what were in effect investment banks (*caisses*), which took the form of limited share partnerships for want of official approval for regular *sociétés anonymes*. But it was only in the 1850's that the corporate

[1] The literature on the banking history of this period is fairly abundant. Among the more useful secondary sources are, for France: R. Bigo, *Les banques françaises au cours du XIXe siècle* (Paris, 1947); A. Courtois fils, *Histoire des banques en France* (2nd ed.; Paris, 1881); P. Dupont-Ferrier, *Le marché financier de Paris sous le Second Empire* (Paris, 1925); E. Kaufmann, *La banque en France* (trans. A. S. Sacker; Paris, 1914); Jean Bouvier, *Le Crédit Lyonnais de 1863 à 1882* (2 vols.; Paris, 1961); and G. Ramon, *Histoire de la Banque de France* (Paris, 1929).

For Germany, see Poschinger, *Bankwesen und Bankpolitik*; A. Krueger, *Das Kölner Bankiergewerbe vom Ende des 18. Jahrhunderts bis 1875* (Essen, 1925); F. Hecht, *Bankwesen und Bankpolitik in den süddeutschen Staaten 1819–1875* (Jena, 1880); K. Jackel, *Gründung und Entwicklung der Frankfurter Bank, 1854–1900* (Leipzig, 1915).

For Belgium, see B. S. Chlepner, *Le marché financier belge depuis cent ans* (Brussels, 1930); A. van Schoubroeck, *L'évolution des banques belges en fonction de la conjoncture de 1850 à 1872* (Gembloux, 1951).

For Holland, H. M. Hirschfeld, *Het Ontstaan van het moderne Bankwezen in Nederland* (Rotterdam, 1922).

[2] W. Zorn, *Handels- und Industriegeschichte Bayerisch-Schwabens 1648–1870* (Augsburg, 1961), p. 129.

[3] Cf. P. Schöller, 'La transformation économique de la Belgique de 1832 à 1844', *Bull. l'Institut de Recherches Economiques et Sociales* (Louvain), XIV (1948).

finance company took hold—first in France, where the brothers Pereire founded the *Crédit Mobilier* (1852) that gave the institution one of its generic names, then in Germany, Austria, Spain, Italy, and Holland, and finally, from the 1860's on, throughout the business world. For only then were the political and economic conditions for easy company formation and flotation satisfied: in France, a new regime anxious to build a counterpoise to older financial interests; in Germany and elsewhere, impecunious governments hungry for outside capital and amenable to pecuniary persuasion; and an easy, indeed, exalted, capital market.[1]

It would be impossible to do justice in a few paragraphs to the contribution of the investment bank to the economic development of these decades. We will have to confine ourselves to a few general points:

(1) The principal virtue of the investment banks lay in their ability to channel wealth into industry. Bigger and richer than the traditional private houses, they were, like the joint-stock commercial banks, an active force for widening and deepening the capital market. They sought out the largest possible clientele for their promotions, which they advertised as one would a patent medicine. And whereas the old private merchant banks viewed industrial credit as a hazardous operation incompatible with the character of their resources, and even the more versatile joint-stock commercial banks looked upon it as an accessory activity at best, the finance companies made it their *raison d'être*.

(2) The contribution of the *crédit mobilier* was manifestly most important where the opportunities for industrial investment were abundant and the supply of capital limited or hard to mobilize. Thus it came late to Britain (1860's) and then did comparatively little for the improvement or expansion of the transport network and manufacturing plant. Rather, it concentrated its activities in the lucrative but risky areas of commodity speculation, secondary short-term financing, overseas trade and investment.

By contrast, Germany is the best illustration of the generous yield of systematic investment in a backward economy of high potential.[2]

---

[1] D. S. Landes, 'Vieille banque et banque nouvelle: la révolution financière du dix-neuvième siècle', *Revue d'histoire moderne et contemporaine*, III (1956), 204–22; R. Cameron, 'The Crédit Mobilier and the Economic Development of Europe', *J. Political Economy*, LXI (1953), 461–88; R. Cameron, 'Founding the Bank of Darmstadt', *Explorations in Entrepreneurial History*, VIII (1955–6), 113–30. A translation of the last, with supporting documents, appeared in *Tradition*, II (1957), 104–31.

[2] Cf. A. Gerschenkron, 'Economic Backwardness in Historical Perspective', in B. Hoselitz, ed., *The Progress of Underdeveloped Areas* (Chicago, 1952), pp. 3–29,

Already in the 1840's, the more far-sighted missionaries of national development were calling for banks to promote industry and transport as well as to perform the traditional functions of commercial credit and exchange. Several of these projects were well advanced when stifled by the economic and political crisis of 1846–8. In the 1850's, however, hard on the heels of the *Crédit Mobilier* and with its assistance, Mevissen founded his *Darmstädter Bank* (1853); Hansemann reorganized the *Discontogesellschaft* (1856); a syndicate of leading Berlin merchant bankers formed the *Handelsgesellschaft* (1856); and so on to the capital sum of over 200 million taler (equal approximately to 740 million francs) in new banks by 1857.[1]

Not all of these were explicitly *crédits mobiliers*. But even those that were nominally commercial banks found it hard to resist the opportunities of industrial finance. Moreover, the investment banks were generally mixed in function, that is, they received deposits and performed the traditional commercial services at the same time as they promoted companies, floated securities, and lent at long term. This was the most revolutionary feature of the new institution. By all that was sacred in good banking practice, sight and demand claims were incompatible with the immobilization of assets in speculative ventures. The mixed bank was in principle an unviable monster; many did in fact collapse when crisis followed boom. But the great majority throve, in large measure because this combination of deposit and investment functions could also be a source of tremendous strength. For it multiplied many times the ability of these institutions to accumulate resources, and this in turn meant greater support for the banks' industrial and commercial protégés, enabling them to expand easily in prosperity and sustaining them in adversity.

The result was a circle of mutual assistance and reinforcement. Under unfavourable circumstances, this interdependence could bring all down together, and many a Cassandra predicted the direst of consequences for all concerned. In an economy growing so rapidly as the German, however, the effect was one of general stimulation. During the decades preceding the First World War, the system seemed to march from success to success, the so-called *Grossbanken* fattening on their

which develops a theme that goes back through Schumpeter and a number of German students of banking history to such contemporary promoters and observers as Mevissen and Horn.

[1] According to Max Wirth, *Geschichte der Handelskrisen* (4th ed., Frankfurt-am-Main, 1890), p. 310. This sum comprises all banks, including the purely commercial institutions. But it is difficult to assemble figures on investment banks specifically because so many firms refused in practice to confine themselves to the activities provided for in their statutes. For purposes of comparison, new railroad shares in this period totalled 140 million taler, plus a substantial sum in bond issues.

triumphs, absorbing competitors, sowing the land with branches and subsidiaries.[1] It is no coincidence that German economists were the first to develop the conception of a new stage of economic organization —finance capitalism.

The French case was strikingly different. They were, after the Belgians, the first to develop joint-stock investment banking; and after the debacle of 1848, nowhere did the new financial era begin with so much *éclat*. Yet the long-run impact of the innovation was small, not so much for lack of means, that is, capital, as of opportunities to use it. Two factors were determining here. First, the French investor—in particular the *rentier* from outside the industrial sector—preferred fixed-interest securities, especially bonds issued or guaranteed by governments, to more speculative industrial shares. Promotional possibilities were biased accordingly. Second and more important, French business firms—the family partnership particularly, but joint-stock companies as well[2]—preferred to finance expansion out of profits, to build on the past rather than anticipate the future, and were willing to have recourse to long-term bank credit only *in extremis*. Hence high-quality borrowers were scarce. The *Crédit Mobilier* of the Pereires found it necessary from the start to look abroad for employment of much of its resources. And this was a development bank. The great commercial and deposit banks—the *Crédit Lyonnais, Société Générale* (1864), and others— made some tentative gestures in the direction of industrial investment in their early years but were rapidly disenchanted. As time passed, their coffers swelled with savings swept in by a growing net of branch banks, savings that might have provided a substantial addition to the capital of French industry; instead they went in large part into the funds of other lands. In the first decade of this century, when French banking was under attack for failing to develop home industry—the comparison was explicitly with Germany—Henri Germain of the *Crédit Lyonnais* put the lender's viewpoint brutally: there were, he said, no industrialists in France worthy of support. There were, of course, but they were not interested in borrowing.

So much for the long run, which resembles somewhat the British

[1] They also drew capital from outside Germany, particularly from France, in the form of short-term advances on their commercial paper. In effect, the same French deposit banks that were reluctant to provide capital for French industry were furnishing it to German producers: not directly—this would have violated good practice; but indirectly, by 'proper' loans to financial intermediaries more enterprising than themselves.

[2] On the entrepreneurial behaviour of the French family firm and its implications for growth, see the sources on p. 360, n. 1, above. On the investment policy of joint-stock companies and its similarity to that of the family firm, see Bouvier, *Le Crédit Lyonnais*, pp. 390–7.

experience. For the period that immediately concerns us, that is, the middle decades of the century, the mobilization of savings initiated by the *Crédit Mobilier* and effected by a variety of Parisian and local *sociétés de crédit* was a significant stimulus to growth. Money that would have been hoarded was put into circulation; and even capital that went abroad often returned in the form of contracts for French enterprises and orders for French manufactures. The push was not so direct or strong as in Germany or in the Belgium of the 1830's and 1840's. In part it was merely psychological, a heightening of euphoria. But it was a major element in the expansive conjuncture of these years.

We are now ready to consider the implications of this conjuncture for technological change and economic development. To save time and space, we shall focus the discussion on three points already adumbrated:

(1) the realization of the economic possibilities of the core innovations of the Industrial Revolution; specifically, the triumph in the more advanced European nations, of mechanization in textile manufacture, of the use of coal in iron-making, and of steam power;

(2) the concentration of production in ever-larger units; and

(3) the rationalization and relocation of industry along new regional lines.

(1) TECHNOLOGICAL ADVANCE

A. *Textiles*

By the middle of the century, Britain had more or less completed the transformation of her major textile industries. This was especially true of cotton, where the self-actor had gained its most obvious victories, the hand-loom weavers had consummated their agony, and those pioneers of the Industrial Revolution, the country water mills, had abandoned the struggle with the chimneyed factories of Lancashire. To be sure, there were survivals: the mule still accounted in 1850 for half the spindles in the industry; one spoke of 'a few thousand' draw looms in 1856; and here and there the big, cool wheels turned as before. But against these holdouts, the new techniques continued their remorseless advance: the self-actor won ground in the face of a steady shift to fine yarn that favoured the mule; the last hand looms vanished in the 1860's and 1870's, no longer because remuneration was inadequate but because there were no young people to carry on a dying trade; spindles and looms worked ever faster and better. Thus the giant steps were past. It was now a question of marginal gains in productivity, of filling in corners, of waiting for mechanical improvements to increase slightly the economic advantage of the new equipment, or for a contraction, cyclical or adventitious—as in the cotton famine of the 1860's—to squeeze out the inefficient producers.[1]

Change continued more important in wool, as might be expected of an industry that, for all its age, was technologically younger than cotton. In the woollen manufacture, the condenser filled in the otherwise complete sequence of mechanized operations: it replaced the hand piecers in taking off the loose strips of wool from the carder, and the old 'slubbing billy' in preparing the roving for the mule. The condenser was invented and perfected in New England around 1830 and was commonplace there by 1850. In Britain, Edward Baines was still speaking of it in 1858 as a 'new machine', but within another decade it was widespread in Yorkshire. Elsewhere it was still almost unknown.

Worsted was, as usual, more enterprising than its sister branch. In spinning, the cap frame began to replace the throstle in the 1840's; this and accessory improvements—more precise machine construction, increased power, better lubrication, more efficient transmission—made it possible to double or more in the 1850's the equipment tended by each worker. In weaving, power achieved from 1840 on the success it had won in cotton from the 1820's; by 1867, there were some 71,500 machine looms and the contest was over. But the biggest gain was in the preparation of the yarn: the machine comber, like the condenser, eliminated the one remaining gap in the sequence of mechanization and was, in its effects on productivity and employment, the last of the great textile inventions. Within a decade of its adoption around the middle of the century, it killed off a large and once-flourishing handicraft that, like the hand weaving of a generation before, had already begun to feel the pressure of the first, rudimentary combers and was shrivelling in anticipation of death. The perfected machines of the 1850's left no room for competition: one of them could turn out over 20,000 kilograms of combed wool a year, as against perhaps 350 kilograms for the best hand worker, with his pots to heat his combs, his oils to minimize breakage of the fibres, and his wife and children to bite out the knots that formed in the skeins of wool. The great beneficiary of the new machine was Britain, and specifically Bradford, the world's greatest centre of worsted manufacture: spindlage for England and Wales as a whole (85 per cent or more of it in Yorkshire) went from

---

[1] We need a history of the British cotton industry in the period after 1780, to link up with G. W. Daniels, *The Early English Cotton Industry*, and A. P. Wadsworth and Julia de L. Mann, *The Cotton Trade and Industrial Lancashire*. The best work is still T. Ellison, *The Cotton Trade of Great Britain* (London, 1886); see also S. J. Chapman, *The Lancashire Cotton Industry: a Study in Economic Development* [a term used half a century too soon] (Manchester, 1904).

864,750 in 1850 to 2,087,000 in 1867.[1] The price of the gain was the displacement of some 21,900 hand combers in the Bradford district alone, less than half of whom found employment in the machine industry.[2]

The continental textile industries had much further to go at mid-century. For them, the innovations discussed above were accessory to more fundamental advances: the diffusion of the self-actor in cotton manufacture; and the substitution of the power loom for the draw loom in cotton and wool. In both areas progress was slow. Both of these innovations were essentially labour-saving and fuel-consuming, hence less remunerative on the Continent; and the self-actor in particular required more force than the ordinary water wheel could provide. Most serious, however, were the human resistances: the determined opposition of factory weavers to increase of the work load, which diminished proportionately the economic advantage of power equipment; and the slow response of conservative enterprises, most of them family-owned and run, to technological opportunity.

As before, it was the centres producing the better—though not the very best—fabrics that were most advanced in method and equipment. In France, Alsace, with its fine prints, and the relatively young industry of the Vosges led the way in cottons: from 10 per cent in 1856, the portion of their spindles that were self-acting rose to 73 per cent in 1868; and by 1870 over 90 per cent of Alsatian looms were powered. The North and Normandy followed suit—the former bravely, the latter painfully. The late 1850's and 1860's were a calvary: contraction, lower tariff protection, cotton famine, and then another contraction followed one another in unremitting succession. The small *cotonnier* cried out his anguish to Paris; he had to wait for the Third Republic to obtain satisfaction.[3]

The worsted centres of Roubaix and Fourmies, in the Nord, and Reims, in Champagne, were the pace-setters of the French wool industry. Modernization was especially rapid in the 1860's, when the American Civil War pushed the price of cotton fabrics up and stimulated enormously the demand for the lighter textile substitutes. Of 450,000 worsted spindles added to national plants from 1862 to 1867, most of them self-acting, some three quarters were installed in the

[1] Since localization is generally promoted by mechanization, which enhances the importance of fuel costs and external economies, it is significant that, at the turn of the century, the West Riding still accounted for only a half of the woollen spindles of the kingdom. Clapham, *The Woollen and Worsted Industries* (London, 1907), p. 20. Compare the 85 % or more of worsted spindlage in this area.

[2] The best source on worsted technology is Sigsworth, *Black Dyke Mills*, pp. 30–4 88–92.

[3] The best source is C. Fohlen, *L'industrie textile au temps de Second Empire* (Paris, 1956).

department of the Nord; in roughly the same years, Roubaix and Reims tripled their power looms, which numbered respectively 12,000 in 1869 and 7000 in 1866. By contrast, a top woollen *fabrique* like Elbeuf had only 370 such looms in 1870; many of the others had none.

In Germany it was the southern centres—Bavaria, Württemberg, and Baden—with their new joint-stock companies and, interestingly enough, their persistent use of water power in conjunction with steam, that took the lead in cotton (72 per cent self-actors in 1867); the Gladbach area (Rhineland) was not far behind. Even so, the spinning mills were unable to satisfy the demand of the weaving section of the industry, favoured as always by the low cost of rural labour. Imports of yarn actually increased. But their share of total consumption fell rapidly and almost uninterruptedly—from 70·6 per cent in 1836–40, to 52·6 per cent in 1851–5, to 22 per cent in 1867–9. This progressive emancipation is the measure of the development in Germany of a modern, all-factory industry.

By comparison with cotton, or even with the French wool industry, the German wool manufacture was poor in resources and hesitant in performance. Production of worsted yarn was little developed: not until the 1870's and 1880's did Germany begin to free herself from dependence on British imports. And woollen spinning, as everywhere, was a stronghold of conservatism. Yet the important branch was weaving, and here, in both worsteds and woollens, the use of power increased sharply, while draw looms began for the first time to decline absolutely as well as relatively, from 74,000 in 1861 to 47,000 in 1875.[1] The figures measure an important industrial advance; but who will translate them into a measure of the puzzlement, pain, and dull resentment of those ground by the wheels of an impersonal progress?

The picture obtained of the continental textile technology in these middle decades is thus far less serene than that of its British counterpart. There are brilliant highlights that recall, in smaller degree, the great strides of Lancashire and Yorkshire; but these are flecked with grey and black, and whole sections of the canvas are dull and even sombre. By comparison with the more homogeneous techniques and advanced localization of the British industries, all is still confusion.

One passes also from a large to a small canvas. Continental progress notwithstanding, Britain's textile manufacture remained far ahead of competitors. Its dominance was most striking in cotton, where it had three-fifths of the spindles in the world at the end of our period, more

---

[1] The most convenient assemblage of statistical material on the development of the German cotton and wool industries in the nineteenth century is to be found in G. Jacobs, *Die deutschen Textilzölle im 19. Jahrhundert* (Braunschweig, 1907).

than half of those in Europe as late as 1913 (see Table 46). Britain's equipment was the latest available; her factories the largest; her labour force the most efficient. Comparisons with the best French and German practice toward the end of the century show Oldham mills using less than half, sometimes less than one-third as many workers per thousand spindles. The margin was presumably even greater around 1870. It is not easy to make the same comparison in weaving because of differences in the final products. Yet where the hand loom had all but disappeared in Britain, France still counted 200,000 of them in 1866, as against 80,000 power looms;[1] while for the Germany of 1875 (not including Alsace) the numbers were 125,000 of the old type and 57,000 of the new. Other things equal, moreover, it would appear that English power looms ran faster and wasted less; while the English weaver minded more machines—generally twice as many as his French or German counterpart.

Table 46. *Cotton Spindlage in Major Countries (in thousands)*

	1834	1852	1861	1867	1913
Great Britain	10,000	18,000	31,000	34,000	55,576
U.S.A.	1,400	5,500	11,500	8,000	30,579
France	2,500	4,500	5,500	6,800	7,400
Germany	626[a]	900	2,235	2,000	10,920
Switzerland	580	900	1,350	1,000	1,389
Belgium	200	400	612	625	1,469
Austria-Hungary	800	1,400	1,800	1,500	4,864[b]

[a] 1836.
[b] Areas of post-war Austria and Czechoslovakia only.
SOURCES. For 1834 and 1861, G. Jacobs, *Die deutschen Textilzölle im 19. Jahrhundert* (Braunschweig, 1907), p. 26, n. 1; P. Benaerts, *Les origines de la grande industrie allemande* (Paris, n.d.), p. 487; Viebahn, *Statistik*, p. 877.
For 1852 and 1867, Mimerel Fils, 'Filature du cotton', in M. Chevalier, ed., *Exposition universelle de 1867 à Paris*, IV, 20.
For 1913, Comm. on Industry and Trade, *Survey of Textile Industries: Cotton, Wool, Artificial Silk [Being Part III of a Survey of Industries]* (London, 1928), p. 151.

Britain's lead in wool was smaller but still substantial: 2,087,000 worsted spindles in 1867, against perhaps 1,750,000 for France; 71,500 worsted power looms against perhaps 20–25,000. Germany, with her

[1] G. Roy, 'Industrie cotonnière—tissage', in M. Chevalier, ed., *Exposition universelle de 1867 à Paris: Rapports du Jury international* (13 vols., Paris, 1868), IV, 39. This volume contains useful data on the other textile industries. It should be remembered that the rate of output of a machine loom was substantially greater than that of a draw loom. Fohlen, *L'industrie textile*, p. 456, gives a ratio of six to one. G. von Viebahn, *Statistik des zollvereinten und nördlichen Deutschland*, p. 926, gives one of slightly over three to one. Much would depend on the kind of looms used, the skill of the workmen, and the type of fabric woven.

320,000 spindles and perhaps 10,000 looms was a poor third. We do not have comparable figures for woollens, but here it would appear that Germany rather than France held second place.

All in all, it was an impressive hegemony. To be sure, Britain's margin diminished with time—as the return of protection closed valuable markets, as the younger textile industries of the Continent grew into a manhood nourished by rising standards of living, as newcomers in distant lands entered the competition. Even so, no other established British industry, perhaps, showed so much vitality and adaptability in the difficult years from 1870 to 1914. But that is another story.

B. *Iron and steel*

It is something of a relief to move on from textiles—heterogeneous and subtle—to metallurgy. The history of iron and steel is simple by comparison with that of woven fabrics: far less diversity of raw material or final product; technological changes uncomplicated by competition between modes of production; an overwhelming primacy of resources in determining location and competitive ability, which contrasts sharply with the subtle interplay of human and material considerations in the lighter industry.

In the middle decades of the nineteenth century the major development in continental metallurgy was the definitive triumph of mineral fuel. Coal had long come to dominate the refining process, and the traditional 'Walloon' or 'Champagne' techniques had given way in most places to the puddling furnace and rolling mill. But smelting remained a stumbling block owing to the direct contact between ore and fuel in the blast furnace, and right past the middle of the century charcoal-blast iron continued to command a premium for quality. For uses demanding special tenacity—axles, for example—it was almost obligatory.

In the long run, however, the inelasticity of the supply of wood and the forced dispersion and limited capacity of wood-burning furnaces made charcoal smelting uneconomic. The Belgians, with their abundant coal deposits and long mining experience, were, as we have seen (above, p. 405), the first on the Continent to make the shift to mineral fuel: by 1845, 90 per cent of their pig iron output, 121,000 out of 134,500 tons, was being made in coke-blast furnaces. (The reader should remember that almost the entire British make was produced with coke by 1800.) By contrast the French, who started on this path even earlier (Le Creusot in the 1780's) and possessed at least as much technical competence in this domain, were slow to accomplish the transition. For one thing, they were perennially short of coal, especially the kind that makes good metallurgical coke; only too often, more-

over, the coal was located far from the ore, and costs of transport in
the pre-railway age were discouragingly high. For another, much of
their iron industry was in the hands of small, technically ignorant
furnacemasters, bound by resources and habit to uneconomic locations and
protected from the incursions of more efficient producers by prohibitive
tariffs, costly transport, and a tacit general avoidance of price competition.

In the early 1850's France's industrial expansion gave the traditional
technique a new lease on life; the make of charcoal pig actually rose,
though nowhere near so fast as that of coke-blast iron. But then the
crisis of 1857 brought a sharp contraction in demand, and the old-
fashioned furnaces were the first to suffer. They settled at a new, lower
level from 1858 to 1860, whereupon the new competition of the low-
tariff 1860's, facilitated by cheap transportation, all but killed them off.
The nature and timing of the shift is apparent from Table 47.

Germany was the last of the three to develop a large coke-blast
smelting industry. As late as 1840 the only furnaces to use mineral fuel
were in Silesia, and even there the great majority burned charcoal. It
was around that time that the coke technique was successfully introduced into the Saar basin; five or six years later it was the turn of the
Rhineland; not until 1849 was the first coke-blast pig poured in the
Ruhr. At that date, barely one-tenth of the make of iron in the
Zollverein was smelted in this manner.

Once the decisive step was taken, however, the new technique took
hold rapidly and drove out the old in a matter of years. For Prussia as a
whole, representing about 90 per cent of the iron output of the *Zollverein*, the proportion of charcoal-blast iron fell from 82 per cent in
1842, to 60 per cent in 1852, to 12·3 per cent in 1862. In a new smelting
industry like that of the Ruhr, the demise of vegetable fuel was even
more rapid; it accounted for 100 per cent of iron output in 1848, 63
per cent in 1850, 4·2 per cent in 1856, 1·3 per cent in 1863.[1]

Along with this went a continued increase in size of equipment and
plant, which was made possible by and stimulated in return the kind of
technological improvements that are not spectacular or revolutionary
in themselves but constitute severally a major transformation. The
blast became more powerful and hotter; cooling, more efficient (the
more heat generated, the more acute the problem of dissipating it), and
smelting runs consequently longer; loading, easier. Other things equal,
the latest-model furnace doubled in height and more than doubled in
capacity from 1850 to 1870; while the shift from charcoal to coke
brought with it an even greater increase in the size of the average furnace.
In France the make per coke-blast furnace rose from 2450 tons in 1846

[1] Benaerts, *Les origines de la grande industrie allemande*, p. 457; Beck, *Geschichte des
Eisens*, IV, 990.

Table 47. *Substitution of Mineral for Vegetable Fuel in Smelting Iron*
(Production in thousands of metric tons)

| | France | | Prussia | | Belgium | |
	Coke or mixed	Charcoal	Coke or mixed	Charcoal	Coke	Charcoal
1825	5	194	—	—	—	—
1830	31	194	—	—	—	—
1835	49	246	—	—	—	—
1837	—	—	9	87	—	—
1840	82	321	—	—	—	—
1842	—	—	18	80	—	—
1845	193	305	—	—	121	13·5
1850	176	230	33	99	131	13·3
1855	488	361	158	123	280	14·1
1856	548	375	225	120	306	15·9
1857	619	373	270	110	288	14·5
1858	546	326	295	110	313	11·5
1859	531	333	281	110	309	9·6
1860	582	316	299	96	315	5·3
1861	691	276	377	73	306	5·9
1862	817	274	461	65	353	3·6
1863	901	256	568	70	386	6·1
1864	989	224	631	75	444	5·5
1865	1010	194	712	60	466	4·6
1866	1076	184	750	54	482	0·6
1867	1074	155	838	78	422	1·4
1868	1104	131	973	80	435	0·9
1869	1262	119	1104	77	532	2·2
1870	1088	90	1086	69	563	1·8
1875	1332	116	1341	57	540	1·3
1880	1670	55	2021	32	—	—
1885	1602	29	2634	31	—	—
1890	1950	12	3269	20	—	—

SOURCES. For France, Jean-Paul Courthéoux, 'Délais d'innovation, états des coûts, évolution des prix dans l'industrie sidérurgique', in Jean Fourastié, ed., *Prix de vente et prix de revient: recherches sur l'évolution des prix en periode de progrés technique* (8e série) (Paris, n.d.), table 1.

For Prussia, Beck, *Geschichte des Eisens*, IV, 714; V, 1069; *Zeitschrift für das Berg-, Hütten-, und Salinenwesen* (1856–71).

For Belgium, I have not been able to obtain figures of actual output of charcoal- and coke-blast furnaces before 1845. There are, however, data on the number of such furnaces which would seem to indicate that output of coke-blast iron passed that of charcoal blast some time around 1833–5 (assuming a ratio of 1 to 4 for the average annual outputs of the two types of furnace: cf. E. Flachat, A. Barrault, and J. Petiet, *Traité de la fabrication du fer et de la fonte* (Paris, 1842), p. 1287). *Exposé de la situation du Royaume, 1840–1850*, part IV, p. 118; ibid. *1850–1860*, III, 114; *1861–1875*, II, 726.

to 5800 in 1870; for all furnaces, from 1250 to 4400 tons over the same period. Prussia began with smaller, less efficient equipment: in 1850 the average furnace produced 720 tons. By 1871, however, the figure was over 5000 for Germany as a whole and slightly higher for Prussia.

The gains in refining were by contrast small. The puddling furnace remained the bottleneck of the industry. Only men of remarkable strength and endurance could stand up to the heat for hours, turn and stir the thick porridge of liquescent metal, and draw off the blobs of pasty wrought iron. The puddlers were the aristocracy of the proletariat, proud, clannish, set apart by sweat and blood. Few of them lived past forty.[1] Numerous efforts were made to mechanize the puddling furnace—in vain. Machines could be made to stir the bath, but only the human eye and touch could separate out the solidifying decarburized metal. The size of the furnace and productivity gains were limited accordingly.

The answer was eventually found in an entirely different direction—in the manufacture of cheap steel and its substitution for wrought iron in all but a handful of uses. The Bessemer process dates from 1856; the Siemens–Martin open-hearth technique from 1864. Yet each, as we shall see, did not make real headway until almost a decade after its introduction. Steel still accounted for less than 15 per cent of the finished iron (cast or refined) produced in Germany around 1870, less than 10 per cent of that made in Great Britain. Its commercial triumph and the revolutionary impact of this triumph on industrial technique belong to the next period of economic development, and we shall accordingly postpone our discussion of these innovations so as not to separate them from their effects.

One final point to place matters in their proper perspective: the spectacular expansion of the continental iron industry in these decades should not blind the reader to the continued progress and dominance of the British manufacture. Her rate of growth (5·2 per cent per year, 1848–70) was not so rapid as that of Germany (10·2 per cent, 1850–69) or even that of France (6·7 per cent, 1850–69), but for an old industrial power it was eminently respectable. Her equipment was bigger than that of her major competitors; her enterprises were larger and stronger. The *most powerful* furnaces in the Ruhr yielded around 250 tons of pig a week in 1870;[2] the *average* British unit did almost as much (183 tons), and the new eighty-foot 'monsters' (the expression is Clapham's) of the Cleveland district, with gas recovery and superheated blast, were

[1] See the fascinating article by J. P. Courthéoux, 'Privilèges et misères d'un métier sidérurgique au XIXe siècle: le puddleur', *Révue d'histoire économique et sociale*, XXXVII (1959), 161–84.
[2] *Z. f. das Berg-, Hütten-, und Salinenwesen*, XIX (1871), Statistischer Theil, 169, 171.

turning out 450–550 tons a week in 1865.[1] Nor were there any firms on the Continent like Dowlais and Gartsherrie, with eighteen and sixteen blast furnaces respectively in the 1850's. By way of comparison the largest German firm, the Hörder Verein, had six furnaces in 1870, averaging 180 tons a week.[2] When all is said and done, the United Kingdom was still manufacturing half the world's pig iron in 1870, three-and-one-half times as much as the United States, more than four times as much as Germany, more than five times as much as France.

C. *Power*

With the diffusion of those new techniques on the Continent went larger power requirements and an increased reliance on the steam-engine as prime mover. It appeared in areas and trades where it had never been used before; it was adopted by firms desirous of supplementing their supply of water power or of replacing their hydraulic installations by something more dependable; and its use spread within enterprises already familiar with it. A large iron or engineering works might employ a dozen or more engines of varying capacity—to drive the blast, turn the rolls, work the hammers, power a diversity of machine tools, and operate lifts, cranes, and other manipulatory devices.

Our figures of steam power in this period are seriously defective: for most countries, including Britain, we have only more or less informed private estimates; and differences in methods of calculating capacity (a difficulty that persists into the twentieth century) make international comparisons especially hazardous.

Such as they are, however (see Tables 48 and 49), the statistics make clear the importance of these years for the adoption of the steam-engine in the continental countries. All the more advanced were by 1840 on the steep middle slope of the 'S-curve' of increasing capacity, which doubled or more every decade until the 1870's. At mid-century, France led by a wide margin in number of fixed engines—more than the rest of continental Europe combined—and clearly no economy had gone so far in adapting steam to a wide variety of uses. But her power units were small compared to those of Belgium and Prussia, with their heavy stress on mining and metallurgy, and the aggregate

---

[1] Beck, *Geschichte des Eisens*, v, 964; I. L. Bell, *Principles of the Manufacture of Iron and Steel* (London, 1884), p. 24. Clapham, *Economic History*, II, 50, incorrectly gives this as output per day. Interestingly, the world leader in this regard was Belgium, whose blast furnaces averaged over 230 tons a week. See C. Reuss, É. Koutny and L. Tychon, *Le progrès économique en sidérurgie: Belgique, Luxembourg, Pays-Bas 1830–1955* (Louvain and Paris, 1960), p. 58 (Table 11). Aggregate Belgian output of pig iron, however, was less than one-tenth of the British make.

[2] *Z. f. das Berg-, Hütten-, und Salinenwesen*, XIX (1871), 168. These were built in 1853 and 1854, and were slightly under 50 feet in height (48 Prussian feet).

Table 48. *Capacity of All Steam-engines (in thousands of horse-power)*

	1840	1850	1860	1870	1880	1888	1896
Great Britain	620	1,290	2,450	4,040	7,600	9,200	13,700
Germany	40	260	850	2,480	5,120	6,200	8,080
France	90	270	1,120	1,850	3,070	4,520	5,920
Austria	20	100	330	800	1,560	2,150	2,520
Belgium	40	70	160	350	610	810	1,180
Russia	20	70	200	920	1,740	2,240	3,100
Italy	10	40	50	330	500	830	1,520
Spain	10	20	100	210	470	740	1,180
Sweden	—	—	20	100	220	300	510
Netherlands	—	10	30	130	250	340	600
Europe	860	2,240	5,540	11,570	22,000	28,630	40,300
U.S.A.	760	1,680	3,470	5,590	9,110	14,400	18,060
World	1,650	3,990	9,380	18,460	34,150	50,150	66,100

SOURCE. Mulhall, *Dictionary of Statistics*, p. 545; Wl. Woytinsky, *Die Welt in Zahlen* (7 vols.; Berlin, 1926), IV, 59. Woytinsky correctly stresses the approximate character of these estimates.

Table 49. *Fixed Steam-engines and Capacity by Country (Capacity in thousands of horse-power)*

	Prussia		France		Belgium	
	Number	Capacity	Number	Capacity	Number	Capacity
1837	419	7	—	—	—	—
1838	—	—	—	—	1,044	25
1839	—	—	2,450	33	—	—
1843	462	16	3,369	43	—	—
1844	—	—	3,645	46	1,448	37
1849	1,445	29	9,949	62	—	—
1850	—	—	5,322	67	2,040	51
1855	3,049	62	8,879	112	—	—
1860	—	—	14,513	178	4,346	99
1861	7,000	143	15,805	191	—	—
1869	—	—	26,221	320	—	—
1870	—	—	27,088	336	8,138	176
1878	34,431	958	37,589	484	—	—
1880	—	—	41,772	544	11,752	273

SOURCES. For Prussia, Engel, 'Das Zeitalter des Dampfes', in *Z. Königlichen Statistischen Landesamtes* (1880), p. 122; also available in Woytinsky, *Die Welt in Zahlen*, IV, 63; for France, *Annu. statistique*, LVII (1946), rés. rétro. p. 116*; for Belgium, *Exposé de la situation du Royaume, 1840–1850*, part IV, p. 113, and Woytinsky, *Die Welt in Zahlen*, IV, 70.

capacity of the Belgian plant, totalling perhaps 25 per cent less than that of France, continued to justify Briavoinne's invidious comparison of the 1830's (see above, p. 410, n. 1).

In the years after 1850 Belgium maintained her rate of advance; French capacity grew faster than before; while Prussia leaped forward at a rate (quintupling from 1849 to 1861, then increasing almost seven times from 1861 to 1878) that took her past Belgium in the mid-1850's and a few years later left France far behind. Together with the spectacular rise in her output of iron and coal, this leap heralded the appearance of a new industrial giant. We have no comparable figures, unfortunately, for Britain, where the *laissez-faire* of the executive power in the nineteenth century has cost the economic historian dear—though he has been more than compensated by the curiosity of Parliament; but if total steam power is a valid indication, the increase of British fixed engine capacity was already beginning to slow in the 1860's.

(2) INCREASING SCALE AND CONCENTRATION

The ever-greater size and cost of industrial equipment and the new competitive pressures produced by cheaper transport and freer trade gave a strong stimulus to two trends already under way—increasing scale and, to a lesser degree, concentration.

The enterprise was growing steadily larger. Some of this was a statistical illusion, for the elimination of marginally inefficient units tended to move the statistical average up. But much of it was real growth, as successful firms expanded and new ones were established on a scale never dreamed of. It is here that the joint-stock company made its greatest contribution. Almost all the new iron-works and coal-mines in Prussia were founded as corporations, as they had long been in Belgium. The same was true in French heavy industry, though often the *commandite par actions* was employed in order to reconcile personal direction and responsibility with widespread ownership. Yet this compromise in itself, which had been resorted to from the 1830's on in an effort to by-pass the government's suspicion of and hostility to the corporation as a business form, was eloquent testimony to the exigencies of increasing scale. Even in Britain, where the accumulation of capital within the enterprise and the efficiency of the money market made recourse to the investment public unnecessary, the trend to joint-stock was strong and growing stronger. From the 1850's on, the larger new firms were established as companies, like the railroads before them, and from the 1860's on, numerous private ventures, especially in capital-intensive industries like metallurgy, converted to the corporate form: thus John Brown in Sheffield, Ebbw Vale in

Wales, Bolckow-Vaughan at Middlesbrough. Some of these reorganiz-
ations reflected the biological problems inherent in individual proprietorship and partnership—death, illness, unwillingness of heirs to
carry on the business; some of them were inspired by a desire, occasionally only too well justified, for the shelter of limited liability;
but many were a response to the increased capital requirements of
production.[1]

The most rapid increase in scale came, as would be expected, in
heavy industry. In 1853 the largest smelting firm in the Ruhr, the
Borbecker Hütte at Essen, with its three blast furnaces and steam-
engines totalling 252 h.p., employed 450 men to make 19,500 tons of
pig iron. By 1870 a dozen enterprises surpassed this output, and the
leader, the Hörder Verein, produced three times as much. (Thanks to
increased productivity, however, growth as measured by number of
employees was slow; the more efficient enterprises of 1870 were
getting as much as 100 tons per man per year or more, as against the
43 of the Borbecker Hütte.)[2] And one could show similar developments in France, where a firm like Wendel saw its output of pig iron
rise from 22,370 tons in 1850 to 134,470 in 1870; or in Britain, where
Schneider, Hannay and Co. (later merged in the Barrow Haematite
Steel Co.) began in Barrow in 1859 with two furnaces and added to its
plant at intervals until by 1871 it had twelve in operation, all in a row
like the pretty maids of the nursery rhyme.[3] The reader may perhaps
object that I have chosen these examples to make my point; as indeed I
have. And he may adduce numerous instances of ventures that did not
grow so quickly, or even failed. Yet the firms mentioned were not
alone; one could cite enterprises like Cockerill in Belgium, Krupp in
Prussia, Schneider in France, John Brown in England, which expanded
if anything faster. And the figures of increasing employment per
firm in a period of rising productivity and capital intensity make the
general tendency manifest.

The trend was not so strong in a light industry like textiles, for
several reasons: technological change had slowed and with it the
increase in optimum size of plant; it is probable that economies of

[1] The best discussion is in J. B. Jeffreys, 'Trends in Business Organization in Great
Britain since 1856' (unpublished Ph.D. thesis, University of London, 1938). See also
the above-cited (p. 426, n. 2) essay by D. S. Landes, 'The Structure of Enterprise in
the Nineteenth Century: the Cases of Britain and Germany', and references given
there.

[2] Z. f. das Berg-, Hütten-, und Salinenwesen, II (1854), A. 286; XIX (187), B. 168–9.

[3] See the illustration in Beck, Geschichte des Eisens, V, 236. The layout was unquestionably unusual in its simplicity. See also J. D. Marshall, Furness and the Industrial
Revolution (Barrow-in-Furness, 1958), pp. 220–2, 249–54, 342, who gives the figure of
sixteen furnaces, against Beck's twelve.

scale were smaller; because non-material and entrepreneurial factors were of more weight than in heavy industry, a small but imaginative firm was better able to compete; and finally, since initial capital requirements were lower, there was less pressure toward the formation of joint-stock enterprises with their built-in penchant for bigness.[1] Generally speaking, the less advanced the industry, the more rapid the growth of scale; or more accurately, average size increases most rapidly in the period of transition from the dispersed shops and tiny man- or animal-powered mills of early mechanization to the steam- or water-driven factory. Thus spindlage per mill in the cotton industry of Great Britain rose by about half from 1850 to 1878; that of firms in northern France about doubled from 1850 to 1870; while in Prussia it increased seven times (828 to 5738) from 1837 to 1861.[2] The same phenomenon may account for the somewhat faster trend to bigness in the British woollen industry, by comparison with cotton, in spite of smaller economies of scale: in the years 1850–75, spindles per mill almost doubled in woollens and increased by 158 per cent in worsteds.[3] On the other hand, the Prussian experience was the reverse—a sixfold increase in wool from 1837 to 1861 (from an average of 103 to one of 587 spindles), as against the sevenfold gain in cotton mentioned above.

Increasing scale is usually accompanied by the concentration of an ever-greater share of the assets or output of industry in the hands of the largest firms. Yet the available statistics, which are discouragingly sparse, do not permit a categorical affirmation on this point. We do not, for example, have data on size or production of individual firms in the textile industry, and even in metallurgy, where the surveillance by government bureaus of equipment and practice at the level of the plant has left the historian a heritage of invaluable information, our coverage is incomplete and not always homogeneous. Still certain inferences seem justified. In the textile manufactures of the Continent, the purge of marginal enterprises in the 1850's and 1860's by easier transport, lower tariffs, and—in cotton—by the interruption of American supplies and a concomitant sharp rise in the requirements of working capital, almost

[1] Jefferys, 'Trends in Business Organization', p. 92 n., gives a figure of £250,000 for an up-to-date iron-and-steel works in the 1870's and 1880's, £75–100,000 for 'the most expensive' new cotton mill.

[2] Ellison, Cotton Trade, p. 72; Fohlen, L'industrie textile, pp. 228–9, 450–1; Amtlicher Bericht über die allgemeine Gewerbe-Ausstellung zu Berlin im Jahre 1844, I, 238; Viebahn, Statistik, p. 877. The figures for France are not complete enough to permit more than an informed guess about the rate of increase. It was apparently faster in Roubaix-Tourcoing than at Lille.

[3] Parl. Papers, 1850, XLII, 458–60, 467–8; 1875, LXXI, 68, 74. See also F. J. Glover, 'The Rise of the Heavy Woollen Trade of the West Riding of Yorkshire in the Nineteenth Century', Business History, IV (1961), 1–21.

surely promoted a higher degree of concentration: the rich got richer, and the poor went under. Britain had nothing like this, save for the travail of the cotton famine; her day of reckoning came after 1873, when the prolonged depression of prices and trade, combined with the loss of some of her finest markets to resurgent protectionism and the energy of younger competitors, effected a comparable catharsis. In the meantime, however, the new ease of company formation and the accumulation of capital in Lancashire favoured the creation of cotton enterprises of an unprecedented size as early as 1860. These were the so-called 'Oldham limiteds'—huge, standardized joint-stock spinning mills established in and around Oldham, outside Manchester, beginning in 1858 and continuing *crescendo* to a spate in the mid-1870's. They were built in large measure with the savings of local shopkeepers, professional men, even workers, who bought shares in denominations as small as one pound. The largest ran well over 100,000 spindles; the average to between 60,000 and 70,000. In the two peak years of 1874-5, about three million spindles were floated in Oldham alone, as much, roughly, as there were in all of France or Germany. The propagation of these giants almost surely meant an increase in concentration. Yet when all is said and done, the textile industry is not one that lends itself to monopolistic tendencies: entry is too easy as we have seen; the economies of scale are not great enough. In 1885 the ten largest public companies in Oldham accounted for only 22 per cent of the assets or spindlage of such joint-stock enterprises in that locality alone; their share of the national totals was far smaller.[1]

One would expect, and one finds, a higher degree of concentration in metallurgy; though the trend is by no means powerful or un-ambiguous. In France, the ten largest firms produced 14 per cent of the total make of wrought iron and steel in 1840-5; in 1869, one company alone, De Wendel, made over 11 per cent, and the top ten together were up to 54 per cent.[2] In Germany, however, these same years saw little movement in this direction. The top ten smelting enterprises made 32·6 per cent of the pig iron in 1852, 35·9 per cent in 1871.[3] And while we do not have the data that would permit a similar analysis of the British iron manufacture, the subsequent pattern would seem to indicate that both assets and output were more evenly

[1] Based on Roland Smith, 'An Oldham Limited Liability Company 1875–1896', *ibid.* pp. 52–3.
[2] On France, see Bertrand Gille, 'Analyse de l'industrie sidérurgique française à la veille de 1830', *Rev. d'hist. de la sidérurgie*, III (1962), 83–111; 'Les plus grandes sociétés métallurgiques françaises en 1845', *ibid.* II (1961), 207–19; J. B. Silly, 'La concentration dans l'industrie sidérurgique en France sous le Second Empire', *ibid.* III (1962), 19–48.
[3] *Z. f. das Berg-, Hütten- und Salinenwesen*, I (1853), A. 157–65; XX (1872), Statistischer Theil, 153–64.

shared than in France and possibly even Germany. As late as 1927, the twelve largest concerns made only 47 per cent of the country's pig iron and 60 per cent of its steel.[1] This lack of concentration was apparently linked to the geographical dispersion of the industry.

In general, the historical experience of concentration is almost *terra incognita*. The fairly abundant literature on the structure of industry in the nineteenth century has concerned itself almost exclusively with such questions as scale, integration (were spinning mills and weaving sheds combined? smelting and refining?), and localization; and even those studies that purport to deal with concentration generally treat rather of these other issues.

(3) NEW REGIONAL PATTERNS

Increasing scale and the forces that brought it about combined to recast the economic map of Europe. The process took two forms: localization, the spatial concentration of industrial activity; and relocation, the rise of new centres of production.

In regard to the first, one can distinguish positive and negative stimulants. On the one hand, bigness gave added weight to the advantages of rational location; the larger the appetite for raw materials, the more important it was to be placed near convenient sources of supply. Moreover, the advance of technology gave rise to new external economies in those branches characterized by a complex interweaving of mutually supporting activities. In short, the rich got richer. On the other hand, we have already noted the dissolving effect of cheaper, easier transport—especially when reinforced by lower barriers to foreign competition—on the mosaic of local autarkies. The poor got poorer, and many were simply snuffed out. The net result was a coalescence of manufacturing activity at a few favoured points and a de-industrialization of the countryside that gave new impetus to the age-old pumping of rural population by urban centres.[2]

Relocation was closely related to the new resource base of heavy industry consequent on the substitution of mineral for vegetable fuel and the invention of new steelmaking techniques (more of these later). Each country had its areas of opportunity. In France, it was the northeast corner (the departments of the Meurthe and the Moselle) and the

---

[1] T. H. Burnham and G. O. Hoskins, *Iron and Steel in Britain, 1870–1930* (London, 1943), p. 210.

[2] See the detailed local study of Ph. Pinchemel, *Structures sociales et dépopulation rurale dans les campagnes picardes de 1836 à 1936* (Paris, 1957). It was not the purely agricultural areas of Picardy that lost by emigration in the mid-nineteenth century, but the regions of declining domestic industry.

northern apex (the Nord and the Pas-de-Calais). The former had the largest, most easily exploited beds of iron ore in Europe—the relatively poor (iron content about 30–33 per cent), once despised *minette*—in reasonable proximity to the coal of the Saar. With the construction of the eastern railway in the late 1840's, new smelting installations were built, and the area swiftly rose from one of the lesser ironmaking districts to the most important in France. Its greatest gains came after 1856, when first the commercial crisis, then low tariffs and cheaper transport put heavy pressure on the antiquated forest furnaces of Champagne, the Franche-Comté, the Nivernais, and Dauphiné. In an economy in which competition was damped by entrepreneurial forbearance and formal *ententes*, no purge was so effective as a forced purge. Output in Lorraine quadrupled (109,000 tons in 1857 to 420,000 in 1869), and where in 1847 the two departments accounted for 10·6 per cent of the nation's make of iron and in 1857 for 11 per cent, the proportion had risen by 1869 to 30·5 per cent.[1] By comparison, the growth of smelting in the Nord and the Pas-de-Calais was far slower, but there the availability of relatively cheap fuel furnished a stronger base for refining, finishing, and that multitudinous family of energy-consuming industries called by the generic name of metalworking. In addition, the area possessed long-established textile trades—heavy consumers of machines, engines, and other metal products—a powerful chemical manufacture, and a prosperous industrial agriculture centring on the sugar beet. The result was a far more diversified economy than in the north-east.

This pattern of balanced growth also characterized the Ruhr, though on a far larger scale; indeed in one sense, the big story of these years is the emergence of Westphalia as the greatest centre of industrial activity in western Europe. The bases of this development were coal and iron: once the extent of local mineral resources became apparent, German bankers and investors, often seconded or anticipated by French and Belgian capital, hastened to create a rash of joint-stock mining and metallurgical corporations. Twenty-seven coke-blast furnaces were built from 1851 to 1857, more than had existed in the entire *Zollverein* at the earlier date; after a short pause during the crisis of 1857–9, the boom resumed and continued until the prolonged depression of the 1870's. From 1851 to 1871 output of pig iron in the Dortmund district increased *over* 35 *times*, to 421,000 tons, almost twice as much as in all of Germany at mid-century. By that time, the Dortmund and Bonn

[1] France, Ministère des Travaux Publics, Direction des Routes, de la Navigation et des Mines, *Statistique de l'industrie minérale*, 1893, p. 10. Twenty years later, in 1888, in spite of the loss of much of this area to Germany, the mills of Lorraine produced 54% of the country's pig iron.

districts combined (the latter included enterprises situated in southern Westphalia) turned out over two thirds of Prussian output and five eighths of that of the entire Empire.[1]

Nevertheless, the spectacular rise of a smelting industry in the Ruhr should not obscure the growth of other forms of manufacture. Here too, cheap coal encouraged all the metalworking and engineering trades, including the long-established manufacture of small hardware— screws, nuts, knives, locks, and the like—whose demand for semi- finished iron and steel further stimulated the furnace and heavy forge sectors. The most striking thing about Westphalia to this day is not so much the thick stacks of the *Hochöfen* or the hoists above the coal pits, as the slender chimneys everywhere. In this regard it resembles, though on a larger scale, the well-named 'Black Country' around Birmingham. Moreover, as in northern France, though again on a larger scale, metallurgy was tied into a broad regional complex that included the textile manufactures of Gladbach-Rheydt and Elberfeld-Barmen and the lusty infant chemical trades of the Frankfort and Cologne areas.

Britain too saw a relocation of her industry, though less drastic in its impact. Staffordshire (with Birmingham and the Black Country) and Wales were merely marking time. Scotland, which had risen in two decades to second place among British iron-producing districts on the strength of blackband and the hot blast, continued to gain slightly and held the first position for a while in the late 1850's and 1860's. But by the end of our period output had levelled off and it was only a matter of time before the rising cost of the blackband ores brought about contraction. Two-thirds of the entire increase of the national make of pig iron (from 2,700,000 tons in 1852 to 5,963,500 in 1869) took place in two new areas: in the north-east (centre Cleveland), which went from about 145,000 tons in 1852 to something over 1,600,000 in 1869; and north-west (Cumberland and north Lancashire), with 16,570 tons in 1855, 169,200 tons in 1860, 678,000 in 1869, 1,045,000 in 1875. (Here was growth even more rapid than that of the Ruhr: an in- crease of 63 times in twenty years!) The first built its prosperity on the proximity of ore and coal in the valley of the Tees; its social expression was the grimy boom town of Middlesbrough. The second was really a creature of the 1860's, when its deposits of haematite iron proved to be the only major source of ore suitable to the acid Bessemer process in the British Isles; it too had its frontier mill town—Barrow-in-Furness.

By 1870 the industrial map of Europe was substantially what it is today. The only major deposits of minerals to enter the pool of resources

[1] Excluding the newly acquired territory of Lorraine, the figures for 1870 were: 799,000 tons in the Bonn and Dortmund districts, 1,156,000 tons in Prussia, 1,391,000 tons in the *Zollverein*. Beck, *Geschichte des Eisens*, v, 254-60.

since then are the northern Swedish ores (opened up by railway transport in the late 1880's), the Briey extension of the Lorraine beds (late 1890's and 1900's), the Lincolnshire ores in England (developed after the First World War), and the Lorraine extension of the Saar coal field (developed on an important scale only since the Second World War). All of these have been essentially ancillary and none has had an impact on location comparable to that of the new fields of the middle decades of the nineteenth century. It is no coincidence that the discovery and exploitation of these in different countries fell so close in time. Prospecting was a reflection of economic pressures and opportunities. The results constituted as much a consummation as a commencement. Individually, each of the new fields marked a new area of growth; together they represented the effective completion of the material base of the Industrial Revolution.

The 1850's and 1860's then were the years when western Europe caught up with Britain. Not in a quantitative sense; that was to come later, and then only in certain areas. Nor even qualitatively, whether in scale and efficiency of production of given industries, or in degree of industrialization of the economy as a whole. Britain, as we have seen, was not standing still. If one envisages development as a sequence of stages—traditional (or pre-industrial) economy, industrial revolution, and maturity—the nations of western Europe were still in the second stage during these decades, that is, they had broken through the 'crust of custom', had cleared away institutional obstacles to growth, and were engaged in transforming the technology of their basic industries; while Britain, which had accomplished this transition around the turn of the century in metallurgy, by the end of the 1830's in cotton, had spent the decades since diffusing the core innovations and their derivatives throughout the economy. Britain achieved maturity by the middle of the century; Germany, not until the 1890's, and even then not to the same degree.

Yet such comparisons are misleading. Stage systems, which go back in economic history to the German historical school (List, Roscher, Bücher and, off to the side, Marx), have their virtues.[1] They clarify and

[1] The latest is that of W. W. Rostow, which refines the traditional tripartite schema into a five-part taxonomy. The pre-industrial stage is divided into traditional and preparatory ('transitional') phases; and the maturity stage, into maturity proper and the affluent age of surplus output (which may be devoted to high mass consumption, armament, or such other goals as the society may choose). Much of Rostow's system consists in calling old flowers by new names. The Industrial Revolution, which he has vividly labelled 'take-off', remains the heart of the process. His 'leading sectors' are Schumpeter's areas of entrepreneurial innovation. The 'backward' and 'lateral' linkages are the derived demand of neoclassical economics; the 'forward linkages' are a

synthesize the inconsiderate confusion of reality. But they also have their weaknesses, the most serious of which is their inability to encompass historical time. The Industrial Revolution in France or Germany was very different from what it was in Britain—and this, not only because of the peculiar circumstances and endowments of each of these countries, but also because they made their moves later and indeed skipped certain moves altogether. So that while taxonomically Britain was still far more advanced than her continental emulators around 1870, was 'mature' where they were 'immature', in terms of capacity to grow her lead had disappeared. As a result of a generation of drastic institutional changes and selective investment, the nations of western Europe now had the knowledge and means to compete with Britain *in certain areas* on an even plane. (The analogy to the rivalry between the Soviet Union and the United States will not fail to strike the reader.) Face to face with opportunities for growth and development, they were as free—perhaps freer—to pick their methods and opportunities. Their very lateness now turned to their advantage. In the jargon of sports, it was a new race.

IV.   Short Breath and Second Wind

The years from 1873 to 1896 seemed to many contemporaries a startling departure from historical experience. Prices fell unevenly, sporadically, but inexorably through crisis and boom—an average of about one-third on all commodities. It was the most drastic deflation in the memory of man. The rate of interest fell too, to the point where economic theorists began to conjure with the possibility of capital so abundant as to be a free good. And profits shrank, while what was now recognized as periodic depressions seemed to drag on interminably. The economic system appeared to be running down.

Then the wheel turned. In the last years of the century, prices began to rise and profits with them. As business improved, confidence returned—not the spotty, evanescent confidence of the brief booms that had punctuated the gloom of the preceding decades, but a general

combination of the traditional notions of response to bottlenecks and of external economies. Aside from such nomenclatorial merits as the system may possess (in my opinion, questionable), it has the virtue of reaffirming the distinctive historical importance of the industrial revolution in the history of any economy. It also has the fault, however, almost inescapable in stage analysis, of oversimplifying and overgeneralizing to the point of discomfort. On all this see Rostow, 'The Take-Off into Self-Sustained Growth', *Econ. J.* LXVI (1956), 25–48; Rostow, *The Stages of Economic Growth* (Cambridge, 1960); above all, Rostow (ed.), *The Economics of Take-off* (cited above, p. 422, note).

euphoria such as had not prevailed since the *Gründerjahre* of the early 1870's. Everything seemed right again—in spite of rattlings of arms and monitory Marxist references to the 'last stage' of capitalism. In all of western Europe, these years live on in memory as the good old days—the Edwardian era, *la belle époque*.

Their memory is brightened by the contrast with the years of death and disenchantment that followed. In every field, the war seems to be the great divide: between optimism and pessimism, parliamentary democracy and fascism, progress and decline. The massive mobilization of people and resources for conflict and their destruction in conflict seemed to throw everything out of kilter, never to be set right again. In economic life, the war saw the introduction of 'temporary' controls and restrictions—of trade, prices, investments, movements of funds and persons—that have persisted in one or another form ever since. The quietly self-adjusting international economy gave way to a sputtering, inefficient mechanism, kept operating only by repeated adjustments and repairs.

Yet a closer examination makes clear that the war was only a catalyst, a precipitant of changes already under way. The signs of a turning from optimism and freedom are apparent well before 1900, in literature and philosophy as well as in politics and economics. This is not to deny the enormous impact of the war, but simply to place it in its context. The system was already undergoing a painful transformation, which was itself more source than consequence of international rivalry and conflict. Here, however, we touch on a subject both complicated and polemical, and we had best put off discussing it for the moment.

Superficially, the intercyclical trends of the European economy in this period have appeared to most analysts to be a repetition of earlier alternations of long-term contraction and expansion. Monetary theorists have pointed to a diminution in the supply of money relative to demand from 1873 to 1896, followed by a sharp increase in the stock of bullion consequent on gold strikes in South Africa and the Klondike. This argument received its fullest analytical development, perhaps, in the work of Simiand, who generalized the nineteenth-century experience and constructed a model of alternating inflationary and deflationary long trends, the former characterized by rapid quantitative growth on a relatively stable technological basis (analogous to what we now call widening of capital), the latter by qualitative improvement (deepening of capital) and the forced elimination of inefficient enterprises.[1]

[1] F. Simiand, *Le salaire, l'évolution sociale et la monnaie* (3 vols., Paris, 1932).

Generally opposed to this interpretation are those economists and historians who see investment as the primary determinant and prices as a symptom. Schumpeter is perhaps the best known of this group, with his model of an economic machine powered by bursts of innovation. Also in this camp is Rostow, with a more nuanced analysis based on shifts of investment among uses with different rates of gestation: the longer the lag between outlay and return (infinite in the case of expenditure on armaments), the greater the immediate inflationary effect.

Between these two positions falls a man like Kondratiev, who argues that the upswing of the long cycle *is associated with* increases in both investment (due to new inventions, resources, and markets) and money supply. Kondratiev does not look upon these concomitants of fluctuation as causes, but rather as products of the conjuncture, and speaks cryptically of 'causes which are inherent in the essence of the capitalistic economy'. It is nevertheless clear—questions of ideology aside—that they hold the same explanatory place in his schema as they do, *mutatis mutandis*, in those of the other writers on the subject.[1]

On one point, however—the periodization of the long trends—all agree. Beginning with the late eighteenth century, they would punctuate the economic history of the industrial era roughly as follows: 1790–1817, inflation; 1817–50, deflation; 1850–73, inflation; 1873–96, deflation; 1896–1914, inflation. (The exact dates will vary from one analysis to another, but the schema and the approximate points of demarcation remain the same.) Moreover, most would agree on the cyclical character of these fluctuations. To be sure, a Marxist like Kondratiev would presumably qualify this (though he does not do so explicitly) by confining the pattern to capitalist economies and subjecting its repetitiveness to the influence of underlying, even longer-range changes in the total system. Similarly, the recent work of Rostow on stages of industrialization would seem to imply the possibility that the rhythm and character of these waves alter with maturation of the economy. Yet these reservations would not affect the accepted periodicity of the nineteenth century.

This picture seems to me inaccurate and leads in my opinion to a misunderstanding of the relationship between the underlying process of industrialization and the other aspects of economic change. The main source of difficulty is the optical illusion produced by the contrast between the boom of the 1850's and the depression of the 1870's: each

[1] His classic article, 'Die langen Wellen der Konjunktur', appeared in the *Archiv für Sozialwissenschaft und Sozialpolitik*, LVI (1926), 573–609. This has been translated in short form as 'The Long Waves in Economic Life', *Rev. Economics and Statistics*, XVII (1935), 105–15; the English version has been reprinted in *Readings in Business Cycle Theory* (Philadelphia, 1944), 20–42.

stands out and seems to usher in a new era, marking off a period of inflationary upswing from 1850 to 1873. In fact, the price series show no such long trend. The long deflation that begins after the Napoleonic wars is momentarily reversed by the influx of bullion and the credit boom of the 1850's. But the inflation lasts no longer than the upturn of the short cycle. Prices break in 1857, and while they have their ups and downs over the next decade and a half, the trend is slightly falling (at most, level in some cases), with a sharp decline setting in from 1873.[1]

In sum, the nineteenth century was marked by a protracted and sharp deflation, stretching from 1817 to 1896 with only one short interruption of some six or seven years. In the long history of money and prices from the Middle Ages to the present, there is nothing like it—with the possible exception of milder declines in the decades following the Black Death and in the seventeenth century. Moreover, unlike these earlier periods, when falling prices were linked to catastrophe, depopulation, and widespread depression, the nineteenth century was a period of peace, of unprecedented increase in numbers and rapid economic expansion. Otherwise, with or without the connivance of kings and governments, the long run is all debasement and inflation.

The explanation for the aberration of the nineteenth century seems to lie precisely in the productivity gains that stimulated and made possible this economic growth. Over the century, real costs dropped steadily, at first mainly in manufacturing, and then—after a revolution in transport that opened vast new lands to commercial cultivation—in food production as well. (It is the harvest of advances in both sectors that accounts for the particularly sharp drop of the years 1873–96.) To be sure, technological improvements and cost economies had occurred before. Why, then, this uniquely persistent deflation? The answer lies of course in the uniqueness of the innovations that constituted the Industrial Revolution; never before had there been a cluster of novelties so general in their application and so radical in their implications.

The price decline of the nineteenth century, then, is the consequence and barometer of European industrialization. Needless to say, this does not imply that, because the course of price changes was more or less the same for all the countries of Europe, the course of industrialization was also the same. Given the commercial and monetary communica-

[1] The path of prices varied somewhat from one country to another, for each felt the impact of boom and bust differently according to political as well as economic circumstances. For all the major economies of western Europe, however—Great Britain, Germany, France, Belgium—the trough of 1873–96 is an extension of the path traced in 1820–50. See Graph no. 1 in Gaston Imbert, *Des mouvements de longue durée Kondratieff* (Aix-en-Provence, 1959), pocket.

tion that prevailed, a synchronization of price trends was inevitable. This is in the nature of a market. But patterns and rates of growth are another matter. Although the same international communication that gave rise to general deflation was also conducive to sympathetic movements of technology, here differences in material resources and institutions and lags in the timing of development were determining. The result was substantial variation from one country to another.

The economy whose career the course of prices fits best is that of Britain. This is hardly surprising. The first nation to industrialize, she remained, into the twentieth century, the bellwether of the international market. Even after she lost her supremacy in critical branches like iron and coal to the United States and Germany in the 1890's, her position as mediator of world trade and finance sustained her predominant influence on commodity prices.

It is not my intention to undertake at this point a detailed examination of the British experience. We may note simply that such calculations as we have of her rates of industrial growth and increase in productivity—and they are confirmed by the major industrial time series—show a distinct falling-off after the mid-century decades of high prosperity. They do not turn up again until after 1900. From 1870 on, with the exception of a branch like steel, which was transformed by a series of fundamental advances in technique, British industry had exhausted the gains implicit in the original cluster of innovations that had constituted the Industrial Revolution. More precisely, it had exhausted the big gains. The established industries did not stand still. Change was built into the system, and innovation was if anything more frequent than ever. But the marginal product of improvements diminished as the cost of equipment went up and the physical advantage over existing techniques fell.

Not until a series of major advances opened new areas of investment around the turn of the century was this deceleration reversed. These years saw the lusty childhood, if not the birth, of electrical power and motors; organic chemistry and synthetics; the internal-combustion engine and automotive devices; precision manufacture and assembly-line production—a cluster of innovations that have earned the name of the Second Industrial Revolution. Conceivably the energetic exploitation of the cost-saving possibilities of these innovations might have yielded a further decline in prices—though, given the state of technology, their relative impact was bound to be smaller than that of the path-breaking advances of the eighteenth century. In the event, however, Britain did not take full advantage of the opportunities offered, and the initial boost to prices imparted by bullion inflows from South Africa (Witwatersrand, 1887), West Australia (1887), and the Klondike

(1896) was relayed and reinforced by a pattern of investment that yielded slow returns in consumable goods and services. And then, of course, came the First World War, bringing with it pressures toward inflation that render comparison with the earlier period impossible.

Even so, this cluster of innovations marked the start of a new upswing, a second cycle of industrial growth which is still in course and whose technological possibilities are still far from exhausted. It is in this context that one may understand the debate about the timing of Britain's 'climacteric'. Change of life there was; the question is, did it take place in the 1870's or 1890's?[1] The answer clearly depends on the point of view. The end of high prosperity after 1873 and the persistent malaise of the following decades signal in effect the evening of the Industrial Revolution; whereas the hinge of the 1890's marks the beginning of a new career.

Germany offers a striking contrast. Hers was an economy that, for all its capabilities, was well behind Britain in 1870 in assimilating and diffusing the technology of the Industrial Revolution. Large sectors of industry remained to be mechanized; domestic manufacture continued to predominate in many branches; the rail network was far from complete; the scale of production, generally small. So that once the setback of the mid-1870's was behind her, Germany resumed her high rate of growth. And she had not yet exhausted this momentum when the new opportunities at the end of the century gave her economy another push. As a result, one has the impression of an uninterrupted rise. For Germany too, however, the 1890's were a watershed.

France presents still another pattern. With Belgium, she had been the first on the Continent to follow the British example. But her overall rate of industrial growth had been the slower for her tentative decades of preparation and experiment, and for the development within her body social of psychological and institutional antibodies to the virus of modernization. 'France', wrote Clapham, 'never went though an industrial revolution.' She did, but it was muffled. The contours of the spurt that accompanied the shift to mechanization, steam power, the factory system, and rail transport are rounded both before and after.

---

[1] Cf. the debate between E. H. Phelps-Brown and S. J. Handfield-Jones, 'The Climacteric of the 1890's: a Study in the Expanding Economy', *Oxford Econ. Papers*, IV (1952), 266-307; and D. J. Coppock, 'The Climacteric of the 1890's: a Critical Note', *The Manchester School*, XXIV (1956), 1-31.

On the general problem of the so-called Great Depression, see the valuable article of A. E. Musson, 'The Great Depression in Britain, 1873-1896: a Reappraisal', *J. Econ. Hist.* XIX (1959), 199-228. Also Coppock, 'The Causes of the Great Depression, 1873-96', *The Manchester School*, XXIX (1961), with critique by J. Saville and reply, *ibid.*, XXXI (1963); and H. Rosenberg, 'Political and Social Consequences of the Depression of 1873-1896 in Central Europe', *Econ. Hist. Rev.* XIII (1943), 58-73.

After the relatively rapid expansion of the Second Empire, the Third
Republic was a period of measured autumnal advance, accelerated
finally by the upturn of 1900–13, which was based partly on the new
technology, partly on the opening of valuable iron ore deposits in
Lorraine. Previous to this revival—and even after, for opinion always
lags in these matters—the somnolence of the French economy called
forth repeated warnings from Cassandras aghast at the increasing gap
between the French and German economies. 'Growthmanship' is by
no means an invention of contemporary American political debate.

Alongside the advanced economies, a number of what we would
call today 'underdeveloped' nations embarked during these years of
technological transition upon their own industrial revolutions. Some
among them, like Sweden and Denmark, effected the change smoothly
and achieved rapid gains in productivity and real income per head.
Others, like Italy, Hungary, and Russia, assimilated only pieces of
modern technology, and these advances, achieved at discrete points of
the economy, were slow to break down the tenacious backwardness of
most branches of economic activity. In these countries, moreover,
industry accounted for so small a fraction of national wealth and
income, that even rapid gains in this sector did relatively little at first
for total output or the standard of living. Nevertheless, their industrial
growth was generally more rapid in this period than that of the more
advanced countries, even Germany. Partly this reflects a statistical
fallacy: their product was so small in these early stages that even
modest increments appear proportionately large. But even more it
reflects the poverty of their technological base and the enriched content
of their industrial revolutions: the gap between what they had and
what they might do was that much greater than it had been for the
early industrializers.[1]

The exhaustion of the technological possibilities of the Industrial
Revolution coincided with changes in the structure and size of the market that aggravated the dampening effect of diminishing autonomous
investment. These changes did not all work in the same direction; but
they added up on balance to a failure of demand to keep up with the
increasing capacity of industry. There were customers for those who
knew how to find and win them; but one had to look for them in new
places and woo them in new ways. And the task was not so easy

---

[1] This statement begs certain questions about the advantages and disadvantages of
an early start that are best left in abeyance at the moment. For statistics of industrial
growth, see S. J. Patel, 'Rates of Industrial Growth in the Last Century, 1860–1958',
Economic Development and Cultural Change, IX (1961), 316–30; R. W. Goldsmith,
'The Economic Growth of Tsarist Russia, 1860–1913', *ibid.* 441–75.

as it had been for the pioneer industrialists of the first half of the century.

The historical relationship of demand to supply over the course of the nineteenth century is not a simple one. We have noted the pressure of rapidly increasing domestic and foreign demand on the industrial system of Britain in the eighteenth century; it was this pressure that gave rise to bottlenecks and tensions resolved finally by a transformation of the means and mode of production. This Industrial Revolution in turn radically altered the terms of the problem. On the one hand, it shifted the emphasis from consumption to investment: capital was needed to build industrial plant and realize the potentialities of the new techniques. On the other, it made foreign outlets that much more important, for even a domestic market whose purchasing power was in no way constrained by a higher rate of saving would have been unable to keep up with the rapid increase in the output of manufactured goods.

In fact aggregate domestic demand did rise substantially in all the industrializing countries, even during the period of most rapid capital formation. How much it increased, however, is hard to say. Here we run into the question of the alleged 'immiseration' of the working classes, which has aroused an extraordinary amount of discussion, particularly with regard to the British experience.[1]

Did the standard of living of the poorer classes fall as a result of the Industrial Revolution during the years, say, from 1780 to 1850? It would be presumptuous to attempt to settle so complicated and emotional an issue in a few lines. The arguments commonly advanced are concerned with the consumption not only of manufactures, but of all goods and services, and rest as much or more on theoretical deductions, political dogma, and sympathy as on empirical data—for what they may be worth. Much of this lies outside our range of interest. What does concern us is first, that average as well as total home demand for *manufactures* rose. Consumption of cotton goods, for example, increased from some 35,600,000 lb. per year in 1819–21 to 149,600,000 in 1844–6 (the Hungry Forties!), a fourfold leap at a time when population rose by somewhat less than a third.[2] And if comparable

---

[1] An extensive bibliography would take too much space. The interested reader may consult R. M. Hartwell, 'Interpretations of the Industrial Revolution in England: a Methodological Inquiry', *J. Econ. Hist.* XIX (1959), 229–49.

[2] Ellison, *Cotton Trade*, p. 59. How much of this rise in demand was due to the substitution effect (that is, to the purchase of cotton in preference to other goods because of its relatively greater fall in price) and how much to increased real income consequent on this fall in price is another question, one directly related to the controversy over the standard of living in these years. But it is not immediately relevant to our concern with the evolution of the market for manufactures, except in so far as the

statistics on other commodities were available, on iron in the form of
consumers' goods, for instance, they would no doubt tell the same story.

Even so, home demand could not keep up with supply. From the
start, Britain had to rely heavily on overseas outlets, and the interruptions of normal trade relations by war and blockade before 1815
and protectionist tariffs after only stirred her to search for new markets
in distant corners of the globe. The picaresque expedition of Popham to
Buenos Aires in 1806 is dramatic evidence of both commercial anxieties
and dynamic response: here was a naval commander who took it upon
himself to sail his squadron across the Atlantic in time of war to pluck
a piece of the Spanish empire for British trade. And when His Majesty's
Navy took umbrage and instituted court martial proceedings, Popham
saved himself by rallying the British mercantile community to his
defence.[1]

As early as the period 1819–21, two-thirds of the cotton yarn produced in Britain were sold abroad either directly or in the form of
cloth; almost three-fifths of the yard goods manufactured were similarly disposed of. Sixty years later, in 1880–2, the respective proportions
were 84·9 and 81·6 per cent. The biggest gains were in the Orient: in
1814 less than a million yards of cloth were shipped to ports east of Suez;
by 1830 the figure had risen to 57 million yards; by 1850, 415 million;
and by 1870, 1402 million, or some 43 per cent of total exports.[2]

To be sure, no other major commodity depended so heavily as
cotton on foreign markets. But almost all manufactures showed the
same trends: a substantial increase in both absolute volume sold abroad
and the proportion of such sales to total output. We do not have
direct estimates of the overall export proportion over time; but
Schlote has calculated a ratio of the *index* of exports of finished goods
to an *index* of industrial production (in both cases, 1913 = 100) that
shows a rise from about 45 per cent in the 1820's to almost 90 per cent
by the early 70's.[3]

---

rise in consumption of cotton was compensated by a fall in that of other textiles. This
does not seem to have happened in Britain, even in the case of linen, which was cotton's
most direct competitor. Cf. Deane and Cole, *British Economic Growth*, p. 204.

[1] H. S. Ferns, *Britain and Argentina in the Nineteenth Century* (Oxford, 1960), ch. 1.

[2] Ellison, *Cotton Trade*, pp. 59, 63; S. B. Saul, *Studies in British Overseas Trade,
1870–1914* (Liverpool, 1960), p. 14.

[3] W. Schlote, *British Overseas Trade from 1700 to the 1930's* (Oxford: Blackwell,
1952), pp. 75–7, 154–5. The export index includes finished goods, metals, coal, and
processed foodstuffs. The source of the index of production is not given, but Schlote
apparently used the index later published by W. Hoffmann in his *Wachstum und Wachs-
tumsformen der englischen Industriewirtschaft von 1700 bis zur Gegenwart* [Kiel, Institut
für Weltwirtschaft, 'Probleme der Weltwirtschaft', Vol. 63] (Kiel, 1939)—see
Schlote's reference, p. 50. Schlote's ratios are useful only as indicators of trend.

This steady extraversion of the economy was the principal motor of the persistent, if spasmodic expansion of British imperialism throughout the century. Until recent years, scholars were inclined to underestimate the scope of this expansion. They allowed themselves to mistake the principles and even the policy embodied in the slogan 'Little England' for performance; and more serious, they neglected what, from an economic point of view, is the most important and lucrative variety of imperial dominion—informal control.[1] The fact was that not only did Britain annex during these years large areas in India, Oceania, and South Africa, but her sphere of commercial influence broadened enormously to embrace most of Latin America, coastal Africa, and south and east Asia.

By the last third of the century, however, the conditions of commercial expansion had altered drastically. Monopoly had given way to competition; Britain no longer stood alone as the workshop of the world. This had always been true of certain articles: the fine cottons of Alsace and Switzerland had held their own with those of Lancashire from the early nineteenth century, while French 'merinos' proved an admittedly inimitable rival of Yorkshire worsteds. But from 1870 on, there was a sharp increase in such competitive exports, particularly from the younger industrial nations—Germany, the United States, even India and Japan.

British commercial observers of the nineteenth century were wont to indulge in a little game, which we may call 'Count the customers', by analogy with chicken counting and similar pastimes. They would estimate the number of people in a given area, note their consumption of British products by comparison with more established markets, and then calculate the gain that would result if sales could be increased to this hypothetical standard. China was a favourite subject for such suppositions. A population of well over 300 millions! If her consumption per capita of British cotton could be raised to the Indian level, Ellison reckoned, sales would total £25 million per annum instead of the £5 million of 1883. Nothing illustrates the commercial implications of the industrial surge of newcomers like India and Japan better than what happened to these daydreams. From 1885 to 1913 British sales of yarn in China fell from 20 million to 2 million pounds. In 1905 India alone sold 200 million pounds there.[2] And in 1913 the Japanese figure was

[1] See J. Gallagher and R. Robinson, 'The Imperialism of Free Trade', *Econ. Hist. Rev.* 2nd ser. VI (1953), 1–15; John S. Galbraith, 'Myths of the "Little England" Era', *Amer. Hist. Rev.* LXVII (1961), 34–48.

[2] From the late 1880's, British exports of cotton cloth to India levelled off, while sales of yarn fell. In the meantime, the proportion of Indian yarn output exported rose from 15 per cent in the 1870's to over 75 per cent by 1913. Saul, *Studies in*

156 millions, and her total export of yarn and thread was worth well over twice as much as that of Germany and about 40 per cent of that of the United Kingdom.[1]

This shift from monopoly to competition was probably the most important single factor in setting the mood for European industrial and commercial enterprise. Economic growth was now also economic struggle—struggle that served to separate the strong from the weak, to discourage some and toughen others, to favour the new, hungry nations at the expense of the old. Optimism about a future of indefinite progress gave way to uncertainty and a sense of agony, in the classical meaning of the word. All of which strengthened and was in turn strengthened by sharpening political rivalries, the two forms of competition merging in that final surge of land hunger and that chase for 'spheres of influence' that have been called the New Imperialism.

From 1876 to 1914, the colonial powers of the world annexed over 11 million square miles of territory. This was the high-water mark of that expansion of Europe that began in the eleventh century on the East Elbian plains, the plateau of Castille, and the waters of the Mediterranean. Politically the gain was a source of gratification to many: the sun never set on the British flag. Economically the results were dis-

British Overseas Trade, p. 189. India's first mechanized cotton mill was founded in the Bombay area in 1851. A decade later she had 338,000 spindles, which became almost 5 million by the turn of the century; by 1913 the number had grown to 6,917,000. In that year, her consumption of 2,177,000 running bales of raw cotton placed her fourth in the world, after the United Kingdom, the United States, and Russia. A. Rai, Die indische Baumwoll-Industrie (Delhi, n.d.), pp. 46–7; Committee on Industry and Trade, Survey of Textile Industries, p. 154. (G. E. Hubbard, Eastern Industrialization and Its Effect on the West [Oxford, 1938], p. 256, gives spindles working in 1913–14 as 5,848,000.)

[1] Committee on Industry and Trade, Survey of Textile Industries, p. 156; J. E. Orchard, Japan's Economic Position (New York, 1930), pp. 93–4. The growth of the Japanese cotton industry may be gauged from the following data:

	Number of spindles (thousands)	Output of yarn (million pounds)	Export of yarn (million pounds)	Export of cloth (thousand sq.yd.)
1880	13	—	—	—
1890	358	42	—	—
1900	1361	268	83	572
1913	2287	672	187	4302

SOURCES. Spindles from Manji Iijima, Nihon bōsekishi [A history of the Japanese spinning industry] (Tokyo, 1949), pp. 489–91; yarn output from Japan, Naikaku Tōkeikyoku [Cabinet Bureau of Statistics], Nihon Teikoku tōkei nenkan [Japanese Imperial Statistical Yearbook], vols. XII, XXIV–XXV, XL; exports of yarn and cloth from Nihon sen'i Kyōgikai [Council of the textile industry of Japan], Nihon sen'i sangyōshi [A history of the Japanese textile industry] (2 vols., Tokyo, 1958), pp. 944–5.

tinctly less impressive. Already by 1870, little but the chaff remained: the best markets had already been formally annexed or informally integrated into Europe's expanding economy. There were still gains to be made in Africa and especially Asia, and indeed, the share of exports that went to these areas increased in subsequent decades. But given the poverty of these countries and their low rates of growth, their demand for manufactures was limited: on the eve of the First World War, the industrial powers of the world were still *each other's* best customers.

Even more, they were *their own* best customers: as the potentialities of overseas outlets diminished, the domestic market acquired increasing importance. And rightly so. Here were the richest consumers in the world; and both their numbers and wealth were increasing faster than those of the more backward areas. From 1870 to 1910 the population of Europe rose from 290 to 435 millions and that of the leading industrial nations (the United Kingdom and Germany) from 72 to 110 millions, while national incomes doubled or tripled. (France, of course, was an exception: her population was just about standing still.) If the days of easy commercial expansion were over and the time had come to cultivate demand in depth, there was no better place to work than at home.

More important than the growth in aggregate purchasing power was the change in the pattern of consumption. The steady rise in income *per capita*, which reached down into the lowest strata of the population, released increasing amounts for the purchase of manufactures as against food, of conveniences as against necessities.[1]

A number of factors reinforced this process. First of all, food

[1] Real wages rose substantially, even allowing for cyclical unemployment. Thus so anticapitalist an author as J. Kuczynski shows gains of the order of two-thirds in Britain from 1850 to 1900; of one-third in Germany from 1870 to 1900. *Die Geschichte der Lage der Arbeiter in England von 1640 bis in die Gegenwart*, Bd. IV, 3. Teil: *Seit 1832* (Berlin, 1955), pp. 132–3; *Die Geschichte der Lage der Arbeiter in Deutschland*, Bd. I, 2. Teil: *1871 bis 1932* (Berlin, 1954), pp. 96–7.

Whether labour's share in national income rose, is another question. Such statistics as we have point to a significant increase in the share of income going to salaried employees and wage-earners combined in France and Germany; in Britain in our period the change is negligible. But there is no way of separating out the higher-salaried brackets from the lower. See S. Kuznets, 'Quantitative Aspects of the Economic Growth of Nations, IV. Distribution of National Income by Factor Shares', *Economic Development and Cultural Change*, VII, no. 3, part II (April 1959), and the sources cited there.

As for equality of distribution of income, our data are incomplete, grossly approximate, and scarcely comparable; the picture is consequently obscure. Cf. Colin Clark, *The Conditions of Economic Progress* (2nd ed., London, 1951), pp. 530–41; also the discussion in Wm. Ashworth, *An Economic History of England, 1870–1939* (London, 1960), pp. 247f.

prices dropped relatively to others after 1875 as a result of massive flows of grain from the great plains and steppes of North America and South Russia and ever larger imports of meat from Argentina and of oils and fruit from tropical and semi-tropical areas. It took a combination of technological improvements to make this radical increase and diversification of Europe's food supply possible: the railroad, which linked interior agricultural regions to the sea; more efficient marine transport, which led to a sharp rise in capacity and a corresponding fall in freight rates; new techniques of cultivation, especially dry farming of open plains; new methods of food conservation, among them canning and refrigeration.

This competition from outside producers called forth in turn a vigorous technological response from certain sectors of European agriculture. Some countries or regions turned to specialization, choosing those products where nature and skill combined to yield differentiated quality that defied competition. Denmark is the best example, with her pork and dairy products (the cream-separator was the vital innovation here). But Switzerland and France had their cheeses and every large city had its ring of market gardens. At the same time cultivators obtained much higher yields per acre for all crops by extensive use of fertilizer, especially the new mineral and artificial varieties and rich organic imports like Peruvian guano (another dividend of the revolution in transportation.) The result was the highest standard of eating that the world had known. For the first time, man could afford to feed his own staff of life, grain, to animals to fatten them for his table.

Secondly, the same improvements in transportation that did so much to diminish the cost of food also worked to reduce the price of manufactures. Not only was shipment less expensive, but the creation of truly national markets conduced to the elimination of local peculiarities of taste and hence to the economies of mass production.

Thirdly, consumer wants increased significantly. There was, to begin with, the steady process of urbanization, which introduced millions of rustics to a more expansive way of life. Nor was this appetite for creature comforts confined solely to those who settled in the cities. It slowly but inexorably seduced the countryside, traditionally self-denying to the point of avarice. Some, who visited the city, largely thanks to the railroad, were never more the same; and some felt the need to emulate city cousins, whether for the sake of self-esteem or to meet the competition of a more comfortable, varied existence for the loyalty of children, girl-friends, and wives. Seen in the large, the process was painfully slow and uneven; the material backwardness of most rural homesteads is a problem even today. And it was inevitably erratic: the same peasant who sold his cheese and ate curd, who raised bees to avoid buying sugar and made a Sunday suit last a lifetime, might buy himself a watch, give a gold bauble to his daughter, let his son visit a vacation resort, or allow his wife to decorate the house.[1] (In all this, the increased influence of women and children on consumption, a tendency that has continued to the present, is obvious.) In the long run, however, this internal 'demonstration effect' has been probably the most important factor—more important than the increase in income—in developing a market of high consumption (to adapt W. W. Rostow's term), that is, a body of consumers able and willing to buy above the line of necessity.

Once again, larger economic and social processes owed much to technological innovation, in this case to the introduction of new methods of retail distribution. It is these decades that saw the spectacular development of the department store and the chain store (multiple shop), with all their associated devices for the temptation of the consumer: fixed prices, right to return purchases without charge, standard packaging, catalogue orders, effective display, periodic sales, advertising.[2] And to these should be added the efforts of merchants and manufacturers to increase their market by cultivating fashion changes and establishing the reputation of trademarks and brand names.

All of this was the more important because of the relationship of the new industrial technology to the character of consumption. As we shall see, the great advances of these decades—cheap steel, precision manufacture, electric power—made possible a whole new range of consumers' goods, what we now call consumers' durables: the sewing machine, cheap clocks, the bicycle, electric lighting and eventually electrical appliances. The consequent expansion of production, after the earlier surge based primarily on capital goods and the complex of demands associated with the railway, was possible only in this new kind of supraminimal market.

[1] Cf. A. G. Manry, 'En Limagne, entre 1865 et 1905', *Annales: Economies, Sociétés, Civilisations*, v (1950), 114–19.
[2] One of the best indirect indicators of this commercial transformation is the spectacular rise in production of plate glass, used extensively for store windows and mirrors. From 1870 to 1901, British imports of plate jumped from some 36,000 to 464,000 cwt., while the output of Britain's largest producer, who entered the field in 1876, rose from 1,078,000 sq. ft. in 1877 to over 5 million in 1903–4, to over 14 million in 1912–13. Barker, *Pilkington Brothers*, pp. 161, 189. The Pilkington figures are for the Cowley Hill works only.
On the significance of the new techniques of retail selling, see J. B. Jefferys, *Retail Trading in Britain, 1850–1950* (Cambridge, 1954); P. Bonnet, *La commercialisation de la vie française du Premier Empire à nos jours* (Paris, 1929); G. d'Avenel, *Le mécanisme de la vie moderne*, 1re série (7th ed.; Paris, 1922), pp. 1–79.

The severity of competition for foreign outlets and concomitantly increasing importance of domestic demand led to a sharp reaction against the economic freedom, hence insecurity, of the mid-century. The liberalization of commerce was barely achieved when the tide changed. In France, agitation against the new policy of low protection never ceased; from the start, the representatives of the manufacturing interest put protocol aside and denounced the agreement with England as an abusive, even fraudulent, act of fiat. (In a sense, the Empire began to die in January 1860.) Every ill of French industry was imputed to 'the Treaty'; every success was achieved in spite of it. The campaign for a return to protection grew stronger with the crisis of 1867, achieved some minor successes in the early years of the Third Republic, and finally attained its goal with the passage of the Méline tariff in 1892. In Germany, the depression of the 1870's and Bismarck's desire for the support of the new alliance of industrialists and Junkers led to a rejection in 1879 of the traditional policy of low duties, which had reached its extreme with the free admission of pig iron in 1873. Italy adopted high protection in 1887; Austria and Russia returned to it in 1874/5 and 1877 respectively; Spain established new rates in 1877 and 1891; and so on throughout Europe. Overseas, American import duties tended to rise with each new tariff law from the Civil War onward. Even Britain, the home of classical economics, saw its faith in free trade shaken. The commercial interdependence of these increasingly specialized economies multiplied the impact of these increases; each action brought its reactions, until tariff rates were established as much for bargaining as for protection. The spiral continued upward with few pauses or reversals until the constraints of war made these earlier restrictions look like freedom.

Along with this encapsulation of national markets went efforts to minimize intranational competition. Cartels for the control of prices and output—an institution that went back to the seventeenth century and beyond (cf. the Newcastle Vend)—began to multiply, especially after periods of prolonged or severe depression. Characteristically they were found in industries like coal, iron, or chemicals, where homogeneity of product facilitated the specification of quotas and prices, and where lumpy capital requirements yielded important economies of scale, the number of competing units was consequently small, and entry was difficult. They were most numerous and effective in Germany, where entrepreneurial psychology, the structure of industry, legal institutions (cartels could enforce their contracts in the courts), and tariff protection against interlopers all combined to promote agreements in restraint of trade.

Cartels were less important in France, for reasons that may be deduced from the analysis of their success in Germany. For one thing, light industry was far more important than heavy, and the family firm, with its attachment to entrepreneurial independence, held a large place, even in capital-intensive branches of manufacture. Secondly, the emphasis on diversity and differentiation of product made group control difficult. Finally and most important, French industry had long maintained tacit limits on competition that were about as effective as formal contracts. Not only the entrepreneur, but labour and indeed society in general looked upon price warfare as essentially unfair (*déloyale*) and subversive. And given the modified oligopoly character-istic of many industries—a few big, efficient enterprises amid a swarm of small, backward ones—these moral sentiments were reinforced by counsels of prudence; vigorous competition could only invite reprisal from rivals just as big and capable as oneself. In short, France did not need cartels. She did develop a few, in iron and steel manufacture particularly. But their role was more one of convenience than influence.

British industry found itself in a mixed position in matters of com-bination. In the first place, conspiracies in restraint of trade were for-bidden by common law; yet cartels went back centuries in Britain, and it was Adam Smith who wrote: 'People of the same trade seldom meet together, even for merriment and diversion, but the conversation ends in a conspiracy against the public, or in some contrivance to raise prices.'[1] Secondly, the absence of a tariff barrier was a serious obstacle to collusive fixing of prices or output; yet costs of transportation or local productive advantages served to protect certain trades, regionally or nationally, and make combination profitable. Finally the structure of the enterprise, unlike that in Germany, was ill-suited to formal co-operation: most firms, even nominally public companies, were private in character and independent in behaviour; moreover there was little vertical integration or bank control. Yet as in France, there was also a strong tendency to the kind of gentleman's agreement that makes cartels unnecessary.

With these contradictory forces in play, Britain developed a mild trend toward mild combination. Cartels appeared in metallurgy, milling, chemicals, glass-making, but they were less rigid than their German analogues, less compulsory in character, less effective in times of contraction, less enduring. The foreign interloper was always a prob-lem. Thus the highly effective British Glass Manufacturers' Association found its efforts to maintain prices at home continually thwarted by Belgian competition. Offers to establish an international agreement were disregarded for decades, until labour troubles in the early 1900's con-vinced the Belgian producers that the security of union more than

[1] *Wealth of Nations*, Book I, ch. x.

compensated for the constraints. As finally established, the Plate Glass Convention of 1904, the most successful of the international glass cartels, included not only the United Kingdom and Belgium, but Germany, France, Italy, Austria-Hungary, and the Netherlands. Similar accords were negotiated in fields like rail-making and tobacco, where, because the bulk of demand lay overseas or because value in proportion to weight was so high that transport costs offered no protection, national agreements were ineffective. Such international cartels worked well on the whole so long as there was agreement but showed little resistance to dissension and rupture; their histories have an on-again-off-again beat.[1]

Aside from cartels, that is, associations of independent enterprises, there were also a number of 'combines', monopolistic or would-be monopolistic concerns that grouped a sizable fraction of the productive units in a given trade in various degrees of amalgamation. In some cases, these coalitions were simply what the Germans call an *Interessengemeinschaft*; each participant retained his autonomy, and centralized direction was provided by a sometimes unwieldy body whose influence depended on the good will of the member firms. The original English Sewing-Cotton Company (1897) and the Calico Printers Association (1899) were of this type. Others were true mergers, like the Salt Union of 1888, which claimed to control 91 per cent of the salt output of the United Kingdom; or the United Alkali Company, formed in 1891 in a last-ditch effort of Leblanc producers to hold their own against the competition of the Solvay process.

The combines were Britain's answer to the integration and concentration of German industry. On the whole, they were a poor answer: they appeared in the wrong industries, or if in the right ones, for the wrong reasons; they were often founded by promoters rather than producers, and the initial over-evaluation of capital burdened subsequent performance; the very multiplicity of their adherents complicated their task; and here too the absence of tariff protection exposed the prosperous ones to the incursions of interlopers—success was almost as dangerous as failure.

The consequences of this new, commercial version of the enclosure movement are not easy to disengage from the multitude of other factors that determined the character and volume of world trade; nor do they lend themselves to easy generalization. The return to protection discouraged some forms of international exchange, but served to stimulate rivalry in open markets. Similarly, cartels worked to restrain competition and stabilize prices and output up to a point; but their very success nourished ambitions that led to eventual rupture and wider

[1] On the glass cartels, see Barker, *Pilkington Brothers*, chs. VIII, IX, and XIII.

fluctuations than before. And even when accord was maintained, the effort of the individual members to secure larger quotas often stimulated a development of capacity more rapid than free competition would have produced or a rational investment policy based on anticipated return warranted. In the last analysis, however, these new institutional arrangements are of interest to us as efforts to cure, hence as indicia of, an internal malaise. That they did not always accomplish their purpose should not surprise.

What, then, is the larger significance of this welter of developments, sometimes mutually reinforcing, sometimes contradictory? The answer would seem to lie in that vivid word of Phelps-Brown, 'climacteric'—applied not to Britain alone, however, but to the world economy as a whole, and conceived primarily in terms of the relations of the component national economies to one another. What we have, in short, is a shift from monarchy to oligarchy, from a one-nation to a multi-nation industrial system; if we want to retain the biological metaphor, from a one-celled to a many-celled organism. That this change of life coincided with an equally fundamental technological transformation only complicated what was intrinsically a difficult adjustment—so difficult, indeed, that the most determined efforts of the wisest men did not avail to appease the resentments and enmities that grew out of the consequentially altered balance of political power. Marxist students of history have been wont to see the international rivalries that preceded the First World War as the thrashing of a system in process of decline and dissolution. *The fact is that these were the growing pains of a system in process of germination.*

It was not the first time that the world economy, as an interacting system, had passed through such a climacteric. A comparable crisis had attended Britain's breakthrough to a modern industrial order. There too, as we have seen, the balance of both economic and political force shifted drastically, posing a severe challenge to all nations pretending to membership in the concert of first-class powers. That the international consequences were not so unhappy as they were to be during the next climacteric reflects *in part* market considerations: on the one hand, the availability in the earlier period of a still untapped, highly elastic world demand for manufactures; on the other, the opportunities for fruitful interaction between the one major centre of production and its still pupillary emulators.

If the climacteric of the late nineteenth century was not the first of this international system, neither has it been the last. In so far as the historian can understand his own age, it would seem that we are now going through still another change of life, once again brought about by the entry into the lists of a new group of industrial and industrializing nations, the most important of which is Soviet Russia. This time, however, the problem of adjustment is complicated by fundamental differences of social structure and organization between old and new. In effect, the newcomers are competing with the older industrial powers not so much economically as politically, and economic efforts are directed not to the pursuit of wealth, with such unfortunate political consequences as that may or may not entail, but to the pursuit of power, with more probably disastrous results. Here a certain wistful and wishful reserve, as well as the historian's customary prudence, counsels against any attempt at prediction.

With that brief allusion to the unhappy present, inserted only to complete the logic of this analysis, we may turn with relief to the anodyne details of the history of technology.

By the last decades of the nineteenth century, technological advance was proceeding within the older industries on so broad a front that the task of the historian is enormously complicated. And this in turn goes far to explain why the subject has been neglected.[1] Broad advance, as Rostow notes, is the hallmark of maturity: the basic innovations spread from the small group of industries that are at the heart of the revolution to the rest of the productive sector. Under the circumstances, we shall have to abandon our concentration on a few selected foci of change. Instead, we shall attempt to organize the data of technological progress along analytical lines, grouping them according to principle rather than area of application: I. New materials and new ways of preparing old materials. II. New sources of energy and power. III. Mechanization and division of labour.

The order chosen is not intended to imply relative importance, since there is no way of assessing the impact of each of these on general productivity. Rather, my intention is to reconcile as much as possible the analytical schema, which is in a sense timeless, with the chronological sequence of technological change, so that the reader will not lose track of economic history *qua* history. For this reason, the bulk of the space will be allotted to topics I and II, for they lend themselves best to description as process, as development through time. More than the others, also, they permit the historian to introduce those general issues of comparative economic growth that are the *leitmotif* of the chapter.

[1] Cf. R. J. Forbes, 'The History of Science and Technology', in XIe Congrès International des Sciences Historiques, *Rapports*, 1, 72.

(I) NEW MATERIALS

The subject of new materials and new ways of making old materials is multifarious and would, were we to pursue it to its limit, take us into every branch of industry. For the sake of economy, however, we shall concentrate on two themes: the invention and diffusion of cheap steel and the transformation of the chemical industry.

A. *The age of steel*

Man is a naming animal. He loves to pin labels on things. And no one is more prolific of nomenclature than the historian, who cannot resist the opportunity to designate each chronological section of his subject by some pithy title—the Age of the Enlightenment, the Era of Good Feeling, the Age of Reform—partly for pedagogic or heuristic convenience, partly for proclamatory effect, partly as a surrogate for understanding.

So we have the Age of Steel. It is one of the better of these slogan-titles. If one were to seek out the primary feature of the technology of the last third of the nineteenth century, it would be the substitution of steel for iron and the concomitant increase in the consumption of metal per head.

It is a commonplace to note that modern industry was built (and indeed continues to be built, even after the development of plastics and concrete) on a framework of metal, particularly ferrous metal. It is worth pausing, however, to consider why this was and is so. The answer lies not so much in the separate characteristics of metal, some of which are duplicated by other materials, but in their combination, which is unique and thus far unapproached by any other product of man's ingenuity.

The salient advantages are three: great strength in proportion to weight and volume; plasticity; and hardness. The first is implicit in the elasticity of metal, that is, its resistance to the various forms of stress-compression (including the variety known as percussion), pull, and bending or torsion. Even so remarkable a material as reinforced or pre-stressed concrete, light in proportion to volume and capable of surprising performances as an enclosing or supporting member of standing structures, cannot compete with metal where economy of space and movement are important considerations. In the earliest days of the Industrial Revolution, when metalworking techniques were rudimentary and craftsmen voluntarily employed whatever substitute materials offered themselves—wood, particularly, but also leather and rope, depending on the use—the most important pieces of the machines, the spindles for example, were already made of iron. And it was not long before everything, including the frame, was so made. No better material for articulated parts has been discovered since.

The superiority of iron in such uses derives from its exceptional strength—greater than that of other metals—and from its plasticity and hardness. It can be shaped without significant loss of elasticity—hammered (malleability); drawn (ductility); cut, stamped, and drilled; filed and ground; melted and cast. And it can be worked with precision: one can make a clean cut in it, a smooth hole, a sharp impression. Finally, it holds its shape well under abrasion and heat: the edge remains straight and, when necessary, keen; the holes remain smooth; the impression stays sharp.

As a result of this intimate connection between ferrous metals and machines, the consumption of iron *per capita* has always been one of the most accurate measures of industrialization. We have already had occasion to note the precociously 'ferruginous temper' of the English in the eighteenth century. The introduction of puddling and rolling accentuated this tendency, which was ever a source of astonishment to visitors from poorer lands. Thus the French ironmaster, Achille Dufaud of Fourchambault, in 1823: 'Internal consumption is said to be 110,000 tons; a frightening quantity, but when one has gone through England, it does not seem incredible.'[1] Only a generation later, in 1849, she was consuming perhaps fifteen times as much.

Steel is a superior variety of iron. It possesses all the advantages attributed above to metal and especially ferrous metal, in higher degree. Chemically, the two are distinguished by carbon content: pig iron, 2·5–4 per cent; steel, 0·1 per cent to about 2 per cent; wrought iron, less than 0·1 per cent. The higher the carbon content, the harder the metal; the less carbon, the softer, more malleable, and more ductile. Tenacity reaches a peak at about 1·2 per cent carbon, in the steel zone, then tapers off rapidly to 3 per cent, where the drop slows. As a result, pig iron is hard, but it is also brittle. It cannot be worked without breaking; to be used at all it must be cast. And it cannot withstand stress; hence it is suited only for the manufacture of such things as pots and pans, radiators, or engine blocks, where compression and torsion are negligible. Wrought iron, on the other hand, can be made so soft it can be worked by hand. In India the farrier tests his nails by bending them on his forehead. By the same token, however, wrought iron is extremely susceptible to wear and tear, is easily altered by shock, and offers low resistance to pull or bending. Where pig iron will crack or snap, wrought iron will yield.

[1] Guy Thuillier, *Georges Dufaud et les débuts du grand capitalisme dans la métallurgie, en Nivernais, au XIXe siècle* (Paris, 1959), p. 230.

Steel combines the advantages of both. It is hard, elastic, and plastic. It can be ground to a sharp edge and then hold it; nothing else is so well suited to cutting and shaping other metals. Its resistance to percussion and abrasion makes it ideal for hammers, anvils, nails, rails and other objects subject to pounding or wear and tear. Its strength in proportion to weight and volume makes possible lighter, smaller, and yet more precise and rigid—hence faster—machines and engines. And the same combination of compactness and strength makes steel an excellent construction material, especially in shipbuilding, where the weight of the vessel and space left for cargo are of primary importance.[1]

Metalworkers were aware of the peculiarities of steel in ancient times. The old bloomery furnace, which made malleable iron directly from the ore, produced a mass of heterogeneous metal whose degree of decarburization varied with the effectiveness of oxidization and contact with the fuel. Most of the bloom was wrought iron (*fer doux*), but some, especially the matter on or near the surface (the *fer fort*), had the quality of steel or even pig iron.

The reaction of the earliest smiths was to reject this recalcitrant material as unworkable. With time, however, the virtues of steel were recognized, especially for the production of edged tools and weapons. Somewhere, sometime in the ancient world, smiths learned to make steel deliberately, rather than accept what the accident of the bloomery yielded. The principal technique employed was carburization of wrought iron by cementation, that is by soaking it at a high temperature in a solid bath of carboniferous matter; the result was what came to be known as blister steel, so called because of the characteristic blistering of the surface when carburization was completed. An alternative method, though less satisfactory, was the direct one of interrupting the refining process before the carbon had burned completely away.

Because of the nature of the cementation process, in which the hot but solid metal absorbed its carbon from outside, blister steel was uneven in quality, ranging from soft steel at the core to iron at the surface. Greater homogeneity could be achieved by breaking the blister steel into small pieces, packing them in a sheath, and pounding them together at welding heat, thereby distributing the carbon more evenly through the mass and yielding what became known as shear steel. The resultant bars could then be bent double and the process of hammering

[1] Within the category of steel, there are mild and hard steels, again distinguished by carbon content. The former (less than 0·25% carbon) are much like wrought iron: they will not take a temper, but are very tough and ductile, and are especially suited to structural uses, rails, and such forge work as riveting. The latter are the high-carbon steels, used for edged and other tools, the moving parts of machines, and structural pieces of unusual strength.

repeated as often as necessary to obtain the quality desired. In Britain, one pounding was deemed sufficient for most purposes, and twice-hammered shear steel was considered the best made. In Germany craftsmanship was pushed further, and the so-called *viermal raffinierter Stahl* consisted of tough, nervy bars that consolidated in their 30-centimetre cross-section some 320 separate layers of charcoal steel.

This kind of work took time: one to two weeks to complete cementation and several days of forge work afterward. Moreover, the alternate heating and hammering called for a prodigal expenditure of fuel. Small wonder that first-quality steel was a costly commodity worth up to several hundred pounds sterling a ton. In effect, this was a metal sold and used by the pound for small objects of high value in proportion to weight: in particular, razors, surgical tools, blades, shears, files and rasps. Even ordinary blister steel was too costly to use in quantity: the blade of the peasant's scythe—when he could afford a scythe—usually consisted of a steel surface welded on to the iron core. The one area in which there was little or no stinting was the manufacture of arms: man has rarely quibbled about the cost of instruments of death.

This was the status of steel technology on the eve of the Industrial Revolution. The first major innovation in this area since the anonymous, dateless invention of cementation was Huntsman's crucible technique (1740–2), which yielded decisive gains in the quality of the product. Huntsman took blister steel, achieved a high enough temperature to melt it in small vessels along with a flux of carbon and other metals, skimmed off the slag and poured. The result was (1) a purer steel, for the natural separation of foreign matter from the molten iron was far more effective than the pounding or squeezing out of drossy juices ever could be; and (2) a more homogeneous steel than could possibly be achieved by hammering solid metal on the anvil (compare the difference between stirring batter and kneading dough).

Crucible steel was harder and tougher than even the best shear steel; its one weakness was that it could not be treated at more than red heat, hence was hard to work, especially with the tools of the eighteenth century. (It could, of course, be cast.) Moreover, in the early days of Huntsman's monopoly or near-monopoly, its price was higher than that of shear steel in spite of the labour economies consequent on the elimination of repetitive forge work. As a result, smiths were hostile, and the use of the new metal was limited to those objects where the price of material was a negligible fraction of total cost—watch and clock parts, for example, and the finest edged tools. It did not really take hold until after 1770.

With time, however, the entry of competitors brought the price down. The effect of monopoly may be judged in part from the French experience: in 1815 cast steel had to be imported from Britain at £700 or £800 per ton; in 1819, after plants had been established at Badevel (Doubs) by Japy and near Saint-Etienne by James Jackson (English, as the name indicates), the price was £140.[1] Improvements in technique conduced to the same result. Producers learned to work with cheaper ingredients, to start with wrought iron, for example, and build up to steel by addition of powdered carbon. By the middle of the nineteenth century, Swedish steelmakers were mixing pig iron and iron ore with charcoal and selling the product at £50–£60 per ton.

The crucible technique had one further advantage, which opened the door to modern steel technology: it made possible—implicitly at first, effectively by the mid-nineteenth century—the manufacture of large pieces. Not that the individual crucibles could be made very big: they were perhaps 9–11 inches tall at first—the size of a vase—and more than a century later (1860) were still only about 16 inches in height; they held perhaps 45 to 60 pounds, though larger sizes were occasionally used. But they could be heated and poured *en masse*, or rather in close succession; and with time manufacturers learned to co-ordinate the labour of a small army of men, teeming hundreds of crucibles, to produce ingots weighing many tons. Krupp was the pioneer here, and his 2¼-ton cylinder was the sensation of the Crystal Palace Exposition; scarcely a generation later, in 1869, Vickers was using 672 crucibles at a time to make pieces ten times as heavy.[2]

The products of these *tours de force* were intended for boring as cannon; at £100 or more a ton, large ingots of crucible steel were far too expensive for ordinary industrial purposes. Yet the advantages of steel over wrought iron were manifest, and considerable money and effort was devoted to discovering a method to produce cheap steel in bulk.

The first step was the development of puddled steel; the major contribution was made in the early 1840's by two German technicians, Lohage and Bremme. The principle was simple: if the puddling process could refine pig iron into carbon-free wrought iron, why not stop it before completion, while there was still enough carbon in the metal to make steel? Execution was another matter. It was particularly difficult to know when the steel was ready and yet not too cooked; and the temperature had to be kept high enough to melt the pig iron, while low enough to let the steel separate out as a pasty mass because of its higher melting point. As a result, puddled steel was rarely as homogeneous and hard as crucible steel, or as tough as shear steel. Often it was simply substituted for blister steel or iron in the crucible process.

---

[1] [W. F. Jackson], *James Jackson et ses fils* (Paris: privately printed, 1893), p. 17, gives a lower figure—£120 per ton in 1818.

[2] Sidney Pollard, *History of Labour in Sheffield*, p. 160.

On the other hand, it was cheap—by the 1850's it was selling in Germany for about £22 a ton—and could be produced in large masses for such peaceful uses as tyres, wheels, gears, and drive shafts. The process was adopted more rapidly on the Continent than in Britain, where the ore apparently yielded pig iron too impure to serve as a base for acieration by puddling.[1] In France the new metal passed all other forms of steel in importance in 1857; the German figures do not permit a similar comparison (puddled and blister steel are combined), but the scissor year probably came at least as early.[2]

For lack of better, puddled steel would have been the nearest approach to mass-production steel—costs were eventually squeezed to around £10 per ton—had it not been for the invention of the Bessemer and Siemens–Martin processes, in their acid and basic variants.

(1) *Bessemer.* Again the inspiration came from armament. Henry Bessemer (1813–98), who was not a metallurgist but rather a kind of high-class tinkerer already wealthy by his ingenuity and versatility, devised in the early 1850's an artillery shell that required an exceptionally long and strong gun. The problem was to make steel cheap enough to render the mass production of such large pieces budgetarily feasible. (Even the military gagged at the cost under existing techniques of acieration.)

Bessemer found one of those solutions that amaze by their simplicity —once they are discovered. Instead of refining the pig iron by the traditional application of heat to its periphery, he blew air into and through the molten metal, using the heat thrown off by the oxidization itself to keep the iron liquid.[3] As a result, decarburization was extremely

[1] See the report of M. Goldenberg in Michel Chevalier, ed., *Exposition Universelle de 1867 à Paris, Rapports du jury international* (14 vols., Paris, 1868), v, 393f.

[2] France, Min. de l'Agric., du Comm., et des Trav. Publics, Direction des Mines, *Statistique de l'industrie minérale; Résumé des travaux statistiques de l'Administration des Mines en 1853, 1854, 1855, 1856, 1857, 1858 et 1859* (Paris, 1861), pp. 484–99; G. Viebahn, *Statistik des zollvereinten Deutschlands*, pp. 439 ff.

[3] Due credit should be given to the earlier invention (c. 1851) of this technique (with minor differences) by William Kelly in the United States. Kelly kept his operations secret until 1856, when his application for a patent ran up against a previous grant to Bessemer. He finally succeeded in getting his priority recognized in 1857—too late, however, to save himself from bankruptcy. It is doubtful, in any event, whether his process was suitable to mass production. See W. Paul Strassmann, *Risk and Technological Innovation: American Manufacturing Methods during the Nineteenth Century* (Ithaca, N.Y., 1959), p. 30. Nor should one overlook the vital contribution of Robert F. Mushet, who corrected the tendency of the converter to produce a 'burned-out' (over-oxidized) iron, by adding *Spiegeleisen*, that is, an iron containing manganese, to the molten metal. This process proved especially valuable in refining British pig iron. Owing to an unfortunate combination of circumstances, Mushet's patent was allowed to lapse before he could reap the fruits of his inventiveness. Cf. R. F. Mushet, *The Bessemer-Mushet Process, or Manufacture of Cheap Steel* (Cheltenham, 1883).

rapid: three to five tons in the early days in ten or twenty minutes, as against perhaps 24 hours for the equivalent amount of puddled steel.[1] A Bessemer converter in blast fairly erupts with the sudden release of energy. It is a little hell. With its flames and its shooting sparks of changing hue, it is also one of the most exciting sights that industry has to offer.

The consequent saving in labour and materials (Bessemer entitled the paper in which he announced his discovery in 1856, 'The Manufacture of Iron without Fuel') made possible the first steel that could compete in price with wrought iron—£7 (including royalty of about £1) per ton as against about £4 per ton. Yet adoption was slow. For one thing, iron-makers and users were reluctant to admit that the greater strength and durability of steel more than made up for the remaining difference in price; indeed, the very advent of cheap steel was enough to put producers of wrought iron on their mettle and stimulate them to more strenuous efforts. For another, the Bessemer process was attended by technical difficulties, some the inevitable concomitants of breaking-in, others inherent in the process itself.

The most serious of these was the inability of the converter to burn off the phosphorus along with other impurities in the pig iron; anything more than a minute proportion of this element made the steel unworkable. It was mere chance that Bessemer was using the right kind of pure pig iron when he invented his technique. (Compare the good fortune of Darby, one hundred and fifty years earlier.) His licensees were less lucky: hardly had they gone into production when they had to stop. The contretemps came, in Bessemer's words, 'as a bolt from the blue'.

A new start was made with haematite ores, which are non-phosphoric. The difficulty was that these were rarer and costlier than ordinary ironstone. In the entire industrial world, only the United States had an adequate supply: about half the Lake Superior basin was non-phosphoric. Britain had a major deposit of haematite in the Cumberland–Furness area, which boomed as a consequence, but almost from the start had to import additional supplies from Spain; the beds of non-phosphoric ironstone in the Bilbao area were probably the richest in Europe. Germany had small amounts in the Siegerland, but had to provide the great bulk of her needs from Spain and Austrian Galicia.

---

[1] Moreover, there was no intrinsic limit to the size of the converter. In puddling, the capacity of the furnace could not exceed the amount of molten iron a strong workman could stir by hand. The usual charge was about 200 kg. In the Bessemer process, by contrast, the only limit was the ability of machines to tilt the container and pour its contents. The early converters ran from 2 to 5 tons; by the end of the century, 20- and 25-ton vessels were common.

France had only scattered outcroppings of haematite in the Centre and had to bring in ore from Elba and Algeria to supplement imports from Spain. Belgium had nothing. Small wonder that the use of the Bessemer technique developed slowly on the Continent, and that for almost a decade after its invention puddled steel continued to predominate.

(2) *Siemens–Martin.* The second major advance in steelmaking simply re-emphasized the ore problem: the Siemens-Martin process also required non-phosphoric iron. As the name implies, the innovation was twofold. The furnace itself was the work of Frederick and William Siemens, brothers and members of a German family that will go down as the most inventive in history. (The main branch of the family were, as we shall see, pioneers in electrical communication and engineering.) The originality of the furnace lay in its utilization of the regenerative principle, by which the waste gases of oxidization were used to heat a honeycomb of bricks that in turn superheated the air and gaseous fuel in combustion; at the same time, the generation in a separate unit of the gas required made possible the employment of low-grade coal. The result was the achievement of far higher temperatures—the only immediate limit was the resistance of the furnace itself—at a substantial saving of fuel.

The potential contribution of the regenerative principle was not confined to metallurgy; it was an efficient method of heat production applicable to any energy-consuming industrial process. Its first appearance in iron manufacture was in the hot-blast stove of E. A. Cowper, an associate of Siemens, in 1857; from the start it yielded a blast of 620° C. and thereby increased the output of pig by 20 per cent.[1] The open-hearth version developed by Charles William Siemens found its first employment in 1861 in a flint-glass works in Birmingham. Early efforts to use it in steelmaking, where along with the Bessemer converter it had the advantage of being able to melt the pig completely (the puddling furnace produced at best a viscous mass), were failures. Commercial success was not achieved until 1864, when Pierre Martin introduced scrap iron into the bath to facilitate the process of decarburization. Even then, diffusion had to wait until the different centres of steel manufacture, each using its own qualities of ore, iron, and coal, learned by trial and error the proper combination of ingredients. Some used a mix that was more than half scrap; others added no more than a seasoning of iron chips; some used old steel as well as, or instead of, iron; Siemens himself used iron ore. The effective use of the open-hearth technique really dates from the 1870's.

(3) *Basic steel.* As a result of her favourable resource position,

[1] H. R. Schubert, 'The Steel Industry', in Singer *et al.*, ed., *History of Technology*, v, 58.

Britain dominated the early age of steel—in spite of the fact that no country had a greater stake in the old way of doing things. To the end of the 1870's she accounted for more than half of the Bessemer and Siemens–Martin production of the four major industrial countries of western Europe. This weakness of the continental countries in a new technological situation was potentially of critical importance both economically and politically. For Germany in particular, the great advances of the 1850's and 1860's were substantially offset and the new balance of power called into question. It is obviously hard to say what would have happened if the ore problem had not been solved (compare the fuel issue in eighteenth-century England). The conjuncture

Table 50. *Production of Bessemer and Siemens–Martin Steel (Flusseisen)* *(in thousand tons)*

	1865	1869	1873	1879
Great Britain	225	275	588	1030
Germany[a]	99·5	161	310	478
France	40·6	110	151	333
Belgium	0·65	2·9	22	111

[a] Includes Luxembourg. New boundaries from 1873.

SOURCE. Beck, *Geschichte des Eisens*, v, 233, 308.

gives no clue. One is tempted to ascribe the severity of the depression of the German iron industry in the 1870's—five years of red ink and a 19 per cent drop in output from peak to trough—to structural reasons: approaching inanition for want of nourishment. Admittedly the decline was shared, though in lesser degree, by Britain, and by France and Belgium as well. Still, it seems most unlikely that the spectacular rise of the Reich to a position of economic pre-eminence in Europe by the end of the century would have been possible without a strong steel industry, and one may doubt whether the steelmakers of the Ruhr could have thrived as they did had they been forced to seek their raw material in the Mediterranean area and northern Spain in competition with British producers, already advantaged by haematite deposits at home.[1] Lorraine, of course, far from good coking coal and dependent on cheap but high-phosphoric *minette*, would have gone out of competition with wrought iron and the puddling furnace.

The answer was found in 1878–9 by two Englishmen: Sidney Gilchrist Thomas, by occupation a clerk in a police court; and his cousin

[1] Beginning in the 1890's, the Ruhr came to rely increasingly on Swedish ores, which averaged about 60% iron content. They were too phosphoric, however, for acid steel, and would have played a far smaller role had technology remained the same as in the 1870's.

Sidney Gilchrist, chemist in a Welsh iron-works. They put basic limestone in the molten iron to combine with the acid phosphorus in a slag that could then be drawn off; and they lined the converter with basic matter in place of the usual acid siliceous bricks in order to prevent this basic slag from eating away the walls and releasing phosphorus back into the metal. The solution was a simple one, founded on a widely known principle. Success lay in the ingenuity of the practical arrangements—the combination of basic flux and lining—and it is probably no coincidence that the idea came to an amateur who approached the problem with an open mind.[1] Thomas is comparable in this regard to Bessemer, who for all his experience as a professional inventor was not a steel man. But whereas Bessemer had done his work a generation earlier when metallurgical chemistry was still in its infancy, Thomas solved a problem that had engaged the attention of some of Europe's most highly trained engineers for years. He was one of the last and perhaps the most important of the line of tinkerers that had made the Industrial Revolution. After him, the professionals just about had the field to themselves.

The invention of basic steel was an event of world import. Thomas was besieged by offers; the petitioners would not even let him eat his breakfast in peace. The story is told that two of the leading German iron firms sent representatives on a Phineas Fogg-like race to Middlesbrough; the one who did not stop for sleep won. The tale may be apocryphal, but it conveys something of the excitement of the occasion. In the end, a handful of industrial giants on the Continent (Schneider in France; Wendel in German Lorraine; the Hörder-Verein and Rheinische Stahlwerke in Germany) leased the patent rights for sums that, though not so inconsequential as tradition would have it, were a wonderful bargain; most of them sublet them in turn to other producers. The commercial manufacture of Thomas steel began in late 1879; within four years there were eighty-four basic converters in operation in western and central Europe (including Austria-Hungary), with a capacity of 755 tons. Output in 1883 totalled over 600,000 tons; compare acid Bessemer output, which took well over a decade to reach that level.[2] The adaptation of the process to the open hearth was almost as rapid.

[1] This twofold character of the innovation is often overlooked. See the discussion in Schubert, 'The Steel Industry', p. 60; similarly, J. Jewkes, D. Sawers and R. Sillerman, *The Sources of Invention* (London, 1960), p. 51.

[2] In the absence of statistics separating converter from open-hearth production for France, 1872 would seem to have been the year when Bessemer output in western and central Europe passed the 600,000-ton mark. Cf. Beck, *Geschichte des Eisens*, v, 967, 1057, 1110, 1134, 1177.

(4) *Steel* v. *wrought iron*. Together, the Bessemer, Siemens–Martin, and basic processes drove the real cost of crude steel down some 80 or 90 per cent between the early 1860's and mid-1890's and opened the iron ore deposits of the earth to fruitful exploitation. The consequences may be followed in the curve of output, which behaves in its steep upward trend like that of a new substance confronted by an extremely elastic demand. The combined production of Britain, France, Germany, and Belgium in 1861—before the Bessemer process had taken hold—was approximately 125,000 tons; in 1870 the total was perhaps 385,000 tons; in 1913 it amounted to 32,020,000 tons, a gain of 83 times (10·8 per cent per year) over the forty-three-year period.

Against this must be set the decline of wrought iron, long the frame of the industrial structure. At first, the older malleable form resisted: it was cheaper, and in countries like Britain there was a fortune invested in puddling plant. Moreover, the homogeneity of early Bessemer steel left something to be desired, and even the open-hearth variety, costlier to begin with, was not good enough for more exacting uses—large rolled plates, for example. Nor should one underestimate the strength of inertia and conservatism in these matters—the scepticism of the British Admiralty, the reluctance of French railway men to admit that steel rails could outlast iron by a factor of six to one. Before long, however, steelmakers learned to correct the flaws in their product; and improvements in efficiency wiped out enough of the price difference to make competition in most uses impossible. The railways were the first major consumer (after the military, of course) to adopt the new metal. The changeover was substantially accomplished in the 1870's; it was stimulated by the diminishing ratio of steel and iron rail prices—2·65 to 1 in 1867, 1·50 in 1871, 1·16 in 1875.[1] Shipbuilding, by contrast, which set higher standards under the watchful eyes of insurers like Lloyd's, began to accept steel in place of iron only in the late 1870's. In 1880 38,000 tons of steel shipping were added to the register of the United Kingdom, against 487,000 of iron. Five years later iron still predominated—308,500 to 185,000 tons—especially in the building of sailing vessels, where initial cost was a decisive consideration. Another five years of savings in the manufacture of open-hearth plates, however, and the tables had turned: 913,000 tons of steel to 46,000 of iron in 1890.[2]

---

[1] This is the French ratio, but the trend was substantially parallel in the other producing countries. Jean Fourastié, ed., *Documents pour l'histoire et la théorie des prix* [Centre d'Etudes Economiques, 'Etudes et Mémoires: Recherches sur l'évolution des prix en période de progrès technique'] (Paris, n.d. [1959]), pp. 122–3.

[2] *Encyclopaedia Britannica*, 11th edition, 'Ship'. These figures differ somewhat from those of the British Iron Trade Association. See W. A. Sinclair, 'The Growth of the British Steel Industry in the Late Nineteenth Century', *Scottish J. Political Economy*, VI (1959), 35, 41 f.

Actually, the high point of wrought-iron manufacture was not reached in Britain and France until 1882 (2,841,000 and 1,073,000 tons respectively) and in Germany until 1889 (1,650,000 tons). As late as 1885 Britain was turning out more puddled iron than steel; in Germany the curves of output do not cross until 1887; and in France, not until 1894.

This Indian summer of growth and achievement in obsolescence is a common economic phenomenon: witness the golden age of coaching after the coming of the railway; or the development of the clipper and the large intercontinental schooners after the introduction of the steamship. It derives from one or more of several factors: (1) a creative technological response to the challenge of the new competitor; (2) a compression of cost and elimination of waste in the struggle for survival; (3) opportunities derived from the demand created by the more efficient technique (cf. the role of coaches as feeders to railway trunk lines in the 1830's and 1840's).

Wrought iron attempted the first without success (above, p. 447). The goal proved a will-o'-the-wisp. Given the qualitative advantages of steel, it is most unlikely that mechanization could have done more than delay the inevitable. More effective was a general rationalization of methods and reduction of wages (compare the compression of wages of hand-loom weavers in earlier decades) that made it possible to cut prices by about half from the early 1870's to mid-1880's.

As for the third, wrought iron and steel were essentially substitutes rather than complementary, especially after the invention of basic steel. To be sure, the general demand for metal—all metals—was increasing, and the income effect of cheap steel may have redounded somewhat to the benefit of the older substance. In the end, however, iron came to be confined to uses where softness was not a handicap and resistance to corrosion was especially desirable: anchors and anchor chains, ornamental grill-work and gates, garden furniture and the like.

(5) *International division of labour and competition.* It would take too long to discuss in detail the different technical characteristics of Bessemer and Siemens–Martin steel, acid and basic, and analyse their implications for industrial development. They are summarized in the accompanying table. Very briefly, Bessemer was cheaper, more approximate in quality, and was produced in larger, more capital-intensive plants; Siemens–Martin steel was more homogeneous, closer to specification, and better suited to custom work. The one found its most important early use in rails; the other in plates. As production standards rose and railway construction slowed, the long-run trend was toward Siemens–Martin; but it was much more rapid in Britain, the world's greatest builder of ships, than in continental Europe (Table 52).

Table 51. *The Manufacture of Cheap Steel in the Nineteenth Century*

	Acid	Technology and economic consequences	Basic	Technology and economic consequences
Bessemer	Uses relatively scarce non-phosphoric ores. Long reputed to produce a tougher steel than the basic process	Half-hour or less for carbonization; rapidity of output compels extensive mechanization; consequently important economies of scale	Uses cheaper ore; costs less. Produces by-product phosphates that make excellent fertilizer. High proportion of slag leads by way of compensation to larger scale of production	Long reputed the poorest of cheap steels. Yet produces metal of high ductility and excellent welding quality—especially good for tubes and wire
Siemens–Martin		Six to eighteen hours for decarbonization; closer quality control; smaller scale of production. Higher cost; but differences mitigated by feasibility of using scrap		Especially abundant supply of scrap iron since most wrought iron was phosphoric

Some of this diversity was due to differences in resources. Britain, with her haematite ores, long remained faithful to the acid process. The continental countries, on the other hand, compelled by the absence of haematite ironstone and encouraged by the abundance of phosphorus-rich ore in Lorraine and Sweden to concentrate on the basic technique, found Thomas steel (that is, basic Bessemer) especially remunerative. Yet one should not underestimate the human factor. Stimulated by necessity, the continental steelmasters worked at the basic process with a scientific will: they achieved and maintained a proper mix and produced a metal of good, uniform quality. The British tinkered and improvised, and the irregularity of their product merely confirmed the doubts of consumers, which in turn discouraged experiment and investment. The whole situation was self-reinforcing. By about 1890, the continental countries were turning out more basic than acid steel; whereas the latter accounted for 92 per cent of Britain's open-hearth make and 73 per cent of her converter output as late as 1897.[1] The respective proportions were 63 and 65 per cent in 1913, and it took the First World War to wean Britain from her allegiance to the older, more costly process.[2]

Table 52. *Percentage of Steel Produced by Siemens–Martin*

	1890	1913	1930
Great Britain	43·6	79·2	94·3
Germany	17·4	40·2	52·3[a]
France	36·8	33·8	27·5
Belgium	Negligible	Negligible	Negligible

[a] Had been as high as 60·6 per cent in 1920.

SOURCE. T. H. Burnham and G. O. Hoskins, *Iron and Steel in Britain 1870–1930* (London, 1943), p. 183.

This specialization by type of process both shaped and was shaped by the growth patterns of the respective national steel industries. Britain had relatively small plants; Germany large. Around the turn of the century, the *biggest* British mills were turning out only as much as the *average* Westphalian works. (Contrast the situation a generation earlier; see above, p. 448.) Nor was this simply a matter of delayed response to opportunity: *new* British plants in the 1890's were a quarter to a third of the size of their German competitors.

The disparity extended backward to the smelting stage: the median member of the German steel cartel (1903) was four times as big as its British analogue (1900), more than twice as big as the median iron firm

[1] See the discussion *ibid.*; also I. F. Gibson, 'The Establishment of the Scottish Steel Industry', *Scottish J. Political Economy*, v (1958), 22–39.

[2] *Iron and Coal Trades Rev.* Diamond Jubilee Issue, 1867–1927 (1927), 134; Burnham and Hoskins, *Iron and Steel in Britain*, pp. 179–80.

in the Cleveland area. And the disadvantage to Britain was cumulative, for Germany put big and big together and Britain left small and small apart. In 1902 only twenty-one open-hearth firms of seventy-two in Britain, with one quarter of the make, had adjacent blast furnaces; whereas integration with smelting was almost universal in the Reich. The same was true of ties to later stages of manufacture: where the tendency of Westphalia was to build rolling mills on to steel works, British rerollers were relying increasingly on outside sources for their crude metal.

Size of plant and integration, moreover, were closely related to technique and productivity. German equipment, originally smaller and less efficient than the British, grew rapidly in size and performance until, by the turn of the century, it outstripped that of her precursor by a wide margin.[1] In 1870 the average British blast furnace made 74 per cent more pig iron than its German counterpart—8700 against 5000 tons. By 1910 the positions were reversed: Germany, 49,000 tons; Britain, 30,000. Similarly in steel: by 1890 the average German open hearth was half again as large as the British—15 against 10 tons—and output was correspondingly higher; and German converters poured out an average of 34,000 tons in 1901, where British equipment produced 21,750.[2]

What is more, the very size of German equipment imposed extensive mechanization. A furnace turning out 3000 tons of pig iron a week consumed 6000–9000 tons of ore, perhaps 1000 tons of limestone, some 4000 tons of coke. It took some six hundred freight trucks, averaging 20 tons capacity, just to bring materials to the mill.[3] (It would have

---

[1] The above is based primarily on the discussion in Burn, *Economic History*, ch. x. The recent article of Sinclair argues that Burn neglected the open-hearth sector, with consequent depreciation of the achievements of British metallurgy by comparison with the German. The reproach, it seems to me, is exaggerated. For one thing, Burn makes a number of salient points about the weaknesses of open-hearth steel—though he tends to pass over the strengths. For another, and more important, the comparison is not so much between sectors of the British steel industry, as between British and foreign manufacture. It would be equally unreasonable to measure the growth of German steel by the Thomas sector alone.

What is more, Sinclair carries his story only into the 1890's; yet the discrepancy between German and British rates of growth is even more striking after that date than before. Even if we measure British open-hearth against German total steel output, we find, taking 1890 as 100, an increase by 1913 to 387 for the former, to 825 for the latter. Taking total output for both countries, the respective indexes are 214 and 825. *Iron and Coal Trades Rev.* Diamond Jubilee Issue, 1867–1927 (1927), 130, 134.

[2] Burnham and Hoskins, *Iron and Steel*, pp. 145, 181; S. J. Chapman, *Work and Wages*, part 1: *Foreign Competition* (London, 1904), p. 89.

[3] British trucks were much smaller, and coal wagons were typically of 10-ton capacity. Cf. K. G. Fenelon, *Railway Economics* (London, 1932), pp. 168–73; S. E. Parkhouse, 'Railway Freight Rolling Stock', *J. Institute of Transport*, xxiv (1951), 213–15.

taken twelve hundred or more of the smaller British trucks.) And once there, these materials had to be fed somehow to the flames. The traditional winch and counterweight systems for hauling small tilt wagons to the lip of the furnace—supplemented on occasion by human brawn and hand shovels—were hopelessly inadequate. In their place appeared continuous conveyors, travelling cranes, and suspended railways powered by electricity.

And then there were the 3000 tons of iron to be tapped, poured into moulds, lifted, and broken for remelting; or better yet, delivered directly to the refinery for conversion into wrought iron or steel. As noted earlier, the rapid Bessemer process required mechanization from the start. By comparison, the lengthier period required for decarburization by Siemens–Martin encouraged a certain tolerance of interruptions for transport and manipulation: with proper facilities it took some $3\frac{1}{2}$ hours to fill a 40-ton hearth by hand.[1] But here too the trend toward mechanization was inexorable. By the end of the century, German steelmakers especially were imitating the best American practice and building tiltable furnaces of 100–300 tons capacity, equipped with hydraulically or electrically powered charging apparatus. The effect of mechanical loading alone was to reduce a work force of 46 skilled and unskilled labourers per hearth to 16 and cut labour costs (allowing for the amortization of the additional capital) by 58 per cent.[2]

Finally, and perhaps more important, there was a strong tendency toward increased automaticity of the forge. The development was along two lines. One, resuming the advance implicit in Cort's combination of puddling and rolling, was to eliminate as much as possible the hammer and have all the work of squeezing and shaping done by the mill. Powerful and fast as the steam hammer was, it was of its nature intermittent in operation and gave rise to a costly and difficult problem in manual manipulation. One has only to look at any of the hundreds of sketches of mid-nineteenth-century forges that have come down to us to appreciate the disadvantages of the old technique: the shop is generally a vaulted cavern, illuminated by the glow of the furnaces and the hot ingots and blooms; the floor is a Vulcanian jungle of puffing steam-driven machines, heaps of incinerating iron, tools momentarily discarded, the suspended vines of the overhead cranes; and in the middle,

[1] 'On Charging Open-hearth Furnaces by Machinery', *J. Iron and Steel Institute*, LI (1897), 90–1. Actually 48 tons of materials were charged per heat in a hearth of this size, 'and that in the face of a furnace radiating a considerable amount of heat'. Four men were used, each charging about 3·4 tons per hour. The 'great physical and constitutional strength' required may easily be imagined.

[2] Von Kammerer, 'Entwicklungslinien der Technik', *Technik und Wirtschaft*, III (1910), 16.

hanging dumb but deadly in its chain sling is the large cylinder or block of white-hot metal, teased and nudged on to the anvil, then twisted and released into a new position, and then another, by the pincers and rods of as many as dozens of black and sweating pygmies. To which one must add what the sketches cannot convey: the clash and clangour, the enervating heat, the burning, dust-filled air that killed.[1]

Around 1870, direct rolling of big masses was confined essentially to rails; otherwise it was thought necessary to 'consolidate the structure' of the ingot by pounding before squeezing. Some of the British began to get away from this intermediary step in the 1860's, and the contraction of the 1870's helped spread the practice by sharpening competition. At John Brown's in Sheffield, one mill and eighteen men did the work of three hammers and fifty-four men.[2]

Note, however, the factor of three: even with the mill it took eighteen men to send the metal on its way, then receive it as it completed its run and send it back for another pass. The task was just as difficult as that of guiding ingots under the hammer; if there was less need for strength and precision, more agility was required to handle the billet or sheet as it spewed from between the rolls. Fatigue could be fatal, and indeed most of the accidents occurred in the early morning hours.[3]

The answer—and this is the second of the two lines of development referred to above—lay in minimizing handling by automating the mill. One improvement, which was first introduced in Britain in 1866, was to apply a reversing engine to the rolls, so that the metal could be run back and forth without leaving the machine. The saving in labour and time was such that capacity was more than doubled; but the strain on the engine, which every few seconds had to fight its momentum and that of the rolls to start back the other way, was tremendous. The American solution, extensively adopted in Germany, was the three-high mill, where a third roll placed above the usual two made it possible to pass the metal back on an 'upper level', shaping it the while.

Faster work called for improvements in feeding techniques, for the task of catching the metal on a three-high mill and lifting or lowering it to send it back on the other track was if anything more arduous and

---

[1] See Pollard, *A History of Labour in Sheffield*, pp. 168-9. The average age at death of rollers and forgers in Sheffield who died in the period 1864-71 (85 cases) was 37 years; the only group that was consumed more rapidly was the puddlers, who averaged a brief 31 years.

[2] Burns, *Economic History*, p. 56, citing *Iron and Coal Trades Review* (1874), 760.

[3] See the analysis of a realistic painting of the forge at Königshütte (Silesia) in the 1870's: K. Kaiser, *Adolph Menzels Eisenwalzwerk* (Berlin: Heuschelverlag, 1953). Compare the jacket illustration of Pollard's *Labour in Sheffield*, which shows sheet rolling at the Atlas Steel Works in 1861.

dangerous than on two-high mills. By the turn of the century, best practice was moving the metal on roller tables, turning it by automatic tumbling bars, raising and lowering it by lifts, putting it into and removing it from the reheating furnaces by hydraulic (later, electric) cranes fitted with giant pincers. Reheating itself was progressively eliminated as the rapidity of the shaping process increased. There were even continuous mills for narrow shapes, with ten or more sets of rolls that stretched and shaped the billet in a single pass. It required great precision to effect such a result: at one end the much reduced, almost finished metal came rushing through the final rolls at forty to sixty miles an hour; while at the other end the same piece of metal, thick and unshapen, was still feeding slowly into the roughing rolls. It also required ingenuity and heavy capital outlays to process the final product: 'flying shears' for cutting, facilities for cooling, stacking, and moving. These were the ancestors of the modern wide strip mill. The continuous system was first invented in Britain, where one or two examples were built in the 1860's to make rods and rails. But it did not find general acceptance, and it was not until the 1890's that the idea was picked up again in the United States and spread thence to Europe. On the whole, the continental engineers, especially the Germans, were quickest to adopt it.[1]

Efficiency promotes efficiency: indeed, it makes it necessary. Just as size and integration facilitated in Germany greater intensity of capital, so capital intensity encouraged a more rational organization of work and a simplification of the product mix. The reader will recall that one of the most serious obstacles to the diffusion of the power loom was the high cost of immobilizing valuable machinery to change patterns; by the same token, the need to change rolls was an impediment to the adoption of longer and faster mills. In order to make the most of their equipment, the Germans were compelled to standardize and in that way stretch their production runs. As early as 1883 the United Societies of German Architects and Engineers drew up a complete set of standard sections for rolled iron in shipbuilding, engineering, and construction.[2]

---

[1] On German 'arrangements for relieving labour of its more exhausting characteristics', see British Iron Trade Association, *The Iron and Steel Industries of Belgium and Germany* (London, 1896), p. 13 and *passim*.

[2] Burn, *Economic History*, p. 199. It is impossible to say what was the effect of such a list on industrial practice. But the very fact of its preparation is significant (Burn notes the preoccupation of German engineers with the advantages of different sections in the 1870's), and the characteristics of the cost curves, to say nothing of the ideological commitment to rationality (see below, pp. 579-81) undoubtedly influenced the German enterprise in this direction. Cf. W. H. Henman, in discussion of W. H. A. Robertson, 'Notes on the Mechanical Design of Rolling Mills', *J. Birmingham Metallurgical Soc.* VII (1919), 40.

And where in 1900 British steelmakers were turning out 122 channel and angle sections as a matter of course, the Germans made 34.

Finally, there was the question of waste. In the eighteenth and early nineteenth centuries, the best British enterprises were internationally renowned for their neatness, their attention to detail, their meticulous inventory controls. Wedgwood was uncompromising on this point; continental visitors to Crawshay's iron mill in Wales, coming as they did from poorer lands, found this one of the most impressive and congenial features of his production organization. By the end of the century, however, the tables had turned. British visitors to German steel plants marvelled at bins to catch oil dripping from the lubrication boxes and steam captured, condensed, and re-used.[1] Above all, they admired the Germans' efficient use of fuel, so often the best criterion of metallurgical performance. The discrepancy here was apparent at every stage—from coking, where continental ovens supplied energy for steam-engines and produced by-product tar and ammonia for the chemical manufacture;[2] to smelting, where the German *mise au mille* was 15–25 per cent lower than good British practice and the hot gases of their blast furnaces drove internal-combustion engines whose output transcended the requirements of the enterprise and furnished electric power to outside consumers; to steelmaking, where German vertical integration made it possible to work their metal hot from start to finish, while the British, whose high pig–scrap ratio made such methods even more profitable, had to move and reheat pigs and blooms at several stages. The statistics on fuel consumption in post-smelting processes are eloquent: 22·5 cwt. per ton of output in Britain in 1929 (31 cwt. in 1920), 4·9 in the average Belgian plant, 3·2 in an integrated Belgian plant, even less in Germany.[3]

The effects of greater capital intensity and more rational organization were apparent in productivity, where output per man-year (a necessarily gross approximation of real productivity) in steel melting and rolling ran to 77 tons in Germany in 1913, against 48 tons in Britain in 1920, when productivity was presumably higher than before the war.[4] It also showed in prices. British rails and plates, originally

[1] See British Iron Trade Assn., *The Iron and Steel Industries of Belgium and Germany*, pp. 36, 42, 45, 47. German superiority in this field continued right through to the war and after. Cf. Robertson, 'Notes'.
[2] The best history of coke technology is F. M. Ress, *Geschichte der Kokereitechnik* (Essen, 1957).   [3] Burn, *Economic History*, p. 439 and n. 4.
[4] *Ibid.* p. 417. The figures are ambiguous and comparison is correspondingly hazardous. Thus we have such statistical anomalies as an output per man-year in Germany in 1913 of 345 tons in steel melting, 104 tons in rolling, but only 77 in melting and rolling combined.
Smelting productivity gives rise to even more serious problems. Chapman, *Work*

the cheapest in the world, became dearer than comparable German products around the turn of the century, both on the respective home markets and for export. On the eve of the war, the difference in quotations on plate at Essen and on the Clyde was 20–25 per cent.

As a result, superior technology went hand in hand (I use the expression advisedly because there was clearly a reciprocal relationship) with industrial expansion. A semi-log graph of iron and steel output offers the most vivid illustration possible of the course of international economic rivalry in the period 1870–1914: the British lines bend over like wilting flowers, while the German continue their steep ascent to the very eve of the conflict. In the early 1870's, Britain was making four times as much iron and twice as much steel as the *Zollverein*. In the quinquennium 1910–14, by contrast, Germany averaged almost twice as much iron, more than twice as much steel. The point of passing was 1893 for steel, 1903 for pig iron.

One more point is worth making about Britain's loss of metallurgical hegemony, which actually dated from 1890, when the United States permanently took over first place in both iron and steel output. For a long time, the painful effects of expansion abroad were somewhat mitigated by the absorption of the great bulk of the incremental make by the markets of the producing countries; both the United States and Germany needed vast quantities of steel for their own economies. By 1910, however, Germany was exporting more iron and steel than Britain, which had been the leading supplier to the world for over a century; worse yet, the steelmasters of the Ruhr were selling some of their production in the United Kingdom itself. The royal crown was slipping, and the doctrines of economic theorists on comparative advantage and international division of labour were cold comfort.

B. *A new chemical industry*

Chemical manufacture, which by definition is the transformation of matter for productive use, is the most miscellaneous of industries. Thus metallurgy is technically a branch of applied chemistry, and among our new materials of the turn of the century (see p. 477 above) would have

and Wages, p. 76, simply asserts that 'no trustworthy figures are obtainable'. The statistics given by Burnham and Hoskins, *Iron and Steel*, pp. 315–17, and Burn, *Economic History*, p. 417, show some brutal variations in productivity from year to year but concur in showing Britain ahead—as much as 40% ahead—before the war. Everything we know about comparative size, capacity, and mechanization of blast furnaces, however, and the relationship of these to productivity throws doubt on these data. The trouble would seem to lie in the count of workers assigned to smelting. (There is also the question of actual hours worked, but this is probably much less important as a source of bias.)

to be alloy steels and non-ferrous metals like aluminium. Similarly, glass-making and paper-making are branches of the chemical trade, and so are cement and rubber manufacture and ceramics.

In all of these areas, the late nineteenth century saw important technological innovations. Of chemical improvements proper, we may note the invention and perfection of wood-pulp paper from about 1855 onward (there are bibliophiles and scholars who would not accept this as an advance); the Hall-Héroult electrolytic process for deriving aluminium from bauxite (1886), which changed a precious metal used for spoons at the table of Napoleon III to a light, non-corrosive industrial substitute for iron and steel in some of their applications; and the development of more refractory materials in the manufacture of furnace brick (magnesite and dolomite, 1860 on), indispensable for the higher temperatures become customary in heat-consuming processes. At least as important, probably, in raising productivity in the chemical trades were mechanical and instrumental innovations: the introduction of the regenerative furnace (late 1850's) and the semi-automatic bottle machine (1859 on) in glass-making; the use of automatic presses, extrusion and hose-making machines in rubber; of the continuous long-chamber kiln, special presses, and extrusion machines in brick-making and ceramics; of the shaft kiln (developed in the 1870's; introduced to Britain from Germany in the 1880's) and rotary kiln (perfected early 1890's) in cement manufacture.

Yet all of these improvements took place in what were still minor areas of industrial activity—the great days of rubber and cement, for example, still lay in the future; or, occurring as they did in the manufacture of final products, their impact on the economy as a whole through indirect savings and derived demand was limited. The great advances in chemical manufacture in our period had these qualities of immediate scope and ramifying consequences. The two most important were the Solvay method of alkali manufacture and the synthesis of organic compounds.

1. L. F. Haber has called the period from 1860 to 1880 'the golden age of the Leblanc soda industry'. The demand for alkalis increased with that for textiles and soap, consumption of which rose with income, improved sanitation, and higher standards of living; and the introduction of esparto grass into paper manufacture, to supplement the manifestly inadequate supply of rags, called for large quantities of bleaching powder. In the generation from 1852 to 1878, British production of soda ash tripled, from 72,000 to 208,000 tons; the make of soda crystals rose almost as fast, from 61,000 to 171,000 tons; and output of bleaching powder increased almost eight times, from 13,000 to 100,000 tons. Most of these alkalis were consumed at home, but a significant and

growing proportion went abroad, first to the United States, and then to France after the commercial treaty of 1860 and to the *Zollverein*. Exports went from 16,500 tons in 1847 to 273,000 in 1876, a leap of over 1500 per cent. The production of the continental countries, though growing, was a small fraction of the British.[1]

This growth evoked several improvements in technique, mostly of an instrumental character and more labour- than material-saving: larger decomposing pans; mechanical roasters; the revolving furnace (late 1860's); and the Shanks vat (1861), which made it possible to extract the black ash by means of hydrostatic pressure rather than by laborious shovelling from tank to tank.[2] Yet when all is said and done, the industry had never used much labour, and the impact of such innovations was correspondingly limited. In 1862, around 10,000 men were employed in the Leblanc manufacture of England and Wales, as against 400,000 in textiles. Of these, a fraction (less than a fifth probably) were needed to perform the chemical process proper; the rest were engaged in packaging, handling, and maintenance.[3]

Even so the supply barely kept ahead of demand. The long-term level of alkali prices during these years was unchanged; bleaching materials alone showed a significant decline, and then only after the crisis of 1873, when general deflation had set in. It was at this point that ammonia soda entered the picture.

The Leblanc technique was an offence to chemist and manufacturer alike. Even after Gossage had developed in 1836 his towers for the condensation of by-product hydrochloric acid, whose fumes were poisoning the countryside in the neighbourhood of every alkali plant, the chlorine therein was lost to industry. Moreover, the process continued to waste valuable sulphur, to say nothing of calcium and large amounts of unchanged coal, in the form of a noisome mud that the inhabitants of Lancashire expressively baptized 'galligu', which added to the injury of loss the insult of costly disposal.

By comparison the ammonia-soda technique was more elegant (in the mathematical sense of neatness and simplicity), and gave every promise of being more profitable. The chemical reaction was discovered by Fresnel as early as 1811: one could obtain sodium bicarbonate and ammonium chloride from concentrated solutions of salt (sodium chloride) and ammonia (NH_3) by treating with carbonic acid (H_2CO_3). The sodium bicarbonate, on heating, yielded the sodium

[1] Haber, *Chemical Industry*, pp. 59, 55.
[2] See T. I. Williams, 'Heavy Chemicals', in Singer *et al.*, eds., *A History of Technology*, v, 235–56.
[3] Cf. D. W. F. Hardie, *A History of the Chemical Industry in Widnes* (n.p., Imp. Chemical Industries, 1950), pp. 118–19.

carbonate (soda) desired, plus water and carbon dioxide. The one practical difficulty—and it proved serious—was the inability to recover the ammonia, a costly compound in those days, from the by-product ammonium chloride.

The problem was essentially one of plant—to build equipment to do what everyone knew should and could be done. Dozens of scientists and empiricists spent tens of thousands of pounds to find a solution. 'Never before was the industrial realisation of any process attempted so frequently and for such a long period of time....'

Ernest Solvay (1838–1922), born in the small Belgian village of Rebecq, inherited his interest in chemical manufacture. His father was a salt refiner, among other things; his uncle, the director of a gas works, the one place where ammonia was almost a free good. It was in his uncle's factory that he first observed its wastage in coal distillation; and it was there he conducted his first experiments in soda manufacture, devised his tower to mix carbon dioxide with ammoniacal brine, built his still to recover the ammonia. In December 1863—he was only 25 years old—Solvay founded with outside assistance the firm that bears his name and remains to this day one of the giants of the world chemical industry.

The years immediately following saw numerous disappointments, continued experiments. It took another decade to perfect the process; but by the mid-1870's, Solvay alkalis, even with the burden of royalty payments, could undersell Leblanc products as then produced by about 20 per cent. The greatest saving was in materials.

There then ensued a struggle that is technologically analogous to that between cheap steel and wrought iron and economically analogous to the competition between the British and German steel industries. The new technique spread rapidly on the Continent, predominantly in the Solvay version but to a small extent in variant forms. In France, less than a quarter of the alkali produced in 1874 was made by the ammonia process; a generation later, in 1905, the figure was 99·65 per cent. Germany was slower at first; of the comparatively small quantity of soda produced in 1878, some 42,500 tons, only 19 per cent was of the ammonia variety. By 1887, however, the proportion was 75 per cent; by 1900, it was over 90 per cent of some 300,000 tons.[1]

Only Britain lagged. She had a large investment in Leblanc plant,

---

[1] On the competition between the two processes, see, in addition to Haber, G. Lunge, *The Manufacture of Sulphuric Acid and Alkali* (3rd ed.; 4 vols.; London, 1911), III, 737–44; R. Hasenclever, 'Ueber die gegenwärtige Lage der Leblanc'schen Soda-fabriken in Concurrenzkampf mit der Ammoniak-Soda', *Die Chemische Industrie*, x (1887), 290–1; *idem*, 'Die Lage der deutschen Sodafabrikation im Jahre 1901', *ibid.* xxv (1902), 73–5.

which entrepreneurs were unwilling to abandon. And these hard-pressed producers squeezed new economies and additional income out of their Leblanc works by closer attention to costs, the introduction of more efficient equipment, and recovery of chlorine from the by-product hydrochloric acid (Weldon's process, 1869–70). Prices of Leblanc alkalis fell by 1890 to about a third of their peak on the eve of Solvay (1872–3).

At these levels, British alkalis were competitive, and the firmness of the price of by-product bleaching powder was an unexpected dividend. British exports more than doubled in tonnage from 1870 to 1883 and remained at almost that high level until 1895. Then the agony began. It was partly technical in origin. The introduction of electrolytic methods of preparing chlorine and caustics in the 1890's hit directly at the Leblanc industry's most profitable operation. Once again, Britain watched other countries take the lead: by 1904 all the American and 65 per cent of the German output of chlorine was electrolytic; the corresponding figures for France and the United Kingdom were 19 and 18 per cent.[1] And it was partly the result of protectionism abroad; the United States Dingley tariff of 1897 was particularly harmful. Total exports fell from 312,400 to 188,500 tons; output decreased by much less, about 10 per cent, but the point is that it decreased—for the first time since the beginning of the Industrial Revolution. German output rose the while and was beginning to compete even in those tropical areas that had always been a British preserve.

Thus disappeared the last resource of the Leblanc manufacture (the gains afforded by the Chance-Claus sulphur recovery process—at last a way to save the sulphur!—were not enough to compensate). The formation in 1890 of the United Alkali Co. Ltd., uniting in one large trust the bulk of the country's Leblanc capacity, and the subsequent negotiation of price and commodity agreements with the major producer of ammonia soda, Brunner, Mond and Co., served only to delay the demise. In spite of all the determination and ingenuity the company could muster, disappointment followed disappointment, dividends stopped, the equity shrank to a fraction of its original value, to the point where there was not enough capital to scrap the old and build anew. In 1920, not quite a century after its introduction, Britain's once great Leblanc industry shut down.

As in steel, differences in technique were reflected in rates of growth. We do not have British figures on alkali manufacture for the years immediately preceding the First World War; and such German statistics as we possess are not comparable because the products are measured at different degrees of purity. But we do have estimates of the respective

[1] Clapham, *Economic History*, III, 173.

outputs of sulphuric acid, 'the most important inorganic chemical for technical purposes'. It is used for the production of such other inorganic compounds as sodium sulphate; in the manufacture of fertilizer, particularly the superphosphates; in petroleum refining, iron and steel, and textiles; in the production of explosives; and in dyemaking and other branches of organic chemistry. As a result, its consumption is a rough yardstick of general industrial development. As late as 1900, British output of sulphuric acid was almost twice the German: about 1 million as against 550,000 tons. Only thirteen years later the positions were almost reversed: Germany, 1,700,000 tons; Britain, 1,100,000.[1]

2. The theoretical and experimental work that lay at the basis of the organic chemical industry was largely German and British. Some of the landmarks are Faraday's isolation of benzene in 1825, Wöhler's discovery of the isomerism of organic compounds (1828), the analysis and fractionation by Hofmann and his pupils of coal tar (Mansfield's historic paper, 'Researches on Coal Tar, Part I', was published in 1849), and Kekulé's theoretical reconstruction of the benzene molecule (1865). The practical discoveries that were the substance of the new industry were the work of Britons, Germans working in Britain, and Frenchmen. In 1856 Perkin fortuitously synthesized the first aniline dye, a purple that took the French name *mauve*; Natanson and Verguin in France perfected aniline red, or magenta, in 1859; in 1863 Martius, building on the researches of Griess, made the first commercially successful azo dye, Bismarck brown;[2] finally, in 1869 Perkin in England and Graebe and Liebermann in Germany produced alizarin, the first artificial dye to replace a natural colourant, in this case madder. This was the last of the great British developments and the first of a long series of major discoveries by German laboratories; it marked a shift in the locus of innovation. It also symbolized the arrival of an era of purposive research: Perkin came upon mauve by accident, but he sought and found alizarin, while Graebe undertook his research on direct orders from his master Baeyer. The two turning-points—in location and character of research—were interrelated.

[1] These figures are derived from W. Woytinsky, *Die Welt in Zahlen*, IV, 316; the *Statistisches Jahrbuch des deutschen Reichs*; Haber, *Chemical Industry*, pp. 104, 122; and League of Nations, Economic and Financial Section, International Economic Conference, Geneva, May 1927, Documentation: *The Chemical Industry* (Geneva, 1927), pp. 23, 127. An effort has been made to convert all figures to acid of 100 % concentration (monohydrate); the indifference of even the most expert writers to this elementary detail does not make the task easy.

[2] Azo dyes are so called because of the presence of nitrogen (French *azote*) in the molecule. Haber notes that they were the first to be produced directly on cloth and became the most fruitful source of artificial colourants—385 out of 681 commercial dyes in 1902, 461 of 1001 in 1922. *Chemical Industry*, p. 83.

One final remark about the scientific background: as in other examples of industrial innovation, so in organic chemicals it is tempting to recall the famous achievements and take the rest for granted. The fact was that experimental syntheses were a far cry from commercial processes. The transfer of these reactions from laboratory to factory called for the development of new sources and patterns of supply, accessory techniques for the inexpensive manufacture of scarce test-tube materials, and the invention of reliable equipment for effecting what could be dangerous reactions. In one early British works, the nitration shed was known as 'the shooting gallery'. At the same time, the utilization of these dyes in textile manufacture called for further innovations: mordants for recalcitrant fabrics; and patterns that would take advantage of the opportunities presented by these new and fast colours. Here the French contribution was decisive.

As this account implies, the first years of the new branch of chemical manufacture belonged to Britain, with France in second place. Not only was the bulk of the early research conducted in English laboratories, but in no other country had the distillation of coal tar for commercial purposes advanced so far. The same enterprises that produced heavy oils for wood preservatives (Bethell patent of 1838) and 'naphtha' for use in the manufacture of rubber and varnish could easily turn out 'light oils' as well. Conditions of supply were therefore especially favourable, and indeed several of the pioneers of the British organic industry went from coal tar to dye-stuffs.

In France, the emphasis on highly coloured, imaginatively designed fabrics provided a ready-made market for the new dyes. Lyons, the home of the silk manufacture (silk took aniline dyes better than other fibres), was one centre. Alsace, with its high-fashion cotton-print industry, an old pioneer in textile chemistry, was another. The Paris area was a third. In 1864 one of the strongest producers joined with the young Crédit Lyonnais to found what was probably the largest dye firm in the world, La Fuchsine, capital 4 million francs.

In both countries, however, this early development was soon blighted. In Britain, the coal-tar amateurs were out of their depth, and the specialists lost their best German scientists to the enterprises of their native country. All but a few firms stagnated or failed. They found themselves undersold at every turn by foreign competitors and in so far as they prospered, they did so on sufferance, by means of price or market agreements. Venture capital was frightened off, accentuating the spiral of decline. In France, many of the producers ruined each other by a costly patent war in the 1860's. La Fuchsine went bankrupt in 1868, doing more than anything else to convince Henri Germain, the crusty director of the Crédit Lyonnais, that there was no industrialist in France worthy of his support.[1]

German output of dyestuffs soared. In the late 1860's, the industry was still small, dispersed, and essentially imitative. Scarcely a decade later, Badische Anilin, Höchst, AGFA, and the others held about half of the world market; by the turn of the century, their share was around 90 per cent. Moreover, this does not take into account the output of subsidiaries and affiliates in other countries. Thus in France, only one of the major dyestuff plants on the eve of the First World War was French-owned and managed; six were German, two Swiss; and the four or five small native firms were dependent on foreign, principally German, firms for intermediate products.

In technical virtuosity and aggressive enterprise, this leap to hegemony, almost to monopoly, has no parallel. It was Imperial Germany's greatest industrial achievement. Of the other nations of the world, only Switzerland succeeded in developing a vigorous dyestuffs manufacture in the face of this competition. By importing raw chemicals and intermediates from north of the border, concentrating on special tints requiring the highest production skills, and offering their customers the latest technical advice, CIBA, Geigy, and the other Basle manufacturers won and held an important share of the international market. Swiss output in 1895 was almost a fifth as large (by value) as the German and just about as big as that of all other countries combined.

In Germany, the organic sector accounted for well over half of the work force and capital investment of the chemical industry by the First World War; other countries, though far slower, were following the same path. For dyes were only one corner of a new world: the scientific principles that lay behind artificial colourants were capable of the widest application. There was the whole range of products derived from cellulose, that remarkable family of carbohydrates that constitutes the chief solid element of plants. Nitrocellulose explosives (Schönbein's gun-cotton, 1846) came first, followed by lacquers, photographic plates and film, celluloid (the first modern plastic, by Hyatt in 1868, and for all its flammability still useful, for the manufacture of table-tennis balls among other things), and artificial fibres (Chardonnet's *soie artificielle*, 1889; C. F. Cross's viscose in 1892). Viscose in turn gave birth to a family of its own, including cellophane (Brandenberger in 1912), sizing compounds, sausage casings, and sundry other items of greater or lesser usefulness. And in 1909 Baekeland patented the first of the synthetic resins, the so-called 'plastic of a thousand uses', bakelite. The point to be noted is the almost incredible

[1] See the account in Bouvier, *Le Crédit Lyonnais*, pp. 374–81, and the sources cited there.

ingenuity of these techniques, their ceaseless ramification in new directions and products. As the title of one history of a chemical firm put it,
One Thing Leads to Another. Here in unexpected form was a surrogate
for the long-sought secret of transmuting and creating matter.

(2) NEW SOURCES OF ENERGY AND POWER

The subject divides itself logically into three parts:

(1) The sources of energy proper: falling water; burning carbon (in
the form of coal, wood, gas, oil, or the like); the sun; chemical substances that liberate heat or electrical current in reaction.

(2) Motors and the conversion of energy into movement.

(3) The distribution of energy. It is under this last rubric that the
economic historian will most conveniently place electricity as a technological innovation. Electricity is not a source but a form of energy.
Electrical dynamos and similar generators are essentially converters,
turning water, steam, or other primary power into current, which can
then be stored in batteries, used directly for illumination, heat, or
communication, or transformed into motion by means of motors.

Because of the inextricable relationship of these three elements,
however, it is not convenient to dissect the historical development
along these lines. Instead, we shall build the story around those areas of
innovation that had the widest economic significance, keeping the
above schema in mind as a guide to the technological rationale.

A. *Steam and steam-engines*

The closing decades of the nineteenth century saw the gradual exhaustion of the technological possibilities of the reciprocating steam-
engine. Earlier advances had shown the way to greater power and
efficiency—first higher pressures, and then compound expansion—and
by the end of our period, the forty-pound pressures of the 1850's had
increased four- and five-fold, while triple- and quadruple-expansion
engines had been developed to channel these concentrations of
energy.

Compounding, known for decades (see above, pp. 410f.) but neglected, came into its own at mid-century. It was adopted most rapidly
for ships, where power plant tended to be larger than on land and fuel
economy was of crucial importance—every foot taken for coal was
lost to cargo. A kind of improvised compound engine was achieved by
McNaught in 1845 when he joined a high-pressure cylinder to the old
low-pressure one and used both to drive the beam. This was a relatively
inexpensive solution to the problem of inadequate power and dozens of
engines were 'M'Naughted' in subsequent years. It was not until 1854,

however, that the first compound engine built as such was installed on a vessel; within the decade they were the rule on large ocean steamers. The triple-expansion variety was introduced in 1874, but did not spread until the 1880's; it was standard for big plant, both on land and at sea, by the end of the century.[1]

The main contribution of these technical improvements was power: compare, for example, the first steamer of the Peninsular and Oriental, launched in 1829 with paddle wheels and a 60 h.p., low-pressure machine, with the *Campania* or *Lucania* of 1893, each equipped with twin screws and triple-expansion engines totalling 30,000 h.p.; or the 10 and 20 h.p. industrial engines of the opening decades of the century with the 3000 h.p. superheated giants of the close. By contrast, the gains in fuel economy were less impressive. Even if one discounts the extraordinary reported performances of the Cornish beam engines in the 1830's and 1840's, it is clear that the great reduction in energy consumption per unit of output had already occurred by the 1850's, when well-run machines were using less than 4 pounds of coal per horsepower-hour. At the end of the century, best performance was down to around $1\frac{1}{2}$ and the curve was running along the asymptote.

Yet still the demand for power grew, especially for high power in proportion to space. The way to get more power was to increase the running speed of the engine, but here the need to convert reciprocating to rotary motion posed a serious difficulty. The assembly of the piston, piston rod, cross-head, and connecting rod had to be started and stopped with each half-turn of the crank; and the force required to reverse this momentum rose with the speed of the stroke. Eventually the stresses were such that the engine broke down. So that although piston velocities had been pushed as high as 1000 feet a minute by the turn of the century, they were beginning to rub against a ceiling of commercial feasibility: one could build bigger and stronger engines, but at disproportionately higher costs for both materials and space.

At this point the steam turbine made possible a new technological breakthrough, both in power and economy. The principle was simple: instead of turning force into reciprocating motion and converting that into rotary, one went directly into rotary by driving against appropriately shaped vanes or buckets branching off a turning axis. Every child who has ever played with a pinwheel is familiar with the technique.

As noted earlier, the water-driven turbine went back as far as 1827 and had been much improved in subsequent decades, particularly in

---

[1] As is so often the case with mechanical improvements, this success owed much to the employment of superior materials—in this instance, high-quality open-hearth steel plate that could withstand greater boiler pressures.

connection with the utilization of high-fall power. A practical steam turbine, however, in spite of experiments going back to the eighteenth century, was not achieved until 1884, when Charles H. Parsons learned to tame the kinetic energy of the steam jet by joining a series of turbines together and letting the pressure drop off by stages. Here again was the principle of the compound engine, in an idealized form: one put almost all the useful heat to work by letting the steam cool by expansion only, driving as it went. Used in tandem in this way, each wheel had an efficiency of between 70 and 80 per cent, as high as that of water turbines and far higher than that of even the best reciprocating steam-engines.

The Parsons machine was more powerful than any motor built up to that time. It had been devised to run electric generators, but no generator could handle it—the maximum speed of existing dynamos was 1200 r.p.m. Parsons therefore developed his own generator, running at 18,000 r.p.m., and patented it at the same time as the turbine. The two together represent the greatest innovation in the use of steam power since Watt's construction of an engine to produce rotary motion; they also made possible an efficient, large-scale electrical power industry.

In subsequent years, a number of variant types of turbine appeared, of which pure impulse machines like those of C. G. Curtis in the United States and of C. G. P. de Laval of Sweden, proved most useful. The latter, a one-stage affair, proved particularly effective for low- and medium-horsepower installations. The Parsons, however, dominated the high-power field. On the eve of the First World War, a few tandem turbo-alternators were generating over 10,000 kW. (13,400 h.p.), and ships like the *Lusitania* and *Mauretania* (1907) were equipped with twin turbine sets totalling 68,000 h.p. each.[1]

B. *Internal combustion and new fuels*

The principle of an internal combustion motor is that of a channelled explosion: the rapid expansion of gases in a confined space, a cylinder for example, drives an object, generally a piston, in the direction desired. The earliest and most elementary form of internal-combustion engine is a gun. This remark may seem facetious to some, or at best a *curiosum*, and indeed single-stroke mechanisms of this type have up to now been of little or no productive use. In recent years, however, it has proved feasible to shape by explosion pieces of metal too large for presses, thereby eliminating the need for costly and intrinsically unreliable

[1] See, among others, R. H. Parsons, *The Development of the Parsons Steam Turbine* (London, 1936), and J. W. French, *Modern Power Generators* (London, 1908).

welds, and if technological change follows its usual pattern, the principle will find an increasing variety of applications in years to come.

The most important use of the internal-combustion engine, of course,
has been in motors. The possibility of such a device, driven by regularly
repeated explosions, was conceived as far back as the seventeenth
century, when the Abbé Hautefeuille proposed (1678) and Huygens
actually constructed an experimental machine powered by gunpowder.
Not until 1859, however, when Etienne Lenoir brought forth a motor
fired by a mixture of gas and air, was a potentially practical version
achieved.

Lenoir's prototype consumed too much gas to be commercially
competitive. But it furnished the pattern, and from then on a large
number of engineers and tinkerers devoted themselves to the problem.
The crucial conceptual contribution was made in 1862 by Beau de
Rochas, whose four-stroke cycle has since become standard. But no
one put this principle to effective use until N. A. Otto combined it in
1876 with precompression of the charge to produce the first practical
gas engine. The Otto 'silent' engine, as it was called, swept the market:
within a few years, more than 35,000 of them were at work all over the
world.[1]

This form of internal combustion offered the industrialist important
advantages over steam. It was more efficient, especially when working
intermittently or at less than full load,[2] conditions frequently found in
small industry. It was cleaner, and the nature of the fuel was such that
it was easy to automate the feed; the saving on labour costs was often
substantial. Finally, gas was often obtainable as a by-product of other
industrial operations—coking and smelting for example—and, so
obtained, was far cheaper than when deliberately distilled from coal,
or than coal itself.[3]

The major weakness of the gas engine was its immobility. It was
tied to its source of supply, whether feeder line or furnace. This was not
a serious handicap for most industrial purposes, but it did make gas less
suitable as a source of power in transportation.[4] The answer was found

[1] D. C. Field, 'Internal Combustion Engines', in Singer et al., A History of Technology, v, 159.
[2] See the figures in William Robinson, Gas and Petroleum Engines (2nd ed.; 2 vols.;
New York, 1902), I, 4, 136, 198, and passim.
[3] Around 1900, a blast furnace would give off 158,000 cubic feet of gas per ton of
iron smelted. It was a dirty gas, which often had to be cleaned for further use, and a
poor one, yielding from 70 to 120 B.Th.U. per cubic foot (as against perhaps 480
B.Th.U. for illuminating gas).
[4] Although man's ingenuity has surmounted this difficulty in times of crisis, when
no other fuel has been available. Frenchmen of the immediate post-war years will not
forget the automobiles circulating with tanks of gas on their roofs. But it should be

in liquid fuels—primarily petroleum and its distilled derivatives. These burned about as efficiently as gas and produced about twice as much work per weight as coal, while taking half as much space;[1] like gas, moreover, they could be fed cleanly and mechanically, with automatic controls. All of this was especially important at sea, for there economy counted double and everything saved on fuel or crew meant that much more income from cargo and passengers. Not least important was the elimination of the stokers, who generally accounted for more than half the crew. It was getting increasingly hard to find men for this back-breaking work, and those hired were not surprisingly notorious for their intractability and their appetites.

The principal objection to oil was its cost—anywhere from four to twelve times that of coal in Britain around 1900. Yet the price of petroleum products fell rapidly as new sources of supply were opened up and the industry perfected its methods of refining and techniques of distribution. The earliest commercially practical oil engines were probably those used in Russia from the 1870's to burn *ostatki* waste from distillation of Baku crude in the manufacture of kerosene and lamp oil. According to Lunge, 'practically all the steam power in South Russia, both for factories and navigation of the inland seas and rivers', was being raised *c.* 1910 from *ostatki* fuel.[2] In the West, however, in spite of widespread and successful experimentation with oil engines, petroleum did not really catch on until the opening of the Borneo (1898) and Texas fields (Spindletop Well, 1901) made available an oil especially suited by chemical composition to serve as fuel. Shortly thereafter (1902) the Hamburg-Amerika Line adopted petroleum in place of coal on its new liners and was followed by one after another of the great steamship companies. At the same time, the navies of the great European powers began the process of conversion: Italy installed an oil burner as early as 1890; Britain began in 1903 with vessels operating in waters near sources of petroleum—the Far East particularly—but within a decade built a world-wide storage network that permitted the use of liquid fuel throughout the fleet.

Acceptance for land use was slower, although some British railways and a few industrial firms on the Thames tried petroleum and abandoned it only when rising prices made it too expensive relative to coal.

noted that even then, such vehicles were most common in the south, near the centre of natural gas production in the Toulouse area, and disappeared rapidly as petrol once again came on the market. I am told that the English resorted to the same expedient.
[1] In most cases, it was possible to free the space given over to coal bunkers entirely and store the oil in the double-bottom spaces once used only for water ballast.
[2] J. Fortescue-Flannery, in article, 'Fuel', *Encyclopaedia Britannica*, 11th ed. A masterly survey.

The one application in which it gained ground steadily was in the form of what contemporaries called petroleum spirit, our present-day petrol or gasoline. Nevertheless, the automobile was still a luxury in pre-World War I Europe, roads were atrocious, breakdowns frequent, and no one could possibly anticipate the enormous expansion in the demand for liquid fuel for road vehicles that has taken place since. The oil companies themselves moved their products by horse and wagon.

C. *Electricity*

From the standpoint of the economic historian, the significance of electricity lay in its unique combination of two characteristics: transmissibility and flexibility. By the first we mean its ability to move energy through space without serious loss. And by the second we mean its easy and efficient conversion into other forms of energy—heat, light, or motion. An electric current can be used to produce any or all of these, separately or together, and the user can switch from one to the other at will. He can also draw precisely the amount of power needed, large or small, and can change it when necessary without time-consuming adjustments or sacrifice of efficiency. And he pays for what he uses.

From these characteristics two major consequences emerge. On the one hand, electricity freed the machine and the tool from the bondage of place; on the other, it made power ubiquitous and placed it within reach of everyone. Both of these—and they are inextricably linked together—merit detailed consideration.

Up to the latter half of the nineteenth century, the machine had always been closely bound to its prime mover. It could not be placed too far off because of the inefficiency of belts and shafting as a method of distributing energy: each gear, joint, or wheel was a source of power loss, and the torsion on long shafts was such that rigidity and smooth rotation could be maintained only by the use of disproportionately heavy materials. Similarly, the machine was rooted to its emplacement or restricted to positions along the path of the shafts, for only there could it draw on the source of energy.

These were not serious disadvantages in such industries as the textile manufacture, where neatly aligned banks of equipment worked side by side at the same pace, although even there shafting longer than 200 feet posed costly problems.[1] But they gave rise to all manner of difficulties in

---

[1] Yet in Coventry, entrepreneurs erected in the 1850's a number of so-called 'cottage-factories', rows or enclosures of weavers' houses, which drew power from a central engine over a distance of several hundred feet. John Prest, *The Industrial Revolution in Coventry* (Oxford, 1960), ch. VI.

trades like iron or engineering, where the work was dispersed, the pace uneven, and much of the equipment was always being moved about. The answer in such cases was a multiplicity of steam-engines, large and small. It was an expensive solution, not only in capital outlays but in operating costs. As we have already seen, these smaller engines, often working at less than full load, were extremely inefficient; by the same token, they had a voracious appetite for labour. Not least important, they were a nuisance, with their piles of coal scattered about, their noise and dirt, their exhaust gases, their need for separate maintenance.

Energy can be transmitted economically over longer distances than a few hundred feet only by fluids or gases, which can be delivered under pressure in rigid pipe or flexible hose, or by electric current. Each technique has its own merits and area of application; all are highly efficient. In the last half of the nineteenth century, all three of these methods began to be used, in the order given.

Fluid systems generally use water—there is no liquid cheaper—or oil, which lubricates as it works; gas systems almost always use air. They are especially suitable to short and medium-range transmission, at distances up to a few miles between prime mover and machine. Their forte is work where incompressibility is an advantage and the mechanical action is direct—in lifts, pumps, presses, punches, and brakes. Their effect in these operations has a certain inexorable quality, and their work is characterized more by force than by motion—as anyone who has ridden in a hydraulic lift will testify.

In principle, water and air pressure may also be used with turbines to produce rotary motion (cf. the windmill). Here, however, they are not so flexible as electricity nor so suitable to heavy work. But compressed air, especially, is excellent with light motors—it has found a new application today in dentistry, where it has proved the most convenient drive for high-speed drills—and is almost indispensable in fields like mining where the presence of inflammable dusts precludes the use of sparking motors.

Historically, pneumatic pressure systems have almost always been the work of the individual enterprise, whereas hydraulic pressure has usually been distributed from central power stations. The development of these installations dates from the invention in 1850 of the accumulator, which made it possible to store pressure and to economize on peak capacity. At first water was obtained simply by tapping public mains. But by the last two decades of the century, the technique had reached the point where private capital was ready to invest in independent pumping works and distribution systems. British enterprise was particularly active in this regard, and as late as the middle 1890's, there were engineers who were convinced that hydraulic pressure was superior to any other means of power transmission. In 1894 Antwerp actually tried to use it to distribute energy to electrical power stations scattered through the city, rather than send current directly from the central power plant. The operation was not profitable.

The fact was that hydraulic and pneumatic power owed much of their success to their priority. They came along first. But once electricity came on the scene, they were bound to lose ground. They were strongest where one or both of two conditions prevailed:

(a) Where the primary power source had been constructed for other purposes and existed independently, as in the case of public water works or of air pumps used in underwater excavation. In such circumstances, the water or air used for motor purposes is a by-product whose marginal cost is very low. The municipal hydraulic systems of Geneva and Lyons, both cities abundantly endowed with flowing water, fall in this category.

(b) Where the industrial operations of the area lent themselves to these techniques—in ports, for example, like Liverpool and London, where there is a great deal of lifting work to be done; or in a cotton town like Manchester, with its hundreds of packing presses.

Otherwise—beginning in the very last years of the nineteenth century—electricity had the field of power transmission to itself. The history of this development is worth following—as an example of scientific and technical co-operation, of multiple invention, of progress by an infinitude of small improvements, of creative entrepreneurship, of derived demand and unanticipated consequences. The symbiotic growth of electric power and electric motors is like that of textile machines and the steam-engine in the eighteenth century: a new technique and system of production were now available, with boundless possibilities. This was once again Genesis.

At the start of the nineteenth century, electricity was a scientific curiosity, a plaything of the laboratory. As the result of widespread investigation and experiment, however, it became a commercially useful form of energy, first in communication,[1] shortly thereafter in light-chemical and metallurgical processes,[2] and finally in illumination.

---

[1] A brief list of the key inventions and landmarks will be helpful: Electromagnetic telegraph, in Britain, by Cooke and Wheatstone, c. 1837; in the United States, by Morse and Vail, c. 1838; undersea cable, across the Channel, 1851; across the Atlantic, by C. W. Field, 1866. Telephone, by A. G. Bell, 1876. Wireless, by Marconi, 1895.

[2] Light industrial electrochemistry went back to the 1830's. It found its principal applications in galvanoplasty, that is, the manufacture of exact moulds of sculptures, engravings, and the like for purposes of reproduction (invention in 1838 by Spencer in England and Jacobi in Russia), and electroplating (John Wright of Birmingham, in 1840, followed by a host of others). These processes, originally effected with batteries,

Of these, the last had the greatest economic impact because of its implications for power technology in general.

The invention of the incandescent filament lamp, especially Edison's high-resistance variety, was crucial here. For the first time electricity offered something useful not only in industry, or in commerce, or on the theatre stage, but in every home. None of the earlier applications had been particularly voracious of energy; and each enterprise, given the scale of its requirements, could profitably generate its own. Now, however, a demand existed—incalculably large *in toto* yet atomized into a multitude of individual needs—that could be satisfied only by a centralized system of power generation and distribution. This too was Edison's conception, and it made all the difference between electric lighting for a wealthy few and for everyone.

The development of central power was the work of the last two decades of the nineteenth century. It was a tremendous technological achievement, made possible only by almost a century of large and small theoretical advances and practical innovations. The landmarks stand out: Volta's chemical battery in 1800; Oersted's discovery of electromagnetism in 1820; the statement of the law of the electric circuit by Ohm in 1827; the experiments of Arago, Faraday, and others, climaxed by Faraday's discovery of electromagnetic induction in 1831; the invention of the self-excited electromagnetic generator (Wilde, Varley, E. W. von Siemens, Wheatstone, *et al.*) in 1866–7; Z. T. Gramme's ring dynamo, the first commercially practical generator of direct current, in 1870; the development of alternators and transformers for the production and conversion of high-voltage alternating current in the 1880's. Less well known but equally vital, however, were advances in the manufacture of cable and insulation, in the details of generator construction, in the operation of prime movers, in the linkage of the component units of the system, in the choice of current characteristics, in the registration of flow and consumption.[1]

The first public power station in Europe was established at Godalming in England by Siemens Brothers in 1881.[2] Within the next decade and a

were greatly stimulated by the availability of cheap, abundant current from central stations. A new range of industrial applications opened up, especially in plating with baser metals (galvanized iron).

[1] The above is based largely on C. M. Jarvis, 'The Generation of Electricity' and 'The Distribution and Utilization of Electricity', in Singer *et al.*, eds., *History of Technology*, v, 177–234. Other treatments sometimes give other dates and even other names. The history of technology has yet to be endowed with a commonly accepted chronology.

[2] G. F. Westcott and H. P. Spratt, *Synopsis of Historical Events: Mechanical and Electrical Engineering* (London: H.M.S.O., 1960), p. 18, give 1882 as the date of the first central station in England (Holborn) and note that it was designed by Edison.

half others sprang up throughout western Europe, a patchwork multitude of market-situated local units, each with its own equipment and
method of transmission. In Britain, particularly, where the Electric
Lighting Act rested on the proposition that each parish should have its
own power station, the resultant multiplicity of techniques was to be a
costly legacy.

Very early, however, entrepreneurs realized that important savings
might be achieved if the generating plant were located at or close to the
source of energy and the current were sent out from there. To be sure,
the longer the lines the greater the loss of power, but this could be
minimized by the use of high-voltage alternating current.[1] The first
large station of this kind was that which Ferranti built in 1887–9 at
Deptford on the Thames to supply London at 10,000 volts. In the
meantime, experiments on the Continent, where there was a great
incentive to use hydro-electric power, were demonstrating the possibility of transmitting energy over even longer distances. In 1885
power was sent from a 150 kW. generator in Creil to Paris, a distance
of 56 km., on an experimental basis; and in 1891 the decisive breakthrough came when Oscar Müller and the Swiss firm of Brown,
Boveri and Co. delivered 225 kW. over 179 km. at 30,000 volts, from
Lauffen on the upper Neckar to Frankfurt-am-Main.[2] Twenty years
later current was being transmitted over lines operating at as high as
100,000 volts, and the principle of regional distribution grids was
established. It was now possible to develop large, integrated power
districts in which agricultural and industrial enterprises of all kinds, to
say nothing of homes and shops, could draw on an efficient energy
source in common. To the substantial economies of scale in the generation of power were thus added the advantages of diversification: the
more heterogeneous the demand, the more favourable the load and
capacity factors.

[1] Both alternating and direct current have their advantages. The latter is cheaper to
generate, among other things, because it is possible to store the surplus current of
periods of low demand in batteries and release it as needed; one thus obtains more
favourable load and capacity factors. On the other hand, alternating current is easier
to transmit over long distances. The reason is that such transmission calls for high
voltages and low amperage (energy losses increase proportionately with amperage),
and alternating current lends itself far more readily than direct to substitutions of
voltage for amperage and vice-versa, which it effects by means of transformers. The
two systems competed fiercely in Britain for many years. In the long run, however,
victory lay with centralized generators and long-distance transmission.
[2] G. Olphe-Galliard, *La force motrice au point de vue économique et sociale* (Paris,
1915), p. 104; A. Menge, 'Distribution of Electrical Energy in Germany', in *Trans.
First World Power Conference, London 1924* (London, n.d.), III, 528. Menge gives the
figure of 135 kW.

The Germans took the lead here. The most rapid development occurred in Westphalia, where the waste heat of the blast furnaces and the gases of the coking ovens constituted an exceptionally cheap source of energy; even so, demand outstripped supply, and huge coal-fired steam generating plants were built to meet the needs of industrial and domestic consumers. The largest producer of current was the Rheinisch-West-fälische Elektrizitäts-A.-G., founded in 1900, whose network of lines ran the length and breadth of the Rhine valley, from Koblenz to the Dutch border; from 2·7 million kWh. in 1900/1, its output leaped to 121·7 million in 1910/11 and 388 million in 1915/16. Other companies were smaller only by comparison; and to these should be added the several coal and iron firms that doubled as independent suppliers of power.[1] In the rest of Europe, however, the realization of these possibilities did not come until a decade or more later.

Yet electrical current was more than a convenient means of distributing established fuels. Thanks to long-distance transmission, falling water once again came into its own as a source of energy, which could now be delivered to the factory as coal to the steam-engine. The addition to the world's resources was enormous: in 1913 world output of water power, most of it used to generate electricity, was 510 million kWh., the equivalent of 800,000 long tons of coal (at a consumption of 3·5 lb. of coal per kWh.); sixteen years later, in spite of a world war, hydro-electric output was over 120 billion kWh., equivalent to slightly over 100 million tons of coal (at a more efficient rate of 1·0 lb. per kWh.) and representing 40 per cent of the total world production of electricity.[2] By that time electric generating plants were taking up about two-thirds of the prime mover capacity of the principal industrial countries.

While the precipitating cause of large-scale generation of power was electrical illumination, this was soon surpassed as a demand factor by other and heavier applications of the new form of energy. The first of these was traction. It was in 1879, at about the same time as the incandescent filament lamp came on the market, that Siemens demonstrated the first electric railway at the Berlin Industrial Exposition. Within the next generation electrical drive had become standard in tramways and subways and had been successfully introduced into full-gauge rail systems. The second was heavy electro-chemistry: both the Hall–Héroult method of aluminium manufacture (1886) and Castner's

[1] Hans Spethmann, *Die Grosswirtschaft an der Ruhr* (Breslau, 1925), pp. 86–91.
[2] These are the figures given by Hugh Quigley in his article on 'Power, Industrial' in the *Encyclopædia of the Social Sciences*. Henri Cavaillès, *La houille blanche* (Paris, 1922), p. 199, gives hydro-electric output at that time as about 104 milliard h.p. per year, which he equates with the energy yielded by 104 million metric tons of coal.

sodium, sodium cyanide, and caustic soda processes (1886 and 1894) required enormous quantities of energy.[1] The third was electro-metallurgy: the key innovation was Sir William Siemens's electric furnace (1878). This technique, whose great virtues are its cleanness and high temperatures, received considerable impetus from the development of special alloy steels around the turn of the century.

The fourth and most important application was fixed motor power. Ironically enough, producers and engineers were long in appreciating its potential. As late as 1894, some six years after Tesla's invention of the a.c. induction motor and polyphase a.c. systems had 'made alternating current as suitable for power purposes as it had been for lighting',[2] the President of the British Institute of Mechanical Engineers was saying that the chief purpose of public generating plants 'was, and probably always would be, to supply energy for lighting purposes'.[3]

He could not have been more mistaken. By its flexibility and convenience, electricity transformed the factory. Now the motor could be fitted to the tool and the tool moved to the job—an especial advantage in engineering and other industries engaged in the manufacture of heavy objects. And now one could clear away the jungle of shafts and belts that had been the most prominent feature of machine rooms since the water mills of the 1770's—a threat to safety, an interference to movement, a source of breakdowns, and a devourer of energy.

But electricity did more than change the techniques and decor of the factory: by making cheap power available outside as well as inside the plant, it reversed the historical forces of a century, gave new life and scope to dispersed home and shop industry, and modified the mode of production. In particular, it made possible a new division of labour between large and small units. Where before the two had almost inevitably been opposed within a given industry—the one using new techniques and thriving, the other clinging to old ways and declining—now a complementarity was possible. Both types could use modern equipment, with the factory concentrating on larger objects or standardized items that lent themselves to capital-intensive techniques, while the shop specialized in labour-intensive processes using light power tools. And often the complementarity became symbiosis: the modern structure of sub-contracting in the manufacture of consumers' durables rests on the technological effectiveness of the small machine shop.

[1] Around 1910 the consumption was 9 kWh. per pound of metal produced.
[2] C. H. Merz, 'The Transmission and Distribution of Electrical Energy', in *Trans. First World Power Conference*, III, 809.
[3] Clapham, *Economic History of Modern Britain*, III, 193, citing A. W. Kennedy, *Trans. Institute of Mechanical Engineers* (1894), 181.

New uses and cheaper power promoted capital formation. The increased efficiency of prime movers was more than compensated by the larger demand for energy and the multiplication of motors and machines, not only in industry but in agriculture and eventually the household. To be sure, the great expansion promised by electrification of the home still lay far ahead: in Europe, the refrigerator, electric heater, washing machine, and similar big power users (by contrast with electric lighting, the radio, and the gramophone, which consume little current) do not come in on a large scale until after the Second World War. As late as the 1950's the overwhelming majority of houses and flats made do with entry circuits of ten amperes or less; the hungriest piece of equipment was the electric iron. Yet this secular proliferation and diffusion of electrical equipment, which is far from exhausted, goes back to these decades before the First World War. There was now no activity that could not be mechanized and powered. This was the consummation of the Industrial Revolution.

Some of this investment represented simply a shift from working to fixed capital, as resources once set aside for fuel supplies and furnace labour were freed for other uses. But by far the greater part of it was new capital, created in response to the opportunities offered by new production functions. In this respect, one should not forget the electrical industry itself—tens of thousands of enterprises generating and distributing current and building and servicing electrical equipment.

Here, as in chemicals, the most striking achievements occurred in Germany. The parallels are numerous: the belated start, the rapid rise based on technological excellence and rational organization, the concentration of production, the strong position on the world market. Up to the very eve of the First World War, Britain was possibly still ahead in consumption of electrical power, though the statistics of the two countries were established on so different a basis that comparison is hazardous.[1] Within less than a decade, however, Germany had over-

[1] The only overall figures we have are those collected by each country in the industrial censuses of 1907. The British returns give capacity of engines and motors; the German, the power produced in regular operation (the instruction explicitly states that this does not mean capacity [*Höchstleistungsfähigkeit*]). The British statistics show total prime mover capacity (including engines producing energy for electric generators) as 10,749,000 h.p., generator capacity as 2,341,900 h.p. German figures of power production are respectively 8,008,405 and 1,830,000 h.p. These last do not include industrial enterprises in the public sector, far more important in Germany than in Britain; the power output here was 733,520 h.p. overall, 151,800 h.p. by electric generators.

On Britain, *Parl. Papers*, 1912–13, CIX (Cd. 6230): Final Report, First Census of Production; on Germany, *Statistik des deutschen Reichs*, N.F. vol. CCXIV, tables 8, 11, 15.

Furthermore, we have reason to believe that the difference in the basis of inquiry biased the results in favour of British power production even more than appears at

taken her rival and left her far behind—in spite of heavy losses of territory due to the war. Thus by 1925, regular output of German prime movers totalled 21,186,825 h.p., as against 16,808,700 in Britain in 1924; the corresponding figures for electric generators were 13,288,800 and 8,510,000 h.p. respectively. What is more, as the higher German capacity factor implies, her stations and distribution nets were on the average larger: her current characteristics more uniform; and her performance more efficient.

Even more impressive was the progress of the German electrical manufacturing industry. It was the largest in Europe—more than twice as big as that of Britain—and second only by a small margin to that of the United States.[1] The firms, as in the chemical industry, were large, well-financed enterprises, strongly supported by the capital market and the great investment banks. The largest, Emil Rathenau's Allgemeine Electricitäts-Gesellschaft (or AEG) and the Siemens-Schuckert combine, were holding companies of extraordinary versatility and complexity. Their products were ingenious, solidly made, competitively priced; financial support made possible generous credit to customers. As a result, German exports on the eve of the war were the largest in the world, more than two-and-one-half times the United Kingdom total, almost three times the American.[2]

Yet one should not overemphasize the importance of capital. As in the chemical manufacture, scientific knowledge, technical skill, and high standards of performance weighed more heavily in the market place than price. Here too a small country like Switzerland was extraordinarily successful, and names like Brown-Boveri, Oerlikon, Eggi-Wyss, and C.I.E.M. (Cie de l'Industrie Electrique et Mécanique)

first examination. We do not have the relevant figures for 1907, but post-war data (1929 for Germany, 1928 for Britain) show that German electrical generator plant had a capacity factor 67 % higher than the British, that is, each unit of German generator capacity produced two-thirds more current in the course of the year. Wilhem Leisse, 'Die Energiewirtschaft der Welt in Zahlen', in Vierteljahrshefte zur Konjunkturforschung, Sonderheft 19 (Berlin, 1930), p. 34. This is the kind of ratio that reflects the pattern of power distribution and the structure of the electrical industry and presumably did not change much in the course of these two decades.

[1] According to the estimates of the British Electrical and Allied Manufacturers' Association, German output of electrical products and equipment in 1913 was worth about £65 million, that of Britain £30 million, that of France £7,700,000. The United States Census of Manufactures gave American output in 1914 as $359 million. Great Britain, Comm. on Industry and Trade, Survey of Metal Industries...Being Part IV of a Survey of Industries (London, 1928), pp. 282, 331. Note that British industry had made substantial gains in the decade before the war: the Census of Production of 1907 returned only £14·4 million for electrical manufactures.

[2] Ibid. pp. 338–9. Because there are statistical difficulties in making this comparison, approximate ratios are preferable to meretricious precision.

acquired international renown. And for the same reasons, even an agrarian economy like that of Hungary could produce an enterprise like Ganz of Budapest.

D. *Some general considerations*

There are two points that deserve emphasis: the underlying stability of the resource base of industrial power; and the continued growth of power consumption. The spectacular contribution of new methods of power production and distribution tends to obscure the continuities of this aspect of industrial history. This is an optical illusion: the eye is always caught by movement. For all the development of new sources of energy—hydro-electricity, oil, gasoline, gas—coal retained its commanding position. It lost ground, to be sure: in 1913 it accounted for about 88½ per cent of the world's energy output; in 1925 75½ per cent; in 1931 only 66½. Yet these figures tend to exaggerate the decline, for a high proportion of the power derived from other sources has always gone to transportation and domestic consumption; by contrast coal holds a much stronger place in industry, either directly by means of steam engines or indirectly through the intermediary of the electric generator.

Table 53. *Proportion of Primary Power Derived from Steam-engines*

	1911 (%)	1925 (%)
Great Britain	92	90
Germany	82	82
France	73	71
Italy	29	22
Switzerland	20	6

SOURCE. G. F. Hiltpold, *Erzeugung und Verwendung motorischer Kraft* (Zürich, 1934), p. 12.

The proportion of energy derived from coal varied in each country with resources. Mineral-rich Britain and Germany relied heavily on the steam-engine as prime mover; Belgium, a flat land with no high-fall streams, even more so. By comparison, France, with a perennial coal deficit but abundant hydro-electric endowment (Alps, Pyrenees, Vosges, Massif Central), made less use of heat engines, while Italy and Switzerland, with almost no coal but lots of mountains, came to depend almost entirely on water power.

To this day coal remains the primary source of industrial energy and thus the basic resource of an industrial economy. How long this will continue is impossible to predict, given the rapidity of technological change, the progressive exhaustion of the more accessible deposits, the competition of cheap petroleum, and the potential competition of nuclear power.[1] Even in ferrous metallurgy, where coal would seem most firmly ensconced because of its role as both source of energy and reducing agent, recent innovations in smelting practice have made it possible to work with natural gas, and it would be rash to predict the course of technique. Even so, coal has the advantage of cheapness and elasticity of supply, for important deposits are yet to be exploited and the ratio of output to reserves remains comparatively low. Coal—one is tempted to say King Coal—is not likely to be dethroned in our lifetime.

Whatever the source, however, the use of power in and out of industry grew rapidly. Even allowing for the egregious shortcomings of our statistical data, particularly resistant to international comparisons, the trend over time is too strong to be missed. World production of commercial sources of energy is estimated to have increased from the equivalent of 1674 million megawatt hours in 1870 to 10,840 million in 1913.[2] As for national developments, we are best informed about the continental countries:

Table 54. *Steam Power in Industry (capacity in thousand horse-power)*

	Germany	France	Belgium
c. 1860[a]	100	169	102
1875	949	401	212
1895	3357	1163	—
1907[b]	6500[c]	2474[d]	1038

[a] 1861 for the *Zollverein*; 1859 for France; 1861 for Belgium.
[b] 1909 for Belgium.
[c] 8,008,000 h.p. from all energy sources.
[d] 3,191,500 h.p. from all energy sources.

SOURCES. Germany: G. Viebahn, *Statistik des zollvereinten und nördlichen Deutschlands*, pp. 1036–7 (his figure does not seem to accord with that of Engel, 'Das Zeitalter des Dampfes', *Z. Königlichen Preussischen Statistischen Landesamtes*, xx [1880], 122, who shows 142,658 h.p. for *Prussian* agriculture and industry in 1861); F. Zweig, *Economics and Technology* (London, 1936), pp. 119–20; G. F. Hiltpold, *Erzeugung und Verwendung*, p. 68.
France. *Annu. statistique*, LVII (1956), *rés. rétro.* pp. 116*–117*.
Belgium: *Exposé de la situation du royaume, 1861–1875*, II, 834–5; *Annu. statistique* (1911–12), p. 349.

[1] Cf. A. P. Usher, 'The Resource Requirements of an Industrial Economy', *J. Econ. Hist.* VII, supplement (1947), 40, 46.
[2] United Nations, Dept. of Economic and Social Affairs, *Acts of the International Conference on the Utilization of Atomic Energy for Peaceful Ends*, vol. I, table xxiii B, p. 28.

We cannot offer comparable statistics for Britain, but here the figures on coal consumption tell the story:

Table 55. *Coal Consumption in Selected Countries (in thousands of tons)*[a]

	United Kingdom		Germany		France		Belgium	
	Amount	Index	Amount	Index	Amount	Index	Amount	Index
1861	77,657	100	13,957[b]	100	15,403	100	6,140	100
1913	189,074	244	187,000[c]	1340	64,834[d]	421	26,032	424

[a] Long tons for the U.K.; metric tons for the rest.
[b] Includes 4522 tons of lignite, deflated at a 9:2 ratio.
[c] Includes 94,160 tons of lignite, deflated at a 9:2 ratio.
[d] To which one might add approximately 10,000 tons consumed in Alsace-Lorraine.

SOURCES. United Kingdom: Finlay A. Gibson, *The Coal Mining Industry of the United Kingdom* (Cardiff, 1922), p. 77, and William Page, *Commerce and Industry* (London, 1919), II, 154, 180.
France: *Annu. statistique* LVII (1946), 230*–31*.
Germany: Bienengräber, *Statistik des Verkehrs und Verbrauchs im Zollverein*, pp. 259, 263, for the year 1861; *Statistisches Jahrbuch für das Deutsche Reich*, XLI (1920), 149, for the year 1913.

It should be noted, moreover, that these figures on coal under-estimate if anything the rapidity of the German industrial advance. In Britain, transportation, in particular shipping, accounted for a large and growing share of energy consumption in the last decades of the nineteenth century. Estimates by Mulhall give power of fixed engines as 20 per cent or less of total steam capacity; other guesses range as high as 33 per cent, but this is still a small fraction.[1] In Prussia, by contrast, shipping engines could provide less than a tenth of total steam power, while fixed plant accounted for about 85 per cent.

We may conclude this discussion with a few thoughts on the wider significance of these somewhat tedious statistics of power production and fuel consumption. They are of interest for their own sake, but even more as indicators of industrial growth and capital formation. The coefficient of correlation between energy consumption and such calculations as have been made of industrial capital stock is astonishingly high—for the United States from 1880 to 1948, 0·9995; for the United Kingdom from 1865 to 1914, 0·96 or 0·99, depending on the series employed.[2] Indeed, one is almost tempted to ask whether direct, composite measurement of capital formation is worth the effort.

At first thought, this parallelism may be surprising: technological

[1] Woytinsky, *Welt in Zahlen*, IV, 66–7.
[2] A. G. Frank, 'Industrial Capital Stocks and Energy Consumption', *Econ. J.* LXIX (1959), 170–4.

improvements have tended to increase the ratio of energy output to input and therefore to diminish capital requirements at a given level of power consumption. But this has been counteracted, as we have seen in the discussion of electricity, by the spread of motors and machinery into activities previously left to hand or animal labour; in effect, every improvement in the efficiency of the production or utilization of energy has encouraged the substitution of fixed for working capital. In a sense, the story of power is the story of industrialization.

(3) MECHANIZATION AND DIVISION OF LABOUR

Any effort to follow the diffusion of mechanization in all its ramifications is bound to welter in a confusion of details. The basic principles, however, established by 1850, were few. As noted above, the machine that will punch metal can be made to punch leather; the die press that will stamp coins can be made to shape pipe or stamp out body parts for automobiles; the knife that will cut cloth can be made to slice metal. The period from 1850 on was rich in new adaptations of this type. One example, chosen for its social as well as its economic significance, will suffice: the sewing machine.

Credit for invention of the sewing machine is not easy to assign: as is frequently the case, there is the distinction to be made between nominal and effective discovery and between inventor and innovator; and in this instance matters are complicated by parallel and not-so-parallel invention. The earliest workable machine was that of Barthélemy Thimonnier of St Etienne, patented in 1830. It was made of wood, was slow and clumsy, but it did take hold in the manufacture of army uniforms, where quality was a secondary consideration and standardization was feasible. In 1841 there were perhaps eighty-one of the machines in operation in a large shop in Paris; they were wrecked by a mob in an almost forgotten outbreak of Luddism. Thimonnier improved his model in subsequent years, but the disturbances arising from the revolution of 1848 and the development of superior techniques by others disappointed his efforts. He died poor and unknown in 1857.

The main line of sewing-machine development runs through Elias Howe (the eye-pointed needle, underthread shuttle, and characteristic lock-stitch in 1846), Isaac Singer (the treadle and the straight needle, in 1851 and later years), and Allen B. Wilson (rotary hook and bobbin, making possible continuous rather than reciprocating motion, and four-motion feed, in 1850 and 1854). Singer was the Arkwright of the industry. He had a vision of the role the new device could have, not only in industry but in the home; it was the first domestic appliance. He advertised it widely, provided courses in its use, made it available on the instalment plan, pioneered the sale-and-service contract. In the face of fierce opposition from tailors and professional seamstresses, the machine caught on rapidly. It was bound to—not only because industry found it so economical but because women found in it liberation from an old bondage. The sewing machine did not mark the end of exploitation and sweating in the clothing manufacture; on the contrary. But it did make needle and thread obsolete and so doing put an end to the 'weary hand' and 'stitch-stitch-stitch' of the dolorous 'song of the shirt'.

The sewing machine gave birth to a family of related devices: machines for band stitching, button-holing, blind-stitching, embroidery, lace-making. Even more important were its applications in other industries: in glove-making, harness work and saddlery, book-binding, above all, in boot- and shoe-making (Blake-McKay machine for sewing uppers to soles, 1860; Goodyear welt machine, 1871 and 1875). Its versatility made it the most radical innovation in the production of consumers' goods since the power loom.

The result was a further extension of the factory system and a sub-stitution of the large shop (often sweatshop) or putting-out arrangements for the seamstress's table and artisan's bench. Machine clothing manu-facture, especially, required relatively little initial capital (a new sewing machine in 1870 cost from £4. 10s. to perhaps £14);[1] the supply of labour, nourished by immigration from central and eastern Europe, was abundant; and production could be dispersed, subcontracted, or given out to home workers. As a result entry was easy; but so was exit.

In the long run demand was elastic and steadily increasing. The early producers of ready-made clothing had confined themselves to sailors' uniforms, army orders, and the plantation market overseas. People of means had their clothes made to taste; the poor made their own. By the end of the century, however, the acceptance of store clothing was widespread, beginning with those articles—coats, shirts, undergarments—where fit was a less important consideration. The 'Sunday suit' was a major factor in this change of attitude: the work-man who had been content to spend his life in corduroy or denim trousers and cotton or knitted pullover now had some dress clothes. And for the more fastidious clientele, there was the special order department, turning out factory garments to personal measure. Unfortunately, we do not have statistics on the output of the clothing industry over time; but such partial and qualitative evidence as we do have testifies to the rapidity of its expansion and to the importance of this new class of commodities for the field of retail trade.

[1] Joan Thomas, A History of the Leeds Clothing Industry [Yorkshire Bulletin of Economic and Social Research, Occasional Paper no. 1] (Leeds, 1955), p. 37.

Shoe manufacture was another story: the equipment was too expensive and bulky for home use and was ill-suited by its functional specialization to dispersed production. Indeed, all the efforts of the industry were directed toward fragmenting the work into steps simple enough to be carried out by single-purpose machines. In 1858 it took one cobbler 1025 hours to produce 100 pairs of women's shoes, at a labour cost of $256.33; in 1895 it took 85 men 80 man-hours to accomplish the same work, at a total labour cost of $18.59.[1]

This was in the United States, where the price of labour was relatively high and consumers were more favourable to mass-produced, standardized clothing. In Europe the advance of the machine shoe industry was slower, that of factory manufacture slower yet. Nevertheless, the example of American development and, in Britain, the pressure of cheap imports from across the Atlantic encouraged the adoption of the new techniques. Between 1890 and 1903 the value of imports of leather footware into the United Kingdom rose by £607,000, while exports fell by £53,000. Even so hard-shelled an opponent of mechanization and a defender of the pristine virtues of the craftsman as the Union of Boot and Shoe Operatives was shaken, and reluctantly reconciled itself to the necessity for change.[2]

The entrepreneurial reaction was appropriately vigorous: 'There can be no doubt that the boot and shoe industry is now in process of a more sudden and complete revolution from a hand to a machine industry than any other great English industry', noted an observer in 1904.[3] The statement was true only of the larger plants, which made up *most* of the technical lag by about 1907. The industrial census of that year showed 75 per cent of the workers in the British shoe trade (105,200 out of 140,500) in 'factories' using some amount of power; the rest were outworkers (13,700) or handicraftsmen in shops (21,600). These factories were for the most part small enterprises using light equipment; total power capacity was only 20,171 h.p., or about $\frac{1}{5}$ h.p. per man.[4] They accounted, however, for 88 per cent of the industry's output.

[1] U.S. Bureau of Labor, *Thirteenth Annual Report of the Commissioner of Labor, 1898: Hand and Machine Labor* [55th Congress, 3rd Session, House Doc. 301] (2 vols.; Washington, D.C.: G.P.O., 1899), I, 28–9.

[2] See the discussion in Alan Fox, *A History of the National Union of Boot and Shoe Operatives 1874–1957* (Oxford, 1958), ch. XXIV.

[3] U.S. Dept. of Labor, *Eleventh Special Report of the Commissioner of Labor: Regulation and Restriction of Output* (Washington, D.C., 1904), p. 841, cited by S. B. Saul, 'The American Impact on British Industry, 1895–1914', *Business History*, III (1960), 20. An important article.

[4] *Parliamentary Papers*, 1912–13, CIX, 420–1 (Final Report, First Census of Production).

German figures are not strictly comparable. But allowing for differences in classification, they show an industry somewhat smaller than the British and probably more mechanized. One thing is clear: the German shoe manufacture relied far more on electrical power.

For all the sewing machine's impressive proliferation in variant forms, its technological significance resides perhaps even more in the conditions of its own production. The introduction of such a complex device into the home offered a great opportunity to manufacturers of machinery, but posed new problems of technique. For one thing, the machine had to work smoothly and quietly: no housewife was going to take the din of the factory into her bedroom or sitting-room if she could help it. For another, repairs had to be simple and cheap: a mill could afford to have a maintenance staff on hand at all times; the individual home, or even small shop, could not. Both these conditions called for precision manufacture with interchangeable parts—a subject we shall come to in a moment.

With mechanization went the pursuit of speed, both in the literal sense of faster movement of machines and in the related sense of greater output per unit of time.

No field saw greater gains in this respect than metalworking and engineering. Not only were machine tools more powerful and convenient, but the development of hard steel alloys put in the hands of the workman cutting edges worthy of the mechanical force at his disposal. The earliest of these special materials was simple high-carbon steel; it could work economically at cutting speeds of about 40 feet a minute. In the 1850's and 1860's, Köller in Austria and Mushet in England developed tungsten, vanadium, and manganese alloys that were self-cooling, outlasted regular tool steel five or six times, and could cut 60 feet a minute. This, moreover, was under unfavourable circumstances: machines of the day were not strong enough to support the speed that the steel made possible. The discrepancy was quickly corrected, however, and by the 1890's tools had been developed that could cut 150 feet of mild steel a minute without lubricants. Finally, in 1900 F. W. Taylor and Maunsel White demonstrated their high-speed chromium-tungsten steel at the Paris Exposition. The metal ran red-hot, yet did not soften or dull. Again it was the machine that lagged, and heavier models had to be built, four to six times as powerful as those using carbon steel, before the possibilities of the new metal could be exploited. By the First World War, speeds of 300 and 400 feet per minute had been achieved on light cuts, and it was common for a single tool to remove twenty pounds of waste a minute. Little remembered now, this innovation was one of the wonders of its day. One senses, reading contemporary accounts, the near incredulity of observers at seeing steel pierced and cut like butter.

Yet metalwork offers but one example, admittedly impressive and important, of a general phenomenon. The improvement of textile machinery in this period consisted primarily in more revolutions or picks per minute. Thus from the 1830's to the 1890's, the time needed fort he mule carriage to run out and back was cut by one- to two-thirds, depending on the fineness of the yarn; the speed of spindle rotation more than doubled from the throstle to the ring frame; similarly, the pace of the simple power loom. In heavy industry, the invention of the steam hammer meant more rapid as well as heavier blows; the progressive substitution of rolling for hammering speeded the output of wrought iron and steel considerably; and increased automaticity of the rolling equipment led, as we have seen, to continuous mills that moved the hot metal along at the speed of a railway train.

And so on. It would take too long to review these numerous and varied gains in detail; what is important is to considei those underlying improvements that made faster driving practicable. Three changes were crucial.

The first was improved lubrication. This is a subject that has been much neglected by observers and students of technology and its history. The great international expositions of the nineteenth century collected and displayed industrial activities and products of man with a comprehensiveness and taxonomic enthusiasm that never fails to astonish. They assembled all manner of tools and machines, the raw materials they worked, the finished articles they made. They did not neglect the products of the soil or the sea, even the take of the hunt. But they took grease for granted.

And yet from the very start of the Industrial Revolution, lubrication was a matter of critical importance. In 1823 the young French ironmaster Achille Dufaud wrote home to Fourchambault that Cyfarthfa was using only first-quality Russian fat as grease. The cost was high—6d. a pound—but in the summer, when the water was low, the use of this fat had gained ten revolutions per minute for the mill wheel; the total annual saving was £3000.[1] And a generation later Fairbairn wrote in his classic *Treatise on Mills and Millwork*: 'In large cotton mills I have known as much as ten to fifteen horses' power absorbed by a change in the quality of oil used for lubrication; and in cold weather, or when the temperature of the mill is much reduced (as is generally the case when standing over Sunday), the power required on a Monday morning is invariably greater than at any other time during the week'.[2]

[1] Thuillier, *Georges Dufaud et les débuts du grand capitalisme dans la métallurgie*, pp. 227, 230.   [2] Second edition; 2 vols.; London 1865, II, 77.

Few manufacturers gave lubrication the attention it deserved—small wonder the historian has ignored it. Fairbairn again notes that in most plants the task of oiling the shafts was given to the sloppiest worker in the enterprise: 'the result is, that every opening for the oil to get to the bearings is plugged up, the brass steps are cut by abrasion, and the necks or journals of the shafts destroyed'. With time, however, the construction of heavier, faster equipment made it impossible to be indifferent to the cost of lost motion and wear and tear. Experience gave rise to an awareness of the numerous facets of what had seemed at first a simple problem. Industrialists and engineers learned to differentiate solid, semi-solid, and liquid lubricants; and to distinguish them by viscosity, oiliness, freezing and melting points, flammability, tendency to gum or thicken, to stain fabrics, or to decompose and deposit acid or carbon. They learned to suit the material to the use, often by mixing two or more types of lubricant to secure the advantages of each; the introduction of mineral oils and greases from the 1850's on opened a whole range of new possibilities. They also invented ingenious ways to maintain the lubrication of rapidly moving parts without interrupting motion: placing the rubbing surfaces in a standing bath; saturating a pad against which parts moved: cutting grooves down which the oil could run by gravity or be siphoned; and installing automatic pumps or spray guns. A major advance was the use from 1890, first in steam-engines and then in other machines, of forced lubrication, which made possible quiet running at high speeds with little wear and without risk of seizing.[1]

The second of our underlying advances was the substitution of steel for wrought iron in the construction of machinery—of a hard, smooth material, resistant to wear, for a comparatively soft metal, nervy in structure and irregular in abrasion. The result was less friction. And the third was greater precision in the manufacture of moving parts (of which more later), with similar gains.

These last two together made possible a major innovation designed to dispense with or diminish the need for lubrication. The principle of the spherical bearing is well known and as old as history; it is the same as that underlying the use of the wheel instead of the sledge in surface transport—the replacement of sliding friction by rolling contact. Benvenuto Cellini set 'four little globes of wood' to this purpose in the base of a statue as far back as the sixteenth century, and he was almost surely not the first to do so. Yet it was not until around 1880 that precision machinery and the development of hard steels made the

[1] The inventor was A. C. Pain, a designer on the staff of Belliss and Morcom, Birmingham, who pioneered the innovation. A. Stowers, 'The Stationary Steam-engine, 1830–1900', in C. Singer et al., eds., A History of Technology, v, 136.

spherical bearing a practical industrial instrument by making possible even distribution of the load and reducing the distortion produced by wear to tolerable proportions. The decisive patent was taken out in 1877 by William Bown of Birmingham, a manufacturer of sewing machine parts and roller skates. The first important application, however, was in the form of ball bearings in the bicycle manufacture—Rudge was advertising their advantages in 1886—and for a time the technique seemed suitable only to light loads. The development of the roller bearing, however, by distributing the pressure over lines rather than points of contact, corrected this shortcoming and made possible savings of as much as 90 per cent of power losses in shaft transmission.[1]

Machines were not only faster; they were also bigger, as was the whole range of manufacturing plant. There is no need to labour the point. We have already observed the trend in the iron and steel industry and in the construction of prime movers. At the same time, and in large measure owing to this growth of the equipment unit, the scale of efficient working increased. The trend to size, already marked in the period from 1850 to 1873, continued.

It was most rapid in Germany, where industry was younger, growth more rapid, and the close ties between manufacturing and finance facilitated company formation, expansion, and mergers. In addition, the very prevalence of cartel arrangements in many fields made it often imperative to integrate vertically, in order to free oneself from the exactions of collusive suppliers or customers; and integration opened the way to new economies of scale. Over the period from 1882 to 1907 the proportion of workers in enterprises employing over fifty persons increased from 26·3 to 45·5 per cent; the number of people in works of over one thousand employees more than quadrupled, from 205,000 to 879,000.

As might be expected, the stronghold of big business was heavy, capital-intensive industry: iron and steel, where almost three-quarters of the men in 1907 worked in enterprises of over a thousand employees; machine construction and engineering, where 84 per cent were employed in what was designated as *Grossbetriebe* (51 or more employees);

[1] For information on the introduction of ball bearings into modern manufacture, I am indebted to Mrs Smith of the University of Birmingham. From the evidence she has collected, it is clear that the discussions in extant published sources are both incomplete and inaccurate. Even so, the reader may consult with profit Hugh P. and Margaret Vowles, *The Quest for Power from Prehistoric Times to the Present Day* (London, 1931), pp. 206–10; J. G. Crowther, *Discoveries and Inventions of the 20th Century* (4th ed., New York, 1955), pp. 118–19; C. F. Caunter, *The History and Development of Cycles*, part I: *Historical Survey* (London: H.M.S.O., for the Science Museum, 1955), p. 15.

the manufacture of heavy electrical equipment (dynamos, generators, motors, transformers), with 96·4 per cent in the 51-plus category; and chemicals, where the alkali, explosives, and organic-dye trades showed proportions ranging from 82·6 to 98·2 per cent in this class. Yet the trend was clearly general, and even an industry like textile manufacture saw the share of the work force in *Grossbetriebe* increase in spinning from 71·1 per cent in 1882 to 89 per cent in 1907; in weaving from 34·3 per cent to 73·5 per cent.[1]

This increase in personnel, moreover, was accompanied by an even greater one in physical output per unit, for productivity was rising. We cannot always measure this growth directly because of variation in product over time, but where we are dealing with a homogeneous commodity, the evidence is clear. Thus in iron and steel, the average annual make of smelting plants increased seven-and-one-half-fold from 1880 to 1910—19,500 to 149,000 tons[2]—while that of Bessemer mills went from 109,000 tons in 1890 to 205,000 in 1905.[3]

What was happening in Germany was also happening in Britain, France, Belgium, and the other countries of Europe—though in lesser degree.[4] Some of this increase in scale is accounted for by new plants, risen full-blown from the soil as Venus from the foam. But much of it, and especially the giantism, consisted in the growth of established enterprises, some young, some old, adding machines, shops, entire buildings and works to their existing plant. Look at the maps that often adorn the proud anniversary histories of business firms—showing them either 'before and after', or distinguishing by colours and dates the stages of their growth.[5] Except for their linearity, they resemble nothing so much as historical maps of the expansion and consolidation of kingdoms and empires—here a frontier straightened out, there a salient established, there an enclave absorbed.

This accretionary character of industrial growth had important technological consequences. There was a certain rationality underlying it all, but opportunism and improvisation were of necessity equally

[1] *Statistik des deutschen Reichs*, N.F. ccxiv, table 11.

[2] Sombart, *Der moderne Kapitalismus*, iii², 889.

[3] Burn, *Economic History*, p. 220.

[4] We cannot follow the process so well in Britain, for lack of censuses comparable to those in Germany in 1861, 1875, 1882, 1895 and 1907. The trend is obvious, however (cf. *inter alia* Pollard, *History of Labour*, pp. 159–63, 224–6), though one must distinguish for our purposes true growth from consolidation. On the comparison of scale of enterprise between France and Germany, see D. S. Landes, 'Social Attitudes, Entrepreneurship, and Economic Development: A Comment', *Explorations in Entrepreneurial History*, vi (1954), 245–72.

[5] Thus the historical map of the Siemens plant at Woolwich in J. D. Scott, *Siemens Brothers 1858–1958: an Essay in the History of Industry* (London, 1958), opp. p. 268.

determining. As a result, the matrix of past arrangements became ever more confining, and at each change of equipment or addition to plant, the gap between 'best possible' and 'best practicable' grew. Nowhere was this legacy a more serious handicap than in the organization of the flow of work—what we may call the logistics of production.

Increased intensity of capital and scale of production made the old demon of logistical strangulation more redoubtable than ever. This was inevitable—implicit in the general discrepancy between anticipation and event. The city is built to handle the population and traffic of today or at best a decade from today; with time the streets are too narrow, the courts inaccessible, the buildings cramped and inconvenient. By the same token, even the well-planned factory begins its obsolescence from the moment its doors open. Changes in technique alter to its disadvantage the relationship between work and environment; increased speed and volume of work press against the confinement of fixed walls and equipment like the agitated molecules of a heated gas in a rigid container. To be sure, ingenuity and powerful handling and moving devices can ease the difficulty—as we shall see. But even these have their limits, and logistical problems of this kind—with the related costs they attach to any given innovation—have been perhaps the greatest single material obstacle to technical change in mature economies. Consider the comment in 1960 of an American steelman confronted with a new process that allegedly more than doubles the output of an open hearth: 'We can do the same thing on any one open hearth on any one day that we want to put on a demonstration. But I'd like to see them do it day in, day out, with all the furnaces in an open-hearth shop. That creates a tremendous congestion and enormous problems of heating the furnaces and keeping them properly heated, getting the metal away, and getting enough charging buggies.'[1]

By the same token, bigness increased the leverage of logistic operations and of workers' performance in general on the pecuniary results of the enterprise. We are often so impressed by the increase in productivity that results from labour-saving innovations, that we forget the other side of the coin—the multiplier effect on the costs of inefficiency. The greater the outlay on plant and equipment, the less one can afford bottlenecks, sloppiness, or slack; worse yet, inefficiency is infectious and tends to contaminate everything around.

The entrepreneurs of the late nineteenth century were thus goaded by necessity and spurred by the prospect of higher returns to find ways, first, to ease the movement of work through the plant, and second, to draw more output from each man with a given body of equipment.

[1] *Wall Street Journal*, Pacific Coast edition, 20 May 1960, p. 22.

The two were interrelated, not only because a smooth flow of work led to higher productivity, but because a change in the organization and character of labour was, in fact, prerequisite to a revision of the traffic pattern within the plant.

Moreover, this drive to efficiency was reinforced by the underlying commercial and technological trends of the period after 1870. As we have seen, competition was growing keener both in national and international markets as capacity began to outstrip demand, and the pressure for economy grew with it. Yet at the same time, innovation in the older industries was slowing down; new equipment cost more and yielded less. So that the one area that offered large opportunities to cut costs was that of organization and administration; the one factor that was compressible was labour.

The actual progress of these efforts to rationalize production and increase efficiency is hard to follow. Other aspects of technological change and industrial development lend themselves to quantification, and we have a rich statistical heritage to work with. But changes in plant layout and organization are not easily measured, and even where this is possible in individual cases, the variation in approach makes standardization and comparison difficult if not impossible. Perhaps for these reasons, these are subjects that have been relatively neglected by scholars. There are no general histories, and most contemporary accounts are concerned with ideal arrangements rather than actual practice. Our knowledge of the latter must be constructed from occasional case studies, passing references, and informed inferences. Most of the research remains to be done.

To clarify the issue, it is useful to divide industries into two classes, those that transform and those that assemble. The former would include most of the textile and chemical manufactures, metallurgy, glass-making, petroleum refining, food processing, and those other trades whose primary purpose is the conversion of a given body of raw material into some other form. The latter comprises fields like machine-building and engineering, clothing and shoe manufacture, and construction industries, all of which may undertake some transformation but whose salient characteristic is that they put their work together.

The distinction has direct implications for technique. The basic principle of industrial organization is smooth and direct work flow from start to finish of the manufacturing process; detours, returns, and halts are to be avoided as much as possible. For transforming industries, the conceptual problem is simple: there is one stream of activity and a sequential spatial arrangement of operations is all that is required. By contrast, the actual movement of the material may give rise to serious difficulties. It may be too hot to handle, as in metallurgy or certain

chemical processes; it may be corrosive or noxious, as in the manufacture of acids and alkalis; it may be bulky or heavy. These problems
stimulated a wide variety of ingenious arrangements for moving solid,
liquid, and gaseous matter at all temperatures: conveyors and belts,
elevators and hoists, pipe and valve systems, pumps, storage bins and
tanks, meters, calibrators, gauges, and controls.

Solids gave the most trouble. To be sure, man is capable of astonishing
feats of strength and adroitness: there are porcelain factories in Limoges
today where porters carry almost one hundred expensive plates at a
time, along corridors, around corners, through doorways and down
steps—two-thirds of their precious burden in their hands, the rest
heaped high on their heads! Moreover, the mechanics of manipulation
have long been familiar; the basic devices—screw, pulley, lever, crank,
and inclined plane—go back to antiquity. Yet the transmission of
power to such machines was beset with difficulties. Moving equipment,
by its very nature, could be tied to shaft-and-belt systems only within
narrowly circumscribed limits. To some extent human strength was
sufficient, if labour was cheap. Matschoss remarks that as late as the
1870's, hand-driven travelling cranes were still the rule in German
industry;[1] and among the new installations in a modernizing French
machine-construction plant in the 1920's were 'four small 2-ton
travelling cranes worked by hand'.[2]

Yet the limitations of human power are obvious: it took four
workers 50 minutes to raise five tons four metres by means of winches;
two workers, $12\frac{1}{2}$ minutes using pulleys. An effort was made to use
small, special-purpose steam-engines; probably the most frequent application of the locomobile—aside from its employment in agriculture—
was in lifting and handling. But this was a wasteful and troublesome
technique: the engines were generally worked well below capacity and
then only intermittently; and the task of keeping the machine fueled was
complicated by its movement. Steam was at its best where bulk was not
a handicap and speed of action not particularly important—in surface
excavation for example—or where weight was a positive advantage, as
in the rolling of asphalt pavement.

The eventual solution was, as we have seen, threefold:

(1) Water or air pressure where the working radius of the machine
was relatively limited and its action direct and simple. These came in
on a large scale in the 1860's and dominated the scene until about 1900.

[1] Matschoss, *Ein Jahrhundert deutscher Maschinenbau*, p. 137.
[2] This was the Soc. Anon. de Constructions Métalliques de Baccarat. International
Labour Office, *The Social Aspects of Rationalisation* [Studies and Reports, Series B
(Economic Conditions), no. 18] (Geneva, 1931), p. 114, citing a report published in
the *Bulletin du Ministère du Travail* from 1924 to 1927.

(2) Electricity where the radius was limited but freedom, rapidity, and versatility of action desirable. It was introduced in the 1890's in the United States, a decade later in Europe.

(3) Petroleum or gasoline where the range of action was very large, in dispersed construction projects for example.

Of these, electricity was the most important. Its most useful area of application was in the driving of 'travellers', where its quickness and responsiveness to control yielded productivity gains of the order of several hundred per cent. The electric crane revolutionized dock work and such industries as metallurgy, where it was often used in conjunction with giant magnets in the lifting of iron and steel objects. The latter technique was particularly effective in handling such things as scrap, the pieces of which were too large for shovels to handle and too irregular and small for claws. Here too, as everywhere, the trend was to size, with machines of 100-ton capacity and more in common use in shipyards and of up to 75 or 100 tons in heavy engineering on the eve of the First World War.

How important was this mechanization of transport and manipulation within the plant? The answer would vary with the nature of the enterprise; in some processes, handling represents more than 85 per cent of the cost of the finished product; in light industries like textiles, very little. Moreover, big gantry cranes or mobile lifts are not in themselves an assurance of economy. Often enterprises were outfitted with equipment too big or elaborate for the work required. And sometimes labour was so cheap that machines were a luxury. It is only too easy to mistake the paraphernalia of modernity for efficiency.

Nevertheless, one may fairly say that handling was a focus of rapid advance in productivity—not so much because of the spectacular realizations in heavy industries like metallurgy, but because of the uncounted small improvements in every branch of manufacture. The backwardness of some enterprises in this period is astonishing: one reads of dozens of men carrying tons of earth or coal on their backs; of chains of workers standing on a ladder passing material from hand to hand. Often a simple hoist, a few small carriages, or the installation of lifting tables or a conveyor system made all the difference. In an age of ever costlier equipment and diminishing returns, this was the one area that repeatedly saw investments pay for themselves in months and even weeks.

Many of these advances were also important in assembling industries, as several of the examples show. Here the nature of the work had given rise to a complex and wasteful pattern of operations. First—and this was really determining—the assembly process was in most trades imprecise, a matter of repeated trial and error and adjustment; this character of the work is still reflected in our vocabularies, in English words like *fitter* and *steam-fitter* or the French term *ajusteur*. Secondly, few of these industries benefited from the long production runs of homogeneous products that characterized metallurgy and the chemical manufacture. Engineering and machine-building in particular did much of their work to order, and even basic components varied with the job. As a result, there was a great deal of repetitious movement of the wrong kind, with a given object going back and forth several times over the same path until it was satisfactory; and little repetitive movement of the right kind, in which object after object follows the same path, undergoes the same processes, and emerges from the production line with the expedition that comes from practice and mechanization.

In such industries two kinds of work arrangements were commonly employed:

(1) Machines were grouped by type—drills, planes, lathes, and so on in engineering and machine construction, for example—and the pieces were moved from one post to another until they were finally brought together for fitting in the assembly shop. This is the German *Platzarbeit*.

(2) If the work was extremely bulky, as in shipbuilding, construction, or heavy engineering, the men and tools would be brought to it, and components would either be prepared on the spot or wrought elsewhere, usually on the first system, and brought over as well.

Thus instead of the linear flow of the transforming industries, a nodal traffic arrangement prevailed, with material zigzagging back and forth between these work posts, different pieces following different paths. The one pattern may be compared to the smooth stream of vehicles on a through highway; the other to the spasmodic, irregular movement of city streets.[1] One may carry the analogy further. Just as an addition to a throughway increases travel time only in proportion, whereas the expansion of an urban complex increases it at a geometric or even exponential rate, so in *Platzarbeit*, the growth of the plant means greater distances between the posts and multiplies the time lost in the repetitive movement of material. The more successful enterprises gave entire floors, or even separate shops, to a single type of tool. Logistic difficulties thus set a low upper limit to economies of scale.

Finally, the same technological problems that gave rise to the nodal pattern—imprecision and variation on the one hand, custom work on the other—called forth and sustained social institutions that were a source of further inefficiencies. The assembling industries were the

[1] For illustrations of plant and equipment layouts characteristic of the two systems, see Vienna, Kammer für Arbeiten und Angestellte in Wien, *Rationalisierung, Arbeitswissenschaft und Arbeiterschutz* (2nd ed., Vienna, 1928), pp. 189–95.

stronghold of skilled craftsmen, for in the period before gauges and automatic machine tools, only a deft hand could make components that were reasonably accurate or fit them together. These men were the aristocracy of the labour force. Masters of their techniques, able to maintain their tools as well as use them, they looked upon their equipment as their own even when it belonged to the firm. On the job they were effectively autonomous. Most of them paid their own assistants, and many played the role of subcontractors within the plant, negotiating the price of each job with management, engaging the men required, and organizing the work to their own taste and convenience. The best of them 'made' the firms they worked for.

Yet their independence was costly. Measured by modern time-and-motion methods, skilled labour tends to be less efficient than directly supervised semi-skilled or unskilled labour; and this is only to be expected, for the skilled worker sets his own pace instead of accommodating to that of the machine. Furthermore, these master craftsmen were proud, umbrageous, and usually well organized. Their vested interest in the *status quo* was an obstacle to innovation, the more so because their skill and virtuosity were incompatible with the fundamental principle of industrial technology—the substitution of inanimate accuracy and tirelessness for human touch and effort.

The drives to mechanization and increased scale, on the one hand, and toward a more rational organization of production, on the other, converged at this point. In order to eliminate skill and push back the logistic barrier, two steps were required: (1) the fragmentation of the job into simple operations susceptible of being performed by single-purpose machines run by unskilled or semi-skilled hands; and (2) the development of methods of manufacture so precise that assembly became routine, in other words, the production of interchangeable parts. Only in this way could one change from a nodal to a linear flow; only in this way could one move the work to the workers at a pre-determined pace, to be processed and put together by a series of simple, repetitive acts. The assembly line was thus far more than just a new technique, a means of obtaining greater output at less cost. In those branches where it took hold, it marked the passage from shop, however big and heavily equipped, to factory.

Coherent sequences of machines and interchangeable parts are easier to establish in some industries than others. The determining consideration is the degree of precision required, which varies not only with the purpose of the product (compare a chronometer, a rifle, a pair of pliers, and the frame of a house), but with the material employed (compare textile fabrics or leather, which give, with metals, which do not). It is largely because of its comfortable tolerances that shoe manufacture was among the earliest assembling industries to develop progressive machining, as it is sometimes called.

Metal devices—the kind that had to be wrought piece by piece and assembled, as opposed to simple objects that could be stamped or pressed out—were another matter. Here margins were often very fine, measured in the hundredths and thousandths of an inch. As a result, interchangeability was costly, and only the achievement of volume manufacture made the effort worth while. (Eventually entrepreneurs learned that the converse was also true: the effort, if successful, made for low prices and a mass market.) It is no coincidence that the first important applications of the principles of interchangeable parts and line assembly were in the manufacture of small arms, which were needed in quantity for military use.

History has traditionally assigned this critical innovation to Eli Whitney, of cotton-gin fame, but his claim will not stand up under scrutiny. Robert S. Woodbury has noted that a Swedish mechanic, Christopher Polhem, was making uniform clock gears as early as the 1720's, and that a Frenchman named Blanc was turning out rifles in the government arsenals on an interchangeable basis before the Revolution. Neither of these early achievements took root, however, and it was not until a number of American gunmakers—among them, Whitney, though he was by no means the first—worked out the principles and developed the requisite tools in the first two decades of the nineteenth century that we have an unbroken record of diffusion.[1] In the beginning the technique found its widest application in the north-eastern United States, in the manufacture not only of small arms, but also of locks, clocks, and agricultural machinery.[2] Not until the 1850's was it introduced into Britain, in the government arms factory at Enfield following a visit of inspection across the Atlantic. Even then, progress was slow: the Birmingham Small Arms Company, founded in 1861 to turn out military rifles at the rate of about 500 a week, did most of its work at first by means of skilled hand labour; the shops were filled with benches and vices, rather than machines.[3]

Yet the rifle and pistol are, so far as articulation is concerned, crude mechanisms. The contribution of the last half of the nineteenth century

[1] R. S. Woodbury, 'The Legend of Eli Whitney and Interchangeable Parts', *Technology and Culture*, 1 (1960), 235–53. John E. Sawyer, President of Williams College, is currently preparing a study of the 'American system of manufacturing' and its French antecedents.

[2] J. E. Sawyer, 'The Social Basis of the American System of Manufacturing', *J. Econ. Hist.* XIV (1954), 361–79; D. L. Burn, 'The Genesis of American Engineering Competition', *Econ. Hist.* [supplement of the *Econ. J.*], II (1931), 292–311; Merle Curti, 'America at the World Fairs, 1851–1893', *Amer. Hist. Rev.* LV (1950), 833–56.

[3] *Proc. Inst. Mech. Engineers* (1910), part III, p. 1324.

lay, first, in the invention of a number of non-military devices—the sewing machine, then the typewriter, bicycle, and finally the automobile —that required a much higher degree of precision and at the same time enjoyed the kind of demand that made the achievement of inter-changeability worth while, if not indispensable; and second, in the development of the equipment and techniques required. Three areas of innovation were crucial: machine tools, grinding, and measurement.

We have already had occasion to discuss the early improvements in machines to make machines. By the middle of the nineteenth century, the essential requirements were all present: the true plane, which sup-plied the uniform standard of reference; the slide rest, which took the cutting tool from the fallible hands of the artisan; and screw-threaded adjustments, which made possible fine work. What the next two generations did was essentially to adapt and elaborate on these tech-niques in developing more efficient forms of the basic tools: drills, lathes, planers, and the rest. There were, however, two major novelties, both connected to the growing demand for what are now consumers' durables:

(1) The turret (eventually automatic) lathe. The machine was equipped with a rotating turret that carried as many as eight cutting tools, each of which could be brought to bear on the work in turn. The next step was automatic rotation, achieved in 1861 if not earlier, and the concurrent invention of a device for gripping and feeding the work reduced the role of the worker to insertion, supervision, and removal. Though the idea came perhaps from Britain, the first extensive use of these machines was in the United States in the 1840's; the Civil War, with its demand for mass-produced metal wares, encouraged their diffusion. By the 1870's they were widely used in Europe.

Toward the end of the century the productivity of these machines was increased four or five times by the use of multiple spindles, which made it possible to work on several pieces simultaneously. Eventually, banks of these machines were set up, using cross-slides as well as turrets, to work away side by side like the array of spindles on a mule. The only labour required was for occasional tool setting and replenishing the supply of raw material.

(2) The milling machine. Its distinguishing characteristic is the use of a revolving multiple cutter, which resembles a small cylinder or truncated cone with saw-toothed sides. It offered several major advant-ages over the usual single-point tools, with their intermittent recipro-cating actions:[1] relatively wide cutting edges; continuous motion; and

---

[1] This was one example of a general principle that has found numerous applications in the history of technology. Some of these are already familiar: the substitution of the rolling mill for the hammer in forge work; of continuous rolling for reversing rolls in

the possibility of profiling the teeth to permit the production of any geometrical shape desired. When the cutter, moreover, was combined with an adjustable swivel headstock to permit attacking the work from all angles or from changing angles, to cut spirals for example, the result was the so-called universal miller (1861), a marvel of versatility. Eventually this was further improved by a kind of compounding process comparable to that which had produced the multi-spindle lathe.[1]

The first milling cutter is said to go back to Vaucanson in the eighteenth century; the first milling machine was built by Eli Whitney in 1818. Again, however, it was the demand arising out of the Civil War that established the device in the United States; by the early 1870's it was standard in the manufacture of sewing machines. Europeans were long sceptical. The British, who had begun to copy American models from about 1875, did not really take it up until the bicycle boom of the 1890's opened a new field of application.

Part of the difficulty was technical: for a long time, machine design and materials were not up to the conception. The wide cutting edges of the miller, more than one of which may be in contact with the work at once, subject the spindle and arbor to extreme stress, and only the stiffest construction will prevent the tool from vibrating and chattering; even then, the reciprocating planer and shaper will do more accurate work, especially on wide surfaces. Furthermore, the continuity and rapidity of milling call for tough metal, the more so because the uneven wear of any of the cutting edges necessitates the regrinding of all; as we have seen, the special tool steels required were invented only at the turn of the century.[2]

The introduction of new and harder alloy steels, not only for tools but for machine parts, intensified the challenge already posed by the

the mill; the replacement of the reciprocating steam-engine by the turbine. Other uses will also come to mind: the circular saw, rotary printing press, cylinder printing of textiles. In machine manufacture itself, we may note the increasing use in the late nineteenth century of high-speed drills, using bits with spiral cutting edges instead of the traditional smooth sides, in place of such tools as the slotting machine. Cf. the discussion of this 'Rotationsprinzip' in Sombart, Der moderne Kapitalismus, III¹, 109–10. On the innovation of the twist drill, see G. A. Fairfield, 'Report on Sewing Machines', in R. H. Thurston, ed., Reports of the Commissioners of the United States to the International Exhibition held at Vienna, 1873, vol. III: Engineering (Washington, D.C., 1876), p. 30.

[1] The best source is R. S. Woodbury, History of the Milling Machine [Technology Monographs, Historical Series, no. 3] (Cambridge, Mass., 1960). It offers a brief but useful bibliography.

[2] The extent of the wear on the cutting tool, even with high-speed steels, was often such as to compel machine makers to sacrifice speed of operation to speed and ease of maintenance and to use milling heads with one tooth. This was a twentieth-century development. Cf. Ludwig Loewe und Co., Actiengesellschaft Berlin, 1869–1929 (Berlin, 1930), pp. 87–8.

drive for speed and precision. Rapid, accurate work called for sharp cutting edges and nice finishing; both of these could be achieved only by grinding.

It is important to distinguish between these two basic functions of grinding—tool maintenance and shaping. Until the turn of the century, the first was by far the more important: grinding was generally confined to the irregular and unsystematic sharpening of tools by the individual workman. Gradually, however, abrasives came to be used as tools themselves. As in most other areas of metal working, the United States led the way: as early as the 1870's, one observer was able to write that 'the grandeur [Grossartigkeit] of the grindstone industry in America astonishes every foreigner'. In these early years, however, the technique was confined to fine finishing. It took a series of related advances in the preparation and manipulation of abrasives plus a creative reinterpretation of the nature and the possibilities of the technique to make possible what has since come to be known as production grinding.[1]

The major material problem was the achievement of a true, efficient abrasive surface of known and uniform characteristics. Up to the end of the nineteenth century, all industrial grinding was done with such natural abrasives as sandstone, emery (an impure aluminium oxide), or, beginning in the 1820's, corundum (almost pure aluminium oxide). The last of these was the hardest, but it was also the most costly, for until the 1870's it had to be imported from lands around the Indian Ocean. At that point, the discovery of large deposits in North America brought the price down, and in the next two decades, corundum largely displaced emery in shaping and finishing. At the same time, the desirability of a true and lasting abrasive surface led to the development of solid grinding wheels, in which the cutting grains were mixed with such bonds as glue, vulcanized rubber, clay, or silicates. The first of these date back at least to 1837 in England, 1843 in France, 1850 in Germany. Along with them went ingenious devices for dressing, that is, renewing the edge of the wheel (1860's on) and truing its shape (roughly the same period).

At the same time, machine builders were putting these wheels into power devices that could operate them as a drill its bit or a miller its cutting head. The earliest of these grinders go back to the Renaissance, if not beyond, and they found considerable use in optical work, watchmaking, and similar light trades in the following centuries; but their improvement and specialization for large-scale manufacturing was the

[1] Again the best source is R. S. Woodbury, *History of the Grinding Machine: A Historical Study in Tools and Precision Production* (Cambridge, Mass., 1959). See also Mildred M. Tymeson, *The Norton Story* (Worcester, Mass., 1953).

work of the Industrial Revolution. British (Whitelaw, Bodmer, Nasmyth, Barker and Holt), German (Krupp), and above all American (David Wilkinson, Bridges, Wheaton, Darling, Poole) mechanics were engaged in this development, which reached its culmination in the work of Joseph Brown of Brown and Sharpe, the conceiver if not designer of the universal grinding machine (1875).

It is no coincidence that these concomitant improvements in abrasive surface and working mechanism quickened toward the end of the century and came to inspire a radically new concept of grinding technique. Once again the revolution in this domain was intimately connected with the growing demand for complex machines smooth and sturdy enough in operation to withstand the abuse of the mechanically incompetent household consumer. The sewing machine gave a foretaste of these derived technological consequences, as did the bicycle with its ball bearings; but neither had anything like the impact of the automobile. It is hard to overestimate this impact, which is comparable to that of the steam-engine in the eighteenth century. The automobile was not the first object of manufacture to call for complicated or delicate or precise work. But nothing before had ever demanded all of these, often in materials too hard to be shaped by traditional means, and in such quantity as to strain the supply of skilled labour. From the start, the automobile industry paid top wages for its craftsmen: it needed to and could afford to. And from the start it was compelled to do new things and find new ways to do old. Moreover, there was the economic carrot as well as the technological stick: the elasticity of demand for private transportation provided an enormous incentive for cost-saving improvements, which, given the nature of the work, almost invariably consisted in the substitution of capital for labour.

The answer to many of the new industry's production problems lay in replacing cutting and scraping by grinding. Not only did the new technique assure the greater precision required by interchangeable parts working at high speeds and temperatures, but it proved invaluable in rough work—in removing stock from crankshafts and camshafts, for example. And it permitted the use of light, hard alloys like vanadium steel, without which an economical automobile for general use would not have been feasible.[1]

The advances that made this kind of production grinding possible were threefold: first, the invention of artificial abrasives, particularly carborundum (first commercial use, 1896), which was harder than the traditional natural materials (always excepting the diamond) and could

---

[1] Cf. P. W. Kingsford, 'The Lanchester Engine Company Ltd., 1899–1904', *Business History*, III (1961), 110; John B. Rae, *American Automobile Manufacturers: the First Forty Years* (Philadelphia and New York, 1959), p. 120, n. 7.

be prepared in varying grits to suit the requirements of the work; second, the development of precision grinding machinery, of heavy, powerful construction, using larger and wider wheels; and finally, the introduction of plunge grinding, in which the wheel was given the shape of the part desired and fed into the work rather than run across it.

As in most areas of metal technology, the United States took the lead in production grinding. In part this was a consequence of creative engineering. Particularly important was the contribution of Charles H. Norton, a giant in the tradition of Maudslay, Nasmyth, and Whitworth. Norton conceived the new technique, called attention to its larger economic implications, designed numerous machines to effect it, and worked out the principles of optimum operation, notably the choice of abrasive and grinding speed to fit the job. But his success and that of the other American pioneers in this area owed much to the entrepreneurial and technological orientation of the American automobile industry—the precocious emphasis on quantity, lightness, and low cost.

European practice was not far behind the American. To be sure, the extensive adoption of production grinding in the manufacture of automotive vehicles did not come in Britain and Germany until during the War or after. On the other hand, both countries anticipated the United States in the application of grinding to the construction and maintenance of locomotives. And in other industries, Europeans were quick to buy American equipment or manufacture machines after American patents; beginning in 1904, for example, Ludwig Loewe and Co. were turning out Norton-type grinders in Berlin. It was not long, moreover, before they and others were designing their own models to suit their own conceptions and the requirements of European manufacture.

In the meantime, the new standards of manufacture called forth a revolution in the other domain of grinding, that of the maintenance of cutting tools. Here the key gains were once again the introduction of improved abrasives and the development of precise, special-purpose machines. The effective utilization of this equipment, however, entailed a reorganization of the shop that often aroused sharp opposition from the highly skilled and correspondingly umbrageous metal workers. In particular, it was now necessary to appoint specialist grinders and create a separate tool room to stock work pieces and keep them in proper condition. This meant the abdication by the worker of control over his tools; it also deprived him of the pleasant relaxation of the grindstone queue—the nineteenth-century equivalent of the coffee break.[1]

[1] See the delightful photograph of such a queue in O. M. Becker, *High-speed Steel* (New York and London, 1910), p. 153.

Along with improved tools went standardized controls—not by means of measuring devices like the rule and calipers, but by instruments independent of the vagaries of the human eye, stable in their accuracy, and calling for little or no skill. Whitworth's plug and ring gauges were the prototypes of a whole family of contrivances—limit (go and no-go) gauges, difference gauges, adjustable gauges, reference disks, end measuring blocks—whose tolerance was sometimes as small as one fifty-thousandth of an inch and whose operation was almost foolproof. Even so, the gain was not in the quality of the final product, but in its cost. The nature of the change is well described by H. F. Donaldson, machine manufacturer from Woolwich and member of the Council of the Institution of Mechanical Engineers, in a lecture of 1909:

When I began to serve my time in the shops, I remember that 'a fine 1/64 of an inch' was about the closest measurement to which any workman, or for the matter of that, his superiors, referred to, but none the less, even with such a coarse nominal dimension, and the use of a pair of ordinary callipers, magnificent work was produced owing to the skill of the individual workmen and the precision of their sense of touch. Neither the workman, nor in many cases his superiors, had any real knowledge of the degree of accuracy to which the work was being done, but the fact remains that work of the highest quality was made and fitted together, having fits at least as close as those secured today by more systematic, and, as we believe, improved and certainly cheaper methods. The great difference which existed between then and now, is that though the work then was of the highest quality as regards each machine put together, the degree of accuracy ruling in each part was quite unknown, and the parts of one such machine were not interchangeable, or capable of mutual substitution in another machine, which was nominally of the same dimensions in all particulars. In other words, the machines were made and 'fitted' then with great care and with a large amount of expensive hand-work, where today, at least in the more progressive shops, machines are 'assembled' from parts made to a known degree of accuracy, and with a minimum of expensive hand-fitting, and with the added advantage that the parts of machines so made are interchangeable one with another if the work is done on a proper system of limits or limit-gauges.[1]

The quotation is as interesting for what it implies as for what it says. Before the First World War, outside those few industries manufacturing mass-market items like the sewing machine, only the more progressive enterprises in Britain worked with interchangeable parts. A team of American automobile mechanics, sent by Cadillac to England in 1906, caused a sensation when they set out the jumbled components of three cars on the floor of a shed at the Brooklands track and assembled

[1] *Proc. Inst. Mech. Engineers* (1909), pp. 254-5.

the vehicles with wrench, screw-driver, hammer, and pliers.[1] Most British firms of this period were caught in a vicious circle: output was not big or uniform enough to warrant heavy outlays for specialized precision equipment and a reorganization of plant layout; yet this was the only way to achieve the lower costs and prices that would yield increased demand and justify longer production runs. Many manufacturers would have plausibly argued that any effort to fix the form and structure of their products would rob them of that flexibility that is the strongest arm of the small or medium enterprise. It took initiative to break this conservative chain of logic, and it was rarely forthcoming. In most cases it took outside pressure, like the increasing inroads of Henry Ford on the British market, or extraordinarily favourable incentives, like the huge government orders of wartime, to induce a change.[2]

If standardization within the firm was difficult, how much harder was it to persuade manufacturers throughout an industry to accept a national norm? The problem was complicated by the peculiarly British institution of the consulting engineer, who tended to design every project as though the manufacturer were a custom tailor working in metal. Here too, however, outside competition made itself felt. The Americans had been the first to adopt uniform shapes and sizes, imposing them by fiat on manufacturing clients and consumers from the eighties on.[3] The Germans had followed suit, in large part for reasons of principle—simplification was rational; moreover, industrial organization facilitated the introduction and enforcement of inter-firm standards. Lagging British sales, both in these countries and in other markets, and the increased concern of technicians finally led in 1901 to the creation in Britain of an Engineering Standards Committee under the auspices of the leading national engineering associations.

The first efforts of the committee were in the field of iron and steel manufacture, where British makers produced 122 angle and channel sections against 33 for the United States, 34 for Germany.[4] Here they achieved considerable success, for the manufacturers wanted to eliminate the waste of diversification and the very existence of standards gave

---

[1] Arthur Pound, *The Turning Wheel: the Story of General Motors through Twenty-five Years* (Garden City, N.Y., 1934), p. 107.

[2] Cf. P. W. S. Andrews and E. Brunner, *The Life of Lord Nuffield: a Study in Enterprise and Benevolence* (Oxford, 1955), pp. 59–71, 87–94.

[3] On the importance of entrepreneurial attitudes—the refusal of producers to supply their clients with special shapes except on payment of a punitively high price—see J. Stephen Jeans, ed., *American Industrial Conditions and Competition: Reports of the Commissioners Appointed by the British Iron Trade Association to Enquire into the Iron, Steel, and Allied Industries of the United States* (London, 1902), p. 256.

[4] Burn, *Economic History*, p. 199. See above p. 495.

them a ready-made reply to the idiosyncratic preferences of the client.[1] By 1914, 95 per cent of the output of five of the largest rolling mills in the United Kingdom was standardized.[2] Similarly, standardization made good progress in a new industry like electrical manufacturing, run by scientifically trained technicians and relatively forward-looking managers, though diversity of current supply complicated matters considerably.

By contrast, the older assembling industries like engineering were slow to change. Each firm took a proprietary pride in its own work, to the point where many were simply not interested in norms and the production techniques that went with them.[3] Moreover, labour in the engineering trades, strongly organized, craft-oriented, and fearful of technological unemployment, fought all changes in conditions of work.[4] Again it was the First World War with its great demand for machines of all kinds and short supply of skilled hands that gave impetus to the struggle against idiosyncrasy; indeed, the descriptions of the gains made after 1914 are our best source—implicit but valid—for the inefficiencies that prevailed before.[5] Even so, progress was slow in many branches, which were described in 1927 as 'still bound by tradition and drift[ing] along with an enormous number of spare parts, making no attempt to simplify'.[6]

By comparison with Britain, then, Germany was distinctly more advanced, though there is a tendency to concentrate on the most striking examples of German achievement in this domain, thereby

[1] Cf. Report of the Tariff Commission [a private body], vol. 1: The Iron and Steel Trades (London, 1904), no. 631.

[2] Commission on Industry and Trade, Factors in Industrial and Commercial Efficiency [Being Part I of a Survey of Industries] (London, 1927), p. 294.

[3] Donaldson, 'Interchangeability', Proc. Inst. Mech. Engineers (1909), pp. 255 f.

[4] The issue was at the heart of dozens of major and minor strikes in the industry from 1897-8 on. Cf. A. Shadwell, The Engineering Industry and the Crisis of 1922 (London, 1922); Pollard, History of Labour in Sheffield, pp. 235 ff.; J. B. Jefferys, The Story of the Engineers, part III. The very existence of this conflict, of course, is evidence that a certain amount of rationalization was taking place.

[5] Cf. the Report of the Board of Trade Engineering Trades Committee of 1916-17: 'Old works have been added to, fresh machinery has been introduced from time to time to balance up old machinery. There has been generally an absence of totally new works with an economic lay-out. Whilst the country can point to many works of the highest class, with the most modern equipment worked at the highest efficiency, there can be no doubt that many of our older works are manufacturing at costs which could be greatly reduced if their works as a whole were on a larger scale, well-planned and equipped with plant, and, therefore, capable of being worked in the most efficient and economical manner.' Commission on Industry and Trade, Survey of Metal Industries [Being Part IV of a Survey of Industries] (London, 1928), p. 149.

[6] Commission on Industry and Trade, Factors in Industrial and Commercial Efficiency, p. 295.

exaggerating the discrepancy. Even so modern a plant as the Loewe machine-tool works in Berlin, built anew in 1898–99 according to the best American practice, did not set up 'Arbeitskreise', that is, switch over from a nodal to a linear-flow pattern, until 1926.[1] Similarly, the Wolf machine works in Magdeburg was turning out interchangeable parts with special-purpose equipment before the war, but these components were then used to mount rows of fixed machines in the assembly hall.[2] For both countries, the new system of mass production was essentially the work of the famous 'rationalization' of the 1920's.

As already implied, reorganization of work entailed reorganization of labour: the relationships of the men to one another and to their employers were implicit in the mode of production; technology and social pattern reinforced each other.

But labour is not a factor like other factors. It is active where equipment and materials are passive. It has a mind of its own; it resists as well as responds. Its performance independent of other considerations —what we may call its efficiency as opposed to its productivity—is not easily calculated except by modern systems of cost accounting, and the historical data are correspondingly impressionistic and sparse. It is especially difficult to separate pure effort, diligence, and skill from organization and supervision, which obviously make a difference. Fortunately, such fine discrimination is not necessary to our analysis, and we may lump these elements together without undue sacrifice of precision.

Our ignorance of the variations of labour efficiency over space and time is the more unfortunate because we have every reason to believe that it was an important determinant of the rate and character of economic development in any given country and as between countries; moreover, that its significance in this regard grew in the course of the Industrial Revolution until, by the turn of the century, this was one of the areas of greatest slack and, by the same token, of greatest potential gain in productivity.

In the days before power machinery, skill and rapidity were decisive differentials. Defoe was well aware of this; comparing wages and work in England and France, he wrote:

I might examine this Article of Wages, and carry it thro' almost every Branch of Business in *England*; and it would appear, that the *English* Poor earn more Money than the same Class of Men or Women can do at the same kind of Work, in any other Nation.

[1] *Ludwig Loewe and Co.*, pp. 94–9.
[2] C. Matschoss, *Die Maschinenfabrik R. Wolf, Magdeburg-Buckau, 1862–1912* (Magdeburg, n.d.), pp. 103 f.

Nor will it be deny'd, but that they do more Work also: So then, if they do more Work, and have better Wages too, they must needs live better, and fare better; and it is true also, that they cannot support their Labour without it.

And here I may grant, that a *French* Man shall do more Work than an *English* Man, if they shall be oblig'd to live on the same Diet; that is to say, the Foreigner shall starve with the *English* Man for a Wager, and will be sure to win: He will live and work, when the *English* Man shall sink and dye; but let them live both the same Way, the *English* Man shall beggar the *French* Man, for tho' the *French* Man were to spend all his Wages, the *English* Man will outwork him.

It is true again, the *French* Man's Diligence is the greatest, he shall work more hours than the *English* Man; but the *English* Man shall do as much Business in the fewer Hours, as the Foreigner who sits longer at it.[1]

In the early decades of the Industrial Revolution, however, when rapidly changing techniques offered large returns and mechanization in particular yielded spectacular gains in productivity over hand work, labour efficiency lost in relative importance and—wisely or not—was neglected. Eric Hobsbawm, in an important article on 'Customs, Wages, and Work-load in Nineteenth-Century Industry',[2] cites the *Carding and Spinning Master's Assistant* of 1832, which warned against rearranging machine installations, even if inefficient, on the grounds that the cost would probably exceed the savings.

Most entrepreneurs and managers in this period preferred fixed wages and relied on 'hard driving' by foremen and master workmen to get them value for their money in the short run, on the quiet effect of technological change to cut labour costs in the long. When the measurement of output was possible, piece wages were sometimes used as an incentive to diligence; but a number of considerations combined to nullify their stimulatory effect. Thus rates were usually calculated on the basis of customary norms and adjusted with changes in technique so as to reserve to capital the greater part of any gains in productivity. Such a division of the incremental product may or may not have been fair, but the effect on the worker was to convince him of the uselessness of assiduity. Moreover, labour, even in the factory, often had the kind of backward-bending supply curve that had always characterized domestic work.[3] Just as wages tended to be customary, so the level of performance was fixed by tradition and income expectations—compare the still persistent ideal of 'a fair day's work for a fair day's pay'—and was enforced against the temptations of ambition by the strongest

[1] [Defoe], *A Plan of the English Commerce* (Oxford, 1928), p. 28.
[2] In Asa Briggs and John Saville, eds., *Essays in Labour History* (London, 1960), pp. 113–39. This is a path-breaking effort to synthesize some of this material historically.
[3] Cf. Pollard, *History of Labour in Sheffield*, p. 130, for this phenomenon in the light metal trades toward the end of the nineteenth century.

group pressure. It is the slack implied by this rationing of effort that goes far to account for the ability of labour to maintain output in the short run whenever hours were cut, as they were repeatedly in the course of the century; and conversely, for the almost universal failure of technological innovations to yield the productivity gains they theoretically made possible.[1]

The tendency of management to let custom set the level of work performance was shaken by adversity. The contractions of the late 1860's (in textiles especially) and mid-1870's (industry-wide), when wages held up better than profits, were crucial in this regard. Employers attempted to cut labour costs by increasing performance, and the question of the nature and size of the work load supplanted wages as the major issue in labour disputes. In textiles the *casus belli* was the attempt of management to increase the number of power looms per weaver; the struggle was particularly bitter on the Continent. In machine construction and engineering a serious bone of contention was the right of management to shift men about as needed, that is, to treat the worker as an interchangeable part of the production process. In all industries, there was general discontent at the replacement of skilled by unskilled and semi-skilled hands, easier to manage and more amenable to pace set from above.

The wage structure reflected the new policy. As the diversified work of the artisan, unmeasurable in homogeneous units of output, gave way to the routine operation of special-purpose machines, time wages gave way to piece wages. The change was felt most keenly in the engineering trades, where time rates had always been the rule. There were numerous protests. That there should have been any was testimony to the tensions and resentments produced by these changes in technique and organization. For labour, and particularly organized labour, ordinarily preferred piece wages. Admittedly, they led some men to overtask themselves (although collective restraints usually prevented this), encouraged hasty, even sloppy work (though it was not difficult to watch against this), and caused some to adopt the rush-slack rhythm that we know to have characterized the putting-out manufacture of the

---

[1] A direct historical measurement of the cost of labour inefficiency and bad organization is impossible, but it does not seem far-fetched to draw, as Hobsbawm does, on the analogy of the cotton textile industry of Latin America in the mid-twentieth century. This was studied in detail in a pioneering attempt to measure the relative importance of determinants of productivity for an entire industry. The conclusion was, contrary to expectations, that the greater part of the excess of labour employed was due to administrative and organizational rather than technological deficiencies—and this in an industry where, far more than most, machines set the pace for labour, rather than vice-versa. United Nations, *Labour Productivity of the Cotton Textile Industry in Five Latin-American Countries* (New York: U.N. Dept. of Econ. Affairs, 1951), p. 10.

eighteenth century. Yet more important than all of these drawbacks was the conviction of most men that piece wages gave them their only assurance of a share of increased output consequent on advances in technique. Even where the employer tried to adjust the rates downwards, there was at least something to negotiate. With time wages, by contrast, the work could and did increase imperceptibly as productivity rose; and even when the process was manifest, the system of remuneration afforded little opportunity for redress.

To the English worker of the late nineteenth century, however, the piece wage seemed an instrument of exploitation rather than a defence. To be sure, it held out the promise of higher pay. But the workers alleged that the rates were set to the performance of the most rapid men; the slow ones followed suit or 'went to the wall'.[1] The higher pay, they felt, was nothing but sweetening to get them to swallow higher work norms; and in fact, the new rates were rarely maintained beyond what was felt to be a reasonable increase—a third or perhaps a half—over customary wages.

Here, as much as in the employer's appetite for gain, lay the heart of the difficulty. The employer, like most Englishmen of the 'propertied classes', took it for granted that his men and their children were destined to remain workers; and 'that the whole social, political, and industrial fabric would fall into a heap' if labourers suddenly became rich, discontented with their lot, and ambitious for higher status.[2] Now there may have been a time, as some assert, when the worker, or at least many a worker, did not believe this, when he honestly thought he could rise and was susceptible to appeals to diligence and 'self-help'. By the last decades of the century, however, disenchantment had clearly set in, partly owing to longer experience with the difficulties of advancement, partly to the heightened class consciousness of an organized labour movement ideologically fortified by militant doctrine. By this time the worker was prepared to see any initiative of the employer as a trap. And to this should be added his fear of technological unemployment. Political economy notwithstanding, he instinctively held to the 'lump-of-labour' doctrine: there was just so much work to go around and what one man gained by faster work took bread out of the mouth of his fellow. As a result, the worker tended to resist, as a member of a group, even those innovations that were to his advantage as an individual; and whereas, in the early nineteenth

Comments of W. G. Bunn at the Industrial Remuneration Conference of 1885. See Industrial Remuneration Conference, *The Report of the Proceedings and Papers* (London, 1885), p. 169. There is a great deal of scattered information on this trend.
[2] U.S. Bureau of Labor, *Twelfth Special Report of the Commissioner of Labor: Regulation and Restriction of Output* (Washington, D.C., 1904), pp. 752–7.

century, the effort of labour to wrest improvements from the employer
was a stimulus to innovation, by the end of our period, the same effort
—more effective, but aimed more at conditions of work than at wages
—may well have been on balance a deterrent to technological change.
Certainly this was often true in the short run; and in history if not in
theory, the long run is often the short run enshrined as practice, tradition, or vested interest.

In the meantime, the effort to maximize the product of labour led to
a careful study of the worker as an animate machine, through the eyes
of a new kind of engineer. The initiative came from the United States,
as always preoccupied with this issue. It was in the Midvale Steel
Works in Pennsylvania in the early 1880's that Frederick W. Taylor
(1865–1915) met and learned, as worker and foreman in the machine
shop, the practice and tricks of ca' canny and developed the system that
came to be known as scientific management or Taylorism. As eventually
elaborated, his method comprised, first, careful observation, analysis,
and timing of workers' movements; second, precise measurement of
the labour cost of each operation; and third, the establishment of norms
based on these calculations. The introduction of these new standards,
almost invariably higher than those customary in the trade, was to be
sweetened by favourable piece rates, premium payments, or other
incentives.

Here the circle came full turn: the effort to improve the worker's
efficiency, an effort which grew out of the increased efficiency of
capital, opened the way to advances in the use of equipment. Scientific
management was logically linked both as cause and effect to the innovations in machine-tool operation, handling of materials, division of
labour in the shop, and organization of work flows discussed above,
for the establishment of norms rested on an analysis of the production
process and inevitably turned up both weaknesses and possibilities of
improvement. What Taylor preached was a substitution of reason for
habit, a new way of looking at familiar things. It is no coincidence that
he discovered high-speed steel; or that he worked out correct tensions
and speeds for power belting and an efficient procedure for the
maintenance of what had always been the responsibility of no one in
particular (like oiling or grinding). The point is that his search for an
optimum pace of work led him to study and set standards of efficiency
for every aspect of production.[1]

[1] See Hugh G. J. Aitken, *Taylorism at Watertown Arsenal: Scientific Management in
Action, 1908–1915* (Cambridge, Mass., 1960), ch. 1; also M. J. Nadworny, *Scientific
Management and the Unions, 1900–1932: a Historical Analysis* (Cambridge, Mass., 1955);
Frank B. Copley, *Frederick W. Taylor, Father of Scientific Management* (2 vols.; New
York, 1923).

Almost as early, however, Europeans were doing their own thinking and writing on plant management, and parallel ideas were finding occasional and discrete application. In 1896 J. Slater Lewis, head of the electrical engineering department of a Manchester steel works, published 'what is apparently the first modern book on factory organization'.[1] By the turn of the century, the leading engineering journals in England and Germany, as well as the United States, were full of the new gospel and supporting their preachments with examples of successful innovation. It is no coincidence, however, that the area of most rapid advance was accounting: it was easier to improve the flow and quality of intelligence than to act upon it. Nevertheless, closer cost controls made possible a more centralized administration of production; it is this, for example, that explains in large part the decline of the so-called 'butty system', in which management subcontracted jobs to master workmen who hired their own assistants on a time basis. The system was generally expensive, but its most serious disadvantages were its nasty implications for discipline and morale: the interposition of an entre-preneur between employer and worker made effective command difficult; and the competition for these contracts gave rise to the kind of wage squeeze that often accompanied the putting-out system. For all this, the butty system was almost indispensable in industries like ship-building, where it enabled management to calculate the costs of complicated jobs in advance. Without prediction, there could be no competitive bidding. From the 1890's on, cost accounting was the answer. The office was beginning, but only beginning, to dominate the shop.

Seen from the hindsight of the mid-twentieth century, scientific management was the natural sequel to the process of mechanization that constituted the heart of the Industrial Revolution: first the sub-stitution of machines and inanimate power for human skills and strength; then the conversion of the operative into an automaton to match and keep pace with his equipment. The third stage is now upon us: automation—the replacement of man by machines that think as well as do. How far and fast the new technique will go; whether, in combination with atomic power, it will mean a second (or third)

[1] L. H. Jenks, 'Early Phases of the Management Movement', *Administrative Science Quart.* v (1960), 428. This is the best brief survey of the subject and offers an extremely useful bibliography on developments in the United States and Britain. On the latter, see also L. Urwick and E. F. L. Brech, *The Making of Scientific Management* (3 vols.; London, 1949), vols. I and II. There is some historical material on the movement in France in G. Bricard, *L'organisation scientifique du travail* (Paris, 1927). Yet these are poor substitutes for a scholarly study, and the best source remains the contemporary engineering periodicals.

Industrial Revolution, it is still too early to say. But it is some consolation to think that it is apparently easier to make machines like man than to turn man into a machine.

Behind this kaleidoscope of change—sometimes marked by brilliant bursts, sometimes tedious in its complex fragmentation, always bewildering in its variety—one general trend is manifest: the ever-closer marriage of science and technology. We have already had occasion to observe the essential independence of these two activities during the Industrial Revolution; and to note that such stimulus and inspiration as did cross the gap went from technology toward science rather than the other way. Beginning in the middle of the nineteenth century, however, a close alliance develops; and if technology continued to pose fruitful problems for scientific research, the autonomous flow of scientific discovery fed a widening stream of new techniques.

How did this marriage come about? The usual answer is that it was the inevitable consequence of increasing knowledge: as the cognitive content and range of both activities grew, they were bound to touch and join forces in certain areas of common concern. Yet in fact, they do not touch, and this is one marriage that requires permanent mediation to work; the gap between science and technology is far too wide for direct communication. The link is provided by two intermediaries: applied science, which has as its aim control rather than knowledge and converts the discoveries of pure science into a form suitable for practical use; and engineering, which takes the generalities of applied science, along with a host of other considerations, economic, legal, and social, and extracts those elements needed to solve a particular technical problem—whether it be building a bridge, designing a plant, or rating a machine.

When one speaks, therefore, of the marriage of science and technology, one really refers to a complex liaison, which was not consecrated at a moment in time but developed slowly and unevenly, and varies to this day from country to country and industry to industry. There are still areas of production that must rely heavily on inspired empiricism. Nevertheless, it was the second half of the nineteenth century that first saw close systematic ties between the two in important branches of industrial activity; and it was success in these areas that set the pattern and provided the incentive for further collaboration.[1]

[1] The precise dating of this progressive marriage of science and technology is a matter of some dispute among students of the subject. There are those who would confine it to the twentieth century, even to the last generation, others who push it back to the nineteenth and in some areas farther. To an outside observer, it would seem that much of the disagreement inheres in the vagueness of the generalizations commonly

The reasons for this development may be sought in both the supply of and demand for knowledge. On the side of supply, the establishment as early as the 1790's of institutions of engineering instruction, staffed in part by men of theoretical preparation and bent, made it possible not only to transmit to the students certain elements of contemporary science (which were sometimes erroneous) but more important, to equip them with the tools of analysis and attitudes of mind that make it possible to pass from the abstract to the concrete, the general to the specific. On the side of demand, the nature of the newer fields of industrial activity—organic chemistry and electrical engineering in particular—tended to diminish reliance on the traditional combination of empiricism and common sense and impose a more scientific approach. For these older methods are capable of handling well only what is susceptible to ordinary sensory perception and formulatable in terms of the familiar: one can see a lever lift a weight and deduce from that an accurate principle of mechanical advantage; it is another matter to infer the nature and possibilities of an electric current from observation of its effects. Admittedly the ingenuity of man as tinkerer and doer almost surpasses belief: note the lead of steam engineering over the theory of thermodynamics.[1] The fact remains that the task of invention was getting steadily more complex, the matter of invention more recondite. As a result, applied science was a more efficient key to the unknown, hence more prolific of innovations.

Nor were these accomplishments limited to the newer branches of industry. Everywhere, the growth of scale turned what once had been negligible elements of cost into potentially serious sources of loss: the smallest economy in a steam plant that consumes a ton of coal a minute can save thousands of pounds a year. The result was steady pressure toward more exact and rational design, a trend reinforced by the greater complexity and precision of manufacturing equipment and the closer control of quality in a period of increasing competition. More than ever, the emphasis was on measurement, and the measuring instruments themselves were among the most ingenious applications of pure scientific principles to industrial needs: thus the modern refracto-

offered. If a chronology must be attempted, it is clear that the evidences of collaboration from before the mid-nineteenth century are exceptional and often adventitious—essentially prodromes. See the discussion in John Jewkes et al., The Sources of Invention (London, 1960), chs. II and III.

[1] Conversely, there is often an enormous lag between applied science and engineering on the one hand and practice on the other. Thomas Savery's steam-engine of 1698 was a perfectly workable concept; but the metalworkers of the day were simply incapable of building it. R. Jenkins, 'Savery, Newcomen, and the Early History of the Steam Engine', Trans. Newcomen Soc. III (1922–3), 96–118; IV (1923–4), 113–30. We have already noted Watt's difficulties in this regard.

meter-goniometer, used in chemical manufacture, and the pyrometer, used in all manner of high-temperature work. Other products of this collaboration between theory and practice were Parsons's steam-turbine, which required a combination of 'all the available resources of mathematics, science, and machine design', and such major innovations in non-ferrous metallurgy as the Hall–Héroult aluminium and Mond nickel processes. Even in iron manufacture, where empiricism and serendipity continued to play a fruitful role into the twentieth century, the need for new materials (as against traditional problems of smelting and refining) made recourse to precise measurement, chemical analysis, and microscopic metallography indispensable.[1] To be sure, these were often simply sharper tools in the service of empiricism. But the emphasis on accurate examination and systematic experiment opened the door to scientific principles, for the man trained to perform the one could often apply the other. And while he could get along without them—and usually did—he could do a lot more with them. Competition took care of the rest.

In general, there was a gradual institutionalization of technological advance. The more progressive industrial enterprises were no longer content to accept innovations and exploit them, but sought them by deliberate, planned experiment. To take just one example: until this century engineers were content to utilize in their work such materials as were readily available from metals producers; but beginning with a branch like the electrical industry, which introduced a whole range of new requirements, the demand for special alloys increased to the point where users were not ready to wait on the pleasure and imagination of suppliers. Laboratory techniques and equipment steadily improved; and increasing amounts were allocated to research. For those who were unable or unwilling to sink capital in permanent plant and staff, scientific and technical consultants were becoming available—division of labour that was evidence in itself of the growth of the market for knowledge. Eventually success nurtured in industry a veritable mystique of the profitability of science—to the point where enterprise began to finance fundamental as well as practical research.

This cognitive tie between science and practice accelerated enormously the pace of invention. Not only did the autonomous expansion of the frontiers of knowledge yield all manner of unanticipated practical fruits, but industry could now order desiderata from the laboratory as a

[1] Cf. J. K. Finch, 'Engineering and Science: a Historical Review and Appraisal', *Technology and Culture*, II (1961), 329–30; J. K. Feibleman, 'Pure Science, Applied Science, Technology, Engineering: an Attempt at Definitions', *ibid*. pp. 313 f.; M. Kerker, 'Science and the Steam Engine', *ibid*. p. 388; Cyril S. Smith, 'The Interaction of Science and Practice in the History of Metallurgy', *ibid*. pp. 363–4.

POLITICAL CONSEQUENCES OF ECONOMIC CHANGE   553

client a shipment from the mill. In a strange way, the importance of technology as a factor in economic change was thus both heightened and diminished. On the one hand, it became more than ever the key to competitive success and growth. The faster the rate of change, the more important to be able to keep up with the pacemakers. On the other, technology was no longer a relatively autonomous determinant. Instead, it had become just another input, with a relatively elastic supply curve at that.

(4) SOME REASONS WHY

It is now time to pull the threads of our story together and ask ourselves why the different nations of western Europe grew and changed as they did. In particular—for lack of space compels us to select our problems—why did industrial leadership pass in the closing decades of the nineteenth century from Britain to Germany?

The larger interest of this question will not escape the reader. It is of concern not only to the student of economic growth but to the general historian who seeks to understand the course of world politics since 1870. The rapid industrial expansion of a unified Germany was the most important development of the half-century that preceded the First World War—more important even than the comparable growth of the United States, simply because Germany was enmeshed in the European network of power and in this period the fate of the world was in Europe's hands.

In 1788 a perceptive French demographer named Messance wrote: 'The people that last will be able to keep its forges going will perforce be the master; for it alone will have arms.'[1] He was somewhat in advance of his times. In subsequent years the Revolutionary armies and then Napoleon were to show what well-directed manpower—a nation in arms—using traditional weapons, could do to traditional armies. By the 1860's, however, Messance's analysis was borne out, first by the American Civil War, and then by the Franco-Prussian War. It was now Blut und Eisen that counted, and all the blood in the world could not compensate for timely, well-directed firepower.

It took a long time for people to adjust to this new basis of power. When the Prussian coalition defeated France in 1870, numerous Britons, including the Queen, rejoiced to see the traditional Gallic enemy and disturber of the peace humbled by the honest, sober Teuton. Within fifteen years, however, the British awoke to the fact that the Industrial Revolution and different rates of population growth had raised Germany to Continental hegemony and left France far behind. This was

[1] M. Messance, Nouvelles recherches sur la population de la France (Lyons, 1788), p. 128.

one of the longest 'double-takes' in history: the British had been fighting the Corsican ogre, dead fifty years and more, while Bismarck went his way.

In subsequent decades, this shift in the balance of power was the dominant influence in European international relations. It underlay the gradual re-forming of forces that culminated in the Triple Entente and Triple Alliance; it nourished the Anglo-German political and naval rivalry, as well as French fears of their enemy east of the Rhine; it made war probable and did much to dictate the membership of the opposing camps. It has, I know, been fashionable for more than a generation to deny this interpretation. In the reaction against Marxist slogans of 'imperialist war' and 'the last stage of capitalism', scholars have leaned over backwards to expunge the slightest taint of economic determinism from their lucubrations. Yet doctrine was never a valid guide to knowledge, at either end of the ideological spectrum, and this effort to rule out material considerations as causes of the World War betrays *naïveté*, or ignorance about the nature of power and the significance of power relations for the definition of national interests.

These political concerns go far to explain Britain's agitated response to German economic expansion. Germany was not, after all, the only country to compete with Britain in the home and foreign markets. American manufactures, particularly machine tools and other devices that placed a premium on ingenuity, invaded the United Kingdom as early as the middle of the century and continued to trouble British producers to the end of our period. And we have already noted the success of Indian and Japanese cottons in the competition for the potentially bottomless Eastern market.

Yet it was Germany that stuck in John Bull's craw. In the decades preceding 1870, she had gradually turned from one of the best markets for British manufactures to a self-sufficient industrial country; one can follow the process in her diminishing dependence on imports of such tell-tale products as cotton yarn (see above, p. 442) and pig iron (57½ per cent of consumption in 1843 at the height of the railway boom, 34 per cent in 1857, 11 per cent a decade later).[1] After 1870, with the home market won, German industry began to make an important place for itself abroad. Actually, the process had begun before, but it is from this point roughly that the increase in the volume of manufactured exports picked up and the British began to awaken to their new rival. From 1875 to 1895, while the value of British exports stood still, though volume rose by some 63 per cent, the value of German exports rose 30 per cent and volume correspondingly more. At the same time, where only 44 per cent of German exports were finished products in

[1] Beck, *Geschichte des Eisens*, IV, 696; Benaerts, *Origines*, pp. 460-1.

1872, 62 per cent fell into this category in 1900 (as against 75 per cent for the United Kingdom).[1]

Moreover, the particulars of the trend were more disturbing than the general tide. There was, for example, the export of German iron and steel to areas that Britain had come to look on as a private preserve—Australia, South America, China, Britain herself. There was the marked superiority of Germany in the newer branches of manufacture: organic chemicals from the 1880's, electrical equipment from the 1890's. Above all, there were the 'unfair' methods allegedly employed by the Teuton: he sold meretricious, shoddy merchandise, often under the guise of British articles; he accepted training engagements with British houses in order to spy out a trade; he pandered to the tastes of the natives and seduced them by concessions to their ignorance—to the point of translating sales catalogues into their language. Complaints reached a peak during what Ross Hoffman called the 'midsummer madness of 1896'.[2] Parliamentary orators exercised their eloquence on government purchases of Bavarian pencils, or the importation of brushes made by German convict labour; newspapers denounced the purchase of cheap German garments, many of them produced from reclaimed British woollens. No item was too small to heap on the flames of indignation: playing-cards, musical instruments, buggy whips.[3]

To be sure, it is easy to demonstrate the exaggeration of these alarms. Germany's gains still left her far behind Britain as a commercial power: the volume of her trade in 1895 was perhaps three-fifths as great; the tonnage of her merchant marine only a sixth as large. British commerce was still growing, losses in one market were generally compensated by gains in another, her industry had not forgotten how to meet competition. Moreover, the difference in overall rates of growth between the two countries was considerably smaller than the discrepancy in rates of industrial growth would lead one to expect. Where British output of manufactured commodities (including minerals and processed food) slightly more than doubled from 1870 to 1913, against a German increase of almost sixfold, the ratio between the rising incomes of the

---

[1] Germany, *Statistisches Jahrbuch* (1908), p. 125; Schlote, *British Overseas Trade*, p. 125. The 1872 figure is from France, *Annu. statistique*, XLVIII (1932), rés. rétro. p. 408, which gives the 1900 German percentage as 65.

[2] *Great Britain and the German Trade Rivalry, 1875–1914* (Philadelphia, 1933).

[3] On all this, see D. S. Landes, 'Entrepreneurship in Advanced Industrial Countries: the Anglo-German Rivalry', in *Entrepreneurship and Economic Growth* (Papers presented at a Conference sponsored jointly by the Committee on Economic Growth of the Social Science Research Council and the Harvard University Research Center in Entrepreneurial History, Cambridge, Mass., 12 and 13 November 1954).

Table 56. *Capital Formation as Share of National Product (in percentages)*

		United Kingdom				Germany[a]		
		NDCF/NDP		NNCF/NNP		NDCF/NNP	NNCF/NNP	
U.K.	Germany	Current prices	Constant prices	Current prices	Constant prices	Current prices	Current prices	Constant prices
	1851–60					8·4	8·6	7·9
1860–9		7·2	8·6	10·0	11·5			
	1861–70					8·5	9·7	10·6
1870–9		8·2	7·3	11·8	10·9			
	1871–80					11·6	13·5	13·0
1880–9		6·4	3·4	10·9	8·1			
	1881–90					11·2	14·0	14·5
1890–9		7·3	3·0	10·1	6·0			
	1891–1900					13·9	15·4	15·9
1895–1904		8·8	4·8	10·5	6·7			
1900–9		8·2	4·1	11·7	7·8			
	1901–13					15·6	16·5	15·9
1905–14		6·7	1·2	13·0	8·0			

[a] 1913 boundaries.

ABBREVIATIONS
NDCF   Net Domestic Capital Formation.
NDP   Net Domestic Product.
NNCF   Net National Capital Formation.
NNP   Net National Product.

SOURCE. S. Kuznets, 'Quantitative Aspects of the Economic Growth of Nations: VI. Long-Term Trends in Capital Formation Proportions', *Economic Development and Cultural Change*, IX, 4, part II (July 1961), 58, 59, 64.

two countries, whether calculated in aggregate or *per capita*, was of the order of 0·7 or 0·8 to 1.[1]

In part this paradox simply reflected a shift in resources. More mature than Germany, Britain was beginning to develop her service sector (distribution, transport, banking and insurance) at the expense of manufacturing industry; so that the share of the latter in national product diminished steadily. The increase in foreign holdings had similar statistical consequences.[2] In part, however, Britain's relatively good

[1] On production of *Sachgüter*, see R. Wagenführ, 'Die Industriewirtschaft: Entwicklungstendenzen der deutschen und internationalen Industrieproduktion 1860 bis 1932', *Vierteljahrshefte zur Konjunkturforschung* (ed. Institut für Konjunkturforschung), Sonderheft 31 (Berlin, 1933), pp. 58, 69.

[2] On the eve of the First World War, Britain earned almost £200 million a year by business services to the rest of the world—just about as much as she derived from her

overall performance was the result of a more efficient allocation of resources. The rapidity of German industrial expansion had left important sectors of the economy behind, protected from the shock of obsolescence and the logic of marginal rationality by human foibles and such institutional devices as protective tariffs. A surprisingly large area of manufacturing, for example, clung tenaciously to hand processes and domestic production;[1] and where Britain had liquidated the less remunerative aspects of her agriculture, a sizable fraction of the German population continued to live on the soil.[2] The German economy, in other words, presented some of those contrasts between advanced and

enormous foreign investments. The two together represented more than a sixth of national income. A. H. Imlah, *Economic Elements in the Pax Britannica: Studies in British Foreign Trade in the Nineteenth Century* (Cambridge, Mass., 1958), table 4, pp. 70–5.

[1] Of 10,873,701 people engaged in mining and manufacture in 1907, almost 30 % (3,166,734) were self-employed or worked in enterprises of five persons or less. Dispersed home production was common in clothing and textiles, leather and woodwork, toy manufacture, food processing and a host of minor metal trades. In these areas Wilhelmian Germany was just beginning to go through the process of modernization that Britain had largely traversed by 1870, as the spate of contemporary studies on the problem of the *Hausarbeiter* testifies.

The best brief introduction to the subject is W. Sombart, 'Verlagssystem (Hausindustrie)', in J. Conrad *et al.*, eds., *Handwörterbuch der Staatswissenschaften* (3rd ed., Jena, 1911), vol. VIII. There is a convenient guide to the literature in Belgium, Ministère du Travail, *Bibliographie générale des industries à domicile* [Supplément à la publication: *Les industries à domicile en Belgique*] (Brussels, 1908). Sombart offers a list of materials published in the years immediately following.

[2] How large the discrepancy was between input and output in agriculture, not only in Germany, but throughout Europe, may be inferred from the following table:

Place of Agriculture in Selected Economies, c. 1891–96 (in percentages)

	Share of population dependent thereon	Share of national wealth	Share of national income
Russia	70	43	32
Austria	62	39	27
Italy	52	45	28
France	42	32	21
Germany	39	31	20
United States	35	25	16
Belgium	25	36	14
Holland	22	33	18
Great Britain	10	15	8

SOURCE. M. G. Mulhall, *Dictionary of Statistics* (4th ed., London, 1909), p. 615.

On the winnowing of British agriculture, see T. W. Fletcher, 'The Great Depression of English Agriculture, 1873–1896', *Econ. Hist. Rev.* XIII (1961), 417–32.

backward sectors that we have come to call dualism and to associate with rapid, unbalanced growth.[1]

Even so, compound interest is a remorseless arbiter. The difference in the rates of growth cannot be blinked: any projection of the trends constitutes a judgment unfavourable to Britain. And this is the more true in that the discrepancy between the two countries applied not only to national income, that is, the yield of today, but also to capital formation, that is, the yield of tomorrow. Here the contrast was particularly striking: as Britain slowed down, Germany speeded up (see Table 56).

Table 57. *Germany and United Kingdom: Foreign Investment as Percentage of Total Net Capital Formation (at current prices)*

Germany		United Kingdom	
1851/5–1861/5	2·2	1855–64	29·1
1861/5–1871/5	12·9	1865–74	40·1
1871/5–1881/5	14·1	1875–84	28·9
1881/5–1891/5	19·9	1885–94	51·2
1891/5–1901/5	9·7	1895–1904	20·7
1901/5–1911/13	5·7	1905–14	52·9

SOURCES. The German series is from a manuscript kindly furnished by Professor Simon Kuznets and based on information from Professor Walter Hoffman. The series for the United Kingdom is based on Imlah's calculation of foreign balance on current account, *Economic Elements in the Pax Britannica*, pp. 70–5, and on estimates of net domestic capital formation kindly communicated by Miss Phyllis Deane.

At this point, moreover, our aggregate statistics join our qualitative and micro-quantitative data. All the evidence agrees on the technological backwardness of much of British manufacturing industry—on leads lost, opportunities missed, markets relinquished that need not have been. These are themes that have recurred in every official

---

[1] In this sense, the pre-First World War German economy was comparable to the Japanese. See Henry Rosovsky, *Capital Formation in Japan, 1868–1940* (Glencoe, Ill., 1960), ch. IV, who argues, however, that the persistence of a labour-intensive traditional sector released resources for the costly installations of the modern sector and thereby promoted Japanese growth. The thesis is a provocative one. It does not seem applicable to the German case.

One should carefully distinguish, incidentally, between this dualism of growth, inherent in the inevitable unevenness of development, and the dualism of the colonial economy, in which the modern installations of foreign administration and enterprise contrast sharply with the primitiveness of indigenous life; or the dualism of a semi-stagnant economy like that of Spain or southern Italy (at least until very recently), in which a few gleaming cities, or merely city districts, and other isolated expressions of modern technology are scattered over a countryside little different from what it was two millennia ago.

inquiry, every report of a travelling delegation, for the last two generations. And the very spurts that certain branches have made from time
to time are evidence of an effort to catch up and of previously unexploited potential. There is no doubt, in short, that British industry was
not so vigorous and adaptable from the 1870's on as it could have
been. Why?

Before attempting to answer this question, it may be useful to clear
the ground by ruling out the usual congenial explanations. Thus
Britain's industrial resources were as good as those of any other European country in the late nineteenth century. In the whole world, only
the United States surpassed her in coal output; and no country possessed
better coal for power, metallurgy, or chemical manufacture. One of the
ironies of economic history is that Germany, which almost mono-
polized the production of coal-tar derivatives, drew much of her tar
from the United Kingdom.[1] Much has been made of the great Lorraine iron deposits and their suitability for the production of Thomas
steel; but England had her own large deposits of phosphoric ores in the
East Midlands, far closer to good coking coal than the Lorraine beds
and just as easily mined. As for those industrial materials which had to
come from the outside—cotton, for example, and almost all wool—
England was better situated than her European competitors. No
nation had so wide a commercial network at its command, and it was
no accident that almost all the major primary commodities had their
central markets in Liverpool and London. To be sure, England's
relative importance as a re-exporter of the world's merchandise
declined somewhat as countries like Germany, France and the United
States learned to buy directly from producing areas; but they—and
other countries still less—never learned to by-pass the British entrepôt
entirely, and the absolute value of this re-export trade continued to rise
right up to the war. Actually, commodities like cotton and wool
tended to be a few pennies cheaper in Liverpool and other British ports
than in Le Havre and Hamburg; and though the difference was not
great, foreign industrialists thought it great enough to buy there.

Nor was the smaller size or slightly slower rate of increase of the
British population a disadvantage. From the standpoint of labour
supply, it was Germany rather than Britain who found it difficult to
meet the needs of growing industries toward the end of the century;

[1] Marshall, *Industry and Trade*, p. 195. On the advantageous resource position of the
British chemical industry, both for organic and inorganic processes, and Germany's
dependence on imports for a significant fraction of her consumption of things like
pitch, tar, and anthracene, cf. *Parliamentary Papers*, 1901, LXXX, no. 2, 'Report on
Chemical Instruction in Germany and the Growth and Present Condition of the
German Chemical Industries', pp. 42, 68.

among other things, she had to move tens of thousands of people from the villages of Pomerania and East Prussia clear across the country to the mills of Westphalia and the Rhineland. As for demand, although the German home market was no doubt growing faster and was potentially greater, British manufacturers actually had most of the known world for an outlet. Here again, their wide-flung, experienced commercial relations gave them an important initial advantage over potential competitors. Even in certain German colonies, British traders and planters long held a pre-eminent position because of their earlier establishment in these areas, their familiarity with the problems and possibilities of backward regions, and the greater willingness of the British investor to put his money into distant ventures.[1]

Finally, Britain had more capital to work with than Germany. Her role as precursor of industrialization had made possible an unprecedented accumulation of wealth, which spilled over her boundaries in increasing abundance from the late eighteenth century on. The first of a series of booms in foreign funds occurred in the 1820's, and by the middle of the century the London Exchange had taken on that cosmopolitan colour that distinguished it from all others. It was and remained, in spite of the rivalry of the Paris Bourse toward the end of the century, the world's most important international securities market, whether for funds, rails, mining shares, or industrial and agricultural ventures.[2]

Germany, by contrast, was a net importer of capital throughout the first two-thirds of the nineteenth century. And even after, the appetite of her burgeoning industry was such that foreign placements never took more than a small fraction of savings available for investment. For a long time indeed, the government discouraged the export of capital on the explicit ground that domestic needs were urgent and should receive priority. This attitude later yielded to other considerations—the desire to develop an empire and to extend German political influence abroad.[3] Even so, and in spite of the rapid ramification of German bank interests throughout the world, the outflow of funds was sporadic and from the 1890's on represented a diminishing portion of net capital formation (Table 57).

This hunger for money was reflected in a continued gap of one to

---

[1] Cf. W. O. Henderson, 'British Economic Activity in the German Colonies, 1884–1914', Econ. Hist. Rev. xv (1945), 55–66.

[2] The best source remains L. H. Jenks, The Migration of British Capital to 1875 (New York, 1928). See also Landes, Bankers and Pashas, chs. i and ii; A. K. Cairncross, Home and Foreign Investment 1870–1913 (Cambridge, 1953); and Imlah, Economic Elements in the Pax Britannica.

[3] The traditional hostility to foreign lending remained strong notwithstanding, and the ministries of Finance and Foreign Affairs were often divided on the issue. See Herbert Feis, Europe the World's Banker, 1870–1914 (New Haven, 1930), ch. vi.

two points between the rate of interest in Berlin and those rates prevailing in the other markets of western Europe. Short-term funds moved back and forth with the business cycle, but the net balance favoured Germany, even *vis-à-vis* a country like France which discouraged lending to a former enemy. French banks may have been reluctant to entrust their funds to domestic industry, as undeserving of confidence; but they thought German banks a good risk, and these passed the money on to their own entrepreneurs. Financially this procedure was unexceptionable; politically it had the makings of a scandal.

No, the reasons for German success in the competition with Britain were not material but rather social and institutional, implicit once again in what has been called the economics of backwardness.

There were, first, certain disadvantages inherent in chronological priority: not so much, however, the oft-cited costs of breaking the path as the so-called 'related costs' of adjustment to subsequent change. The former have been much overemphasized. Admittedly a pioneer in any field incurs additional expense owing to ignorance and inexperience; and in theory those who follow may profit by his mistakes. Yet this assumes on the part of the imitators a wisdom that historical experience belies. If the pioneer often sins on the side of excessive modesty, the follower often suffers from excessive ambition; if the one does not quite know where he is going, the other knows too well and undoes himself by his eagerness. There is such a thing, as technicians of the late nineteenth century were careful to point out, as machines that are too big, engines too powerful, plants that are too capital-intensive.

Far more serious are the burdens imposed by interrelatedness, that is, the technical linkage between the component parts of the industrial plant of an enterprise or economy. In principle, the entrepreneur is free to choose at any time the most remunerative technique available. In fact, his calculus is complicated by his inability to confine it to the technique under consideration. For one thing—and here we shall stress the point of view of the enterprise—no piece of equipment works in a void: the engine, the machine it drives, and the means by which it transmits its power are all built to fit; similarly the number and kinds of machines employed, as well as the capacity and type of channels for supply, transfer, and removal of raw and finished material are rationally calculated in relation to one another. As a result, the replacement of one unit of equipment by another, or the introduction of a new device, can rarely if ever be considered in isolation. What is more, the decision on a given change does not always lie entirely within the enterprise but will depend rather, in greater or lesser degree, on the co-operation of outside units. New assembly techniques, for example, may require new standards of accuracy, hence new equipment, in the plants of subcontractors; more rapid loading facilities may yield far less than their possibilities if carriers do not adjust their methods to the new tempo. In such cases, the allocation of cost and risk poses a serious obstacle, not only because calculation is objectively difficult but even more because human beings are typically suspicious and stubborn in this kind of bargaining situation.[1]

On the other hand—and here we are considering the problem from the standpoint of the economy—large-scale, mechanized manufacture requires not only machines and buildings, but a heavy investment in what has been called social capital: in particular, roads, bridges, ports, and transportation systems; and schools for general and technical education. Because these are costly, because the investment required is lumpy and far exceeds the means of the individual enterprise, and because, finally, the return on such outlays is often long deferred, they constitute a heavy burden for any pre-industrial economy condemned by its technological backwardness to low productivity. Moreover, the burden has tended to grow with the increasing size of industrial plant, so that today many of the so-called underdeveloped countries are trapped in a vicious circle of poverty and incapacity. The much-vaunted freedom of the latecomer to choose the latest and best equipment on the basis of the most advanced techniques has become a myth.

There are thus two kinds of related costs: the one, micro-economic, falls most heavily on the early industrializer; the other, essentially macro-economic, falls most heavily on the follower country. The relative weights of the two have never been measured historically, nor is it likely that the information at our command will ever permit such a calculation. It would seem, however, that the ratio has varied over time. If the balance today favours the advanced countries, whose lead in output and in standard of living continues to grow, the advantage lay the other way in the middle and late nineteenth century. By that time Germany had built up a more productive stock of social capital than Britain (she was never so far behind as the 'backward' countries of today), while the related costs of growth fell to the enterprises of the unhappy pioneer. All of British industry suffered from the legacy of precocious urbanization; the cities of the early nineteenth century were

[1] On the comparative advantages and disadvantages of priority, see F. R. J. Jervis, 'The Handicap of Britain's Early Start', *The Manchester School*, XVI (1947); M. Frankel, 'Obsolescence and Technological Change', *Amer. Econ. Rev.* XLV (1955), 296–319; and an exchange between D. F. Gordon and Marvin Frankel on the same subject, *ibid.* XLVI (1956), 646–56. Also W. E. G. Salter, *Productivity and Technical Change* (Cambridge, 1960); and C. P. Kindelberger, 'Obsolescence and Technical Change', *Bull. Oxford University Institute of Statistics*, XXIII (1961), 281–97.

not built to accommodate the factories of the twentieth (logistics again!). Steel plants, especially, with cramped, ill-shaped sites, found it difficult to integrate backward to smelting or forward to finishing; and lack of integration in turn inhibited adoption of a number of important innovations, among them by-product coking. Similarly, railways and colliery owners were long unable to agree on the adoption of larger freight trucks; and the electrical industry was crippled for decades by the initial diversity of methods of supply. The very sight of the spacious arrangements of the Homestead plant in the United States made Windsor Richards wish he 'could pull down the whole works at Bolckow's and start afresh'.[1] If wishes were horses, beggars would ride.

Where, then, the gap between leader and follower is not too large to begin with, that is, where it does not give rise to self-reinforcing poverty, the advantage lies with the latecomer. And this is the more so because the effort of catching up calls forth entrepreneurial and institutional responses that, once established, constitute powerful stimuli to continued growth.

The French, among others, have a saying: 'It is easier to become rich than to stay rich' (compare the related apothegm, 'shirtsleeves to shirtsleeves in three generations'). However sceptical those of us who have not had the opportunity to test this aphorism may be of its general validity, it clearly rests on empirical observation of the rise and fall of fortunes. On the one hand, prosperity and success are their own worst enemies; on the other, there is no spur like envy.

Thus the Britain of the late nineteenth century basked complacently in the sunset of economic hegemony. In many firms, the grandfather who started the business and built it by unremitting application and by thrift bordering on miserliness had long died; the father who took over a solid enterprise and, starting with larger ambitions, raised it to undreamed-of heights, had passed on the reins; now it was the turn of the third generation, the children of affluence, tired of the tedium of trade and flushed with the bucolic aspirations of the country gentleman. (One might more accurately speak of 'shirtsleeves to hunting jacket—or dress coat, or ermine robes—in three generations'.) Many of them retired and forced the conversion of their firms into joint-stock companies. Others stayed on and went through the motions of entrepreneurship between the long weekends; they worked at play and played at work. Some of them were wise enough to leave the management of their enterprises to professionals, comparable in privilege and function to the steward of the medieval domain. Yet such an arrangement is at best a poor substitute for interested ownership; at its worst, it is an invitation to conflict of interests and misfeasance. The annals of

[1] In the *J. Iron and Steel Institute*, LI (1897), 106.

history are full of enriched and ennobled stewards, bailiffs, *Meier*, valets, and the like.

Nor were corporate enterprises significantly better. For one thing, family considerations often determined their selection of managing personnel. For another, such scanty and impressionistic evidence as we have indicates that private and public companies alike recruited too many of their executives from the counting room rather than from the shop.[1] And such production men as were elevated to high responsibility were more likely than not to be 'practical' people who had learned on the job and had a vested interest in the established way of doing things.

The weaknesses of British enterprise reflected this combination of amateurism and complacency. Her merchants, who had once seized the markets of the world, took them for granted; the consular reports are full of the incompetence of British exporters, their refusal to suit their goods to the taste and pockets of the client, their unwillingness to try new products in new areas, their insistence that everyone in the world ought to read English and count in pounds, shillings, and pence. Similarly, the British manufacturer was notorious for his indifference to style, his conservatism in the face of new techniques, his reluctance to abandon the individuality of tradition for the conformity implicit in mass production.

By contrast, the German entrepreneur of the late nineteenth century was generally a *novus homo*; he was almost bound to be, given the lateness and rapidity of the country's industrialization. Often he was a technician, formally trained for his work; trained or not trained, however, he was utterly serious. He worked long hours and expected his subordinates to do likewise; he watched every *pfennig*, knew every detail of his firm's operations. The observers of the day join in picturing him as supple, ingenious, aggressive to the point of pushingness, and occasionally unscrupulous. He had no antiquated veneration of quality for its own sake, was skilled in meretricious presentation, accommodating on terms of sale, energetic in prospecting for new customers and tenacious in serving them.

Yet these unflattering comparisons, which ring true and conform to the historical experience of similar rivalries (compare the inflexibility of the declining Italian cloth industry of the seventeenth and eighteenth centuries),[2] also contain a great deal of caricature. For one thing, a

[1] Cf. Charlotte Erickson, *British Industrialists: Steel and Hosiery, 1850–1950* (Cambridge, 1959), ch. VIII, esp. p. 194.

[2] See the interesting article by Carlo Cipolla, 'The Decline of the Italian Cloth Manufacture: the Case of a Fully Matured Economy', *Econ. Hist. Rev.* 2nd ser. v (1952), 178–87.

certain amount of exaggeration is built into any contrast of this kind. For another, the evidence is biased, to a degree that is hard to assess. Contemporary observers emphasized the failures of British entrepreneurship and the imminent dangers of German competition much as a newspaper cries up the morbid aspects of the news. That was the way one sold articles or attracted the notice of officials in London. Besides, there is such a thing as fashion in opinions, and this was clearly one of the popular dirges of the day.

The question is a complicated one. Berrick Saul has shown that a number of British enterprises in fields like engineering reacted vigorously and imaginatively to foreign competition in the years before the First World War. He cites an American consular report of 1906: 'No one who has not lived in England during the last seven or eight years can realize how great has been the awakening here nor how changed the British mental attitude is regarding new ways of doing things. There has been much wise and clever adaptation to British cheaper labor of American machinery ideas.'[1]

In certain fields, then, the lag was probably diminishing. Yet there was still a great deal to be accomplished, as the wartime inquiries into these same industries were to show. Moreover, this very irregularity of pace and this uneven distribution of technological advance pose important questions for the economic historian. If many older enterprises were complacent, why did younger units not take advantage of the opportunity to push them aside? In other words, why did not change diffuse more rapidly? And what of new industries like electrical engineering and organic chemicals, where hardening of the arteries had not set in?

A number of considerations suggest themselves. There were the usual market frictions. Macro-economic change is rarely abrupt, simply because the system works imperfectly. The nature of the competitive imperfections of the British economy before 1914 is a subject well worth investigating. This was in principle the freest market in the world—no barrier to outside products and, as we have seen, a limited movement toward formal cartelization. Yet only a close study of actual buying and selling practices will show the extent to which habit, personal ties, and sheer inertia distorted the play of competition.

A second support of conservatism was increasing difficulty of entry. This was most severe in heavy industry, especially in branches like metallurgy, where site and ready access to scarce mineral resources were critically important; but the increase in the scale of enterprise and consequently in initial capital requirements was general, and it was no

[1] S. B. Saul, 'The American Impact on British Industry 1895–1914', *Business History*, III (1960), 28.

longer an easy matter for an individual or even a group of partners to undertake the manufacture of a mass-market commodity.

There were exceptions. Trades like clothing, where taste played a role, the vagaries of fashion limited standardization, and equipment was inexpensive and shop production feasible, continued to beckon to new-comers. And there was a steady proliferation of small repair and maintenance units, not only in the older machine trades, but in new fields like bicycle and electrical repair. A few of these firms became giants—one has only to think of the beginnings of the British or, for that matter, any motor car industry. The bulk, however, performed modestly; economies of scale were limited, and with them the scope for entrepreneurial ability; and while the rate of entry was high, so was the death rate.

All of this was connected with a general turning away of talent from the older branches of manufacture, whose inadequacy of reward at once justified and was aggravated by this abandonment. The area of greatest opportunity for new men lay in catering to the needs of a long-enriched business class freed of the habit and necessity of abstinence, of a labour force enjoying for the first time an income above the minimum of decency, of a growing rentier class reposing on the returns from home and overseas investments. Mass leisure had become a powerful market force, for the first time in European history, and the service sector grew apace—not only banking, insurance and the professions, but the whole range of activities that provide for recreation and travel. It began to look as though Britons would soon be living by transferring back and forth the income received from the work of others. The image was caricature, but it testified to the direction of economic change. The situation offers some interesting analogies to that of eighteenth-century Holland.[1]

Finally, there were two difficulties that afflicted the entire industrial sector, but above all its newest branches: scarcity of skills and scarcity of venture capital.

Skills are learned. And the supply of skills to industry is essentially dependent on education. To observe this, however, is merely to state a truism. To do more, one must begin by breaking down this omnibus word 'education' and relating its content to the requirements of production.

By education we really mean the imparting of four kinds of know-ledge, each with its own contribution to make to economic perfor-

[1] Cf. the studies of Charles Wilson: 'The Economic Decline of the Netherlands', *Econ. Hist. Rev.* IX (1939), 111–27; and *Anglo-Dutch Commerce and Finance in the Eighteenth Century* (Cambridge, 1941).

mance: (1) the ability to read, write, and calculate; (2) the working skills of the craftsman and mechanic; (3) the engineer's combination of scientific principle and applied training; and (4) high-level scientific knowledge, theoretical and applied. In all four areas, Germany represented the best that Europe had to offer; in all four, with the possible exception of the second, Britain fell far behind.

The first raises special problems of evaluation. It is not easy to define and assess the relationship of primary education to industrial efficiency. The more obvious connections are probably the least important. Thus, although certain workers—supervisory and office personnel in particular—must be able to read and do the elementary arithmetical operations in order to perform their duties, a large share of the work of industry can be performed by illiterates; as indeed it was, especially in the early days of the Industrial Revolution. Probably the main economic advantages of an extensive, well-run system of compulsory elementary education, therefore, are first, the foundation it provides for more advanced work, and second, its tendency to facilitate and stimulate mobility and to promote thereby a selection of talent to fit the needs of the society. It helps optimize, in short, the allocation of human resources.

Yet it is one thing to point out the significance of this mechanism and another to measure its effectiveness. No empirical studies of the relationships between education and selection on the one hand, between selection and industrial performance on the other, exist for our period. All we have is qualitative observations, plus data on length and generality of schooling and on some of the more elementary cognitive consequences of instruction—notably percentages of literacy. The rest we are obliged to infer.

For what these data are worth—and they are subject to serious caution when used for international comparisons—they show an enormous gap between British and German achievements in this area. On the one hand, we have a nation that until the closing decades of the century preferred to leave schooling to the zeal, indifference, or exploitation of private enterprise. It was not only a question of laissez-faire. For every idealist or visionary who saw in education the path of an enlightened citizenry, there were several 'practical' men who felt that instruction was a superfluous baggage for farm labourers and industrial workers. These people, after all, had been ploughing fields or weaving cloth since time beyond recall without knowing how to read or write; not only was there no reason to change now, but in the last analysis, all they would learn in school was discontent. As a result of this indifference and resistance, it was not until 1870 that local boards were empowered to draft by-laws of compulsory attendance; and not until 1880 was primary instruction made obligatory throughout the kingdom.

Under the circumstances, Britain did well to have roughly half of her school-age children receiving some kind of elementary instruction around 1860. At least this was the finding of the Newcastle Commission, which was exceptionally tolerant of hearsay evidence and tended to view the situation with invincible optimism.[1] There was good reason to believe that many if not most of these students honoured their classrooms by their absence more than their presence; and that in some of the large industrial centres, attendance was lower in the 1860's than it had been a generation before.[2] Even granting the accuracy of the Newcastle estimates, one notes that only two-fifths of these children went to schools inspected by the state; and only one quarter of these remained long enough to enter the upper classes, the only ones that were 'reasonably efficient'.

The situation improved considerably in later years. At least attendance increased sharply from 1870 on and the content of elementary education was enriched by the simple act of assimilating the instruction of the generality of schools to the modest standards of the inspected institutions. Even so, the system remained sterilized by invidious prejudice and the constraints of pathological social conditions. Thus it was widely assumed that aptitude for instruction—or more subtly, ability to use instruction—was a function of class, and that the content and level of training should be suited to the student's station in life. 'The Education Act of 1870,' wrote H. G. Wells, 'was not an Act for common universal education, it was an Act to educate the lower classes for employment on lower class lines, and with specially trained, inferior teachers who had no university quality.'[3] In short, it was not intended to find and advance talent. But one could go further: whatever the ostensible aims of compulsory elementary education, its essential function (what Robert Merton might call its latent function) was not even to instruct. Rather it was to discipline a growing mass of disaffected proletarians and integrate them into British society. Its object was to civilize the barbarians; as Her Majesty's Inspector for London put it, 'if it were not for her five hundred elementary schools London would be overrun by a horde of young savages'.[4]

Compulsory elementary education goes back in parts of Germany to

---

[1] See *Parliamentary Papers*, 1861, XXI (Cd. 2794).

[2] Frank Smith, *A History of English Elementary Education, 1760–1902* (London, 1931), pp. 280–1.

[3] In his *Experiment in Autobiography*, cited by G. A. N. Lowndes, *The Silent Social Revolution: an Account of the Expansion of Public Education in England and Wales, 1895–1935* (London, 1937), p. 5.   [4] *Ibid.* p. 19.

the sixteenth century; in Prussia, Frederick the Great issued his *General Landschulreglement* in 1763. The quality of the instruction was often poor—teaching posts were long looked upon as excellent places for old soldiers—but improved with time. By the early nineteenth century, the school systems of Germany were famed throughout Europe, and travellers like Madame de Staël and observers like Victor Cousin made it a point to visit and examine this greatest achievement of a knowledge-hungry people.

The obligation of children to attend primary school was enforced— as laws usually are in Germany: in Prussia in the 1860's, the proportion of children of school age attending class was about $97\frac{1}{2}$ per cent;[1] in Saxony, it was actually over 100 per cent.[2] More important than quantitative results, however, were the character and content of the system. To begin with, it was the expression of a deep-rooted conviction that schooling was a cornerstone of the social edifice; that the state not only had an obligation to instruct its citizenry, but found its advantage therein, since an educated people is a moral and strong people. Secondly, the very antiquity of the system obviated the emphasis on debarbarization that marked the first generation of compulsory education in Britain. Observers from abroad were impressed by the neatness and decorum of German schoolchildren, from whatever class; the schools were consequently free to concentrate their efforts on instruction. Thirdly, schooling tended to last longer than in Britain, and the elementary classes were linked to so-called 'middle' and secondary grades in such a way that some selection of talent occurred. The process was only moderately effective; in large areas, particularly rural districts, it was inoperative. Yet even in the middle decades of the nineteenth century, visitors were impressed by the catholicity of recruitment of the continuation (as well as the elementary) schools: 'They are generally very well attended by the children of small shopkeepers,' wrote Joseph Kay in 1850, 'and contain also many children from the poorest ranks of society.'[3]

[1] It had been 43% in 1816, 68% in 1846. Prussia, *Mittheilungen des Statistischen Bureaus in Berlin* (ed. Dieterici), 1847, p. 47.
[2] The excess is to be accounted for by children under six or over fourteen years of age, and by a number of foreign students. France, Min. de l'Agriculture, du Commerce et des Travaux Publics, *Enquête sur l'enseignement professionnel* (2 vols.; Paris, 1865), II, 7f.
[3] J. Kay, *The Social Condition and Education of the People in England and Europe* (2 vols.; London, 1850), II, 227. Kay returns to this theme repeatedly: '...I *constantly* found the children of the highest and of the lowest ranks sitting at the same desk....' *Ibid.* p. 209; also pp. 74–5, 80.
Compare the introduction of universal education in Japan in the 1870's, which was hastened and facilitated by similarly deep-rooted social values. According to

It hardly needs saying that the above discussion does some violence to the complexity of the contrast between the two countries. One can find some striking bright spots in the British achievement—certain elementary and grammar schools, for example, which provided excellent instruction to poor scholars and children of well-to-do parents alike; just as one can find among the Junkers of East Elbia instances of a benighted hostility to education to match anything in Britain.[1] Similarly, one could discuss endlessly the merits of the educational philosophies of the two countries, not only because the subject is intrinsically open to contention, but because it is almost impossible to reconcile the contradictory mass of impressionistic evidence. Was one system of elementary instruction more given to 'cramming' than another? one more practical, the other more liberal? one more devoted to facts, the other to ability to think? No categorical answer is possible.

The link between formal vocational, technical, and scientific education on the one hand and industrial progress on the other is more direct and evident. Moreover, it became closer in the course of the nineteenth century, for reasons that can be deduced from our earlier discussion of technology. To begin with, the greater complexity and precision of manufacturing equipment and the closer control of quality, in conjunction with the growing cost of inefficiency and pressure of competition, conduced to higher standards of technical knowledge and proficiency, especially on the upper levels of the productive hierarchy and among the designers of industrial plant. Secondly, the high cost of equipment made on-the-job training increasingly expensive and helped break down an apprenticeship system that had long been moribund. And finally, the changed scientific content of technology compelled supervisory employees and even workers to familiarize themselves with new concepts, and enhanced enormously the value of personnel trained to keep abreast of scientific novelty, appreciate its economic significance, and adapt it to the requirements of production.

It would serve no useful purpose to paint in detail the familiar

Ronald Dore, the acceptance of the Confucian principle that virtue consists in knowledge of one's station and respect for one's superiors, implied the necessity of education for all, but especially for the lower classes, who had that much more virtue to acquire. (See his essay on 'The Legacy of Tokugawa Education', to be published in one of the forthcoming volumes of the Association of Asian Studies Conferences on the Modernization of Japan. I am indebted to Henry Rosovsky for this reference.) The system ostensibly aimed, then, at least before the Meiji period, at reducing ambition and mobility. Yet latent functions are often more important than manifest ones, and history is full of unanticipated consequences.

[1] Cf. R. H. Samuel and R. H. Thomas, *Education and Society in Modern Germany* (London, 1949), pp. 6–7.

chiaroscuro of the late and stunted growth of technical and scientific education in Britain as against the vigorous, precociously developed German system. Briefly, where Britain left technical training, like primary education, to private enterprise, which led in the event to a most uneven and inadequate provision of facilities, the German states generously financed a whole gamut of institutions, erecting buildings, installing laboratories, and above all maintaining competent and, at the highest level, distinguished faculties. Until the middle of the century, Britain had nothing but the young University of London, the good, bad, and indifferent mechanics' institutes, occasional evening lectures or classes, and courses in the rudiments of science in a few enlightened secondary and grammar schools. After that, improvement came slowly, though the pace picked up measurably after about 1880. The first gains came around the middle of the century in scientific education (Royal College of Chemistry in 1845; Government School of Mines, 1851; Owen's College, Manchester, 1851; university degrees in science, 1850's); they came at the highest level and for many years were partially vitiated by the above-mentioned failure of the primary and secondary schools to find and prepare recruits. Technical and vocational training had to wait another generation and suffered right through the inter-war period from the same handicap. On the eve of the First World War, the British system still had a long way to go to catch up with the German—at least from the standpoint of economic productivity. (There were social and psychological aspects of the Teutonic system that gave outsiders pause.) The long chorus of anguish from otherwise sober savants, writing in the press, addressing the public, or testifying before a remarkable series of parliamentary commissions from 1867 on bears witness to the high cost of this educational backwardness.

More important than the lag itself are the reasons. Essentially they boil down to demand, for a free society generally gets the educational system it wants, and demand was once again a function in part of British industrial priority and German emulation.

As we have seen, even elementary education encountered suspicion and resistance in England; *a fortiori*, technical instruction. There were those industrialists who feared it would lead to the disclosure of or diminish the value of trade secrets. Many felt that 'book learning' was not only misleading but had the disadvantage of instilling in its bene-ficiaries or victims—depending on the point of view—an exaggerated sense of their own merit and intelligence. Here management was joined by foremen and master craftsmen who, products of on-the-job apprenticeship, despised or feared—in any case, resented—the skills and knowledge of the school-trained technician. Still other employers could not see spending money on anything that did not yield an immediate return, the more so as the notions imparted by these classes and institutes almost invariably called for new outlays of capital.

A few were afraid of raising up competition.[1] But most would have snorted at the very idea: they were convinced the whole thing was a fraud, that effective technical education was impossible, scientific instruction unnecessary. Their own careers were the best proof of that: most manufacturers had either begun with a minimum of formal education and come up through the ranks or had followed the traditional liberal curriculum in secondary and sometimes higher schools. Moreover, this lesson of personal experience was confirmed by the history of British industry. Here was a nation that had built its economic strength on practical tinkerers—on a barber like Arkwright, a clergyman like Cartwright, an instrument-maker like Watt, a professional 'amateur inventor' like Bessemer, and thousands of nameless mechanics who suggested and effected the kind of small improvements to machines and furnaces and tools that add up eventually to an industrial revolution. She was proud of these men—listen to Lowthian Bell citing in reply to criticism of British technical shortcomings the names of Darby and Cort.[2]

In many trades there developed a mystique of practical experience. Consider the implications of the following question at the Parliamentary Inquiry of 1885:

You know perfectly well that in every mill there is one man who can spin very much better than anyone else, and if you wanted a finer number, that was the man that was put on. Without a technical school you have always some man of that kind; do you think any technical school would turn out any number of those men in a mill?[3]

And one manufacturer in the tinplate trade, denying the importance of trained engineers, remarked that what was needed was 'practical men who were in sympathy with their rolls and everything else. They could do a lot with their machinery if they were in sympathy with it.'[4]

Moreover, even when employers did come to recognize the need for trained technical personnel, they yielded grudgingly. The underpaid

---

[1] In 1884 Huxley stigmatized this 'miserable sort of jealous feeling about the elevation of their workmen'. Cited in S. F. Cotgrove, *Technical Education and Social Change* (London, 1958), p. 24.

[2] *J. Iron and Steel Institute*, 1878, p. 315.

[3] *Parliamentary Papers*, 1886, XXI: 'Commission...on Depression of Trade and Industry', Q. 5173.

[4] W. E. Minchinton, 'The Tinplate Maker and Technical Change', *Explorations in Entrepreneurial History*, VII (1954–5), 7.

'scientists' were put in sheds, reclaimed workrooms, and other improvised quarters that hardly permitted controlled conditions and accurate tests. Their work was one cut above the rule-of-thumb techniques of the skilled workman; it was far below that of the German laboratory researcher.[1]

In sum, job and promotion opportunities for graduates in science and technology were few and unattractive. The most remunerative field, in spite of what has been said, was chemistry, and even there the best positions were often reserved for men trained abroad; undoubtedly the mediocre quality of many British graduates served to reinforce the scepticism of management. There was just about nothing for physicists until the last decade of the nineteenth century. The worst situation was in the lower ranks, on the level of vocational training, where students occasionally suffered for their ambition: a witness before the Committee on Scientific Education of 1868 testified that only one in four of those who attended vocational classes of the Science and Art Department in the 1850's got back into his trade.[2] In 1884 the Royal Commission on Technical Instruction reported:[3] 'We believe that many workmen are disposed to attach too little value to the importance of acquiring knowledge of the principles of science, because they do not see their application.' No wonder. No wonder also that the most gifted of those few young men who had the means to pursue their education beyond the intermediate level followed the traditional liberal curriculum to careers in the civil service, to pursuit of the genteel county life, or to the kind of post in industry or trade—and there were many—that called for a gentleman and not a technician.

The contrast with German attitudes is hard to exaggerate. For an ambitious nation, impatient to raise its economy to the level of the British, vexed if not humiliated by its dependence on foreign experts, an effective system of scientific and technical training was the foundation and promise of wealth and aggrandizement. A veritable cult of *Wissenschaft* and *Technik* developed. The kings and princes of central Europe vied with one another in founding schools and research institutes and collected savants (even humanistic scholars like historians!) as their predecessors of the eighteenth century had collected musicians and composers; or as the courts of the Italy of the *cinquecento*, artists and

---

[1] Cf. J. E. Stead, *J. Iron and Steel Institute*, XLIX (1896), 119; Burn, *Economic History*, p. 178; *Final Report of the Committee on Industry and Trade* (Cd. 3282; London: H.M.S.O., 1929), pp. 214f.

[2] *Parliamentary Papers*, 1867-8, Comm. on Scientific Instruction, pars. 301-28, cited by Cotgrove, *Technical Education*, p. 51, n. 1.

[3] *Parliamentary Papers*, 1884, XXIX: Royal Commission on Technical Instruction, Second Report, I, 523; cited *ibid.* p. 40.

sculptors. The people came to gape at the *Hochschulen* and universities with the awe usually reserved for historical monuments. Most important, entrepreneurs prized the graduates of these institutions and often offered them respected and often powerful positions—not only the corporate giants with their laboratory staffs of up to a hundred and more, but the small firms also, who saw in the special skills of the trained technician the best defence against the competition of large-scale production.

There is keen irony in all this. We have noted how a British observer of the mid-nineteenth century was impressed by the 'social democracy' of the German classroom; yet this is precisely what had struck continental travellers of the eighteenth century as one of the peculiar virtues of the British society of that period. To be sure, higher schooling in those days was confined to a very small fraction of the population; even the children of wealthy families often received little formal instruction; so that such equality as prevailed was as much or more one of ignorance than of knowledge. But that is the point: it did not make that much difference in the eighteenth century how much instruction a man had received. The recruitment of talent was on other grounds; wide avenues of mobility were open to the unschooled as well as the schooled; and many a man taught himself or learned by experience the knowledge and skills he required for his work.

With industrialization and the proliferation of bureaucracy in business as well as government, however, formal education took on steadily increasing importance as the key to occupational, hence social, preferment. This is not to say that the system or content of instruction was well suited to the requirements of the economy and polity; merely that schooling came more and more to govern recruitment of talent.

This is a task that a school system is in theory ideally equipped to perform. It is of its essence objective, grading and advancing students on the basis of ability and work—except where competition has been deliberately excluded from the classroom. Yet in fact, the selective efficiency of the system depends directly on its own circumstances and principles of recruitment, and these reflect in turn the values and attitudes of its creators and clientele.

Once again, timing and intent are crucially important. In Britain, where technological change came early, a new industrial society had already taken shape by the time the schools were built; so that these embodied not only the prejudices and cleavages of the established order, but the material inequalities. For members of the poorer classes, it was not only presumptuous to covet a more than minimal education; it was pecuniarily impossible—not so much because of the direct outlays required (though these were often a serious deterrent) as because of the earnings that would have to be foregone. It was the opportunity cost of instruction that made it the almost exclusive prerogative of the well-to-do. The school system, in other words, which might have been the great force for social mobility and advancement by talent, became a powerful crystallizer, defending the positions of a newly entrenched Establishment by giving it a quasi-monopoly of such knowledge and manners (including speech pattern) as the society valued.

Some of this was also true of German education, but to a much smaller degree—and differences in history are almost always a question of degree. The Germans developed their schools in advance of and in preparation for industrialization. The system was meant to strengthen the polity and economy not only by instruction, but also by finding and training talent, and while it necessarily fell short of its objectives, the elements of intent and direction were critically important. Hence one of the strangest paradoxes in modern history: that on the one hand, a liberal society standing out from all others in the eighteenth century for equality and mobility of status, should have lost something of these during the very period of its progressive political democratization; while on the other, a far more authoritarian society, characterized in its pre-industrial period by a clearly defined, fairly rigid hierarchy of rank, should have developed a more open structure, without corresponding political change.[1]

Needless to say, this contrast between two forms of social organization is not meant to imply an invidious moral judgement. Education and mobility are not virtuous ends in themselves, but means to ends, and their consequences, intended or not, may as easily be evil as good. One could easily argue that the *élite* produced by the British system— obnoxiously sure at times of its place and prerogatives but endowed with a keen sense of traditional morality and *noblesse oblige*—was in every way to be preferred to the hard, opportunistic, end-justifies-means specimens promoted by the German *cursus honorum*. But such a comparison would take us well beyond the limits of our subject.

Britain's relative lack of skills and knowledge (who could have imagined this eventuality in the first half of the nineteenth century?) was accompanied by, and contributed to, an equally astonishing inadequacy of venture capital. This statement may well strike the reader as inconsistent with our earlier discussion of Britain's plethora of wealth. But savings are not necessarily investment, and there are all kinds of investment—foreign and domestic, speculative and safe, rational and irrational. The British had the capital. But those who channelled and dispensed it were not alert to the opportunities offered

[1] Cf. Kay, *Social Condition*, II, 74–5; also G. M. Trevelyan, *British History in the Nineteenth Century* (1st ed., London, 1922), p. 353.

by modern technology; and those who might have used it did not want or know enough to seek it out.

The supply side first: the British banking system had grown more or less like industry—step by step, from the ground up, along with its clientele. Its greatest virtue was its remarkable ability to transfer resources from suppliers to demanders of capital through such traditional instruments as the bill of exchange, the open credit, the overdraft. Its greatest weakness, which became apparent only after the middle of the nineteenth century, was its inability to initiate or encourage the kind of industrial enterprise that would call for large amounts of outside capital. It was passive rather than active, responsive rather than creative.

Moreover, in so far as the capital market did direct the flow of funds, habit and predilection combined to give the preference to overseas governments and to public utilities, foreign and domestic. These were London's stock in trade, and London controlled the bulk of the country's liquid capital.[1] Industry was left to local markets: Manchester had its cotton enterprises; Birmingham, arms and hardware; Newcastle, coal and metallurgy. In such fields London itself was no more than a regional centre, trading the shares of shipyards on the Thames, a machine construction firm at Ipswich, local breweries, and the great department stores and hotels of the capital. As a result, the British corporation was often simply a partnership writ large—parochial in resources, direction, control, and scope. It was bigger than its predecessors of the first half of the century; but it was no match for the *Konzerne* and *Interessengemeinschaften* that were mushrooming across the North Sea.[2]

The sharply contrasting structure of German credit and finance is once again understandable only in terms of the economics of priority and backwardness. We have already observed that whereas British industry could build its resources from the ground up, the Germans found it necessary from the start to create institutions to mobilize scarce capital and channel it to a productive system taking its departure on an advanced level of technique and organization. These were the joint-stock investment banks, and their increasingly intimate collaboration with manufacturing enterprise was to have major consequences for the rate and character of German development.

For one thing, it meant planned promotion and development of the individual firm. The banks had to learn to evaluate the possibilities for

[1] Cf. John Saville, 'A Comment on Professor Rostow's British Economy of the 19th Century', *Past and Present*, no. 6 (November 1954), pp. 77–8.
[2] Cf. C. W. von Wieser, *Der finanzielle Aufbau der englischen Industrie* (Jena, 1919), pp. 134–5; Lord Aberconway, *The Basic Industries of Great Britain* (London, 1927), p. 346.

profit in a given business situation before undertaking to issue securities. To this end they not only consulted outside technicians, but developed their own specialists to examine and advise on industrial matters. There were some banks, to be sure, which were less careful than others, or less scrupulous. Germany had her *Gründerzeit*, and there were always financiers who felt that the only significant question in any promotion was its speculative potentialities. Yet most banks did not float and unload; they stayed with their creations, held on to some of their stock, kept an eye on their performance, and encouraged their growth as lucrative clients.

For another, bank financing implied continuing expansion of the industrial sector as a whole. If the profitability of *any given* promotional transaction depended on careful appreciation of the elements involved and on influence over later developments, the *total return* of this very important branch of the bank's operations depended on finding or inventing promotions. Thus the specialists in industrial finance were as concerned with discovering possibilities for growth or reorganization as with helping them come about. This was especially true from 1880 on, after the decline in railway construction and nationalization had deprived the market of its most popular staple. In the following years, the banks played an important role in stimulating as well as in supporting the growth of German heavy industry and its integration along vertical and horizontal lines. Throughout, their influence was on the side of a more thorough utilization of resources and a more effective combination of the factors of production.[1]

Yet it is easy to exaggerate the importance of these differences in the structure and behaviour of the capital markets of the two countries. Students of British economic history in particular have offered on occasion a simpler answer: they have assumed a straightforward inverse relationship between domestic and overseas investment; when the one waxed, the other waned.[2] More careful examination of the data has forced the abandonment of this simple model for a more complex, more accurate, but less comfortable analysis.[3] Even so, many scholars have continued to take for granted that, *grosso modo*, the scale of British foreign investment was such as to deprive domestic industry of nourishment.

[1] One of the best studies of this relationship is O. Jeidels, *Das Verhältnis der deutschen Grossbanken zur Industrie* (Leipzig, 1905).
[2] This point of view is implicit in W. W. Rostow's *British Economy of the Nineteenth Century* (Oxford, 1948), though nowhere does he state it so plainly as A. K. Cairncross, who affirms 'that in the *long* run foreign investment was largely at the expense of home investment or vice versa'. *Home and Foreign Investment* (Cambridge, 1953), p. 187.
[3] Cf. S. B. Saul, *Studies in British Overseas Trade*, pp. 90f.

I am not persuaded by this thesis. It rests, first, on a misapprehension. Without going so far as Professor Rostow, who saw the period 1873–98 as one of a general shift from foreign placements toward 'intensive investment at home', one may note that there were times during these years when Britain sank large sums into domestic industry. In 1885 Goschen waxed fairly rapturous on the subject:

Never before has there been so keen a desire on the part of the whole community to invest every reserve shilling they may have in some remunerative manner. There is a competition between men who have a few tens of pounds and a few hundreds of pounds to put them into business, and into business they are put. Joint-stock enterprise has swept up all these available resources. Like a gigantic system of irrigation it first collects and then pours them through innumerable conduit pipes right over the face of the country, making capital accessible in every form at every point.[1]

Yet from the macro-economic standpoint, the results were a disappointment. Clearly, it is not money that counts, but what one does with it.[2]

Secondly, there is good reason to believe that capital flows to opportunity, that if there are borrowers who know what to do with it and seek it, there will be lenders to meet their needs. Admittedly such a generalization does violence to the facts of many individual cases and even perhaps to the experience of certain nations. And it slights the contribution that an imaginative, active banking system can make to industrial development—as we have seen. Yet it seems valid on balance for the major sectors, *qua* sectors, of the advanced industrial economies.[3]

This consideration, moreover, is reinforced here by the fact that, barring non-economic deterrents—lack of security, confiscatory exchange controls, and the like—home enterprise has first claim on the resources of an economy. It has all the advantage of the familiar, whereas foreign ventures are difficult to appreciate, relatively immune from verification and control, and intrinsically more speculative. Indeed the differences between the two are sufficient to give rise to a substantial gap in the expectations of return required to attract investment to each of the two sectors—a gap analogous to the cost of moving

---

[1] *Addresses on Economic Questions* (London, 1905), quoted in Rostow, *British Economy*, p. 70.

[2] In this connection, it is interesting to note that a recent comparison of production functions in different countries shows differences in the efficiency of capital as well as in the better known efficiency of labour. Indeed the two seem to be related.

[3] Cf. Alec K. Cairncross, 'The Place of Capital in Economic Progress', in Leon H. Dupriez, ed., *Economic Progress* (Louvain, 1955), pp. 235–48.

labour from one job to another. In sum, if Britain sent so much money abroad, it was partly for lack of initiative on the part of lenders, but even more because borrowers at home did not want it.

This brings us to the demand side of the equation, which, given the rough equality of the two economies in material resources, was essentially a function of entrepreneurship, that is, of those human elements— imagination, energy, aspiration—that shaped investment decisions in the two systems. Here again, the contrast is sharp enough to transcend the intrinsic limitations of qualitative evidence. The British manufacturer, strong in his admiration for experience and his preference for empiricist tinkering as against bookish experiment, was inclined to be suspicious of novelty. Riley, describing his finally successful efforts to introduce the use of hot pig in Scottish open-hearth mills to the Iron and Steel Institute in 1900, declared that 'the want of confidence in success and the passive resistance often met with in such cases was perhaps more discouraging than any possible difficulties which might arise in actual working, or in working out practical methods'. The conservatism of the tinplate trade was notorious: 'Generally speaking,' said one manufacturer in the years before the war, 'when anything new is introduced into any work, if it is not right away a success out it goes'. The response to something new was to ask 'if any other fool had tried it yet'.[1] One could cite similar examples from other branches of industry.

In the meantime the German system had institutionalized innovation: change was built in. There was no assurance of major discoveries— it is worth noting, for example, that the great advances in metallurgy in the second half of the century were English (Bessemer, Siemens, Thomas–Gilchrist), French (Martin, Carvès), or Belgian (Coppée). But there was some assurance that inventions of whatever origin would be tested and exploited; and there was within industry itself a steady flow of small improvements which cumulatively constituted a technological revolution.[2] The six largest German firms for coal-tar products took out 948 patents between 1886 and 1900, as compared with 86 by the corresponding English firms.[3] And as Schumpeter put it in his description of the German electrical industry, the variety and frequency of innovation under the impulse of the technical departments of the big

[1] Minchinton, 'The Tinplate Maker', *Explorations*, VII (1954–5), 6.
[2] Cf. the discussion of W. N. Parker, 'Entrepreneurial Opportunities and Response in the German Economy', *Explorations*, VII (1954–5), 27: 'Economic opportunity in Germany has been an opportunity for the technologist of ingenious and limited range, and for the production engineer. It has not been aimed at devising striking new types of machinery....' On p. 29 he speaks of 'German possibilities and their introduction in small and incessant doses into existing technology...'.
[3] Cotgrove, *Technical Education*, pp. 20f.

concerns gave rise to a race which 'though never displaying the formal properties of perfect competition, yet produces all the results usually attributed to perfect competition'.[1]

Furthermore—and again we come up against the complexity and inextricability of multiple factors in historical explanation—these contrasts in receptivity to innovation were strengthened by differences in entrepreneurial rationality. The British manufacturer remained faithful to the classical calculus: he attempted to maximize return by making those investments which, given anticipated costs, risks, and sales, yielded the greatest margin over what existing equipment could provide. He was handicapped, as we have seen, by the burden of related costs, which often made otherwise interesting outlays unprofitable. He often made the mistake of tying investment to current operations and returns rather than to expectations of what the future might reasonably bring. Either his tacit assumption was that tomorrow would be the same as today or, as Kindleberger suggests,[2] he was unconsciously trying to minimize the need to make decisions—as always, the most demanding and disagreeable duty of the entrepreneur. Finally, he was sometimes unreasonable enough to neglect one of the cardinal precepts of economics, that sunk costs are sunk, and cling to antiquated equipment because it worked. The theorist is reluctant to admit that people often behave this way, because irrationality does not lend itself to logical analysis; but they do. The weight of earlier advance and growth lay heavy on many a British producer. As Lowthian Bell put it in a comparison of British and American practice: 'The English ironmaster stood in a somewhat different position, inasmuch as if he spent £25,000 to effect [a] saving, he would have to sacrifice the £25,000 he had already laid out.'[3] And another remarked: 'One wants to be thoroughly convinced of the superiority of a new method before condemning as useless a large plant that has hitherto done good service.'[4] The latter statement, of course, may have been nothing more than an affirmation of the need for accuracy in comparing the profitability of old and new equipment—though one is troubled by the reference to past rather than future returns. Even when the British entrepreneur was rational, however, his calculations were distorted by the shortness of his time horizon, and his estimates were on the conservative side.

[1] J. A. Schumpeter, *Business Cycles: a Theoretical, Historical and Statistical Analysis of the Capitalist Process* (2 vols.; New York, 1939), I, 440.

[2] Kindleberger, 'Obsolescence and Technical Change', *Bull. Oxford Univ. Inst. of Statistics*, XXIII (1961), 296, 298.

[3] *J. Iron and Steel Institute*, LIX (1901), no. 1, p. 123.

[4] Alfred Baldwin, in his Presidential Address to the British Iron Trade Association, as reported in *Engineering*, 6 May 1898, p. 569; cited in Burn, *Economic History*, p. 186. Cf. Kindleberger, 'Obsolescence', p. 295.

The significance of this pecuniary approach is best appreciated when it is contrasted with the technological rationality of the Germans. This was a different kind of arithmetic, which maximized, not returns, but technical efficiency. For the German engineer, and the manufacturer and banker who stood behind him, the new was desirable, not so much because it paid, but because it worked better. There were right and wrong ways of doing things, and the right was the scientific, mechanized, capital-intensive way. The means had become end. The economist, to be sure, considering the situation *ex post*, will simply distinguish between two pecuniary calculations: the German entrepreneur simply had a longer time-horizon and included in his estimates exogenous variables of technological change that his British competitor held constant. But this would miss the crucial difference in *ex ante* motivation that made the German behave as he did.

Given this non-rational motivation, there was of course no *a priori* reason why the German pattern should have paid better. It is clear that there can be such a thing as overmodernization—an excessive substitution of capital for labour—just as there can be overemphasis on one or two branches of economic activity at the expense of the rest. Here, however, Germany was fortunate, in that the long wave of technological change favoured science- and capital-intensive methods and industries, while the nature of her own human and material resources were such as to enable her to take advantage of the opportunities offered. In short, she took the right path, though in part for the wrong, or more exactly, irrelevant reasons.

Here some words of caution are in order. I have rested much of this discussion of Anglo-German economic competition on what sociologists call the analysis of ideal types, in this case, two contrasting types of entrepreneurs. This is inevitably a dangerous technique of historical comparison, because it rests on the averaging of the unmeasurable, hence unaverageable, and does violence to the complexity and variety of human behaviour. The economist would be the first to point out that it does not matter in the long run how backward the techniques or how inefficient the performance of the great majority of entrepreneurs, so long as a few are energetic enough to introduce change and force the rest to follow suit. And this is true enough—of the long run. The observation of Lord Keynes has been so often repeated that it has lost much of its pungency; but its correctness remains: In the long run, we are all dead. In the long run, under the pressure of American and German competition, British industry did change many of its ways. But in the meantime it lost ground; one war and then another intervened; new economic rivals appeared; and much talent and capital flowed in other channels. The world does not stand still for anyone, and the short-run weakness contributes, in ways that we are as yet unable to define and measure, to the long-run lag.

One final point. Even if one grants the importance of this human factor—the success of entrepreneurial and technological creativity on one side, the failure on the other—perhaps it was itself nothing more than a reflection of economic determinants. There is, for example, what we may call the 'feedback approach', which sees the growth of an economy or even an industry in any period as a function of its growth in the preceding period: the rate of expansion itself elicits the material and human responses required to sustain it. A succinct statement of this position is to be found in Svennilson:[1]

It may be assumed that the new capacity added in an expanding industry will be built in accordance with the latest technical knowledge, while the rest of the industry, representing the earlier capacity, will lag behind in moderniza- tion. The proportion of modern equipment in an industry will thus increase in proportion to the rapidity of the industry's growth. This leads to the conclusion that, *ceteris paribus*, the efficiency of an industry increases according to the rapidity of its expansion.

This line of explanation has been applied to the Anglo-German rivalry by Professor Habakkuk in his study of *American and British Technology*.[2] To begin with, he is inclined to depreciate the gap between British and German performance: he lays stress, for example, on the British bright spots of open-hearth steel and shipbuilding, the one related to the other. And while he concedes the backwardness of other branches, old and new, he lays great stress on related costs of change, on the burden of established plant and vested interest (for example, the obstacle posed by a widespread gas network to electrification), and above all, on the slow rate of expansion. This last, he feels, explains not only the lack of opportunity to build up-to-date plant, but also such entrepreneurial short-comings as may in fact have existed (here too, Habakkuk feels that the usual indictment is exaggerated): 'Great generals are not made in time of peace; great entrepreneurs are not made in non-expanding industries.' Even the weakness of British scientific training and technical performance (once again, Habakkuk contends that it has been overdrawn) can be largely accounted for in analogous terms: 'the English industry failed to attract or retain the

---

[1] Svennilson, *Growth and Stagnation*, p. 10.

[2] H. J. Habakkuk, *American and British Technology in the Nineteenth Century: The Search for Labour-saving Inventions* (Cambridge, 1962). It would have been desirable to consider this work at a number of other points. Unfortunately, the original manuscript was in the hands of the printer at the time Professor Habakkuk's volume appeared. The present discussion has been added in galley because of the fundamental importance of the general issue.

available scientific ability, and lacked the desire to train its own scientists, because its prospects deteriorated for reasons independent of the supply of scientific skills'. In sum, 'such lags as there were in the adoption of new methods in British industry can be adequately explained by economic circumstances, by the complexity of her industrial structure and the slow growth of her output, and ultimately by her early and long-sustained start as an industrial power'.[1]

I disagree. Not that the argument is wrong; it is simply incomplete and does justice to the behaviour of neither adversary.[2] In regard to Britain, there is the evidence that even the new investment of older industries was characterized by excessive caution and short horizons; and it is also necessary to account for the generally weak performance of the new science-based branches of manufacture. Moreover, it would be wrong to dismiss as incorrect or irrelevant a great mass of contemporary evidence not only testifying to entrepreneurial and technological shortcomings but attributing them to social values and forces independent of the economic system.

The explanation is equally incomplete for the German side of the rivalry. Here too, the analysis has much truth in it: the economic achievements of the *Zollverein* and then the Reich, in conjunction with the military triumphs of Prussia, promoted an atmosphere of euphoric confidence and thereby reinforced the material stimuli to investment and growth. But this is not all one has to explain. There is the question in particular, why the pattern of German investment deviates from what relative factor costs would lead one to expect. Until the last quarter of the nineteenth century, this was not the case: new German plant was less capital-intensive than British plant; equipment was smaller, often less advanced—and this in spite of a far higher rate of growth than in Britain, from 1850 certainly and perhaps from 1834. There is also the objective evidence of technological fecundity deriving from good and widespread scientific training; nowhere is this more obvious than in organic chemicals, where the opportunities for research are in large measure independent of the character or volume of current production. Finally, there is again an abundance of concurrent contemporary testimony about the influence of entrepreneurial attitudes and technical standards on business performance that one would be ill-advised to dismiss except on the strongest grounds.

[1] The quotations are to be found *ibid.* pp. 212, 216, 220.
[2] Our concern here is specifically with the feedback part of the analysis, that is, the contention that Britain's slower rate of growth 'adequately' (perhaps 'substantially' would be more accurate) accounts for those aspects of her economic performance not explained by such direct limitations on entrepreneurial decisions as related costs. On these, already discussed above (see p. 561), one would find general agreement.

In other words, the feedback approach offers an explanation for one side of economic behaviour, that of the stimulus to economic activity which comes from the side of demand. But it slights the supply side and thereby truncates historical reality. Nothing succeeds like success ...but why do some succeed and others fail? Why do some front runners fade and laggards pick up?

Such questions take us into the most difficult problem of economic history, that of explaining why—not simply how or what—change occurs. This is not the place to undertake a discussion of the causation of development and growth, a subject that has already provoked a library of debate, much of it concerned explicitly with the issue posed by the Anglo-German rivalry, that is, the relative importance of human and non-human determinants. But one brief *wissenschaftsoziologische* observation is worth making: when all is said and done, neither empirical evidence nor theoretical reasoning is likely to settle the dispute. Sharp differences of opinion will always remain. For one thing, so complex is the matter of history and so unamenable to the replicated analysis of the laboratory, that the precise imputation of weights to each of the many determinants of economic development— even in a limited situation, *a fortiori* in general—is impossible and likely to remain so. For another, this very complexity and imprecision precludes demonstration that any given explanation of events, however plausible, is the only possible explanation. And since scholars are human, with many, if not all, of the predilections and biases of other humans, they tend to choose and will no doubt go on choosing those interpretations that they find not only plausible but congenial.

This element of congeniality must not be underestimated. Economic development is a great drama. It is the puberty of nations, the passage that separates the men from the boys. It therefore carries with it, in a world that admires power and covets material prosperity, connotations of success and virility. Now some societies have effected this passage earlier than others and have consequently achieved greater wealth; some, though later starters, have been growing faster than some of their predecessors and promise (or threaten, depending on the point of view) to pass them; others have not yet been able to enter on the path of development at all. Because of the profound implications of this drama for the status of the participants, the explanations offered for success or failure are themselves crucial to the self-esteem of these societies and their members. Under the circumstances, the identification of the scholar with the problem he studies has often been as important a determinant of his approach as the objective data.

V. *Conclusion*

Economic history has always been in part the story of international competition for wealth; witness the literature and politics of mercantilism—or the title of Adam Smith's classic study. The Industrial Revolution gave this competition a new focus—wealth through industrialization—and turned it into a chase. There was one leader, Britain, and all the rest were pursuers. The lead has since changed hands, but the pursuit goes on in what has become a race without a finishing line. To be sure, there are only a few contestants sufficiently endowed to vie for the palm. The rest can at best follow along and make the most of their capacities. But even these are far better off than those who are not running. No one wants to stand still; most are convinced that they dare not.

The laggards have good reason to be concerned: the race is getting faster all the time, and the rich get richer while the poor have children. It took man hundreds of thousands of years to learn to grow crops and domesticate livestock and, in so doing, to raise himself above the level of subsistence of a beast of prey, however efficient. The increased food supply that this neolithic revolution provided made possible a substantial growth of population and a new pattern of concentrated settlement with specialization of labour that had the most fertile consequences for man's intellectual development.

It took another ten thousand years or so to make the next advance of comparable magnitude: the industrial breakthrough that we call the Industrial Revolution and its accompanying improvements in agricultural production. Once again the results have been a huge increase in numbers, more and bigger agglomerations of people, greater specialization of labour, and rapid intellectual progress, at least in the domain of science and technology.

Thanks to this progress it has taken man less than two hundred years to leap to atomic power and automation; and in the course of this time, the pace of change has speeded in every domain: compare the centuries of development of the steam-engine with the decades of internal-combustion engines, jet propulsion, and rocket motors. The point, as we have noted, is that man can now order technological and scientific advance as one orders a commodity. This acceleration has produced such interesting anomalies as newly graduated engineers who are paid almost as much as men with decades of experience. It was once thought that this preferential treatment of beginners reflected a temporary maladjustment of the market, a lag in the response of supply to increased demand. There is good reason to believe, however, that this imbalance will persist and even increase, and that it is due in large part to the superior knowledge of men who have received the latest instruction, who have been trained in schools whose curriculum depreciates and is transformed faster than the human products it turns out. Even more must teachers of scientists and engineers labour under the threat of accelerated obsolescence: a man who does not retool constantly is unfit to teach graduate students after ten years, advanced under-graduates after twenty.[1]

The historical experience of western and central Europe provides us with some of our best insights into the nature of this race after wealth and the power that goes with it: into the sources and dynamics of industrial development; stimulants and deterrents; the implications of precedence and backwardness; the effect of non-economic values and institutions on economic performance. Nowhere else is the course so long: one can see the runners coast as well as sprint, follow them from youthful ardour to maturity, observe the working out of at least two technological revolutions. And within this course, one can see such a variety of institutional forms as facilitates the kind of comparison and contrast that is the historian's strongest asset in disentangling and appraising the determinants of complex phenomena.

Needless to say, it is impossible in the present state of our knowledge to evaluate the parameters of economic development. Even the European experience, the one we have studied longest and presumably know best, is still in many areas *terra incognita*. It is perhaps premature, therefore, to proffer generalizations. Yet an end calls for conclusions, and this may serve to exculpate my temerity.

It will be helpful to begin by defining the methodological context of these remarks. The interest of economic theorists and historians in growth has led to the invention of a large number of schemas designed to conceptualize and elucidate this process. Some of these schemas are true models, that is, they take a group of interacting variables and trace a cause-and-effect sequence of changes in these variables to an end result. Others are essentially taxonomies, that is, they classify the stages that an economy or some aspect of an economy passes through on the path of development and growth, without analysing the mechanism of passage from one stage to another. Others combine both of these features.

Some of these conceptions pretend to universal application: they may be essentially imaginary constructions, tied to historical experience only by the most diffuse common sense; or inductive derivations from a sample of historical experience. Other schemas are what Robert

[1] Thomas Stelson, 'Education for Oblivion; or, Change: Grow, or Perish', *Carnegie Alumnus* (April 1961), summarized in *What the Colleges Are Doing* (Ginn and Co. Newsletter), no. 119 (Autumn 1961), p. 2.

Merton has called middle-range hypotheses, that is, generalizations about a closely specified phenomenon or relationship based on a given body of empirical data; as such, they are essentially explanatory or descriptive, though they may have predictive implications. Some of these, such as Professor Gerschenkron's model of the conquest of backwardness, we have encountered at various points in the discussion. Others, like the 'staples theory' of growth, are relevant to patterns of development other than those described by the nations of western Europe.

For obvious reasons, historians are more sympathetic to these limited inductive analyses than to the more ambitious universal abstractions. In this they are mistaken, for the two approaches perform different functions and both are indispensable. A model is not worthless or anathema because it is not empirically anchored. If well constructed, it offers the scholar an analytical pattern against which to hold the experiences of history and appreciate their elements of uniqueness and uniformity. The value of such a model is thus heuristic rather than informative: it does not *tell* what happened but helps one to find and understand what happened.

There is no question here of attempting to catalogue this multiplicity, indeed this plethora, of schemas and evaluate them *seriatim* in the light of the evidence. At most I have space for a small number of middle-range conclusions of my own that modify some widely accepted generalizations. The reader will note that the tone of these remarks is fundamentally negative; in view of our ignorance, it is often easier to say no, or maybe, than yes.

1. It has often been asserted that backward economies develop faster than their predecessors, that given what one writer has called the tension between their existing state and their potentialities, their industrialization takes the form of an eruption.[1] There is some truth in this. The retarded nation, once it has overcome those social and institutional forces that have held it back, can move ahead more quickly for the experience and advances of others. If it has the means, it can make use of the latest equipment, teach the newest techniques; it can even attract the capital and talent of richer economies in proportion to the opportunities it offers.

On the other hand, the assumption on which this thesis is based—like most such assumptions—tends to beg the question. Once retardative forces are overcome…but that is a long and difficult job, and that is why the backward economy was backward to begin with. German industrial growth looks extremely rapid if one dates it from 1850. It is

[1] Thus Gerschenkron, *Economic Backwardness in Historical Perspective*, pp. 5–30.

much slower, slower at first than the British for example, if 1815 is the starting-point. Too often it is assumed that non-economic obstacles simply melt in the face of economic opportunity.[1] In fact, they are extraordinarily resistant, and it is the tension building up behind this resistance that accounts in large measure for the rapidity of development once the spring is released. As a result there is an initial spurt of growth, a making-up of lost time. But there is no reason to assume, as some do, that this pace can be maintained indefinitely.[2] Follower countries also have their fluctuations in rate of growth. And they too mature.

2. It is sometimes asserted that follower countries, unlike Britain, base their breakthrough to industrialization on heavy rather than light manufactures—on iron and steel, mining, chemicals. The Belgian, German, American, and Russian examples all seem to justify the generalization. The argument is twice wrong. First, it confuses the increasing importance of heavy industry in the economy—any economy —and the specific characteristics of backwardness. In western Europe the critical period of expansion and development was the second third of the nineteenth century. These were also the years of what Schumpeter called 'railroadization', and the economies of Germany, Belgium and France showed it in the place assumed by metallurgy and engineering; but then so did that of Britain in this period. And second, the argument ignores the historical validity of the law of comparative advantage. Heavy industry, for example, was far more important in Belgium and Germany than in France and Switzerland— or, for that matter, Japan. And a country like Denmark developed by rationalizing her agriculture. As for subsequent experience—that of the under-developed countries of the twentieth century—it goes without saying that their obsession with heavy industry has only a coincidental connection with economic vocation. The historian should never make the mistake of taking political choice for material necessity.

3. One frequently assumes that follower countries will adopt the most advanced techniques and equipment available. Sometimes this assumption is based on a deceptive kind of common sense: if one is going to buy machinery, one might as well buy the best. Sometimes it

---

[1] Cf. *ibid.*, pp. 68–9.

[2] Cf. Surendra J. Patel, 'Rates of Industrial Growth in the Last Century, 1860–1958', *Economic Development and Cultural Change*, IX (April 1961), 316–60. This is essentially a declaration of faith in the power of compound interest. But Patel remarks, p. 330: 'A more appropriate strategy of growth for these [newly industrializing] countries would be to attain very high rates of growth in the earlier phase and cumulate the enlarged mass of output at somewhat lower rates.'

is based on the more subtle argument that, while there may be an apparent superabundance of labour in the backward country and relative factor costs seem to militate against capital-intensive techniques, skilled workers are in fact scarce and labour-saving devices more necessary even than in advanced economies.

Here, too, the historical facts will not support so simple a generalization. As we have seen, continental industry of the first half of the nineteenth century developed largely with equipment that was already obsolete across the Channel. Two considerations were determining here: first, for all the scarcity of certain kinds of skills, relative factor costs in the follower countries favoured labour-intensive techniques; and secondly, the choice of production functions was not always governed by the rational calculations of theory. Habit, social prejudice, and entrepreneurial caution all conduced to a relatively conservative investment policy.

In the second half of the century this pattern changed, though the shift to ultra-modernity was by no means so extensive as the customary discussion would lead one to believe. It was most marked in heavy industry and in the younger, more scientific branches of manufacture. Even there, however, there were important differences between countries. French and Belgian enterprise adhered in large measure to earlier policies of labour-intensive production and prolonged obsolescence. Cost of production and consequent limitations on the size of the market clearly played a role: hence the modest equipment installed in the infant Dutch steel industry on the eve of the First World War.[1] On the other hand, Germany took the lead in European technology, though both skilled and unskilled labour were cheaper than in Britain and often even France; and Russia, wretchedly poor in domestic capital and rich in manpower, was building its iron and steel industry by the turn of the century on some of the largest blast furnaces in Europe.[2]

[1] R. M. Westebbe, 'The Iron Age in the Netherlands', Explorations in Entrepreneurial History, IX (1956–7), 172–7.

[2] The modernity and gigantism of the Russian iron and steel industry has been somewhat exaggerated. The old iron manufacture of the Urals was notoriously backward, and the first efforts of an outsider to build a modern plant in the Donetz basin (John Hughes in the 1870's) rested on techniques that, while superior to anything yet seen in Russia, were far behind those employed in western Europe. Methods and equipment improved markedly in the 1890's when there was a massive infusion of Belgian and French money and enterprise. Even so, the scale of production was well behind that of even the more conservative producers in the West. M. Goldman, 'The Relocation and Growth of the Pre-Revolutionary Russian Ferrous Metal Industry', Explorations in Entrepreneurial History, IX (1956–7), 19–36; L. Beck, Geschichte des Eisens, V, 1223–24.

This late nineteenth-century pattern of mottled modernity can be explained only partially in terms of relative factor costs. Heavy weight must be given, as we have seen, to non-economic considerations, in particular the technological rationality of engineers, who could hardly be expected to deviate from best practice as they had learned it. Germany here represents almost an ideal type. She had no shortage of skilled hands. Her wages and salaries for equivalent work were distinctly lower than those of Britain and often even of France. To be sure, capital for investment in heavy industry was relatively abundant thanks to the banking system and an interested capital market. Yet it was not so cheap as in Britain, and, in the last analysis, the decisive consideration was one of attitudes and values.[1]

It should be noted, however, that modernity is often meretricious, and that even in technologically oriented industries, the law of relative factor costs was operative—either in the positive sense of determining ratios of factor inputs, or in the negative one of punishing deviations from the rational. The best evidence of the former is to be found, first, in the relatively high labour intensity of processes utilizing modern equipment: the Russian iron plants, for example, used more men per furnace or per ton than German or British enterprises with comparable equipment; just as German cotton manufacturers employed far more men per thousand spindles than the British.[2] It is also to be found in the generous use of labour in auxiliary processes, particularly in the handling and movement of materials and finished goods. The evidence for the latter—the penalization of irrationality—is less clear because of the difficulty of separating out the causes of poor performance. Yet it is worth noting that with the exception of German industry, where technological and pecuniary rationality coincided in the long run, the performance of capital-intensive industry in labour-rich underdeveloped countries tended to be well below theoretical capacity. Much of this was due, no doubt, to inefficient organization and lack of skills; but

---

[1] The ratio of factor costs would seem to have had more influence on Russian development; perhaps not so much on the ground usually adduced, that skilled industrial labour was scarce, as for the opposite reason, that risk capital was in fact abundant—in certain sectors. Thus the foreign entrepreneurs of the Donetz basin were generally iron and steel men from older centres in the West. They had funds to invest and had no intention of turning banker and placing their money in perhaps more remunerative but also less familiar and, inferentially, riskier operations. Had the new Russian iron industry confined itself substantially to domestic capital, the technological pattern might have been drastically different. Yet even in the Russian case non-economic considerations, in particular the predilections of imported entrepreneurs and technicians, played a significant role.

[2] Cf. G. von Schulze-Gaevernitz, *The Cotton Trade in England and on the Continent* (London and Manchester, 1895), pp. 97f.

much also reflected demand limited by high prices due to the poor combination of factors.[1]

The extent and cost of such deviations from the rational has tended to increase over time, as ever more backward economies have been drawn into the stream of industrialization. On the one hand, these newer candidates have been poorer in capital and richer in manpower than their European predecessors. On the other, they have been more dependent on imported technical expertise, hence more subject to the influence of technological rationality. Moreover, they have been slower to develop a machine-construction industry of their own to fabricate equipment suitable to their circumstances; or what amounts to the same thing, they have been far quicker to develop certain machine-using branches than the producers' goods industries to supply them. They have therefore been compelled to import their equipment and have had little choice but to purchase the models made and used in more advanced countries.[2] It is this combination of material and non-material considerations that accounts for such apparent anomalies as more modern spinning machinery in India, Japan, and parts of Latin America than in Britain, in spite of factor-cost ratios far more favourable to labour-intensive techniques.[3]

If there is some general conclusion to be drawn from all this, it is the complexity of economic development. This is a process that, particularly when it takes the form of industrialization, affects all aspects of social life and is affected in turn by them. The remark may seem an empty truism, a typical flight of the historian into the refuge of multiple interrelationship. Yet it has content, as the denial of a sociologist like Herbert Blumer makes clear.[4] And the serious empirical basis of this

[1] The allusion is specifically to heavy industry: cf. the gap between capacity and output in Russian iron manufacture, which accounts in part for the contradiction between its reputation for gigantism and the statistical evidence of performance. The same discrepancy characterized Dutch iron production between the wars, although much of the difficulty there lay in the inadequate absorptive capacity of the home market.
In light industry, on the other hand, one is often struck by use of equipment beyond rated capacity, aggravating wear and tear and increasing maintenance costs substantially.

[2] This element of compulsion is apparent in the tendency to keep this modern equipment in use an inordinately long time—up to and beyond the point that cheap labour (for maintenance and repair of damage caused by worn machinery) makes advisable.

[3] On much of the above, see V. V. Bhatt, 'Capital Intensity of Industries: a Comparative Study of Certain Countries', *Bull. Oxford University Institute of Statistics*, XVIII (1956), 179–94; also United Nations, Dept. of Economic Affairs, *Labour Productivity of the Cotton Textile Industry in Five Latin-American Countries* (1951), p. 9.

[4] H. Blumer, 'Early Industrialization and the Laboring Class', *The Sociological Quarterly*, I (1960), 5–14; *Idem*, 'Industrialization as Agent of Social Change' (MS.), *passim*.

denial, as well as the weighty implications of such a relationship between industrialization and the social order, were it to be proved, justifies, indeed calls for, some serious consideration of the subject.

Economic theory has traditionally been interested in one half of the problem—the determinants of economic change—rather than its non-economic effects; and it long vitiated that half by holding non-economic variables constant, for reasons that, as we have seen, often have little to do with the empirical evidence. Professor Blumer has come to his conclusions from the other direction. Rather than deny or affirm *a priori*, whether for analytical convenience or out of logical conviction, the influence of the non-economic on the economic (and vice versa), he has looked at the wide variety of human experience in this regard and induced therefrom that the relationship is so diverse and free in its working and that so much of what is often derived from economic development, population growth for example, is in fact autonomous, that one is not justified in speaking of uniform causal ties or influences. Indeed he goes beyond this purely negative position to argue that economic development and even industrialization are 'neutral' and have no specific or necessary effect on social institutions.

It seems to me that such an affirmation overdoes a salutary reaction to the abstractions of sociological system makers. Clearly there are no rigid compulsory relationships between a modern industrial economy and the entirety of its complex, multifaceted environment. Rather there is a wide range of links, direct and indirect, tight and loose, exclusive and partial, and each industrializing society develops its own combination of elements to fit its traditions, possibilities, and circumstances. The fact that there is this play of structure, however, does not mean that there is no structure; by the same token, the fact that many of the non-economic institutions of a society are of autonomous origin does not mean that their subsequent development is unrelated to economic change.

Let us try briefly to consider the European experience in the light of these remarks, looking first for the proximate concomitants of industrialization and proceeding by degrees to institutions less tightly confined by the logic or requirements of economic growth. The former, by implication, will have a kind of universal application, transcending time and place. By the same token, the latter will be distinctively European, or British or continental, as the case may be, and will in effect represent one society's or one area's choice of the range of possibilities offered.

When all the complicating circumstances are stripped away—changing technology, shifting ratios of factor costs, diverse market structures in diverse economic and political systems—two things remain and characterize any modern industrial system: rationality, which is the spirit of the institution, and change, which is rationality's logical corollary, for the appropriation of means to ends that is the essence of rationality implies a process of continuous adaptation. These fundamental characteristics have had in turn explicit consequences for the values and structure of the economy and society, consequences that centre in the principle of selection by achievement.

The significance of this principle is obvious: just as the industrial system tries to combine non-human factors of production efficiently, so it will seek to maximize its return from wages and salaries by putting the right man in the right place. This 'universalistic' standard of selection contrasts sharply with the so-called 'particularistic' criteria of the pre-industrial society, dominated by agriculture, landed property, and an Establishment resting on interlaced family ties and hereditary privileges. Men are chosen, not for who they are or whom they know, but for what they can do.

The logical concomitant of such selection is mobility: otherwise, how make the choice effective? A competitive industrial system—whether the competition takes place internally, between productive units, or externally, with rival systems, or both—will therefore place a premium on easy movement of labour power, technical skills, and managerial talent. It will encourage geographical mobility, separating men and women from their ancestral homes and families, to work in strange places; and it will increase social mobility, raising the gifted, ambitious, and lucky, and lowering the inept, lazy, and ill-fortuned. This is the kind of thing one sees in eighteenth- and nineteenth-century Germany, dissolving the bonds of serfdom and the privileges of guilds so as to create a free market for labour and a free field for enterprise; or in nineteenth- and twentieth-century Japan, making extensive use of adoption as a device to recruit talent into the tight familial framework of enterprise: or in France, where the so-called *politique des gendres* has much the same motivation; or in the India of today, striving to break down the once inexorable boundaries of caste. Industrialization is, in short, a universal solvent, and its effects are the more drastic the greater the contrast between the old order and the new.

At this point, the reader impatient with this somewhat theoretical discussion may protest. How much, he may ask, have objective principles of selection really governed the assignment of position and responsibility in societies like England, where higher education has been the prerogative of a favoured few and where personal connections, in business as well as in social intercourse and politics, have been an open sesame to success? And how effective have geographical and social mobility been in the industrializing nations of Europe—or of the world, for that matter? The existence, throughout the Industrial Revolution, of chronically depressed areas and trades is eloquent testimony to the reluctance of people to move, even in the face of necessity.

The answer is that no economic and social system, at least historically, has ever been pushed to its extreme logical consequences. No one will pretend that the Industrial Revolution gave rise, even momentarily, to perfect mobility or created a paradise of universal opportunity. Man is too perverse a creature to admit of absolute systematization, even that of absolutely rugged individualism. Fortunately. And vested interests, especially in a free society, have ways and means to preserve something of their advantages.

The point made here is an entirely different one. It says, first, that industrialization promoted certain social consequences; and there is no blinking the fermentation produced by this drastic economic change in traditionalistic, sluggish agrarian societies. But second and more important, it says that in so far as different countries effected these related social adjustments, they advanced the process of industrialization; and conversely, that in so far as they failed to adjust, their economic growth was retarded. The analogy is complete with the role of rationality in economic theory. Just as all enterprises fall short of absolute rationality yet survive and even flourish thanks to the imperfections of the market place, so societies live and even prosper in spite of the contradictions of their structure. By the same token, however, just as deviations from rationality have their price and if pushed too far can result in elimination of the enterprise, so deviations from economic and social logic entail costs, and if pushed too far can have analogous consequences for an entire nation.

Less universal only by comparison are the social stigmata of backwardness-in-emulation, for this after all is a category that embraces all industrializing nations but the first. One of these we have already considered in detail: the development of a system of general education, whose function is partly to provide training in the skills and sciences required by industry, but even more, as we have seen, to facilitate the selection and recruitment of talent. But I have said little or nothing about two other frequent concomitants of emulation: government intervention and ideological exaltation—for the simple reason that these have been characteristic, not so much of the early industrializers of western and central Europe, as of the rushing laggards like Japan and Russia.

Each of these deserves a moment's attention here. First, political structure: even a cursory consideration of the comparative government of industrialized and industrializing nations makes it clear that a wide variety of institutional arrangements have been compatible with this course of development. Britain has been a parliamentary democracy; the United States, a presidential democracy; France has lived under a diversity of regimes; Russia has passed from autocracy to totalitarianism; Japan effected her industrial revolution under the rule of an alliance of military and plutocrats whose closest parallel was the Junker-industrialist oligarchy of the German empire. Moreover, there has been only a loose correlation between the degrees of political and economic freedom. There was as much intervention in the economy in parliamentary Belgium as in imperial Austria; more intervention in France under the *monarchie censitaire* than under the Second Empire; and more everywhere in the twentieth century than in the nineteenth.

One can, of course, speak of minimal political requisites: security, first, in the widest sense that transcends mere physical safety of persons and possessions and implies the ability to assume the working out of economic decisions without arbitrary non-economic interference—no security, no prediction; and second, effective management of the affairs of government. The latter is the kind of thing that European nations have more or less taken for granted since the city- and nation-states of the late Middle Ages developed bureaucracies and, drawing in part on the Church, a corps of professional civil servants. But as anyone who has tried to get something done in the underdeveloped countries of the twentieth century can testify, administrative competence is not easily acquired and is adequately appreciated only in its absence.

The critical importance of effective government in the twentieth century is due to the increased responsibility for economic development assumed by or devolving upon the State. Here the argument of Gerschenkron is persuasive: the more backward a country—the bigger the gap between its economic performance and possibilities—the more necessary the intervention of authority in promoting growth. One of the ironies of history is that the nations of western and central Europe, with their long experience of centralized government and mercantilistic policy, largely eschewed economic management. It was not only that it was not required, that these societies were ready and able to mobilize voluntarily the resources required and utilize them on the basis of free choice. The fact was that, given Europe's limited experience with industrialization in the nineteenth century and the shortcomings of the economic science of the time, no superior authority could have effected an industrial revolution so rapidly and efficiently as the impersonal market. Under the best of circumstances, the governments of the day were ignorant; in addition, they were usually perverse in their judgments and inconsistent in their actions. As we have seen, such efforts. as authoritarian regimes were ready to make to develop their economies were liable to promote misallocation of resources or lose their force amid contradictory measures in support of the *status quo*. It is no coincidence that the areas of most rapid industrial growth in the eighteenth and nineteenth centuries were those free of supervision and constraints—the textile centres of the Rhineland, for example, rather than the hothouse factories of Frederick II.

The apparently perverse reliance on planning and management by the industrializing nations of the twentieth century, who lack even the rudiments of administrative competence, is explained only in part by the even more serious scarcity of private capital and enterprise. The heart of the choice is ambition, a hunger for growth (which is assumed to mean industrialization) and the fruits of growth that chafes at delay, has no patience for the workings of the free market, and sees in authority a means of forcing the gates of time. To a degree the calculation is correct: in so far as the attitudes and values of the society are such that its members will not respond rationally to opportunity, direction and stimulation from above are indispensable. But to an even greater degree the calculation is ideological, based on value judgments about the contrast between stereotypes of capitalism—exploitive, unjust, enriching a few at the expense of the many—and socialism—egalitarian, placing the resources of the society in the hands of the representatives of the society, for the benefit of all.

There is neither point nor space here to examine the merits of this value judgment. Suffice it to point out that that is what it is, and that as such, its empirical justification is necessarily adventitious. Moreover, the choice of the authoritarian way in no wise exempts an economy from the iron laws of growth: that one never gets anything for nothing and must save first in order to enjoy more later on; and that growth is most rapid when resources are allocated to the area of highest return. The former is inviolable, except in so far as an economy can obtain gifts or loans from outside; and the pain of saving is even more severe in economies that are in a hurry than in those that depend on voluntary abstinence. All the sufferings endured by the English and European working classes during their decades of incipient industrialization bulk little alongside the hardships, insecurity, and death imposed on the proletariats and peasantries of Soviet Russia and Communist China in the name of 'singing tomorrows'. The second law is violated all the time—always at a price—though generally more in authoritarian societies than in free. For where deviations from rationality in market economies generally reflect the aberrations of tradition or prejudice and are penalized to the degree that the market is free and competition effective, they are often the result of deliberate choice in the planned economy, where they are sanctioned and sustained by the exigencies of ideology.

The role of ideology, like that of government, tends to increase with degree of backwardness; and indeed the two go hand in hand. Here, too, there is a functional justification: some kind of psychological reassurance and inspiration is necessary to comfort the members of a society in their years of privation and stimulate them to labour for better times to come; and they are the more necessary, the more difficult the effort, the more ambitious the goal, the greater the sacrifices demanded.

But ideology has roots of its own, and the economy is as much its servant as its master. The great religion of today is nationalism, with its companions of pride (which starts as self-respect) and ambition (which starts as hope). It is nationalism, working through authoritarian government, that directs the economic planning of the under-developed countries of today and has dictated the choice of industrialization as the path to wealth and power; and it is nationalism that justifies this decision and the sacrifices it entails to the people who bear them.

One cannot generalize about the consequences of nationalist ideology for economic growth. Admittedly it can inspire to labour, but its influence may or may not be well directed. It tends to encourage a preference for industry rather than agriculture, for heavy rather than light industry, for monuments rather than utilitarian investments. The price of such a bias will vary with the endowment and vocation of an economy; often it will far surpass the compensating gain of stimulation received.

For the industrializing nations of western and central Europe, ideology, whether nationalist or otherwise, played a less obvious, more subtle role than it does today. It was of modest significance in Britain, though even there, a certain precocious chauvinism, linked to a long history of naval exploits and successful imperial conquests, contributed to the confidence and drive of British trade. It had even less influence in small countries like Belgium, Holland, and Switzerland, where the realities of power precluded patriotic fancies; on the other hand, the ready acceptance by the small countries of a commercial-industrial vocation and their relative immunity to the temptations of what we may call the politics of *gloire* was in itself an aid to effective enterprise. It is no coincidence, for example, that the Belgian aristocracy, more than any other on the Continent, was intensely venal, alert to business opportunity, and ready, like the British gentry, to shift its capital wherever most remunerative.[1]

[1] See the fascinating study of G. Jacquemyns, *Langrand-Dumonceau, promoteur d'une puissance financière catholique* (2 vols.; Brussels, 1960); also any of the literature dealing with Leopold II and his entourage, especially with their appropriation of the Congo.

The reverse is apparent in a country like France, victim in a way of past glories and too much inclined to cherish the predilections and prejudices of the pre-industrial society. The France of Louis XIV and then again of Napoleon had dominated Europe, awed the rest of the world by her pomp and circumstance, scintillated by her artistic and intellectual achievements. She had developed in the process, especially at the upper levels of society, a highly integrated set of values, suffused with a sense of satisfaction and superiority. As is characteristic in such cases of identification between way of life and values on the one hand and self-esteem on the other, her reaction to those areas of activity in which she could not achieve pre-eminence was simply to reject them as unworthy. Britain was more successful commercially? What else could one expect from a nation of shopkeepers?

The successive military and naval defeats by Britain, from Blenheim and Ramillies through Plassey and Quebec to Trafalgar and Waterloo, did not shake this conviction of superior virtue. On the contrary, they reinforced Britain's position as France's traditional rival and enemy and confirmed the French in their hostility to what was viewed as a competitive way of life. Especially after 1815 there was a tendency—alongside a powerful current of cultural and intellectual Anglophilia—to seek comfort for defeat by noting the evils that industrialism had brought to England: the periodic crises, the hordes of blanched children slaving in the mills, the excrescent slums. Along with this went a tacit surrender of economic aspirations: France would never be able to compete with Britain in an industrial world based on coal and iron; hence the need for high protection and even prohibition to preserve a different kind of economy—a more humane economy based on family units of enterprise, a market place free of cannibalistic competition, a healthful balance between agriculture and industry. The consequences of this rejection of the new industrial civilization for both public policy and entrepreneurial behaviour are not easy to measure, if only because this factor blends in with many others. It was nevertheless extremely important in fixing dispositions and justifying them; for it was this value judgment that furnished the moral sanction for economic retardation.

Finally there was Germany, which faced the rest of Europe at the start of the nineteenth century enfeebled by division and still impoverished by the wars of the seventeenth century. The low point was reached in 1805, when, after the battle of Jena, the largest and most powerful German state, Prussia, was threatened with dissolution. At that point there was nothing to look backward to; only the present to take urgent steps in to remake the society and bolster the polity, and the future to build toward. The increasingly close identification of this future, envisioned as one of national rehabilitation, international power and, with time, of a united Germany, on the one hand, and economic growth, on the other, was a powerful support for the new industry, especially for those branches of manufacture that were directly or indirectly linked to power: coal, iron, engineering, eventually chemicals and electricity. The chimney aristocracy could claim a prestige based not only on wealth—for new wealth is always resented—but on their contribution to national aggrandizement. At the same time, German enterprise in general became imbued with a chauvinism that found expression, first, in confidence in its ability to overtake its British precursor and, later on, in an aggressive determination to establish its supremacy throughout the world. The tone was sharply different from that prevailing in France, and while it is easy to point out that the discouragement of the one and assurance of the other were simply based on the realities of economic life, the fact remains—as any athlete will testify—that attitude is an important fraction, win or lose, of any performance.

Ideology is only one of many non-economic factors autonomous in origin but closely connected both as cause and effect with the Industrial Revolution. We could not possibly try to resume all of these here, but two—demographic change and urbanization—are worthy of special notice, not only for their intrinsic interest, but also for the light they throw on the general problem of analysing complex historical inter-relationships.

Look again at the growth of population in the eighteenth and nineteenth centuries. It is clear that its source was in large measure independent of the Industrial Revolution, as Ireland alone suffices to demonstrate. The key factor was a more abundant, regular food supply, which led to a lower death rate, principally by mitigating the periodic winnows of famine and disease.[1] As a result, by the end of the eighteenth century population was already beginning to exert severe pressure on resources in certain parts of western Europe, which was threatened in principle with the kind of general fall in the standard of living that has attended similar discrepancies between growth of numbers and growth of social product in other areas of the world. That such a disaster did not occur was the work partly of major improvements in agricultural

[1] The elimination of what have been called 'dismal peaks' of mortality was probably of least importance in England where, even before the eighteenth century, the supply of food to local areas seems to have been more regular and responsive to demand than in other countries. Indeed, the increase of population there may have been due more to a higher birth rate, the result of earlier age of marriage, than to a lower death rate; and population growth may well have been a response to the opportunities created by expanding industry. But the data are most uncertain, and the matter is still a subject of controversy.

productivity but even more of the industrialization of western Europe and the creation of a surplus of manufactures that could be traded for nourishment from outside.[1] What is more, by creating opportunities for employment, industrial growth almost surely encouraged the long persistence of a high birth rate, which might otherwise have been expected to adjust fairly rapidly to a higher rate of survival (as it did in fact in France), and thereby turned an increase in numbers into an explosion.

The same combination of autonomous origins, at least in part, and subsequent interaction may be seen in the case of urbanization. There is nothing in industrialization itself that will account for the growth of the giant capitals of Europe, which have remained essentially administrative, financial, commercial, and 'cultural' in character. Cities like London, Paris, and Berlin had and have their industry, often based on the availability of cheap labour (crowded immigrants in sweatshops) or highly skilled labour (the woodworking artisans of the Faubourg St-Antoine or the imaginative craftsmen who make *articles de Paris*), or on the preferences of technicians and management who want to live and work in the centre of intellectual, economic, and political activity. But their manufactures are rarely the stuff industrial revolutions are made of; and if they engage in the heavier, more capital-intensive branches, they are compelled with time to expel them—to the outskirts or farther, where land costs are commensurate with industrial use.

But industrialization does tend to the development of another type of city, based on locational advantages and the external economies of proximity in interdependence. Just as the craftsmen of the Middle Ages found it convenient and profitable to work in the company of their trade—their very concentration was a form of advertising that drew the customers to their place of work—so the modern factory often gains by working alongside competitors, not only because the site may be convenient, but also because the presence of a number of producers makes possible the existence of accessory specialists who are indispensable to the efficient working of the branch as a whole. It is this combined process of growth by expansion and diversification that accounts for the massive localization of the textile industry in Lancashire and of metalworking trades in the Ruhr and the Birmingham area.

These centres of factory manufacture may be small or large, depending on size of market, vocation of the area, and technology. The last factor merits a moment's special attention. We have seen that so long as industry was compelled or well advised to rely on water for power, the

---

[1] On the expansion of western Europe's food supply by the opening of new areas of specialized cultivation trading with the industrial zone, there is an excellent essay by Karl Helleiner (ed.), in his introduction to his *Readings in European Economic History* (Toronto, 1946), pp. 24–37.

development of manufacture led, not to urbanization, but to a new kind of rural settlement. The coming of the rotary steam-engine changed this; but the subsequent invention of electric power and the development of cheap local transport (tramways and automobiles) altered once again the technological basis of location and made possible competitive dispersed production. It even gave, as we have seen, a new vitality to craft and domestic manufacture. Nevertheless, the external economies of localization are such that although the advantages of site have diminished and the ecological pattern of the manufacturing city has changed, with industry moving more and more to the suburbs, the tie between factory production and urban concentration has never been broken and is not likely to be.

The convolution of the above discussion may discourage the reader, the more so because it gives at best an incomplete and oversimplified picture of a complex phenomenon. How much more agreeable it would be to reduce everything to a handful of aspects and explain these by a handful of causes! And how comforting it would be to be able to draw unambiguous lessons from this rich tapestry of human experience and present them for the guidance of the industrializers of today, that they may avoid the mistakes of their predecessors. History, after all, is a sacrifice on the altar of hope—hope that man will one day know more about man and be able to master himself as he now masters nature.

In the meantime, the industrialization of the world proceeds, for better or worse. This world, which has never before been ready to accept universally any of the universal faiths offered for its salvation, is apparently prepared to embrace the religion of science and technology without reservation. There are some in the more advanced industrial countries who have qualms about this worship of material achievement; but they are wealthy and can afford this critical posture. The overwhelming majority of the inhabitants of this world, especially the great mass of the hungry and unwashed, take it for granted that food, clothing, and other creature comforts are not only good for both body and soul but lie within reach.

The reason for the optimism is the assumption that man's capacity to know and do is infinite; we have here the millennial heresy of man's worship of himself. The trouble is that no one wants to wait to know before doing. If there is one positive lesson to be drawn from the history of economic development, it is that nations, like people, usually have eyes bigger than their stomachs; further, that they have no patience with those who caution them about their goals and even less for those who complain about their means. All of which should not discourage the scholar—for history is still its own justification.